Writing about Writing

A College Reader

Writing about Writing

A College Reader

Elizabeth Wardle
University of Central Florida

Doug Downs
Montana State University

Bedford/St. Martin's
Boston • New York

FOR BEDFORD/ST. MARTIN'S

Senior Executive Editor: Leasa Burton
Senior Developmental Editor: Alexis Walker
Production Editor: Jessica Skrocki Gould
Production Supervisor: Samuel Jones
Marketing Manager: Molly Parke
Art Director: Lucy Krikorian
Text Design: Brian Salisbury
Copy Editor: Virginia Perrin
Indexer: Leoni Z. McVey
Photo Research: Naomi Kornhauser
Cover Design: Marine Miller
Composition: Glyph International
Printing and Binding: Haddon Craftsmen, Inc., an RR Donnelley & Sons Company

President: Joan E. Feinberg
Editorial Director: Denise B. Wydra
Editor in Chief: Karen S. Henry
Director of Development: Erica T. Appel
Director of Marketing: Karen R. Soeltz
Director of Production: Susan W. Brown
Associate Director, Editorial Production: Elise S. Kaiser
Managing Editor: Shuli Traub

Library of Congress Control Number: 2010932997

For information, write: Bedford/St. Martin's, 75 Arlington Street, Boston, MA 02116   (617-399-4000)

ISBN: 978-0-312-53493-6

Acknowledgments

Acknowledgments and copyrights appear at the back of the book on pages 735–37, which constitute an extension of the copyright page.

It is a violation of the law to reproduce these selections by any means whatsoever without the written permission of the copyright holder.

Preface for Instructors

Writing about Writing is part of a movement that has been growing quietly for years. As composition instructors, we have always focused on teaching students how writing works and helping them develop ways of thinking that would enable them to succeed as writers in college. We found ourselves increasingly frustrated, however, teaching traditional composition courses based on topics that had nothing to do with writing. It made far more sense to us to have students really engage with *writing* in the writing course; the best way to do this, we decided, was to adopt a "writing about writing" approach, introducing students directly to what writing researchers have learned about writing and challenging them to respond by writing and doing research of their own. After years of experimenting with readings and assignments, and watching our colleagues do the same, we eventually developed *Writing about Writing*, a reader for first-year composition students that presents the subjects of composition, discourse, and literacy as its content. Here's why we think *Writing about Writing* is a smart choice for composition courses:

Writing about Writing *engages students in a relevant subject.* One of the major goals of the writing course, as we see it, is to move students' ideas about language and writing from the realm of the automatic and unconscious to the forefront of their thinking. In conventional composition courses, students are too often asked to write about either an arbitrary topic unrelated to writing or, conversely, about anything at all. In our experience, when students are asked to read and interact with academic scholarly conversations about writing and test their opinions through their own research, they become more engaged with the goals of the writing course and, most important, they learn more about writing.

Writing about Writing *engages students' own areas of expertise.* By the time they reach college, students are expert language users with multiple literacies: They are experienced student writers, and they're engaged in many other discourses as well—blogging, texting, instant messaging, posting to social networking sites like Facebook and YouTube, and otherwise using language and writing on a daily basis. *Writing about Writing* asks students to work from their own experience to consider how writing works, who they are as writers, and how they use (and don't use) writing. Students might wonder, for example, why they did so poorly on the SAT writing section or why some groups of people use writing that is so specialized it seems intended to leave others out. This book encourages students to discover how others—including Sondra Perl, Mike Rose, James Paul Gee, their instructors, and their classmates—have answered these questions and then to find out more by doing meaningful research of their own.

Writing about Writing *helps students transfer what they learn.* Teachers often assume that students can automatically and easily "apply" what they learn in a writing course to all their other writing—or at the very least, to other college writing.

This assumption sees writing and reading as "basic," universal skills that work the same regardless of situation. Yet research on transfer of learning suggests that there is nothing automatic about it: David Perkins and Gavriel Salomon found that in order to transfer knowledge, students need to explicitly *create general principles* based on their own experience and learning; *be self-reflective*, so that they keep track of what they are thinking and learning as they do it; and *be mindful*, that is, alert to their surroundings and what they are doing rather than just doing things automatically and unconsciously. A writing course that takes language, writing, reading, and literacy as its subjects can help students achieve these goals by teaching them to articulate general principles such as "Carefully consider what your audience needs and wants this document to do." In addition, it teaches them to reflect on their own reading, writing, and research processes.

Writing about Writing *has been extensively class tested—and it works.* The principles of this writing-about-writing approach have been well tested and supported by the experience of writing instructors and thousands of students across the country. *Writing about Writing* itself has been formally class tested in a pilot at the University of Central Florida, which yielded impressive outcomes in comparative portfolio assessment with more traditional composition courses. Assessment results suggest, among other things, that the writing-about-writing approach had a statistically significant impact on higher-order thinking skills—rhetorical analysis, critical thinking about ideas, and using and integrating the ideas of others. The writing-about-writing approach also had a significant impact on how students and teachers engaged in writing as a process.

Features of *Writing about Writing*

Topics That Matter to Writers

Writing about Writing is organized around concepts and principles from Writing Studies with which we think students should become familiar: how texts in general, and ideas about writing in particular, are constructed; what writing processes are and how they work; what "literacy" means and how people become literate (or multiliterate); how communities use and are shaped by discourse; and how writers can gain authority when writing in college. These issues are framed in the text as questions, each of which forms the basis of one chapter:

- Chapter 1: Texts/Constructs: How Do Readers Read and Writers Write?
- Chapter 2: Writing Processes: How Do *You* Write?
- Chapter 3: Literacies: How Have You Become the Reader and Writer You Are Today?
- Chapter 4: Discourses: How Do Communities Shape Writing?
- Chapter 5: Authority: How Do You Make Yourself Heard as a College Writer?

By asking students to find their own answers to these questions, we encourage them to reflect on past literacy experiences and to be mindful of present ones, making them directly responsible, in the end, for their own learning.

Challenging but Engaging Readings

Because our intention in putting this book together was to invite students directly into scholarly conversations about writing, most readings in the book are articles by rhetoric and composition scholars. In deciding which articles to include, we looked for work that was readable, relevant to student experience, effective in modeling how to research and write about writing, and useful for helping students frame and analyze writing-related issues. We drew not only on our own experience with students but also on feedback from a growing nationwide network of faculty using writing-about-writing approaches to composition and on the feedback of teachers using an early version of the text at the University of Central Florida in the fall of 2009. The articles that made the final cut expose students to some of the most interesting work in our field and encourage them to wrestle with questions we're all trying to figure out.

Of course, we don't expect first-year students to read these texts like graduate students would—that is, with a central focus on the content of the readings, with the purposes of critiquing them and extending their ideas. Instead, we intend for them to be used as springboards to exploration of their own writing and reading experiences. The readings—and thus this book—are not the center of the course; instead, they help students develop language and ideas for talking about what *is* the center: their own experiences with writing, discourse, and literacy, and their (and the field's) open questions on these issues.

While most readings are scholarly, notable exceptions appear in a Chapter 2 interlude called "What Writers Say." These texts are short and pithy commentaries about writing from popular authors with whom students may be familiar, including Stephen King and Junot Díaz. These readings let students see how non-academic writers think and write about what they do and compare that to other research findings in the book.

Real Student Writing

Writing about Writing also includes as many student voices as we could reasonably fit in: Comments from students who have completed a writing-about-writing course are included throughout, and each chapter includes at least one annotated student paper that responds to one of the assignments included in the text. These papers are actual student writing, not rewritten by us. They are not, therefore, perfect papers, but rather the in-progress work of writers who have ideas worth considering. Our annotations highlight some of their ideas and ask questions about the pieces' strengths and weaknesses. As much as possible, we have tried to avoid making direct judgments about the student texts and have instead asked your students to make those judgments for themselves as mindfully as they can. In other words, we have tried to stay true to the spirit of the book by encouraging students to abstract principles and apply them, to be reflective, and to act out of their own knowledge as readers and writers.

Scaffolded Support for Learning

The material presented in this book is undeniably challenging. We've found that students need guidance in order to engage with it constructively, and many instructors appreciate support in teaching it. Therefore, we've extensively scaffolded the material in ways that help make individual readings more accessible to students and that help them build toward mastery of often complex rhetorical concepts.

- The book begins with an introduction for students that explains what the book does and why, provides some reading strategies, and offers two readings that allow students to practice reading and introduce them to the guiding tenets of the book.
- Each chapter begins with a chapter introduction that summarizes its content and goals and overviews each reading and its central ideas.
- Each reading begins with a *Framing the Reading* section offering background on the author and the text and *Getting Ready to Read* suggestions for activities to do *before* reading and questions to ask *during* reading.
- Each reading is followed by two sets of questions: *Questions for Discussion and Journaling*, which can be used in class or for homework, and *Applying and Exploring Ideas*, which recommends reading-related writing activities (both individual and group). These questions and activities are designed to make teachers' jobs easier the first time they teach the book, by providing a variety of prompts that have been class tested by others.
- Each chapter ends with "major" assignment options. Building on one or more of the readings from the chapter, assignments are designed to help the student achieve the goals outlined in the chapter introduction. Though these assignments hardly scratch the surface of what's possible, these have proven to be favorites with us, our students, and other teachers.
- The book includes a glossary of technical terms in composition that students will encounter in their readings. Terms in the glossary, such as **rhetorical situation** and **discourse**, are noted in the reading via bold print as shown.

We've sequenced the chapters in the book to begin with foundational concepts (most notably, that of the *rhetorical situation*) and then to move through various aspects of writing, from personal to public, individual to social. However, there are many alternate arrangements, and we encourage you to discover them.

A note on citation styles. While student writings reflect current MLA or APA style guides in citation and documentation, other material in the book, all previously published, remains written in the citation styles used by the journals and books in which they were originally published, current at those times. This means you should expect to see a great deal of variation from current MLA, APA, or *Chicago* style guidelines—a decision that we hope will provide many instructors with an excellent starting point for conversation about how citation actually works in the "real world" of academic publication over time.

The Instructor's Edition of *Writing about Writing* (ISBN 978-0-312-65681-2)

Some teachers won't need any supplements at all, including the discussion questions and major assignment options. But we have designed the book to be as accessible as possible to all of the kinds of people teaching composition, including new graduate students and very busy adjuncts. Toward that end, we provide instructor's resource material written by Deborah Weaver and Lindee Owens, two long-time teacher-trainers at the University of Central Florida, who themselves piloted an early version of this book and taught the material in it to a number of other composition teachers there. This material, bound together with the student text in a special Instructor's Edition, includes the following:

- sample course calendars
- lists of key vocabulary for each chapter
- key outcomes for each chapter
- a list of readings that can help teach the various outcomes
- summaries and take-home points for each reading, and
- supplemental activities that help teach to each outcome.

Digital Resources for *Writing about Writing*

Writing about Writing doesn't stop with a book. Online, you'll find both free and affordable premium resources to help students get more out of the book and your course. You'll also find convenient instructor resources, such as downloadable sample syllabi, classroom activities, and even a nationwide community of teachers. To learn more about or order any of the products below, contact your Bedford/St. Martin's sales representative, e-mail sales support (sales_support@bfwpub.com), or visit the Web site at bedfordstmartins.com/writingaboutwriting/catalog.

Student Resources

Send students to free and open resources, upgrade to an expanding collection of innovative digital content, or package a standalone CD-ROM for free with *Writing about Writing*.

- **Re:Writing**, the best *free* collection of online resources for the writing class, offers clear advice on citing sources in *Research and Documentation Online* by Diana Hacker, 30 sample papers and designed documents, and over 9,000 writing and grammar exercises with immediate feedback and reporting in *Exercise Central*. Updated and redesigned, *Re:Writing* also features five free videos from *VideoCentral* and three new visual tutorials from our popular *ix visual exercises* by Cheryl Ball and Kristin Arola. *Re:Writing* is completely free and open (no codes required) to ensure access to all students. To learn more, visit bedfordstmartins.com/rewriting.
- **VideoCentral** is a growing collection of videos for the writing class that captures real-world, academic, and student writers talking about how and why they write. Writer and teacher Peter Berkow interviewed hundreds of people—from Michael Moore to Cynthia Selfe—to produce 50 brief videos about topics such as revising and getting feedback. *VideoCentral* can be packaged with *Writing about Writing* at a significant discount. An activation code is required. To learn more, visit bedfordstmartins.com/videocentral. To

order *VideoCentral* packaged with *Writing about Writing*, use ISBN 978-0-312-56044-7.

- **Re:Writing Plus** gathers all of Bedford/St. Martin's premium digital content for composition into one online collection. It includes hundreds of model documents, the first ever peer-review game, and *VideoCentral*. *Re:Writing Plus* can be purchased separately or packaged with *Writing about Writing* at a significant discount. An activation code is required. To learn more, visit bedfordstmartins.com/rewriting. To order *Re:Writing Plus* packaged with *Writing about Writing*, use ISBN 978-0-312-56043-0.

Instructor Resources

You have a lot to do in your course. Bedford/St. Martin's wants to make it easy for you to find the support you need—and to get it quickly. To find everything available with *Writing about Writing*, visit bedfordstmartins.com/writingaboutwriting/catalog.

- The **Instructor's Manual for Writing about Writing** is available in PDF that can be downloaded from the Bedford/St. Martin's online catalog. In addition to sample syllabi, the manual provides lists of key vocabulary and key outcomes for each chapter, summaries and take-home points for each reading, supplemental activities that help teach to each outcome, and a list of readings that can help teach the various outcomes.
- **TeachingCentral** offers the entire list of Bedford/St. Martin's print and online professional resources in one place. You'll find landmark reference works, sourcebooks on pedagogical issues, award-winning collections, and practical advice for the classroom—all free for instructors.
- **Bits** collects creative ideas for teaching a range of composition topics in an easily searchable blog. Elizabeth Wardle and Doug Downs will contribute ideas relevant to *Writing about Writing*; the wider community of teachers—other leading scholars, authors, and editors—will provide their own takes on revision, research, grammar and style, technology, peer review, and much more. Take, use, adapt, and pass the ideas around. Then, come back to the site to comment or share your own suggestion.
- **Content cartridges** for the most common course management systems—Blackboard, WebCT, Angel, and Desire2Learn—allow you to easily download digital materials from Bedford/St. Martin's for your course.

Acknowledgments

We came to writing-about-writing independently of one another, in different ways, and became better at it as a result of working together. David Russell was a mentor for us both. Elizabeth came to writing-about-writing as a result of her dissertation research, which Russell chaired and supported. Doug came to it as a result of questions about building better research pedagogy, directly fueled by Russell's work on the history of college research-writing instruction and his chapter in Petraglia's *Reconceiving Writing*.

Initially, Elizabeth's interest was theoretical ("this might be an interesting idea") while Doug's was quite practical (he designed and studied a writing-about-writing class for his dissertation). We discovered each other's common interest through dialog on the WPA-L listserv and a long-term collaboration was born. It is fair to say that neither of us would have written this book without the other, as we both seem to get a lot more done when working collaboratively. (There is a vividly remembered two hours in the sunshine at the University of Delaware, at the 2004 WPA conference, where we took our first steps at figuring out collaboration.) So, if it's not too corny, we would like to acknowledge collaboration in general, our collaboration in particular, and tenure systems at our institutions that have recognized collaborative work for the valid, challenging, and rewarding process it is.

To many, many people—colleagues, mentors, and friends—we owe a deep debt of gratitude for putting the ideas grounding *Writing about Writing* "in the air." In addition, over the five years that it took to build this book, we met many wonderful teacher-scholars who inspired us to keep going. Over many dinners, SIGs, conference panels, e-mail discussions, and drinks, we learned and are still learning a lot from them. We surely won't remember to name all of our influential colleagues, but a partial list includes: Anis Bawarshi, Barb Bird, Shannon Carter, Deb Dew, Heidi Estrem, Elizabeth Fogle-Young, Mark Hall, Deb Holdstein, Amy Krug, Catherine MacDonald, Laurie McMillan, Michael Michaud, Andrew Moss, Michael Murphy, Sarah Read, Amy Reed, David Russell, Betsy Sargent, David Slomp, Susan Thomas, Linda Turk, Scott Warnock, Kathi Yancey, and Leah Zuidema.

Many of these people are now on the FYC as Writing Studies listserv; members of the Writing about Writing Network founded by Betsy Sargent; or participants in the annual CCCC Special Interest Group, The Subject Is Writing: FYC as Introduction to Writing Studies. Through such intercommunication, they continue to develop research projects, create conference presentations and workshops, and inspire us—and one another—with their curricular creativity. Writing-about-writing students have also been given a national platform to publish their work, thanks to the editorial board of the national, peer-reviewed undergraduate journal of Writing Studies, *Young Scholars in Writing*. Editor Laurie Grobman created a First-year Writing Feature (continued as the Spotlight on First-year Writing under the editorship of Jane Greer) co-edited over time by Shannon Carter, Doug Downs, Heidi Estrem, and Patti Hanlon-Baker. Carter has also created another venue for the writing of first-year students in the National Conversation on Writing (http://ncow.org/site/).

In fall 2009, a group of instructors and teaching assistants at the University of Central Florida piloted an early, ugly, and un-edited coursepack version of this book. Their feedback, both during and at the end of the semester, improved the final version immeasurably. For their remarkable and giving work as guinea pigs, we thank Matthew Bryan, Ed Bull, Lynn Casmier-Paz, Katie Beth Curtis, Kathryn Dunlap, Marcy Galbreath, Edie Kindle, Scott Launier, Jessica Masri, Lindee Owens, Adele Richardson, Sonia Stephens, Mary Tripp, Laurie Uttich, Daniel Valencia, Erin Waddell, Heather Wayne, and Debbie Weaver.

Debbie Weaver, composition coordinator at the University of Central Florida, proved a powerful motivating force in helping us get the coursepack version finished in time for the start of that semester. She also trained all of the graduate teaching assistants in how to use it and finally delivered her enthusiastic verdict on the teachability of the curriculum, which was an immense relief to us both.

We owe a massive thank you to Bedford/St Martin's, and to Leasa Burton and Joan Feinberg in particular, who had the vision to believe that this book might really find an audience if they published it. To all the Bedford crew who made it real—Alexis Walker, Karrin Varucene, Karita dos Santos, Denise Wydra, Jimmy Fleming, Nick Carbone, Harriet Wald, Alanya Harter, and doubtless many others—you guys rock. And to the numerous reviewers of proposals, drafts, and near-final versions of the book, as well as Bedford's TA Advisory Group, we offer thanks both for the formative feedback and for assuring everyone involved that there would be people interested in using this book. It wouldn't exist without that affirmative feedback.

We also thank Marilyn Moller at W. W. Norton, whose early and lengthy interest in the idea of this book helped us understand more about what we wanted it to do. For her time, effort, and interest, we remain grateful.

Nkosi Shanga helped us figure out how to frame the first chapter when we were both out of ideas.

Ultimately, our students deserve the most acknowledgement. They have inspired us to keep teaching writing about writing. They have demonstrated that the focus is one that continues to excite and motivate, and their papers and projects continue to inspire and teach us.

Elizabeth Wardle

Doug Downs

About the Authors

Elizabeth Wardle is an associate professor and Director of Writing Outreach Programs in the Department of Writing and Rhetoric at the University of Central Florida. Her research interests center on genre theory, the transfer of writing-related knowledge, and composition pedagogy. She is currently conducting a study examining the impact of smaller class size on the learning of composition students, as well as a study examining the impact of the writing-about-writing pedagogy on student writing and attitudes about writing.

Doug Downs is an assistant professor of rhetoric and composition in the Department of English at Montana State University. His research interests center on research-writing pedagogy both in first-year composition and across the undergraduate curriculum. He continues to work extensively with Elizabeth Wardle on writing-about-writing pedagogies and is currently studying problems of researcher authority in undergraduate research in the humanities.

Contents

CHAPTER 2

Writing Processes: How Do *You* Write?   170

CHAPTER 5

Authority: How Do You Make Yourself Heard as a College Writer?   578

Writing about Writing

A College Reader

Introduction to the Conversation

Let go of all previous convictions about what an English class is "supposed" to be. In high school English, classes tend to focus primarily on literature and touch briefly on literary style. This English class is more correctly a seminar that looks deeply into rhetoric and the actual process of writing.

—**Elizabeth Grauel, Student**

This book does not tell you how to write. It does not contain step-by-step advice about how to draft your paper or how to conduct research. Instead, it introduces you to the research about writing conducted in the field of writing studies, much as your textbooks in biology or psychology introduce you to the research of those fields. *Writing about Writing* asks you to think about writing as something we *know* about, not just something we *do*. It offers you these kinds of learning:

- Deeper understanding of what's going on with your own writing and how writing works
- Knowledge about writing that you can take with you to help you navigate other writing situations
- Experience engaging with scholarly articles and other research
- The ability to conduct inquiry-driven research on unanswered questions

Have you ever wondered why every teacher seems to have a different set of rules for writing? Or why writing seems to be more difficult for some people than for others? Or why some people use big words when they don't have to? *Writing about Writing* invites you to compare your own writing and reading experiences to research others have done on questions like these and to find your own answers by conducting research of your own.

In order to do something correctly you first need to know what is expected. In sports, for instance, you would need to know the rules, customs, and expectations of both the sport and your particular position before you could begin playing. How would you learn these? You would read the rules and watch professionals play and attempt to mimic their movements. The same is true for this course. In order to learn how to write well you must read the rules, see how the professionals do it, and then mimic them.

—**Matt Craven, Student**

Why Study Writing?

Basically, this course will teach you how to become a better writer by learning about the theories of writing and reading the products of good writers so that you may incorporate these into your own writing process.

—**Matt Craven, Student**

You might wonder why it is more helpful to learn *about* writing than to simply be told *how* to write. What good will this do you as a writer? We think the answer to this question is that changing what you know *about* writing can change the way you *write*. Much of the research in this book questions everyday assumptions about writing—like the idea that you can't use your own **voice** in writing for school, or that writing is just easy for some people and hard for others, or that **literacy** is only about how well you can read. If you change your ideas about what writing is *supposed* to be, you're likely to do different things—better things—with your writing.

There are additional advantages to studying writing in a writing course:

- Writing is *relevant* to all of us. Most of us do it every day, and all of us live in a world in which writing, reading, and other related uses of language are primary means of communication.
- What you learn about writing now will be directly *useful* to you long after the class ends. In college, at work, and in everyday life, writing well can have a measurable impact on your current and future success.
- You already have a great deal of *experience* with writing and reading, so you are a more knowledgeable investigator of these subjects than you might be of a lot of others.
- Doing research on writing will give you the opportunity to *contribute new knowledge* about your subject, not simply gather and repeat what lots of other people have already said.

Making Sense of the Readings

The first step is to learn how to approach the readings. Do not let the big words intimidate you. . . . After some practice and class discussion, you will learn how to pull the important topics out of the piece. The readings . . . will help you to think of topics in writing that need to be addressed and greatly assist you in research. The readings build a frame of reference and train you in deciphering academic literature.

—Elizabeth Grauel, Student

Understanding the "Framing the Reading" section that's placed before the article is very useful. This passage prepares me for what I should know about the author and briefly states what the article is going to be about. I also find annotating an article helpful for me while I'm reading. I highlight or underline important words or phrases that I need to understand for my English class and assignments.

—Natasha Gumtie, Student

The scholarly articles collected in this reader are written by expert researchers for an audience of other experts. Reading such texts is sometimes not easy even for your professors, and they won't be easy or quick for you to read at first either. We've created the reader to make sure that the time you spend with the articles is rewarded with new ideas that you'll understand and value, and we have some advice on how to use the book to make sure your time is well spent.

- Very consciously connect at least *some* part of each piece you read to your own experience as a writer; the readings have been chosen specifically to allow you to do that.
- Read the backstory of each piece, which you'll find in the "Framing the Reading" sections. These introductions give you background necessary to more fully understand the pieces themselves.
- Use the activities and questions in the "Getting Ready to Read," "Questions for Discussion and Journaling," "Applying and Exploring Ideas," and "Meta Moment" sections to help you focus your reading on the most important concepts in the pieces.
- Apply the readings to your own writing experience as you work on any of the projects from the end-of-chapter "Writing Assignments and Advice" sections. Use the sample student papers throughout the book as models and inspiration for your own writing.

- Read more deeply on subjects that especially interest you by using the "Suggested Additional Readings and Resources" in each chapter.

Although I found some of the readings difficult . . ., I found that actively reading the material helped me to make sense of the content. I was sure to identify where the author writes of others' research, the "gap" [the author identified], and how the author intends to fill the gap. I also highlighted the conclusions that the author drew [and] took notes in the margin as well. . . .

—**Casey Callahan, Student**

As you are reading the articles in the book, try to read them with an open mind. Some of them may seem intimidating at first . . . but don't worry . . . there is still much to learn from the readings if you actually give them a chance. As you are going through the articles, try jotting down the concepts you don't understand. If they still aren't clear, after the lecture, ask your instructor. Most instructors are more than willing to help.

—**Jillian Loisel, Student**

A Different Kind of Research and Argument

Research is asking questions on a topic that interests you, examining what questions have already been answered by others, and then developing a method to answer the questions that you have that have been unanswered. The most integral part of the process is choosing a topic that truly interests you. . . . I found my own personal research to be extremely enjoyable and it barely felt like work. I found myself thinking about my research outside of class and my work. Some of my best ideas came when I was out with my friends and [my topic] . . . came up in conversation.

—**Casey Callahan, Student**

You may not be very familiar with the kind of research—scholarly inquiry—you encounter in this book. Scholarly inquiry is imperfect, incomplete, inconclusive, and provisional. It doesn't offer easy or full answers. It is question- and problem-driven. It includes a lot of personal opinion rather than clear, objective facts. How can this be? Scholarly inquiry doesn't stand on *existing* knowledge; rather, in scholarly inquiry, researchers come together to try a lot of different approaches to the same problem, and then, through argument *as conversation*, gradually develop consensus about what the best explanation of or solution to the problem is.

Before you turn to Chapter 1, we'd like to offer three "foundational" selections that will help you understand the rest of what you'll encounter in *Writing about Writing*: a summary of John Swales's **"Create a Research Space" (CARS) model** of research introductions (pp. 6–8); the article "Argument as Conversation" by Stuart Greene (pp. 9–21); and another article, "What Is It We Do When We Write Articles Like This One—and How Can We Get Students to Join Us?," by Michael Kleine (pp. 22–30).

The summary of Swales's CARS model will help you understand how academic writers construct the introductions to their research articles; Greene's article will help you see how the selections in the rest of the book argue differently from texts you might be more familiar with; and Kleine's article will suggest why academic writers write the way they do. We offer these selections as an introduction to the ongoing scholarly conversations about writing, research, and inquiry—conversations in which they—and now *you*—are an essential part.

Do not expect to be treated like a freshman [in this book]. Many first-year college courses will baby you. . . . In this course, however, you will be treated as a member of academia. . . . This course gives you the opportunity to go above and beyond the expectations of a first-year college student, and it is a valuable and shaping experience. As an undergraduate I completed close to fifty courses; out of fifty courses, [the composition] class that I took for four months at the very beginning is one that I can recall most clearly and was able to actually apply to my major studies. Apply yourself and work hard; this class is worth it.

—**Elizabeth Grauel, Student**

"Create a Research Space" (CARS) Model of Research Introductions[1]

JOHN SWALES

Sometimes getting through the introduction of a research article can be the most difficult part of reading it. In his CARS model, Swales describes three "moves" that almost all research introductions make. We're providing a summary of Swales's model here as a kind of shorthand to help you in both reading research articles and writing them. Identifying these moves in introductions to the articles you read in this book will help you understand the authors' projects better from the outset. When you write your own papers, making the same moves yourself will help you present your own arguments clearly and convincingly. So read through the summary now, but be sure to return to it often for help in understanding the selections in the rest of the book.

Move 1: Establishing a Territory

In this move, the author sets the context for his or her research, providing necessary background on the topic. This move includes one or more of the following steps:

Step 1: Claiming Centrality

The author asks the **discourse community** (the audience for the paper) to accept that the research about to be reported is part of a lively, significant, or well-established research area. To claim centrality the author might write:

"Recently there has been a spate of interest in . . ."

"Knowledge of X has great importance for . . ."

This step is used widely across the academic disciplines, though less in the physical sciences than in the social sciences and the humanities.

and/or

Step 2: Making Topic Generalizations

The author makes statements about current knowledge, practices, or phenomena in the field. For example:

---

[1]Adapted from John M. Swales's *Genre Analysis: English in Academic and Research Settings*. Cambridge: Cambridge UP, 1990.

"The properties of X are still not completely understood."

"X is a common finding in patients with . . ."

and/or

Step 3: Reviewing Previous Items of Research

The author relates what has been found on the topic and who found it. For example:

"Both Johnson and Morgan claim that the biographical facts have been misrepresented."

"Several studies have suggested that . . . (Gordon, 2003; Ratzinger, 2009)."

"Reading to children early and often seems to have a positive long-term correlation with grades in English courses (Jones, 2002; Strong, 2009)."

In citing the research of others, the author may use *integral citation* (citing the author's name in the sentence, as in the first example above) or *non-integral citation* (citing the author's name in parentheses only, as in the second and third examples above). The use of different types of verbs (e.g., *reporting verbs* such as "shows" or "claims") and verb tenses (past, present perfect, or present) varies across disciplines.

Move 2: Establishing a Niche

In this move, the author argues that there is an open "niche" in the existing research, a space that needs to be filled through additional research. The author can establish a niche in one of four ways:

Counter-claiming

The author refutes or challenges earlier research by making a counter-claim. For example:

"While Jones and Riley believe X method to be accurate, a close examination demonstrates their method to be flawed."

Indicating a Gap

The author demonstrates that earlier research does not sufficiently address all existing questions or problems. For example:

"While existing studies have clearly established X, they have not addressed Y."

Question-raising

The author asks questions about previous research, suggesting that additional research needs to be done. For example:

"While Jones and Morgan have established X, these findings raise a number of questions, including . . ."

Continuing a Tradition

The author presents the research as a useful extension of existing research. For example:

"Earlier studies seemed to suggest X. To verify this finding, more work is urgently needed."

Move 3: Occupying a Niche

In this move, the author turns the niche established in Move 2 into the *research space* that he or she will fill; that is, the author demonstrates how he or she will substantiate the counter-claim made, fill the gap identified, answer the question(s) asked, or continue the research tradition. The author makes this move in several steps, described below. The initial step (1A or 1B) is obligatory, though many research articles stop after that step.

Step 1A: Outlining Purposes

The author indicates the main purpose(s) of the current article. For example:

"In this article I argue . . ."

"The present research tries to clarify . . ."

or

Step 1B: Announcing Present Research

The author describes the research in the current article. For example:

"This paper describes three separate studies conducted between March 2008 and January 2009."

Step 2: Announcing Principal Findings

The author presents the main conclusions of his or her research. For example:

"The results of the study suggest . . ."

"When we examined X, we discovered . . ."

Step 3: Indicating the Structure of the Research Article

The author previews the organization of the article. For example:

"This paper is structured as follows . . ."

Argument as Conversation:
The Role of Inquiry in Writing a Researched Argument

STUART GREENE

Greene, Stuart. "Argument as Conversation: The Role of Inquiry in Writing a Researched Argument." *The Subject Is Research*. Ed. Wendy Bishop and Pavel Zemliansky. Portsmouth, NH: Boynton/Cook, 2001. 145–64. Print.

Framing the Reading

In "Argument as Conversation," Stuart Greene explains how scholarly inquiry is a different kind of research and argument from the kinds we encounter in our everyday lives or (for most of us) in earlier schooling. The principles that Greene discusses—research as *conversational inquiry*, where an *issue* and *situation* contribute to *framing* a problem a particular way and researchers seek not to collect information but to generate new knowledge in *a social process*—are the ideas and activities that drive the entire college or university where you're study-ing right now. They work in every field where scholarly research is happening, from anthropology to zoology.

In this book, you'll apply these principles specifically in terms of research on writing, literacy, language, communica-tion, and related fields. As Greene suggests in his discussion of context, you'll "weave" your experiences with research that's already been done on questions and issues related to them. The research you do on your own may even offer new insights into long-running questions about these subjects.

Getting Ready to Read

Before you read, do at least one of the following activities:

- Think about how you define *argument*. How is the word used in everyday conversation? What do you think the word means in an academic setting? What's the difference between the two?
- Have a conversation with a classmate on the following topic: How would you say *argument* and *conversation* relate to each other? Can some arguments be

conversational and some conversations argumentative, or is no crossover possible? Provide examples, and be sure to explain your terms as precisely as possible.

As you read, consider the following questions to help you focus on particularly important parts of the article:

- Who is Greene's audience? Who, in other words, is the "you" he addresses? How do you know?
- How does Greene structure his article? If you were to pull out the major headings, would the outline created from them be useful in any way?
- What kinds of support does Greene use for his claims? What other texts does he refer to? Is this support relevant to his claims and sufficient to prove them?

A rgument is very much a part of what we do every day: We confront a pub-   1
lic issue, something that is open to dispute, and we take a stand and support what we think and feel with what we believe are good reasons. Seen in this way, argument is very much like a conversation. By this, I mean that making an argument entails providing good reasons to support your viewpoint, as well as counterarguments, and recognizing how and why readers might object to your ideas. The metaphor of conversation emphasizes the social nature of writing. Thus inquiry, research, and writing arguments are intimately related. If, for example, you are to understand the different ways others have approached your subject, then you will need to do your "homework." This is what Doug Brent (1996) means when he says that research consists of "the looking-up of facts in the context of other worldviews, other ways of seeing" (78).

In learning to argue within an academic setting, such as the one you probably   2
find yourself in now, it is useful to think about writing as a form of inquiry in which you convey your understanding of the claims people make, the questions they raise, and the conflicts they address. As a form of inquiry, then, writing begins with problems, conflicts, and questions that you identify as important. The questions that your teacher raises and that you raise should be questions that are open to dispute and for which there are not prepackaged answers. Readers within an academic setting expect that you will advance a scholarly conversation and not reproduce others' ideas. Therefore, it is important to find out who else has confronted these problems, conflicts, and questions in order to take a stand within some ongoing scholarly conversation. You will want to read with an eye toward the claims writers make, claims that they are

> The questions that your teacher raises and that you raise should be questions that are open to dispute and for which there are not prepackaged answers.

making with respect to you, in the sense that writers want you to think and feel in a certain way. You will want to read others' work critically, seeing if the reasons writers use to support their arguments are what you would consider good reasons. And finally, you will want to consider the possible counterarguments to the claims writers make and the views that call your own ideas into question.

Like the verbal conversations you have with others, effective arguments 3 never take place in a vacuum; they take into account previous conversations that have taken place about the subject under discussion. Seeing research as a means for advancing a conversation makes the research process more *real*, especially if you recognize that you will need to support your claims with evidence in order to persuade readers to agree with you. The concept and practice of research arises out of the specific social context of your readers' questions and skepticism.

Reading necessarily plays a prominent role in the many forms of writing 4 that you do, but not simply as a process of gathering information. This is true whether you write personal essays, editorials, or original research based on library research. Instead, as James Crosswhite suggests in his book *The Rhetoric of Reason*, reading "means making judgments about which of the many voices one encounters can be brought together into productive conversation" (131).

When we sit down to write an argument intended to persuade someone to 5 do or to believe something, we are never really the first to broach the topic about which we are writing. Thus, learning how to write a researched argument is a process of learning how to enter conversations that are already going on in written form. This idea of writing as dialogue—not only between author and reader but between the text and everything that has been said or written beforehand—is important. Writing is a process of balancing our goals with the history of similar kinds of communication, particularly others' arguments that have been made on the same subject. The conversations that have already been going on about a topic are the topic's historical context.

Perhaps the most eloquent statement of writing as conversation comes from 6 Kenneth Burke (1941) in an oft-quoted passage:

> Imagine that you enter a parlor. You come late. When you arrive, others have long preceded you, and they are engaged in a heated discussion, a discussion too heated for them to pause and tell you exactly what it is about. In fact the discussion had already begun long before any of them got there, so that no one present is qualified to retrace for you all the steps that had gone before. You listen for a while, until you decide that you have caught the tenor of the argument; then you put in your oar. Someone answers; you answer him; another comes to your defense; another aligns himself against you, to either the embarrassment or gratification of your opponent, depending on the quality of your ally's assistance. However, the discussion is interminable. The hour grows late, you must depart, with the discussion still vigorously in progress. (110–111)

As this passage describes, every argument you make is connected to other arguments. Every time you write an argument, the way you position yourself will depend on three things: which previously stated arguments you share, which previously stated arguments you want to refute, and what new opinions and supporting information you are going to bring to the conversation. You may, for example, affirm others for raising important issues, but assert that they have not given those issues the thought or emphasis that they deserve. Or you may raise a related issue that has been ignored entirely.

Entering the Conversation

To develop an argument that is akin to a conversation, it is helpful to think of 7 writing as a process of understanding conflicts, the claims others make, and the important questions to ask, not simply as the ability to tell a story that influences readers' ways of looking at the world or to find good reasons to support our own beliefs. The real work of writing a researched argument occurs when you try to figure out the answers to the following:

- What topics have people been talking about?
- What is a relevant problem?
- What kinds of evidence might persuade readers?
- What objections might readers have?
- What is at stake in this argument? (What if things change? What if things stay the same?)

In answering these questions, you will want to read with an eye toward identifying an *issue*, the *situation* that calls for some response in writing, and framing a *question*.

Identify an Issue

An issue is a fundamental tension that exists between two or more conflicting 8 points of view. For example, imagine that I believe that the best approach to educational reform is to change the curriculum in schools. Another person might suggest that we need to address reform by considering social and economic concerns. One way to argue the point is for each writer to consider the goals of education that they share, how to best reach those goals, and the reasons why their approach might be the best one to follow. One part of the issue is (*a*) that some people believe that educational reform should occur through changes in the curriculum; the second part is (*b*) that some people believe that reform should occur at the socioeconomic level. Notice that in defining different parts of an issue, the conflicting claims may not necessarily invalidate each other. In fact, one could argue that reform at the levels of curriculum and socioeconomic change may both be effective measures.

Keep in mind that issues are dynamic and arguments are always evolving. 9 One of my students felt that a book he was reading placed too much emphasis on school-based learning and not enough on real-world experience. He framed the issue in this way: "We are not just educated by concepts and facts that we learn in school. We are educated by the people around us and the environments that we live in every day." In writing his essay, he read a great deal in order to support his claims and did so in light of a position he was writing against: "that education in school is the most important type of education."

Identify the Situation

It is important to frame an issue in the context of some specific situation. Whether curricular changes make sense depends on how people view the problem. One kind of problem that E. D. Hirsch identified in his book *Cultural Literacy* is that students do not have sufficient knowledge of history and literature to communicate well. If that is true in a particular school, perhaps the curriculum might be changed. But there might be other factors involved that call for a different emphasis. Moreover, there are often many different ways to define an issue or frame a question. For example, we might observe that at a local high school, scores on standardized tests have steadily decreased during the past five years. This trend contrasts with scores during the ten years prior to any noticeable decline. Growing out of this situation is the broad question, "What factors have influenced the decline in standardized scores at this school?" Or one could ask this in a different way: "To what extent have scores declined as a result of the curriculum?"

The same principle applies to Anna Quindlen's argument about the homeless in her commentary "No Place Like Home," which illustrates the kinds of connections an author tries to make with readers. Writing her piece as an editorial in the *New York Times*, Quindlen addresses an issue that appears to plague New Yorkers. And yet many people have come to live with the presence of homelessness in New York and other cities. This is the situation that motivates Quindlen to write her editorial: People study the problem of homelessness, yet nothing gets done. Homelessness has become a way of life, a situation that seems to say to observers that officials have declared defeat when it comes to this problem.

Frame a Good Question

A good question can help you think through what you might be interested in writing; it is specific enough to guide inquiry and meets the following criteria:

- It can be answered with the tools you have.
- It conveys a clear idea of who you are answering the question for.
- It is organized around an issue.
- It explores "how," "why," or "whether," and the "extent to which."

A good question, then, is one that can be answered given the access we have to certain kinds of information. The tools we have at hand can be people or other texts. A good question also grows out of an issue, some fundamental tension that you identify within a conversation. Through identifying what is at issue, you should begin to understand for whom it is an issue—who you are answering the question for.

Framing as a Critical Strategy for Writing, Reading, and Doing Research

Thus far, I have presented a conversational model of argument, describing writing   13
as a form of dialogue, with writers responding to the ways others have defined
problems and anticipating possible counterarguments. In this section, I want to
add another element that some people call framing. This is a strategy that can help
you orchestrate different and conflicting voices in advancing your argument.

Framing is a metaphor for describing the lens, or perspective, from which   14
writers present their arguments. Writers want us to see the world in one way as
opposed to another, not unlike the way a photographer manipulates a camera
lens to frame a picture. For example, if you were taking a picture of friends in
front of the football stadium on campus, you would focus on what you would
most like to remember, blurring the images of people in the background. How
you set up the picture, or frame it, might entail using light and shade to make
some images stand out more than others. Writers do the same with language.

For instance, in writing about education in the United States, E. D. Hirsch   15
uses the term *cultural literacy* as a way to understand a problem, in this case
the decline of literacy. To say that there is a decline, Hirsch has to establish
the criteria against which to measure whether some people are literate and
some are not. Hirsch uses *cultural literacy* as a lens through which to discrimi-
nate between those who fulfill his criteria for literacy and those who do not.
He defines *cultural literacy* as possessing certain kinds of information. Not
all educators agree. Some oppose equating literacy and information, describing literacy as an *event* or as a *practice* to argue that literacy is not confined
to acquiring bits of information; instead, the notion of literacy as an *event* or
practice says something about how people use what they know to accomplish
the work of a community. As you can see, any perspective or lens can limit
readers' range of vision: readers will see some things and not others.

In my work as a writer, I have identified four reasons to use framing as a   16
strategy for developing an argument. First, framing encourages you to name
your position, distinguishing the way you think about the world from the ways
others do. Naming also makes what you say memorable through key terms
and theories. Readers may not remember every detail of Hirsch's argument,
but they recall the principle—cultural literacy—around which he organizes his
details. Second, framing forces you to offer both a definition and description
of the principle around which your argument develops. For example, Hirsch
defines *cultural literacy* as "the possession of basic information needed to thrive
in the modern world." By defining your argument, you give readers something
substantive to respond to. Third, framing specifies your argument, enabling
others to respond to your argument and to generate counterarguments that
you will want to engage in the spirit of conversation. Fourth, framing helps you
organize your thoughts, and readers', in the same way that a title for an essay,
a song, or a painting does.

To extend this argument, I would like you to think about framing as a strat-   17
egy of critical inquiry when you read. By critical inquiry, I mean that reading

entails understanding the framing strategies that writers use and using framing concepts in order to shed light on our own ideas or the ideas of others. Here I distinguish *reading as inquiry* from *reading as a search for information*. For example, you might consider your experiences as readers and writers through the lens of Hirsch's conception of cultural literacy. You might recognize that schooling for you was really about accumulating information and that such an approach to education served you well. It is also possible that it has not. Whatever you decide, you may begin to reflect upon your experiences in new ways in developing an argument about what the purpose of education might be.

Alternatively, you might think about your educational experiences through a very different conceptual frame in reading the following excerpt from Richard Rodriguez's memoir, *Hunger of Memory*. In this book, Rodriguez explains the conflicts he experienced as a nonnative speaker of English who desperately sought to enter mainstream culture, even if this meant sacrificing his identity as the son of Mexican immigrants. Notice how Rodriguez recalls his experience as a student through the framing concept of "scholarship boy" that he reads in Richard Hoggart's 1957 book, *The Uses of Literacy*. Using this notion of "scholarship boy" enables him to revisit his experience from a new perspective.

As you read this passage, consider what the notion of "scholarship boy" helps Rodriguez to understand about his life as a student. In turn, what does such a concept help you understand about your own experience as a student?

Motivated to reflect upon his life as a student, Rodriguez comes across Richard Hoggart's book and a description of "the scholarship boy."

His initial response is to identify with Hoggart's description. Notice that Rodriguez says he used what he read to "frame the meaning of my academic success."

For weeks I read, speed-read, books by modern educational theorists, only to find infrequent and slight mention of students like me. . . . Then one day, leafing through Richard Hoggart's *The Uses of Literacy*, I found, in his description of the scholarship boy, myself. For the first time I realized that there were other students like me, and so I was able to frame the meaning of my academic success, its consequent price—the loss.

Hoggart's description is distinguished, at least initially, by deep understanding. What he grasps very well is that the scholarship boy must move between environments, his home and the classroom, which are at cultural extremes, opposed. With his family, the boy has the intense pleasure of intimacy, the family's consolation in feeling public alienation. Lavish emotions texture home life. *Then*, at school, the instruction bids him to trust lonely reason primarily. Immediate needs set the pace of his parents' lives. From his mother and father the boy learns to trust spontaneity and nonrational ways of knowing. *Then*, at school, there is mental calm. Teachers emphasize the value of

The scholarship boy moves between school and home, between moments of spontaneity and reflectiveness.

a reflectiveness that opens a space between thinking and immediate action.

Years of schooling must pass before the boy will be able to sketch the cultural differences in his day as abstractly as this. But he senses those differences early. Perhaps as early as the night he brings home an assignment from school and finds the house too noisy for study.

Rodriguez uses Hoggart's words and idea to advance his own understanding of the problem he identifies in his life: that he was unable to find solace at home and within his working-class roots.

He has to be more and more alone, if he is going to 'get on.' He will have, probably unconsciously, to oppose the ethos of the health, the intense gregariousness of the working-class family group. . . . The boy has to cut himself off mentally, so as to do his homework, as well as he can. (47)

In this excerpt, the idea of framing highlights the fact that other people's 20 texts can serve as tools for helping you say more about your own ideas. If you were writing an essay using Hoggart's term *scholarship boy* as a lens through which to say something about education, you might ask how Hoggart's term illuminates new aspects of another writer's examples or your own—as opposed to asking, "How well does Hoggart's term *scholarship boy* apply to my experience?" (to which you could answer, "Not very well"). Further, you might ask, "To what extent does Hirsch's concept throw a more positive light on what Rodriguez and Hoggart describe?" or "Do my experiences challenge, extend, or complicate such a term as *scholarship boy?*"

Now that you have a sense of how framing works, let's look at an excerpt 21 from a researched argument a first-year composition student wrote, titled "Learning 'American' in Spanish." The assignment to which she responded asked her to do the following:

Draw on your life experiences in developing an argument about education and what it has meant to you in your life. In writing your essay, use two of the four authors (Freire, Hirsch, Ladson-Billings, Pratt) included in this unit to frame your argument or any of the reading you may have done on your own. What key terms, phrases, or ideas from these texts help you teach your readers what you want them to learn from your experiences? How do your experiences extend or complicate your critical frames?

In the past, in responding to this assignment, some people have offered an overview of almost their entire lives, some have focused on a pivotal experience, and others have used descriptions of people who have influenced them. The important thing is that you use those experiences to argue a position: for example, that even the most well-meaning attempts to support students can actually hinder learning. This means going beyond narrating a simple list of experiences, or simply asserting an opinion. Instead you must use—and analyze—your experiences, determining which will most effectively convince your audience that your argument has a solid basis.

As you read the excerpt from this student's essay, ask yourself how the writer uses two framing concepts—"transculturation" and "contact zone"—from Mary Louise Pratt's article "Arts of the Contact Zone." What do these ideas help the writer bring into focus? What experience do these frames help her to name, define, and describe?

The writer has not yet named her framing concept; but notice that the concrete details she gathers here set readers up to expect that she will juxtapose the culture of Guayabal and the Dominican Republic with that of the United States.

Exactly one week after graduating from high school, with thirteen years of American education behind me, I boarded a plane and headed for a Caribbean island. I had fifteen days to spend on an island surrounded with crystal blue waters, white sandy shores, and luxurious ocean resorts. With beaches to play on by day and casinos to play in during the night. I was told that this country was an exciting new tourist destination. My days in the Dominican Republic, however, were not filled with snorkeling lessons and my nights were not spent at the blackjack table. Instead of visiting the ritzy East Coast, I traveled inland to a mountain community with no running water and no electricity. The bus ride to this town, called Guayabal, was long, hot, and uncomfortable. The mountain roads were not paved and the bus had no air-conditioning. Surprisingly, the four-hour ride flew by. I had plenty to think about as my mind raced with thoughts of the next two weeks. I wondered if my host family would be welcoming, if the teenagers would be friendly, and if my work would be hard. I mentally prepared myself for life without the everyday luxuries of a flushing toilet, a hot shower, and a comfortable bed. Because Guayabal was without such basic commodities, I did not expect to see many reminders of home. I thought I was going to leave behind my American ways and immerse myself into another culture. These thoughts filled my head as the bus climbed the rocky hill toward Guayabal. When I finally got off the bus and stepped into the town square, I realized that I had thought wrong: There was no escaping the influence of the American culture.

In a way, Guayabal was an example of what author Mary Louise Pratt refers to as a contact zone. Pratt defines a contact zone as "a place where cultures

The writer names her experience as an example of Pratt's conception of a "contact zone." Further, the writer expands on Pratt's quote by relating it to her own observations. And finally, she uses this frame as a way to organize the narrative (as opposed to ordering her narrative chronologically).

The writer provides concrete evidence to support her point.

The writer offers an illustration of what she experienced, clarifying how this experience is similar to what Pratt describes. Note that Pratt's verb *clash*, used in the definition of *contact zone*, reappears here as part of the author's observation.

The author adds another layer to her description, introducing Pratt's framing concept

meet, clash, and grapple with each other, often in contexts of highly asymmetrical relations of power" (76). In Guayabal, American culture and American consumerism were clashing with the Hispanic and Caribbean culture of the Dominican Republic. The clash came from the Dominicans' desire to be American in every sense, and especially to be consumers of American products. This is nearly impossible for Dominicans to achieve due to their extreme poverty. Their poverty provided the "asymmetrical relation of power" found in contact zones, because it impeded not only the Dominican's ability to be consumers, but also their ability to learn, to work, and to live healthily. The effects of their poverty could be seen in the eyes of the seven-year-old boy who couldn't concentrate in school because all he had to eat the day before was an underripe mango. It could be seen in the brown, leathered hands of the tired old man who was still picking coffee beans at age seventy.

The moment I got off the bus I noticed the clash between the American culture, the Dominican culture, and the community's poverty. It was apparent in the Dominicans' fragmented representation of American pop culture. Everywhere I looked in Guayabal I saw little glimpses of America. I saw Coca-Cola ads painted on raggedy fences. I saw knockoff Tommy Hilfiger shirts. I heard little boys say, "I wanna be like Mike" in their best English, while playing basketball. I listened to merengue house, the American version of the traditional Dominican merengue music. In each instance the Dominicans had adopted an aspect of American culture, but with an added Dominican twist. Pratt calls this transculturation. This term is used to "describe processes whereby members of subordinated or marginal groups select and invent from materials transmitted by a dominant or metropolitan culture" (80). She claims that transculturation is an identifying feature of contact zones. In the contact zone of Guayabal, the marginal group, made up of impoverished Dominicans, selected aspects of the dominant American culture, and invented a unique expression of a culture combining both Dominican and American styles. My most vivid memory of this transculturalization was on a hot afternoon when I of "transculturation." Here again she quotes Pratt in order to bring into focus her own context here. The writer offers another example of transculturation.

heard some children yelling, "Helado! Helado!" or "Ice cream! Ice cream!" I looked outside just in time to see a man ride by on a bicycle, ringing a hand bell and balancing a cooler full of ice cream in the front bicycle basket. The Dominican children eagerly chased after him, just as American children chase after the ice-cream truck.

Although you will notice that the writer does not challenge the framing 22 terms she uses in this paper, it is clear that rather than simply reproducing Pratt's ideas and using her as the Voice of Authority, she incorporates Pratt's understandings to enable her to say more about her own experiences and ideas. Moreover, she uses this frame to advance an argument in order to affect her readers' views of culture. In turn, when she mentions others' ideas, she does so in the service of what she wants to say.

Conclusion: Writing Researched Arguments

I want to conclude this chapter by making a distinction between two differ- 23 ent views of research. On the one hand, research is often taught as a process of collecting information for its own sake. On the other hand, research can also be conceived as the discovery and purposeful use of information. The emphasis here is upon *use* and the ways you can shape information in ways that enable you to enter conversations. To do so, you need to demonstrate to readers that you understand the conversation: what others have said in the past, what the context is, and what you anticipate is the direction this conversation might take. Keep in mind, however, that contexts are neither found nor located. Rather, context, derived from the Latin *contexere*, denotes a process of weaving together. Thus your attempt to understand context is an active process of making connections among the different and conflicting views people present within a conversation. Your version of the context will vary from others' interpretations.

Your attempts to understand a given conversation may prompt you to do 24 research, as will your attempts to define what is at issue. Your reading and inquiry can help you construct a question that is rooted in some issue that is open to dispute. In turn, you need to ask yourself what is at stake for you and your reader other than the fact that you might be interested in educational reform, homelessness, affirmative action, or any other subject. Finally, your research can provide a means for framing an argument in order to move a conversation along and to say something new.

If you see inquiry as a means of entering conversations, then you will under- 25 stand research as a social process. It need not be the tedious task of collecting information for its own sake. Rather, research has the potential to change readers' worldviews and your own.

Works Cited

Bartholomae, David, and Anthony Petrosky. 1996. *Ways of Reading: An Anthology for Writers.* New York: Bedford Books.

Brent, Doug. 1996. "Rogerian Rhetoric: Ethical Growth Through Alternative Forms of Argumentation." In *Argument Revisited; Argument Redefined: Negotiating Meaning in a Composition Classroom*, 73–96. Edited by Barbara Emmel, Paula Resch, and Deborah Tenney. Thousand Oaks, CA: Sage Publications.

Burke, Kenneth. 1941. *The Philosophy of Literary Form.* Berkeley: University of California Press.

Crosswhite, James. 1996. *The Rhetoric of Reason: Writing and the Attractions of Argument.* Madison, WI: University of Wisconsin Press.

Freire, Paulo. 1970. *Pedagogy of the Oppressed.* New York: Continuum.

Hirsch, E. D. 1987. *Cultural Literacy.* New York: Vintage Books.

Ladson-Billings, Gloria. 1994. *The Dreamkeepers: Successful Teachers of African American Children.* New York: Teachers College Press.

Pratt, Mary Louise. "Arts of the Contact Zone." *Profession* 91 (1991): 33–40.

Quindlen, Anna. 1993. "No Place Like Home." In *Thinking Out Loud: On the Personal, the Public, and the Private*, 42–44. New York: Random House.

Rodriguez, Richard. 1983. *Hunger of Memory: The Education of Richard Rodriguez.* New York: Bantam Books.

Acknowledgment

I wish to thank Robert Kachur and April Lidinsky for helping me think through the notions of argument as conversation and framing.

Questions for Discussion and Journaling

1. What role, according to Greene, does reading play in the kind(s) of writing you will be asked to do in college?

2. Take another look at the "oft-quoted passage" by Kenneth Burke in paragraph 6. Why does Greene quote it yet again? Explain the extended metaphor that Burke uses. How would you describe the way it presents writing? What other ideas about writing might it challenge?

3. Explain the concept of *framing*. What metaphor underlies it? Why is the concept important for Greene? What does framing allow a writer to do?

Applying and Exploring Ideas

1. What, if anything, does Greene's article leave you wondering? That is, along with whatever questions he answers, what questions does he *raise* in your mind? Pair up with another student and make a list of your questions.

2. Does Greene's article itself represent a "conversation"? If so, with whom? How does he frame his argument? Would you say, in short, that Greene practices what he preaches in "Argument as Conversation"?

3. Take another look at the passages in which Greene describes Richard Rodriguez's use of "scholarship boy" (para. 19) and a first-year college student's use of "transculturation" and "contact zone" (para. 21) as framing concepts to illuminate their own experiences. Think about some of the new concepts you've recently learned in your other classes; browse your class notes or textbooks to refresh your memory. Try to find a concept that works as a frame that illuminates your own experience, and explain how it works. After completing this exercise, consider: Why do you think Greene considers framing so significant in the process of writing and inquiry? Did you find the exercise useful?

What Is It We Do When We Write Articles Like This One—and How Can We Get Students to Join Us?

MICHAEL KLEINE

Kleine, Michael. "What Is It We Do When We Write Articles Like This One—and How Can We Get Students to Join Us?" *The Writing Instructor* 6 (1987): 151–61. Print.

Framing the Reading

Kleine's article opens with a scene you might recognize yourself: a library full of students gathering information to put into a research paper. Kleine walks in on this scene and wonders, is this what the students' professors do when they engage in research? He realizes that he doesn't really know; at the time Kleine was writing (1987), few studies existed that actually examined the way professional researchers in various disciplines do research and write about it. So he decided to try to find out.

Kleine builds a hypothesis about a **heuristic** (a problem-solving pattern) that he thinks researchers might be using to do their research, and he interviews a number of researchers to test his theory: Are they really doing what he thinks they are? Once he considers the resulting data from the interviews carefully, Kleine draws some conclusions that come back around to the central question: How can we teach students to research more like researchers do?

Read this article both for the research it contains *and* for the challenge it offers you. What could you do with your own research to make it less just a process of collecting existing information and more an attempt to answer real questions that matter to you and others?

Getting Ready to Read

Before you read, do at least one of the following activities:

- Compare with a friend your most recent experiences of writing using sources. How did you find the sources, and how did you use them in your writing?

- Look through your syllabi for courses this semester: How many of them require researched writing? Right now, how do you imagine doing the research for those projects? Make a list of what you think you'll need to do to accomplish the projects.

As you read, consider the following questions to help you focus on particularly important parts of the article:

- What is Kleine's research question—that is, what is he trying to find out?
- Which mode of research sounds more attractive to you, the "hunter" or the "gatherer"?
- Have you done any research or writing like the kinds described by Kleine's colleagues?
- How trustworthy or reliable would you say Kleine's research is? What might make it more reliable?
- How does Kleine arrive at the five 'pedagogical [teaching] implications" at the end of the article?

It was night, but I went to the college library anyhow. I was hoping to find in the library everything I needed to write this article on the research and writing processes of academics. But, perhaps because it was late at night and perhaps because I felt weary and depressed. I experienced a nightmare vision. Even though it was a Sunday, students were everywhere—high school students and college students working in small groups at scattered tables, segregated by age: they were all writing RESEARCH PAPERS. I knew they were writing research papers because they were talking and laughing, but not about their work. In a sense, the work was present, scattered across the various tables, but the work was not the focus. Really, the work was not work, just a jumble of texts: notebooks filled with doodling and copied textual fragments, encyclopedias, a few books. When the students were not talking, they were transcribing sections of encyclopedia text into the text of their own writing, into the notebooks. I knew they were writing research papers because they were not writing at all—merely copying. I imagined, then, that they saw their purpose as one of lifting and transporting textual substance from one location, the

> I knew they were writing research papers because they were not writing at all—merely copying.

library, to another, their teachers' briefcases. Not only were they not writing, but they were not reading: I detected no searching, analyzing, evaluating, synthesizing, selecting, rejecting, etc. No time for such reading in the heated bursts of copying that interrupted the conversations. The horror. The horror.

The nightmare vision deepened when I realized that I knew the high school 2 and college students were writing research papers mainly because I was about to do the same thing myself—only at a more sophisticated level—and I saw myself mirrored back and forth by the student faces; I recognized the transcribing behaviors; I was one of them. And again the vision deepened: I was in that night library just then, watching in horror, but I had been in the same night library many times before. Years ago, I sat at one of the high school tables, copying. Some years later, I sat at one of the college tables, paraphrasing, summarizing, and quoting. Sometimes, still, I go to the night library, building my own authority by using the texts of others, carefully documenting.

I fled from the night library and decided, in the cool darkness outside, that 3 this article would need to answer some questions that had suddenly gained meaning for me: do college-level academics—teachers, I mean, who actually *do* academic writing—really live in the night library? Or do they participate in a rich process of discovery and communication, a process that might have both private and public value?

Research Procedure

I knew that in order to answer my questions I would need to talk to academic 4 writers, probe with still more questions to discover what it is we academics do, and what distinguishes us from each other across the disciplines. In the beginning, however, I was not sure what sort of data, precisely, I wanted to get from colleagues in my own and other departments.

I decided, then, to guide my own research with a process model that two 5 of my colleagues in the English department here (Steve Anderson and Barry Maid) and I developed to teach advanced writing classes. Steve, who teaches technical writing mainly, and Barry and I, who teach upper-level expository writing classes, had all become disenchanted with linear stage models of the writing process: not only do they fail to account for the role of data-gathering and reading in academic and professional writing, but they also, in their linearity, suggest that planning and inventing ("pre-writing") guides a writer through subsequent acts of text production and revision. All three of us agreed that academic and professional writing is a complex, recursive process that includes both research, or data-gathering, and reading from start to finish. Moreover, we agreed that academic and professional writers develop a sense of rhetorical purpose as the process unfolds, not strictly before the acts of researching and writing. Thus writing that includes research of any kind must be seen as being both "strategic" and "heuristic." Not only do researchers/writers need to collect data and write with an established and focused sense of their goal (strategic work), but they also need to accommodate and consider unexpected data and insights that are *discovered* during the process (heuristic work).[1]

Thus, the three of us decided that our own model needed to be bimodal 6 (to account for both the strategic and heuristic aspects of the process), and segmented into stages that are both non-linguistic, or research-based, and linguistic, or writing-based. Thinking of Joseph Campbell's *Primitive Mythology*, we developed a metaphor for the strategic and heuristic modes of work. Campbell distinguishes between primitive "hunters" and "gatherers." A hunter must go into the world with a strong sense of purpose and direction, and employ deliberate strategies and technologies to kill his game, while a gatherer must look about widely, making sense and use of the food he discovers fortuitously. A hunter *finds* what he is looking for; a gatherer *discovers* that which might be of use. We agreed that in our own work we were alternately hunters and gatherers, whether collecting data, reading. or actually writing: clear purpose at times helped guide our work strategically; the surprise of heuristic discovery acted as a force of change and revision.

We then segmented the process into four stages that accorded with our own 7 rough sense of linearity: researchers/writers need to *collect* data; then they need to *sift* the data rhetorically, keeping that which is relevant to audience and purpose, and throwing out that which is irrelevant; then they need to *seek* patterns in the data—and use those patterns to either make or confirm hypotheses; and finally they need to *translate* their findings into writing. Implicit in this segmentation is the notion that research/writing is a form of discourse that includes both epistemology and rhetoric: its ultimate goal is not only the private discovery of new knowledge, but also the effective transmission of that knowledge to a community of interested others. Collecting data and seeking pattern in it seemed to us to be more intrinsically *epistemic*, while sifting the data and translating knowledge into text seemed more intrinsically *rhetorical*.

Although our model (drawn below in eight cells) seems static and linear, we 8 knew, when contriving it, that it was at best a good fiction, an effort to segment and schematize our own intuitive sense of a recursive process that is, at bottom, cognitive and invisible. When we actually began to use the model in our classes to design assignments, teach, and guide work in progress, and found that the quality of student work and writing improved. we decided to maintain the fiction.

In my own research, then, the hunting/gathering model became a kind of 9 heuristic that helped me discover what my colleagues really did when they were at work. I decided to interview a total of eight professors at the University of Arkansas at Little Rock, and attempt to trace and characterize their research/writing routes through the eight-celled model. Because I wanted to understand both my own colleagues in the English department, and others across the disciplines, I carefully chose my subjects: three from my own English department, two from the natural sciences, two from the social sciences, one from history. Although this sampling obviously does not include all instructional

	Collecting	Rhetorical Sifting	Pattern Seeking	Translating
HUNTING				
GATHERING				

Figure 1 A Metaphor for the Research/Writing Process

units (business comes to mind), it does represent significant and diverse areas of academic inquiry—the sciences, social sciences, and humanities.

During the interviews, I asked the subjects to remember a recent academic   10 writing experience. I told them to begin with their initial sense of exigence and then, in a narrative, recall the entire experience, attempting to remember the nature of the research, attitudes about the research, sense of audience and purpose, attempts to organize and interpret data, the writing itself, attitudes about writing, etc. Usually, I let the subjects develop the narrative on their own, but when the narrative seemed superficial or failed to consider some aspect of our model—pattern seeking, say—I'd ask a pointed question: "At some point did you worry about either finding a pattern in the data, or imposing an organizational design on that data?" As the subjects talked, I attempted to code their narrative sequentially into the eight-celled grid. If, as was the case with a creative writer I interviewed, the process began with something other than "collecting" (the creative writer said his process always begins with language itself, with writing) I would enter a "1" into the grid square I deemed appropriate. Thus, with the creative writer, I entered a 1 into the gathering/translating square, and continued to listen and code from there. My assumption was that the narrative would reveal not only the salient aspects of a subject's process, but also a kind of linearity that would help characterize the research/writing process.

Even as I conducted the interviews, I realized the limitations and problems   11 inherent in such a procedure. Obviously, I was not doing composing research: never did I watch the subjects at work, or even interrupt them during a working experience. Quite simply, my procedure was incapable of uncovering what the subjects actually *did* during the process; instead, it helped me, and them, understand their own sense, and memory, of what it was they did when they wrote academically. Moreover, from the beginning I was aware of the highly interpretive nature of my coding: time and time again I heard things that didn't fall neatly into the hunting/gathering model. For instance, many of the subjects talked about the role of reading in their research/writing process, and I was forced to categorize and code their statements about reading out of my own sense of its relationship to the model. In most cases, reading seemed to be a kind of gathering/collecting act, so I coded that act accordingly. This is why I say I used our model heuristically: it helped me make my own subjective sense of what I heard from the subjects.

After the subjects finished recalling their processes, I told them about our   12 model, what I was trying to do, and showed them how I had coded what they had told me. I then asked each one to react to the model itself. Is it comprehensive? Is it capable of characterizing your sense of what you did? Does this sequence, or route, somehow capture your memory of what you did? Can you think of problems with the coding and my own attempt to trace the sequence of your work? In all cases, I found the postnarrative interview to be the most useful aspect of the procedure, as I'll explain later.

Despite the limitations of my own collecting procedure, I think that the inter-   13 views helped me gain at least a superficial understanding of what we academics *think* we do when we research and write. The news I will report next is, from my own perspective, happy and even exciting.

Findings

From the beginning of my research on. I was astounded by my subjects' eager- 14
ness to talk about their work. Each of the eight had not only recently done research and writing, but wanted to talk about the work at length. I expected to encounter some resistance and defensiveness, but the subjects seemed delighted by both my interest in them and the nature of my project once I explained it. In fact, now that the interviews are over, the subjects still return to me: "I just remembered something else," they will say, and away we go: still another narrative about some aspect of their experience. At first when these "return visits" occurred, I attempted to recode the forms, but now I have given up. The more the subjects talk to me, the more I realize the depth of what they have to tell me about their work. In all eight cases, then, the coding form was not capable of capturing the complexity of what the subjects did, their ability to recall their experiences, or their enthusiasm about their work.

In all eight cases, too, I discovered other shared recollections of academic 15
writing that I found heartening. All of the subjects recalled writing out of inter-est, not because of some external compulsion. Never did a subject say, "I wrote because I had to get tenure" or "My chairman made me do it." The exigence, in all cases, was personal interest and dissonance: some problem, some ques-tion, some contradiction, some opposition, some surprise was worth exploring, thinking about, writing about. The remembered motivation to write academi-cally was internal, not externally imposed.

Moreover, all eight recalled starting points for their work that evinced their 16
involvement in genuine research communities. The starting points included conversations with peers, reading the work of a peer, listening to a paper by a peer, and the use of language with a community of careful readers in mind. Never did a subject remember writing for an authority figure, a critic, or a subordinate: always, the subjects gestured at a concerned community of peers and found starting points within the ongoing discourse of such a community. Typical memories of starting points went like this: "I was reading an interesting book by . . ." or "I was talking to another person in my department . . ." or "I was at a conference and I heard . . ."

Finally, all eight subjects recalled complex academic processes and talked 17
about both the sloppiness and richness of their processes: they remembered struggling with both the research and the writing. In terms of "hunting" and "gathering," they remembered moving freely and flexibly between strategic hunting and heuristic gathering, and described moments of purposeful control mixed with moments of dissonance, discovery, and revision of both plan and material. Tom K., the historian, characterized the entire group's memory of the research/writing struggle: "As I see it, it's a dialectical process. I go back and forth between *all* of the cells in your model, working toward a final sense of things and, of course, the book I am writing." In fact, the word "process" is not

one that I have imposed upon this interpretation of what I heard: the subjects themselves freely used the word in their own narratives; they recalled rethinking and revising their work.

There were, of course, some pronounced differences across the disciplines, 18 and I will now attempt to characterize those differences according to patterns I myself found while in a gathering mode. What follows is, of course, my personal interpretation of the narrative data.

The scientists (a physicist and a biologist), the social scientists (a psycholo- 19 gist and a communications researcher), and one member of the English department (a composition theorist) remembered far more about the research process itself—about procedures, methodology, empirical data-gathering, etc.—than they did about the rhetorical implications of their work. On the other hand, the Americanist and creative writer in my own department, and the historian, talked quite a bit about audience and purpose, about problems of establishing authority, about the rhetorical dimension of their thinking and writing. Another way of saying this is: the subjects who were located in the sciences and social sciences recalled an epistemic orientation, and methods of inquiring relatively divorced from rhetorical implications; the subjects in the humanities recalled a rhetorical orientation, where the knowledge, the attitudes, beliefs, and values of the audience seriously affected their own inquiry and writing. Interestingly, though, on a continuum between epistemic and rhetorical polarities, the scientists talked more about audience than did the social scientists. For some reason, the two social scientists—the communications researcher and the psychologist—seemed more concerned with methodology, less with rhetoric and writing itself as a process of discovery, than the natural scientists.

Too, the division between the sciences and social sciences, and the humani- 20 ties, was reflected in the focus of the work. Subjects in the humanities recalled research that was "text-centered," that is, work that involved their own interaction, through reading and writing, with other texts. Among the scientists and social scientists, research was recalled more as a long process of gathering data and subjecting that data to established procedures of quantitative analysis ("bench work," the biologist called it). Perhaps this division explains differences in attitudes about research and writing. The scientists and social scientists tended to regard research as a process of observing and quantifying that is prior to writing. Research itself is what leads to understanding, and the purpose of writing is, mainly, to clearly communicate the results of that research to the appropriate community. The subjects in the humanities tended to view writing and reading as activities inseparable from the research process: in a sense, writing and reading *are* the research. The creative writer, for instance, says that his process always begins with writing itself, though it includes reading. And while the Americanist and the historian talked about reading first, all three remembered more interaction between research and writing throughout the total experience than did the other five.

Perhaps because they view research as being prior to writing, and as an 21 activity that needs to be performed and considered by itself, the scientists and social scientists tended to talk about writing formats instead of the strategic organization of information in a rhetorical context. Thus, the physicist, after selecting a particular journal for his article, knew that he would need to "first review the literature, then state the problem, then discuss his observational and quantitative procedure, then present the results, and finally discuss those results." The Americanist, on the other hand, tended to view organization as a process of understanding what her audience already knew, what they needed to know, and then revised her own text accordingly.

If the individual narratives and coding forms alone were used to develop a [22] theory of academic writing across the curriculum, the disciplines considered might be located on James Kinneavy's discourse triangulation. In *A Theory of Discourse*, Kinneavy proposes that a discourse might be classified according to its purpose, and by the element of the total discourse situation that it emphasizes. Hence, discourse that emphasizes the encoder is "expressive"; discourse that emphasizes the decoder is "persuasive"; discourse that emphasizes reality, or the world, is "referential"; and discourse that emphasizes the signal, or language itself, is "literary."

During each interview, however, I found the postnarrative discussion to be [23] more useful than the narrative itself. When I attempted to discuss my own interpretations of what I was hearing, and present my perceptions of patterns across the disciplines, the subjects were quick to offer some important reservations. For instance, when I told the scientists that I found their work more epistemic (from Kinneavy's perspective, "referential") than rhetorical, they strongly asserted that underlying their research was a sense of the general knowledge of their own research community. In a way, then, all of their work was done within a context of potential readers and was from the beginning "rhetorical." Those in the humanities reminded me that while their work might be rhetorical in nature (ultimately "persuasive"), they still struggled with notions like "validity," with an effort to gather factual content objectively, epistemically. It may well be the case, then, that all academic research is both epistemic and rhetorical.

Moreover, the actual writing that academics do may well be both expressive [24] and transactional, a form of effective communication and a mode of learning.[2] When I asked if the research-before-writing approach of the scientists led to a kind of direct and strategic translating, or writing, the physicist told me that he uses writing expressively, instrumentally, to help him understand what he is trying to say. So even though he postpones the writing, it is, for him both heuristic and strategic—both a mode of learning and a form for communicating what he has learned. Thus, the function of academic writing cannot be regarded as only one of clearly transmitting knowledge (hunting mode). Nor can it be regarded as only one of discovering knowledge (gathering mode): it is too rich, when it is done well and sincerely, to categorize—even by discipline.

The subjects also voiced some reservation about my effort to code the narratives. Though they all agreed that the hunting/gathering model is capable of elegantly explaining the sorts of things academic writers do, they were unanimous in questioning a rigid effort to categorize and code: when I showed the psychologist my effort to code her narrative, she said, "Yes, sort of. But I think that I go [25] back and forth between the cells even more than the coding shows. And, during different projects, I might take different routes." In short, then, the postnarrative discussion led me, at last, to a relatively simple truth: among academics, the research/writing process is recursive, too complicated to code, and incredibly rich; although there might be some trends in different disciplines, an individual academic writer needs to be characterized independently, and probably characterized differently during different research and writing occasions.

I am left, at last, with a strange contradiction: my subjects were all signifi- 26 cantly alike—and significantly different. Alike in that they worked out of interest and sense of community. Different in that they recalled processes that varied not only according to discipline, but also according to personality and task.

Pedagogical Implications

My interviews across the disciplines did indeed help me answer my own 27 questions, and they convinced me that academic writing is worth doing and teaching. For me, there are strong implications now for both writing-across-the-curriculum projects and the teaching of academic writing.

1. A hunting/gathering model of the research-writing process, while it has categorical limitations, has tremendous potential as a heuristic. Those who are interested in conducting writing-across-the-curriculum workshops might do well to use the model as I have used it: to help academics remember, and recall, what it is they do, and value, as they research and write. Not only does such self-examination help the content teacher remember what academic writing really is (certainly *not* the research paper as it is usually taught), but it also provides the groundwork for developing a university-wide pedagogy: if we can better understand what it is that we do when we inquire and write, then we might be capable of leading our students away from the night library.

2. All of us who teach academic writing need to work on building, in our classes, genuine research communities. This would involve downplaying our own teacher-as-audience roles, and instead encouraging writing to and for peers. The classroom would become a place of researching, reading, writing, and talking, and its focus would become an area of common investigation. Thus, the starting point for research and writing might be a shared question, a problem, a gap in the collective knowledge of the community, preferably student-generated, not teacher-assigned.

   Such restructuring of a writing class, whether it be the second semester of freshman composition or a writing course in a specified content area, implies not just a new set of assumptions about the research paper and how to teach it, but a new set of assumptions about education itself. Students would be researching and writing to broaden their own knowledge and the knowledge of their own community rather than to transcribe the knowledge already generated by academicians (and teachers) in external communities.

3. We need to promote genuine reading in our classrooms and allow for research that might not involve the library alone. Rather than suggesting definite research procedures, we need to encourage students to select, intelligently and critically, research procedures relevant to their own questions and problems. We need to help them see that academic research, reading, and writing is a constructive, personal process—one worth sharing with others.

4. We need to invite students to participate in a range of research tasks— some that would be more characteristic of the natural and social sciences, some more characteristic of the humanities. By moving toward writing across the curriculum, we could extend the range of academic writing invitations and experiences. If students wrote in different disciplines, and if content-area teachers modeled genuine research and writing, and invited their students to do what they really do, then students would participate in both epistemology and rhetoric. Their ability to think would be enhanced by different approaches to knowledge and its construction; their rhetorical competency would be enhanced because they would write for a wide range of academic peer audiences.

5. Finally, we need to help students who are already writing across the curriculum enrich their own processes. In my research, I discovered that academic writers in a variety of disciplines see their own writing as not just a vehicle for clear communication, but as a learning process as well. Students need to learn to both hunt and gather—to work with a sense of focus and purpose, but to change direction and accommodate new data when they encounter the unexpected—and they need to develop the sort of flexibility and resourcefulness I discovered among my colleagues: perhaps it is the *absence of a direct and linear route* through the research/ writing process that is most characteristic of solid, and honest, work.

As I conclude my writing here, I realize that my own work was influenced by   28
what I heard from others. Indeed, the scientists and social scientists rubbed off on me: like them, I did some research first, and only then began to write. Like them, I attempted to rely more on what I did, empirically, than on what I read. Like them, I even divided this article up into a procedures/results/implications format. But at some point during my own academic writing process I talked to my friend, the creative writer, and told him what was happening to me. He said he thought it was very unfortunate that writing was not a part of my process from start to finish: "Research *is* writing," he said, meaning, I think, that there is no such thing as knowledge that is dissociated from discourse. I learned from what he said—or from what I thought he meant. When I did begin to draft and rewrite, I decided to at least give the writing a chance to teach me something new, to change my sense of the research I had done. So I wrote at first in the "gathering mode," expressively, even though I used a transactional and well-defined format and later revised extensively. The effort to "write to learn" convinced me anew that writing brings with it, always, new knowledge, change, growth. The physicist had told me the same thing, really, when he said

that no matter how objective his research, the process of writing always gave him a slightly different view of what he had discovered empirically.

In the end, I am left with this: my colleagues are men and women who   29
seriously inquire and who write both to learn and to share their knowledge. I learned a good deal from them, and I think all of us, across the disciplines, have much to learn from one another. What we do when we write academically can be enriched by learning what others do, by expanding our discourse. I believe, now, that the next step for me, and for my colleagues, is to invite our students to join in what we really do when we write articles like this one.

Notes

1. Throughout this article I will associate the words (and concepts) "discovery" and "change" with the kind of research and writing I am here calling "heuristic" and will later describe as a "gathering" activity. My thinking grows from Young, Becker, and Pike's development of a new rhetoric, one that emphasizes epistemology and human cooperation more than effective (and strategic) persuasion.
2. Those familiar with the work of James Britton and Janet Emig will recognize the language I am using here. For Britton, a writer's development can be characterized as a movement from private "expression" to public "transaction." Expressive writing, though it may not evince a writer's awareness of a public audience and an effort to strategically meet that audience's needs, not only drives that writing which *is* transactional, but may result in the kind of writing that surprises the writer herself, and lead to discovery. Janet Emig, though she does not use Britton's language, seems to be suggesting the same thing: writing can be regarded as not only a form of communication, but also as an instrument with which to construct new knowledge, as a "mode of learning."

Works Cited

Britton, James, et al. *The Development of Writing Abilities* (11–18). London: Schools Council Project, 1975. Print.

Campbell, Joseph. *Primitive Mythology*. New York: Penguin, 1976. Print.

Emig, Janet. "Writing as a Mode of Learning." *College Composition and Communication* 28.2 (1977): 122–28. Print.

Kinneavy, James. *A Theory of Discourse*. Englewood Cliffs, NJ: Prentice-Hall, 1971. Print.

Young, Richard, Alton Becker, and Kenneth Pike. *Rhetoric: Discovery and Change*. New York: Harcourt, Brace, and World, 1970. Print.

Questions for Discussion and Journaling

1. How does what Kleine is talking about line up with your own experiences? Does it sound like he's describing the way you write and research, or not?

2. At some moments, Kleine's article reads almost like a story. Does it surprise you that a research article could be written as a narrative? Have you ever tried writing research in this fashion?

3. How big a role do sources play in the research of the professionals Kleine interviews? What role have they played in your past research efforts? How can you explain the differences?

4. What would change about how you do research if you did what Kleine talks about?

Applying and Exploring Ideas

1. Kleine gathers data by interviewing h s research participants. What other methods of gathering data are you aware of? Create a list and compare it with two other students' lists; add to yours, if appropriate. Keep your list and see how many of these methods show up in other chapters in this reader.

2. If Kleine's study showed up on national news or in major newspapers, what would be the news? Write the headline and the first paragraph of that imaginary news story, and then explain why you wrote it the way you did.

3. What, if anything, does Kleine's research leave you wondering? That is, along with whatever questions he answers, what questions does he *raise* in your mind? Pair up with another student and make a list of your questions.

1 | Texts/Constructs: How Do Readers Read and Writers Write?

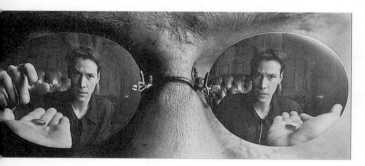

Do you remember the movie *The Matrix*? In that movie, people did not realize they were living in a fantasy until they took a red pill that enabled them to see the world as it was. Well, taken together, the articles you'll read in this chapter are kind of like that red pill. The authors of the articles suggest that many of the things we believe about reading and writing aren't exactly right. According to these authors, we walk around with a lot of misconceptions about writing, reading, and the ways we interact with texts generally, and our lives as readers and writers would make a lot more sense if we could see these misconceptions for what they are.

Here are some conceptions (ideas) about writing that the "red pills" in this chapter encourage you to rethink:

- The rules of writing are universal and do not change based on the situation.
- Writing can convey facts without "spin" and thus transmit information without changing it.
- Texts inherently "mean" something—the same "something"—regardless of who's reading them.
- You can write without putting yourself in your text—that is, you can write "impersonally."
- It is easy to distinguish which ideas are a writer's own and which they "borrowed" from others, and failing to make this distinction is plain and simple plagiarism.

- "Writing" is mostly about getting the grammar right, and good writing is therefore about a grasp of simple and basic rules of English syntax.
- Grammar rules are fixed, inviolable, and not subject to interpretation or disagreement—and there is one authoritative set of such rules.

The readings in this chapter challenge these ideas; they suggest that the reality is much more complicated when we actually pay close attention to how texts work and what readers and writers are doing when they engage with them.

A key word we want you to keep in mind for this chapter is **construct**. One common way to describe writing is as a *construction*—that is, writers *construct* texts by using words and images to develop ideas. The writers you'll read in this chapter demonstrate and discuss various aspects of the construction of texts. In "All Writing Is Autobiography," for example, Donald Murray argues that who we are bleeds into our texts even if we strive to write "objectively" or "factually." In "Rhetorical Reading Strategies and the Construction of Meaning," Christina Haas and Linda Flower demonstrate that, like writing, the act of reading also requires us to construct meaning: Different readers bring different experiences and understandings to texts and, as a result, they construct different meanings from them.

But *construct* is not only a verb (conSTRUCT); it is also a noun (CONstruct). *Constructs* are mental frameworks that people build in order to make sense of the world around them. One of the key features of an effective construct is that it quickly begins to seem "natural" or inevitable, rather than made-up. The world people saw in *The Matrix* was a construct. Many of the things we believe about writing are constructs, too—and that's why we are prescribing the "red pill" that is this chapter: so that you can see constructs *as* constructs instead of assuming them to be "truth" or "reality."

We encounter several constructs in this chapter. One is the notion of **plagiarism**, which governs how people think about building new texts out of existing ones. Our thinking about plagiarism is a set of ideas we've built up over time rather than the *only* way of thinking about correct ways of using source material. For example, in many schools in the United States, students are taught always to write independently, never to use their previous writing in a subsequent paper, and never to use other students' work in their own papers. In many U.S. workplaces, however, texts are often written collaboratively, and they are frequently based on texts written previously by other employees, who may receive little or no credit. In this chapter, James Porter discusses questions of **authorship** and **originality** that are raised by such seeming contradictions between our culture's notion of writing as the work of unassisted writers creating original ideas and the ways in which most writers actually work.

Another construct we encounter in this chapter is the idea of **error**—the popular idea that the quality of writing is mostly dependent on the absence of grammatical and mechanical mistakes in a text. In "The Phenomenology of Error," Joseph Williams explores the notion that this concept of error is not natural or inevitable—rather, it's a concept that was at some point created by people with a particular set of values.

Not all constructs are negative misconceptions. Several readings in this chapter touch on a construct we call **rhetoric**. *Rhetoric* is typically used to describe both the language speakers and writers (or **rhetors**) use to communicate and get things done, and the study of that language. **Rhetorical** theory helps us understand how readers interpret texts, how rhetors construct texts persuasively, how readers and writers construct meaning from texts, and how the rules for writing vary with writers' and readers' situations and needs. The ideas from rhetorical theory that you'll encounter in this chapter contradict nearly all the simple myths about how writing works, and so rhetoric becomes an important construct for you to carry with you through the rest of the book as you explore and research writing in your world.

Perhaps the most important related term you will encounter is **rhetorical situation**. In this chapter, Keith Grant-Davie calls an activity, an event, or a situation *rhetorical* when it's shaped by language or communication that tries to get people to *do* something, whether that something is to change their minds or to change something in the world around them. According to this definition, an advertisement can be understood as rhetorical, as can a political speech, a protest in front of City Hall, an intervention, or a conversation between a college counselor and a student. A rhetorical situation includes the entire **context** for the activity, event, or situation—the motivating factors for speaking or writing, as well as the people, places, and things involved. All of these factors impact what people do, what they say, what they believe, and how their rhetoric looks and sounds.

Chapter Goals

- To understand how writers construct texts persuasively (or not)
- To understand how readers construct meaning(s) from texts
- To understand what it means to say that knowledge is *constructed*
- To understand plagiarism and error as constructs
- To understand the concept of the *rhetorical situation* and be able to apply it to writing and reading situations

The Phenomenology of Error

JOSEPH M. WILLIAMS

Williams, Joseph M. "The Phenomenology of Error." *College Composition and Communication* 32.2 (1981): 152–68. Print.

Framing the Reading

Be forewarned: Your teacher will know f you do not read beyond the first three pages of Joseph Williams's "The Phenomenology of Error." Once you reach the end, you'll understand why.

Error, in composition theory, is a technical term, referring to a specific set of mistakes that writers make with syntax and the mechanics and conventions of writing. Errors include using *I* where you should use *me*, spelling words incorrectly, and ending a sentence with a comma instead of a period. If you follow baseball, you might think of errors in writing just as you do errors n baseball, as mistakes in a standard, almost automatic procedure that most people usually get right.

The interesting thing about error in writing is that many people believe the things you can make errors on—grammar, punctuation, spelling—are *all that writing is*. They think that if they learn grammar, punctuation, and spelling, they've learned to write. Compare that to baseball: nobody thinks you know everything you need to know about how to play baseball just because you can catch the ball and throw it to the right base to tag a runner out. Just as there's a lot more to the game of baseball than catching and throwing, there's a lot more to the game of writing than avoiding grammar, punctuation, and spelling errors.

Of course, you would lose a lot of baseball games if you made a lot of errors, and the same is true of writing: numerous errors in grammar, punctuation, and spelling can really drag down a piece of writing. That explains why so much of your writing instruction in earlier levels of school tried to help you eliminate errors from your writing. But did you ever wish that teachers would have paid a little more attention to what you were trying to say and a little less attention to how you messed up in getting it said? Did you ever feel like maybe they cared a little *too* much about the errors and not nearly enough about everything else there was to care about in your writing? Did you ever feel the difference between having your writing *read* and having it *corrected*? Williams has certainly felt this way, as you will see from his introduction.

In the end, Williams concludes that error is a **construct**, a set of ideas woven together over time until they seem inevitable, the only way of thinking about a problem, when in fact they are not at all inevitable but simply choices in thinking that are *constructed* to look unavoidable. The concept of error in writing that most people hold is one that people have become accustomed to, but it is *not* one that is necessarily universally "true."

Getting Ready to Read

Before you read, do at least one of the following activities:

- Make a list of the errors you most commonly make in your writing. What makes avoiding them difficult for you—why do you still make them even though you know about them?
- Grab your writing or grammar handbook and see if it has a list of "most common errors." See if you can find another handbook, or do a search online, and compare the lists. How similar are they?
- Think about what your writing teacher has said (or not said) so far in your class about error. What do you think his or her attitude is toward error?

As you read, consider the following questions:

- What does Williams mean by the *phenomenology* of error? Do you think a more straightforward title would have been more effective?
- Judging from his introduction, what would you say are the *research problem* and *question* that Williams means to address?
- If an idea we take for granted is in fact a construct, that means we can and should revise it if we come up with a better idea. What is Williams's "better idea"? What do you think of it?

I am often puzzled by what we call errors of grammar and usage, errors 1
such as *different than, between you and I,* a *which* for a *that,* and so on. I am puzzled by what motive could underlie the unusual ferocity which an *irregardless* or a *hopefully* or a singular *media* can elicit. In his second edition of *On Writing Well* (New York, 1980), for example, William Zinsser, an otherwise amiable man I'm sure, uses, and quotes not disapprovingly, words like *detestable vulgarity* (p. 43), *garbage* (p. 44), *atrocity* (p. 46), *horrible* (p. 48); *oaf* (p. 42), *idiot* (p. 43), and *simple illiteracy* (p. 46), to comment on usages like *OK, hopefully,* the affix *-wise,* and *myself* in *He invited Mary and myself to dinner.*

The last thing I want to seem is sanctimonious. But as I am sure Zinsser 2
would agree, what happens in Cambodia and Afghanistan could more reasonably be called horrible atrocities. The likes of Idi Amin qualify as legitimate oafs.

Idiots we have more than enough of in our state institutions. And while simply illiteracy is the condition of billions, it does not characterize those who use *disinterested* in its original sense.[1]

I am puzzled why some errors should excite this seeming fury while others, not obviously different in kind, seem to excite only moderate disapproval. And I am puzzled why some of us can regard any particular item as a more or less serious error, while others, equally perceptive, and acknowledging that the same item may in some sense be an "error," seem to invest in their observation no emotion at all.

> I am puzzled why some errors should excite this seeming fury while others, not obviously different in kind, seem to excite only moderate disapproval.

3

At first glance, we ought to be able to explain some of these anomolies by subsuming errors of grammar and usage in a more general account of defective social behavior, the sort of account constructed so brilliantly by Erving Goffman.[2] But errors of social behavior differ from errors of "good usage": Social errors that excite feelings commensurate with judgments like "horrible," "atrocious," "oaf(ish)," and "detestable" are usually errors that grossly violate our personal space: We break wind at a dinner party and then vomit on the person next to us. We spill coffee in their lap, then step on a toe when we get up to apologize. It's the Inspector Clouseau routine. Or the error metaphorically violates psychic space: We utter an inappropriate obscenity, mention our painful hemorrhoids, tell a racist joke, and snigger at the fat woman across the table who turns out to be our hostess. Because all of these actions crudely violate one's personal space we are justified in calling them "oafish"; all of them require that we apologize, or at least offer an excuse.

This way of thinking about social error turns our attention from error as a discrete entity, frozen at the moment of its commission, to error as part of a flawed transaction, originating in ignorance or incompetence or accident, manifesting itself as an invasion of another's personal space, eliciting a judgment ranging from silent disapproval to "atrocious" and "horrible," and requiring either an explicit "I'm sorry" and correction, or a simple acknowledgment and a tacit agreement not to do it again.[3]

To address errors of grammar and usage in this way, it is also necessary to shift our attention from error treated strictly as an isolated item on a page, to error perceived as a flawed verbal transaction between a writer and a reader. When we do this, the matter of error turns less on a handbook definition than on the reader's response, because it is that response—"detestable," "horrible"—that defines the seriousness of the error and its expected amendment.

But if we do compare serious nonlinguistic gaffes to errors of usage, how can we not be puzzled over why so much heat is invested in condemning a violation whose consequence impinges not at all on our personal space? The language some use to condemn linguistic error seems far more intense than the language they use to describe more consequential social errors—a hard bump on the arm, for example—that require a sincere but not especially effusive apology.

But no matter how "atrocious" or "horrible" or "illiterate" we think an error like *irregardless* or a *like* for an *as* might be, it does not jolt my ear in the same way an elbow might; a *between you and I* does not offend me, at least not in the ordinary sense of offend. Moreover, unlike social errors, linguistic errors do not ordinarily require that we apologize for them.[4] When we make *media* a singular or dangle a participle, and are then made aware of our mistake, we are expected to acknowledge the error, and, if we have the opportunity, to amend it. But I don't think that we are expected to say, "Oh, I'm sorry!" The objective consequences of the error simply do not equal those of an atrocity, or even of clumsiness.

It may be that to fully account for the contempt that some errors of usage 8 arouse, we will have to understand better than we do the relationship between language, order, and those deep psychic forces that perceived linguistic violations seem to arouse in otherwise amiable people.[5] But if we cannot yet fully account for the psychological source of those feelings, or why they are so intense, we should be able to account better than we do for the variety of responses that different "errors" elicit. It is a subject that should be susceptible to research. And indeed, one kind of research in this area has a long tradition: In this century, at least five major surveys of English usage have been conducted to determine how respondents feel about various matters of usage. Sterling Leonard, Albert Marckwardt, Raymond Crisp, the Institute of Education English Research Group at the University of Newcastle upon Tyne, and the *American Heritage Dictionary* have questioned hundreds of teachers and editors and writers and scholars about their attitudes toward matters of usage ranging from *which* referring to a whole clause to split infinitives to *enthuse* as a verb.[6]

The trouble with this kind of research, though, with asking people whether 9 they think *finalize* is or is not good usage, is that they are likely to answer. As William Labov and others have demonstrated,[7] we are not always our own best informants about our habits of speech. Indeed, we are likely to give answers that misrepresent our talking and writing, usually in the direction of more rather than less conservative values. Thus when the editors of the *American Heritage Dictionary* asks its Usage Panel to decide the acceptability of *impact* as a verb, we can predict how they will react: Merely by being asked, it becomes manifest to them that they have been invested with an institutional responsibility that will require them to judge usage by the standards they think they are supposed to uphold. So we cannot be surprised that when asked, Zinsser rejects *impact* as a verb, despite the fact that *impact* has been used as a verb at least since 1601.

The problem is self-evident: Since we can ask an indefinite number of ques- 10 tions about an indefinite number of items of usage, we can, merely by asking, accumulate an indefinite number of errors, simply because whoever we ask will feel compelled to answer. So while it may seem useful for us to ask one another whether we think X is an error, we have to be skeptical about our answers, because we will invariably end up with more errors than we began with, certainly more than we ever feel on our nerves when we read in the ways we ordinarily do.

In fact, it is this unreflective feeling on the nerves in our ordinary reading 11
that interests me the most, the way we respond—or not—to error when we
do not make error a part of our conscious field of attention. It is the difference between reading for typographical errors and reading for content. When
we read for typos, letters constitute the field of attention; content becomes
virtually inaccessible. When we read for content, semantic structures constitute the field of attention; letters—for the most part—recede from our consciousness.

I became curious about this kind of perception three years ago when I was 12
consulting with a government agency that had been using English teachers to
edit reports but was not sure they were getting their money's worth. When I
asked to see some samples of editing by their consultants, I found that one
very common notation was "faulty parallelism" at spots that only by the most
conservative interpretation could be judged faulty. I asked the person who had
hired me whether faulty parallelism was a problem in his staff's ability to write
clearly enough to be understood quickly, but with enough authority to be taken
seriously, He replied, "If the teacher says so."

Now I was a little taken aback by this response, because it seemed to me 13
that one ought not have to appeal to a teacher to decide whether something
like faulty parallelism was a real problem in communication. The places where
faulty parallelism occurred should have been at least felt as problems, if not
recognized as a felt difficulty whose specific source was faulty parallelism.

About a year later, as I sat listening to a paper describing some matters of 14
error analysis in evaluating compositions, the same thing happened. When I
looked at examples of some of the errors, sentences containing alleged dangling participles, faulty parallelism, vague pronoun reference, and a few other
items,[8] I was struck by the fact that, at least in some of the examples, I saw
some infelicity, but no out-and-out grammatical error. When I asked the person
who had done the research whether these examples were typical of errors she
looked for to measure the results of extensive training in sentence combining, I
was told that the definition of error had been taken from a popular handbook,
on the assumption, I guess, that that answered the question.

About a year ago, it happened again, when a publisher and I began circulat- 15
ing a manuscript that in a peripheral way deals with some of the errors I've
mentioned here, suggesting that some errors are less serious than others. With
one exception, the reviewers, all teachers at universities, agreed that an intelligent treatment of error would be useful, and that this manuscript was at least
in the ballpark. But almost every reader took exception to one item of usage
that they thought I had been too soft on, that I should have unequivocally condemned as a violation of good usage. Unfortunately, each of them mentioned
a different item.

Well, it is all very puzzling: Great variation in our definition of error, great 16
variation in our emotional investment in defining and condeming error, great
variation in the perceived seriousness of individual errors. The categories of
error all seem like they should be yes-no, but the feelings associated with the
categories seem much more complex.

If we think about these responses for a moment we can identify one source   17
of the problem: We were all locating error in very different places. For all of
us, obviously enough, error is in the essay, on the page, because that is where
it physically exists. But of course, to be in the essay, it first has to be in the student. But before that, it has to be listed in a book somewhere. And before that
in the mind of the writer of the handbook. And finally, a form of the error has
to be in the teacher who resonated—or not—to the error on the page on the
basis of the error listed in the handbook.

This way of thinking about error locates error in two different physical   18
locations (the student's paper and the grammarian's handbook) and in three
different experiences: the experience of the writer who creates the error; in the
experience of the teacher who catches it; and in the mind of the grammarian—
the E. B. White or Jacques Barzun or H. W. Fowler—who proposes it. Because
error seems to exist in so many places, we should not be surprised that we do
not agree among ourselves about how to identify it, or that we do not respond
to the same error uniformly.

But we might be surprised—and perhaps instructed—by those cases where   19
the two places occur in texts by the same author—and where all three experiences reside in the same person. It is, in fact, these cases that I would like to
examine for a moment, because they raise such interesting questions about the
experience of error.

For example, E. B. White presumably believed what he (and Strunk) said in   20
Elements of Style (New York, 1979) about faulty parallelism and *which* vs. *that*:

> Express coordinate ideas in similar form. This principle, that of parallel con-
> struction, requires that expressions similar in content and function be outwardly
> similar. (p. 26)

> *That, which. That* is the defining or restrictive pronoun, *which* the non-defining
> or non-restrictive . . . The careful writer . . . removes the defining *whiches,* and by
> so doing improves his work. (p. 59)

Yet in the last paragraph of "Death of a Pig," [9] White has two faulty parallelisms, and according to his rules, an incorrect *which:*

> . . . the premature expiration of a pig is, I soon discovered, a departure which
> the community marks solemnly on its calendar . . . I have written this account
> in penitence and in grief, as a man who failed to raise his pig, and to explain
> my deviation from the classic course of so many raised pigs. The grave in
> the woods is unmarked, but Fred can direct the mourner to it unerringly and
> with immense good will, and I know he and I shall often revisit it, singly and
> together, . . .

Now I want to be clear: I am not at all interested in the trivial fact that   21
E. B. White violated one or two of his own trivial rules. That would be a
trivial observation. We could simply say that he miswrote in the same way he
might have mistyped and thereby committed a typographical error. Nor at the
moment am I interested in the particular problem of parallelism, or of *which*

vs. *that,* any more than I would be interested in the particular typo. What I am interested in is the fact that no one, E. B. White least of all, seemed to notice that E. B. White had made an error. What I'm interested in here is the noticing or the not noticing by the same person who stipulates what should be noticed, and why anyone would surely have noticed if White had written,

> I knows me and him will often revisit it, . . .

Of course, it may be that I am stretching things just a bit far to point out   22
a trivial error of usage in one publication on the basis of a rule asserted in another. But this next example is one in which the two co-exist between the same covers:

> *Were* (sing.) is, then, a recognizable subjunctive, & applicable not to past facts, but to present or future non-facts. (p. 576)

> Another suffix that is not a living one, but is sometimes treated as if it was, is *-al* . . . (p. 242)

> H. W. Fowler. *A Dictionary of Modern English Usage.* Oxford, 1957.

Now again, Fowler may have just made a slip here; when he read these entries, certainly at widely separate intervals, the *was* in the second just slipped by. And yet how many others have also read that passage, and also never noticed?

The next example may be a bit more instructive. Here, the rule is asserted in   23
the middle of one page:

> In conclusion, I recommend using *that* with defining clauses except when stylistic reasons interpose. Quite often, not a mere pair of *that's* but a threesome or foursome, including the demonstrative *that,* will come in the same sentence and justify *which* to all writers with an ear. (p. 68)

and violated at the top of the next:

> Next is a typical situation which a practiced writer corrects for style virtually by reflex action. (p. 69)

> Jacques Barzun. *Simple and Direct.* New York, 1976.

Now again, it is not the error as such that I am concerned with here, but rather the fact that after Barzun stated the rule, and almost immediately violated it, no one noticed—not Barzun himself who must certainly have read the manuscript several times, not a colleague to whom he probably gave the manuscript before he sent it to the publisher, not the copy editor who worked over the manuscript, not the proof reader who read the galleys, not Barzun who probably read the galleys after them, apparently not even anyone in the reading public, since that *which* hasn't been corrected in any of the subsequent printings. To characterize this failure to respond as mere carelessness seems to miss something important.

This kind of contradiction between the conscious directive and the unre-   24
flexive experience becomes even more intense in the next three examples,

examples that, to be sure, involve matters of style rather than grammar and usage:

> Negative constructions are often wordy and sometimes pretentious.
>
> 1. wordy   Housing for married students is not unworthy of consideration.
>
>   concise   Housing for married students is worthy of consideration.
>
>   better   The trustees should earmark funds for married students' housing. (Probably what the author meant)
>
> 2. wordy   After reading the second paragraph you aren't left with an immediate reaction as to how the story will end.
>
>   concise   The first two paragraphs create suspense.
>
> The following example from a syndicated column is not untypical:
>
> Sylvan Barnet and Marcia Stubbs. *Practical Guide to Writing.* Boston, 1977, p. 280.

Now Barnet and Stubbs may be indulging in a bit of self-parody here. But I don't think so. In this next example, Orwell, in the very act of criticising the passive, not only casts his proscription against it in the passive, but almost all the sentences around it, as well:

> I list below, with notes and examples, various of the tricks by means of which the work of prose construction is habitually dodged . . . *Operators* or *verbal false limbs.* These save the trouble of picking out appropriate verbs and nouns, and at the same time pad each sentence with extra syllables which give it an appearance of symmetry . . . the passive voice is wherever possible used in preference to the active, and noun constructions are used instead of gerunds . . . The range of verbs if further cut down . . . and the banal statements are given an appearance of profundity by means of the *not un* formation. Simple conjunctions are replaced by . . . the ends of sentences are saved by . . .
>
> "Politics and the English Language"

Again, I am not concerned with the fact that Orwell wrote in the passive or used nominalizations where he could have used verbs.[10] Rather, I am bemused by the apparent fact that three generations of teachers have used this essay without there arising among us a general wry amusement that Orwell violated his own rules in the act of stating them.

And if you want to argue (I think mistakenly) that Orwell was indulging in 25 parody, then consider this last example—one that cannot possibly be parodic, at least intentionally:

> Emphasis is often achieved by the use of verbs rather than nouns formed from them, and by the use of verbs in the active rather than in the passive voice.
>
> *A Style Manual for Technical Writers and Editors,* ed. S. J. Reisman. New York, 1972. pp. 6-11.

In this single sentence, in a single moment, we have all five potential locations of error folded together: As the rule is stated in a handbook, it is simultaneously violated in its text; as the editor expresses in the sentence that is part of the handbook a rule that must first have existed in his mind, in his role as writer he simultaneously violates it. And in the instant he ends the sentence, he becomes a critical reader who should—but does not—resonate to the error. Nor, apparently, did anyone else.

The point is this: We can discuss error in two ways: we can discuss it   26
at a level of consciousness that places that error at the very center of our consciousness. Or we can talk about how we experience (or not) what we popularly call errors of usage as they occur in the ordinary course of our reading a text.

In the first, the most common way, we separate the objective material text   27
from its usual role in uniting a subject (us) and that more abstract "content" of the object, the text, in order to make the sentences and words the objects of consciousness. We isolate error as a frozen, instantiated object. In the second way of discussing error, a way we virtually never follow, we must treat error not as something that is simply on the surface of the page, "out there," nor as part of an inventory of negative responses "in here," but rather as a variably experienced union of item and response, controlled by the intention to read a text in the way we ordinarily read texts like newspapers, journals, and books. If error is no longer in the handbook, or on the page, or in the writer—or even purely in the reader—if instead we locate it at an intersection of those places, then we can explain why Barzun could write—or read—one thing and then immediately experience another, why his colleagues and editors and audience could read about one way of reflexively experiencing language and then imme- diately experience it in another.

But when I decided to intend to read Barzun and White and Orwell and   28
Fowler in, for all practical purposes, the way they seem to invite me to read—as an editor looking for the errors they have been urging me to search out—then I inform my experience, I deliberately begin reading, with an intention to experi- ence the material constitution of the text. It is as if a type-designer invited me to look at the design of his type as he discussed type-design.

In short, if we read any text the way we read freshman essays, we will find   29
many of the same kind of errors we routinely expect to find and therefore do find. But if we could read those student essays unreflexively, if we could make the ordinary kind of contract with those texts that we make with other kinds of texts, then we could find many fewer errors.

When we approach error from this point of view, from the point of view   30
of our pre-reflexive experience of error, we have to define categories of error other than those defined by systems of grammar or a theory of social class. We require a system whose presiding terms would turn on the nature of our response to violations of grammatical rules.

At the most basic level, the categories must organize themselves around   31
two variables: Has a rule been violated? And do we respond? Each of these variables has two conditions: A rule is violated or a rule is not violated. And to either of those variables, we respond, or we do not respond. We thus have four possibilities:

1a. A rule is violated, and we respond to the violation.

1b. A rule is violated, and we do not respond to its violation.

2a. A rule is not violated, and we do not respond.

2b. A rule is not violated, and we do respond.

	[+ response]	[– response]
[+ violation]		
[– violation]		

Now, our experiencing or noticing of any given grammatical rule has to be ₃₂ cross-categorized by the variable of our noticing or not noticing whether it is or is not violated. That is, if we violate rule X, a reader may note it or not. But we must also determine whether, if we do **not** violate rule X, the same reader will or will not notice that we have violated it. Theoretically, then, this gives us four possible sets of consequences for any given rule. They can be represented on a feature matrix like this:

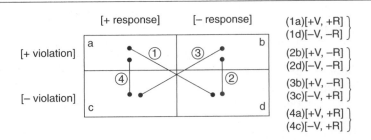

That is, the first kind of rule, indicated by the line marked ①, is of the following kind: When violated, [+V], we respond to the violation, [+R]. When it is not violated, [–V], we do not respond, [–R]. Thus the same rule results in combinations of features indicated by (a-d). Rule type ② is characterized by a rule that when violated, [+V], we do not notice, [–R]. But when we do not violate it, [–V], we do not notice it either, [–R]. Thus the single rule combines features indicated by (b-d). The other rules follow the same kind of grid relationships. (As I will point out later, the problem is actually much more complex than this, but this will do as a first approximation.)

I do not assert that the particular items I will list as examples of these rules ₃₃ are universally experienced in the way indicated. These categories are based on personal responses, and it is possible that your responses are quite different than mine. But in fact, on the basis of some preliminary research that I shall report later, I would argue that most readers respond in the ways reflected by these categories, regardless of how they might claim they react.

The most obviousest set of rules be those whose violation we instantly notes, ₃₄ but whose observation we entirely ignore. They are the rules that define bedrock standard English. No reader of this journal can fail to distinguish these two passages:

> There hasn't been no trainees who withdrawed from the program since them and the Director met to discuss the instructional methods, if they met earlier, they could of seen that problems was beginning to appear and the need to take care of them immediate. (+V, +R)

> There haven't been any trainees who have withdrawn from the program since they and the Director met to discuss the instructional methods. If they had met earlier, they could have seen that problems were beginning to appear and that they needed to take care of them immediately. (–V, –R)

Among the rules whose violation we readily note but whose observance we do not are double negatives, incorrect verb forms, many incorrect pronoun forms, pleonastic subjects, double comparatives and superlatives, most subject-verb disagreements, certain faulty parallelisms,[11] certain dangling modifiers,[12] etc.

The next most obvious set of rules are those whose observation we also 35 entirely ignore, but whose violation we ignore too. Because we note neither their observation nor their violation, they constitute a kind of folklore of usage, rules which we can find in some handbook somewhere, but which have, for the most part, lost their force with our readers. For most readers, these two passages differ very little from one another; for many readers, not at all:

> Since the members of the committee had discussed with each other all of the questions which had been raised earlier, we decided to conduct the meeting as openly as possible and with a concern for the opinions of everyone that might be there. And to ensure that all opinions would be heard, it was suggested that we not limit the length of the meeting. By opening up the debate in this way, there would be no chance that someone might be inadvertently prevented from speaking, which has happened in the past. (+V, –R)

> Because the members of the committee had discussed with one another all the questions that had been raised earlier, we decided to conduct the meeting in a way that was as open as possible and concerned with the opinion of everyone who might be there. To ensure that all opinions would be heard, someone suggested that we not limit the length of the meeting. By opening up the debate in this way, we would not take the chance that someone might be inadvertently prevented from speaking, something which has happened in the past. (–V, –R)

I appreciate the fact that some readers will view my lack of sensitivity to some of these errors as evidence of an incorrigibly careless mind. Which errors go in which category, however, is entirely beside the point.[13] The point is the existence of a *category* of "rules" to whose violation we respond as indifferently as we respond to their observance.

A third category of rules includes those whose violation we largely ignore 36 but whose observance we do not. These are rules which, when followed, impose themselves on the reader's consciousness either subliminally, or overtly and specifically. You can sense the consequence of observing these rules in this next "minimal pair":

I will not attempt to broadly defend specific matters of evidence that one might rest his case on. If it was advisable to substantially modify the arguments, he would have to re-examine those patients the original group treated and extend the clinical trials whose original plan was eventually altered. (+V, –R)

I shall not attempt broadly to defend specific matters of evidence on which one might rest one's case. Were it advisable substantially to modify the arguments, one should have to re-examine those patients whom the original research group treated and extend the clinical trials the original plan of which was eventually altered. (–V, +R)

I appreciate that many of you believe that you notice split infinitives as quickly as you notice a subject-verb error, and that both should be equally condemned in careful prose. At the end of this paper, I will try to offer an argument to the contrary—that in fact many—not all—of you who make that claim are mistaken. 37

The exceptions are probably those for whom there is the fourth category of error, that paradoxical but logically entailed category defined by those rules whose violation we note, and whose observance we also note. I think that very few of us are sensitive to this category, and I think for those very few, the number of items that belong in the category must, fortunately, be very small. Were the number of items large, we would be constantly distracted by noticing that which should not be noticed. We would be afflicted with a kind of linguistic hyperesthesia, noticing with exquisite pleasure that every word we read is spelled correctly, that every subject agrees with its verb, that every article precedes its noun, and so on. Many of us may be surprised when we get a paper with no mispelled words, but that pleasure does not derive from our noticing that each word in turn is correctly spelled, but rather in the absence of mispelled words. 38

In my own case, I think I note equally when an infinitive is split, and when it is not. In recent months, I also seem to be noticing when someone uses *that* in the way that the "rule" stipulates, and I notice when a writer uses *which* in the way which the "rule" prohibits. I hope I add no more. 39

I suspect that some readers put into this category the *regardless/irregardless* pair, *media* as a singular and as a plural, perhaps *disinterested/uninterested*. I offer no pair of contrasting examples because the membership of the category is probably so idiosyncratic that such a pair would not be useful. 40

Now in fact, all this is a bit more complicated than my four categories suggest, albeit trivially so. The two-state condition of response: [+/–], is too crude to distinguish different qualities of response. Responses can be unfavorable, as the ordinary speaker of standard English would respond unfavorably to 41

Can't nobody tell what be happening four year from now.

if it appeared in a text whose conventions called for standard English. A response can be favorable, as in the right context, we might regard as appropriate the formality of

Had I known the basis on which these data were analyzed, I should not have attempted immediately to dissuade those among you whom others have . . .

(We could, of course, define a context in which we would respond to this unfavorably.)

Since only the category of [+response] can imply a type of response, we 42 categorize favorable and unfavorable response, [+/–favorable], across only [+response]. This gives us four more simple categories:

[+violate, –favorable]

[–violate, +favorable]

[+violate, +favorable]

[–violate, –favorable]

The first two I have already illustrated

[+v, –f]: He knowed what I meaned.

[–v, +f]: Had I known the basis on which . . . : should not etc.

This leaves two slightly paradoxical categories, which, like Category IV: those 43 rules whose violations we notice and whose observations we notice too, are populated by a very small number of items, and function as part of our responses only idiosyncratically. In the category [–violate, –favorable], I suspect that many of us would place *It is I,* along with some occurrences of *whom,* perhaps.

The other paradoxical category, [+violate, +favorable] is *not* illustrated by 44 *It's me,* because for most of us, this is an unremarked violation. If it elicits a response at all, it would almost invariably be [–favorable], but only among those for whom the *me* is a bête noir. In fact, I can only think of one violation that I respond to favorably: It is the *than* after *different(ly)* when what follows is a clause rather than a noun:

This country feels differently about the energy crisis than it did in 1973.

I respond to this favorably because the alternative,

This country feels differently about the energy crisis from the way it did in 1973.

is wordier, and on principles that transcend idiosyncratic items of usage, I prefer the two less words and the more certain and direct movement of the phrase. My noticing any of this, however, is entirely idiosyncratic.

As I said, though, these last distinctions are increasingly trivial. That is why I 45 refrain from pursuing another yet more finely drawn distinction: Those responses, favorable or unfavorable, that we consciously, overtly, knowingly experience, and those that are more subliminal, undefined, and unspecific. That is, when I read

It don't matter.

I know precisely what I am responding to. When most of us read a *shall* and a shifted preposition, I suspect that we do not consciously identify those items as the source of any heightened feeling of formality. The response, favorable or unfavorable, is usually less specific, more holistic.

Now what follows from all this? One thing that does **not** follow is a rejection 46 of all rules of grammar. Some who have read this far are undoubtedly ready to call up the underground grammarians to do one more battle against those who would rip out the Mother Tongue and tear down Civilized Western Values. But need I really have to assert that, just because many rules of grammar lack practical force, it is hardly the case that none of them have substance?

Certainly, how we mark and grade papers might change. We need not believe 47 that just because a rule of grammar finds its way into some handbook of usage, we have to honor it. Which we honor and which we do not is a problem of research. We have to determine in some unobtrusive way which rules of grammar the significant majority of careful readers notice and which they do not. One way to do this research is to publish an article in a journal such as this, an article into which have been built certain errors of grammar and usage. The researcher would then ask his readers to report which errors jumped out at them **on the first reading**. Those that you did not notice should then not be among those we look for first when we read a student's paper.

One curious consequence of this way of thinking about error is that we no 48 longer have to worry about defining, rejecting, quibbling over the existence of a rule. We simply accept as a rule anything that anyone wants to offer, no matter how bizarre or archaic. Should anyone re-assert the 19th-century rule against the progressive passive, fine. Upon inspection it will turn out that the rule belongs in the category of those rules whose violation no one notices, and whose observation no one notices either. As I said, it may be that you and I will find that for any particular rule, we experience its violation in different ways. But that is an empirical question, not a matter of value. Value becomes a consideration only when we address the matter of which errors we should notice.

Done carefully, this kind of classification might also encourage some diction- 49 ary makers to amend their more egregious errors in labeling points of usage. The *AHD*, for example, uses "non-standard" to label

> . . . forms that do not belong in any standard educated speech. Such words are recognized as non-standard not only by those whose speech is standard, but even by those who regularly use non-standard expressions.

The *AHD* staff has labeled as non-standard, *ain't, seen* as the past tense of *see*, and *don't* with a singular subject. It has also labeled as non-standard *irregardless, like* for *as, disinterested for uninterested*, and *see where*, as in the construction, *I see where* . . . Thus we are led to believe that a speaker who would utter this:

> I see where the President has said that, irregardless of what happens with the gasoline shortage, he'll still be against rationing, just like he has been in the past. He seems disinterested in what's going on in the country.

would be just as likely to continue with this:

> I ain't sure that he seen the polls before he said that. He don't seem to know that people are fed up.

Indeed, we would have to infer from this kind of labeling that a speaker who said "I ain't sure he seen . . . " would also be sensitive to mistakes such as *disinterested* for *uninterested* or *like* for *as*. In matters such as this, we see too clearly the very slight scholarly basis upon which so much of this labeling rests.

Finally, I think that most of this essay is an exercise in futility. In these mat- 50 ters, the self-conscious report of what should be counted as an error is certainly an unreliable index to the unself-conscious experience. But it is by far a more satisfying emotion. When those of us who believe ourselves educated and liter-ate and defenders of good usage think about language, our zealous defense of "good writing" feels more authentic than our experience of the same items in unreflective experience of a text. Indeed, we do not experience many of them at all. And no matter how wrong we might discover we are about our unreflective feelings, I suspect we could be endlessly lectured on how we do not respond to a *less* in front of a count noun, as in *less people*, but we would still express our horror and disgust in the belief that *less* is wrong when used in that way. It simply feels more authentic when we condemn error and enforce a rule. And after all, what good is learning a rule if all we can do is obey it?

If by this point you have not seen the game, I rest my case. If you have, I invite 51 you to participate in the kind of research I suggested before. I have deposited with the Maxine Hairston of the University of Texas at Austin (Austin, Texas 78712), a member of the Editorial Board of this journal, a manuscript with the errors of grammar and usage that I deliberately inserted into this paper specifi-cally marked. How can I ask this next question without seeming to distrust you? If you had to report right now what errors you noticed, what would they be? Don't go back and reread, looking for errors, at least not before you recall what errors you found the first time through. If you would send your list (bet-ter yet, a copy of the article with errors noted on first reading circled in red) to Professor Hairston, she will see that a tally of the errors is compiled, and in a later issue will report on who noticed what.

If you want to go through a second time and look for errors, better yet. Just 52 make clear, if you would, that your list is the result of a deliberate search. I will be particularly interested in those errors I didn't mean to include. There are, incidentally, about 100 errors.

Notes

1. I don't know whether it is fair or unfair to quote Zinsser on this same matter:

   OVERSTATEMENT. "The living room looked as if an atomic bomb had gone off there," writes the inexperienced writer, describing what he saw on Sunday morning after a Saturday night party that got out of hand. Well, we all know that he's exaggerat-ing to make a droll point, but we also know that an atomic bomb didn't go off there, or any other bomb except maybe a water bomb. . . . These verbal high jinks can get just so high—and I'm already well over the limit—before the reader feels an overpowering drowsiness. . . . Don't overstate. (p. 108)

2. Erving Goffman, *Frame Analysis: An Essay on the Organization of Experience.* (New York: Harper and Row, 1974).

3. Some social errors are strictly formal and so ordinarily do not require an apology, even though some might judge them "horrible": a white wedding gown and a veil on a twice-divorced and eight-month pregnant bride, brown shoes with a dinner jacket, a printed calling card.

4. Some special situations do require an apology: When we prepare a document that someone else must take responsibility for, and we make a mistake in usage, we are expected to apologize, in the same way we would apologize for incorrectly adding up a column of figures. And when some newspaper columnists violate some small point of usage and their readers write in to point it out, the columnists will often acknowledge the error and offer some sort of apology. I think William Safire in *The New York Times* has done this occasionally.

5. Two other kinds of purely linguistic behavior do arouse hostile feelings. One kind includes obscenities and profanities. It may be that both are rooted in some sense of fouling that which should be kept clean: obscenities foul the mouth, the mouth fouls the name of a deity. The other kind of linguistic behavior that arouses hostility in some includes bad puns and baby talk by those who are too old for it. Curiously, Freud discusses puns in his *Wit and the Relation to the Unconscious* (under "Technique of Wit") but does not in "The Tendencies of Wit" address the faint sense of revulsion we feel at a bad pun.

6. Sterling Leonard, *Current English Usage,* English Monograph No. 1 (Champaign, Ill.; National Council of Teachers of English. Chicago, 1932); Albert H. Marckwardt and Fred Walcott, *Facts About Current English Usage,* English Monograph No. 7 (Champaign, Ill.: National Council of Teachers of English. New York, 1938); Raymond Crisp. "Changes in Attitudes Toward English Usage," Ph.D. dissertation, University of Illinois, 1971; W. H. Mittins, Mary Salu, Mary Edminson, Sheila Coyne, *Attitudes to English Usage* (London: Oxford University Press, 1970); *The American Heritage Dictionary of the English Language* (New York: Dell, 1979). Thomas J. Cresswell's *Usage in Dictionaries and Dictionaries of Usage,* Publication of the American Dialect Society, Nos. 63–64 (University, Alabama: University of Alabama Press 1975), should be required reading for anyone interested in these matters. It amply demonstrates the slight scholarly basis on which so much research on usage rests.

7. William Labov, *The Social Stratification of English in New York City* (Washington, D.C.: Center for Applied Linguistics, 1966), pp. 455–81.

8. Elaine P. Maimon and Barbara F. Nodine, "Words Enough and Time: Syntax and Error One Year After," in *Sentence Combining and the Teaching of Writing,* eds. Donald Daiker, Andrew Kerek, Max Morenberg (Akron, Ohio: University of Akron Press, 1979) pp. 101–108. This is considered a dangling verbal: *For example, considering the way Hamlet treats Ophelia, there is almost corruptness in his mind.* Clumsy yes, but *considering* is an absolute, or more exactly, meta-discourse. See footnote 12. This is considered a vague pronoun reference: *The theme of poisoning begins with the death of old King Hamlet, who was murdered by his brother when a leperous distillment was poured into his ear while he slept.* Infelicitous, to be sure, but who can possibly doubt who's pouring what in whose ear (p. 103)? Counting items such as these as errors and then using those counts to determine competence, progress, or maturity would seem to raise problems of another, more substantive, kind.

9. *Essays of E. B. White* (New York: Harper and Row, 1977), p. 24.

10. Orwell's last rule: *Break any of these rules sooner than say anything outright barbarous,* does not apply to this passage. Indeed, it would improve if it had conformed to his rules:

> I list below, with notes and examples, various of the tricks by means of which a writer can dodge the work of prose construction . . . such writers prefer wherever possible the passive voice to the active, and noun constructions instead of gerunds . . . they further cut down the range of verbs . . . they make their banal statements seem profound by means of the *not un-*formation. They replace simple conjunctions by . . . they save the ends of sentences . . .

Should anyone object that this is a monotonous series of sentences beginning with the same subject, I could point to example after example of the same kind of thing in good modern prose. But perhaps an example from the same essay, near the end, will serve best (my emphasis):

> When *you* think of a concrete object, *you* think wordlessly, and then, if *you* want to describe the thing *you* have been visualizing, *you* probably hunt about till *you* find the exact *words that* seem to fit it. When *you* think of something abstract *you* are more inclined to use words from the start, and unless *you* make a conscious effort to prevent it, the existing dialect will come rushing in and do the job for you . . .

Nine out of ten clauses begin with *you*, anc n a space much more confined than the passage I rewrote.

11. Virtually all handbooks overgeneralize about faulty parallelism. Two "violations" occur so often in the best prose that we could not include them in this Category I. One is the kind illustrated by the E. B. White passage: the coordination of adverbials: . . . *unerringly and with immense good will.* The other is the coordination of noun phrases and WH-clauses: *We are studying the origins of this species and why it died out.* Even that range of exceptions is too broadly stated, but to explain the matter adequately would require more space than would be appropriate here.

12. Handbooks also overgeneralize on dangling constructions. The generalization can best be stated like this: When the implied subject of an introductory element is different from the overt subject of its immediately following clause, the introductory element dangles. Examples in handbooks are always so ludicrous that the generalization seems sound:

> Running down the street, the bus pulled away from the curb before I got there.

> To prepare for the wedding, the cake was baked the day before.

Some handbooks list exceptions, often called absolutes:

> Considering the trouble we're in, it's not surprising you are worried.

> To summarize, the hall is rented, the cake is baked, and we're ready to go.

These exceptions can be subsumed into a more general rule: When either the introductory element *or* the subject of the sentence consists of meta-discourse, the introductory element will not always appear to dangle. By meta-discourse I mean words and phrases that refer not to the primary content of the discourse, to the reference "out there" in the world, the writer's subject matter, but rather to the process of discoursing, to those directions that steer a reader through a discourse, those filler words that allow a writer to shift emphasis (*it, there, what*), and so on, words such as *it is important to note, to summarize, considering these issue, as you know, to begin with, there is*, etc. That's why an introductory element such as the following occurs so often in the prose of educated writers, and does not seem to dangle (meta-discourse is in bold face):

> To succeed in this matter, **it is important** for you to support as fully as possible . . .

> Realizing the seriousness of the situation, **it can be seen** that we must cut back on . . .

As I will point out later, the categories I am suggesting here are too broadly drawn to account for a number of finer nuances of error. Some violations, for example, clearly identify social and educational background:

> He didn't have no way to know what I seen.

But some violations that might be invariably noted by some observers do not invariably, or even regularly, reflect either social or educational background. Usages such as *irregardless, like* for *as, different than*, etc. occur so often in the speech and writing of entirely educated speakers and writers that we cannot group them with double negatives and non-standard verb forms, even if we do unfailingly respond to both kinds of errors. The usage note in the *American Heritage Dictionary* (Dell Paperback Edition, 1976; third printing, November, 1980) that *irregardless* is non-standard and "is only acceptable when the intent is clearly humorous" is more testimony to the problems of accurately representing the speech and writing of educated speakers. On February 20, 1981, the moderator on *Washington Week in Review,* a Public Broadcasting System news program, reported that a viewer had written to the program, objecting to the use of *irregardless* by one of the panelists. To claim that the person who used *irregardless* would also use *knowed* for *knew* or an obvious double negative would be simply wrong. (I pass by silently the position of *only* in that usage note. See footnote 13, item 9.) The counter-argument that the mere occurrence of these items in the speech and writing of some is sufficient testimony that they are not in fact educated is captious.

13. Here are some of the rules which I believe belong in this Category II: (1) Beginning sentences with *and* or *but*; (2) beginning sentences with *because* (a rule that appears in no handbook that I know of, but that seems to have a popular currency); (3) *which/that* in regard to restrictive

relative clauses; (4) *each other* for two, *one another* for more than two; (5) *which* to refer to a whole clause (when not obviously ambiguous); (6) *between* for two, *among* for more than two. These next ones most readers of this journal may disagree with personally; I can only assert on the basis of considerable reading that they occur too frequently to be put in any other category for most readers: (7) *less* for *fewer*; (8) *due to* for *because*; (9) the strict placement of *only*; (10) the strict placement of *not only, neither,* etc. before only that phrase or clause that perfectly balances the *nor*. The usage of several disputed words must also suggest this category for most readers: *disinterested/uninterested, continuous/continual, alternative* for more than two. Since I have no intention of arguing which rules should go into any category, I offer these only as examples of my observations. Whether they are accurate for you is in principle irrelevant to the argument. Nor is it an exhaustive list.

14. The rules that go into Category III would, I believe, include these. Again, they serve only to illustrate. I have no brief in regard to where they should go. (1) *shall/will,* (2) *who/whom,* (3) unsplit infinitives, (4) fronted prepositions, (5) subjunctive form of *be,* (6) *whose/of which* as possessives for inanimate nouns, (7) repeated *one* instead of a referring pronoun *he/his/him,* (8) plural *data* and *media,* singular verb after none.

Questions for Discussion and Journaling

1. Return to our earlier question about the title: What does Williams mean by the "phenomenology" of error? What do you think was his purpose in choosing this title instead of a more straightforward one?

2. What have been some of your own experiences with the construct of *error*? Why do they stand out in your mind? How might you react to those experiences now, having read Williams's piece?

3. What, if anything, did you disagree with in this article? Did Williams make any arguments that conflict with your experience or with your sense, as a writer, of how things should be done?

4. Two of Williams's claims are that (a) if we read expecting to find errors, we tend to find them, whereas if we aren't looking for them we are less likely to notice them, and (b) if we were to read student papers as we read "ordinary" texts, we would find far fewer errors in them. If you take these two ideas together, what does Williams seem to be saying? What do you think of what he's saying?

5. How would you describe Williams's **tone** in this piece—that is, if he were reading it aloud, how would he sound? Note how often he repeats the words *puzzled* and *puzzling*. Do you think he really was puzzled?

6. What would you say Williams's text *does*? It might be helpful for you to think about why Williams wrote it, where it was published, and who was meant to read it. We think that Williams's article *indicts* someone or something. (If you aren't sure what *indict* means, then you should look it up.) If this is true, then what or whom does it indict, and why?

7. Of the various observations that Williams makes in this article, what was most *surprising* to you? Which did you *like* most? Why?

Applying and Exploring Ideas

1. Compile your own list of writing errors that people criticize in others while ignoring in themselves. What will you use to come up with this list? Will you look in handbooks or in the writing of other students? Or will you think back to errors that your teachers have emphasized? Though this is a short assignment, gathering the information for your list can be considered a mini research project.

2. See how many errors you can find in Williams's piece: mark it up with a red pen—and then make a list of the errors you find. Next, compare your list with those of three of your classmates. Which errors did you all notice? Which ones did only some, or just one, of you notice? Do these results tell you anything about one of Williams's main questions—which errors are bigger problems than others?

3. Write a few informal paragraphs to share with your classmates regarding the research Williams did for this article. What did he study? What data did he collect? How did he analyze the data he collected? Now brainstorm a few research questions of your own that would prompt you to collect and analyze data like these. Why are these interesting questions to you?

Meta Moment

Why do you think your teacher and the authors of this textbook are asking you to consider error as a construct? Do you think your relationship to writing would be different if all of your previous teachers had understood error as a construct and taught it to you that way?

All Writing Is Autobiography

DONALD M. MURRAY

Murray, Donald M. "All Writing Is Autobiography." *College Composition and Communication* 42.1 (1991): 66–74. Print.

Framing the Reading

By the time you've gotten to college, it's very likely that at least one teacher has told you not to use "I" in your school papers. Push the question, and you might be told that academic writing (especially if it uses research) isn't supposed to be "personal"—rather, you should strive to be as objective as possible. The paper, after all, isn't about you—so you shouldn't be in it.

Donald Murray probably had the same voices echoing in his head when he wrote this article for the writing teachers who read *College Composition and Communication*. Having made his living as a writer (including winning a Pulitzer prize as a newspaper columnist, writing textbooks, and publishing a range of poetry and fiction), Murray disagreed. Writing, he thought, is *always* personal, whatever else it is. So he sat down to catalog the various ways that writing of any sort *includes the writer*—the ways that, in a sense, all writing is **autobiography**. This article is one result of his thinking on this topic.

Some readers object to Murray's argument because they misunderstand his use of the term *autobiography*, assuming he's referring to all writing as books in which people tell the stories of their lives. Murray makes it clear, though, that he's not thinking that research papers and workplace memos are autobiographies. Rather, Murray is referring to the autobiographical *nature* of texts, all of which necessarily contain traces of their creators. If you understand autobiography in this sense, it will be easier to fairly weigh Murray's arguments.

This chapter is about how careful research on writing— attempting to explain how writing works on the basis of actual examples of that writing, and the people doing it—actually challenges many of the commonsense "rules" we're taught about writing as young people—like, in this case, "Don't use *I* in your writing" or "Research writing is purely factual and objective." Research like Murray's tells a more complicated story that does a better job explaining the actual writing we see around us.

Getting Ready to Read

Before you read Murray's article, try the following activity:

- Think back to what you've been taught about how "personal" your school or work writing (that is, not your diary, journal, poetry, songwriting, or other "expressive" writing) can be. What kinds of rules or guidance did you get? If you have friends or classmates around, compare notes with them.

As you read this article, consider the following questions:

- What reasons does Murray give for his contention that all writing is autobiography?
- What **genres** (kinds) of writing does Murray discuss? Why? Does he leave any out?
- How does Murray relate writing and reading?
- Why did Murray choose to write *as* he did (for example, by using poetry), *where* he did (in the scholarly journal *College Composition and Communication*), and *for whom* he did? (You may need to do some research to answer this question.) What did he hope to accomplish?

I publish in many forms—poetry, fiction, academic article, essay, newspaper column, newsletter, textbook, juvenile nonfiction and I have even been a ghost writer for corporate and government leaders—yet when I am at my writing desk I am the same person. As I look back, I suspect that no matter how I tuned the lyre, I played the same tune. All my writing—and yours—is autobiographical. 1

To explore this possibility, I want to share a poem that appeared in the March 1990 issue of *Poetry*. 2

At 64, Talking Without Words

The present comes clear when rubbed
with memory. I relive a childhood
of texture; oatmeal, the afternoon rug,
spears of lawn, winter finger tracing
frost on window glass, August nose
squenched against window screen. My history
of smell: bicycle oil, leather catcher's
mitt, the sweet sickening perfume of soldiers
long dead, ink fresh on the first edition.
Now I am most alone with others, companioned
by silence and the long road at my back,
mirrored by daughters. I mount the evening
stairs with mother's heavy, wearied

step, sigh my father's long complaint.
My beard grows to the sepia photograph
of a grandfather I never knew. I forget
if I turned at the bridge, but arrive
where I intended. My wife and I talk
without the bother of words. We know Lee
is 32 today. She did not stay twenty
but stands at each room's doorway. I place
my hand on the telephone. It rings.

What is autobiographical in this poem? I was 64 when I wrote it. The child- 3
hood memories were real once I remembered them by writing. I realized I was
mirrored by daughters when the line arrived on the page. My other daughter
would have been 32 on the day the poem was written. Haven't you all had the
experience of reaching for the phone and hearing it ring?

There may even be the question of autobiographical language. We talk 4
about our own language, allowing our students their own language. In going
over this draft my spellcheck hiccupped at "squenched" and "companioned."
As an academic I gulped; as a writer I said, "Well they are now."

Then Brock Dethier, one of the most perceptive of the test readers with whom 5
I share drafts, pointed out the obvious—where all the most significant information is often hidden. He answered my question, "What is autobiographical in
this poem?" by saying, "Your thinking style, your voice." Of course.

We are autobiographical in the way 6
we write; my autobiography exists in
the examples of writing I use in this
piece and in the text I weave around
them. I have my own peculiar way of
looking at the world and my own way
of using language to communicate what
I see. My voice is the product of Scot-
tish genes and a Yankee environment,
of Baptist sermons and the newspaper
city room, of all the language I have heard and spoken.

> We are autobiographical in the way we write; my autobiography exists in the examples of writing I use in this piece and in the text I weave around them.

In writing this paper I have begun to understand, better than I ever have 7
before, that all writing, in many different ways, is autobiographical, and that
our autobiography grows from a few deep taproots that are set down into our
past in childhood.

Willa Cather declared, "Most of the basic material a writer works with is 8
acquired before the age of fifteen." Graham Greene gave the writer five more
years, no more: "For writers it is always said that the first 20 years of life contain the whole of experience—the rest is observation."

Those of us who write have only a few topics. My poems, the novel I'm 9
writing, and some of my newspaper columns keep returning to my family
and my childhood, where I seek understanding and hope for a compassion
that has not yet arrived. John Hawkes has said, "Fiction is an act of revenge."

I hope not, but I can not yet deny the importance of that element in my writing. Revenge against family, revenge against the Army and war, revenge against school.

Another topic I return to is death and illness, religion and war, a great tangle 10 of themes. During my childhood I began the day by going to see if my grandmother had made it through the night; I ended my day with, "Now I lay me down to sleep, I pray the Lord my soul to keep. If I should die before I wake, I pray the Lord my soul to take."

I learned to sing "Onward Christian Soldiers Marching as to War," and still 11 remember my first dead German soldier and my shock as I read that his belt buckle proclaimed God was on *his* side. My pages reveal my obsession with war, with the death of our daughter, with that territory I explored in the hours between the bypass operation that did not work and the one that did.

Recently, Boynton/Cook/Heinemann published *Shoptalk*, a book I began in 12 Junior High School that documents my almost lifelong fascination with how writing is made. I assume that many people in this audience are aware of my obsession with writing and my concern with teaching that began with my early discomfort in school that led to my dropping out and flunking out. My academic writing is clearly autobiographical.

Let's look now at a Freshman English sort of personal essay, what I like to 13 call a reflective narrative. I consider such pieces of writing essays, but I suppose others think of them in a less inflated way as newspaper columns. I write a column, *Over Sixty*, for the *Boston Globe*, and the following one was published October 10th of 1989. It was based on an experience I had the previous August.

Over sixty brings new freedoms, a deeper appreciation of life and the time to celebrate it, but it also brings, with increasing frequency, such terrible responsibilities as sitting with the dying.

Recently it was my turn to sit with my brother-in-law as he slowly left us, the victim of a consuming cancer.

When I was a little boy, I wanted—hungered—to be a grown-up. Well, now I am a grown-up. And when someone had to sit with the dying on a recent Saturday, I could not look over my shoulder. I was the one. My oldest daughter will take her turn. She is a grown-up as well, but those of us over sixty have our quota of grown-upness increase. Time and again we have to confront crisis: accident, sickness, death. There is no one else to turn to. It is our lonely duty.

Obligation has tested and tempered us. No one always measures up all the time. We each do what we can do, what we must do. We learn not to judge if we are wise, for our judgments boomerang. They return. At top speed and on target.

Most of us, sadly and necessarily, have learned to pace ourselves. We have seen friends and relatives destroyed by obligation, who have lost themselves in serving others. There is no end to duty for those who accept it.

And we have seen others who diminish by shirking responsibility. When we call them for help the door is shut. We hear silence.

We grow through the responsible acceptance of duty, obligation balanced by self-protection. We teeter along a high wire trying to avoid guilt or sancrimoniousness as we choose between duty and avoidance.

And so my mind wanders as Harry sleeps, blessedly without pain for the moment, moving steadily toward a destination he seems no longer to fear.

He would understand that as we mourn for him, we mourn for ourselves. Of course. We are learning from his dying how to live. We inevitably think of what he did that we can emulate and what we should try to avoid.

And we learn, from his courage and his example, not to fear death. I remember how horrified I was years ago when a mother of a friend of mine, in her late eighties, feeling poorly in the middle of the night, would get up, change into her best nightgown, the one saved for dying, and go back to sleep.

Now I understand. During my last heart attack I had a volcanic desire to live but no fear of dying. It was not at all like my earlier trips to the edge.

Harry continues my education. He did not want trouble while he lived and now he is dying the same way, causing no trouble, trying to smile when he wakes, trying to entertain me.

He needs the comfort of sleep and I leave the room, turning outside his door to see how quickly his eyes close. He wants nothing from us now. Not food, not drink, not, we think, much companionship. He accepts that his road is lonely and he does not even show much impatience at its length.

It is not a happy time, alone in the house with a dying man, but it is not a dreadful time either. I pat the cat who roams the house but will not go to the room where Harry lies; I read, write in my daybook, watch Harry, and take time to celebrate my living.

This house, strange to me, in an unfamiliar city, is filled with silence. No music, no TV, just the quiet in which I can hear his call. But he does not call. I cannot hear his light breathing. Every few minutes I go to the door to see if the covers still rise and fall.

He would understand as I turn from him to watch the tree branch brush the roof of the house next door, as I spend long moments appreciating the dance of shadows from the leaves on the roof, then the patterns of sunlight reflected up on the ceiling of the room where I sit, as I celebrate my remaining life.

Again I stand at the edge of the door watching, waiting, and take instruction from his dying. We should live the hours we have in our own way, appreciating their passing. And we should each die in our own way. I will remember his way, his acceptance, his not giving trouble, his lonely, quiet passing.

This is simple narrative with the facts all true, but it is really not that simple; 14 few things are in writing or in life. The details are selective. A great deal of family history is left out. A great many details about the day, the illness, where it was taking place and why were left out. In fact, I wrote it in part for therapy, and it began as a note to myself several weeks after the experience to help me cut through a jungle of thoughts and emotions, to try to recover for myself what was happening that day. Later I saw that it might speak to others, give comfort or form to their own autobiographies. I did not write the whole truth of that day, although the facts in the piece are accurate; I wrote a limited truth seeking a limited understanding, what Robert Frost called "a momentary stay of confusion."

Yes, I confess it, I wrote, and write, for therapy. Writing autobiography is my 15 way of making meaning of the life I have led and am leading and may lead.

Let's look at another autobiographical poem, one of my favorites, which, 16 I suppose, means that it was one I especially needed to write for no autobiographical reason I can identify. It has not yet been published, although a great many of the best poetry editors in the country have failed in their obligation to Western culture by rejecting it.

Black Ice

On the first Saturday of winter, the boy
skated alone on Sailor's Home Pond, circling
from white ice to black, further each time
he rode the thin ice, rising, dipping, bending
the skin of the water until the crack raced
from shore to trick him but he heard bent
his weight to the turn, made it back in time.

That winter he saw the fish frozen in ice,
its great unblinking eye examining him
each time he circled by. He dreamt that eye
all summer, wondered if Alex had seen
the fish eye before he rode the black ice,
did not hear the crack sneak out from shore,
imagined he learned to skate on water.

At night, after loving you, I fall back
to see that fish eye staring down, watch
Alex in shoe skates and knickers from below
as he skates overhead, circling faster, faster,
scissor legs carrying him from white ice
to black. His skates sing their cutting song,
etching larger, larger circles in my icy sky.

It is true that the boy, myself, skated on thin ice and that he skated at Sailor's 17 Home Pond in Quincy, Massachusetts, although the thin ice may not have been on that pond. He did not, however, see a fish in the ice until he wrote the poem, although he was obsessed with the eyes of the fish, haddock and cod, that followed him when he went to Titus's fish store in Wollaston. Readers believe that Alex is my brother, although I was an only child. There was no Alex; no one I knew had drowned by falling through the ice until I received the poem; I did not, after loving, stare up to see him skating above me until after I wrote the poem. I do now. The poem that was for a few seconds imaginary has become autobiographical by being written.

Ledo Ivo, the Latin American writer, said, "I increasingly feel that my writ- 18 ing creates me. I am the invention of my own words" (*Lives on the Line,* Ed.

Doris Meyer, U of California P, 1988). Don DeLillo explains, "Working at sentences and rhythms is probably the most satisfying thing I do as a writer. I think after a while a writer can begin to know himself through his language. He sees someone or something reflected back at him from these constructions. Over the years it's possible for a writer to shape himself as a human being through the language he uses. I think written language, fiction, goes that deep. He not only sees himself but begins to make himself or remake himself" (*Anything Can Happen,* Ed. Tom LeClair and Larry McCaffery, U of Illinois P, 1988).

We become what we write. That is one of the great magics of writing. I am   19 best known as a nonfiction writer, but I write fiction and poetry to free myself of small truths in the hope of achieving large ones. Here are the first pages from a novel I am writing.

> Notebook in his lap, pen uncapped, Ian Fraser sat in the dark green Adirondack chair studying the New Hampshire scene that had so often comforted him as he put in his last years in his Washington office. The green meadow sloping unevenly over granite ledge to the lake and the point of land with its sentinel pine that marked the edge of his possession, and across the lake the hills rising into mountains touched with the reds, oranges, yellows that would flame into autumn this week or next. He was settled in at last and ready to begin the book he had so long delayed, but he could not write until he scanned this quiet scene with his infantryman's eyes for it still was, as were all his landscapes, a field of fire.
>
> He had to know where to dig in, where the enemy would attack, what was at his back. He supposed it was what had attracted him to this old farmhouse, he could hold this position, he had a good field of fire. First he scanned the lake. Left to right, far edge to near, not one boat or canoe, nothing breaking the surface, no wind trail or wake. Now right to left to see what might be missed. Nothing.
>
> The point of land, his furthest outpost. Scraggly pines, hulking ledge, ideal cover. He studied it close up, knew the pattern of shadows, where the ledge caught the light, where crevice was always dark. This is ridiculous, he thought, an old man whose wars are all over, but he could not stop the search for the enemies that had been there at the edge of other fields so long ago, so recent in memory.
>
> The woods left, on the other side from sentinel point. Sweep his eyes at the woods a half a field away, open ground any enemy would have to cross. He made himself still; anyone watching would not know his eyes were on patrol. He could have hidden a platoon in these woods, tree and bush, ledge and rock wall, but there was no shadow that moved, no unexpected sound, no leaves that danced without wind.
>
> And yet, Ian felt a presence as if he, the watcher, were being watched. He scanned the woods on the left again, moving from lake edge up. Nothing.
>
> Now the woods on the right, he had cut back from the house when he bought it, saying he needed sun for vegetables. He needed open field. More hardwoods here, more openness, the road unseen beyond. It was where someone would come in. His flood lights targeted these woods, but it was not night. He examined these familiar woods, suddenly looking high in the old oak where a pileated wood-

pecker started his machine gun attack. Ian studied squirrel and crow, the pattern of light and dark, followed the trail of the quiet lake breeze that rose through the woods and was gone.

Now the field of fire itself, where a civilian would think no-one could hide. He smiled at the memory of a young paratrooper, himself, home on leave, telling Claire, who would become his first wife, to stand at the top of the field and spot him if she could as he crept up the slope, taking cover where there seemed no cover. She was patient with his soldiering—then. She knew her quarry and did not laugh as this lean young man crawled up the slope moving quickly from ledge to slight hollow to the cover of low bush blueberries that July in 1943.

He never knew if she saw him or not.

Do I have a green lawn that reaches down to a New Hampshire lake? No. 20 Do I still see when I visit a new place, forty-six years after I have been in combat, a good field of fire? Yes. Did I have another wife than Minnie Mae? Yes. Was her name Claire? No. Did I play that silly game in the field when I was home on leave? Yes. Is the setting real? Let Herman Melville answer, "It is not down on any map: true places never are."

What is true, what is documentally autobiographical, in the novel will not 21 be clear to me when I finish the last draft. I confess that at my age I am not sure about the source of most of my autobiography. I have written poems that describe what happened when I left the operating table, looked back and decided to return. My war stories are constructed of what I experienced, what I heard later, what the history books say, what I needed to believe to survive and recover—two radically different processes.

I dream every night and remember my dreams. Waking is often a release 22 from a greater reality. I read and wear the lives of the characters I inhabit. I do not know where what I know comes from. Was it dreamt, read, overheard, imagined, experienced in life or at the writing desk? I have spun a web more coherent than experience.

But of course I've been talking about fiction, a liar's profession, so let us turn 23 to the realistic world of nonfiction. That novel from which I have quoted is being written, more days than not, by a technique I call layering that I describe in the third edition of *Write to Learn:*

> One technique, I've been using, especially in writing the novel, is to layer my writing. Once I did quite a bit of oil painting and my pictures were built up, layer after layer of paint until the scene was revealed to me and a viewer. I've been writing each chapter of the novel the same way, starting each day at the beginning of the chapter, reading and writing until the timer bings and my daily stint is finished. Each day I lay down a new layer of text and when I read it the next day, the new layer reveals more possibility.
>
> There is no one way the chapters develop. Each makes its own demands, struggles towards birth in its own way. Sometimes it starts with a sketch, other times the first writing feels complete [next day's reading usually shows it is not]; sometimes I race ahead through the chapter, other times each paragraph is honed before I go on to the next one. I try to allow the text to tell me what it needs.

I start reading and when I see—or, more likely, hear—something that needs doing, I do it. One day I'll read through all the written text and move it forward from the last day's writing; another time I'll find myself working on dialogue; the next day I may begin to construct a new scene [the basic element of fiction]; one time I'll stumble into a new discovery, later have to set it up or weave references to it through the text; I may build up background description, develop the conflict, make the reader see a character more clearly; I may present more documentation, evidence, or exposition, or hide it in a character's dialogue or action.

Well, that is academic writing, writing to instruct, textbook writing. It 24 is clearly nonfiction, and to me it is clearly autobiography. And so, I might add, is the research and scholarship that instructs our profession. We make up our own history, out own legends, our own knowledge by writing our autobiography.

This has enormous implications for our students, or should have. In *Note-* 25 *books of the Mind* (U of New Mexico P, 1985), a seminal book for our discipline, Vera John-Steiner documents the importance of obsession. "Creativity requires a *continuity of concern*, an intense awareness of one's active inner life combined with sensitivity to the external world." Again and again she documents the importance of allowing and even cultivating the obsessive interest of a student in a limited area of study. I read that as the importance of encouraging and supporting the exploration of the autobiographical themes of individual students—and the importance of allowing ourselves to explore the questions that itch our lives.

I do not think we should move away from personal or reflective narrative in 26 composition courses, but closer to it; I do not think we should limit reflective narrative to a single genre; I do not think we should make sure our students write on many different subjects, but that they write and rewrite in pursuit of those few subjects which obsess them.

But then, of course, I am writing autobiographically, telling other people to 27 do what is important to me.

And so all I can do is just rest my case on my own personal experience. I 28 want to read my most recent poem in which the facts are all true. I had not seen as clearly before I wrote the poem the pattern of those facts, the way I—and a generation of children in the United States and Germany and Britain and Japan and China and Spain and France and Italy and Russia and so many other countries—was prepared for war. This piece of writing is factually true but watch out as you hear it. Writing is subversive and something dangerous may happen as you hear my autobiography.

A woman hearing this poem may write, in her mind, a poem of how she was 29 made into a docile helpmate by a society that had its own goals for her. A black may write another autobiography as mine is heard but translated by personal history. A person who has been mistreated in childhood, a person who is a Jew, a person whose courage was tested at the urging of jeering peers on a railroad bridge in Missouri, will all hear other poems, write other poems in their mind as they hear mine.

Winthrop 1936, Seventh Grade

December and we comb our hair wet,
pocket our stocking caps and run,
uniformed in ice helmets,

to read frost etched windows:
castle, moat, battlements, knight,
lady, dragon, feel our sword

plunge in. At recess we fence
with icicles, hide coal in
snow balls, lie freezing

inside snow fort, make ice balls
to arc against the enemy; Hitler.
I lived in a town of Jews,

relatives hidden in silences,
letters returned, doors shut,
curtains drawn. Our soldier

lessons were not in books taught
by old women. In East Boston,
city of Mussolinis, we dance

combat, attack and retreat, sneak,
hide, escape, the companionship
of blood. No school, and side

staggered by icy wind we run
to the sea wall, wait
for the giant seventh wave

to draw back, curl mittens
round iron railing, brace
rubber boots, watch

the entire Atlantic rise
until there is no sky. Keep
mittens tight round iron rail,

prepare for the return of ocean,
that slow, even sucking back,
the next rising wave.

    I suspect that when you read my poem, you wrote your own autobiography. 30
That is the terrible, wonderful power of reading: the texts we create in our own
minds while we read—or just after we read—become part of the life we believe
we lived. Another thesis: all reading is autobiographical.

Questions for Discussion and Journaling

1. Remember that one of the goals of this chapter is to help you consider **constructs** about writing that poorly describe how writing actually works. What construct is Murray asking you to reconsider?

2. In what ways, according to Murray, is writing autobiography? Can you categorize the ways that Murray believes writing is autobiography?

3. Murray's article was published in a peer-reviewed, scholarly journal, yet it does not share the typical features of that genre. Murray's writing is more informal, more "creative," and easier to read in some ways. Make a list of the ways that Murray's article is different from the other scholarly articles in this chapter. Then consider some reasons why Murray would have wanted to break out of the usual "rules" for writing in the scholarly article genre.

4. If you've answered the third question, you have already considered the ways in which this piece is unusual for a scholarly article. Now consider the opposite question: Make a list of the features that mark Murray's article as belonging to the genre of "scholarly article."

5. Consider the implications of Murray's arguments: If he's right, how do his ideas change the way you think about writing? Would they encourage you to write any differently than you currently do?

6. Consider the last few texts that you have written, whether for school, work, or personal reasons. Consider the ways that these texts are—or are not—autobiography in the sense that Murray describes.

Applying and Exploring Ideas

1. Write a one- to two-page response to Murray that explains your reaction to his piece and gives reasons for your thinking. You could write this piece a number of different ways: as a letter to Murray, or to a friend; as an article in the same style as Murray's; or as a review of the article (like a review of a new album or film).

2. If you've heard before that writing—especially academic writing—should be impersonal and keep the writer out, Murray's article might inspire you to argue against that point of view. Take one to two pages and freewrite comments you might make to a teacher or other authority figure who told you in the past to write "objectively" and keep yourself out of the text.

Meta Moment

Quickly name two or three ways that understanding Murray's claims here can have a positive impact on you as a writer and/or on your attitude about writing.

Helping Students Use Textual Sources Persuasively

MARGARET KANTZ

Kantz, Margaret. "Helping Students Use Textual Sources Persuasively." *College English* 52.1 (1990): 74–91. Print.

Framing the Reading

Several articles in this chapter suggest that writing and reading are not just about transmitting and receiving information, and that texts don't mean the same things to every reader: Rather, we *interact* with texts, putting something of ourselves into them and drawing meaning from their **context**.

Margaret Kantz's work takes us to the next logical step, in discussing how it is that we write a new text from other existing texts. In Kantz's article we follow the learning experiences of a particular student, Shirley. Whereas Shirley had been taught in high school that "research" meant compiling facts and transmitting them to a teacher, she must now learn to use a variety of conflicting sources to make an original **argument** on the subject she's researching. Kantz analyzes how Shirley has moved from the realm of *reporting* "just the facts" to the more sophisticated world of *arguing about what the facts might be*, and she shows readers how many new ideas are involved in that change.

A key concept in this change is learning to recognize that facts aren't so much inherently true statements as they are **claims**—that is, assertions that most of a given **audience** has *agreed* are true because for that audience sufficient proof has already been given. You, like most people, would probably classify the statement "the Earth is round" as a "fact." Its status as a fact, however, depends on our mutual agreement that "round" is an adequate description of the Earth's actual, imperfectly spherical shape. What Kantz wants us to see is that what makes the statement a fact is not how "true" the statement is but that most people have *agreed* that it's true and treat it as true. Statements about which we haven't reached this consensus remain *claims*, statements that people *argue* about. Kantz's work here demonstrates why it's so important to read texts—even "factual" works like textbooks and encyclopedias—as consisting of claims, not facts.

This idea that textbooks and other "factual" texts aren't inherently true but instead simply represent a *consensus of*

opinion is a major conceptual change from the way most students are taught in school before college. Like the ideas that writing is always personal (not purely factual or objective) and that error is very much in the eye of the beholder (not simply inherent in a text), this idea requires us to revise our thinking about writing and move from the notion of writing as transmitting "information" to making and supporting claims.

While Kantz wrote this piece as a professor at Central Missouri State University, she conducted the research for it while a graduate student at Carnegie Mellon University. One of her professors there was Linda Flower and one of her classmates was Christina Haas, whose names you will encounter elsewhere in this chapter (and, if you pay close attention, in Kantz's Works Cited list). We make this point to remind you that texts are authored by real people, and these people are often connected both inside and outside of their texts.

Getting Ready to Read

Before you read, do at least one of the following activities:

- Think about an argument you've had recently in which people disagreed about the facts of the issue. How did you resolve the factual dispute? Did the arguers ever agree on what the facts were? If not, how was the argument resolved?
- Write down, in a few quick sentences, how *you* define these terms: *fact, claim, opinion*, and *argument*.
- Watch three TV commercials (you might want to record them) and count the number of *facts* and the number of *claims* in each. Then think about what's most persuasive in the ads: the facts, the claims, or the combination of the two?

As you read Kantz's article, consider the following questions:

- How does Kantz know what she knows? What is the basis for her claims?
- What is Kantz's research question or problem? What does she want to know, or what is she trying to solve?
- What challenges do the students about whom Kantz writes face in making sense of conflicting sources?

Although the researched essay as a topic has been much written about, it has been little studied. In the introduction to their bibliography, Ford, Rees, and Ward point out that most of the over 200 articles about researched essays published in professional journals in the last half century describe classroom methods. "Few," they say, "are of a theoretical nature or based on research, and almost none cites even one other work on the subject" (2). Given Ford and Perry's finding that 84% of freshman composition programs and 40% of advanced composition programs included instruction in writing research papers, more theoretical work seems needed. We need a theory-based explanation, one grounded in the findings of the published research on the nature and reasons for our students' problems with writing persuasive researched papers. To understand how to teach students to write such papers, we also need a better understanding of the demands of synthesis tasks.

> We need a theory-based explanation, one grounded in the findings of the published research on the nature and reasons for our students' problems with writing persuasive researched papers.

2

As an example for discussing this complex topic, I have used a typical college sophomore. This student is a composite derived from published research, from my own memories of being a student, and from students whom I have taught at an open admissions community college and at both public and private universities. I have also used a few examples taken from my own students, all of whom share many of Shirley's traits. Shirley, first of all, is intelligent and well-motivated. She is a native speaker of English. She has no extraordinary knowledge deficits or emotional problems. She comes from a home where education is valued, and her parents do reading and writing tasks at home and at their jobs. Shirley has certain skills. When she entered first grade, she knew how to listen to and tell stories, and she soon became proficient at reading stories and at writing narratives. During her academic life, Shirley has learned such studying skills as finding the main idea and remembering facts. In terms of the relevant research, Shirley can read and summarize source texts accurately (cf. Spivey; Winograd). She can select material that is relevant for her purpose in writing (Hayes, Waterman, and Robinson; Langer). She can make connections between the available information and her purpose for writing, including the needs of her readers when the audience is specified (Atlas). She can make original connections among ideas (Brown and Day; Langer). She can create an appropriate, audience-based structure for her paper (Spivey), take notes and use them effectively while composing her paper (Kennedy), and she can present information clearly and smoothly (Spivey), without relying on the phrasing of the original sources (Atlas; Winograd). Shirley is, in my experience, a typical college student with an average academic preparation.

Although Shirley seems to have everything going for her, she experiences difficulty with assignments that require her to write original papers based on textual sources. In particular, Shirley is having difficulty in her sophomore-level writing class. Shirley, who likes English history, decided to write about the Battle of Agincourt (this part of Shirley's story is biographical). She found half a dozen histories that described the circumstances of the battle in a few pages each. Although the topic was unfamiliar, the sources agreed on many of the facts. Shirley collated these facts into her own version, noting but not discussing discrepant details, borrowing what she assumed to be her sources' purpose

3

of retelling the story, and modelling the narrative structure of her paper on that of her sources. Since the only comments Shirley could think of would be to agree or disagree with her sources, who had told her everything she knew about the Battle of Agincourt, she did not comment on the material; instead, she concentrated on telling the story clearly and more completely than her sources had done. She was surprised when her paper received a grade of C–. (Page 1 of Shirley's paper is given as Appendix A.)

Although Shirley is a hypothetical student whose case is based on a real 4 event, her difficulties are typical of undergraduates at both private and public colleges and universities. In a recent class of Intermediate Composition in which the students were instructed to create an argument using at least four textual sources that took differing points of view, one student, who analyzed the coverage of a recent championship football game, ranked her source articles in order from those whose approach she most approved to those she least approved. Another student analyzed various approaches taken by the media to the Kent State shootings in 1970, and was surprised and disappointed to find that all of the sources seemed slanted, either by the perspective of the reporter or by that of the people interviewed. Both students did not understand why their instructor said that their papers lacked a genuine argument.

The task of writing researched papers that express original arguments pre- 5 sents many difficulties. Besides the obvious problems of citation format and coordination of source materials with the emerging written product, writing a synthesis can vary in difficulty according to the number and length of the sources, the abstractness or familiarity of the topic, the uses that the writer must make of the material, the degree and quality of original thought required, and the extent to which the sources will supply the structure and purpose of the new paper. It is usually easier to write a paper that uses all of only one short source on a familiar topic than to write a paper that selects material from many long sources on a topic that one must learn as one reads and writes. It is easier to quote than to paraphrase, and it is easier to build the paraphrases, without comment or with random comments, into a description of what one found than it is to use them as evidence in an original argument. It is easier to use whatever one likes, or everything one finds, than to formally select, evaluate, and interpret material. It is easier to use the structure and purpose of a source as the basis for one's paper than it is to create a structure or an original purpose. A writing-from-sources task can be as simple as collating a body of facts from a few short texts on a familiar topic into a new text that reproduces the structure, tone, and purpose of the originals, but it can also involve applying abstract concepts from one area to an original problem in a different area, a task that involves learning the relationships among materials as a paper is created that may refer to its sources without resembling them.

Moreover, a given task can be interpreted as requiring an easy method, a 6 difficult method, or any of a hundred intermediate methods. In this context, Flower has observed, "The different ways in which students [represent] a 'standard' reading-to-write task to themselves lead to markedly different goals and strategies as well as different organizing plans" (*Role* iii). To write a synthesis,

Shirley may or may not need to quote, summarize, or select material from her sources; to evaluate the sources for bias, accuracy, or completeness; to develop original ideas; or to persuade a reader. How well she performs any of these tasks—and whether she thinks to perform these tasks—depends on how she reads the texts and on how she interprets the assignment. Shirley's representation of the task, which in this case was easier than her teacher had in mind, depends on the goals that she sets for herself. The goals that she sets depend on her awareness of the possibilities and her confidence in her writing skills.

Feeling unhappy about her grade, Shirley consulted her friend Alice. Alice, who is an expert, looked at the task in a completely different way and used strategies for thinking about it that were quite different from Shirley's. 7

"Who were your sources?" asked Alice. "Winston Churchill, right? A French couple and a few others. And they didn't agree about the details, such as the sizes of the armies. Didn't you wonder why?" 8

"No," said Shirley. "I thought the history books would know the truth. When they disagreed, I figured that they were wrong on those points. I didn't want to have anything in my paper that was wrong." 9

"But Shirley," said Alice, "you could have thought about why a book entitled *A History of France* might present a different view of the battle than a book subtitled *A History of British Progress*. You could have asked if the English and French writers wanted to make a point about the history of their countries and looked to see if the factual differences suggested anything. You could even have talked about Shakespeare's *Henry V*, which I know you've read—about how he presents the battle, or about how the King Henry in the play differs from the Henrys in your other books. You would have had an angle, a problem. Dr. Boyer would have loved it." 10

Alice's representation of the task would have required Shirley to formally select and evaluate her material and to use it as proof in an original argument. Alice was suggesting that Shirley invent an original problem and purpose for her paper and create an original structure for her argument. Alice's task is much more sophisticated than Shirley's Shirley replied, "That would take me a year to do! Besides, Henry was a real person. I don't want to make up things about him." 11

"Well," said Alice, "You're dealing with facts, so there aren't too many choices. If you want to say something original you either have to talk about the sources or talk about the material. What could you say about the material? Your paper told about all the reasons King Henry wasn't expected to win the battle. Could you have argued that he should have lost because he took too many chances?" 12

"Gee," said Shirley, "That's awesome. I wish I'd thought of it." 13

This version of the task would allow Shirley to keep the narrative structure of her paper but would give her an original argument and purpose. To write the argument, Shirley would have only to rephrase the events of the story to take an opposite approach from that of her English sources, emphasizing what she perceived as Henry's mistakes and inserting comments to explain why his decisions were mistakes—an easy argument to write. She could also, if she wished, write a conclusion that criticized the cheerleading tone of her British sources. 14

As this anecdote makes clear, a given topic can be treated in more or less   15
sophisticated ways—and sophisticated goals, such as inventing an original purpose and evaluating sources, can be achieved in relatively simple versions of a
task. Students have many options as to how they can fulfill even a specific task
(cf. Jeffery). Even children can decide whether to process a text deeply or not,
and purpose in reading affects processing and monitoring of comprehension
(Brown). Pichert has shown that reading purpose affects judgments about what
is important or unimportant in a narrative text, and other research tells us that
attitudes toward the author and content of a text affect comprehension (Asch;
Hinze; Shedd; Goldman).

One implication of this story is that the instructor gave a weak assignment   16
and an ineffective critique of the draft (her only comment referred to Shirley's
footnoting technique; cf. Appendix A). The available research suggests that
if Dr. Boyer had set Shirley a specific rhetorical problem such as having her
report on her material to the class and then testing them on it, and if she had
commented on the content of Shirley's paper during the drafts, Shirley might
well have come up with a paper that did more than repeat its source material
(Nelson and Hayes). My teaching experience supports this research finding.
If Dr. Boyer had told Shirley from the outset that she was expected to say
something original and that she should examine her sources as she read them
for discrepant facts, conflicts, or other interesting material, Shirley might have
tried to write an original argument (Kantz, "Originality"). And if Dr. Boyer
had suggested that Shirley use her notes to comment on her sources and make
plans for using the notes, Shirley might have written a better paper than she
did (Kantz, *Relationship*).

Even if given specific directions to create an original argument, Shirley might   17
have had difficulty with the task. Her difficulty could come from any of three
causes: 1) Many students like Shirley misunderstand sources because they read
them as stories. 2) Many students expect their sources to tell the truth; hence,
they equate persuasive writing in this context with making things up. 3) Many
students do not understand that facts are a kind of claim and are often used
persuasively in so-called objective writing to create an impression. Students
need to read source texts as arguments and to think about the rhetorical contexts in which they were written rather than to read them merely as a set of
facts to be learned. Writing an original persuasive argument based on sources
requires students to apply material to a problem or to use it to answer a question, rather than simply to repeat it or evaluate it. These three problems deserve
a separate discussion.

Because historical texts often have a chronological structure, students believe   18
that historians tell stories, and that renarrating the battle casts them as a historian. Because her sources emphasized the completeness of the victory/defeat and
its decisive importance in the history of warfare, Shirley thought that making
these same points in her paper completed her job. Her job as a reader was thus
to learn the story, i.e., so that she could pass a test on it (cf. Vipond and Hunt's
argument that generic expectations affect reading behavior. Vipond and Hunt
would describe Shirley's reading as story-driven rather than point-driven).

Students commonly misread texts as narratives. When students refer to a textbook as "the story," they are telling us that they read for plot and character, regardless of whether their texts are organized as narratives. One reason Shirley loves history is that when she reads it she can combine her story-reading strategies with her studying strategies. Students like Shirley may need to learn to apply basic organizing patterns, such as cause-effect and general-to-specific, to their texts. If, however, Dr. Boyer asks Shirley to respond to her sources in a way that is not compatible with Shirley's understanding of what such sources do, Shirley will have trouble doing the assignment. Professors may have to do some preparatory teaching about why certain kinds of texts have certain characteristics and what kinds of problems writers must solve as they design text for a particular audience. They may even have to teach a model for the kind of writing they expect.

The writing version of Shirley's problem, which Flower calls "writer-based 19 prose," occurs when Shirley organizes what should be an expository analysis as a narrative, especially when she writes a narrative about how she did her research. Students frequently use time-based organizing patterns, regardless of the task, even when such patterns conflict with what they are trying to say and even when they know how to use more sophisticated strategies. Apparently such common narrative transitional devices such as "the first point" and "the next point" offer a reassuringly familiar pattern for organizing unfamiliar material. The common strategy of beginning paragraphs with such phrases as "my first source," meaning that it was the first source that the writer found in the library or the first one read, appears to combine a story-of-my-research structure with a knowledge-telling strategy (Bereiter and Scardamalia, *Psychology*). Even when students understand that the assignment asks for more than the fill-in-the-blanks, show-me-you've-read-the-material approach described by Schwegler and Shamoon, they cling to narrative structuring devices. A rank ordering of sources, as with Mary's analysis of the football game coverage with the sources listed in an order of ascending disapproval, represents a step away from storytelling and toward synthesizing because it embodies a persuasive evaluation.

In addition to reading texts as stories, students expect factual texts to tell 20 them "the truth" because they have learned to see texts statically, as descriptions of truths, instead of as arguments. Shirley did not understand that nonfiction texts exist as arguments in rhetorical contexts. "After all," she reasoned, "how can one argue about the date of a battle or the sizes of armies?" Churchill, however, described the battle in much more detail than Shirley's other sources, apparently because he wished to persuade his readers to take pride in England's tradition of military achievement. Guizot and Guizot de Witt, on the other hand, said very little about the battle (beyond describing it as "a monotonous and lamentable repetition of the disasters of Crecy and Poitiers" [397]) because they saw the British invasion as a sneaky way to take advantage of a feud among the various branches of the French royal family. Shirley's story/study skills might not have allowed her to recognize such arguments, especially because Dr. Boyer did not teach her to look for them.

When I have asked students to choose a topic and find three or more sources   21
on it that disagree, I am repeatedly asked, "How can sources disagree in different ways? After all, there's only pro and con." Students expect textbooks and
other authoritative sources either to tell them the truth (i.e., facts) or to express
an opinion with which they may agree or disagree. Mary's treatment of the
football coverage reflects this belief, as does Charlie's surprise when he found
that even his most comprehensive sources on the Kent State killings omitted
certain facts, such as interviews with National Guardsmen. Students' desire for
truth leads them to use a collating approach whenever possible, as Shirley did
(cf. Appendix A), because students believe that the truth will include all of the
facts and will reconcile all conflicts. (This belief may be another manifestation
of the knowledge-telling strategy [Bereiter and Scardamalia, *Psychology*] in
which students write down everything they can think of about a topic.) When
conflicts cannot be reconciled and the topic does not admit a pro or con stance,
students may not know what to say. They may omit the material altogether,
include it without comment, as Shirley did, or jumble it together without any
plan for building an argument.

The skills that Shirley has practiced for most of her academic career—find-   22
ing the main idea and learning content—allow her to agree or disagree. She
needs a technique for reading texts in ways that give her something more to
say, a technique for constructing more complex representations of texts that
allow room for more sophisticated writing goals. She also needs strategies for
analyzing her reading that allow her to build original arguments.

One way to help students like Shirley is to teach the concept of rhetorical   23
situation. A convenient tool for thinking about this concept is Kinneavy's triangular diagram of the rhetorical situation. Kinneavy, analyzing Aristotle's description of rhetoric, posits that every communicative situation has three parts: a
speaker/writer (the Encoder), an audience (the Decoder), and a topic (Reality)
(19). Although all discourse involves all three aspects of communication, a given
type of discourse may pertain more to a particular point of the triangle than to
the others, e.g., a diary entry may exist primarily to express the thoughts of the
writer (the Encoder); an advertisement may exist primarily to persuade a reader
(the Decoder). Following Kinneavy, I posit particular goals for each corner of the
triangle. Thus, the primary goal of a writer doing writer-based discourse such as
a diary might be originality and self-expression; primary goals for reader-based
discourse such as advertising might be persuasion; primary goals for topic-based
discourse such as a researched essay might be accuracy, completeness, and mastery of subject matter. Since all three aspects of the rhetorical situation are present
and active in any communicative situation, a primarily referential text such as
Churchill's *The Birth of Britain* may have a persuasive purpose and may depend
for some of its credibility on readers' familiarity with the author. The term "rhetorical reading," then (cf. Haas and Flower), means teaching students to read a
text as a message sent by someone to somebody for a reason. Shirley, Mary, and
Charlie are probably practiced users of rhetorical persuasion in non-academic
contexts. They may never have learned to apply this thinking in a conscious and
deliberate way to academic tasks (cf. Kroll).

The concept of rhetorical situation offers insight into the nature of students'   24
representations of a writing task. The operative goals in Shirley's and Alice's
approaches to the term paper look quite different when mapped onto the points
on the triangle. If we think of Shirley and Alice as Encoders, the topic as Reality, and Dr. Boyer as the Decoder, we can see that for Shirley, being an Encoder
means trying to be credible; her relationship to the topic (Reality) involves a
goal of using all of the subject matter; and her relationship to the Decoder
involves an implied goal of telling a complete story to a reader whom Shirley
thinks of as an examiner—to use the classic phrase from the famous book by
Britton et al.—i.e., a reader who wants to know if Shirley can pass an exam
on the subject of the Battle of Agincourt. For Alice, however, being an Encoder
means having a goal of saying something new; the topic (Reality) is a resource
to be used; and the Decoder is someone who must be persuaded that Alice's
ideas have merit. Varying task representations do not change the dimensions of
the rhetorical situation: the Encoder, Decoder, and Reality are always present.
But the way a writer represents the task to herself does affect the ways that she
thinks about those dimensions—and whether she thinks about them at all.

In the context of a research assignment, rhetorical skills can be used to read   25
the sources as well as to design the paper. Although teachers have probably
always known that expert readers use such strategies, the concept of rhetorical reading is new to the literature. Haas and Flower have shown that expert
readers use rhetorical strategies "to account for author's purpose, context, and
effect on the audience . . . to recreate or infer the rhetorical situation of the
text" (176; cf. also Bazerman). These strategies, used in addition to formulating
main points and paraphrasing content, helped the readers to understand a text
more completely and more quickly than did readers who concentrated exclusively on content. As Haas and Flower point out, teaching students to read
rhetorically is difficult. They suggest that appropriate pedagogy might include
"direct instruction . . . modeling, and . . . encouraging students to become contributing and committed members of rhetorical communities" (182). One early
step might be to teach students a set of heuristics based on the three aspects of
the communicative triangle. Using such questions could help students set goals
for their reading.

In this version of Kinneavy's triangle, the Encoder is the writer of the source   26
text, the Decoder is the student reader, and Reality is the subject matter. Readers
may consider only one point of the triangle at a time, asking such questions as
"Who are you (i.e., the author/Encoder)?" or "What are the important features
of this text?" They may consider two aspects of the rhetorical situation in a
single question, e.g., "Am I in your intended (primary) audience?"; "What do I
think about this topic?"; "What context affected your ideas and presentation?"
Other questions would involve all three points of the triangle, e.g., "What are
you saying to help me with the problem you assume I have?" or "What textual
devices have you used to manipulate my response?" Asking such questions gives
students a way of formulating goals relating to purpose as well as content.

If Shirley, for example, had asked a Decoder-to-Encoder question—   27
such as "Am I in your intended audience?'"—she might have realized that

Churchill and the Guizots were writing for specific audiences. If she had asked a Decoder-to-Reality question—such as "What context affected your ideas and presentation?"—she might not have ignored Churchill's remark, "All these names [Amiens, Boves, Bethencourt] are well known to our generation" (403). As it was, she missed Churchill's signal that he was writing to survivors of the First World War, who had vainly hoped that it would be a war to end all wars. If Shirley had used an Encoder-Decoder-Reality question—such as "What are you saying to help me with the problem you assume I have?"—she might have understood that the authors of her sources were writing to different readers for different reasons. This understanding might have given her something to say. When I gave Shirley's source texts to freshmen students, asked them to use the material in an original argument, and taught them this heuristic for rhetorical reading, I received, for example, papers that warned undergraduates about national pride as a source of authorial bias in history texts.

A factual topic such as the Battle of Agincourt presents special problems 28 because of the seemingly intransigent nature of facts. Like many people, Shirley believes that you can either agree or disagree with issues and opinions, but you can only accept the so-called facts. She believes that facts are what you learn from textbooks, opinions are what you have about clothes, and arguments are what you have with your mother when you want to stay out late at night. Shirley is not in a position to disagree with the facts about the battle (e.g., "No, I think the French won"), and a rhetorical analysis may seem at first to offer minimal rewards (e.g., "According to the Arab, Jewish, and Chinese calendars the date was really . . .").

Alice, who thinks rhetorically, understands that both facts and opinions are 29 essentially the same kind of statement: they are claims. Alice understands that the only essential difference between a fact and an opinion is how they are received by an audience. (This discussion is derived from Toulmin's model of an argument as consisting of claims proved with data and backed by ethical claims called warrants. According to Toulmin, any aspect of an argument may be questioned by the audience and must then be supported with further argument.) In a rhetorical argument, a fact is a claim that an audience will accept as being true without requiring proof, although they may ask for an explanation. An opinion is a claim that an audience will not accept as true without proof, and which, after the proof is given, the audience may well decide has only a limited truth, i.e., it's true in this case but not in other cases. An audience may also decide that even though a fact is unassailable, the interpretation or use of the fact is open to debate.

For example, Shirley's sources gave different numbers for the size of the Brit- 30 ish army at Agincourt; these numbers, which must have been estimates, were claims masquerading as facts. Shirley did not understand this. She thought that disagreement signified error, whereas it probably signified rhetorical purpose. The probable reason that the Guizots give a relatively large estimate for the English army and do not mention the size of the French army is so that their French readers would find the British victory easier to accept. Likewise, Churchill's relatively small estimate for the size of the English army and his high estimate for the French army magnify the brilliance of the English victory. Before Shirley could create an argument about the Battle of Agincourt, she needed to understand that, even in her history textbooks, the so-called facts are claims that may or may not be supported, claims made by writers who work in a certain political climate for a particular audience. She may, of course, never learn this truth unless Dr. Boyer teaches her rhetorical theory and uses the research paper as a chance for Shirley to practice rhetorical problem-solving.

For most of her academic life, Shirley has done school tasks that require her 31 to find main ideas and important facts; success in these tasks usually hinges on agreeing with the teacher about what the text says. Such study skills form an essential basis for doing reading-to-write tasks. Obviously a student can only use sources to build an argument if she can first read the sources accurately (cf. Brown and Palincsar; Luftig; Short and Ryan). However, synthesizing tasks often require that readers not accept the authors' ideas. Baker and Brown have pointed out that people misread texts when they blindly accept an author's ideas instead of considering a divergent interpretation. Yet if we want students to learn to build original arguments from texts, we must teach them the skills needed to create divergent interpretations. We must teach them to think about facts and opinions as claims that are made by writers to particular readers for particular reasons in particular historical contexts.

Reading sources rhetorically gives students a powerful tool for creating a 32 persuasive analysis. Although no research exists as yet to suggest that teaching students to read rhetorically will improve their writing, I have seen its effect in successive drafts of students' papers. As mentioned earlier, rhetorical reading allowed a student to move from simply summarizing and evaluating her sources on local coverage of the championship football game to constructing a rationale for articles that covered the fans rather than the game. Rhetorical analysis enabled another student to move from summarizing his sources to understanding why each report about the Kent State shootings necessarily expressed a bias of some kind.

As these examples suggest, however, rhetorical reading is not a magical 33 technique for producing sophisticated arguments. Even when students read their sources rhetorically, they tend merely to report the results of this analysis in their essays. Such writing appears to be a college-level version of the knowledge-telling strategy described by Bereiter and Scardamalia (*Psychology*) and may be, as they suggest, the product of years of exposure to pedagogical practices that enshrine the acquisition and expression of information without a context or purpose.

To move students beyond merely reporting the content and rhetorical orien- 34 tation of their source texts, I have taught them the concept of the rhetorical gap and some simple heuristic questions for thinking about gaps. Gaps were first described by Iser as unsaid material that a reader must supply to infer from a text. McCormick expanded the concept to include gaps between the text and the reader; such gaps could involve discrepancies of values, social conventions, language, or any other matter that readers must consider. If we apply the concept of gaps to Kinneavy's triangle, we see that in reading, for example, a gap may occur between the Encoder-Decoder corners when the reader is not a member of the author's intended audience. Shirley fell into such a gap. Another gap can occur between the Decoder-Reality corners when a reader disagrees with or does not understand the text. A third gap can occur between the Encoder-Reality points of the triangle if the writer has misrepresented or misunderstood the material. The benefit of teaching this concept is that when a student thinks about a writer's rhetorical stance, she may ask "Why does he think that way?" When a student encounters a gap, she may ask, "What effect does it have on the success of this communication?" The answers to both questions give students original material for their papers.

Shirley, for example, did not know that Churchill began writing *The Birth* 35 *of Britain* during the 1930s, when Hitler was rearming Germany and when the British government and most of Churchill's readers ardently favored disarmament. Had she understood the rhetorical orientation of the book, which was published eleven years after the end of World War II, she might have argued that Churchill's evocation of past military glories would have been inflammatory in the 1930s but was highly acceptable twenty years later. A gap between the reader and the text (Decoder-Reality) might stimulate a reader to investigate whether or not she is the only person having this problem; a gap between other readers and the sources may motivate an adaptation or explanation of the material to a particular audience. Shirley might have adapted the Guizots' perspective on the French civil war for American readers. A gap between the author and the material (Encoder-Reality) might motivate a refutation.

To discover gaps, students may need to learn heuristics for setting rhetori- 36 cal writing goals. That is, they may need to learn to think of the paper, not as a rehash of the available material, but as an opportunity to teach someone, to solve someone's problem, or to answer someone's question. The most salient questions for reading source texts may be "Who are you (the original audience of Decoders)?"; "What is your question or problem with this topic?"; and "How have I (the Encoder) used these materials to answer your question or solve your problem?" More simply, these questions may be learned as "Why," "How," and "So what?" When Shirley learns to read sources as telling not the eternal truth but a truth to a particular audience and when she learns to think of texts as existing to solve problems, she will find it easier to think of things to say.

For example, a sophomore at a private university was struggling with an 37 assignment that required her to analyze an issue and express an opinion on it, using two conflicting source texts, an interview, and personal material as sources. Using rhetorical reading strategies, this girl discovered a gap between Alfred Marbaise, a high school principal who advocates mandatory drug testing of all high school students, and students like those he would be testing:

> Marbaise, who was a lieutenant in the U.S. Marines over thirty years ago . . . makes it very obvious that he cannot and will not tolerate any form of drug abuse in his school. For example, in paragraph seven he claims, "When students become involved in illegal activity, whether they realize it or not, they are violating other students . . . then I become very, very concerned . . . and I will not tolerate that."

Because Marbaise has not been in school for nearly forty years himself, he does not take into consideration the reasons why kids actually use drugs. Today the social environment is so drastically different that Marbaise cannot understand a kid's morality, and that is why he writes from such a fatherly but distant point of view.

The second paragraph answers the So what? question, i.e., "Why does it matter that Marbaise seems by his age and background to be fatherly and distant?" Unless the writer/reader thinks to ask this question, she will have difficulty writing a coherent evaluation of Marbaise's argument.

The relative success of some students in finding original things to say about their topics can help us to understand the perennial problem of plagiarism. Some plagiarism derives, I think, from a weak, nonrhetorical task representation. If students believe they are supposed to reproduce source material in their papers, or if they know they are supposed to say something original but have no rhetorical problem to solve and no knowledge of how to find problems that they can discuss in their sources, it becomes difficult for them to avoid plagiarizing. The common student decision to buy a paper when writing the assignment seems a meaningless fill-in-the-blanks activity (cf. Schwegler and Shamoon) becomes easily understandable. Because rhetorical reading leads to discoveries about the text, students who use it may take more interest in their research papers. 38

Let us now assume that Shirley understands the importance of creating an original argument, knows how to read analytically, and has found things to say about the Battle of Agincourt. Are her troubles over? Will she now create that A paper that she yearns to write? Probably not. Despite her best intentions, Shirley will probably write another narrative/paraphrase of her sources. Why? Because by now, the assignment asks her to do far more than she can handle in a single draft. Shirley's task representation is now so rich, her set of goals so many, that she may be unable to juggle them all simultaneously. Moreover, the rhetorical reading technique requires students to discover content worth writing about and a rhetorical purpose for writing; the uncertainty of managing such a discovery task when a grade is at stake may be too much for Shirley. 39

Difficult tasks may be difficult in either (or both of) two ways. First, they may require students to do a familiar subtask, such as reading sources, at a higher level of difficulty, e.g., longer sources, more sources, a more difficult topic. Second, they may require students to do new subtasks, such as building notes into an original argument. Such tasks may require task management skills, especially planning, that students have never developed and do not know how to attempt. The insecurity that results from trying a complex new task in a high-stakes situation is increased when students are asked to discover a problem worth writing about because such tasks send students out on a treasure hunt with no guarantee that the treasure exists, that they will recognize it when they find it, or that when they find it they will be able to build it into a coherent argument. The paper on Marbaise quoted above earned a grade of D because the writer could not use her rhetorical insights to build an argument presented 40 in a logical order. Although she asked the logical question about the implications of Marbaise's persona, she did not follow through by evaluating the gaps in his perspective that might affect the probable success of his program.

A skillful student using the summarize-the-main-ideas approach can set 41 her writing goals and even plan (i.e., outline) a paper before she reads the sources. The rhetorical reading strategy, by contrast, requires writers to discover what is worth writing about and to decide how to say it as or after they read their sources. The strategy requires writers to change their content goals and to adjust their writing plans as their understanding of the topic develops. It requires writers, in Flower's term, to "construct" their purposes for writing as well as the content for their paper (for a description of constructive planning, see Flower, Schriver, Carey, Haas, and Hayes). In Flower's words, writers who construct a purpose, as opposed to writers who bring a predetermined purpose to a task, "create a web of purposes . . . set goals, toss up possibilities . . . create a multidimensional network of information . . . a web of purpose . . . a bubbling stew of various mental representations" (531–32). The complex indeterminacy of such a task may pose an intimidating challenge to students who have spent their lives summarizing main ideas and reporting facts.

Shirley may respond to the challenge by concentrating her energies on a famil- 42 iar subtask, e.g., repeating material about the Battle of Agincourt, at the expense of struggling with an unfamiliar subtask such as creating an original argument. She may even deliberately simplify the task by representing it to herself as calling only for something that she knows how to do, expecting that Dr. Boyer will accept the paper as close enough to the original instructions. My students do this frequently. When students decide to write a report of their reading, they can at least be certain that they will find material to write about.

Because of the limits of attentional memory, not to mention those caused by 43 inexperience, writers can handle only so many task demands at a time. Thus, papers produced by seemingly inadequate task representations may well be essentially rough drafts. What looks like a bad paper may well be a preliminary step, a way of meeting certain task demands in order to create a basis for thinking about new ones. My students consistently report that they need to marshal all of their ideas and text knowledge and get that material down on the page (i.e., tell their knowledge) before they can think about developing an argument (i.e., transform their knowledge). If Shirley's problem is that she has shelved certain task demands in favor of others, Dr. Boyer needs only to point out what Shirley should do to bring the paper into conformity with the assignment and offer Shirley a chance to revise.

The problems of cognitive overload and inexperience in handling complex 44 writing tasks can create a tremendous hurdle for students because so many of them believe that they should be able to write their paper in a single draft. Some students think that if they can't do the paper in one draft that means that something is wrong with them as writers, or with the assignment, or with us for giving the assignment. Often, such students will react to their drafts with anger and despair, throwing away perfectly usable rough drafts and then coming to us and saying that they can't do the assignment.

The student's first draft about drug testing told her knowledge about her   45
sources' opinions on mandatory drug testing. Her second draft contained the rhetorical analysis quoted above, but presented the material in a scrambled order and did not build the analysis into an argument. Only in a third draft was this student able to make her point:

> Not once does Marbaise consider any of the psychological reasons why kids turn away from reality. He fails to realize that drug testing will not answer their questions, ease their frustrations, or respond to their cries for attention, but will merely further alienate himself and other authorities from helping kids deal with their real problems.

This comment represents Terri's answer to the heuristic "So what? Why does the source's position matter?" If we pace our assignments to allow for our students' thoughts to develop, we can do a great deal to build their confidence in their writing (Terri raised her D + to an A). If we treat the researched essay as a sequence of assignments instead of as a one-shot paper with a single due date, we can teach our students to build on their drafts, to use what they can do easily as a bridge to what we want them to learn to do. In this way, we can improve our students' writing habits. More importantly, however, we can help our students to see themselves as capable writers and as active, able, problem-solvers. Most importantly, we can use the sequence of drafts to demand that our students demonstrate increasingly sophisticated kinds of analytic and rhetorical proficiency.

Rhetorical reading and writing heuristics can help students to represent tasks   46
in rich and interesting ways. They can help students to set up complex goal structures (Bereiter and Scardamalia, "Conversation"). They offer students many ways to think about their reading and writing texts. These tools, in other words, encourage students to work creatively.

And after all, creativity is what research should be about. If Shirley writes   47
a creative paper, she has found a constructive solution that is new to her and which other people can use, a solution to a problem that she and other people share. Creativity is an inherently rhetorical quality. If we think of it as thought leading to solutions to problems and of problems as embodied in questions that people ask about situations, the researched essay offers infinite possibilities. Viewed in this way, a creative idea answers a question that the audience or any single reader wants answered. The question could be, "Why did Henry V win the Battle of Agincourt?' or, "How can student readers protect themselves against nationalistic bias when they study history?" or any of a thousand other questions. If we teach our Shirleys to see themselves as scholars who work to find answers to problem questions, and if we teach them to set reading and writing goals for themselves that will allow them to think constructively, we will be doing the most exciting work that teachers can do, nurturing creativity.

Appendix A: Page 1 of Shirley's paper

The battle of Agincourt ranks as one of England's greatest military triumphs. It was the most brilliant victory of the Middle Ages, bar none. It was fought on October 25, 1414, against the French near the French village of Agincourt.

Henry V had claimed the crown of France and had invaded France with an army estimated at anywhere ~~between~~ *from* 10,000[1] ~~and~~ *to* 45,000 men[2]. During the seige of Marfleur dysentery had taken 1/3 of them[3], his food supplies had been depleted[4], and the fall rains had begun. In addition the French had assembled a huge army and were marching toward him. Henry decided to march to Calais, where his ships were to await him[5]. He intended to cross the River Somme at the ford of Blanchetaque[6], but, falsely informed that the ford was guarded[7], he was forced to follow the flooded Somme up toward its source. The French army was shadowing him on his right. Remembering the slaughters of Crecy and Poictiers, the French constable, Charles d'Albret, hesitated to fight[8], but when Henry forded the Somme just above Amiens[9] and was just

---

1. Carl Stephinson, Medieval History, p. 529.
2. Guizot, Monsieur and Guizot, Madame, World's Best Histories-France, Volume II, p. 211.
3. Cyrid E. Robinson, England-A History of British Progress, p. 145.
4. Ibid.
5. Winston Churchill, A History of the English-Speaking Peoples, Volume I: The Birth of Britain, p. 403.
6. Ibid.
7. Ibid.
8. Robinson, p. 145.
9. Churchill, p. 403.

You footnote material that does not need to be footnoted.

Works Cited

Asch, Solomon. *Social Psychology.* New York: Prentice, 1952.

Atlas, Marshall. *Expert-Novice Differences in the Writing Process.* Paper presented at the American Educational Research Association, 1979. ERIC ED 107 769.

Baker, Louise, and Ann L. Brown. "Metacognitive Skills and Reading." *Handbook of Reading Research*. Eds. P. David Person, Rebecca Barr, Michael L. Kamil, and Peter Mosenthal. New York: Longman, 1984.

Bazerman, Charles. "Physicists Reading Physics: Schema-Laden Purposes and Purpose-Laden Schema." *Written Communication* 2.1 (1985): 3–24.

Bereiter, Carl, and Marlene Scardamalia. "From Conversation to Composition: The Role of Instruction in a Developmental Process." *Advances in Instructional Psychology*. Ed. R. Glaser. Vol. 2. Hillsdale, NJ: Lawrence Erlbaum Associates, 1982. 1–64.

———. *The Psychology of Written Composition*. Hillsdale, NJ: Lawrence Erlbaum Associates, 1987.

Briscoe, Terri. "To test or not to test." Unpublished essay. Texas Christian University, 1989.

Britton, James, Tony Burgess, Nancy Martin, Alex McLeod, and Harold Rosen. *The Development of Writing Abilities (11–18)*. Houndmills Basingstoke Hampshire: Macmillan Education Ltd., 1975.

Brown, Ann L. "Theories of Memory and the Problem of Development: Activity, Growth, and Knowledge." *Levels of Processing in Memory*. Eds. Laird S. Cermak and Fergus I. M. Craik. Hillsdale, NJ: Laurence Erlbaum Associates, 1979. 225–258.

———, Joseph C. Campione, and L. R. Barclay. *Training Self-Checking Routines for Estimating Test Readiness: Generalizations from List Learning to Prose Recall*. Unpublished manuscript. University of Illinois, 1978.

——— and Jeanne Day. "Macrorules for Summarizing Texts: The Development of Expertise." *Journal of Verbal Learning and Verbal Behavior* 22.1(1983): 1–14.

——— and Annmarie S. Palincsar. *Reciprocal Teaching of Comprehension Strategies: A Natural History of One Program for Enhancing Learning*. Technical Report #334. Urbana, IL: Center for the Study of Reading, 1985.

Churchill, Winston S. *The Birth of Britain*, New York: Dodd, 1956. Vol. 1 of *A History of the English-Speaking Peoples*. 4 vols. 1956–58.

Flower, Linda. "The Construction of Purpose in Writing and Reading." *College English* 50.5 (1988): 528–550.

———. *The Role of Task Representation in Reading to Write*. Berkeley, CA: Center for the Study of Writing, U of California at Berkeley and Carnegie Mellon. Technical Report, 1987.

———. "Writer-Based Prose: A Cognitive Basis for Problems in Writing." *College English* 41 (1979): 19–37.

Flower, Linda, Karen Schriver, Linda Carey, Christina Haas, and John R. Hayes. *Planning in Writing: A Theory of the Cognitive Process*. Berkeley, CA: Center for the Study of Writing, U of California at Berkeley and Carnegie Mellon. Technical Report, 1988.

Ford, James E., and Dennis R. Perry. "Research Paper Instruction in the Undergraduate Writing Program." *College English* 44 (1982): 825–31.

Ford, James E., Sharla Rees, and David L. Ward. *Teaching the Research Paper: Comprehensive Bibliography of Periodical Sources*, 1980. ERIC ED 197 363.

Goldman, Susan R. "Knowledge Systems for Realistic Goals." *Discourse Processes* 5 (1982): 279–303.

Guizot and Guizot de Witt. *The History of France from Earliest Times to 1848*. Trans. R. Black. Vol. 2. Philadelphia: John Wanamaker (n.d.).

Haas, Christina, and Linda Flower. "Rhetorical Reading Strategies and the Construction of Meaning." *College Composition and Communication* 39 (1988): 167–84.

Hayes, John R., D. A. Waterman, and C. S. Robinson. "Identifying the Relevant Aspects of a Problem Text." *Cognitive Science* 1 (1977): 297–313.

Hinze, Helen K. "The Individual's Word Associations and His Interpretation of Prose Paragraphs." *Journal of General Psychology* 64 (1961): 193–203.

Iser, Wolfgang. *The act of reading: A theory of aesthetic response*. Baltimore: The Johns Hopkins UP, 1978.

Jeffery, Christopher. "Teachers' and Students' Perceptions of the Writing Process." *Research in the Teaching of English* 15 (1981): 215–28.

Kantz, Margaret. "Originality and Completeness: What Do We Value in Papers Written from Sources?" Conference on College Composition and Communication. St. Louis, MO, 1988.

———. *The Relationship Between Reading and Planning Strategies and Success in Synthesizing: It's What You Do with Them that Counts.* Technical report in preparation. Pittsburgh: Center for the Study of Writing, 1988.

Kennedy, Mary Louise. "The Composing Process of College Students Writing from Sources," *Written Communication* 2.4 (1985): 434–56.

Kinneavy, James L. *A Theory of Discourse.* New York: Norton, 1971.

Kroll, Barry M. "Audience Adaptation in Children's Persuasive Letters." *Written Communication* 1.4 (1984): 407–28.

Langer, Judith. "Where Problems Start: The Effects of Available Information on Responses to School Writing Tasks." *Contexts for Learning to Write: Studies of Secondary School Instruction.* Ed. Arthur Applebee. Norwood, NJ: ABLEX Publishing Corporation, 1984. 135–48.

Luftig, Richard L. "Abstractive Memory, the Central-Incidental Hypothesis, and the Use of Structural Importance in Text: Control Processes or Structural Features?" *Reading Research Quarterly* 14.1 (1983): 28–37.

Marbaise, Alfred. "Treating a Disease." *Current Issues and Enduring Questions.* Eds. Sylvan Barnet and Hugo Bedau. New York: St. Martin's, 1987. 126–27.

McCormick, Kathleen. "Theory in the Reader: Bleich, Holland, and Beyond." *College English* 47.8 (1985): 836–50.

McGarry, Daniel D. *Medieval History and Civilization.* New York: Macmillan, 1976.

Nelson, Jennie, and John R. Hayes. *The Effects of Classroom Contexts on Students' Responses to Writing from Sources: Regurgitating Information or Triggering Insights.* Berkeley, CA: Center for the Study of Writing, U of California at Berkeley and Carnegie Mellon. Technical Report, 1988.

Pichert, James W. "Sensitivity to Importance as a Predictor of Reading Comprehension." *Perspectives on Reading Research and Instruction.* Eds. Michael A. Kamil and Alden J. Moe. Washington, D.C.: National Reading Conference, 1980. 42–46.

Robinson, Cyril E. *England: A History of British Progress from the Early Ages to the Present Day.* New York: Thomas Y. Crowell Company, 1928.

Schwegler, Robert A., and Linda K. Shamoon. "The Aims and Process of the Research Paper." *College English* 44 (1982): 817–24.

Shedd, Patricia T. "The Relationship between Attitude of the Reader Towards Women's Changing Role and Response to Literature Which Illuminates Women's Role." Diss. Syracuse U, 1975. ERIC ED 142 956.

Short, Elizabeth Jane, and Ellen Bouchard Ryan. "Metacognitive Differences between Skilled and Less Skilled Readers: Remediating Deficits through Story Grammar and Attribution Training." *Journal of Education Psychology* 76 (1984): 225–35.

Spivey, Nancy Nelson. *Discourse Synthesis: Constructing Texts in Reading and Writing.* Diss. U Texas, 1983. Newark, DE: International Reading Association, 1984.

Toulmin, Steven E. *The Uses of Argument.* Cambridge: Cambridge UP, 1969.

Vipond, Douglas, and Russell Hunt. "Point-Driven Understanding: Pragmatic and Cognitive Dimensions of Literary Reading." *Poetics* 13, (1984): 261–77.

Winograd, Peter. "Strategic Difficulties in Summarizing Texts." *Reading Research Quarterly* 19 (1984): 404–25.

Questions for Discussion and Journaling

1. Kantz writes that Shirley "believes that facts are what you learn from textbooks, opinions are what you have about clothes, and arguments are what you have with your mother when you want to stay out late at night" (para. 28). What does Kantz contend that facts, opinions, and arguments actually are?

2. Make a list of the things Kantz says students don't know, misunderstand, or don't comprehend about how texts work. Judging from your own experience, do you think she's correct? How many of the things she lists do you feel you understand now?

3. As its title indicates, Kantz's article has to do with using sources *persuasively*. Did her article teach you anything new about the persuasive use of sources to support an argument? If so, what?

4. Do you think Kantz contradicts herself when she says that we should think of sources neither as stories nor as repositories of truth? Explain why or why not.

5. Which of the students in Kantz's article do you most identify with, and why?

6. Do you think Kantz's ideas will change your own approach to doing research and writing with sources? If so, how?

Applying and Exploring Ideas

1. Kantz places some blame for students' writing difficulties on poorly written assignments that don't clearly explain what teachers want. Conduct your own mini review of college writing assignments you've received. How many do you think gave sufficient explanation of what the professor was looking for? As you look at assignments that did give good directions, what do they have in common? That is, based on those assignments, what did you need to be told in order to have a good understanding of what you were being asked to write? Write one to two pages about what you find, and share what you write in class.

2. Write a short reflection on the relationship between creativity and research as you've learned to understand it prior to this class, and as Kantz talks about it. Where do your and her ideas overlap? Where does her thinking influence yours? And where does it not seem to work for you?

Meta Moment

One of the goals for this chapter is considering constructs of or conceptions about writing that don't survive close scrutiny. What constructs or conceptions is Kantz trying to analyze? Why would it be useful for you to understand her findings and claims?

Intertextuality and the Discourse Community

JAMES E. PORTER

Porter, James E. "Intertextuality and the Discourse Community." *Rhetoric Review* 5.1 (1986): 34–47. Print.

Framing the Reading

Two of the deepest conceptions of writing that our culture holds are (1) that writing must be *original* and (2) that if a writer "borrows" ideas from other writing without acknowledging that borrowing, the writer is *plagiarizing*. In the following study, James Porter argues that these common ideas about originality and plagiarism don't account for how texts actually work and how writers actually write. Porter calls into question how original writers can actually be in constructing texts and, following from that question, also wonders how we should define plagiarism if true originality is so difficult to find.

The principle Porter explores in asking these questions is **intertextuality**— that is, the idea that *all* texts contain "traces" of other texts and that there can be no text that does not draw on *some* ideas from some other texts. You may rightly be skeptical of a claim so broad, so follow along carefully as Porter explains why he thinks this is true. You may be particularly interested in the section in which Porter demonstrates his argument by looking at how the Declaration of Independence was written, as he claims, collaboratively, by a number of different authors.

The implications of Porter's study are significant for how you understand writing and how you understand yourself as a writer. Most of us have been taught that writers are *autonomous*—that is, that they're free do to whatever they want with their texts, and also that they're solely responsible for what's in those texts. Porter's research on actual writing and writers challenges this construct. If Porter is correct, then we need a *different* construct of the *author*, one that acknowledges the extent to which communities shape what a writer chooses to say; the extent to which writers say things that have already been said (even when they believe they're being original); and the extent to which texts are constructed by many different people along the way, as readers feed ideas back to the writer.

Getting Ready to Read

Before you read, do at least one of the following activities:

- Write a paragraph on what, in your mind the difference between an *author* and a *writer* is. When would you choose the first term to describe the person/people behind a text, and when would you choose the second?
- Make a list of all the ways you get "help," of any kind, in your writing. Where do you get ideas, advice, feedback, and assistance?
- Find one or two friends or family members who write a great deal, either for a living, as a major part of their jobs, or as a hobby. Interview them about who or what they see contributing to their writing. To what extent do they see themselves doing their writing "on their own"?

As you read, consider the following questions:

- Watch for how Porter poses questions about writers' *autonomy* and *originality*: Does he finally decide that autonomy and originality are impossible?
- Do you think Porter is *criticizing* the Declaration of Independence? Thomas Jefferson? Explain your answer.
- If you haven't seen the Pepsi commercial that Porter discusses, try to find a version of it to watch online. Does Porter's reading of the commercial match yours, or do you understand it differently?

At the conclusion of Eco's *The Name of the Rose*, the monk Adso of   1
Melk returns to the burned abbey, where he finds in the ruins scraps of parchment, the only remnants from one of the great libraries in all Christendom. He spends a day collecting the charred fragments, hoping to discover some meaning in the scattered pieces of books. He assembles his own "lesser library . . . of fragments, quotations, unfinished sentences, amputated stumps of books" (500). To Adso, these random shards are "an immense acrostic that says and repeats nothing" (501). Yet they are significant to him as an attempt to order experience.

We might well derive our own order from this scene. We might see Adso   2
as representing the writer, and his desperate activity at the burned abbey as a model for the writing process. The writer in this image is a collector of fragments, an archaeologist creating an order, building a framework, from remnants of the past. Insofar as the collected fragments help Adso recall other, lost texts, his experience affirms a principle he learned from his master, William of Baskerville: "Not infrequently books speak of books" (286). Not infrequently, and perhaps ever and always, texts refer to other texts and in fact rely on them for their meaning. All texts are interdependent: We understand a text only insofar as we understand its precursors.

This is the principle we know as intertextuality, the principle that all writ-   3
ing and speech—indeed, all signs—arise from a single network: what Vygotsky
called "the web of meaning"; what post-
structuralists label Text or Writing (Barthes, *écriture*); and what a more distant
age perhaps knew as *logos*. Examining
texts "intertextually" means looking
for "traces," the bits and pieces of Text
which writers or speakers borrow and

> All texts are interdependent: We
> understand a text only insofar as
> we understand its precursors.

sew together to create new discourse.[1] The most mundane manifestation of intertextuality is explicit citation, but intertextuality animates all discourse and goes
beyond mere citation. For the intertextual critics, Intertext is Text—a great seamless textual fabric. And, as they like to intone solemnly, no text escapes intertext.

Intertextuality provides rhetoric with an important perspective, one cur-   4
rently neglected, I believe. The prevailing composition pedagogies by and large
cultivate the romantic image of writer as free, uninhibited spirit, as independent, creative genius. By identifying and stressing the intertextual nature of
discourse, however, we shift our attention away from the writer as individual
and focus more on the sources and social contexts from which the writer's
discourse arises. According to this view, authorial intention is less significant
than social context; the writer is simply a part of a discourse tradition, a member of a team, and a participant in a community of discourse that creates its
own collective meaning. Thus the intertext *constrains* writing.

My aim here is to demonstrate the significance of this theory to rhetoric, by   5
explaining intertextuality, its connection to the notion of "discourse community," and its pedagogical implications for composition.

The Presence of Intertext

Intertextuality has been associated with both structuralism and poststructural-   6
ism, with theorists like Roland Barthes, Julia Kristeva, Jacques Derrida, Hayden
White, Harold Bloom, Michel Foucault, and Michael Riffaterre. (Of course, the
theory is most often applied in literary analysis.) The central assumption of these
critics has been described by Vincent Leitch: "The text is not an autonomous or
unified object, but a set of relations with other texts. Its system of language, its
grammar, its lexicon, drag along numerous bits and pieces—traces—of history
so that the text resembles a Cultural Salvation Army Outlet with unaccountable
collections of incompatible ideas, beliefs, and sources" (59). It is these "unaccountable collections" that intertextual critics focus on, not the text as autonomous entity. In fact, these critics have redefined the notion of "text": Text *is*
intertext, or simply Text. The traditional notion of the text as the single work of
a given author, and even the very notions of author and reader, are regarded as
simply convenient fictions for domesticating discourse. The old borders that we
used to rope off discourse, proclaim these critics, are no longer useful.

We can distinguish between two types of intertextuality: iterability and pre-   7
supposition. Iterability refers to the "repeatability" of certain textual fragments,

to citation in its broadest sense to include not only explicit allusions, references, and quotations within a discourse, but also unannounced sources and influences, clichés, phrases in the air, and traditions. That is to say, every discourse is composed of "traces," pieces of other texts that help constitute its meaning. (I will discuss this aspect of intertextuality in my analysis of the Declaration of Independence.) Presupposition refers to assumptions a text makes about its referent, its readers, and its context—to portions of the text which are read, but which are not explicitly "there." For example, as Jonathan Culler discusses, the phrase "John married Fred's sister" is an assertion that logically presupposes that John exists, that Fred exists, and that Fred has a sister. "Open the door" contains a practical presupposition, assuming the presence of a decoder who is capable of being addressed and who is better able to open the door than the encoder. "Once upon a time" is a trace rich in rhetorical presupposition, signaling to even the youngest reader the opening of a fictional narrative. Texts not only refer to but in fact *contain* other texts.[2]

An examination of three sample texts will illustrate the various facets of intertextuality. The first, the Declaration of Independence, is popularly viewed as the work of Thomas Jefferson. Yet if we examine the text closely in its rhetorical milieu, we see that Jefferson was author only in the very loosest of senses. A number of historians and at least two composition researchers (Kinneavy, *Theory* 393–49; Maimon, *Readings* 6–32) have analyzed the Declaration, with interesting results. Their work suggests that Jefferson was by no means an original framer or a creative genius, as some like to suppose. Jefferson was a skilled writer, to be sure, but chiefly because he was an effective borrower of traces. 8

To produce his original draft of the Declaration, Jefferson seems to have borrowed, either consciously or unconsciously, from his culture's Text. Much has been made of Jefferson's reliance on Locke's social contract theory (Becker). Locke's theory influenced colonial political philosophy, emerging in various pamphlets and newspaper articles of the times, and served as the foundation for the opening section of the Declaration. The Declaration contains many traces that can be found in other, earlier documents. There are traces from a First Continental Congress resolution, a Massachusetts Council declaration, George Mason's "Declaration of Rights for Virginia," a political pamphlet of James Otis, and a variety of other sources, including a colonial play. The overall form of the Declaration (theoretical argument followed by list of grievances) strongly resembles, ironically, the English Bill of Rights of 1689, in which Parliament lists the abuses of James II and declares new powers for itself. Several of the abuses in the Declaration seem to have been taken, more or less verbatim, from a *Pennsylvania Evening Post* article. And the most memorable phrases in the Declaration seem to be least Jefferson's: "That all men are created equal" is a sentiment from Euripides which Jefferson copied in his literary commonplace book as a boy; "Life, Liberty, and the pursuit of Happiness" was a cliché of the times, appearing in numerous political documents (Dumbauld). 9

Though Jefferson's draft of the Declaration can hardly be considered his in any exclusive sense of authorship, the document underwent still more 10 expropriation at the hands of Congress, who made eighty-six changes (Kinneavy, *Theory* 438). They cut the draft from 211 lines to 147. They did considerable editing to temper what they saw as Jefferson's emotional style: For example, Jefferson's phrase 'sacred & undeniable" was changed to the more restrained "self-evident." Congress excised controversial passages, such as Jefferson's condemnation of slavery. Thus, we should find it instructive to note, Jefferson's few attempts at original expression were those least acceptable to Congress.

If Jefferson submitted the Declaration for a college writing class as his own . 11 writing, he might well be charged with plagiarism.[3] The idea of Jefferson as author is but convenient shorthand. Actually, the Declaration arose out of a cultural and rhetorical milieu, was composed of traces—and was, in effect, team written. Jefferson deserves credit for bringing disparate traces together, for helping to mold and articulate the milieu, for creating the all-important draft. Jefferson's skill as a writer was his ability to borrow traces effectively and to find appropriate contexts for them. As Michael Halliday says, "[C]reativeness does not consist in producing new sentences. The newness of a sentence is a quite unimportant—and unascertainable—property and 'creativity' in language lies in the speaker's ability to create new meanings: to realize the potentiality of language for the indefinite extension of its resources to new contexts of situation. . . . Our most 'creative' acts may be precisely among those that are realized through highly repetitive forms of behaviour" (*Explorations* 42). The creative writer is the creative borrower, in other words.

Intertextuality can be seen working similarly in contemporary forums. 12 Recall this scene from a recent Pepsi commercial: A young boy in jeans jacket, accompanied by dog, stands in some desolate plains crossroads next to a gas station, next to which is a soft drink machine. An alien spacecraft, resembling the one in Spielberg's *Close Encounters of the Third Kind*, appears overhead. To the boy's joyful amazement, the spaceship hovers over the vending machine and begins sucking Pepsi cans into the ship. It takes *only* Pepsi's, then eventually takes the entire machine. The ad closes with a graphic: "Pepsi. The Choice of a New Generation."

Clearly, the commercial presupposes familiarity with Spielberg's movie or, at 13 least, with his pacific vision of alien spacecraft. We see several American clichés, well-worn signs from the Depression era: the desolate plains, the general store, the pop machine, the country boy with dog. These distinctively American traces are juxtaposed against images from science fiction and the sixties catchphrase "new generation" in the coda. In this array of signs, we have tradition and counter-tradition harmonized. Pepsi squeezes itself in the middle, and thus becomes the great American conciliator. The ad's use of irony may serve to distract viewers momentarily from noticing how Pepsi achieves its purpose by assigning itself an exalted role through use of the intertext.

We find an interesting example of practical presupposition in John Kifner's 14 *New York Times* headline article reporting on the Kent State incident of 1970:

> Four students at Kent State University, two of them women, were shot to death this afternoon by a volley of National Guard gunfire. At least 8 other students were wounded.

The burst of gunfire came about 20 minutes after the guardsmen broke up a noon rally on the Commons, a grassy campus gathering spot, by lobbing tear gas at a crowd of about 1,000 young people.

From one perspective, the phrase "two of them women" is a simple state- 15 ment of fact; however, it presupposes a certain attitude—that the event, horrible enough as it was, is more significant because two of the persons killed were women. It might be going too far to say that the phrase presupposes a "sexist attitude ("women aren't supposed to be killed in battles"), but can we imagine the phrase "two of them men" in this context? Though equally factual, this wording would have been considered odd in 1970 (and probably today as well) because it presupposes a cultural mindset alien from the one dominant at the time. "Two of them women" is shocking (and hence it was reported) because it upsets the sense of order of the readers, in this case the American public.

Additionally (and more than a little ironically), the text contains a num- 16 ber of traces which have the effect of blunting the shock of the event. Notice that the students were not shot by National Guardsmen, but were shot "by a volley of . . . gunfire"; the tear gas was "lobbed"; and the event occurred at a "grassy campus gathering spot." "Volley" and "lobbed" are military terms, but with connections to sport as well; "grassy campus gathering spot" suggests a picnic; "burst" can recall the glorious sight of bombs "bursting" in "The Star-Spangled Banner." This pastiche of signs casts the text into a certain context, making it distinctively American. We might say that the turbulent milieu of the sixties provided a distinctive array of signs from which John Kifner borrowed to produce his article.

Each of the three texts examined contains phrases or images familiar to its 17 audience or presupposes certain audience attitudes. Thus the intertext exerts its influence partly in the form of audience expectation. We might then say that the audience of each of these texts is as responsible for its production as the writer. That, in essence, readers, not writers, create discourse.

The Power of Discourse Community

And, indeed, this is what some poststructuralist critics suggest, those who pre- 18 fer a broader conception of intertext or who look beyond the intertext to the social framework regulating textual production: to what Michel Foucault calls "the discursive formation," what Stanley Fish calls "the interpretive community," and what Patricia Bizzell calls "the discourse community."

A "discourse community" is a group of individuals bound by a common 19 interest who communicate through approved channels and whose discourse is regulated. An individual may belong to several professional, public, or personal discourse communities. Examples would include the community of engineers whose research area is fluid mechanics; alumni of the University of Michigan; Magnavox employees; the members of the Porter family; and members of the Indiana Teachers of Writing. The approved channels we can call "forums." Each forum has a distinct history and rules governing appropriateness to which members are obliged to adhere. These rules may be more or less apparent, more or less institutionalized, more or less specific to each community. Examples of forums include professional publications like *Rhetoric Review, English Journal,* and *Creative Computing;* public media like *Newsweek* and *Runner's World;* professional conferences (the annual meeting of fluid power engineers, the 4C's); company board meetings; family dinner tables; and the monthly meeting of the Indiana chapter of the Izaak Walton League.

A discourse community shares assumptions about what objects are appro-   20 priate for examination and discussion, what operating functions are performed on those objects, what constitutes "evidence" and "validity," and what formal conventions are followed. A discourse community may have a well-established *ethos*; or it may have competing factions and indefinite boundaries. It may be in a "pre-paradigm" state (Kuhn), that is, having an ill-defined regulating system and no clear leadership. Some discourse communities are firmly established, such as the scientific community, the medical profession, and the justice system, to cite a few from Foucault's list. In these discourse communities, as Leitch says, "a speaker must be 'qualified' to talk; he has to belong to a community of scholarship; and he is required to possess a prescribed body of knowledge (doctrine). . . . [This system] operates to constrain discourse; it establishes limits and regularities. . . . who may speak, what may be spoken, and how it is to be said; in addition [rules] prescribe what is true and false, what is reasonable and what foolish, and what is meant and what not. Finally, they work to deny the material existence of discourse itself" (145).

A text is "acceptable" within a forum only insofar as it reflects the commu-   21 nity episteme (to use Foucault's term). On a simple level, this means that for a manuscript to be accepted for publication in the *Journal of Applied Psychology*, it must follow certain formatting conventions: It must have the expected social science sections (i.e., review of literature, methods, results, discussion), and it must use the journal's version of APA documentation. However, these are only superficial features of the forum. On a more essential level, the manuscript must reveal certain characteristics, have an *ethos* (in the broadest possible sense) conforming to the standards of the discourse community: It must demonstrate (or at least claim) that it contributes knowledge to the field, it must demonstrate familiarity with the work of previous researchers in the field, it must use a scientific method in analyzing its results (showing acceptance of the truth-value of statistical demonstration), it must meet standards for test design and analysis of results, it must adhere to standards determining degree of accuracy. The expectations, conventions, and attitudes of this discourse community—the readers, writers, and publishers of *Journal of Applied Psychology*—will influence aspiring psychology researchers, shaping not only how they write but also their character within that discourse community.

The poststructuralist view challenges the classical assumption that writ-   22 ing is a simple linear, one-way movement: The writer creates a text which produces some change in an audience. A poststructuralist rhetoric examines how audience (in the form of community expectations and standards) influences textual production and, in so doing, guides the development of the writer.

This view is of course open to criticism for its apparent determinism, for 23 devaluing the contribution of individual writers and making them appear merely tools of the discourse community (charges which Foucault answers in "Discourse on Language"). If these regulating systems are so constraining, how can an individual emerge? What happens to the idea of the lone inspired writer and the sacred autonomous text?

Both notions take a pretty hard knock. Genuine originality is difficult within 24 the confines of a well-regulated system. Genius is possible, but it may be constrained. Foucault cites the example of Gregor Mendel, whose work in the nineteenth century was excluded from the prevailing community of biologists because he "spoke of objects, employed methods and placed himself within a theoretical perspective totally alien to the biology of his time. . . . Mendel spoke the truth, but he was not *dans le vrai* (within the true)" (224). Frank Lentricchia cites a similar example from the literary community: Robert Frost "achieved magazine publication only five times between 1895 and 1912, a period during which he wrote a number of poems later acclaimed . . . [because] in order to write within the dominant sense of the poetic in the United States in the last decade of the nineteenth century and the first decade of the twentieth, one had to employ a diction, syntax, and prosody heavily favoring Shelley and Tennyson. One also had to assume a certain stance, a certain world-weary idealism which took care not to refer too concretely to the world of which one was weary" (197, 199).

Both examples point to the exclusionary power of discourse communities 25 and raise serious questions about the freedom of the writer: chiefly, does the writer have any? Is any writer doomed to plagiarism? Can any text be said to be new? Are creativity and genius actually possible? Was Jefferson a creative genius or a blatant plagiarist?

Certainly we want to avoid both extremes. Even if the writer is locked into a 26 cultural matrix and is constrained by the intertext of the discourse community, the writer has freedom within the immediate rhetorical context.[4] Furthermore, successful writing helps to redefine the matrix—and in that way becomes creative. (Jefferson's Declaration contributed to defining the notion of America for its discourse community.) Every new text has the potential to alter the Text in some way; in fact, every text admitted into a discourse community changes the constitution of the community—and discourse communities can revise their discursive practices, as the Mendel and Frost examples suggest.

Writing is an attempt to exercise the will, to identify the self within the con- 27 straints of some discourse community. We are constrained insofar as we must inevitably borrow the traces, codes, and signs which we inherit and which our discourse community imposes. We are free insofar as we do what we can to encounter and learn new codes, to intertwine codes in new ways, and to expand our semiotic potential—with our goal being to effect change and establish our identities within the discourse communities we choose to enter.

The Pedagogy of Intertextuality

Intertextuality is not new. It may remind some of Eliot's notion of tradi- 28
tion, though the parameters are certainly broader. It is an important concept,
though. It counters what I see as one prevailing composition pedagogy, one
favoring a romantic image of the writer, offering as role models the creative
essayists, the Sunday Supplement freelancers, the Joan Didions, E. B. Whites,
Calvin Trillins, and Russell Bakers. This dashing image appeals to our need for
intellectual heroes; but underlying it may be an anti-rhetorical view: that writers are born, not made; that writing is individual, isolated, and internal; not
social but eccentric.

This view is firmly set in the intertext of our discipline. Our anthologies 29
glorify the individual essayists, whose work is valued for its timelessness and
creativity. Freshman rhetorics announce as the writer's proper goals personal
insight, originality, and personal voice, or tell students that motivations for
writing come from "within." Generally, this pedagogy assumes that such a
thing as the writer actually exists—an autonomous writer exercising a free,
creative will through the writing act—and that the writing process proceeds
linearly from writer to text to reader. This partial picture of the process can all
too readily become *the* picture, and our students can all too readily learn to
overlook vital facets of discourse production.

When we romanticize composition by overemphasizing the autonomy of the 30
writer, important questions are overlooked, the same questions an intertextual
view of writing would provoke: To what extent is the writer's product itself a
part of a larger community writing process? How does the discourse community influence writers and readers within it? These are essential questions, but
are perhaps outside the prevailing episteme of composition pedagogy, which
presupposes the autonomous status of the writer as independent *cogito*. Talking about writing in terms of "social forces influencing the writer" raises the
specter of determinism, and so is anathema.

David Bartholomae summarizes this issue very nicely: "The struggle of the 31
student writer is not the struggle to bring out that which is within; it is the
struggle to carry out those ritual activities that grant our entrance into a closed
society" (300). When we teach writing only as the act of "bringing out what
is within," we risk undermining our own efforts. Intertextuality reminds us
that "carrying out ritual activities" is also part of the writing process. Barthes
reminds us that "the 'I' which approaches the text is already itself a plurality of
other texts, of codes which are infinite" (10).

Intertextuality suggests that our goal should be to help students learn to write 32
for the discourse communities they choose to join. Students need help developing out of what Joseph Williams calls their "pre-socialized cognitive states."
According to Williams, pre-socialized writers are not sufficiently immersed in
their discourse community to produce competent discourse: They do not know
what can be presupposed, are not conscious of the distinctive intertextuality
of the community, may be only superficially acquainted with explicit conventions. (Williams cites the example of the freshman whose paper for the English
teacher begins "Shakespeare is a famous Elizabethan dramatist.") Our imme-

diate goal is to produce "socialized writers," who are full-fledged members of their discourse community, producing competent, useful discourse within that community. Our long-range goal might be "post-socialized writers," those who have achieved such a degree of confidence, authority, power, or achievement in the discourse community so as to become part of the regulating body. They are able to vary conventions and question assumptions—i.e., effect change in communities—without fear of exclusion.

Intertextuality has the potential to affect all facets of our composition peda- 33 gogy. Certainly it supports writing across the curriculum as a mechanism for introducing students to the regulating systems of discourse communities. It raises questions about heuristics: Do different discourse communities apply different heuristics? It asserts the value of critical reading in the composition classroom. It requires that we rethink our ideas about plagiarism: Certainly *imitatio* is an important stage in the linguistic development of the writer.

The most significant application might be in the area of audience analysis. 34 Current pedagogies assume that when writers analyze audiences they should focus on the expected flesh-and-blood readers. Intertextuality suggests that the proper focus of audience analysis is not the audience as receivers per se, but the intertext of the discourse community. Instead of collecting demographic data about age, educational level, and social status, the writer might instead ask questions about the intertext: What are the conventional presuppositions of this community? In what forums do they assemble? What are the methodological assumptions? What is considered "evidence," "valid argument," and "proof"? A sample heuristic for such an analysis—what I term "forum analysis"—is included as an appendix.

A critical reading of the discourse of a community may be the best way to 35 understand it. (We see a version of this message in the advice to examine a journal before submitting articles for publication.) Traditionally, anthologies have provided students with reading material. However, the typical anthologies have two serious problems: (1) limited range—generally they overemphasize literary or expressive discourse; (2) unclear context—they frequently remove readings from their original contexts, thus disguising their intertextual nature. Several recently published readers have attempted to provide a broader selection of readings in various forums, and actually discuss intertextuality. Maimon's *Readings in the Arts and Sciences*, Kinneavy's *Writing in the Liberal Arts Tradition*, and Bazerman's *The Informed Writer* are especially noteworthy.

Writing assignments should be explicitly intertextual. If we regard each 36 written product as a stage in a larger process—the dialectic process within a discourse community—then the individual writer's work is part of a web, part of a community search for truth and meaning. Writing assignments might take the form of dialogue with other writers: Writing letters in response to articles is one kind of dialectic (e.g., letters responding to *Atlantic Monthly* or *Science* articles). Research assignments might be more community oriented rather than topic oriented; students might be asked to become involved in communities of researchers (e.g., the sociologists examining changing religious attitudes in American college students). The assignments in Maimon's *Writing in the Arts and Sciences* are excellent in this regard.

Intertextual theory suggests that the key criteria for evaluating writing   37
should be "acceptability" within some discourse community. "Acceptability"
includes, but goes well beyond, adherence to formal conventions. It includes
choosing the "right" topic, applying the appropriate critical methodology,
adhering to standards for evidence and validity, and in general adopting the
community's discourse values—and of course borrowing the appropriate
traces. Success is measured by the writer's ability to know what can be presupposed and to borrow that community's traces effectively to create a text that
contributes to the maintenance or, possibly, the definition of the community.
The writer is constrained by the community, and by its intertextual preferences
and prejudices, but the effective writer works to assert the will against those
community constraints to effect change.

The Pepsi commercial and the Kent State news article show effective uses of   38
the intertext. In the Kent State piece, John Kifner mixes picnic imagery ("grassy
campus gathering spot," "young people") with violent imagery ("burst of gunfire") to dramatize the event. The Pepsi ad writers combine two unlikely sets
of traces, linking folksy depression-era American imagery with sci-fi imagery
"stolen" from Spielberg. For this creative intertwining of traces, both discourses
can probably be measured successful in their respective forums.

Coda

Clearly much of what intertextuality supports is already institutionalized (e.g.,   39
writing-across-the-curriculum programs). And yet, in freshman comp texts and
anthologies especially, there is this tendency to see writing as individual, as
isolated, as heroic. Even after demonstrating quite convincingly that the Declaration was written by a team freely borrowing from a cultural intertext, Elaine
Maimon insists, against all the evidence she herself has collected, that "Despite
the additions, deletions, and changes in wording that it went through, the Declaration is still Jefferson's writing" (*Readings* 26). Her saying this presupposes
that the reader has just concluded the opposite.

When we give our students romantic role models like E. B. White, Joan Didion,   40
and Lewis Thomas, we create unrealistic expectations. This type of writer has
often achieved post-socialized status within some discourse community (Thomas
in the scientific community, for instance). Can we realistically expect our students
to achieve this state without first becoming socialized, without learning first what
it means to write within a social context? Their role models ought not be only
romantic heroes but also community writers like Jefferson, the anonymous writers of the Pepsi commercial—the Adsos of the world, not just the Aristotles. They
need to see writers whose products are more evidently part of a larger process
and whose work more clearly produces meaning in social contexts.

Notes

1. The dangers of defining intertextuality too simplistically are discussed by Owen Miller in
   "Intertextual Identity," *Identity of the Literary Text,* ed. Mario J. Valdés and Owen Miller

(Toronto: U of Toronto P, 1985), 19–40. Miller points out that intertextuality "addresses itself to a plurality of concepts" (19).

2. For fuller discussion see Jonathan Culler, *The Pursuit of Signs* (Ithaca: Cornell UP, 1981), 100–16. Michael Halliday elaborates on the theory of presupposition somewhat, too, differentiating between exophoric and endophoric presupposition. The meaning of any text at least partly relies on exophoric references, i.e., external presuppositions. Endophoric references in the form of cohesive devices and connections within a text also affect meaning, but cohesion in a text depends ultimately on the audience making exophoric connections to prior texts, connections that may not be cued by explicit cohesive devices. See M. A. K. Halliday and Ruqaiya Hasan, *Cohesion in English* (London: Longman, 1976).

3. Miller cautions us about intertextuality and *post hoc ergo propter hoc* reasoning. All we can safely note is that phrases in the Declaration also appear in other, earlier documents. Whether or not the borrowing was intentional on Jefferson's part or whether the prior documents "caused" the Declaration (in any sense of the word) is not ascertainable.

4. Robert Scholes puts it this way: "If you play chess, you can only do certain things with the pieces, otherwise you are not playing chess. But those constraints do not in themselves tell you what moves to make." See *Textual Power* (New Haven: Yale UP, 1985), 153.

Works Cited

Barthes, Roland. *S/Z*. Trans. Richard Miller. New York: Hill and Wang, 1974.

Bartholomae, David. "Writing Assignments: Where Writing Begins." *fforum*. Ed. Patricia L. Stock. Upper Montclair, NJ: Boynton/Cook, 1983.

Bazerman, Charles. *The Informed Writer*. 2nd ed. Boston: Houghton Mifflin, 1985.

Becker, Carl. *The Declaration of Independence*. 2nd ed. New York: Random, Vintage, 1942.

Bizzell, Patricia. "Cognition, Convention, and Certainty: What We Need to Know about Writing." *PRE/TEXT* 3 (1982): 213–43.

Culler, Jonathan. *The Pursuit of Signs*. Ithaca: Cornell UP, 1981.

Dumbauld, Edward. *The Declaration of Independence*. 2nd ed. Norman: U of Oklahoma P, 1968.

Eco, Umberto. *The Name of the Rose*. Trans. William Weaver. San Diego: Harcourt Brace Jovanovich, 1983.

Fish, Stanley. *Is There a Text in This Class?* Cambridge: Harvard UP, 1980.

Foucault, Michel. *The Archaeology of Knowledge and the Discourse on Language*. Trans. A. M. Sheridan Smith. New York: Harper & Row, 1972.

Halliday, M. A. K. *Explorations in the Functions of Language*. New York: Elsevier, 1973.

Halliday, M. A. K., and Ruqaiya Hasan. *Cohesion in English*. London: Longman, 1976.

Kifner, John. "4 Kent State Students Killed by Troops." *New York Times* 5 May 1970: 1.

Kinneavy, James L. *A Theory of Discourse*. Englewood Cliffs: Prentice-Hall, 1971.

———, et al. *Writing in the Liberal Arts Tradition*. New York: Harper & Row, 1985.

Kuhn, Thomas S. *The Structure of Scientific Revolutions*. 2nd ed. Chicago: U of Chicago P, 1970.

Leitch, Vincent B. *Deconstructive Criticism*. New York: Cornell UP, 1983.

Lentricchia, Frank. *After the New Criticism*. Chicago: U of Chicago P, 1980.

Maimon, Elaine P., et al. *Readings in the Arts and Sciences*. Boston: Little, Brown, 1984.

———, *Writing in the Arts and Sciences*. Cambridge: Winthrop, 1981.

Miller, Owen. "Intertextual Identity." *Identity of the Literary Text*. Ed. Mario J. Valdés and Owen Miller. Toronto: U of Toronto P, 1985, 19–40.

Scholes, Robert. *Textual Power*. New Haven: Yale UP, 1985.

Williams, Joseph. "Cognitive Development, Critical Thinking, and the Teaching of Writing." Conference on Writing, Meaning, and Higher Order Reasoning, University of Chicago, 15 May 1984.

Appendix

Forum Analysis

Background

—Identify the forum by name and organizational affiliation.

—Is there an expressed editorial policy, philosophy, or expression of belief? What purpose does the forum serve? Why does it exist?

—What is the disciplinary orientation?

—How large is the forum? Who are its members? Its leaders? Its readership?

—In what manner does the forum assemble (e.g., newsletter, journal, conference, weekly meeting)? How frequently?

—What is the origin of the forum? Why did it come into existence? What is its history? Its political background? Its traditions?

—What reputation does the forum have among its own members? How is it regarded by others?

Discourse Conventions

Who Speaks/Writes?

—Who is granted status as speaker/writer? Who decides who speaks/writes in the forum? By what criteria are speakers/writers selected?

—What kind of people speak/write in this forum? Credentials? Disciplinary orientation? Academic or professional background?

—Who are the important figures in this forum? Whose work or experience is most frequently cited?

—What are the important sources cited in the forum? What are the key works, events, experiences that it is assumed members of the forum know?

To Whom Do They Speak/Write?

—Who is addressed in the forum? What are the characteristics of the assumed audience?

—What are the audience's needs assumed to be? To what use(s) is the audience expected to put the information?

—What is the audience's background assumed to be? Level of proficiency, experience, and knowledge of subject matter? Credentials?

—What are the beliefs, attitudes, values, prejudices of the addressed audience?

What Do They Speak/Write About?

—What topics or issues does the forum consider? What are allowable subjects? What topics are valued?

—What methodology or methodologies are accepted? Which theoretical approach is preferred: deduction (theoretical argumentation) or induction (evidence)?

—What constitutes "validity," "evidence," and "proof" in the forum (e.g., personal experience/observation, testing and measurement, theoretical or statistical analysis)?

How Do They Say/Write It?

Form

—What types of discourse does the forum admit (e.g., articles, reviews, speeches, poems)? How long are the discourses?

—What are the dominant modes of organization?

—What formatting conventions are present: headings, tables and graphs, illustrations, abstracts?

Style

—What documentation form(s) is used?

—Syntactic characteristics?

—Technical or specialized jargon? Abbreviations?

—Tone? What stance do writers/speakers take relative to audience?

—Manuscript mechanics?

Other Considerations?

Questions for Discussion and Journaling

1. After reading the first page of the article, define *intertextuality*. When you're finished reading the entire article, define it again. How, if at all, do your two definitions differ?

2. Do you agree with Porter that *intertext*—the great web of texts built on and referring to each other—makes individual writers less important? Why or why not?

3. Why does Porter call the idea of an autonomous writer "romantic"?

4. Porter argues that the key criterion for evaluating writing should be its "acceptability" within the reader's community. How is this different from the way you might have assumed writing should be evaluated prior to reading his article? How is it different from the way(s) your own writing has been evaluated in the past?

5. If Porter is right about intertextuality and its effects on originality, then his article must not be "original," and he must not be writing as an "autonomous individual." How does his own work reflect—or fail to reflect—the principles he's writing about?

6. What harm is there, according to Porter, in imagining writing "as individual, as isolated, as heroic" (para. 39)? What problems does it cause?

Applying and Exploring Ideas

1. Choose a commercial or advertisement you've seen recently and search for traces of intertextuality in it. How many texts can you find represented in it? How do you find *cultural* intertext represented in it?

2. If we accept Porter's argument, then the typical school definition of *plagiarism* seems oversimplified or inaccurate. Rewrite the plagiarism policy for the course you're in now so that it accounts for Porter's notion of plagiarism but still keeps students from cheating. When you're finished, compare the original and your revised version. How much and in what ways do they differ?

Meta Moment

Many of us have been taught to imagine "writers" as people who work more or less alone to get their ideas down in print. Has Porter's study changed the way *you* imagine writers and writing? Would adopting his notion of writers and writing change the way you write?

Rhetorical Situations and Their Constituents

KEITH GRANT-DAVIE

Grant-Davie, Keith. "Rhetorical Situations and Their Constituents." *Rhetoric Review* 15.2 (1997): 264–79. Print.

Framing the Reading

Keith Grant-Davie is an English professor at Utah State University in Logan, "a rural town in the Rocky Mountains." He has studied how readers and writers interact from a number of angles: what readers say writers are trying to do, how writers repeat themselves to make themselves clearer to readers, and how writing and speech are shaped by the context in which they take place and the context(s) to which they respond. When he wrote this article, Grant-Davie was directing the graduate program in USU's English department.

We briefly defined the term **rhetorical situation** in the chapter introduction, and you've encountered it in questions for many of the other articles in this chapter. The term is not an easy one to pin down, however, so you may still be wondering exactly what a rhetorical situation is. Composition theorists like Grant-Davie call an activity, an event, or a situation *rhetorical* when it's shaped by language or communication—also called **discourse**—that tries to get people to *do* something. In order to understand rhetoric, it's necessary to understand the motivations—the purposes, needs, values, and expectations—of the **rhetors**—that is, the people who generate it.

Advertisements are prime examples of rhetorical communication. In advertising, a business communicates with its **audience**—potential customers—in order to persuade them to buy a product: for example, the Coca-Cola corporation hires basketball star Kobe Bryant to command us, "Obey your thirst—drink Sprite!" But rhetorical situations don't have to be strategically planned and constructed *as* rhetoric: in fact, we encounter them every day, in ordinary, unplanned, un-self-conscious interactions. Imagine, for example, sitting in your kitchen with a friend who says, "Boy, I'm really cold." In both the advertisement and your friend's declaration, language *does* things: it convinces us to buy something or to turn up the heat. Such communication is therefore *rhetorical*—that is, it's persuasive or *motivated* communication—and the situations in which it happens would be *rhetorical situations*.

Grant-Davie's article examines the elements of rhetorical situations and may help you better understand and respond to their rhetoric. Why, for example, didn't the Coca-Cola corporation simply bypass the celebrity and the ad agency and issue a statement telling us they'd like us to drink Sprite? Why didn't your chilly friend ask directly, "Can you please turn up the heat?" We need to explore the rhetorical situations of both examples in order to respond intelligently. To use an everyday example: if your little sister walks into your room yelling at the top of her lungs, you won't know how to respond until you understand what's happened and why she's yelling—is she angry, hurt, or excited? Understanding the rhetorical situation of her outburst will help you understand what's at stake and guide you in making an appropriate response.

The idea of a rhetorical situation might not be completely clear to you right away—most people need to encounter the idea in several different ways before they really start to get a handle on it. In particular, it might take you a few tries to understand the idea of **exigence**. Grant-Davie explains this term a few different ways, but the simplest explanation for it is a *problem* or *need* that can be addressed by communication. In the case of the Sprite ad, the exigence of the communication is complex: it includes the corporation's desire to sell and the consumer's desire for a product that will fill one or more needs (thirst quenching but also identification with a popular celebrity). In the case of your chilly friend, the exigence is more straightforward: Your friend wants to be warmer, but doesn't want to appear pushy or offend you by directly stating her desire for a thermostat adjustment.

You'll also encounter the term **stases**, which is a pattern or set of questions that helps explain what's at issue in a given rhetorical situation—a problem of *fact*, of *value*, or of *policy*. (The classic journalist's questions—Who? What? Where? When? How? Why?—are actually stases that attempt to establish fact.) Finally, you'll encounter the concept of **constraints**, which are factors that limit or focus the response to the exigence (problem or need) in a given situation. (In the case of your chilly friend, her desire to be perceived as friendly, not pushy, is a primary constraint.) These and other concepts in Grant-Davie's article will become clearer as you see them used in other readings.

Remember, when we identify language or communication as rhetorical, we're saying that it is *doing* something. So we could ask of Grant-Davie's article, what does it *do*? Keep that question in mind as you read.

> Keith Grant-Davie's article "Rhetorical Situations and Their Constituents" was the most interesting and useful article. . . . I understood terminology such as *exigence, rhetors, audience*, and *constraints* used to describe a rhetorical situation. These descriptive terms are also useful outside of the academic environment.
>
> **—Natasha Gumtie, Student**

Getting Ready to Read

Before you read, do at least one of the following activities:

- Ask one or more roommates or friends to describe the last serious argument or debate they had. Get them to describe the situations in which the debates took place in as much detail as they can. Make a list of what was "in the situation," following the reporter's "five Ws": Who was there? What was it about? When and where did it happen? Why did it happen (that is, what were the motivations of the arguers)?

- Watch a television commercial and look for how it "sets the scene"—how it very quickly puts viewers in the middle of one situation or another (like a family riding in a car or people eating in a restaurant or a sick person talking with a doctor). Make some notes about how the commercial uses scenery, particular language, or text to help explain "where you are" as a viewer, and ask yourself how important understanding that "scene" or situation is to understanding what's being advertised.

As you read, consider the following questions:

- What rhetorical situation gave rise to Grant-Davie's article—that is, why did he write it in the first place? Who is his intended audience? Who else has been talking about this problem/question? What text(s) is he responding to?
- How does the article move from its introduction through the defining work it does to its concluding example? Why is it divided into sections?
- Can you use the examples Grant-Davie gives to help you find examples of rhetorical situations and their components (*exigence*, *rhetors*, *audience*, and *constraints*) in your own life?

Every student in a college English class should know about the concept of rhetorical situations. When reading, as students we typically ask ourselves, "What is happening?" and in order to analyze the rhetorical situation at a fundamental level, then we need to ask ourselves, "Why did this happen?" I was never taught this in high school so being introduced to it was intimidating and somewhat frightening. The definition of a rhetorical situation is something that is hard to grasp but I believe that Lloyd Bitzer (the first to define it) does an efficient job explaining it. He argues that "rhetorical discourse comes into existence as a response to situation, in the same sense that an answer comes into existence in response to a question, or a solution in response to a problem" (qtd. in Grant-Davie 105). Specifically when writing, rhetorical situations and analysis are used to connect with the audience. The first thing to always consider is the relationship between the author, topic, and audience. One must always ask oneself what key factors are present in this relationship. It is also important to ask what the audience expects from you as the author.

—**Sam Greenberg, Student**

Ken Burns's documentary film, *The Civil War*, has mesmerized viewers since   1
it first aired on PBS in 1990. Among its more appealing features are the
interviews with writers and historians like Shelby Foote and Barbara Fields,
who provide the background information and interpretation necessary to
transform battles, speeches, and letters from dry historical data into a human
drama of characters, intentions, and limitations. In effect, their commentaries
explain the rhetorical situations of the events, pointing out influential factors
within the broader contexts that help explain why decisions were made and
why things turned out as they did. Their analyses of these rhetorical situations
show us that some events might easily have turned out otherwise, while the
outcomes of other events seem all but inevitable when seen in light of the situations in which they occurred. When
we study history, our first question
may be "what happened?" but the
more important question, the question whose answer offers hope of
learning for the future as well as
understanding the past, is "why did
it happen?" At a fundamental level,
then, understanding the rhetorical
situations of historical events helps
satisfy our demand for causality—
helps us discover the extent to which
the world is not chaotic but ordered,
a place where actions follow patterns and things happen for good reasons.
Teaching our writing students to examine rhetorical situations as sets of interacting influences from which rhetoric arises, and which rhetoric in turn influences, is therefore one of the more important things we can do. Writers who
know how to analyze these situations have a better method of examining causality. They have a stronger basis for making composing decisions and are better able, as readers, to understand the decisions other writers have made.

> When we study history, our first
> question may be "what happened?"
> but the more important question, the
> question whose answer offers hope
> of learning for the future as well as
> understanding the past, is "why did
> it happen?"

Scholars and teachers of rhetoric have used the term *rhetorical situation*   2
since Lloyd Bitzer defined it in 1968. However, the concept has remained largely
underexamined since Bitzer's seminal article and the responses to it by Richard
Vatz and Scott Consigny in the 1970s. We all use the term, but what exactly do
we mean by it and do we all mean the same thing? My purpose in this essay is
to review the original definitions of the term and its constituents, and to offer
a more thoroughly developed scheme for analyzing rhetorical situations. I will
apply the concept of a rhetorical situation to reading or listening situations
as well as to writing or speaking situations, and to what I call "compound"
rhetorical situations—discussions of a single subject by multiple rhetors and
audiences.[1]

Bitzer defines a rhetorical situation generally as "the context in which speakers   3
or writers create rhetorical discourse" (382).[2] More specifically he defines it as

"a complex of persons, events, objects, and relations presenting an actual or potential exigence which can be completely or partially removed if discourse, introduced into the situation, can so constrain human decision or action as to bring about the significant modification of the exigence" (386).[3] In other words, a rhetorical situation is a situation where a speaker or writer sees a need to change reality and sees that the change may be effected through rhetorical discourse. Bitzer argues that understanding the situation is important because the situation invites and largely determines the form of the rhetorical work that responds to it. He adds that "rhetorical discourse comes into existence as a response to situation, in the same sense that an answer comes into existence in response to a question, or a solution in response to a problem" (385–86). Richard Vatz challenges Bitzer's assumption that the rhetor's response is controlled by the situation. He contends that situations do not exist without rhetors, and that rhetors create rather than discover rhetorical situations (154). In effect, Vatz argues that rhetors not only answer the question, they also ask it.[4]

Scott Consigny's reply to Bitzer and Vatz suggests that each of them is both   4 right and wrong, that a rhetorical situation is partly, but not wholly, created by the rhetor. Supporting Vatz, Consigny argues that the art of rhetoric should involve "integrity"—the ability to apply a standard set of strategies effectively to any situation the rhetor may face. On the other hand, supporting Bitzer, he argues that rhetoric should also involve "receptivity"—the ability to respond to the conditions and demands of individual situations. To draw an analogy, we could say that carpentry has integrity inasmuch as carpenters tackle most projects with a limited set of common tools. They do not have to build new tools for every new task (although the evolution of traditional tools and the development of new ones suggest that integrity is not a static property). Conversely, carpentry might also be said to have receptivity if the limited set of tools does not limit the carpenter's perception of the task. A good carpenter does not reach for the hammer every time.

Looking at these articles by Bitzer, Vatz, and Consigny together, we might   5 define a rhetorical situation as a set of related factors whose interaction creates and controls a discourse. However, such a general definition is better understood if we examine the constituents of situation. Bitzer identifies three: exigence, audience, and constraints. Exigence is "an imperfection marked by urgency; it is a defect, an obstacle, something waiting to be done, a thing which is other than it should be" (386). A rhetorical exigence is some kind of need or problem that can be addressed and solved through rhetorical discourse. Eugene White has pointed out that exigence need not arise from a problem but may instead be cause for celebration (291). Happy events may create exigence, calling for epideictic rhetoric. Bitzer defines the audience as those who can help resolve the exigence: "those persons who are capable of being influenced by discourse and of being mediators of change" (387), while constraints are "persons, events, objects, and relations which are parts of the situation because they have the power to constrain decision and action needed to modify the exigence" (388).

Bitzer's three-way division of rhetorical situations has been valuable, but to   6 reveal the full complexity of rhetorical situations, I think we need to develop his scheme further. I propose three amendments. First, I believe exigence, as the motivating force behind a discourse, demands a more comprehensive analysis. Second, I think we need to recognize that rhetors are as much a part of a rhetorical situation as the audience is. Bitzer mentions in passing that when a speech is made, both it and the rhetor become additional constituents of the situation (388), but he does not appear to include the rhetor in the situation that exists *before* the speech is made. And third, we need to recognize that any of the constituents may be plural. Bitzer includes the possibility of multiple exigences and constraints, but he seems to assume a solitary rhetor and a single audience. In many rhetorical situations, there may be several rhetors, including groups of people or institutions, and the discourse may address or encounter several audiences with various purposes for reading. The often complex interaction of these multiple rhetors and audiences should be considered. What follows, then, are definitions and discussions of the four constituents I see in rhetorical situations: exigence, rhetors, audiences, and constraints.

Exigence—The Matter and Motivation of the Discourse

Bitzer defines rhetorical exigence as the rhetor's sense that a situation both calls   7
for discourse and might be resolved by discourse. According to this definition, the essential question addressing the exigence of a situation would be "Why is the discourse needed?" However, in my scheme I propose that this question be the second of three that ask, respectively, what the discourse is about, why it is needed, and what it should accomplish. I derive the logic for this order of questions from the version of stasis theory explained by Jeanne Fahnestock and Marie Secor, who argue that the stases provide a natural sequence of steps for interrogating a subject. This sequence proceeds from questions of fact and definition (establishing that the subject exists and characterizing it) through questions of cause and effect (identifying the source of the subject and its consequences) and questions of value (examining its importance or quality) to questions of policy or procedure (considering what should be done about it) ("The Stases in Scientific and Literary Argument" 428–31; "The Rhetoric of Literary Criticism" 78–80). Sharon Crowley, too, has suggested stasis theory as a good tool for analyzing rhetorical situations (33).

   What is the discourse about? This question addresses the first two stases,   8
fact and definition, by asking what the discourse concerns. The question may be answered at quite a concrete level by identifying the most apparent topic. A speech by a politician during an election year may be about mandatory school uniforms, Medicare, an antipollution bill, the fight against terrorism, or any of a host of other topics. However, what the discourse is about becomes a more interesting and important question, and a source of exigence, if asked at more abstract levels—in other words, if the question becomes "What fundamental issues are represented by the topic of the discourse?" or "What values are at stake?" Political speeches often use specific topics to represent larger, more enduring issues such as questions of civil rights, public safety, free enterprise, constitutionality, separation of church and state, morality, family values, progress,

equality, fairness, and so forth. These larger issues, values, or principles motivate people and can be invoked to lead audiences in certain directions on more
specific topics. A speech on the topic of requiring school uniforms in public
schools may engage the larger issue of how much states should be free from
federal intervention—an issue that underlies many other topics besides school
uniforms. In the first episode of *The Civil War,* historian Barbara Fields draws
a distinction between the superficial matter of the war and what she sees as the
more important, underlying issues that gave it meaning:

> For me, the picture of the Civil War as a historic phenomenon is not on the battle-
> field. It's not about weapons, it's not about soldiers, except to the extent that
> weapons and soldiers at that crucial moment joined a discussion about something
> higher, about humanity, about human dignity, about human freedom.

On the battlefield, one side's ability to select the ground to be contested has
often been critical to the outcome of the engagement. In the same way, rhetors
who can define the fundamental issues represented by a superficial subject
matter—and persuade audiences to engage in those issues—is in a position
to maintain decisive control over the field of debate. A presidential candidate
may be able to convince the electorate that the more important issues in a
debate about a rival's actions are not the legality of those specific actions but
questions they raise about the rival's credibility as leader of the nation ("He
may have been exonerated in a court of law, but what does the scandal suggest
about his character?"). Attorneys do the same kind of thing in a courtroom,
trying to induce the jury to see the case in terms of issues that favor their client.
Granted, these examples all represent traditional, manipulative rhetoric—the
verbal equivalent of a physical contest—but I believe the same principle is
critical to the success of the kind of ethical argument Theresa Enos describes,
where the aim is not victory over the opponent but a state of identification,
where writer and reader are able to meet in the audience identity the writer has
created within the discourse (106–08) In these kinds of argument, establishing
acceptable issues would seem to be an essential stage, creating an agenda that
readers can agree to discuss.

I am proposing stasis theory be used as an analytic tool, an organizing   9
principle in the sequence of questions that explore the exigence of a situation, but defining the issues of a discourse also involves determining the stases
that will be contested in the discourse itself. The presidential candidate in the
example mentioned above is abandoning the stasis of definition and choosing instead to take a stand at the stasis of value. Asking what the discourse is
about, then, involves identifying the subject matter or topic at the most obvious level, but also determining issues that underlie it and the stases that should
be addressed—in short, asking "what questions need to be resolved by this
discourse?"

Why is the discourse needed? The second question about exigence addresses   10
both the third and fourth stases (cause and value). It addresses cause by asking
what has prompted the discourse, and why *now* is the right time for it to be
delivered. This aspect of exigence is related, as Bill Covino and David Jolliffe

have observed, to the concept of *kairos*—"the right or opportune time to speak or write" (11, 62). Exigence may have been created by events that precede the discourse and act as a catalyst for it; and the timing of the discourse may also have been triggered by an occasion, such as an invitation to speak. A presidential speech on terrorism may be prompted both by a recent act of terrorism but also by a timely opportunity to make a speech. In the case of letters to the editor of a newspaper, the forum is always there—a standing invitation to address the newspaper's readership. However, letter writers are usually prompted by a recent event or by the need to reply to someone else's letter.

While addressing the stasis of cause, the question "why is the discourse   11 needed?" also addresses the value stasis in the sense that it asks why the discourse matters—why the issues are important and why the questions it raises really need to be resolved. The answer to this question may be that the issues are intrinsically important, perhaps for moral reasons. Alternatively, the answer may lie in the situation's implications. Exigence may result not from what has already happened but from something that is about to happen, or from something that might happen if action is not taken—as in the case of many speeches about the environment.

What is the discourse trying to accomplish? Finally, exigence can be revealed   12 by asking questions at the stasis of policy or procedure. What are the goals of the discourse? How is the audience supposed to react to the discourse? I include objectives as part of the exigence for a discourse because resolving the exigence provides powerful motivation for the rhetor. The rhetor's agenda may also include primary and secondary objectives, some of which might not be stated in the discourse. The immediate objective of a presidential campaign speech might be to rebut accusations made by a rival, while a secondary objective might be to clarify the candidate's stance on one of the issues or help shape his image, and the broader objective would always be to persuade the audience to vote for the candidate when the time comes.

Rhetor(s)—Those People, Real or Imagined, Responsible for the Discourse and Its Authorial Voice

Bitzer does not include the rhetor as a constituent of the rhetorical situation   13 before the discourse is produced, although he includes aspects of the rhetor under the category of constraints. Vatz only points out the rhetor's role in defining the situation, yet it seems to me that rhetors are as much constituents of their rhetorical situations as are their audiences. Their roles, like those of audiences, are partly predetermined but usually open to some definition or redefinition. Rhetors need to consider who they are in a particular situation and be aware that their identity may vary from situation to situation. Neither Bitzer nor Vatz explores the role of rhetor in much depth, and an exhaustive analysis of possible roles would be beyond the scope of this essay, too; but in the following paragraphs, I will touch on some possible variations.

First, although for syntactic convenience I often refer to the rhetor as sin-   14 gular in this essay, situations often involve multiple rhetors. An advertisement may be sponsored by a corporation, written and designed by an advertising agency, and delivered by an actor playing the role of corporate spokesperson. Well-known actors or athletes may lend the ethos they have established through their work, while unknown actors may play the roles of corporate representatives or even audience members offering testimony in support of the product. We can distinguish those who originated the discourse, and who might be held legally responsible for the truth of its content, from those who are hired to shape and deliver the message, but arguably all of them involved in the sales pitch share the role of rhetor, as a rhetorical team.

Second, even when a rhetor addresses a situation alone, the answer to the question "Who is the rhetor?" may not be simple. As rhetors we may speak in some professional capacity, in a volunteer role, as a parent, or in some other role that may be less readily identifiable—something, perhaps, like Wayne Booth's "implied author" or "second self"—the authorial identity that readers can infer from an author's writing (70–71). Roger Cherry makes a contrast between the ethos of the historical author and any persona created by that author (260–68). Cherry's distinction might be illustrated by the speech of a presidential candidate who brings to it the ethos he has established through his political career and uses the speech to create a persona for himself as president in the future. Then again, a rhetor's ethos will not be the same for all audiences. It will depend on what they know and think of the rhetor's past actions, so the "real" or "historical" author is not a stable "foundation" identity but depends partly on the audience in a particular rhetorical situation. Like exigence, then, audience can influence the identity of the rhetor.

Rhetors may play several roles at once, and even when they try to play just one role, their audience may be aware of their other roles. A Little League baseball umpire might, depending on his relationship with local residents, receive fewer challenges from parents at the game if he happens also to be the local police chief. The range of roles we can play at any given moment is certainly constrained by the other constituents of the rhetorical situation and by the identities we bring to the situation. However, new rhetorical situations change us and can lead us to add new roles to our repertoire. To use Consigny's terms, rhetors create ethos partly through integrity—a measure of consistency they take from situation to situation instead of putting on a completely new mask to suit the needs of every new audience and situation; and they also need receptivity—the ability to adapt to new situations and not rigidly play the same role in every one.

Audience—Those People, Real or Imagined, with Whom Rhetors Negotiate through Discourse to Achieve the Rhetorical Objectives

Audience as a rhetorical concept has transcended the idea of a homogenous body of people who have stable characteristics and are assembled in the rhetor's presence. A discourse may have primary and secondary audiences, audiences that are present and those that have yet to form, audiences that act collaboratively or as individuals, audiences about whom the rhetor knows little, or audiences that exist only in the rhetor's mind. Chaïm Perelman and Lucie Olbrechts-Tyteca point out that unlike speakers, writers cannot be certain who their audiences are, and that rhetors often face "composite" audiences consisting either of several factions or of individuals who each represent several different groups (214–17).

In Bitzer's scheme audience exists fairly simply as a group of real people within a situation external to both the rhetor and the discourse. Douglas Park has broadened this perspective by offering four specific meanings of audience: (1) any people who happen to hear or read a discourse, (2) a set of readers or listeners who form part of an external rhetorical situation (equivalent to Bitzer's interpretation of audience), (3) the audience that the writer seems to have in mind, and (4) the audience roles suggested by the discourse itself. The first two meanings assume that the audience consists of actual people and correspond to what Lisa Ede and Andrea Lunsford have called "audience addressed" (Ede and Lunsford 156–65). Park's third and fourth meanings are more abstract, corresponding to Ede and Lunsford's "audience invoked." Park locates both those meanings of audience within the text, but I would suggest that the third resides not so much in the text as in the writer before and during composing, while the fourth is derived from the text by readers. Since writers are also readers of their own texts, they can alternate between the third and fourth meanings of audience while composing and rereading; so they might draft with a sense of audience in mind, then reread to see what sense of audience is reflected in the text they have created. In some instances writers may be their own intended audiences. One example would be personal journals, which writers may write for themselves as readers in the future, or for themselves in the present with no more awareness of audience as separate from self than they have when engaging in internal dialogue.

Instead of asking "Who is the audience?", Park recommends we ask how a discourse "defines and creates contexts for readers" (250). As an example of such a context, he offers Chaïm Perelman's notion of the universal audience, which Perelman defines in *The New Rhetoric* as an audience "encompassing all reasonable and competent men" (157). Appealing to the universal audience creates a forum in which debate can be conducted. Likewise, Park argues, a particular publication can create a context that partly determines the nature of the audience for a discourse that appears in it.

Like the other constituents of rhetorical situations, the roles of rhetor and audience are dynamic and interdependent. As a number of theorists have observed, readers can play a variety of roles during the act of reading a discourse, roles that are not necessarily played either before or after reading. These roles are negotiated with the rhetor through the discourse, and they may change during the process of reading (Ede and Lunsford 166–67; Long 73, 80; Park 249; Perelman and Olbrechts-Tyteca 216; Phelps 156–57; Roth 182–83). Negotiation is the key term here. Rhetors' conceptions of audiences may lead them to create new roles for themselves—or adapt existing roles—to address those audiences. Rhetors may invite audiences to accept new identities for themselves, offering readers a vision not of who they are but of who they could be. Readers who begin the discourse in one role may find themselves persuaded to adopt a new role, or they may refuse the roles suggested by the discourse. I may open a letter from a charity and read it not as a potential donor but as a rhetorician, analyzing the rhetorical strategies used by the letter writer. In that case I would see my exigence for reading the letter, and my role in the negotiation, as quite different from what the writer appeared to have had in mind for me.[5]

Rhetorical situations, then, are not phenomena experienced only by rhetors. As Stephen Kucer and Martin Nystrand have argued, reading and writing may be seen as parallel activities involving negotiation of meaning between readers and writers. If reading is a rhetorical activity too, then it has its own rhetorical situations. So, if we prefer to use *writing situation* as a more accessible term than *rhetorical situation* when we teach (as some textbooks have—e.g., Pattow and Wresch 18–22; Reep 12–13), we should not neglect to teach students also about "reading situations," which may have their own exigences, roles, and constraints. 21

Constraints—Factors in the Situation's Context That May Affect the Achievement of the Rhetorical Objectives

Constraints are the hardest of the rhetorical situation components to define neatly because they can include so many different things. Bitzer devotes just one paragraph to them, defining them as 'persons, events, objects, and relations which are parts of the situation because they have the power to constrain decision and action needed to modify the exigence." Since he assumes that rhetors are largely controlled by situations and since he observes "the power of situation to constrain a fitting response" (390), his use of the term *constraints* has usually been interpreted to mean limitations on the rhetor—prescriptions or proscriptions controlling what can be said, or how it can be said, in a given situation. A rhetor is said to work within the constraints of the situation. However, this commonly held view of constraints as obstacles or restrictions has obscured the fact that Bitzer defines constraints more as aids to the rhetor than as handicaps. The rhetor "harnesses" them so as to constrain the audience to take the desired action or point of view. This view of constraints seems useful, so I see them as working either for or against the rhetor's objectives. I refer to the kind that support a rhetor's case as positive constraints, or assets, and those that might hinder it as negative constraints, or liabilities. 22

Bitzer goes on to divide constraints along another axis. Some, which he equates with Aristotle's inartistic proofs, are "given by the situation." These might be "beliefs, attitudes, documents, facts, traditions, images, interests, motives and the like"—presumably including beliefs and attitudes held by the audience. Other constraints, equivalent to Aristotle's artistic proofs, are developed by the rhetor: "his personal character, his logical proofs, and his style" (388). To paraphrase, Bitzer defines constraints very broadly as all factors that may move the audience (or disincline the audience to be moved), including factors in the audience, the rhetor, and the rhetoric. Such an all-inclusive definition would seem to threaten 23 the usefulness of constraints as a distinct constituent of rhetorical situations, so I propose excluding the rhetor and the audience as separate constituents and making explicit the possibility of both positive and negative constraints. I would define constraints, then, as all factors in the situation, aside from the rhetor and the audience, that may lead the audience to be either more or less sympathetic to the discourse, and that may therefore influence the rhetor's response to the situation—still a loose definition, but constraints defy anything tighter.

With the rhetor and the audience excluded from the category of constraints, 24 it is tempting to exclude the other artistic proofs too, thereby simplifying the category further by drawing a distinction between the rhetorical situation and the discourse that arises from it. However, clearly the situation continues after the point at which the discourse begins to address it. A rhetor continues to define, shape, reconsider, and respond to the rhetorical situation throughout the composing process, and at any given point during that process, the rhetor may be highly constrained by the emerging discourse. If we are to be coherent, what we have already written must constrain what we write next.

If constraints are those other factors in rhetorical situations, besides rhetors 25 and audiences, that could help or hinder the discourse, what might they be? I have already included the emerging text of the discourse as a constraint on what a rhetor can add to it. To this we can add linguistic constraints imposed by the genre of the text or by the conventions of language use dictated by the situation. Other constraints could arise from the immediate and broader contexts of the discourse, perhaps including its geographical and historical background. Such constraints could include recent or imminent events that the discourse might call to readers' minds, other discourses that relate to it, other people, or factors in the cultural, moral, religious, political, or economic climate—both local and global—that might make readers more or less receptive to the discourse. Foreign trade negotiations, a domestic recession, a hard winter, civil disturbances, a sensational crime or accident—events like these might act as constraints on the rhetorical situation of an election campaign speech, suggesting appeals to make or avoid making. Every situation arises within a context—a background of time, place, people, events, and so forth. Not all of the context is directly relevant to the situation, but rhetors and audiences may be aware of certain events, people, or conditions within the context that *are* relevant and should be considered part of the situation because they have the potential to act as positive or negative constraints on the discourse. The challenge for the rhetor is to decide which parts of the context bear on the situation enough to be considered constraints, and what to do about them—for instance, whether the best rhetorical strategy for a negative constraint would be to address it directly and try to disarm it—or even try to turn it into a positive constraint—or to say nothing about it and hope that the audience overlooks it too.

Some of my examples have complicated the roles of rhetor and audience, 26 but all so far have looked at discourses in isolation and assumed that situations are finite. It seems clear that a situation begins with the rhetor's perception of exigence, but when can it be said to have ended? Does it end when the exigence has been resolved or simply when the discourse has been delivered? I favor the latter because it establishes a simpler boundary to mark and it limits rhetorical situations to the preparation and delivery of discourses, rather than extending them to their reception, which I consider to be part of the audience's rhetorical situation. Also, as I have tried to show, exigence can be quite complex and the point at which it can be said to have been resolved may be hard to identify. The same exigence may motivate discourses in many quite different situations without ever being fully resolved. Major sources of exigence, like civil rights, can continue to motivate generations of rhetors.

To say that a rhetorical situation ends when the discourse has been delivered   27
still leaves us with the question of how to describe discourse in a discussion. Dialogue challenges the idea of rhetorical situations having neat boundaries. When participants meet around a table and take turns playing the roles of rhetor and audience, are there as many rhetorical situations as there are rhetors—or turns? Or should we look at the whole meeting as a single rhetorical situation? And what happens when the participants in a discussion are not gathered together at one place and time, engaged in the quick give and take of oral discussion, but instead debate a topic with each other over a period of weeks—for example, by sending and replying to letters to the editor of a newspaper? To look at a meeting as a single rhetorical situation recognizes that many of the constituents of the situation were common to all participants, and it emphasizes Bitzer's view that situations are external to the rhetor; whereas to look at each person involved in the discussion as having his or her own rhetorical situation—or each contribution to the discussion having its own situation—would seem to lean toward Vatz's view that rhetorical situations are constructed by rhetors. Both views, of course, are right. Each rhetor has a different perspective and enters the debate at a different time (especially in the case of a debate carried on through a newspaper's editorial pages), so each addresses a slightly different rhetorical situation; but the situations may interlace or overlap extensively with those addressed by other rhetors in the discussion. It may be useful, then, to think of an entire discussion as a compound rhetorical situation, made up of a group of closely related individual situations. Analyzing a compound situation involves examining which constituents were common to all participants and which were specific to one or two. For example, some sources of exigence may have motivated all participants, and in these common factors may lie the hope of resolution, agreement, or compromise. On the other hand, the divisive heat of a debate may be traced to a fundamental conflict of values—and thus of exigence—among the participants.

Examples of this kind of compound rhetorical situation can be found when-   28
ever public debate arises, as it did recently in the editorial pages of a local newspaper in a rural community in the Rocky Mountains. The debate was sparked when the newspaper printed a front-page story about a nearby resort hotel, Sherwood Hills, that had erected a 46-foot, illuminated Best Western sign at the entrance to its property. Such a sign on a four-lane highway would not normally be remarkable, but the setting made this one controversial. Sherwood Hills lies hidden in trees at the end of a long driveway, off a particularly scenic stretch of the highway. There are no other residences or businesses nearby,

and the area is officially designated a forest-recreation zone, which usually prohibits businesses and their signs. Several months earlier, the resort owners had applied to the county council for a permit and been told that some kind of sign on the road might be allowed, but the application had not been resolved when the sign went up.

The newspaper ran several stories reporting the resort owners' rationale 29 (they felt they had applied in good faith and waited long enough) and the council members' reaction (they felt indignant that the owners had flouted the law and were now seeking forgiveness rather than permission). The newspaper also berated the resort owners' actions in an editorial. What might have been a minor bureaucratic matter resolved behind closed doors turned into a town debate, with at least 15 letters to the editor printed in the weeks that followed. From a rhetorical perspective, I think the interesting question is why the incident sparked such a brushfire of public opinion, since not all controversial incidents covered by the newspaper elicit so many letters to the editor. Looking at the debate as a compound rhetorical situation and examining its constituents helps answer that question.

The rhetors and audiences included the resort owners, the county council, the 30 county planning commission, the Zoning Administrator, the newspaper staff, and assorted local citizens. Their debate was nominally about the sign—whether it was illegal (a question at the stasis of definition) and what should be done about it (a question at the policy stasis). These questions were sources of exigence shared by all participants in the debate. However, even greater exigence seems to have come from questions at the stasis of cause/effect—what precedent might the sign create for other businesses to ignore local ordinances?—and at the stasis of value—were the sign and the act of erecting it without a permit (and the ordinance that made that act illegal) good or bad? For most of the letter writers, the debate revolved around the issue of land use, one of the more frequently and hotly contested issues in the western United States, where the appropriate use of both public and private land is very much open to argument.

Critics of the sign generally placed a high value on unspoiled wilderness. For 31 them the sign symbolized the commercial development of natural beauty and challenged laws protecting the appearance of other forest-recreation zones in the area. Those in favor of the sign, on the other hand, saw it not as an eyesore but as a welcome symbol of prosperity erected in a bold and justified challenge to slow-moving bureaucracy and unfair laws, and as a blow struck for private property rights. Underlying the issue of land use in this debate, then, and providing powerful exigence, was the issue of individual or local freedom versus government interference—another issue with a strong tradition in the western U.S. (as in the case of the "sagebrush rebellions"—unsuccessful attempts to establish local control over public lands). The tradition of justified—or at least rationalized—rebellion against an oppressive establishment can of course be traced back to the American Revolution, and in the 1990s we have seen it appear as a fundamental source of exigence in a number of antigovernment disputes in various parts of the nation.

Exigence and constraints can be closely related. For the critics of Sherwood 32
Hills, the breaking of the law was a source of exigence, motivating them to
protest, but the law itself was also a positive constraint in the situation, giving
them a reason to argue for the removal of the sign. Certainly the law constrained the council's response to the situation. On the other hand, the law was
apparently a less powerful constraint for the owners of Sherwood Hills and for
many of their supporters who felt that the law, not the sign, should be changed.
For many on that side of the debate, the tradition of rebelling against what are
perceived to be unfair government restrictions provided both exigence and a
positive constraint. The feeling that private property owners' rights had been
violated was what motivated them to join the discussion, but it also gave them
an appeal to make in their argument. The rhetor's sense of exigence, when
communicated successfully to the audience, can become a positive constraint,
a factor that helps move the audience toward the rhetor's position.

Precedents always create constraints. In the Sherwood Hills debate, sev- 33
eral participants mentioned comparable business signs, including one recently
erected at another local resort, also in a forest-recreation area. The existence of
that sign was a positive constraint for supporters of the Sherwood Hills sign.
However, it was also a negative constraint since the other resort had followed
the correct procedure and received a permit for its sign, and since the sign was
smaller and lower than the Sherwood Hills sign, had no illumination, and had
been designed to harmonize with the landscape.

Other constraints emerged from local history. The highway past Sherwood 34
Hills had recently been widened, and the dust had not yet settled from the
dispute between developers and environmentalists over that three-year project.
Even before the road construction, which had disrupted traffic and limited
access to Sherwood Hills, the resort had struggled to stay in business, changing hands several times before the present owners acquired it. The sign, some
supporters suggested, was needed to ensure the new owners' success, on which
the prosperity of others in the community depended too. The owners were
also praised as upstanding members of the community, having employed local
people and contributed to local charities. Two letter writers argued from this
constraint that the community should not bite the hand that feeds.

This analysis of the Sherwood Hills sign debate as a compound situation 35
only scratches the surface, but understanding even this much about the situation goes a long way toward explaining why the incident generated such an
unusual wave of public opinion. The conclusion of a compound rhetorical situation may be harder to determine than the end of a single-discourse situation,
particularly if the subject of discussion is perennial. This particular dispute
ended when the exchange of letters stopped and the Sherwood Hills owners
reached a compromise with the county council: Both the sign and the ordinance remained in place, but the sign was lowered by ten feet.

As my discussion and examples have shown, exigence, rhetor, audience, and 36
constraints can interlace with each other, and the further one delves into a situation the more connections between them are likely to appear. However, while
the boundaries between the constituents will seldom be clear and stable, I do

think that pursuing them initially as if they were discrete constituents helps a rhetor or a rhetorician look at a situation from a variety of perspectives. My efforts in the preceding pages have been to discuss the possible complexities of rhetorical situations. Teaching student writers and readers to ask the same questions, and to understand why they are asking them, will help them realize their options, choose rhetorical strategies and stances for good reasons, and begin to understand each other's roles.[6]

Notes

1. I thank *Rhetoric Review* readers John Gage and Robert L. Scott, whose careful reviews of earlier drafts of this essay helped me improve it greatly.
2. Bitzer's definition does not distinguish *situation* from *context*. The two terms may be used interchangeably, but I prefer to use *context* to describe the broader background against which a rhetorical situation develops and from which it gathers some of its parts. I see situation, then, as a subset of context.
3. In "The Rhetorical Situation" and "Rhetoric and Public Knowledge," Bitzer uses the terms *exigence* and *exigency* synonymously. I have used *exigence* in this essay mostly for reasons of habit and consistency with the original Bitzer/Vatz/Consigny discussion. I consider it an abstract noun like *diligence, influence,* or *coherence.* While cohesion can be located in textual features, coherence is a perception in the reader. In the same way, exigence seems to me to describe not so much an external circumstance as a sense of urgency or motivation within rhetors or audiences. It is they who recognize (or fail to recognize) exigence in a situation and so the exigence, like the meaning in literary works, must reside in the rhetor or audience as the result of interaction with external circumstances. Although Bitzer calls those circumstances exigences, I prefer to think of them as *sources* of exigence.
4. This fundamental disagreement between Bitzer and Vatz parallels the debate within literary theory over the location of meaning: whether meaning exists in the text, independent of the reader, or whether it is largely or entirely brought by the reader to the text. Bitzer's view looks toward formalism, Vatz's toward reader-response theories, and mine toward the position that meaning is a perception that occurs in the reader but is (or should be) quite highly constrained by the text.
5. Taking poststructuralist approaches to the roles of rhetor and audience, Louise Wetherbee Phelps and Robert Roth further challenge any assumption of a static, divided relationship between the two. Phelps uses Mikhail Bakhtin's idea of heteroglossia to deconstruct the idea of a boundary between author and audience. She argues that the other voices an author engages through reading and conversation while composing are inevitably present in the text, inextricably woven with the author's voice, and that this intertextuality of the text and the author makes a simple separation of text and author from audience impossible (158–59). Roth suggests that the relationship between writers and readers is often cooperative, not adversarial (175), and that a writer's sense of audience takes the form of a shifting set of possible reading roles that the writer may try on (180–82). Neither Phelps nor Roth argue that we should abandon the terms *rhetor* and *audience*. Phelps acknowledges that although author and audience may not be divisible, we routinely act as if they were (163), and she concludes that we should retain the concept of audience for its heuristic value "as a usefully loose correlate for an authorial orientation—whoever or whatever an utterance turns toward" (171). Like Phelps, Roth recognizes that the free play of roles needs to be grounded. "What we really need," he concludes, "is a continual balancing of opposites, both openness to a wide range of potential readers and a monitoring in terms of a particular sense of audience at any one moment or phase in the composing process" (186).
6. I have summarized my analysis in a list of questions that might be used by writers (or adapted for use by audiences) to guide them as they examine a rhetorical situation. Space does not allow this list to be included here, but I will send a copy to anyone who mails me a request.

Works Cited

Bitzer, Lloyd F. "The Rhetorical Situation." *Philosophy and Rhetoric* 1 (1968): 1–14. Rpt. *Contemporary Theories of Rhetoric: Selected Readings*. Ed. Richard L. Johannesen. New York: Harper, 1971. 381–93.

———. "Rhetoric and Public Knowledge." *Rhetoric, Philosophy, and Literature: An Exploration*. Ed. Don M. Burks. West Lafayette, IN: Purdue UP, 1978. 67–93.

Booth, Wayne C. *The Rhetoric of Fiction*. 2nd ed. Chicago: U of Chicago P, 1983.

Cherry, Roger D. "Ethos Versus Persona: Self-Representation in Written Discourse." *Written Communication* 5 (1988): 251–76.

Consigny, Scott. "Rhetoric and Its Situations." *Philosophy and Rhetoric* 7 (1974): 175–86.

Covino, William A., and David A. Jolliffe. *Rhetoric: Concepts, Definitions, Boundaries*. Boston: Allyn, 1995.

Crowley, Sharon. *Ancient Rhetorics for Contemporary Students*. New York: Macmillan, 1994.

Ede, Lisa, and Andrea Lunsford. "Audience Addressed/Audience Invoked: The Role of Audience in Composition Theory and Pedagogy." *College Composition and Communication* 35 (1984): 155–71.

Enos, Theresa. "An Eternal Golden Braid: Rhetor as Audience, Audience as Rhetor." Kirsch and Roen 99–114.

Fahnestock, Janne, and Marie Secor. "The Rhetoric of Literary Criticism." *Textual Dynamics of the Professions*. Ed. Charles Bazerman and James Paradis. Madison: U of Wisconsin P, 1991. 76–96.

———. "The Stases in Scientific and Literary Argument." *Written Communication* 5 (1988): 427–43.

Fields, Barbara. Interview. *The Civil War*. Dir. Ken Burns. Florentine Films, 1990.

Kirsch, Gesa, and Duane H. Roen, eds. *A Sense of Audience in Written Communication*. Newbury Park, CA: Sage, 1990.

Kucer, Stephen L. "The Making of Meaning: Reading and Writing as Parallel Processes." *Written Communication* 2 (1985): 317–36.

Long, Russell C. "The Writer's Audience: Fact or Fiction?" Kirsch and Roen 73–84.

Moore, Patrick. "When Politeness Is Fatal: Technical Communication and the Challenger Accident." *Journal of Business and Technical Communication* 6 (1992): 269–92.

Nystrand, Martin. "A Social-Interactive Model of Writing." *Written Communication* 6 (1988): 66–85.

Park, Douglas. "The Meanings of 'Audience.'" *College English* 44 (1982): 247–57.

Pattow, Donald, and William Wresch. *Communicating Technical Information: A Guide for the Electronic Age*. Englewood Cliffs, NJ: Prentice, 1993.

Perelman, Chaïm. *The New Rhetoric: A Theory of Practical Reasoning*. Trans. E. Griffin-Collart and O. Bird. *The Great Ideas Today*. Chicago: Encyclopedia Britannica, Inc., 1970. Rpt. *Professing the New Rhetorics: A Sourcebook*. Ed. Theresa Enos and Stuart C. Brown. Englewood Cliffs, NJ: Prentice, 1994, 145–77.

Perelman, Chaïm, and L. Olbrechts-Tyteca. *The New Rhetoric*. Trans. John Wilkinson and Purcell Weaver. U. of Notre Dame P, 1969: 1–26. Rpt. *Contemporary Theories of Rhetoric: Selected Readings*. Ed. Richard L. Johannesen. New York: Harper, 1971. 199–221.

Phelps, Louise Wetherbee. *Audience and Authorship: The Disappearing Boundary*. Kirsch and Roen 153–74.

Reep, Diana C. *Technical Writing: Principles, Strategies, and Readings*. 2nd ed. Boston: Allyn, 1994.

Roth, Robert G. *Deconstructing Audience: A Post-Structuralist Rereading*. Kirsch and Roen 175–87.

Vatz, Richard. "The Myth of the Rhetorical Situation." *Philosophy and Rhetoric* 6 (1973): 154–61.

White, Eugene E. *The Context of Human Discourse: A Configurational Criticism of Rhetoric.* Columbia: U of South Carolina P, 1992.

Questions for Discussion and Journaling

1. Have you ever thought of writers as negotiating with their audiences? As a writer, what is the difference between imagining yourself *talking* to and *negotiating* with your audience? What would you do differently if you were doing the latter?

2. How would you define *exigence*? Why does exigence matter in rhetorical situations? (What difference does it make?)

3. Grant-Davie opens with a discussion of historical documentaries and the difference between asking "What happened?" and asking "Why did it happen?" Which question, in your view, does analyzing rhetorical situations answer? What makes you think so?

4. What are *constraints*? To help you work this out, consider what Grant-Davie's constraints might have been in drafting this piece. Bitzer, you learned in this piece, argues that we should think of constraints as *aids* rather than *restrictions*. How can that be?

5. As a writer, how would it help you to be aware of your rhetorical situation and the constraints it creates?

6. Grant-Davie seems to want us to use the idea of rhetorical situation mostly in an *analytical* way, to understand why existing discourses have taken the shape they have. In other words, he seems to be talking to us as *readers*. In what ways is the idea also useful for writers? That is, how is it useful to understand the rhetorical situation you're "writing into"?

7. Grant-Davie suggests that we have to ask three questions to understand the exigence of a rhetorical situation: what a discourse is about, why it's needed, and what it's trying to accomplish. What's the difference between the second question and the third question?

8. What happens if we imagine everyone in a rhetorical situation to be *simultaneously* a rhetor and an audience? How does imagining a *writer* as simultaneously rhetor and audience make you think differently about writing?

9. Based on the rhetorical situation for which Grant-Davie was writing, would you say you are part of the audience he imagined, or not? Why?

10. Other writers (Bitzer, Vatz, Consigny) have tried to explain the concept of the *rhetorical situation* before. Why does Grant-Davie think more work is needed?

Applying and Exploring Ideas

1. a) Write a brief (one- to two-page) working definition of *rhetorical situation*. Be sure to give some examples of rhetorical situations to illustrate your definition.

    b) Complicate your working definition by examining how Grant-Davie, Bitzer, Vatz, and Consigny see the rhetorical situation similarly or differently from one another. You may write this as a straightforward compare-and-contrast discussion if you would like, or, to spice things up a little, write it as a dialogue and create the situation in which it occurs. (Is it an argument? A dinner-table discussion? A drunken brawl?) Where does it happen, how does it go, and what do the participants say?

2. Write a two- to three-page analysis of the rhetorical situation of Grant-Davie's own article, using the elements the article explains.

3. Identify an argument that's currently going on at your school. (Check your school newspaper or Web site if nothing springs to mind.) In a short (two- to three-page) analysis, briefly describe the argument. After describing the argument, analyze the rhetorical situation. Then conclude by noting whether or how your understanding of the argument changed after you analyzed the rhetorical situation.

4. Look at three course syllabi and/or three academic handouts you've received this semester or in previous semesters. What rhetorical situation does each instructor seem to be imagining? Why do you think so? Do the instructors seem to imagine their rhetorical situations differently? If so, why do you think they do this?

5. Watch a few TV commercials and notice how quickly they establish a rhetorical situation *within* the ad. (Not, that is, the rhetorical situation of you as audience and the company as rhetor, but the rhetorical situation inside the commercial, where actors or characters play the roles of rhetors and audiences.) Write a two- to three-page analysis that describes three commercials, the rhetorical situations they create, and whether or not you consider them to be persuasive.

Meta Moment

Why do you think that your teacher assigned this article? How might this article help you achieve the goals of this chapter? How can understanding the concept of *rhetorical situation* potentially be useful to you in school and in your life?

Rhetorical Reading Strategies and the Construction of Meaning

Linda Flower

CHRISTINA HAAS

LINDA FLOWER

Haas, Christina, and Linda Flower. "Rhetorical Reading Strategies and the Construction of Meaning." *College Composition and Communication* 39.2 (1988): 167–83. Print.

Framing the Reading

In the late 1980s and early 1990s, Christina Haas and Linda Flower were doing research on how reading contributes to writing at Carnegie Mellon University's Center for the Study of Writing. Specifically, they were trying to understand what experienced readers do differently from less-experienced ones. What they found was that more-experienced readers used what they called **rhetorical** reading strategies to come more efficiently to an understanding of difficult texts.

Haas and Flower's research makes use of a somewhat imperfect method of investigation called a *think-aloud protocol*. Because we can't see what people think, we can at least try to hear some of what they're thinking by asking them to "think out loud." So research participants are asked first to read aloud and then to describe what they're thinking while they try to understand what the text means. The researchers make tapes of this talk, which are later transcribed for further study. The method is a good way of capturing some of what's going on in people's heads, but you may be able to see potential drawbacks to it as well.

If you read Keith Grant-Davie's article on rhetorical situations, you'll remember our discussion of the term **rhetoric** as descriptive of texts that *accomplish* or *do* things (like get you to buy a car or get you married or get you into war). Haas and Flower help us think about another angle of rhetoric: the *motivation* of the **rhetors** (speakers and writers) and the **context** in which the texts they create are written and read.

It may help you to know, in reading this piece, that Carnegie Mellon has been the scene of a lot of research on artificial intelligence—how to make machines able to think like humans. In research conducted around the time the article was written, human brains were often thought of as "information processors" much like computers—working with memory, central processors, inputs and outputs, and sensory data. Because this way of understanding the human mind was "in the air" (everyone was talking more or less this way) at that time, Haas and Flower's article carries some of that sense, too, and they tend to talk about minds as quite machine-like (for better or for worse). Knowing that, you understand a little more of the context of this article, and (Haas and Flower would say) that means you're a little better equipped to make sense of it.

Getting Ready to Read

Before you read, do at least one of the following activities:

- Ask a couple of friends how they read: When do they pay attention to who is the writer of what they're reading? When do they look up information like definitions or background on the subject? What strategies do they use to keep track of what they're reading, like highlighting, notes in the margins, or a reading notebook? When they encounter material they don't understand, what do they do to try to understand it? Keep notes of your friends' answers and compare them to what you do as a reader.

- Use an audio recorder of some sort to record yourself reading an unfamiliar and hard-to-read text aloud, and talk aloud as you try to figure out what it means. When you play back the recording, make notes about what you heard that you didn't expect to and what you learn about yourself as a reader from doing this.

- Make a quick self-assessment of your reading abilities by answering the following questions: What are you good at, as a reader? What do you think you're not good at when it comes to reading? Is there anything you wish you had been taught better or differently?

According to Haas and Flower, reading is a constructive, rhetorical process. Different readers use certain strategies to find meaning in the text, and the way students use these different techniques lets us know how experienced they are. Haas and Flower conducted an experiment on college students in which data were collected on these techniques. The three main strategies that the students used were identified as Content, Function/Feature, and Rhetorical. On average, 77 percent of the reading protocol was devoted to Content strategies, 22 percent to Function strategies, and only 1 percent to Rhetorical reading (Haas and Flower 130). Reading rhetorically is quite similar to writing rhetorically. In order to fully comprehend what is written, the reader must always account for the author's purpose, context, and effect on the audience. In doing so, one can greatly increase one's knowledge and understanding of the topic at hand.

—Sam Greenberg, Student

As you read, consider the following questions:

- How does the reading style that Haas and Flower recommend compare to your own habits of reading and understanding texts?
- What does it mean to *construct* the meaning of a text rather than to "extract" it or find it "in" the text?
- What, according to Haas and Flower, are more-experienced readers doing that less-experienced readers aren't?
- How do Haas and Flower actually study their question? What do you think of their methods?

There is a growing consensus in our field that reading should be thought of as a constructive rather than as a receptive process: that "meaning" does not exist in a text but in readers and the representations they build. This constructive view of reading is being vigorously put forth, in different ways, by both literary theory and cognitive research. It is complemented by work in rhetoric which argues that reading is also a discourse act. That is, when readers construct meaning, they do so in the context of a discourse situation, which includes the writer of the original text, other readers, the rhetorical context for reading, and the history of the discourse. If reading really is this constructive, rhetorical process, it may both demand that we rethink how we teach college students to read texts and suggest useful parallels between the act of reading and the more intensively studied process of writing. However, our knowledge of how readers actually carry out this interpretive process with college-level expository texts is rather limited. And a process we can't describe may be hard to teach. 1

> There is a growing consensus in our field that reading should be thought of as a constructive rather than as a receptive process: that "meaning" does not exist in a text but in readers and the representations they build.

We would like to help extend this constructive, rhetorical view of reading, which we share with others in the field, by raising two questions. The first is, how does this constructive process play itself out in the actual, thinking process of reading? And the second is, are all readers really aware of or in control of the discourse act which current theories describe? In the study we describe below, we looked at readers trying to understand a complex college-level text and observed a process that was constructive in a quite literal sense of the term. Using a think-aloud procedure, we watched as readers used not only the text but their own knowledge of the world, of the topic, and of discourse conventions, to infer, set and discard hypotheses, predict, and question in order to construct meaning for texts. One of the ways readers tried to make meaning of the text was a strategy we called "rhetorical reading," an active attempt at 2 constructing a rhetorical context for the text as a way of making sense of it. However, this valuable move was a special strategy used only by more experienced readers. We observed a sharp distinction between the rhetorical process these experienced readers demonstrated and the processes of freshman readers. It may be that these student readers, who relied primarily on text-based strategies to construct their meanings, do not have the same full sense of reading as the rhetorical or social discourse act we envision.

Some of the recent work on reading and cognition gives us a good starting 3 point for our discussion since it helps describe what makes the reading process so complex and helps explain how people can construct vastly different interpretations of the same text. Although a thinking-aloud protocol can show us a great deal, we must keep in mind that it reveals only part of what goes on as a reader is building a representation of a text. And lest the "constructive" metaphor makes this process sound tidy, rational, and fully conscious, we should emphasize that it may in fact be rapid, unexamined, and even inexpressible. The private mental representation that a reader constructs has many facets: it is likely to include a representation of propositional or content information, a representation of the structure—either conventional or unique—of that information, and a representation of how the parts of the text function. In addition, the reader's representation may include beliefs about the subject matter, about the author and his or her credibility, and about the reader's own intentions in reading. In short, readers construct meaning by building multifaceted, interwoven representations of knowledge. The current text, prior texts, and the reading context can exert varying degrees of influence on this process, but it is the reader who must integrate information into meaning.

We can begin to piece together the way this constructive, cognitive process 4 operates based on recent research on reading and comprehension, and on reading and writing. Various syntheses of this work have been provided by Baker and Brown; Bransford; Flower ("Interpretive Acts"); and Spivey. To begin with, it is helpful to imagine the representations readers build as complex networks, like dense roadmaps, made up of many nodes of information, each related to others in multiple ways. The nodes created during a few minutes of reading would probably include certain content propositions from the text. The network might also contain nodes for the author's name, for a key point in the text, for a personal experience evoked by the text, for a striking word or phrase, and for an inference the reader made about the value of the text, or its social or personal significance. The links between a group of nodes might reflect causality, or subordination, or simple association, or a strong emotional connection.

The process of constructing this representation is carried out by both highly 5 automated processes of recognition and inference *and* by the more active problem-solving processes on which our work focuses. For instance, trying to construct a well-articulated statement of the "point" of a text may require active searching, inferencing, and transforming of one's own knowledge. The reason such transformations are constantly required can be explained by the "multiple-representation thesis" proposed by Flower and Hayes ("Images" 120). It suggests that readers' and writers' mental representations are not limited to verbally well-formed ideas and plans, but may include information coded as visual images, or as emotions, or as linguistic propositions that exist just above the level of specific words. These representations may also reflect more abstract schema, such as the schema most people have for narrative or for establishing credibility in a conversation. Turning information coded in any of these forms into a fully verbal articulation of the "point," replete with well-specified connections between ideas and presented according to the standard conventions of a given discourse, is constructive; it can involve not only translating one kind of representation into another, but reorganizing knowledge and creating new knowledge, new conceptual nodes and connections. In essence, it makes sense to take the metaphor of "construction" seriously.

It should be clear that this image of "meaning" as a rich network of dispa- 6 rate kinds of information is in sharp contrast to the narrow, highly selective and fully verbal statement of a text's gist or "meaning" that students may be asked to construct for an exam or a book review. Statements of that sort do, of course, serve useful functions, but we should not confuse them with the multi-dimensional, mental structures of meaning created by the cognitive and affective process of reading.

If reading, then, is a process of responding to cues in the text and in the 7 reader's context to build a complex, multi-faceted representation of meaning, it should be no surprise that different readers might construct radically different representations of the same text and might use very different strategies to do so. This makes the goals of teacher and researcher look very much alike: both the teacher and the researcher are interested in the means by which readers (especially students) construct multi-faceted representations, or "meaning." The study we are about to describe looks at a practical and theoretical question that this constructive view of reading raises: namely, what strategies, other than those based on knowing the topic, do readers bring to the process of understanding difficult texts—and how does this translate into pedagogy?

Seeing reading as a constructive act encourages us as teachers to move from 8 merely *teaching texts* to *teaching readers*. The teacher as co-reader can both model a sophisticated reading process and help students draw out the rich possibilities of texts and readers, rather than trying to insure that all students interpret texts in a single, "correct" way—and in the same way. Yet this goal— drawing out the rich possibilities of texts and of readers—is easier to describe than to reach.

What Is "Good Reading"?

The notion of multiple, constructed representations also helps us understand a 9 recurring frustration for college teachers: the problem of "good" readers who appear to miss the point or who seem unable or unwilling to read critically. Many of our students are "good" readers in the traditional sense: they have large vocabularies, read quickly, are able to do well at comprehension tasks involving recall of content. They can identify topic sentences, introductions and conclusions, generalizations and supporting details. Yet these same students often frustrate us, as they paraphrase rather than analyze, summarize rather than criticize texts. Why are these students doing less than we hope for?

To interpret any sophisticated text seems to require not only careful reading 10 and prior knowledge, but the ability to read the text on several levels, to build multi-faceted representations. A text is understood not only as content and information, but also as the result of someone's intentions, as part of a larger discourse world, and as having real effects on real readers. In an earlier study, we say that experienced readers made active use of the strategy of rhetorical reading not only to predict and interpret texts but to solve problems in comprehension (Flower, "Construction of Purpose.") Vipond and Hunt have observed a related strategy of "point-driven" (vs. "story-driven") reading which people bring to literary texts.

If we view reading as the act of constructing multi-faceted yet integrated 11 representations, we might hypothesize that the problem students have with critical reading of difficult texts is less the representations they *are* constructing than those they *fail to construct*. Their representations of text are closely tied to content: they read for information. Our students may believe that if they understand all the words and can paraphrase the propositional content of a text, then they have successfully "read" it.

While a content representation is often satisfactory—it certainly meets the 12 needs of many pre-college read-to-take-a-test assignments—it falls short with tasks or texts which require analysis and criticism. What many of our students *can* do is to construct representations of content, of structure, and of conventional features. What they often *fail* to *do* is to move beyond content and convention and construct representations of texts as purposeful actions, arising from contexts, and with intended effects. "Critical reading" involves more than careful reading for content, more than identification of conventional features of discourse, such as introductions or examples, and more than simple evaluation based on agreeing or disagreeing. Sophisticated, difficult texts often require the reader to build an equally sophisticated, complex representation of meaning. But how does this goal translate into the process of reading?

As intriguing as this notion of the active construction of meaning is, we really 13 have no direct access to the meanings/representations that readers build. We cannot enter the reader's head and watch as the construction of meaning proceeds. Nor can we get anything but an indirect measure of the nature, content, and structure of that representation. What we can do, however, is to watch the way that readers go about building representations: we can observe their use of *reading strategies* and so infer something about the representations they build.

In order to learn something about the construction of meaning by readers, 14 we observed and analyzed the strategies of ten readers. Four were experienced college readers, graduate students (aged 25 to 31 years), three in engineering and one in rhetoric; six were student readers, college freshmen aged 18 and 19, three classified "average" and three classified "above average" by their freshman composition teachers.

We were interested in how readers go about "constructing" meaning and 15 the constructive strategies they use to do so. However, we suspected that many academic topics would give an unfair advantage to the more experienced readers, who would be able to read automatically by invoking their knowledge of academic topics and discourse conventions. This automaticity would, however, make their constructive reading harder for us to see. We wanted a text that would require equally active problem solving by both groups. So, in order to control for such knowledge, we designed a task in which meaning was under question for all readers, and in which prior topic knowledge would function as only one of many possible tools used to build an interpretation. Therefore, the text began *in medias res*, without orienting information about author, source, topic, or purpose. We felt that in this way we could elicit the full range of constructive strategies these readers could call upon when the situation demanded it.

The text, part of the preface to Sylvia Farnham-Diggory's *Cognitive Processes* 16 *in Education,* was like many texts students read, easy to decode but difficult to interpret, with a high density of information and a number of semi-technical expressions which had to be defined from context. The readers read and thought aloud as they read. In addition, they answered the question "how do you interpret the text now?" at frequent intervals. The question was asked of readers eight times, thus creating nine reading "episodes." The slash marks indicate where the question appeared, and also mark episode boundaries, which we discuss later. To see the effect of this manipulation on eliciting interpretive strategies, you might wish to read the experimental text before going further. (Sentence numbers have been added.)

But somehow the social muddle persists.[s1] Some wonderful children come from appalling homes; some terrible children come from splendid homes.[s2] Practice may have a limited relationship to perfection—at least it cannot substitute for talent.[s3] Women are not happy when they are required to pretend that a physical function is equivalent to a mental one.[s4] Many children teach themselves to read years before they are supposed to be "ready."[s5] / Many men would not dream of basing their self-esteem on "cave man" prowess.[s6] And despite their verbal glibness, teenagers seem to be in a worse mess than ever.[s7] /

What has gone wrong?[s8] Are the psychological principles invalid?[s9] Are they too simple for a complex world?[s10] /

Like the modern world, modern scientific psychology is extremely technical and complex.[s11] The application of any particular set of psychological principles to any particular real problem requires a double specialist: a specialist in the scientific area, and a specialist in the real area.[s12] /

Not many such double specialists exist.[s13] The relationship of a child's current behavior to his early home life, for example, is not a simple problem—Sunday Supplement psychology notwithstanding.[s14] / Many variables must be understood and integrated: special ("critical") periods of brain sensitivity, nutrition, genetic factors, the development of attention and perception, language, time factors (for example, the amount of time that elapses between a baby's action and a mother's smile), and so on.[s15] Mastery of these principles is a full-time professional occupation.[s16] / The professional application of these principles—in, say a day-care center—is also a full-time occupation, and one that is foreign to many laboratory psychologists.[s17] Indeed, a laboratory psychologist may not even recognize his pet principles when they are realized in a day care setting.[s18] /

What is needed is a coming together of real-world and laboratory specialists that will require both better communication and more complete experience.[s19] / The laboratory specialists must spend some time in a real setting; the real-world specialists must spend some time in a theoretical laboratory.[s20] Each specialist needs to practice thinking like his counterpart.[s21] Each needs to practice translating theory into reality, and reality into theory.[s22]

The technique of in-process probing tries to combine the immediacy of concurrent reporting with the depth of information obtained through frequent questioning. It can of course give us only an indirect and partial indication of the actual representation. What it does reveal are gist-making strategies used at a sequence of points during reading, and it offers a cumulative picture of a text-under-construction. 17

Aside from our manipulation of the presentation, the text was a typical college reading task. Part of the author's introduction to an educational psychology textbook, it presented an array of facts about the social reality of learning, problems of education, and the aims of research. *Our* reading of the text, obviously also a constructed one, but one constructed with the benefit of a full knowledge of the source and context, included two main facts and two central claims. In a later analysis, we used these facts and claims to describe some of the transactions of readers and text. 18

> Fact: Social problems exist and psychological principles exist, but there's a mismatch between them.
>
> Fact: There are two kinds of educational specialists—real-world and laboratory.
>
> Claim (explicit in text): The two kinds of specialists should interact.
>
> Claim (implicit): Interaction of the two specialists is necessary to solve social problems.

The differences in "readings" subjects constructed of the text were striking and were evidenced immediately. For instance, the following descriptions of three readers' readings of the text suggest the range of readers' concerns and begin to offer hints about the nature of their constructed representations of the text. These descriptions were what we called "early transactions" with the text—an analysis based on readers' comments during reading of the first two paragraphs, or ten sentences, of the text. 19

Seth, a 27-year old graduate student in Engineering, by his own account a voracious reader of literature in his own field, of travel books, history, and contemporary novels, is initially confused with the concepts "physical function and mental one" (sentence 4). He then explains his confusion by noting the nature of the materials: "well, that's got some relationship with something that came before this business." 20

Kara, a freshman who does average college work, also thinks the text is confusing; specifically, she says "I don't know what glibness means" (sentence 7). 21

But whereas Seth sets up a hypothesis about both the content of the text and its source—"I think it's part of an article on the fact that the way you turn out is not a function of your environment"—and reads on to confirm his hypothesis, Kara's reading proceeds as a series of content paraphrases—"It's talking about children coming from different homes . . . and women not being happy." She continues to interpret the text a chunk at a time, paraphrasing linearly with little attempt to integrate or connect the parts. She reacts positively to the text—"I love the expression 'what has gone wrong'" (sentence 8)—and, despite her initial confusion with "glibness," she seems satisfied with her simple reading: "I just feel like you're talking about people—what's wrong with them and the world."

Not all the freshman student readers' transactions with the text were as superficial and oversimplified as Kara's—nor were they all as contented with their readings of the text. Bob—an above-average freshmen with a pre-med major—paraphrases content linearly like Kara, but he also sets up a hypothetical structure for the text: "It seems that different points are being brought out and each one has a kind of a contradiction in it, and it seems like an introduction . . . ." Unlike Kara, however, he becomes frustrated, unable to reconcile his own beliefs with what he's reading: "Well, I don't think they're too simple for a complex world. I don't think these are very simple things that are being said here. I think the situations—women, children, and men—I think they're pretty complex . . . so I don't understand why it said 'too simple for a complex world'" (sentence 10). 22

Our more experienced reader, Seth, also sets up a hypothesis about the text's structure: "Maybe he's [the author] contrasting the verbal glibness with caveman instinct." But Seth goes further: "I think the author is trying to say that it's some balance between your natural instinct and your surroundings but he's not sure what that balance is." These hypotheses try to account for not only the propositional content of the text, but also the function of parts ("contrasting"), the author's intent, and even the author's own uncertainty. 23

Seth continues to read the text, noting his own inexperience with the area of psychology—"I'm thinking about Freud and I really don't know much about psychology"—and trying to tie what he has just read to the previous paragraph: "I guess the psychological principles have something to do with the way children turn out. But I don't know if they are the physical, environmental things or if they're a function of your surroundings and education." 24

In these "early transactions" with the text, we see a range of readings and vast differences in the information contained in the readers' representations: Kara is uncertain of the meaning of a word and somewhat confused generally; she paraphrases content and is satisfied with the text and her reading of it. If we have a hint about the representations of text that Kara is building it is that they are focused primarily on content and her own affective responses and that they are somewhat more limited than those of the other readers. Bob's comments suggest that he may be building representations of structure as well as content, and that he is trying to bring his own beliefs and his reading of the text into line. 25

Seth is concerned with the content, with possible functions—both for parts 26 of the text and for the text as a whole—with the author's intentions, with the experimental situation and with missing text; he also attends to his own knowledge (or lack of it) and to his prior reading experiences. What this suggests is that Seth is creating a multi-dimensional representation of the text that includes representations of its content, representations of the structure and function of the text, representations of author's intention and his own experience and knowledge as a reader of the text.

The "texts" or representations of meaning that the readers created as they were 27 wrestling with the text and thinking aloud were dramatically different in both quantity—the amount of information they contained—and quality—the kinds of information they contained and the amount of the original text they accounted for. However, with no direct access to the internal representations that readers were building, we looked instead at the overt strategies they seemed to be using.

Strategies for Constructing Meaning

The initial transactions with text suggested some differences among readers. 28 Our next move was to more systematically analyze these differences. Each protocol contained two kinds of verbalizations: actual reading of the text aloud and comments in which the readers were thinking aloud. About half of these comments were in response to the question, "How do you interpret the text now?" and the rest were unprompted responses. Each comment was sorted into one of three categories, based on what the readers seemed to be "attending to." This simple, three-part coding scheme distinguished between Content, Function/Feature, and Rhetorical reading strategies. These strategies are readily identifiable with some practice; our inter-rater reliability, determined by simple pair-wise comparisons, averaged 82%. Later, after about 20 minutes' instruction in the context of a college reading classroom, students could identify the strategies in the reading of others with close to 70% reliability.

Comments coded as *content strategies* are concerned with content or topic 29 information, "what the text is about." The reader may be questioning, interpreting, or summing content, paraphrasing what the text "is about" or "is saying." The reader's goal in using content strategies seems to be getting information from the text. Some examples of comments coded as content strategies:

> "So we're talking about psychological principles here."
>
> "I think it's about changing social conditions, like families in which both parents work, and changing roles of women."
>
> "I don't know what glibness is, so it's still confusing."

As Table 1 shows, both student and more experienced readers spent a large proportion of their effort using content strategies. On the average, 77% of the reading protocol was devoted to content strategies for students, 67% for the older readers. Building a representation of content seems to be very important for all of the readers we studied.

Table 1

Mean Proportion of Strategies Used

	STUDENTS		EXPERIENCED READERS	
Content Strategies	77%	(58.1)	67%	(58.0)
Feature Strategies	22%	(15.8)	20%	(18.0)
Rhetorical Strategies	1%*	(.3)	13%*	(9.3)

*Difference significant at .05 level. Numbers in parentheses indicate the mean number of protocol statements in each category.

Function/feature strategies were used to refer to conventional, generic func- 30 tions of texts, or conventional features of discourse. These strategies seemed closely tied to the text: readers frequently named text parts, pointing to specific words, sentences, or larger sections of text—"This is the main point." "This must be an example," "I think this is the introduction." While content strategies seemed to be used to explain what the text was "saying," function/ feature strategies were often used to name what the text was "doing": "Here he's contrasting," "This part seems to be explaining. . . ." In short, the use of these strategies suggests that readers are constructing spatial, functional, or relational structures for the text. Some examples of comments coded as function/ feature strategies:

"I guess these are just examples."

"Is this the introduction?"

"This seems to be the final point."

Predictably, these strategies accounted for less of the protocol than did the content strategies: 22% for students, 20% for more experienced readers (see Table 1). And the groups of readers looked similar in their use of this strategy. This, too, may be expected: Identifying features such as introductions, examples, and conclusions is standard fare in many junior high and high school curricula. In addition, these students are of at least average ability within a competitive private university. We might ask if more basic readers—without the skills or reading experiences of these students—might demonstrate less use of the function/feature strategies. Further, these readers were all reading from paper; people reading from computer screens—a number which is rapidly increasing—may have difficulty creating and recalling spatial and relational structures in texts they read and write on-line (Haas and Hayes 34–35).

Rhetorical strategies take a step beyond the text itself. They are concerned 31 with constructing a rhetorical situation for the text, trying to account for author's purpose, context, and effect on the audience. In rhetorical reading strategies readers use cues in the text, and their own knowledge of discourse situations, to re-create or infer the rhetorical situation of the text they are reading. There is some indication that these strategies were used to help readers uncover the actual "event" of the text, a unique event with a particular author and actual effects. One reader likened the author of the text to a contemporary rhetorician: "This sounds a little like Richard Young to me." Readers seem to be constructing a rhetorical situation for the text and relating *this* text to a larger world of discourse. These examples demonstrate some of the range of rhetorical strategies: comments concerned with author's purpose, context or source, intended audience, and actual effect. Some examples of rhetorical reading strategies:

> "So the author is trying to make the argument that you need scientific specialists in psychology."
>
> "I wonder if it [the article] is from *Ms.*"
>
> "I don't think this would work for the man-in-the-street."
>
> "I wonder, though, if this is a magazine article, and I wonder if they expected it to be so confusing."

While the groups of readers employed content and function/feature strate-   32
gies similarly, there is a dramatic difference in their use of the rhetorical strategy category. Less than 1% (in fact, one statement by one reader) of the students' protocols contained rhetorical strategies, while 13% of the experienced readers' effort went into rhetorical strategies. This is particularly striking when we consider the richness and wealth of information contained in these kinds of comments. For instance, setting this article into the context of *Ms.* magazine brings with it a wealth of unstated information about the kind of article that appears in that source, the kind of writers that contribute to it, and the kind of people who read it.

Rhetorical reading appears to be an "extra" strategy which some readers   33
used and others did not. Mann-Whitney analyses show no significant differences in the use of content or function/feature strategies, and an interesting— $p < 0.5$—difference between the two groups in use of rhetorical strategies. The small numbers in parentheses indicate the mean number of protocol statements in each category for each group of readers; the significance tests, however, were performed on the proportions of strategies used by each reader.

An example of two readers responding to a particularly difficult section of   34
text reveals the differences in the use of strategies even more clearly than do the numbers.

> *Student Reader*: Well, basically, what I said previously is that there seems to be a problem between the real-world and the laboratory, or ideal situation versus real situation, whatever way you want to put it—that seems to be it.
>
> *Experienced Reader*: Ok, again, real world is a person familiar with the social influences on a person's personality—things they read or hear on the radio. . . . And laboratory specialists is more trained in clinical psychology. And now I think this article is trying to propose a new field of study for producing people who have a better understanding of human behavior. This person is crying out for a new type of scientist or something. (Ph.D. Student in Engineering)

While the student reader is mainly creating a gist and paraphrasing content, the experienced reader does this and more—he then tries to infer the author's purpose and even creates a sort of strident persona for the writer. If readers can only build representations for which they have constructive tools or strategies, then it is clear that this student reader—and in fact all of the student readers we studied—are not building rhetorical representations of this text. In fact, these student readers seem to be focused almost exclusively on content. The student reader above is a case in point: her goal seems to be to extract information from the text, and once that is done—via a simple paraphrase—she is satisfied with her reading of the text. We called this type of content reading "knowledge-getting," to underscore the similarity to the knowledge-telling strategy identified by Bereiter and Scardamalia (72) in immature writers. In both knowledge-getting and knowledge-telling, the focus is on content; larger rhetorical purposes seem to play no role.

It is useful to see rhetorical reading not as a separate and different strategy   35 but as a progressive enlargement of the constructed meaning of a text. These student readers seldom "progressed" to that enlarged view. Reading for content is usually dominant and crucial—other kinds of strategies build upon content representations. Functions and features strategies are generic and conventional— easily identified in texts and often explicitly taught. Rhetorical strategies include not only a representation of discourse as discourse but as *unique* discourse with a real author, a specific purpose, and actual effects. This possible relationship between strategies may point to a building of skills, a progression which makes intuitive sense and is supported by what we know about how reading is typically taught and by teachers' reports of typical student reading problems.

The difference in the use that experienced and student readers make of   36 these strategies does not in itself make a convincing case for their value. Rhetorical reading strategies certainly *look* more sophisticated and elaborate, but an important question remains: What does rhetorical reading *do* for readers? We might predict that constructing the additional rhetorical representation— requiring more depth of processing—would be an asset in particularly problematic reading tasks: texts in a subject area about which the reader knows little, or texts complex in structure. It might also be important in those reading tasks in which recognizing author's intention is crucial: propaganda, satire, even the interpretation of assignments in school.

However, let us consider a rival hypothesis for a moment: maybe rhetori-   37 cal strategies are simply "frosting on the cake." Maybe good readers use these strategies because reading for information is easier for them, and they have extra cognitive resources to devote to what might be largely peripheral concerns of the rhetorical situation.

We suspect that this was not the case, that rhetorical reading is not merely   38 "frosting on the cake" for several reasons: first, in the absence of a rhetorical situation for the text, *all* experienced readers constructed one. Second, the more experienced readers seemed to be using all the strategies in tandem; i.e., they used the rhetorical strategies to help construct content, and vice versa. They did not "figure out" the content, and then do rhetorical reading as an "embellishment." Rhetorical reading strategies were interwoven with other strategies as the readers constructed their reading of the texts.

And third, in the "tug of war" between text and reader which characterizes   39 constructive reading (Tierney and Pearson 34), we found that the rhetorical readers seemed to recognize and assimilate more facts and claims into their reading of the text. Recall that there were two facts and two claims which we felt constituted a successful reading of this text. We used readers' recognition of these facts and claims to gauge and to describe the kind of representation they had constructed.

Fact: Social problems exist and psychological principles exist, but there's a mismatch between them.

Fact: There are two kinds of educational specialists—real-world and laboratory.

Claim (explicit in text): The two kinds of specialists should interact.

Claim (implicit): Interaction of the two specialists is necessary to solve social problems.

In recognizing facts in the text, both groups of readers did well. But there were very interesting differences in the patterns of recognition of claims in the text. Readers who used the rhetorical strategies, first, recognized more claims, and second, identified claims sooner than other readers. As we described earlier, our presentation of the text to the readers created nine reading episodes; each asked for the readers' interpretation of "the text so far" at the end of the episode. This allowed us some measure of constructed meaning by plotting the points at which readers recognized each fact or claim. We said that readers recognized a claim when they mentioned it as a possibility. This "recognition" was often tentative; readers made comments such as "So maybe this section is saying the two kinds of scientists should communicate," or "I guess this could solve the stuff at the beginning about social muddle." 40

The "episode line" in Figure 1 shows the points at which two readers (a student and a more-experienced reader) recognized Claim 1, plotted in relation to 41

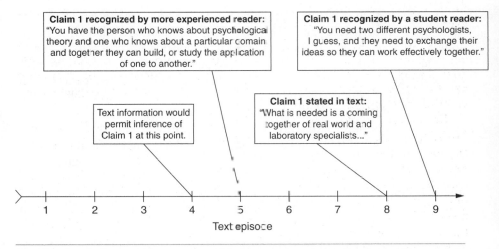

Figure 1 When did a reader recognize Claim 1: "The two kinds of specialists should interact."

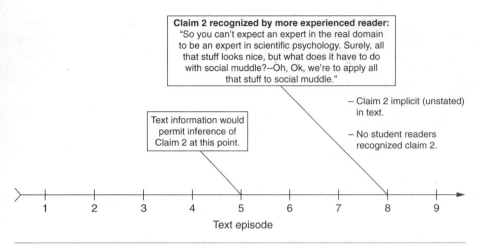

Figure 2 When did a reader recognize Claim 2? "Interaction of two kinds of specialists is necessary to solve social problems."

the point at which the text would reasonably permit such recognition. Figure 2 shows this information for the same readers recognizing Claim 2. Claim 2 is never explicitly stated, it only becomes easy to infer in the final episode. Of all the implicit meanings the text *could* convey, we saw this second claim as central to the coherence of the argument.

As Figure 3 illustrates, all student readers got Claim 1, but only at episode 9, 42 where it was explicitly stated—for the second time—in the text. (Claim 1 is first stated in episode 8.) More experienced readers, on the other hand, had all inferred Claim 1 much earlier—by episode 7. In addition, student readers did not recognize the unstated second claim at all, although all experienced readers inferred it, some as early as episode 8.

At episode 4 (the first point at which it would be possible to infer Claim 1), 43 25% of the experienced readers had inferred and mentioned this idea. At episode 5, 50% of these readers recognized it, at episode 6, 75% saw it, and by episode 7 all of the experienced readers had inferred Claim 1. In contrast, none of the student readers recognized this claim until episode 8, when it was cued in the text. At that point, 33% of the students noted it. At episode 9, when Claim 1 was restated, the rest of the students recognized it.

Claim 2 was never explicitly stated in the text, but half the experienced 44 readers had inferred this claim at episode 8 and all had inferred it at episode 9. None of the student readers offered any hints that they had recognized this implicit claim. It seems that the rhetorical readers were better able to recognize an important claim that was *never explicitly spelled out in the text*. In sophisticated texts, many important high-level claims—like Claim 2—remain implicit, but are crucial nonetheless.

This study, because it is observational rather than experimental, does not 45 allow us to conclude that the rhetorical reading we observed in the more experienced readers—and only in the more experienced readers—was the only or

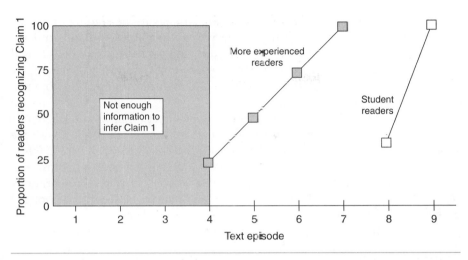

Figure 3 Readers' Recognition of Claim 1

even the dominant cause for their ability to recognize claims. However, it makes sense that readers who are trying to make inferences about author, context, purpose, and effect, who are trying to create a representation of the text as the result of a purposeful action, would be more likely to recognize the claims—both implicit and explicit—within a text.

The Role of Rhetorical Reading

This study suggests that the strategy of rhetorical reading may be an impor- 46 tant element in the larger process of critical reading. The constructive process we observed in readers actively trying to understand the author's intent, the context, and how other readers might respond appears to be a good basis for recognizing claims, especially unstated ones the reader must infer. Speaking more generally, this act of building a rich representation of text—larger than the words on the page and including both propositional content and the larger discourse context within which a text functions—is the kind of constructive reading we desire our students to do.

However, is rhetorical reading a strategy students could easily adopt if cued 47 to do so? Being able to see one's own text and the texts of others as *discourse acts*—rather than bodies of facts and information—is desirable, useful, and important for reading and writing of all kinds. This is the kind of meaning building we would like students to do, and rhetorical reading is one strategy that may help them do it. In saying this, however, we recognize that this knowledge will do us little good if we can't use it to help students. People must be *able* to construct elaborate representations of meaning, and they must have the strategies to do so. How this is to come about is not clear.

Our first attempt at "suggestive" teaching—introducing the students to the 48 concept of rhetorical reading and encouraging them to use it—found that while students could identify the rhetorical reading strategy in the reading of others, they were less successful at using it. Can we expect merely to hand students tools for building rich representations of text and set them to work? Or will rhetorical reading require active teaching—teaching by direct instruction, by modelling, and by encouraging students to become contributing and committed members of rhetorical communities?

Although the answers to these questions are not yet clear, we offer here our own reading of these results: first, some readers are actively concerned with the situations from which texts arise. These readers seemed to expend some effort in representing the rhetorical situation of a text they are reading. However, reading is a complex cognitive activity. It involves constructing representations on several levels, and student readers, even good students, seem to be bogged down in content: they focus on knowledge-getting while reading. 49

We believe that teaching students to read rhetorically is genuinely difficult. It is difficult in the way that teaching students to *write* rhetorically is difficult. In fact, this work with student and experienced *readers* provides a potential parallel to research results with student and expert *writers*. While expert writers, like those Flower, Hayes, Shriver, Carey, and Haas have studied, work within a rhetorical framework—imagining audience response, acknowledging context, and setting their own purposeful goals—students writers often concentrate on content and information—they "knowledge tell," in Bereiter and Scardamalia's terms. Similarly, these student readers seem to concentrate on knowledge, content, what the text is about—not taking into account that the text is the product of a writer's intentions and is designed to produce an effect on a specific audience. 50

While experienced readers may understand that both reading and writing are context-rich, situational, constructive acts, many students may see reading and writing as merely an information exchange: knowledge-telling when they write, and "knowledge-getting" when they read. Helping students move beyond this simple, information-exchange view to a more complex rhetorical model—in both their reading and their writing—is one of the very real tasks which faces us as teachers. And research with real readers and writers continues to offer insights into the equally complex ways all of us construct meaning. 51

Works Cited

Baker, Linda, and Ann L. Brown. "Metacognitive Skills and Reading." *Handbook of Reading Research*. Ed. R. Barr, Michael L. Kamil, and Peter Mosenthal. New York: Longman, 1984. 353–94.

Bereiter, Carl, and Marlene Scardamalia. "Cognitive Coping Strategies and the Problem of Inert Knowledge." *Learning and Thinking Skills: Research and Open Questions*. Ed. Susan Chipman, J. Segal, and Robert Glaser. Hillsdale, NJ: Lawrence Erlbaum Associates, 1985. 65–80.

Bransford, John. *Cognition: Learning, Understanding and Remembering*. Belmont, CA: Wadsworth Publishing Company, 1979.

Farnham-Diggory, Sylvia. *Cognitive Processes in Education: A Psychological Preparation for Teaching and Curriculum Development*. New York: Harper and Row, 1972.

Flower, Linda. "The Construction of Purpose in Writing and Reading." *College English* 50 (1988): 528–50.

Flower, Linda. "Interpretive Acts: Cognition and the Construction of Discourse." *Poetics* 16 (April 1987): 109–30.

Flower, Linda, and John R. Hayes. "Images, Plans, and Prose: The Representation of Meaning in Writing." *Written Communication* 1 (January 1984): 120–60.

Flower, Linda, John R. Hayes, Karen Shriver, Linda Carey, and Christina Haas. *Planning in Writing: A Theory of the Cognitive Process.* ONR Technical Report # 1. Pittsburgh: Carnegie Mellon, 1987.

Haas, Christina, and John R. Hayes. "What Did I Just Say? Reading Problems in Writing with the Machine." *Research in the Teaching of English* 20 (February 1986): 22–35.

Scardamalia, Marlene. "How Children Cope with the Cognitive Demands of Writing." *Writing: The Nature, Development, and Teaching of Written Communication (Vol. 2).* Ed. Carl Frederiksen, M. F. Whiteman, and J. F. Dominic. Hillsdale, NJ: Lawrence Erlbaum Associates, 1981. 81–103.

Spivey, Nancy N. "Construing Constructivism: Reading Research in the United States." *Poetics* 16 (April 1987): 169–93.

Tierney, Robert, and P. David Pearson. "Toward a Composing Model of Reading." *Composing and Comprehending.* Ed. Julie M. Jensen. Urbana, IL: NCTE, 1984. 33–45.

Vipond, Douglas, and Russell Hunt. "Point-driven Understanding: Pragmatic and Cognitive Dimensions of Literary Reading." *Poetics* 13 (June 1984): 261–77.

Questions for Discussion and Journaling

1. What are Haas and Flower trying to find out by doing this research? Why do they want to find it out?

2. Haas and Flower spend a lot of time pointing out that readers "construct" "representations" of a text's content and what it means. Why is this particular language of construction and representation so important to them? How is it different from the ways in which we usually talk about what happens when readers read?

3. One claim this article makes is that when readers try to understand texts, they bring their own knowledge to them. What kinds of knowledge did you bring to this article that helped you make sense of it?

4. Haas and Flower seem to criticize reading that's merely for "information exchange." Why? What do they consider inadequate about using readings simply to convey information?

5. What does it mean to see texts "as purposeful actions" (see para. 12)? What are some examples you've seen of texts that serve as actions?

6. Consider how Haas and Flower went about answering their research questions. What were some advantages and some drawbacks to their methods? What do you think might be the biggest weakness of their approach? How would you have done it?

7. Think back to the last time someone gave you some instruction in how to read. When was it? What were you taught? What differences are there between

what you were taught and what Haas and Flower say is important to teach about reading?

8. Can you identify instances in the past where you've been a rhetorical reader? If so, what were you reading? How was it similar to and different from your usual reading practice?

Applying and Exploring Ideas

1. Use a text your teacher gives you to conduct your own read-aloud/think-aloud experiment. After recording yourself reading the text and stopping at predetermined points to talk about how you understand the text at that moment, listen to your recording and try to find patterns that describe how you read and understand while reading. Then write a three- to four-page report discussing what you've learned.

2. Write a summary of Haas and Flower's article that discusses the following: Why was it written? Who was meant to read it (and how can you tell)? What do Haas and Flower seem to be trying to *do* with the article? If you have read Grant-Davie, you will recognize that part of what you are being asked to do here is identify the *rhetorical situation*. How can your understanding of the text be improved by identifying the rhetorical situation?

3. Make a list of the rhetorical reading strategies that Haas and Flower discuss, trying to include even those they only imply without explicitly stating. Use this list to help you write a set of instructions on reading rhetorically for the next group of students who will take the class you're in now. What should they look for in texts? What questions should they ask about texts to ensure they're reading rhetorically?

4. Locate a text that seems to be purely *informational* (like an instruction manual or directions for taking the SAT). Reading it rhetorically—that is, trying to understand the motivation of the writer and the audience's needs—can you find aspects of the text that go beyond information to claims, opinion, and argument?

Meta Moment

How can you benefit from knowing the results of Haas and Flower's study? How does reading and understanding this article help you achieve the goals of this chapter?

Teaching Punctuation as a Rhetorical Tool

JOHN DAWKINS

Dawkins, John. "Teaching Punctuation as a Rhetorical Tool." *College Composition and Communication* 46.4 (1995): 533–48. Print.

Framing the Reading

John Dawkins focuses on problems with how people understand punctuation rules. (If you read Joseph Williams earlier in the chapter, you will see some similarities). Dawkins loads his article with examples (sixty-nine in all) that make it pretty difficult to deny that how good writers actually write makes handbook rules seem more like guidelines and less like laws. Dawkins offers a solution to the ways people construct "rules": He uses his research across many sample texts to describe a *deeper* and more basic set of rules that seem more widely in use than the narrower handbook rules. You'll be tempted to skim or even skip all the examples Dawkins offers as they begin to pile up. Try to resist that temptation, and you'll learn a lot about how English works.

Dawkins wants us to think about grammar as **rhetorical**. If you've read Haas and Flower or Grant-Davie in this chapter, you should start to have a feel for what the word *rhetorical* means: it has to do with choices that writers make to influence readers.

Stop and think about this for a moment: Dawkins is saying that grammar involves *choices*.

If you're like most students, you learned grammar as a set of inflexible rules that had to be memorized and never violated. At best, you might have had a teacher who told you, when you pointed out how many grammar rules are violated by professional writers, that "you have to *know* the rules before you can break them" or who said, "When you're a best-selling novelist, then you can break the rules, too." Dawkins, however, raises the possibility that there are different sets of "rules" at work and that we might be better off studying actual writing and actual writers instead of slavishly following handbooks.

Getting Ready to Read

Before you read, do at least one of the following activities:

- Combine and rewrite the following two sentences in three different ways, by conveying the information from number 2 at the beginning, middle, and end of number 1.

1. My sister's treehouse made a great place to play with her friends.
2. The treehouse was made of wood scraps and cardboard.

Once you've written the three versions of the sentence, try to explain the grammar rules you used in writing each.

- Poll your friends to see what they learned about grammar rules and how "bendable" they are, or aren't, from their earlier instruction in English or writing.
- Try writing a definition of what aspects of writing count as "grammar." For example, is punctuation grammar? What about the rule in the first sentence of this activity that puts the period inside the quotation mark? Is that grammar, or something else? What about spelling—is that grammar? How about syntax—word order and how phrases hook together? In short, what counts as grammar in your mind?

As you read, consider the following questions:

- According to Dawkins, if we want to know how writing works, where should we look? Who is likely to disagree with Dawkins here? Why?
- What should we conclude, in Dawkins's view, about writing that doesn't seem to follow one set of rules?
- What does Dawkins believe about rules as they relate to writing? Are there, in his view, universal rules that apply to writing? If so, what are they?
- Is there, in your opinion, any value to handbooks that reduce writing to a set of hard-and-fast rules?

Punctuation—just one of the "mechanics" of writing, after all—is perhaps not the first thing you turn to after checking the CCC table of contents, but you are here now, so let me try to keep you here by announcing, quickly, the not unimportant claims to be made. First, manuals of style and college handbooks have it all wrong when it comes to punctuation (good writers don't punctuate that way); there is, I propose, a system underlying what good writers, in fact, do; it is a surprisingly simple system; it is a system that enables writers to achieve important—even subtle—rhetorical effects; it is, even, a system that teachers can teach far more easily than they can teach the poorly systematized rules in our handbooks and style manuals.

It takes only a little study of the selections in our college readers to realize that the punctuation rules in handbooks and style manuals are not sacred texts for a great many good writers. Fragments and comma splices, violations of the coordinate clause and elliptical coordinate clause rules for commas,

> It takes only a little study of the selections in our college readers to realize that the punctuation rules in handbooks and style manuals are not sacred texts for a great many good writers.

and inconsistencies in use of the comma with introductory word, phrase, and clause—these and other failures to follow the rules are frequent enough to raise questions about the rules themselves. Quirk et al. have examined statistical data on the use of the comma to mark coordination and concluded: "These results show we are dealing with tendencies which, while clear enough, are by no means rules. In such cases, it is probable that the general truth that punctuation conforms to grammatical rather than rhetorical considerations is in fact overridden" (1060).

Moreover, handbook rules provide no instruction for use of the comma in the following:

(1) Slowly, he walked to the store.

(2) He walked, slowly, to the store.

(3) He walked to the store slowly.

And when we produce a sequence of three or more independent clauses, punctuation questions often cross sentence (or independent clause) boundaries, and handbooks do not offer help for such interdependent problems. Consider a sequence of three simple independent clauses:

(4) it caught my eye—I swiveled around—and the next instant, inexplicably, I was looking down at a weasel—

There weren't any handbook rules to tell Annie Dillard to use a semicolon rather than a period or a dash or a colon or a comma splice between the first two clauses; or to follow that with a dash rather than a comma or a period or, yes, a colon between the last two.

And what do handbooks tell students about Orwell's punctuation of the following sentences from "Marrakech"?

(5) It was very hot and the men had marched a long way. They slumped under the weight of their packs and the curiously sensitive black faces were glistening with sweat.

(6) When a family is travelling it is quite usual to see a father and a grown-up son riding ahead on a donkey, and an old woman following on foot, carrying the baggage.

According to the handbooks, Orwell is wrong, for their rules are essentially a right-or-wrong approach, providing little—if any—basis for considering options according to rhetorical intentions. Such instruction is negative in that it tells students what not to do and how not to do it; better instruction—in any skill, I assume—is going to tell students what to do and how to do it, it is going to encourage the "good" behaviors, not discourage the bad.

Sentences and Independent Clauses

Conventional punctuation is grammar based—marks are prescribed in terms of grammatical structure—but what "good writers" do, writers like Orwell, is punctuate according to their intended meaning, their intended emphasis.[1] It is an approach to use of the functional punctuation marks that follows "principles" rather than "rules."[2] To understand the principles, however, one grammatical element must be recognized—the independent clause. And the reason for this requirement is clear enough: all prose, written or spoken, consists of concatenations of independent clauses, and punctuation is a matter of showing appropriate relationships between them (some get punctuated as sentences, some do not). It is a mistake to assume that the sentence is the basic element in prose; it is also confusing, for it is the wrong basis for analyzing written language.[3]

To repeat: all discourse, written or spoken, consists of independent clauses or   6 underlying independent clauses. The principle for "underlying" structures is well known: in spite of the missing element(s) in the surface structure, a clause is independent if the missing element(s) can be readily provided by a native speaker:

(7) Where are you going? Home.

(8) Mary read the book. John too.

(9) We went to the beach. Enjoyed the sun.

Sentences, therefore, are but one way of punctuating independent clauses:

(10) First it was rain. Then it was snow.

(11) First it was rain; then it was snow.

(12) First it was rain, then it was snow.

And so on—there are a number of other options for marking this boundary between independent clauses.

Sentences like (10)–(12) suggest a hierarchy of functional punctuation marks.   7 The complete hierarchy is shown in Table 1 with the marks and their different degrees of separation (or connection, if you prefer) within independent clauses as well as between independent clauses.

As [Table 2] suggests, the colon and dash have functions in addition to the   8 hierarchical (to be explained later). The differences in the marks are made still more clear by categorizing them according to basic functions, which reveals a top two, middle two, and bottom two. The functions in Table 2 are general and basic; in addition, they are used by writers—as my discussion of raising and lowering will explain—to gain separation (emphasis) by using an appropri-

Table 1

Hierarchy of Functional Punctuation Marks

MARK	DEGREE OF SEPARATION
sentence final (. ? !)	maximum
semicolon (;)	medium
colon (:)	medium (anticipatory)
dash (—)	medium (emphatic)
comma (,)	minimum
zero (Ø)	none (that is, connection)

Table 2

Basic Functions

TOP (. ;)	separate independent clauses
MIDDLE (: —)	separate independent clauses, or separate non-independent clause element(s) from the independent clause
BOTTOM (, Ø)	separate non-independent clause elements from the independent clauses

ate higher mark, a mark not limited to the next one up; and writers gain con-nectedness (under-emphasis) by using an appropriate lower mark, a mark not limited to the next one down.

Punctuating Single Independent Clauses

Sentences can be analyzed as single independent clauses with or without attachments or as multiple independent clauses with or without attachments. With a single independent clause, possible attachments create three patterns: pre-clausal, post-clausal, and medial. In each case, the writer must decide: *Do I punctuate or don't I?* [See Table 3.] In Pattern III the interruption may of course occur elsewhere within the independent clause.   9

Three of the four "rules" required by this principle-based approach to punc-tuation are needed to punctuate these patterns (rules that literate students will know or quickly learn without instruction). [See Table 4.]   10

As these tables indicate, the writer has choices, so there arises the ques-tion of how one goes about making these choices. The answer, theoretically, is simple, for it is found in anyone's principle of good writing; that is, it is found in the effort to get sentences to say what one means with the kind of emphasis one intends. The principle is general. All writers, evidently, want a sentence to say what they intend it to say. It is, of course, the same principle   11

Table 3

Patterns

I	(word/phrase/clause) + *pct?* + John laughed aloud.
II	John laughed aloud + *pct?* + (word/phrase/clause).
III	John + *pct?* + (word/phrase/clause) + *pct?* – laughed aloud.

Table 4

Rules

Rule 1 (for Pattern I)	Only zero, comma, dash, or colon are permissible.
Rule 2 (for Pattern II)	All functional marks are permissible.
Rule 3 (for Pattern III)	Only paired marks (commas, dashes, zeros, and parentheses) are permissible.

that guides choices among word and syntactic options; one chooses among the options the best one can. A little imaginative effort will suggest how, in the following examples, choices might be made according to "meaning and intended emphasis" (Summey 4):

(13) Surely (zero, comma, dash) the kid will come clean.

(14) The kid will come clean (any functional mark) and go home for a good night's sleep.

(15) The kid (zero, comma, dash, parenthesis) who has a guilty conscience (zero, comma, dash, parenthesis—each paired with the first) will come clean.

In ordinary contexts, one would expect the following:

(16) Today John went to school.

But one can easily create a context (John having been hospitalized for a year) which suggests:

(17) Today, John went to school.

The non-independent clause element in Pattern I might, of course, be greatly expanded:

(18) When Mary sat at her desk and gave careful attention to it and decided, finally, that John wasn't as foolish as he had acted, she . . .

But the principle is the same: meaning and emphasis.

For pattern II the problem is the same—does one want to mark a separation 12 at the boundary or not? And the principle that guides the decision maker is, again, the same:

(19) John wanted the money (*pct?*) which he was owed.

(20) John wanted the money (*pct?*) which was right for him.

(21) John wanted the money (*pct?*) thinking he'd take Mary to dinner.

(22) John wanted the money (*pct?*) even though he hadn't earned it.

For pattern III, the problem is different only in that the choice is "two marks or none":

(23) The student (*pct?*) who was too sick to play (*pct?*) watched on TV.

(24) The candidate (*pct?*) deemed unfit for public office (*pct?*) won 70% of the vote.

Insertions in Pattern III can, of course, occur elsewhere: The candidate won 70% (*pct?*) according to his figures (*pct?*) of the vote.

Raising and Lowering

Within a sentence having a single independent clause, the basic marks are zero 13 and comma:

(25) John asked for a date when he got the nerve.

(26) John asked for a date, when he got the nerve.

The comma gains some emphasis for the attachment. And, because of the nature of the hierarchy, the higher the mark the greater the emphasis:

(27) John asked for a date—when he got the nerve.

(28) John asked for a date. When he got the nerve.

Thus, justification for the sentence fragment.

Pressure to use a mark higher in the hierarchy I call *raising*. It develops 14 naturally when commas within a sentence boundary mark different degrees of separation; thus meaning can be made more clear by using a higher mark at the major boundary. In the following sentence by James Baldwin, pressure for raising will be felt where Baldwin used the semicolons:

(29) I don't think the Negro problem in America can be even discussed coherently without bearing in mind its context; its context being the history, traditions, customs, the moral assumptions and preoccupations of the country; in short, the general social fabric.

Some writers might have resisted the pressure for the first semicolon and stayed with a comma; most, I think, would have used a dash instead of the second semicolon. In either case, the sentence illustrates conditions for raising.

Raising, obviously, calls attention to itself, and thus gains emphasis. And it is 15 this emphasis that Frost evidently felt a need for in the next example.

(30) I once heard of a minister who turned his daughter—his poetry-writing daughter—out on the street to earn a living, because he said there should be no more books written . . .

Raising is thus a device for gaining rhetorical effect. In (31) Alice Walker uses a comma instead of zero to gain emphasis; and in (32) Ellen Goodman chooses an even higher mark to gain even more emphasis:

(31) White men and women continued to run things, badly.

(32) Date rape, after all, occurs in a context, a culture that—still—expects men to be assertive and women to be resistant.

And why does Dillard want commas in the next example?

(33) I think it would be well, and proper, and obedient, and pure, to grasp your one necessity and not let it go.

Pressure for raising accounts for two rules in our handbooks—a semicolon 16 rule and a dash rule. If one or more of the items in a series has internal commas or if the individual items are lengthy, a semicolon at the major boundaries is needed for clarity, as in a sentence by Forster:

(34) We read that the Franks built it in the thirteenth century and called it Misithras or Mistia; that it became the chief fortress in the Peloponnese during

an uninteresting period; that it was taken from the Franks by the Byzantines, and from the Byzantines by the Turks; that it was governed by a long succession of tyrants whose lives were short and brutal.

If the interrupting material contains commas, there is need for a higher mark at the major boundaries, and the dash is appropriate because, unlike the semicolon, it can be used in pairs, as in a Lewis Thomas sentence.

> (35) Although we are by all odds the most social of all social animals—more interdependent, more attached to each other, more inseparable in our behavior than bees—we do not often feel our conjoined intelligence.

I propose that the hierarchy and raising account for these rules systematically—if you know the system, you know how to do it—and more effectively than the disconnected, essentially unsystematized rules in handbooks.

Notice, finally, that *lowering*—the opposite of raising—is also a natural consequence of understanding the hierarchical system. The semicolon in most of its uses, the comma splice, and the avoidance of a comma with a coordinator between independent clauses are common examples of lowering. Raising seems to be required, in certain contexts, to satisfy the need for clarity—as in (29), (34), (35). Lowering, on the other hand, does not seem to be required by a contextual need for clarity, except in a more subtle sense of this need, as in a good comma splice. 17

Multiple Independent Clauses

Discourse consists of multiple independent clauses, and the good writer marks the junctures between them according to an intended meaning and emphasis. Punctuating between independent clauses is different from punctuating within the clause, but the answer is based on the same principle (meaning and emphasis) and on the same knowledge (recognition of the independent clauses). 18

There are but two devices for marking the juncture between independent clauses: the hierarchy of punctuation marks (Table 1) and a set of coordinate conjunctions (*and, but, or, nor, for, so, yet, then*). Let me emphasize that these are the only devices for marking the juncture between independent clauses—in spite of what handbooks and style manuals and workbook exercises tell us, or seem to tell us.[4] Writers use these devices to convey semantic intent, and as they use them, they use the differences inherent in each group as well as combinations among them (more numerous than the brief list suggests) to produce their intended semantic effects. 19

Punctuation Alone

Table 5 is a further representation of the hierarchy as indicated in Tables 1 and 2. The "meaning" of these markings ranges from maximum separation to no separation (or connection)—but see the remarks on the dash and colon below. And since we use punctuation to clarify our meaning and gain appropriate emphasis, it is reasonable that, for ease of reading, the two marks of 20

Table 5

Degrees of Separation Between Clauses

MAXIMUM:	I gravitated to the random. I swung with the nonsequential.—Joan Didion
	I gravitated to the random; I swung with the nonsequential.
MEDIUM:	The fire is dying, the sparks scattering over the sand and stone: there is nothing to do but go.
	The fire is dying, the sparks scattering over the sand and stone—there is nothing to do but go.—Edward Abbey
MINIMUM:	And it is true that all of us write within traditions, we all have a history and a context.—Donald Murray
	And it is true that all of us write within traditions we all have a history and a context.

minimum separation between independent clauses are not as effective as the marks of medium or maximum separation. Zero, of course, is even confusing (and found only in experimental writing or certain kinds of poetry where, however, it is used for the very reasons indicated by the hierarchy—to show connection where, normally, separation would be shown). The comma splice, however, is an intentional mark in the writing of most "good" writers and, as indicated by the hierarchy, shows less of a separation than the higher marks—thus the purpose, an absolutely legitimate purpose, of the comma splice, as illustrated in another sentence by E. M. Forster (a fearless comma splicer):

(36) He could not stand the insecurities that are customary between officials, he refused to make use of the face-saving apparatus that they so liberally provide and employ.

There is a similar difference between the period and semicolon—the significance of the hierarchy, after all, is pretty straightforward. Look at the following ways of punctuating some words by E. B. White: 21

(37) The great days have faded. The end is in sight.

(38) The great days have faded; the end is in sight.

White actually used a comma splice here—forgive the deception, a way to make two points at once.

The dash and the colon are similar in function and, sometimes, even in meaning (see Tables 2 and 5). For example, which one would you choose for E. M. Forster's well-known sentence: 22

(39) So Two Cheers for Democracy (pct?) one because it admits variety and two because it permits criticism.

Forster used a colon, but I suppose that many of us would choose a dash (and if your background is British, you'd be tempted by a semicolon).

Coordination Alone

According to our handbooks, marking the boundary between independent 23
clauses with a coordinator alone is not done—unless the clauses are short and
clear:

> (40) The hare slept and it lost the race.

But we note that sentences like the following are not infrequently found in the
nonfiction prose of good contemporary writers:

> (41) Well—the sun will be up in a few minutes and I haven't even begun to make
> coffee.—Edward Abbey

> (42) He told them very badly but you could see there was something there if he
> could get it out.—Ernest Hemingway

> (43) I could write a syndicated column for teenagers under the name "Debbie
> Lynn" or I could smuggle gold into India or I could become a $100 call girl, and
> none of it would matter.—Joan Didion

What, then, is the meaning signaled by coordinator alone? The answer lies
in the hierarchical function of punctuation marks—to mark a separation (or
degree of connection, if you will). Thus, in the absence of a separating mark, as
in (41)–(43), the signal is just that: as close a connection as the system allows.

Punctuation with Coordinator

What happens when we combine a mark with a coordinator is what the hier- 24
archy predicts: more of a separation. A long sentence by Didion illustrates both
coordinator alone and coordinator with punctuation:

> (44) But after a while the signs thin out on Carnelian Avenue, and the houses
> are no longer the bright pastels of the Springtime Home owners but the faded
> bungalows of the people who grow a few grapes and keep a few chickens out
> here, and then the hill gets steeper and the road climbs and even the bungalows
> are few, and here—desolate, roughly surfaced, lined with eucalyptus and lemon
> groves—is Banyan Street.

One can see clearly, in that sentence, the difference between the two possibilities with independent clauses: coordinator plus comma creates greater separation, greater emphasis, than coordinator alone; the options provided by these
devices are needed—and used by good writers. To oversimplify and suggest
that one should use a comma whenever a coordinator is used between independent clauses—or not use one when the second clause is elipted—is to falsify
the description of written English and to misinform the student. As a matter
of fact, we commonly enough find coordinators between independent clauses
with any of the punctuation marks:

> (45) I wish good fortune to both sides, good will to all. Or conversely, depending
> on my mood of the moment, damn both houses and *pox vobiscum*.—Edward
> Abbey.

(46) Find them, and clone them. But there is no end to the protocol.—E. B. White

(47) Whether or not our old drainboard was a guardian of our health I will never know; but neither my wife nor I have enjoyed as good health since the back kitchen got renovated.—E. B. White

(48) Since then I have walked, and prefer walking to horseback riding—but I had forgotten the depth of feeling one could see in horses' eyes.—Alice Walker

(49) . . . the job in Burma had given me some understanding of the nature of imperialism: but these experiences were not enough to give me an accurate political orientation.—George Orwell

Even more options are available with ellipsis in the second or third clause, the most common form of which is the ellipted subject; the "rule" tells us to punctuate as follows:

(50) This is called "anchoring the mall" and represents seminal work in shopping-center theory.

But the system here allows the writer some options:

(51) This is called "anchoring the mall," and represents seminal work in shopping-center theory.

(52) This is called "anchoring the mall"—and represents seminal work in shopping-center theory.

(53) This is called "anchoring the mall": and represents seminal work in shopping-center theory.

Didion chose (50), but the other choices must be considered as "correct," and perhaps as reasonable as well. Sometimes a writer will even choose maximum separation:

(54) But all I could do was to try to rein him out of it. Or hug his back.—Alice Walker

(55) It is made; not described.—Ernest Hemingway

The ellipted independent clause in the following example by Updike could be punctuated with any mark but zero, making five options:

(56) [Doris Day's] third picture, strange to say, ended with her make-believe marriage to Errol Flynn. A heavenly match, in the realm where both are lovable.

Yet five more options were available for Updike if he considered the deleted *It was.* And with coordinator plus *It was* there are—considering just *and*—probably four more. A total of fourteen options for a writer to consider.

Notice that (51)–(56) are in fact examples of raising and represent options that good writers know how to exploit. Notice also that teaching a "rule" actually denies these options, for a rule indicates—at least for students—only one way of doing something, the "right" way; the rule thus denies students the opportunity to learn an important writing strategy. Which raises the question of pedagogy.

Pedagogy

Because the choices are limited (rules 1, 2, and 3) and the knowledge base spe- 26
cific (tables 1, 2, 3, and awareness of the independent clause), the punctuation
system here is not difficult to learn. It is to be learned by doing—the way all
language skills are learned, which means a lot of doing, of course. So instruction
consists of enough examples for discussion (numerous in college readers) and
enough opportunities in writing to develop the experience needed for making
good choices. In providing these opportunities the teacher will realize one of
the strengths of the approach: it encourages students to analyze their semantic
and rhetorical intentions. The student doesn't try to match his or her sentence
with a rule in a handbook, then respond in a behavioral sense; instead, the
student reads and considers her or his intentions and the reader's needs, then
decides according to an intended meaning and emphasis. We like to say, in our
discussions of the writing process, that writing is thinking. Indeed! In contrast
to the rule-matching process required by a handbook, this approach to punctuating is an expression of the writing-is-thinking premise, for it provides the
occasion and the tools for thinking.

To teach the system one needs a few handouts (like tables 1, 2, 3, and 4) and 27
a feeling for student needs in sequencing the material along with reading and
writing assignments. For example, with basic writers one might want to present the hierarchy but limit initial practice to the period, comma, and zero (one
can write a flawless paper with just these marks). Good instruction will then
sequence the introduction of writing problems according to student needs. Of
course, learning a system well takes lots of practice. Good writers get lots of
practice; students should too.

As should be clear by now, learning to punctuate effectively requires only a 28
little knowledge of grammar, much less than most English teachers will grant.
One needs to recognize an independent clause in one's writing, which requires
bringing to a conscious level what one knows intuitively. All native speakers
have what linguists call a "competence" that includes the ability to speak and
comprehend independent clauses; so students who are native speakers quickly
enough master the consciousness-raising task of identifying subject and finite
verb (irregular syntax obviously requires additional work).

An appealing aspect of this meaning-based approach to punctuation is 29
that it allows for individual differences in its application. (The fifth-grader,
for example, should use his or her knowledge of the hierarchy—which may
be incomplete, of course—according to his or her intentions.) A good writer
chooses to *do* something (to choose a word, to begin a sentence adverbially,
to punctuate). In choosing to do there is a positive, a constructive, a meaning-
creating approach to writing; in contrast, in obeying a negatively worded rule,
there comes a negative attitude, a negative approach to the process, for the
student is punctuating to avoid error rather than to create meaning. Learning
theory, as I understand it, suggests that learning to use a systematic procedure
is far easier than learning to use a list of poorly ordered rules defined by a
technical terminology with exceptions and footnotes and meager examples—

all made more difficult because a behavioristic response is expected from very uncertain stimuli (the student's own sentences).

Let me illustrate these general remarks on pedagogy with some examples of raising and lowering, punctuation practices that can and should be analyzed and practiced during reading and writing assignments. Reading how a good writer punctuates helps anyone grasp more surely some small yet significant point as well as, on occasion, a major point; and such study will thus help anyone punctuate more tellingly. So, consider what some good writers have done.

The following is raising to a comma (the fourth one) where a handbook asks for zero because the compounding is not of independent clauses:

> (57) The business of being out for a walk, coming across something of fascinating interest and then dragged away from it by a yell from the master, like a dog jerked onwards by the leash, is an important feature of school life, and helps to build up the conviction, so strong in many children, that the things you most want to do are always unattainable.—George Orwell.

This sentence, with its long independent clause with three commas, would become confusing if zero were used at the major point of separation within the sentence, even though zero would follow the handbook rule. Raising thus is important for clarity of meaning.

Raising from zero to a comma is common because it produces a simple yet clear emphasis, as in this:

> (58) I was driving down the Thruway in Vermont to consult a doctor in New York, and hit a deer.—Edward Hoagland

The following illustrates raising from commas to periods:

> (59) They float on the landscape like pyramids to the boom years, all those Plazas and Malls and Esplanades. All those Squares and Fairs. All those Towns and Dales . . . —Joan Didion

Didion clearly uses raising here to gain emphasis.

The effective sentence fragment also gains emphasis when an expected colon is raised to a period:

> (60) I can recall that I hated [Southern black country life] generally. The hard work in the fields, the shabby houses . . . —Alice Walker

When the fragment shows raising from an expected comma, there is—as the system predicts—even more emphasis:

> (61) The very name hallucinates. Man's country. Out where the West begins. —Joan Didion

The first fragment is raised from a colon, the second from a comma.

Teaching the punctuation of fragments and when to use them teaches students how to write—quite different from the usual textbook instruction in how not to write. Teaching how teaches judgment—sensitivity to context—important in the development of taste. How else do we learn that some fragments work and others do not?

Consider an example of lowering, first punctuated as it might have been a hundred years ago and next punctuated as it typically is today: 35

(62) He searches for the lamppost with his cane, like a tennis player swinging backhand, and, if he loses his bearings and bumps against something, he jerks abruptly back, like a cavalier insulted, looking gaunt and fierce.

(63) He searches for the lamppost with his cane like a tennis player swinging backhand, and if he loses his bearings and bumps against something, he jerks abruptly back like a cavalier insulted, looking gaunt and fierce.—Edward Hoagland

The modern style (comma lowered to zero) better reflects the meaning, better reinforces the meaning, by more clearly reflecting what goes together and what does not. He "searches . . . like a tennis player swinging backhand"—a comma between those words separates what meaningfully goes together. And the same can be said for "he jerks abruptly back like a cavalier insulted." One may be in the habit of marking off such similes with commas—and one has that option, of course—yet it is clear, I think, that the relationship is better expressed without the commas. Moreover, if *and* is separated from *if* with a comma, the suggestion is that *and* relates to "he jerks abruptly back" (the independent clause); however, *and* is more meaningfully understood as relating all that follows it with all that goes before—the two halves of the sentence.

Lowering is a device that reveals more connection between words, phrases, or clauses than the expected punctuation would; it is most commonly illustrated by lowering from a period to semicolon: 36

(64) The term "scientific literacy" has become almost a cliché in educational circles. Graduate schools blame the colleges; colleges blame the secondary schools; the high schools blame . . . —Lewis Thomas

A frequent example of lowering is the common violation of the handbook rule that tells us, unless the clauses are short, to use a comma between independent clauses:

(65) They are brimming with good humor and the more daring swell with pride when I stop to speak with them.—James Baldwin

And what effect is achieved in the following by lowering commas to zero?

(66) They asked it in New York and Los Angeles and they asked it in Boston and Washington and they asked it in Dallas and Houston and Chicago and San Francisco.—Joan Didion

Lowering justifies the effective comma splice (and, of course, suggests that teachers teach it). A couple of examples: 37

(67) But even so [Harvey] had his consolations, he cherished his dream.—Virginia Woolf

(68) I did not know that the British empire is dying, still less did I know that it is a great deal better than the younger empires that are going to supplant it.—George Orwell

Handbooks I have seen do not discuss the problem of punctuating three or more independent clauses as a single sentence, but according to the rule for "punctuating compound sentences" one should use two commas in the following: 38

(69) The debate might well have been little more than a healthy internal difference of opinion, but the press loves the sensational and it could not allow the issue to remain within the private domain of the movement.
—Martin Luther King, Jr.

King, however, was clearly sensitive to the major and minor boundaries and followed the hierarchical principle by lowering (comma to zero) at the minor boundary—accurately reflecting his semantic intent.

A long while ago, in a long-neglected book, George Summey told us what was wrong with style manuals and handbooks: "The notion that there is only one correct way of punctuating a given word pattern is true only in limited degree. Skillful writers have learned that they must make alert and successful choices between periods and semicolons, semicolons and commas, and commas and dashes, dashes and parentheses, according to meaning and intended emphasis" (4). By teaching raising and lowering, we will be adding to our students' repertoire of skills; we will be encouraging students to clarify the meaning of sentences and to gain intended emphasis. Such instruction illustrates what in our composition classes we like to proclaim but don't always demonstrate: writing is thinking.   39

Acknowledgments

I want to thank Pat Belanoff and Joseph Williams for many valuable comments on the drafts of this manuscript; and I want especially to thank Jim Sledd for his original comments and ongoing support.

Notes

1. "Good" writers is in reference to nonfiction by writers of recognized stature, whose work can be found in college readers. If fiction were included, the evidence would be only more evident. For more on this topic, see my *Rethinking Punctuation*.
2. Functional marks are those marks regularly and typically used to mark syntactic functions. I neglect parentheses, perhaps too arbitrarily, but unlike the other marks, parentheses are limited to pairs, giving them a unique and typically non-rhetorical function, suggesting that the primary use of parentheses is for "non-text" information.
3. For plentiful and convincing diachronic evidence for the claim that the basic unit in prose is the independent clause and that the sentence is simply one way to mark this clause, the reader should see Levinson's dissertation (1985) and derived article (1989).
4. Subordinate conjunctions are not used to join independent clauses; they form "dependent" elements (phrases or clauses), elements which function as the attachments in patterns I, II, and III—and are punctuated accordingly. Similarly, conjunctive adverbs are simply dependent

words and phrasal words ("on the other hand") that function as the same kinds of attachments: "However, they played the next day" (pattern I). "They played the next day, however" (pattern II). "They played, however, the next day" (pattern III).

Works Cited

Dawkins, John. *Rethinking Punctuation*. ERIC ED 340 048. 1992.

Levinson, Joan Persily. *Punctuation and the Orthographic Sentence*. Diss. City U of New York, 1985.

———. "The Linguistic Status of the Orthographic (Text) Sentence." *CUNY Forum* 14 (1989): 113–17.

Quirk, Randolph, Sidney Greenbaum, Geoffrey Leech, and Jan Svartvic. *A Comprehensive Grammar of the English Language*. London: Longman, 1985.

Summey, George. *American Punctuation*. New York: Ronald, 1949.

Questions for Discussion and Journaling

1. What conceptions about writing is Dawkins challenging?

2. Dawkins claims that "manuals of style and college handbooks have it all wrong when it comes to punctuation" (para. 1). How so? Make a list of the things Dawkins says handbooks get wrong. (We'll take the easy one: "Good writers don't punctuate that way.")

3. Explain the principle of "raising and lowering." What does it have to do with, and how does it impact, your choice of punctuation?

4. Why does Dawkins call his way of thinking about punctuation *rhetorical*? You might return to Grant-Davie and Haas and Flower to help you with this question.

5. What do you know about punctuation now that you didn't know before reading Dawkins?

6. How do you usually think about punctuation when you write—do you worry about it, fixate on it, or mostly ignore it? Has reading Dawkins done anything to change your thinking about it?

Applying and Exploring Ideas

1. Look in a weekly periodical (like *Time* or *Newsweek*) for three complex sentences. Rewrite each of them using different punctuation. Then explain how the tone, emphasis, or meaning changes along with the punctuation.

2. Collect an obituary, an editorial, and a set of directions. Look carefully at the various punctuation marks, the length of the sentences, and the word choice. Describe the patterns you see, and try to explain the distinctions among them.

3. Make a "playbook" in which you write down interesting sentences and rebuild them with different punctuation to see what changes. Start with some examples from Dawkins—like numbers 33, 36, 42, 55, 56, 61, and 64. Find and rebuild several other examples from the texts around you—textbooks, what you're reading on the Web, e-mails, and so on. What conclusions can you draw from your work?

4. Think about your experiences as a writer in high school or middle school. Can you think of rules or directions you were given that just didn't make sense to you, and still don't? Write a letter to a past teacher creating an argument for why one or two common rules seem unnecessary. Remember to say not only what you think but why, giving the best reasons and examples you can think of.

Meta Moment

Why do you think your teacher wants you to read an article asserting that punctuation is rhetorical rather than just explaining that it is? What do you gain by reading the article?

A Rhetorical Analysis of Authors on the CIA Torture Inquiry

ZACHARY TALBOT

Framing the Paper

Zachary Talbot, a student at the University of Central Florida, wrote this essay in his English Composition 1101 course in Fall 2009. It responds to the "Navigating Sources That Disagree" assignment at the end of this chapter. As you can see, Talbot selected a current issue in public debate and practiced rhetorical reading in order to understand the views that three writers with opposing perspectives brought to the issue. Talbot worked on this piece in the first month of his course, creating a draft and then revising the piece to appear in his final portfolio. Because it takes time and practice to fully grasp the concepts required to conduct this kind of analysis, Talbot's piece isn't perfect; if he were to return to the piece after thinking further, he would undoubtedly write some things differently. Nevertheless, we think there's a lot you can learn from this draft.

Talbot 1

Zachary Talbot
Professor Bryan
English Composition 1101
2 December 2009

A Rhetorical Analysis of Authors on the CIA Torture Inquiry

The release of a special report on CIA torture operations under the Bush administration has motivated Attorney General Eric Holder to issue an investigation to determine whether the CIA is guilty of war crimes. Many journalists and political activists have had much to say about this decision by the Obama administration, and many have differing opinions on the matter. The authors' conflicting views of political values between

Talbot 2

human rights and national security spark a difference in opinion, arguing whether it is wise to be investigating a large part of our national security, the CIA.

As I write rhetorically about this argument, I will use specific techniques and strategies from authors of very insightful handouts. Grant-Davie's "Rhetorical Situations and Their Constituents" mentions the term *exigence*, better known as motivation. The exigence is fittingly essential in my three sources as it appears that each rhetor has a hidden agenda to persuade their audience to think a certain way. Grant-Davie mentions how key the presentation of exigence is in discourse and debate. He argues, "A rhetor who can define fundamental issues represented by superficial subject matter—and persuade audiences to engage those issues—is in position to maintain decisive control over the field of debate" (267). I plan on tuning in to the exigence of my sources to determine how and why they differ in opinion. To do this properly I wish to use Haas and Flower's technique of reading rhetorically. It is vital to view the texts as purposeful actions coming from the work, and seeing it with their intended effects (170). As I have learned from Kantz, I will create an original argument based on how the authors disagree and use their implied exigence to explain why.

My first source is written by Thomas Barnett, whose article "Obama Targets Jack Bauer, but Who Takes the Fall?" was written for *Esquire.com*. He starts off by scrutinizing the Obama administration for their stance and actions on the accusations of torture aimed toward the CIA. He takes a distinctive approach to his discourse, poking fun at Obama and his administration's decisions in a childlike manner, creating a friendly relationship with his audience and giving the text a very easy-going

Talbot's understanding of rhetorical concepts is still developing. Based on Grant-Davie, how might Talbot better define exigence? How does exigence relate to motivation?

In this paragraph, Talbot uses a lot of metadiscourse— that is, he talks about what he's going to talk about. What are the strengths and weaknesses of this strategy?

Does Talbot describe his three sources neutrally? Explain your answer by closely analyzing his language.

feeling. My second source, "The Torture Trap: Can Obama Really Ease Up?" by John Richardson, was also published by *Esquire.com*, but takes a different approach to the investigations. Richardson explains how it is a good thing for these investigations to take place. He relishes the fact that someone has stepped up and revealed this problem to our country. However, Richardson remains skeptical that the guilty members involved will be punished due to the extreme circumstances that decisions were made under. My third source, "CIA Torture Investigation Declassified," was written by Thomas Eddlem and published in *The New American*. His tone throughout the entire article is ruthless and harsh. Eddlem wants fast and swift justice, and he wants it immediately. He is dead set that war crimes have been committed by the Bush administration without a trial date even set.

Heroes or Villains?

To whom is Talbot referring when he writes "you"? Is "you" the reader; a non-specific "anyone"; or someone else? How could you change this wording to increase clarity?

Based on your values and position on the argument, you consider one side of the argument as the heroes and the opposing side as the villains. You can tell a lot about an author's stance in a debate by analyzing who they're rooting for with regard to individuals and groups on either side. Richardson claims that the individuals who came out and exposed the information about the ongoing tortures, directly initiating an investigation on the CIA, should be honored as heroes. Richardson deems them this privileged title to demonstrate that coming forth with information on such a touchy subject is difficult and takes courage. They are ground-breakers who open the door for new reforms of interrogation to be constructed. He argues, "We should honor the noisy Americans who brought the torture issue to light, from military officers, journalists, our modern Woodward and Bernsteins, heroes all" (Richardson).

Talbot 4

Barnett believes the heroes are the men and women of the CIA trying to keep our nation safe, not the people who are trying to keep them from doing their job. As he emphasizes, "The Agency was under pressure to do everything possible to prevent additional terrorist attacks" (Barnett). He believes in the safety of the nation first. He imparts the feeling in his article that you sacrifice your rights the second you pose a threat to our country. Once in this category of individuals, the line becomes transparent and may be crossed for the sole purpose of saving American lives. These authors are in disagreement due to their values. Are the human rights of a few possible terrorists more important than the prevention of another attack on American soil?

Eddlem's view comes from a different realm where everyone who was involved is guilty. He believes the hero is Attorney General Eric Holder for having the courage to issue an investigation despite Obama voicing that we should move forward, not look back. Eddlem illustrates to his audience that breaking the law should not go unpunished. He criticizes, "A handful of other neo-conservatives have crawled out of the sewers to defend an executive branch that is above the law" (Eddlem). He even says former Vice President Cheney should be put on trial to prove completely to his audience that the conservative view of flexible laws is wrong no matter who you are or what position you hold. We gain a good understanding of these authors and their values simply by noting for whom they are showing their support, and we begin to catch sight of the exigence for their discourse.

Exigence

Each writer uses persuasion to convince their audience of their point of view. However, each has different motive or exigence for doing so. Barnett's exigence, or need, is to illustrate how futile the investigations

> Note that Talbot uses "heroes and villains" as a consistent "unit of analysis," in order to understand each author's values. Could he make this analysis work any better? Why do you think he concentrates so much on the authors' values to begin with?

of the CIA are and the detrimental effects of putting them on the hot seat, hindering their ability to act swiftly to defend the nation in a time of threat. As he insists, "Yes, our public ethics must be observed, but the end result will likely be a CIA too chilled to do its clandestine job" (Barnett). In contrast, we can see the other two authors are both dead set on the law as a concrete set of rules without any transparency. Yet we see that Barnett feels the need to show that when threats to our nation are elevated we must use extremes, sometimes going above the law to keep order and safety for the people of our country. In addition, Barnett would also infer that rhetors like Eddlem are writing their articles to divert attention from Obama's dropping polls and his administration's failing policies.

Richardson's exigence is the desire to establish a line or set of rules regarding interrogation to prevent any future torture or violations of human rights. He asks his audience to reflect where the line should be drawn in the future. As Richardson argues, "A single bucket of freezing water is cruelty. Fifty is torture. Where did it cross the line?" (n. pag.). We are aware that Barnett is opposed to this idea because of his emphasis on letting the CIA do their job as efficiently as possible by any means. We reflect on Richardson's exigence and deduce that he is truly the happy medium among the three authors, taking the ideas of both extremes. He is aware that the crimes are wrong and human rights are important. On the other hand he knows, based on the times and circumstances, no real convictions will be made. However, the investigations are not futile because now new reform can be made and lines can be drawn to what is acceptable for interrogation.

Eddlem's exigence is a need to rally the support of many other liberals, trying to push the investigation further without any possible cover-up,

Talbot 6

so that the main parties involved do not go unpunished. Although his liberal ideology is similar to Richardson's, Eddlem couldn't care less about preventing torture in the future; he craves blood immediately. He truly wants everyone involved brought to justice from top to bottom, as he clearly shows throughout the article. Eddlem argues, "The fact that these unauthorized torture practices happened over extended periods of time at multiple U.S. detention facilities suggests that a permissive command environment existed across theatres and at several levels in the chain-of-command" (n. pag.). He continues. "This climate allowed both authorized and unauthorized techniques to be practiced, apparently without consequence" (n. pag.). Eddlem's outrage most likely emerges from his outlook on conservatives who think they are above the law and constitution. Neither Barnett nor Richardson think this type of justice will be carried out, deeming that the people involved who may be guilty of these crimes will most likely go unpunished due to varied circumstances of the times. Conservatives like Barnett suggest that the main reason for the attention to this issue is to divert attention from Obama's falling poll numbers. Although this may not be his intention, Eddlem's intensity certainly indicates he is searching desperately for support for the Democratic Party and its new way of running things.

Why do you think Talbot chose to interrupt two quotations here, instead of just writing them as a single continuous quotation? How could he have combined them?

Applied Symbolism

Barnett compares the CIA investigators to the TV character Jack Bauer. Bauer is a special agent on an anti-terrorist unit featured in the TV series *24*. He is extremely heroic and is the epitome of patriotism. In some instances Bauer will interrogate terrorists harshly, threatening and torturing them much like the charges against the CIA now. However, Jack always gets his job done and retrieves vital intelligence that saves countless

Talbot could have written the first two sentences here more fluently by combining them. Do you see other places in this paper where Talbot could do the same thing?

Talbot 7

American lives. Barnett compares the CIA to Bauer, conveying that they are more often than not heroes, and even though we don't see it on TV, they are saving lives every day. He stresses that the only outcome of this overdramatic ordeal will be a negative and harmful block on the CIA's ability to protect the nation. As our real Jack Bauers attempt to carry out their jobs, they will now have to look over their shoulder and wonder if the next thing they are asked to do will be called into question later on down the road by the very people they protect. As Barnett remarks, "Jack Bauer goes back in his cage—until we decide we need him again" (n. pag.).

Richardson also makes a reference to Jack Bauer. He responds, "Just because he is closing down Guantanamo doesn't mean the new president can reform the entire real world of Jack Bauers" (n. pag.). This may have to do with the two authors writing for the same source, *Esquire.com*. You can tell the two are in conversation, and in a way Richardson is intentionally responding to Barnett by mentioning Bauer. He, like Barnett, doesn't believe the investigations will result in any convictions. Due to desperate times and crucial circumstances we need people to be real life Jack Bauers. Richardson's purpose for mentioning Jack may be to show that although he is opposed to torture, he knows these types of people have a place in our national security; they just need proper guidelines to follow in order to maintain human rights.

Writers often have difficulty remembering that their audience doesn't know everything they do. Can you as a reader really tell that Richardson and Barnett are "in conversation"? What could Talbot do to clue his readers in?

Conclusion

Why does Talbot use the phrase "We are aware that"? What does it add to his piece, and what would be different if he took it out?

Reading these three sources rhetorically with the help of Haas and Flower has helped me find the exigence and key points of disagreement between these three authors. We are aware that Barnett, Richardson, and Eddlem disagree because of conflicting views of political values between human rights and national security, and whether it is right to be investigating the

Talbot 8

CIA. I have answered why my authors disagree and why they take their particular stance, yet with the answers to these and more, new questions emerge. Why is our liberal author Eddlem attempting so hard to put down the CIA and the former administration that it operated under? With this we ask, why does Richardson, also an obvious liberal, take more of a middle road on the issue, opposed to Eddlem? Perhaps Richardson is just a bit more of a rhetorical thinker. However, what if Richardson is just scared to take a stance on one side of the fence, not taking a true position in the fear of being wrong? Indeed he does sit on the fence agreeing with both sides, being right no matter the outcome.

As we question the left in this manner, it is only fair to pose the same questions to the right. Is our friend Barnett defending something that is obviously ethically wrong? Why is he so calm and friendly as he writes as opposed to Eddlem who sounds desperate to force his ideas on his audience? Other questions arise such as: how will the different authors' views of the constraints on post-9/11 situational circumstances come into play? We realize that the views of these authors are all different, with the two extremes of the left and right, and the rational voice of reason that is our happy medium. We know they will never agree, but that's why we enjoy them. The controversy brings excitement and permits the reader to ask questions, allowing us to make inferences of our own about the rhetors' exigence, truly illustrating the meaning of the discourse.

Talbot uses the metaphor of a "fence" here and seems to argue that any position not clearly on one side of this fence is not a "true position." Do you agree, or do you think this conclusion might come from the limitation of his metaphor? Are there other metaphors that would allow for three or more positions on a complex issue?

Has Talbot ever actually shown us the differences in tone ("calm," "desperate," etc.) he sees in these writings? How could he help us see what he sees?

Where in this paper would you say is Talbot's clearest statement of his personal opinion on this issue?

Works Cited

Barnett, Thomas P. M. "Obama Targets Jack Bauer, But Who Takes the Fall?" *Esquire*. Hearst Magazines, 24 Aug. 2009. Web. 9 Sept. 2009.

Eddlem, Thomas R. "CIA Torture Investigation Declassified." *The New American*. The John Birch Society, 26 Sept. 2009. Web. 29 Sept. 2009.

Grant-Davie, Keith. "Rhetorical Situations and Their Constituents." Wardle and Downs 262–77.

Haas, Christina, and Linda Flower. "Rhetorical Reading Strategies and the Construction of Meaning." Wardle and Downs 164–80.

Kantz, Margaret. "Helping Students Use Textual Sources Persuasively." Wardle and Downs 122–40.

Richardson, John H. "The Torture Trap: Can Obama Really Ease Up?" *Esquire*. Hearst Magazines, 26 Aug. 2009. Web. 9 Sept. 2009.

Wardle, Elizabeth, and Doug Downs, eds. *I Am a Writer in the World: Researching Personal and Academic Literacies*. Acton, MA: Copley-Xanedu Custom, 2009. Print.

Some Other Questions to Consider

- If you've read the "Writing Assignments" at the end of this chapter and the readings in this chapter that Talbot draws on, then you're equipped to see how well this paper responds to the assignment. If you were to grade this draft, what grade would you give it, and why?
- Can you see from Talbot's paper why "*Navigating* Sources That Disagree" is a fitting name for this assignment? In what ways is Talbot *navigating* among his sources (as if they were islands in a sea he's sailing?)
- Does Talbot's paper have a main point or central claim? Where does Talbot state it, and how clearly does he do so? Given the material he has to work with, could he make a "better" claim?
- What other rhetorical principles from Kantz, Haas and Flower, or Grant-Davie could Talbot have brought into his paper? Where and how could he have done so?

Writing about Texts/Constructs: Assignments and Advice

To help you learn and explore the ideas in this chapter, we are suggesting three Assignment Options for larger writing projects: Navigating Sources That Disagree, Considering Constructs about Writing, and Rhetorical Reflection.

Assignment Option 1. Navigating Sources That Disagree

In this chapter you have considered how writers and readers play an active role in constructing texts and making meaning. Grant-Davie, Kantz, and Haas and Flower have demonstrated that understanding the rhetorical situation is central to actively engaging and creating texts. To explore this idea further, for this assignment you will examine texts that appear to disagree and analyze them rhetorically in order to understand how and why their authors disagree.

> My strategy for writing the essays in this class was not to procrastinate. Everyone does it, and it is a hard habit to break, but it is one of the key reasons for my success in the class. I made it a personal goal to have a completed draft for peer reviews; this way I wasn't cramming the night before the due date. I also scheduled an appointment with my professor within two weeks of getting back a graded paper. That way it was still fresh in my mind and I didn't get behind.
>
> —Jillian Loisel, Student

Brainstorming Find an issue that is currently being debated publicly, either in your local campus community or in a larger state or national arena. Make sure that this is a complex issue rather than a simple black-and-white problem. The more nuanced or more difficult the debate is, the more useful your analysis will be—to you as well as others.

Researching and Analyzing After you've settled on a debate, follow these steps:

- Carefully choose three different sources within your debate that do not agree. Look for texts that demonstrate nuanced kinds of disagreement rather than just settling for obvious "pro" and "con" sources. (Remember that the point of this assignment is to help you learn something about how texts are constructed and how meaning is made. If you choose obvious texts to analyze, you won't learn nearly as much as you could have—and your paper will be much harder to write.)
- Once you have chosen your three sources, begin to analyze them. An obvious place to begin would be by sketching out the rhetorical situations for each text, as well as for the larger context of the debate in which they exist. You might also ask who the authors (or *rhetors*) are and what their values, motivations, and constraints might be.

‎

- Next, you should analyze the arguments that the authors are making. What are their points? Do they disagree on everything? What kinds of evidence do they use? Do they seem to believe that the same things even count as evidence?
- Take notes as you analyze your text and find ways to organize your notes. You might consider making a chart of questions with space for answers about each text.

Planning   Now that you have conducted the research and analyzed the texts, take a step back and ask yourself what you found. Go back to your original question and try to answer it: How and why do the authors of these texts disagree? You might have one clear answer to this question, and you might have several potential ideas regarding why they can't agree. Go ahead and make some claims in answer to the question and start marshalling the evidence from your notes to support your claims.

Drafting   Write an analytical, research-based essay in which you provide an answer to the question: Why do authors of texts in the debate on X disagree? Be sure to do the following in your essay:

- Provide background information on the debate and the three texts you chose to analyze.
- Make your claim(s) in answer to the question, and provide the textual evidence from your analysis to support your claims.
- End your essay with some sort of "so what?" Tell your readers, who are most likely your teacher and classmates, why it would be useful to have this analysis and why it is important to understand how texts are constructed and how meaning is made—or not.

Revising   Good, thoughtful work usually takes time, planning, and reconsideration. What you've been asked to do in this activity is not easy, and you are more likely to write an effective text if you take the time to get feedback from some other writers you trust. Work with one or more classmates or a writing center tutor, and ask them if they think that you have effectively completed the assignment. For example, ask them the following:

- Have you given thoughtful reasons for why the sources disagree?
- Do they think you need more evidence?
- Do they believe your claims?
- Are they persuaded by the evidence that you provide?
- As readers, are they helped by the organization you chose for your paper? If not, what changes would help them?

Consider your peers' feedback and make appropriate revisions. Note that at this point in the drafting process, you would do well to focus your revisions on global issues rather than fixating on eliminating "errors" or finding bigger words to use. This assignment asks you to conduct a careful analysis, and that is what your revision should focus on strengthening.

What Makes It Good?   Your essay will be evaluated in terms of how well it accomplishes the goals set out. Remember that your essay should answer the following question: Why do authors of texts in the debate on X disagree? And how?

A strong essay will do the following:

- Orient the reader by initially providing enough background information on the debate and the three texts you chose to analyze;
- make clear claim(s) in answer to the question;
- provide textual evidence that is convincing and clear to the reader;
- be organized in such a way that the reader can follow along without having to work to figure out where you are going; and
- be polished and edited so that the reader understands what you are arguing and is not distracted from your claims.

Assignment Option 2. Considering Constructs about Writing

The introduction to this chapter focuses on the idea of constructs about writing: "*Constructs* are mental frameworks that people build in order to make sense of the world around them. One of the key features of an effective construct is that it quickly begins to seem 'natural' or inevitable, rather than made-up" (p. 35). Another way to think about this is to recognize that many of our conceptions, or common-sense understandings, of writing are actually *misconceptions* that don't hold up under close scrutiny. In this chapter, you have read about error, plagiarism, and "objectivity" as constructs commonly understood in a way that does not hold up when people like Williams, Porter, and Murray study them.

For this assignment, you will take on a *construct* or *conception* about writing and analyze it yourself. Depending on your teacher's instructions, you might choose any construct or conception about writing, or you might look at particular conceptions such as "good writing," "writer," or 'literacy/literate."

Brainstorming   Whatever construct or conception you choose, you should begin brainstorming by mining your own experiences. If you choose "good writing," for example, you might ask yourself

- What is your idea of good writing?
- Where do your preconceptions of good writing come from?
- Can you think of a time when your conception of good writing didn't work or seem "right" in the context?
- Is your conception of good writing limiting in any way?
- Would you behave differently as a writer, or understand yourself differently as a writer, if you conceived of "good writing" in a different way?

Researching and Analyzing   Now conduct some outside research to help you understand whether others share your conceptions and where those conceptions might have come from. You have several options for research, which you should discuss with your teacher. Some possibilities include

- surveying or interviewing your classmates;
- setting up an online survey on a social networking site like Facebook; and/or
- conducting historical research to see how your construct has been portrayed in the popular media over time. (For example, there are numerous moments in American history when news media have announced a "literacy crisis." The stories around those "literacy crises" clearly construct "literacy" to mean certain things and not others, and the meaning of the term seems to shift over time. By analyzing these articles, you could see how news media have defined literacy in ways that shape public understanding.)

Planning   Take some time to plan what you will write and how you will write it. By now you should realize that texts take shape differently depending on their rhetorical situations and purposes. You and your teacher should discuss with whom you want to share your reflection and research, and what the most appropriate forms (*genres*) are for reaching that audience. Here are some possibilities:

- Do you want to tell your high school teacher about your new understanding of "good writing"? If so, how could you best communicate with her? Via letter? If so, what are the characteristics of a formal letter?
- Do you want to write a news article to share your findings with a broader audience? If so, for what media outlet? Who are the readers of that publication? What is their prior knowledge? What is their attention span? How do they expect sources to be used?

Once you determine who you want to share your findings with, and what the appropriate genre is for reaching them, you should find and analyze numerous examples of that genre. What's their typical length? Tone? What language do they use? How do they cite sources (or not)?

Drafting   Given your findings, audience, and genre, what claims do you want to make? What support will you provide for those claims? How much detail should you go into regarding that support? These answers hinge entirely on the expectations and conventions of your audience and genre.

Revising   Once you settle on workable answers to these questions, compose a rough draft of your text and share it with a classmate. Be sure to tell your classmate what your rhetorical situation is, and what genre you are attempting to write, so that your peer can provide you with useful feedback for your revision. Revise your draft and then submit it to your teacher for additional feedback.

Note that this assignment asks you to take on a difficult topic and consider it in a complex and thoughtful way. It will take some time to work out your ideas carefully and then to write about them in ways that are effective and appropriate for your audience and genre, so be prepared to talk with your teacher and classmates multiple times and to revise your text over a longer period of time than you might be used to.

What Makes It Good?   Consider this text a "red pill" that you could give to a friend, parent, or teacher in order to help them see a writing-related concept as a construct and understand it in a new way. What makes this assignment good is your ability to do this. This is not an easy task. You are being asked to get people to reexamine something that they may not believe can or should be reexamined. Your text is "good" if the person who reads it puts it down and is somehow changed for having read it.

Assignment Option 3. Rhetorical Reflection

You will write a number of texts in this class, both short and long. You will revise these texts over the course of the semester and turn them in via a portfolio at the end of the semester. If you do, you will frame that portfolio with a rhetorical reflection of your work for the semester. In that rhetorical reflection, you should return to the material in this chapter. What were the rhetorical situations for the papers you have included in the portfolio? What were the constraints? Exigence? What rhetorical strategies did you use to respond to them? How effective were these rhetorical strategies? And look at the bigger picture: What conceptions of writing did this class try to teach? How is your understanding of writing different than it was? Return to the course and textbook goals, and demonstrate how you have reached them.

Suggested Additional Readings and Resources

Adler-Kassner, Linda, Chris M. Anson, and Rebecca Moore Howard. "Framing Plagiarism." *Originality, Imitation, and Plagiarism: Teaching Writing in the Digital Age*. Ed. Caroline Eisner and Martha Vicinus. Ann Arbor, MI: Digital Culture Books, 2008. 231–45. Print.

Foss, Sonja. *Rhetorical Criticism*. Long Grove, IL: Waveland Press, 2004. Print.

Howard, Rebecca Moore. "Understanding Internet Plagiarism." *Computers and Composition* 24.1 (2007): 3–15. Print.

Lethem, Jonathan. "The Ecstasy of Influence: A Plagiarism." *Harper's Magazine* Feb. 2007: 59–71. Print.

Roberts, Sam. "Celebrating the Semicolon in a Most Unlikely Location." *New York Times* 18 Feb. 2008. Print.

Selzer, Jack. "Rhetorical Analysis: Understanding How Texts Persuade Readers." *What Writing Does and How It Does It*. Ed. Charles Bazerman and Paul Prior. New York: Lawrence Erlbaum, 2004. 279–308. Print.

Spivey, Nancy Nelson. "Transforming Texts: Constructive Processes in Reading and Writing." *Written Communication* 7.2 (1990): 256–87. Print.

Yagoda, Ben. "What Writers Talk about When They Talk about Style." *The Sound on the Page: Style and Voice in Writing*. New York: Harper, 2004. 130–49. Print.

2 | Writing Processes: How Do *You* Write?

Answering the question "How do I write?" isn't as easy as it seems. How well do you really understand how you get things written? How would you describe your writing process if asked to do so right now? And is what you *think* you do actually what you *do*?

While many people are quite conscious of "what works for them" in order to get a text written, they tend not to be able to explain why it works—or even what they're doing, beyond some basic details like "I write down a lot of ideas until I feel like I know what I want to say and then I just start typing it up." Such a description doesn't actually tell us a lot. Yet it would seem that if you want to become a more versatile, capable, powerful writer, you need to be pretty aware of which activities, behaviors, habits, and approaches lead to your strongest writing—and which don't.

Understanding yourself as a writer is complicated by popular conceptions (or, more accurately, misconceptions) of what writing is and how it gets done. As you learned if you read the first chapter of this book, many popular conceptions related to writing (like **error** and **plagiarism**) are inaccurate. These inaccurate conceptions are not harmless; they can impact what we do and don't do, what we are willing to try or not, and how we feel about ourselves and our writing. In the case of writing processes, two popular conceptions seem to be that some people are born writers

---

The photo above, taken on September 9, 2009, shows President Barack Obama holding the heavily revised text to a speech on health care.

and others are not, and that good writers write alone, guided by a mysterious force called "inspiration." If we understand writing in these ways, we might be less likely to try to write better, assuming that we just aren't "natural writers," or we might not ask other people for feedback, assuming that good writers should be able to produce something in isolation.

This chapter draws on actual research about writing in order to demonstrate that these popular conceptions about writing are inaccurate and to replace them with useful, concrete ideas about what writers do when they write. Writing researchers have collected solid, generalizable data on what people are doing when they write, so that they can show novice writers what experienced writers are doing and get them to practice it, finding their own groove along the way.

Across the wide range of articles in this chapter, you will see a common focus on construction and **process**. As you learned if you read Chapter 1, readers and writers construct texts and build meaning together. In this chapter, Robert Tierney and P. David Pearson build on this theme, exploring composing processes as they appear in both writing and reading and suggesting that any attempt to construct texts involves planning, drafting, aligning, revising, and monitoring.

Construction obviously must entail some process or processes. Beginning in the late 1960s, it became clear to writing researchers that understanding "writing" required studying and understanding not simply the finished product—the text the writer created—but the act of creation (construction) itself. At even the quickest glance, it is obvious that a lot more is going on with the act of writing than "Well, I just sat down and wrote it." But for a long time researchers didn't understand what actually happened when people "sat down and wrote."

In this chapter, Sondra Perl and Carol Berkenkotter go about exploring writing-related processes from two different perspectives. Perl studies "unskilled" college students as they draft responses to a standard prompt and concludes that even poor writing is the result of consistent, predictable processes in prewriting, writing, and **editing**. In doing so, she highlights some areas where "unskilled" writers have trouble and thus provides some potentially helpful advice for writers who feel that they are struggling.

Berkenkotter goes to the opposite extreme, studying the revision strategies and decision-making processes of a professional, prize-winning author, Donald Murray (who then writes a response to Berkenkotter's findings). Berkenkotter finds that the writing process loops back on itself, with revision of one draft being indistinguishable from the planning of the next. She also finds that writers are highly idiosyncratic and that very good writers often have procedures and rituals particular to them that they rely on to help them write.

Writing researchers are generally writers themselves, as well as teachers of writing students. Thus they know that even when text construction is going well, writers can suddenly stop, finding themselves blocked and unable to write. Mike Rose is one of many such researchers who have tried to understand why this occurs. For his article in this chapter, Rose interviews a range of writers to see how their "rules for writing" (such as, "You have to have a strong opening paragraph") correlate with their experiences of writer's block. He analyzes which rules seem to help writers and which paralyze them.

While rules can block writers, their commonsense conceptions about writing can block them, too. Writers' commonsense conceptions often show up in how they talk about writing, even in the metaphors they use to describe writing and revision. One writing researcher, Barbara Tomlinson, conducted a study of metaphors used by professional writers to describe the act of revising. What do we know about writing, she asks, if revising it can be seen as both sewing and metal-working?

Tomlinson's study, reprinted in this chapter, brings up an interesting question: How do professional writers' understandings of their own writing processes compare to the research findings about writing processes? To help explore this question, we have added a short "interlude" to this chapter called "What Writers Say." This section is filled with short commentaries on various aspects of writing and revision by famous published writers, including Stephen King, Junot Díaz, and Anne Lamott. These writers don't use the language of research, but much of what they say about what makes writing effective, how they cope with writer's block, and how they revise should resonate with what you learn from the researchers. For example, Susan Sontag reminds us, like Berkenkotter, that good writers revise and revise again, just forging ahead:

> Writing is finally a series of permissions you give yourself to be expressive in certain ways. To invent. To leap. To fly. To fall. To find your own characteristic way of narrating and insisting; that is, to find your own inner freedom. To be strict without being too self-excoriating. Not stopping too often to reread. Allowing yourself, when you dare to think it's going well (or not too badly), simply to keep rowing along. No waiting for inspiration's shove. (p. 316)

Allegra Goodman echoes Mike Rose in encouraging writers to silence their inner critic and just write:

> Ultimately every writer must choose between safety and invention. . . . You must decide which you like better, the perfectionist within or the flawed pages at hand. (p. 310)

Finally, Kent Haruf gives glimpses into the writing rituals that work for him and in so doing invites us to become reflective about our own writing rituals. While it may not help you to write with the skull of a Hereford bull staring at you, as Haruf does, you should take some time to seriously consider the trappings and context of your writing.

Writing researchers and writers themselves are fascinated by where a writer's ideas come from and how they develop over time. So studies of composing processes seriously examine what classical rhetoricians called *inventio* (**invention**), or how writers think up ideas over time, whether through multiple drafts, or outlines, or lots of mulling and percolating and interaction with other people. The readings in this chapter have a lot to say about **planning** and **revision**. Perhaps the most important idea is that composing is only partly the "transcribing" act of writing down an idea. In many cases, the act of putting words on paper (or on the computer screen) is actually the act of coming up with ideas. Sometimes writing works like driving in the dark with headlights: you can only see two hundred yards at a time, so you have to *drive* if you want to see where you'll ultimately end up.

Because writing is in the realm of thought and ideas, we're dealing with the mental or **cognitive** aspect of writing when we think about process. You'll see a number of the researchers in this chapter thinking about, theorizing about, modeling, and testing problem-solving patterns, or **heuristics**, and other guesses about how our brains process ideas in order to construct meaning in texts (both as writers and readers). Along with the cognitive domain, some researchers consider the affective domain—that is, what goes on with the body (or, as some people put it, in *meatspace*—that is, the realm of the physical and the opposite of *cyberspace*). This is where **context** comes in: writing depends not only on the ideas in your brain but on whether you're trying to write in a journal under a tree on a gorgeous sunny afternoon or in a fluorescent-lit cubicle with a boss breathing over your shoulder who needs your memo on budget cuts right away. Our environment shapes our thoughts, so the cognitive domain never stands apart from what's outside our brains.

Still, writing is ultimately the meaning we make in our heads, so to understand composing processes, we have to somehow look inside our heads. This is the tough part of writing research, as you'll see reflected in the numerous **methodologies** (procedures for conducting research) these readings demonstrate. The basic problem is this: researchers can't directly access what's happening in your brain; they have to *infer* what's happening by looking for external signs. You could tell them what you're thinking, but (1) you can't talk as fast as you think and (2) the talking inevitably changes what you're thinking. They could look at the mistakes you make and try to explain the rules you're following (which you're probably not even aware of). They could interview you and study the words you use to express yourself. But they would still never know *exactly* what's going on in there. (Not even you know that, really.)

This chapter prompts you to be reflective about yourself as a writer; if you really engage in the material, you should attain some **mindfulness** about yourself as a writer. Researchers have learned that mindfulness is one of the practices that help you to use later what you are learning now—that is, to **transfer** your writing-related knowledge to new situations. Some of the activities you are asked to engage in here might seem strange—keeping a log of all your writing in a week, talking out loud while you write, and so on. If you can suspend your cynicism about these activities, though, we think you will come out on the other end a more *aware* writer—and maybe even a better one.

This chapter also invites you to explore how other writers write—or don't—and what helps them be successful—or not. We hope, in short, that the work you do in this chapter helps you thoughtfully explore both your own writing processes and those of others around you, so that you continue to get a better sense of how writing works, what processes and practices promote effective writing, and who you are as a writer.

Chapter Goals

- To acquire vocabulary for talking about writing processes and yourself as a writer
- To actively consider your own writing processes and practices and shift them if you wish
- To understand writing and research as processes requiring planning, incubation, revision, and collaboration
- To improve as a reader of complex, research-based texts

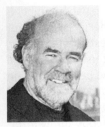

Toward a Composing Model of Reading

ROBERT J. TIERNEY

P. DAVID PEARSON

Tierney, Robert J., and P. David Pearson. "Toward a Composing Model of Reading." *Language Arts* 60.5 (1983): 568–80. Print.

Framing the Reading

Most people don't imagine that when they read a text, they're actually composing its meaning. Some researchers, however, would argue that this is exactly how we should understand reading. Robert Tierney and P. David Pearson make this argument in the article that follows. As they make their case, they show us something else that makes their piece a fitting first reading in a chapter entitled "How Do *You* Write?": what's involved in our attempts to build *written* texts that send particular messages or offer particular meanings to our readers. The authors give us not only an intriguing model of the various functions in a typical composing process but also the reminder that texts' meanings are constructed in a complex negotiation between writers and readers.

Tierney and Pearson wrote their article in 1983, during a particularly active period for research on composing processes in writing and reading. Tierney was at the time a reading researcher, part of the movement asserting that readers don't "find" meaning in texts but instead texts guide readers in how to *build* meaning using what they already know and new information the text provides. Around the same time, Pearson had been intensively researching "reading-writing connections." In this article, their combined ideas about making texts, and making meaning of them, culminated in a fuller model of the composing process than most researchers had used previously.

Getting Ready to Read

Before you read, do at least one of the following activities:

- Consider a time when you read something and then talked to someone else about it, only to realize he or she had understood it in a completely different way than you. Why do you think this happened?
- How do you read? Consider what you do and what happens in your mind when you read.

As you read, consider the following questions:

- How are reading and writing "negotiations" of meaning between the writers and readers of a text?
- What are the five elements of the "composing model of reading," and what does each involve? How do these elements connect to ideas you've already encountered elsewhere in this book?
- Where do you see each of these elements happening in your own reading and writing processes? What does it mean if you *don't* see an element happening?

We believe that at the heart of understanding reading and writing connections one must begin to view reading and writing as essentially similar processes of meaning construction. Both are acts of composing. From a reader's perspective, meaning is created as a reader uses his background of experience together with the author's cues to come to grips both with what the writer is getting him to do or think *and* what the reader decides and creates for himself. As a writer writes, she uses her own background of experience to generate ideas and, in order to produce a text which is considerate to her idealized reader, filters these drafts through her judgements about what her reader's background of experience will be, what she wants to say, and what she wants to get the reader to think or do. In a sense both reader and writer must *adapt* to their perceptions about their partner in negotiating what a text means. 1

Witness if you will the phenomenon which was apparent as both writers and readers were asked to think aloud during the generation of, and later response to, directions for putting together a water pump (Tierney et al., 1987; Tierney 1983). As Tierney (1983) reported: 2

> At points in the text, the mismatch between readers' think-alouds and writers' think-alouds was apparent: Writers suggested concerns which readers did not focus upon (e.g., I'm going to have to watch my pronouns here. . . . It's rather stubborn—so I better tell how to push it hard . . . he should see that it looks very much like a syringe), and readers expressed concerns which writers did not

appear to consider (I'm wondering why I should do this . . . what function does it serve). As writers thought aloud, generated text, and moved to the next set of sub-assembly directions, they would often comment about the *writers' craft* as readers might (e.g., no confusion there. . . . That's a fairly clear descriptor . . . and we've already defined what that is). There was also a sense in which writers marked their compositions with an "okay" as if the "okay" marked a movement from a turn as reader to a turn as writer. Analyses of the readers' *think alouds* suggested that the readers often felt frustrated by the writers' failure to explain why they were doing what they were doing. Also the readers were often critical of *the writer's craft,* including writers' choice of words, clarity, and accuracy. There was a sense in which the readers' *think alouds* assumed a reflexive character as if the readers were rewriting the texts. If one perceived the readers as craftpersons, unwilling to blame their tools for an ineffective product, then one might view the readers as unwilling to let the text provided stand in the way of their successful achievement of their goals or pursuit of understanding. (p. 150)

These data and other descriptions of the reading act (e.g., Bruce 1981; Collins, Brown, and Larkin 1980; L. M. Rosenblatt 1976; Tomkins 1980) are consistent with the view that texts are written and read in a tug of war between authors and readers. These think-alouds highlight the kinds of internal struggles that we all face (whether consciously or unconsciously) as we compose the meaning of a text in front of us. 3

Few would disagree that writers compose meaning. In this paper we argue that readers also compose meaning (that there is no meaning on the page until a reader decides there is). We will develop this position by describing some aspects of the composing process held in parallel by reading and writing. In particular, we will address the essential characteristics of effective composing: planning, drafting, aligning, revising, and monitoring. 4

Planning

As a writer initially plans her writing, so a reader plans his reading. Planning involves two complementary processes: goal-setting and knowledge mobilization. Taken together, they reflect some commonly accepted behaviors, such as setting purposes, evaluating one's current state of knowledge about a topic, focussing or narrowing topics and goals, and self-questioning. 5

Flower and Hayes (1981) have suggested that a writer's goals may be procedural (e.g., how do I approach this topic), substantive (e.g., I want to say something about how rockets work), or intentional (e.g., I want to convince people of the problem). So may a reader's goals be procedural (e.g., I want to get a sense of this topic overall), substantive (e.g., I need to find out about the relationship between England and France), or intentional (e.g., I wonder what this author is trying to say) or some combination of all three. These goals can be embedded in one another or addressed concurrently; they may be conflicting or complementary. As a reader reads (just as when a writer writes) goals may emerge, be discovered, or change. For example, a reader or writer may broaden, fine tune, redefine, 6 delete, or replace goals. A fourth-grade writer whom we interviewed about a project he had completed on American Indians illustrates these notions well: As he stated his changing goals, ". . . I began with the topic of Indians but that was too broad. I decided to narrow my focus on Hopis, but that was not what I was really interested in. Finally, I decided that what I really wanted to learn about was medicine men . . . I really found some interesting things to write about." In

> Texts are written and read in a tug of war between authors and readers.

coming to grips with his goals our writer suggested both procedural and substantive goals. Note also that he refined his goals prior to drafting. In preparation for reading or writing a draft, goals usually change; mostly they become focussed at a level of specificity sufficient to allow the reading or writing to continue. Consider how a novel might be read. We begin reading a novel to discover the plot, yet find ourselves asking specific questions about events and attending to the author's craft—how she uses the language to create certain effects.

The goals that readers or writers set have a symbiotic relationship with the knowledge they mobilize, and together they influence what is produced or understood in a text (Anderson, Reynolds, Schallert and Goetz 1977; Anderson, Pichert and Shirey 1979; Hayes and Tierney 1982; Tierney and Mosenthal 1981). A writer plans what she wants to say with the knowledge resources at her disposal. Our fourth-grade writer changed his goals as a function of the specificity of the knowledge domain to which he successively switched. Likewise readers, depending on their level of topic knowledge and what they want to learn from their reading, vary the goals they initiate and pursue. As an example of this symbiosis in a reader, consider the following statement from a reader of *Psychology Today.*

> I picked up an issue of *Psychology Today.* One particular article dealing with women in movies caught my attention. I guess it was the photos of Streep, Fonda, Lange, that interested me. As I had seen most of their recent movies I felt as if I knew something about the topic. As I started reading, the author had me recalling my reactions to these movies (Streep in "Sophie's Choice," Lange in "Tootsie," Fonda in "Julia"). At first I intended to glance at the article. But as I read on, recalling various scenes; I became more and more interested in the author's perspective. Now that my reactions were nicely mobilized, this author (definitely a feminist) was able to convince me of her case for stereotyping. I had not realized the extent to which women are either portrayed as the victim, cast with men, or not developed at all as a character in their own right. This author carried me back through these movies and revealed things I had not realized. It was as if I had my own purposes in mind but I saw things through her eyes.

What is interesting in this example is how the reader's knowledge about films and feminism was mobilized at the same time as his purposes became gradually welded to those of the author's. The reader went *from* almost free association, *to* reflection, *to* directed study of what he knew. It is this directed study of what one knows that is so important in knowledge mobilization. A writer does not just throw out ideas randomly; she carefully plans the placement of ideas in text so that each idea acquires just the right degree of emphasis in text. A successful reader uses his knowledge just as carefully; at just the right moment he accesses just the right knowledge structures necessary to interpret the text at hand in a way consistent with his goals. Note also how the goals a reader sets can determine the knowledge he calls up; at the same time, that knowledge, especially as it is modified in conjunction with the reader's engagement of the text, causes him to alter his goals. Initially, a reader might "brainstorm" his store of knowledge and maybe organize some of it (e.g., clustering ideas using general questions such as who, what, when, where, or, why *or* developing outlines). Some readers might make notes; others might merely think about what they know, how this information clusters, and what they want to pursue. Or, just as a writer sometimes uses a first draft to explore what she knows and what she wants to say, so a reader might scan the text as a way of fine tuning the range of knowledge and goals to engage, creating a kind of a "draft" reading of the text. It is to this topic of drafting that we now turn your attention.

Drafting

We define drafting as the refinement of meaning which occurs as readers and writers deal directly with the print on the page. All of us who have had to write something (be it an article, a novel, a memo, a letter, or a theme), know just how difficult getting started can be. Many of us feel that if we could only get a draft on paper, we could rework and revise our way to completion. We want to argue that getting started is just as important a step in reading. What every reader needs, like every writer, is a first draft. And the first step in producing that draft is finding the right "lead." Murray (*Learning*, 1982) describes the importance of finding the lead:

> The lead is the beginning of the beginning, those few lines the reader may glance at in deciding to read or pass on. These few words—fifty, forty, thirty, twenty, ten-establish the tone, the point of view, the order, the dimensions of the article. In a sense, the entire article is coiled in the first few words waiting to be released.
>
> An article, perhaps even a book, can only say one thing and when the lead is found, the writer knows what is included in the article and what is left out, what must be left out. As one word is chosen for the lead another rejected, as a comma is put in and another taken away, the lead begins to feel right and the pressure builds up until it is almost impossible not to write. (p. 99)

From a reader's perspective, the key points to note from Murray's description are these: 1) "the entire article is coiled in these first few words waiting to be released," and 2) "the lead begins to feel right. . . ." The reader, as he reads, has that same feeling as he begins to draft his understanding of a text. The whole point of hypothesis-testing models of reading like those of Goodman (1967) and Smith (1971) is that the current hypothesis one holds about what a text means creates strong expectations about what succeeding text ought to address. So strong are these hypotheses, these "coilings," these drafts of meaning a reader creates that incoming text failing to cohere with them may be ignored or rejected.

Follow us as we describe a hypothetical reader and writer beginning their 10 initial drafts.

A reader opens his or her textbook, magazine, or novel; a writer reaches 11 for his pen. The reader scans the pages for a place to begin; the writer holds the pen poised. The reader looks over the first few lines of the article or story in search of a sense of what the general scenario is. (This occurs whether the reader is reading a murder mystery, a newspaper account of unemployment, or a magazine article on underwater life.) Our writer searches for the lead statement or introduction to her text. For the reader, knowing the scenario may involve knowing that the story is about women engaged in career advancement from a feminist perspective, knowing the murder mystery involves the death of a wealthy husband vacationing abroad. For the writer, establishing the scenario involves prescribing those few ideas which introduce or define the topic. Once established, the reader proceeds through the text, refining and building upon his sense of what is going on; the writer does likewise. Once the writer has found the "right" lead, she proceeds to develop the plot, expositions, or descriptions. As the need to change scenarios occurs, so the process is repeated. From a schema-theoretic perspective, coming to grips with a lead statement or, if you are a reader, gleaning an initial scenario, can be viewed as schema selection (which is somewhat equivalent to choosing a script for a play); filling in the slots or refining the scenario is equivalent to schema instantiation.

As our descriptions of a hypothetical reader suggest, what drives reading 12 and writing is this desire to make sense of what is happening—to make things cohere. A writer achieves that fit by deciding what information to include and what to withhold. The reader accomplishes that fit by filling in gaps (it must be early in the morning) or making uncued connections (he must have become angry because they lost the game). All readers, like all writers, ought to strive for this fit between the whole and the parts and among the parts. Unfortunately, some readers and writers are satisfied with a piecemeal experience (dealing with each part separately), or, alternatively, a sense of the whole without a sense of how the parts relate to it. Other readers and writers become "bogged down" in their desire to achieve a perfect text or "fit" on the first draft. For language educators our task is to help readers and writers to achieve the best fit among the whole and the parts. It is with this concern in mind that we now consider the role of alignment and then revision.

Aligning

In conjunction with the planning and drafting initiated, we believe that the align- 13 ment a reader or writer adopts can have an overriding influence on a composer's ability to achieve coherence. We see alignment as having two facets: stances a reader or writer assumes in collaboration with their author or audience, and roles within which the reader or writer immerse themselves as they proceed with the topic. In other words, as readers and writers approach a text they vary the nature of their stance or collaboration with their author (if they are a reader) or audience (if they are a writer) and, in conjunction with this collaboration, immerse themselves in a variety of roles. A writer's stance toward her readers might be intimate, challenging, or quite neutral. And, within the contexts of these collaborations she might share what she wants to say through characters or as an observer of events. Likewise, a reader can adopt a stance toward the writer which is sympathetic, critical, or passive. And, within the context of these collaborations, he can immerse himself in the text as an observer or eyewitness, participant, or character.

As we have suggested, alignment results in certain benefits. Indeed, direct and 14 indirect support for the facilitative benefits of adopting alignments comes from research on a variety of fronts. For example, schema theoretic studies involving an analysis of the influence of a reader's perspective have shown that if readers are given different alignments prior to or after reading a selection, they will vary in what and how much they will recall (Pichert 1979; Spiro 1977). For example, readers told to read a description of a house from the perspective of a homebuyer or burglar tend to recall more information and are more apt to include in their recollections information consistent with their perspective. Furthermore, when asked to consider an alternative perspective these same readers were able to generate information which they previously had not retrieved and which was important to the new perspective. Researchers interested in the effects of imaging have examined the effects of visualizing—a form of alignment which we would argue is equivalent to eyewitnessing. Across a number of studies it has been shown that readers who are encouraged to visualize usually perform better on comprehension tasks (e.g., Sadoski 1983). The work on children's development of the ability to recognize point of view (Hay and Brewer 1982; Applebee 1978) suggests that facility with alignment develops with comprehension maturity. From our own interviews with young readers and writers we have found that the identification with characters and immersion in a story reported by our interviewees accounts for much of the vibrancy, sense of control, and fulfillment experienced during reading and writing. Likewise, some of the research analyzing proficient writing suggests that proficient writers are those writers who, when they read over what they have written, comment on the extent to which their story and characters are engaging (Birnbaum 1982). A number of studies in both psychotherapy and creativity provide support for the importance of alignment. For purposes of generating solutions to problems, psychotherapists have found it useful to encourage individuals to exchange roles (e.g., mother with daughter). In an attempt to generate discoveries, researchers have had experts identify with the experiences of inanimate objects (e.g., paint on metal) as a means of considering previously inaccessible solutions (e.g., a paint which does not peel).

Based upon these findings and our own observations, we hypothesize that 15 adopting an alignment is akin to achieving a foothold from which meaning can be more readily negotiated. Just as a filmmaker can adopt and vary the angle from which a scene is depicted in order to maximize the richness of a filmgoer's experience, so too can a reader and writer adopt and vary the angle from which language meanings are negotiated. This suggests, for language educators, support for those questions or activities which help readers or writers take a stance on a topic and immerse themselves in the ideas or story. This might entail having students read or write with a definite point of view or attitude. It might suggest having students project themselves into a scene as a character, eyewitness, or object (imagine you are Churchill, a reporter, the sea). This might occur at the hands of questioning, dramatization, or simply role playing. In line with our hypothesis, we believe that in these contexts students almost spontaneously acquire a sense of the whole as well as the parts.

To illustrate how the notion of alignment might manifest itself for different 16 readers, consider the following statement offered by a professor describing the stances he takes while reading an academic paper:

> When I read something for the first time, I read it argumentatively. I also find later that I made marginal notations that were quite nasty like, "You're crazy!" or "Why do you want to say that?" Sometimes they are not really fair and that's why I really think to read philosophy you have to read it twice. . . . The second time you read it over you should read it as sympathetically as possible. This time you read it trying to defend the person against the very criticisms that you made the first time through. You read every sentence and if there is an issue that bothers you, you say to yourself, "This guy who wrote this is really very smart. It sounds like what he is saying is wrong; I must be misunderstanding him. What could he really want to be saying?" (Freeman 1982, p. 11)

Also, consider Eleanor Gibson's description of how she approaches the work of Jane Austen:

> Her novels are not for airport reading. They are for reading over and over, savoring every phrase, memorizing the best of them, and getting an even deeper understanding of Jane's "sense of human comedy. . . ." As I read the book for perhaps the twenty-fifth time, I consider what point she is trying to make in the similarities and differences between the characters. . . . I want to discover for myself what this sensitive and perceptive individual is trying to tell me. Sometimes I only want to sink back and enjoy it and laugh myself. (Gibson and Levin 1975, pp. 458-460)

Our professor adjusted his stance from critic to sympathetic coauthor across different readings. Our reader of Austen was, at times, a highly active and sympathetic collaborator and, at other times, more neutral and passive.

Obviously, the text itself prompts certain alignments. For example, consider 17 how an author's choice of words, arguments, or selection of genre may invite a reader to assume different stances and, in the context of these collaborations, different roles.[1] The opening paragraph of Wolfe's *Electric Kool-Aid Acid Test*

---

[1] It is not within the scope of this paper to characterize the various mechanisms by which writers engage readers. We would encourage readers to examine different texts for themselves and some of the analytic schemes generated by Bruce (1981) and Gibson and Levin (1975), among others.

(1977) illustrates how the use of first person along with the descriptive power of words (e.g., cramped . . . metal bottom . . . rising . . . rolling . . . bouncing) compels the reader to engage in a sympathetic collaboration with an author and be immersed as an active participant in a truck ride across the hills of San Francisco.

> That's good thinking there, Cool Breeze. Cool Breeze is a kid with 3 or 4 days' beard sitting next to me on the cramped metal bottom of the open back part of the pickup truck. Bouncing along. Dipping and rising and rolling on these rotten springs like a boat. Out the back of the truck the city of San Francisco is bouncing down the hill, all those endless staggers of bay windows, slums with a view, bouncing and streaming down the hill. One after another, electric signs with neon martini glasses lit up on them, the San Francisco symbol of "bar"—thousands of neon-magenta martini glasses bouncing and streaming down the hill, and beneath them thousands of people wheeling around to look at this freaking crazed truck we're in, their white faces erupting from their lapels like marshmallows—streaming and bouncing down the hill—and God knows they've got plenty to look at. (p. 1)

Also, consider the differences in collaboration and role taking the following text segments invite. While both texts deal with the same information, in one text, the information is presented through a conversation between two children, and in the other text, the information is presented in a more "straightforward" expository style.

> FLY
> Lisa and Mike were bored. It was Saturday and they did not know what to do until Lisa had an idea. "I know a game we can play that they play in some countries . . .

> FLY
> All over the world children like to play different games. In some countries, children enjoy playing a game called "Fly."

We have found that readers of the first text usually assume a sympathetic collaboration with the writer and identify with the characters. They view the game through the eyes of the children and remain rather neutral with respect to the author. Our readers of the second text tend to have difficulty understanding the game at the same time as they are critical of the author. They adopt a role more akin to an observer who, lacking a specific angle, catches glimpses of the game without acquiring an overall understanding. Some of us have experienced a similar phenomenon as viewers of an overseas telecast of an unfamiliar sport (e.g., the game of cricket on British television). The camera angles provided by the British sportscasters are disorienting for the native viewer.

Clearly a number of factors may influence the nature of a reader's alignment and the extent to which his resulting interpretation is viable. A reader, as 18 our last example illustrated, might adopt an alignment which interferes with how well he will be able to negotiate an understanding. Sometimes a reader might adopt an alignment which overindulges certain biases, predispositions, and personal experiences. Doris Lessing (1973) described this phenomenon in a discussion of readers' responses to her *The Golden Notebook:*

> Ten years after I wrote [it], I can get, in one week, three letters about it. . . . One letter is entirely about the sex war, about man's inhumanity to woman, and woman's inhumanity to man, and the writer has produced pages and pages all about nothing else, for she—but not always a she—can't see anything else in the book.
>
> The second is about politics, probably from an old Red like myself, and he or she writes many pages about politics, and never mentions any other theme.
>
> These two letters used, when the book was—as it were—young, to be the most common.
>
> The third letter, once rare but now catching up on the others, is written by a man or a woman who can see nothing in it but the theme of mental illness.
>
> But it is the same book.
>
> And naturally these incidents bring up again questions of what people see when they read a book, and why one person sees one pattern and nothing at all of another pattern, and how odd it is to have, as author, such a clear picture of a book, that is seen so very differently by its readers. (p. xi)

Such occurrences should not be regarded as novel. It is this phenomenon of reader-author engagement and idiosyncratic response which has been at the center of a debate among literary theorists, some of whom (e.g., Jakobson and Levi-Strauss 1962) would suggest that a "true" reading experience has been instantiated only when readers assume an alignment which involves close collaboration with authors. Others would argue that readers can assume a variety of alignments, whether these alignments are constrained by the author (Iser 1974) or initiated freely by the reader (Fish 1970). They would rarely go so far as to suggest the destruction of the text, but instead, as Tompkins (1980) suggested, they might begin to view reading and writing as joining hands, changing places, "and finally becoming distinguishable only as two names for the same activity" (p. ii). We do not wish to debate the distinctions represented by these and other theorists, but to suggest that there appears to be at least some consensus that effective reading involves a form of alignment which emerges in conjunction with a working relationship between readers and writers. In our opinion, this does not necessitate bridling readers and writers to one another. Indeed, we would hypothesize that new insights are more likely discovered and appreciations derived when readers and writers try out different alignments as they read and write their texts. This suggests spending time rethinking, reexamining, reviewing, and rereading. For this type of experience does not occur on a single reading; rather it emerges only after several rereadings, reexaminations, and drafts. It is to this notion of reexamination and revision that we now turn.

Revising

While it is common to think of a writer as a reviser it is *not* common to think   20
of a reader as someone who revises unless perhaps he has a job involving some
editorial functions. We believe that this is unfortunate. We would like to suggest that revising should be considered as integral to reading as it is to writing.
If readers are to develop some control over and a sense of discovery with the
models of meaning they build, they must approach text with the same deliberation, time, and reflection that a writer employs as she revises a text. They must
examine their developing interpretations and view the models they build as
draft-like in quality—subject to revision. We would like to see students engage
in behaviors such as rereading (especially with different alignments), annotating the text on the page with reactions, and questioning whether the model
they have built is what they really want. With this in mind let us turn our attention to revising in writing.

We have emphasized that writing is not merely taking ideas from one's head   21
and placing them onto the page. A writer must choose words which best represent these ideas; that is, she must choose words which have the desired impact.
Sometimes this demands knowing what she wants to say and how to say it. At
other times, it warrants examining what is written or read to discover and clarify one's ideas. Thus a writer will repeatedly reread, reexamine, delete, shape,
and correct what she is writing. She will consider whether and how her ideas fit
together, how well her words represent the ideas to be shared and how her text
can be fine tuned. For some writers this development and redevelopment will
appear to be happening effortlessly. For others, revision demands hard labor
and sometimes several painful drafts. Some rework the drafts in their head
before they rewrite; others slowly rework pages as they go. From analyses of
the revision strategies of experienced writers, it appears that the driving force
behind revision is a sense of emphasis and proportion. As Sommers (1980) suggested, one of the questions most experienced writers ask themselves is "what
does my essay as a *whole* need for form, balance, rhythm, and communication?" (p. 386). In trying to answer this question, writers proceed through revision cycles with sometimes overlapping and sometimes novel concerns. Initial
revision cycles might be directed predominately at topical development; later
cycles might be directed at stylistic concerns.

For most readers, revision is an unheard of experience. Observations of   22
secondary students reveal that most readers view reading competency as the
ability to read rapidly a single text once with maximum recall (Schallert and
Tierney 1982). It seems that students rarely pause to reflect on their ideas or
to judge the quality of their developing interpretations. Nor do they often
reread a text either from the same or a different perspective. In fact, to suggest that a reader should approach text as a writer who crafts an understanding across several drafts—who pauses, rethinks, and revises—is almost
contrary to some well-established goals readers proclaim for themselves (e.g.,
that efficient reading is equivalent to maximum recall based upon a single
fast reading).

Suppose we could convince students that they ought to revise their readings 23
of a text; would they be able to do it? We should not assume that merely allowing time for pausing, reflecting, and reexamining will guarantee that students
will revise their readings. Students need to be given support and feedback at so
doing. Students need to be aware of strategies they can pursue to accomplish
revisions, to get things restarted when they stall, and to compare one draft or
reading with another. The pursuit of a second draft of a reading should have
a purpose. Sometimes this purpose can emerge from discussing a text with the
teacher and peers; sometimes it may come from within; sometimes it will not
occur unless the student has a reason or functional context for revision as well
as help from a thoughtful teacher.

Monitoring

Hand in hand with planning, aligning, drafting, and revising, readers and writ- 24
ers must be able to distance themselves from the texts they have created to
evaluate what they have developed. We call this executive function monitoring.
Monitoring usually occurs tacitly, but it can be under conscious control. The
monitor in us keeps track of and control over our other functions. Our monitor
decides whether we have planned, aligned, drafted, and/or revised properly. It
decides when one activity should dominate over the others. Our monitor tells
us when we have done a good job and when we have not. It tells us when to go
back to the drawing board and when we can relax.

The complexity of the type of juggling which the monitor is capable of has 25
been captured aptly in an analogy of a switchboard operator, used by Flower
and Hayes (1981) to describe how writers juggle constraints:

> She has two important calls on hold. (Don't forget that idea.)
> Four lights just started flashing. (They demand immediate attention or they'll be
> lost.)
> A party of five wants to be hooked up together. (They need to be connected
> somehow.)
> A party of two thinks they've been incorrectly connected. (Where do they go?)
> And throughout this complicated process of remembering, retrieving, and con-
> necting, the operator's voice must project calmness, confidence, and complete
> control. (p. 33)

The monitor has one final task—to engage in a dialogue with the inner 26
reader.

When writers and readers compose text they negotiate its meaning with 27
what Murray ("Teaching," 1982) calls the other self—that inner reader (the
author's first reader) who continually reacts to what the writer has written, is
writing, and will write or what the reader has read, is reading, and will read.
It is this other self which is the reader's or writer's counsel, and judge, and
prompter. This other self oversees what the reader and writer is trying to do,
defines the nature of collaboration between reader and author, and decides
how well the reader as writer or writer as reader is achieving his or her goals.

A Summary and Discussion

To reiterate, we view both reading and writing as acts of composing. We see   28
these acts of composing as involving continuous, recurring, and recursive
transactions among readers and writers, their respective inner selves, and
their perceptions of each other's goals and desires. Consider the reader's role
as we envision it. At the same time as the reader considers what he perceives to
be the author's intentions (or what the reader perceives to be what the author
is trying to get the reader to do or think), he negotiates goals with his inner
self (or what he would like to achieve). With these goals being continuously
negotiated (sometimes embedded within each other) the reader proceeds to
take different alignments (critic, co-author, editor, character, reporter, eyewitness, etc.) as he uses features from his own experiential arrays and what he
perceives to be arrayed by the author in order to create a model of meaning for the text. These models of meaning must assume a coherent, holistic
quality in which everything fits together. The development of these models
of meaning occurs from the vantage point of different alignments which the
reader adopts with respect to these arrays. It is from these vantage points
that the various arrays are perceived, and their position adjusted such that
the reader's goals and desire for a sense of completeness are achieved. Our
diagrammatic representation of the major components of these processes is
given in Figure 1.

    Such an account of reading distinguishes itself from previous descriptions of   29
reading and reading-writing relationships in several notable ways:

    1. Most accounts of reading versus writing (as well as accounts of how
       readers develop a model of meaning) tend to emphasize reading as a

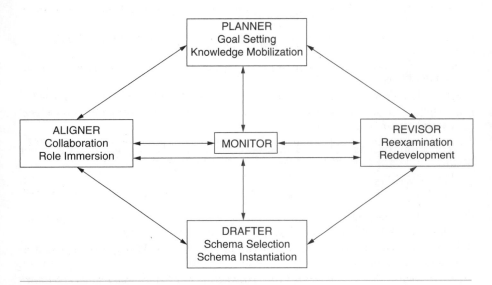

Figure 1 **Some Components of the Composing Model of Reading**

receptive rather than productive activity. Some, in fact, regard reading as the mirror image of writing.

2. Most language accounts suggest that reading and writing are interrelated. They do not address the suggestion that reading and writing are multi-dimensional, multi-modal processes—both acts of composing.

3. The phenomenon of alignment as integral to composing has rarely been explored.

4. Most descriptions of how readers build models of meaning fail to consider how the processes of planning, drafting, aligning, and revising are manifested.

5. Previous interactional and transactional accounts of reading (Rosenblatt 1978; Rumelhart 1980) give little consideration to the transaction which occurs among the inner selves of the reader and writer.

What our account fails to do is thoroughly differentiate how these composing behaviors manifest themselves in the various contexts of reading and writing. Nor does it address the pattern of interactions among these behaviors across moments during any reading and writing experience. For example, we give the impression of sequential stages even though we believe in simultaneous processes. We hope to clarify and extend these notions in subsequent writings.

References

Anderson, R. C.; Pichert, J. W.; and Shirey, L. L. *Effects of the Reader's Schema at Different Points in Time*. Technical Report No. 119. Urbana, IL: Center for the Study of Reading, University of Illinois, April 1979. (ERIC Document Reproduction Service No. ED 169 523)

Anderson, R. C.; Reynolds, R. E.; Schallert, D. L.; and Goetz, E. T. "Frameworks for Comprehending Discourse." *American Educational Research Journal* 14 (1977): 367–382.

Applebee, A. N. *The Child's Concept of Story*. Chicago: University of Chicago Press, 1978.

Birnbaum, J. C. "The Reading and Composing Behavior of Selected Fourth and Seventh Grade Students." *Research in the Teaching of English* 16 (1982): 241–260.

Bruce, B. "A Social Interaction Model of Reading." *Discourse Processes* 4 (1981): 273–311.

Collins, A.; Brown, J. S.; and Larkin, K. M. "Inference in Text Understanding." In *Theoretical Issues in Reading Comprehension,* edited by R. J. Spiro, B. C. Bruce, and W. F. Brewer. Hillsdale, NJ: Erlbaum, 1980.

Fish, S. "Literature in the Reader: Affective Stylistics." *New Literary History* 2 (1970): 123–162.

Flower, L. and Hayes, J. R. "A Cognitive Process Theory of Writing." *College Composition and Communication* 32 (1981): 365–387.

Freeman, M. "How to Read a Philosophical Text." Unpublished paper, Harvard University, 1982.

Gibson, E. J. and Levin, H. *The Psychology of Reading*. Cambridge: M.I.T. Press, 1975.

Gibson, W. *Persona*. New York: Random House, 1969.

Goodman, K. S. "Reading: A Psycholinguistic Guessing Game." *Journal of the Reading Specialist* 6 (1967): 126–135.

Hay, A. and Brewer, W. F. *Children's Understanding of the Narrator's Point of View in Prose*. Urbana, IL: Center for the Study of Reading, University of Illinois, 1982.

Hayes, D. and Tierney, R. "Developing Readers' Knowledge Through Analogy." *Reading Research Quarterly* 17 (1982): 256–280.

Iser, W. *The Implied Reader: Patterns in Communication in Prose Fiction from Bunyan to Beckett*. Baltimore: John Hopkins University Press, 1974.

Jakobson, R. and Levi-Strauss, C. "Les Chats de Charles Baudelave." *L'Homme* 2 (1962): 5–21.

Lessing, D. *Introduction to The Golden Notebook*. New York: Bantam Books, 1973.

Murray, D. *Learning by Teaching*. Montclair, NJ: Boynton/Cook Publishers, Inc., 1982.

Murray, D. "Teaching the Other Self: The Writer's First Reader." *College Composition and Communication* 33 (1982): 140–147.

Pichert, J. W. *Sensitivity to What Is Important in Prose*. Technical Report No. 149. Urbana, IL: Center for the Study of Reading, University of Illinois, November 1979. (ERIC Document Reproduction Service No. ED 179 946)

Rosenblatt, L. M. *Literature As Exploration*, 3rd edition. New York: Noble and Noble, 1976 (originally published 1939).

Rosenblatt, L. *The Reader, the Text, the Poem: The Transactional Theory of the Literary Work*. Carbondale, IL: Southern Illinois University Press, 1978.

Rumelhart, D. "Schemata: The Building Blocks of Cognition." In *Theoretical Issues in Reading Comprehension*, edited by R. J. Spiro, B. Bruce, and W. Brewer. Hillsdale, NJ: Erlbaum, 1980.

Sadoski, M. "An Exploratory Study of the Relationships Between Reported Imagery and the Comprehension and Recall of a Story." *Reading Research Quarterly* 19 (1983): 110–123.

Schallert, D. and Tierney, R. J. *Learning from Expository Text: The Interaction of Text Structure with Reader Characteristics*. Final report. National Institute of Education, 1982.

Smith, F. *Understanding Reading*. New York: Holt, Rinehart & Winston, 1971.

Sommers, N. I. "Revision Strategies of Student Writers and Experienced Adult Writers." *College Composition and Communication* 31 (1980): 378–388.

Spiro, R. J. "Remembering Information from Text: The 'State of Schema' Approach." *In Schooling and the Acquisition of Knowledge*, edited by R. C. Anderson, R. J. Spiro, and W. E. Montague. Hillsdale, NJ: Erlbaum, 1977.

Tierney, R. J. "Writer-Reader Transactions: Defining the Dimensions of Negotiation." In *Forum: Essays on Theory and Practice in the Teaching of Writing*, edited by P. Stock. Montclair, NJ: Boynton/Cook, 1983.

Tierney, R. J.; LaZansky, J.; Raphael, T.; and Cohen, P. "Author's Intentions and Reader's Interpretation." In *Understanding Readers Understanding*, edited by R. J. Tierney, P. Anders, and J. Mitchell. Hillsdale, NJ: Erlbaum, 1987.

Tierney, R. J. and Mosenthal, J. *The Cohesion Concept's Relationship to the Coherence of Text*. Technical Report No. 221. Urbana, IL: Center for the Study of Reading, University of Illinois, October 1981. (ERIC Document Reproduction Service No. ED 212 991)

Tompkins, J. P. *Reader-Response Criticism*. Baltimore: John Hopkins University Press, 1980.

Wolfe, T. *Electric Kool-Aid Acid Test*. New York: Bantam, 1977.

Questions for Discussion and Journaling

1. In the introduction to their article, Tierney and Pearson claim, "In a sense both reader and writer must *adapt* to their perceptions about their partner in negotiating what a text means" (para. 1). Based on the rest of the article, what do you think led them to this conclusion? Can you think of a case from your own experience where such "adaptations" came into play?

2. Given Tierney and Pearson's descriptions of composing process functions such as **drafting** and alignment, what can you say about the role of *expectations* in

reading and writing? If Tierney and Pearscn are right, what do we need and use our own expectations for as we compose texts? Having read the piece, do you now think about the role of expectations differently?

3. Many people aren't aware of the extent to which writing and reading are essentially the same activity. Was this idea a complete surprise to you, or had you already realized it, at least somewhat? Do you think this awareness will (or already does) influence your own processes of reading and writing?

4. Tierney and Pearson pose the construction of texts (both as writers and readers) as a very "mindful" or *reflective* process where the maker of the text thinks a lot about what she's trying to do and how to do it—not just in, say, planning and monitoring, but even n drafting, aligning, and revising. In what ways are you mindful, as a reader and as a writer, and in what ways are you not? Based on your experience, how realistic is Tierney and Pearson's sense of this mindfulness?

5. What are some ways you could *disagree* with the authors' contention that reading is actually a composing process? Are there aspects of their argument that you don't buy, based on your own experience?

6. As a writer, have you experienced the "tug of war" between writers and readers that Tierney and Pearson describe? If so, what do you think of it? If not, why do you think you haven't noticed it before?

7. How is *alignment* different from *planning* in Tierney and Pearson's model? Why isn't alignment just a special kind of planning?

Applying and Exploring Ideas

1. Tierney and Pearson suggest that what writers and readers do in composing texts can be summed up by the five functions they describe: *planning, drafting, aligning, revising,* and *monitoring.* Can you think of anything you do as you write or read texts that isn't covered by one of these functions? How would you change Tierney and Pearson's list—either its order or what's on it?

2. One of Tierney and Pearson's closing suggestions is that, at the time they were writing, researchers were not paying enough attention to the "inner selves" of writers and readers. This is research you can pursue fairly easily. First, listen: Do you find yourself having an "internal" conversation or a running monologue as you read and write? When are you aware of that effect? How does this stream of language, or meaning, help you construct the text? Check in with some of your friends: What is this "inner voice," monologue, or dialogue like for them, and what differences do you discover in how different people describe it?

3. Reflect on how you accomplished your last significant piece of writing (one that took you more than a few minutes to complete). Did you use each of the five functions Tierney and Pearson describe? If not, which did you not use? Can you say why it didn't seem necessary?

4. Keep a record, as you encounter texts that you must read or write, of all the roles you adopt as you produce the text. Try to be especially sensitive to how the texts you read position you as a particular *kind of* person or reader. For example, what roles do a *Seventeen* magazine article and a newspaper article seem to try to get their readers to adopt?

Meta Moment
In what ways is actively considering reading as a process useful to you?

The Composing Processes of Unskilled College Writers

SONDRA PERL

Perl, Sondra. "The Composing Processes of Unskilled College Writers." *Research in the Teaching of English* 13.4 (1979): 317–36. Print.

Framing the Reading

Writing this article in 1979, Sondra Perl argued "To date no examination of composing processes has dealt primarily with unskilled writers. As long as 'average' or skilled
writers are the focus, it remains unclear as to how process research will [help unskilled
writers]" (para. 4). Much of the nature of this article is captured in that brief passage.

With the study reported here, Perl attempted to accomplish two important
and quite distinct projects in advancing writing research. The first was to create
a brand-new way to study writers writing. In the first few pages you'll read Perl's
description of the problem with previous research on the writing process: It relied
almost entirely on stories researchers told about what they observed. Perl tried to
create a more objective system for describing what writers were doing.

The second was to study a group of writers that previous research had ignored.
Writers who aren't very good at writing probably aren't the best test subjects for
"how writing works," and so they had not been studied much by researchers trying
to learn about "the composing process" (which is how composition was described
in those times—as a single kind of process writers either mastered or didn't). Yet,
as Perl argued, studying people who are already proficient writers would probably
not "provide teachers with a firmer understanding of the needs of students with
serious writing problems" (para. 4).

Like many of the articles in this chapter, Perl's is close to thirty years old. It
reflects a time of great interest, among writing researchers,
about processes writers use to compose texts. That interest
waned a few years later; even though there was still much to
be discovered and understood (most process research findings
were provisional at best and needed to be followed up with
larger-scale studies that have never been done), the attention of writing researchers went in other directions. Thus the
majority of research on the writing process tends to be at least
twenty years old.

Perl's article had a particularly great impact on the field
because of her combined focus on a standardized method for

observing, recording, and reporting on writers' behaviors while writing and her attention to "basic" writers whose writing was difficult to read and understand. Work such as this has made Perl one of the most significant researchers the field has seen. She went on to study how writers imagine what to say before they quite *know* what they want to say. (In 2004 she published a book called *Felt Sense: Writing with the Body*, which includes a CD that offers "meditations" for writers. It's quite different from the work you'll read here, which we hope might motivate you to look it up.)

Getting Ready to Read

Before you read, do at least one of the following activities:

- Ask yourself how you view yourself as a writer. Do you think you are a skilled or unskilled writer? Is writing easy or hard for you?
- Write down exactly what you think you do when you have to write something for school. Have you ever thought about this consciously before?
- Watch a roommate or friend write something for school, and make note of the things he or she does while writing.

As you read, consider the following questions:

- What arguments does Perl make about what research methods are necessary for good studies of writing?
- What attitudes and assumptions does Perl seem to bring to her study that you might not agree with, or at least might question?
- What conclusions is Perl able to reach about the major aspects of the composing process—prewriting, writing, and editing—that she identifies?
- How are Tony's processes as an "unskilled" writer different from those of skilled writers?

This paper presents the pertinent findings from a study of the composing 1 processes of five unskilled college writers (Perl, 1978). The first part summarizes the goals of the original study, the kinds of data collected, and the research methods employed. The second part is a synopsis of the study of Tony, one of the original five case studies. The third part presents a condensed version of the findings on the composing process and discusses these findings in light of current pedagogical practice and research design.

Goals of the Study

This research addressed three major questions: (1) How do unskilled writers 2 write? (2) Can their writing processes be analyzed in a systematic, replicable manner? and (3) What does an increased understanding of their processes suggest about the nature of composing in general and the manner in which writing is taught in the schools?

In recent years, interest in the composing process has grown (Britton et al., 1975; Burton, 1973; Cooper, 1974; Emig, 1967, 1971). In 1963, Braddock, Lloyd-Jones, and Schoer, writing on the state of research in written composition, included the need for "direct observation" and case study procedures in their suggestions for future research (pp. 24, 31–32). In a section entitled "Unexplored Territory," they listed basic unanswered questions such as, "What is involved in the act of writing?" and "Of what does skill in writing actually consist?" (p. 51). Fifteen years later, Cooper and Odell (1978) edited a volume similar in scope, only this one was devoted entirely to issues and questions related to research on composing. This volume in particular signals a shift in emphasis in writing research. Alongside the traditional, large-scale experimental studies, there is now widespread recognition of the need for works of a more modest, probing nature, works that attempt to elucidate basic processes. The studies on composing that have been completed to date are precisely of this kind; they are small-scale studies, based on the systematic observation of writers engaged in the process of writing (Emig, 1971; Graves, 1973; Mischel, 1974; Pianko, 1977; Stallard, 1974).

> How do unskilled writers write?

For all of its promise, this body of research has yet to produce work that would insure wide recognition for the value of process studies of composing. One limitation of work done to date is methodological. Narrative descriptions of composing processes do not provide sufficiently graphic evidence for the perception of underlying regularities and patterns. Without such evidence, it is difficult to generate well-defined hypotheses and to move from exploratory research to more controlled experimental studies. A second limitation pertains to the subjects studied. To date no examination of composing processes has dealt primarily with unskilled writers. As long as "average" or skilled writers are the focus, it remains unclear as to how process research will provide teachers with a firmer understanding of the needs of students with serious writing problems.

The present study is intended to carry process research forward by addressing both of these limitations. One prominent feature of the research design involves the development and use of a meaningful and replicable method for rendering the composing process as a sequence of observable and scorable behaviors. A second aspect of the design is the focus on students whose writing problems baffle the teachers charged with their education.

Design of the Study

This study took place during the 1975–76 fall semester at Eugenio Maria de Hostos Community College of the City University of New York. Students were selected for the study on the basis of two criteria: writing samples that qualified them as unskilled writers and willingness to participate. Each student met with the researcher for five 90-minute sessions (see Table 1). Four sessions were devoted to writing with the students directed to compose aloud, to externalize their thinking processes as much as possible, during each session. In one additional session, a writing profile on the students' perceptions and memories of writing was developed through the use of an open-ended interview. All of the sessions took place in a soundproof room in the college library. Throughout each session, the researcher assumed a noninterfering role.

The topics for writing were developed in an introductory social science 7 course in which the five students were enrolled. The "content" material they were studying was divided into two modes: extensive, in which the writer was directed to approach the material in an objective, impersonal fashion, and reflexive, in which the writer was directed to approach similar material in an affective, personalized fashion. Contrary to Emig's (1971) definitions, in this study it was assumed that the teacher was always the audience.

Data Analysis

Three kinds of data were collected in this study: the students' written products, 8 their composing tapes, and their responses to the interview. Each of these was studied carefully and then discussed in detail in each of the five case study presentations. Due to limitations of space, this paper will review only two of the data sets generated in the study.

Coding the Composing Process

One of the goals of this research was to devise a tool for describing the move- 9 ments that occur during composing. In the past such descriptions have taken the form of narratives which detail, with relative precision and insight, observable composing behaviors; however, these narratives provide no way of ascertaining the frequency, relative importance, and place of each behavior within an individual's composing process. As such, they are cumbersome and difficult to replicate. Furthermore, lengthy, idiosyncratic narratives run the risk of leaving underlying patterns and regularities obscure. In contrast, the method created in this research provides a means of viewing the composing process that is:

1. Standardized—it introduces a coding system for observing the composing process that can be replicated;
2. Categorical—it labels specific, observable behaviors so that types of composing movements are revealed;
3. Concise—it presents the entire sequence of composing movements on one or two pages;
4. Structural—it provides a way of determining how parts of the process relate to the whole; and
5. Diachronic—it presents the sequences of movements that occur during composing as they unfold in time.

In total, the method allows the researcher to apprehend a process as it unfolds. It lays out the movements or behavior sequences in such a way that if patterns within a student's process or among a group of students exist, they become apparent.

Table 1
Design of the Study

	SESSION 1 (S1)	SESSION 2 (S2)	SESSION 3 (S3)	SESSION 4 (S4)	SESSION 5 (S5)
Mode	Extensive	Reflexive		Extensive	Reflexive
Topic	Society & Culture	Society & Culture	Interview: Writing Profile	Capitalism	Capitalism
Directions	Students told to compose aloud; no other directions given	Students told to compose aloud; no other directions given		Students told to compose aloud; also directed to talk out ideas before writing	Students told to compose aloud; also directed to talk out ideas before writing

The Code

The method consists of coding each composing behavior exhibited by the stu-   10
dent and charting each behavior on a continuum. During this study, the coding
occurred after the student had finished composing and was done by working
from the student's written product and the audiotape of the session. It was possible to do this since the tape captured both what the student was saying and
the literal sound of the pen moving across the page. As a result, it was possible
to determine when students were talking, when they were writing, when both
occurred simultaneously, and when neither occurred.

The major categorical divisions in this coding system are talking, writing,   11
and reading; however, it was clear that there are various kinds of talk and
various kinds of writing and reading operations, and that a coding system
would need to distinguish among these various types. In this study the following operations were distinguished:

1. General planning [PL]—organizing one's thoughts for writing, discussing how one will proceed.
2. Local planning [PLL]—talking out what idea will come next.
3. Global planning [PLG]—discussing changes in drafts.
4. Commenting [C]—sighing, making a comment or judgment about the
   topic.
5. Interpreting [I]—rephrasing the topic to get a "handle" on it.
6. Assessing [A(+); A(−)]—making a judgment about one's writing; may be
   positive or negative.
7. Questioning [Q]—asking a question.
8. Talking leading to writing [T→W]—voicing ideas on the topic, tentatively finding one's way, but not necessarily being committed to or using
   all one is saying.
9. Talking and writing at the same time [TW]—composing aloud in such a
   way that what one is saying is actually being written at the same time.
10. Repeating [re]—repeating written or unwritten phrases a number of
    times.
11. Reading related to the topic:
    (a) Reading the directions [R_D]
    (b) Reading the question [R_q]
    (c) Reading the statement [R_s]
12. Reading related to one's own written product:
    (a) Reading one sentence or a few words [R^a]
    (b) Reading a number of sentences together [R^{a-b}]
    (c) Reading the entire draft through [R^{W1}]
13. Writing silently [W]
14. Writing aloud [TW]
15. Editing [E]
    (a) adding syntactic markers, words, phrases, or clauses [Eadd]
    (b) deleting syntactic markers, words, phrases, or clauses [Edel]
    (c) indicating concern for a grammatical rule [Egr]

(d) adding, deleting, or considering the use of punctuation [Epunc]
(e) considering or changing spelling [Esp]
(f) changing the sentence structure through embedding, coordination or subordination [Ess]
(g) indicating concern for appropriate vocabulary (word choice) [Ewc]
(h) considering or changing verb form [Evc]

16. Periods of silence [s]

By taking specific observable behaviors that occur during composing and supplying labels for them, this system thus far provides a way of analyzing the process that is categorical and capable of replication. In order to view the frequency and the duration of composing behaviors and the relation between one particular behavior and the whole process, these behaviors need to be depicted graphically to show their duration and sequence.   12

The Continuum

The second component of this system is the construction of a time line and a numbering system. In this study, blank charts with lines like the following were designed:

```
- - - - - - - - - - - - - - - - - - - - - - - - - - - - - - - - - - - - - -
     10          20          30          40          50          60          70
```

A ten-digit interval corresponds to one minute and is keyed to a counter on a tape recorder. By listening to the tape and watching the counter, it is possible to determine the nature and duration of each operation. As each behavior is heard on the tape, it is coded and then noted on the chart with the counter used as a time marker. For example, if a student during prewriting reads the directions and the question twice and then begins to plan exactly what she is going to say, all within the first minute, it would be coded like this: 13

Prewriting
<u>RDRQRDRQPLL</u>
- - - - - - - - - -
10

If at this point the student spends two minutes writing the first sentence, during which time she pauses, rereads the question, continues writing, and then edits for spelling before continuing on, it would be coded like this:

1
<u>TW_1 /s/RQ TW_1[Esp]TW_1</u>
- - - - - - - - - - - - - - - - - - -
20   30

At this point two types of brackets and numbering systems have appeared. The initial sublevel number linked with the TW code indicates which draft the student is working on. TW_1 indicates the writing of the first draft; TW_2 and TW_3 indicate the writing of the second and third drafts. Brackets such as [Esp] separate these operations from writing and indicate the amount of time the operation takes.   14

The upper-level number above the horizontal bracket indicates which sentence in the written product is being written and the length of the bracket indicates the amount of time spent on the writing of each sentence. All horizontal brackets refer to sentences, and from the charts it is possible to see when sentences are grouped together and written in a chunk (adjacent brackets) or when each sentence is produced in isolation (gaps between brackets). (See Appendix for sample chart.)

The charts can be read by moving along the time line, noting which behaviors occur and in what sequence. Three types of comments are also included in the charts. In bold-face type, the beginning and end of each draft are indicated; in lighter type-face, comments on the actual composing movements are provided; and in the lightest type-face, specific statements made by students or specific words they found particularly troublesome are noted. 15

From the charts, the following information can be determined: 16

1. the amount of time spent during prewriting;
2. the strategies used during prewriting;
3. the amount of time spent writing each sentence;
4. the behaviors that occur while each sentence is being written;
5. when sentences are written in groups or "chunks" (fluent writing);
6. when sentences are written in isolation (choppy or sporadic writing);
7. the amount of time spent between sentences;
8. the behaviors that occur between sentences;
9. when editing occurs (during the writing of sentences, between sentences, in the time between drafts);
10. the frequency of editing behavior;
11. the nature of the editing operations; and
12. where and in what frequency pauses or periods of silence occur in the process.

The charts, or *composing style sheets* as they are called, do not explain what students wrote but rather *how* they wrote. They indicate, on one page, the sequences of behavior that occur from the beginning of the process to the end. From them it is possible to determine where and how these behaviors fall into patterns and whether these patterns vary according to the mode of discourse. 17

It should be noted that although the coding system is presented before the analysis of the data, it was derived from the data and then used as the basis for generalizing about the patterns and behavioral sequences found within each student's process. These individual patterns were reported in each of the five case studies. Thus, initially, a style sheet was constructed for each writing session on each student. When there were four style sheets for each student, it was possible to determine if composing patterns existed among the group. The summary of results reported here is based on the patterns revealed by these charts. 18

Analyzing Miscues in the Writing Process

Miscue analysis is based on Goodman's model of the reading process. Created in 1962, it has become a widespread tool for studying what students do when they 19 read and is based on the premise that reading is a psycholinguistic process which "uses language, in written form, to get to the meaning" (Goodman, 1973, p. 4). Miscue analysis "involves its user in examining the observed behavior of oral readers as an interaction between language and thought, as a process of constructing meaning from a graphic display" (Goodman, 1973, p. 4). Methodologically, the observer analyzes the mismatch that occurs when readers make responses during oral reading that differ from the text. This mismatch or miscueing is then analyzed from Goodman's "meaning-getting" model, based on the assumption that "the reader's preoccupation with meaning will show in his miscues, because they will tend to result in language that still makes sense" (Goodman, 1973, p. 9).

In the present study, miscue analysis was adapted from Goodman's model in 20 order to provide insight into the writing process. Since students composed aloud, two types of oral behaviors were available for study: encoding processes or what students spoke while they were writing and decoding processes or what students "read"[1] after they had finished writing. When a discrepancy existed between encoding or decoding and what was on the paper, it was referred to as miscue.

For encoding, the miscue analysis was carried out in the following manner: 21

1. The students' written products were typed, preserving the original style and spelling.
2. What students said while composing aloud was checked against the written products; discrepancies were noted on the paper wherever they occurred,
3. The discrepancies were categorized and counted.

Three miscue categories were derived for encoding: 22

1. Speaking complete ideas but omitting certain words during writing.
2. Pronouncing words with plural markers or other suffixes completely but omitting these endings during writing.
3. Pronouncing the desired word but writing a homonym, an approximation of the word or a personal abbreviation of the word on paper.

For decoding, similar procedures were used, this time comparing the words 23 of the written product with what the student "read" orally. When a discrepancy occurred, it was noted. The discrepancies were then categorized and counted.

Four miscue categories were derived for decoding: 24

1. "Reading in" missing words or word endings;
2. Deleting words or word endings;
3. "Reading" the desired word rather than the word on the page;
4. "Reading" abbreviations and misspellings as though they were written correctly.

A brief summary of the results of this analysis appears in the findings.

---

[1] The word "read" is used in a particular manner here. In the traditional sense, reading refers to accurate decoding of written symbols. Here it refers to students' verbalizing words or endings even when the symbols for those words are missing or only minimally present. Whenever the term "reading" is used in this way, it will be in quotation marks.

Synopsis of a Case Study

Tony was a 20-year-old ex-Marine born and raised in the Bronx, New York. 25
Like many Puerto Ricans born in the United States, he was able to speak
Spanish, but he considered English his native tongue. In the eleventh grade,
Tony left high school, returning three years later to take the New York State
high school equivalency exam. As a freshman in college, he was also working
part-time to support a child and a wife from whom he was separated.

Behaviors

The composing style sheets provide an overview of the observable behaviors 26
exhibited by Tony during the composing process. (See Appendix for samples of
Tony's writing and the accompanying composing style sheet.) The most salient
feature of Tony's composing process was its recursiveness. Tony rarely produced a sentence without stopping to reread either a part or the whole. This
repetition set up a particular kind of composing rhythm, one that was cumulative in nature and that set ideas in motion by its very repetitiveness. Thus, as
can be seen from any of the style sheets, talking led to writing which led to
reading which led to planning which again led to writing.

The style sheets indicated a difference in the composing rhythms exhibited 27
in the extensive and reflexive modes. On the extensive topics there was not
only more repetition within each sentence but also many more pauses and repetitions between sentences, with intervals often lasting as long as two minutes.
On the reflexive topics, sentences were often written in groups, with fewer
rereadings and only minimal time intervals separating the creation of one sentence from another.

Editing occurred consistently in all sessions. From the moment Tony began 28
writing, he indicated a concern for correct form that actually inhibited the
development of ideas. In none of the writing sessions did he ever write more
than two sentences before he began to edit. While editing fit into his overall
recursive pattern, it simultaneously interrupted the composing rhythm he had
just initiated.

During the intervals between drafts, Tony read his written work, assessed 29
his writing, planned new phrasings, transitions or endings, read the directions
and the question over, and edited once again.

Tony performed these operations in both the extensive and reflexive modes 30
and was remarkably consistent in all of his composing operations. The style
sheets attest both to this consistency and to the densely packed, tight quality of
Tony's composing process—indeed, if the notations on these sheets were any
indication at all, it was clear that Tony's composing process was so full that
there was little room left for invention or change.

Fluency

Table 2 provides a numerical analysis of Tony's writing performance. Here 31
it is possible to compare not only the amount of time spent on the various

Table 2

Tony: Summary of Four Writing Sessions (Time in Minutes)

		S1 TW$_1$			S4 T→W	
	Drafts	Words	Time	Drafts	Words	Time
Extensive mode			Prewriting: 7.8			Prewriting: 8.0
	W1	132	18.8	W1	182	29.0
	W2	170	51.0	W2	174	33.9
	Total	302	Total composing: 91.2*	Total	356	Total composing: 82.0*
		S2 TW$_1$			S5 T→W	
	Drafts	Words	Time	Drafts	Words	Time
Reflexive mode			Prewriting: 3.5			Prewriting: 5.7
	W1	165	14.5	W1	208	24.0
	W2	169	25.0	W2	190	38.3
	W3	178	24.2	W3	152	20.8
	Total	512	Total composing: 76.0*	Total	550	Total composing: 96.0*

* Total composing includes time spent on editing and rereading, as well as actual writing.

composing operations but also the relative fluency. For Sessions 1 and 2 the data indicate that while Tony spent more time prewriting and writing in the extensive mode, he actually produced fewer words. For Sessions 4 and 5, a similar pattern can be detected. In the extensive mode, Tony again spent more time prewriting and produced fewer words. Although writing time was increased in the reflexive mode, the additional 20 minutes spent writing did not sufficiently account for an increase of 194 words. Rather, the data indicate that Tony produced more words with less planning and generally in less time in the reflexive mode, suggesting that his greater fluency lay in this mode.

Strategies

Tony exhibited a number of strategies that served him as a writer whether the mode was extensive or reflexive. Given any topic, the first operation he performed was to focus in and narrow down the topic. He did this by rephrasing the topic until either a word or an idea in the topic linked up with something in his own experience (an attitude, an opinion, an event). In this way he established a connection between the field of discourse and himself and at this point he felt ready to write.   32

Level of Language Use

Once writing, Tony employed a pattern of classifying or dividing the topic into manageable pieces and then using one or both of the divisions as the basis for   33 narration. In the four writing sessions, his classifications were made on the basis of economic, racial, and political differences. However, all of his writing reflected a low level of generality. No formal principles were used to organize the narratives nor were the implications of ideas present in the essay developed.

In his writing, Tony was able to maintain the extensive/reflexive distinction. 34 He recognized when he was being asked directly for an opinion and when he was being asked to discuss concepts or ideas that were not directly linked to his experience. However, the more distance between the topic and himself, the more difficulty he experienced, and the more repetitive his process became. Conversely, when the topic was close to his own experience, the smoother and more fluent the process became. More writing was produced, pauses were fewer, and positive assessment occurred more often. However, Tony made more assumptions on the part of the audience in the reflexive mode. When writing about himself, Tony often did not stop to explain the context from which he was writing; rather, the reader's understanding of the context was taken for granted.

Editing

Tony spent a great deal of his composing time editing. However, most of this 35 time was spent proofreading rather than changing, rephrasing, adding, or evaluating the substantive parts of the discourse. Of a total of 234 changes made in all of the sessions, only 24 were related to changes of content and included the following categories:

1. Elaborations of ideas through the use of specification and detail;
2. Additions of modals that shift the mood of a sentence;
3. Deletions that narrow the focus of a paper;
4. Clause reductions or embeddings that tighten the structure of a paper;
5. Vocabulary choices that reflect a sensitivity to language;
6. Reordering of elements in a narrative;
7. Strengthening transitions between paragraphs;
8. Pronoun changes that signal an increased sensitivity to audience.

The 210 changes in form included the following: 36

Additions	19	Verb changes	4
Deletions	44	Spelling	95
Word choice	13	Punctuation	35
		Unresolved problems	89

The area that Tony changed most often was spelling, although, even after completing three drafts of a paper, Tony still had many words misspelled.

Miscue Analysis

Despite continual proofreading, Tony's completed drafts often retained a look 37 of incompleteness. Words remained misspelled, syntax was uncorrected or overcorrected, suffixes, plural markers, and verb endings were missing, and often words or complete phrases were omitted.

The composing aloud behavior and the miscue analysis derived from it provide 38 one of the first demonstrable ways of understanding how such seemingly incomplete texts can be considered "finished" by the student. (See Table 3 for a summary of Tony's miscues.) Tony consistently voiced complete sentences when composing aloud but only transcribed partial sentences. The same behavior occurred in relation to words with plural or marked endings. However, during rereading and even during editing, Tony supplied the missing endings, words, or phrases and did not seem to "see" what was missing from the text. Thus, when reading his paper, Tony "read in" the meaning he expected to be there which turned him into a reader of content rather than form. However, a difference can be observed between the extensive and reflexive modes, and in the area of correctness Tony's greater strength lay in the reflexive mode. In this mode, not only were more words produced in less time (1,062 vs. 658), but fewer decoding miscues occurred (38 vs. 46), and fewer unresolved problems remained in the text (34 vs. 55).

Table 3

Tony—Miscue Analysis

	ENCODING			
	Speaking complete ideas but omitting certain words during writing	Pronouncing words with plural markers or other suffixes completely out omitting these endings during writing	Pronouncing the desired word but writing a homonym, an approximation of the word or a personal abbreviation of the word on paper	Total
S1	1	4	11	16
S2	8	0	14	22
S4	4	0	16	20
S5	3	1	15	19
	16	5	56	77

	DECODING			
	Reading in missing words or word endings	Deleting words or word endings	Reading the desired word rather than the word on the page	Reading abbreviations and misspellings as though they were written correctly	Total
S1	10	1	1	15	27
S2	5	1	2	10	18
S4	3	3	0	13	19
S5	7	1	2	10	20
	25	6	5	48	84

When Tony did choose to read for form, he was handicapped in another 39 way. Through his years of schooling, Tony learned that there were sets of rules to be applied to one's writing, and he attempted to apply these rules of form to his prose. Often, though, the structures he produced were far more complicated than the simple set of proofreading rules he had at his disposal. He was therefore faced with applying the rule partially, discarding it, or attempting corrections through sound. None of these systems was completely helpful to Tony, and as often as a correction was made that improved the discourse, another was made that obscured it.

Summary

Finally, when Tony completed the writing process, he refrained from com- 40 menting on or contemplating his total written product. When he initiated writing, he immediately established distance between himself as writer and his discourse. He knew his preliminary draft might have errors and might need revision. At the end of each session, the distance had decreased if not entirely disappeared. Tony "read in" missing or omitted features, rarely perceived syntactic errors, and did not untangle overly embedded sentences. It was as if the semantic model in his head predominated, and the distance with which he entered the writing process had dissolved. Thus, even with his concern for revision and for correctness, even with the enormous amount of time he invested in rereading and repetition, Tony concluded the composing process with unresolved stylistic and syntactic problems. The conclusion here is not that Tony can't write, or that Tony doesn't know how to write, or that Tony needs to learn more rules: Tony is a writer with a highly consistent and deeply embedded recursive process. What he needs are teachers who can interpret that process for him, who can see through the tangles in the process just as he sees meaning beneath the tangles in his prose, and who can intervene in such a way that untangling his composing process leads him to create better prose.

Summary of the Findings

A major finding of this study is that, like Tony, all of the students studied dis- 41 played consistent composing processes; that is, the behavioral subsequences prewriting, writing, and editing appeared in sequential patterns that were recognizable across writing sessions and across students.

This consistency suggests a much greater internalization of process than has 42 ever before been suspected. Since the written products of basic writers often look arbitrary, observers commonly assume that the students' approach is also arbitrary. However, just as Shaughnessy (1977) points out that there is "very little that is random . . . in what they have written" (p. 5), so, on close observation, very little appears random in *how* they write. The students observed had stable composing processes which they used whenever they were presented with a writing task. While this consistency argues against seeing these students as beginning writers, it ought not necessarily imply that they are proficient writers. Indeed, their lack of proficiency may be attributable to the way in which premature and rigid attempts to correct and edit their work truncate the flow of composing without substantially improving the form of what they have written. More detailed findings will be reviewed in the following subsections which treat the three major aspects of composing: prewriting, writing, and editing.

Prewriting

When not given specific prewriting instructions, the students in this study began   43
writing within the first few minutes. The average time they spent on prewriting in sessions 1 and 2 was four minutes (see Table 4), and the planning strategies they used fell into three principal types:

1. Rephrasing the topic until a particular word or idea connected with the student's experience. The student then had "an event" in mind before writing began.
2. Turning the large conceptual issue in the topic (e.g., equality) into two manageable pieces for writing (e.g., rich vs. poor; black vs. white).
3. Initiating a string of associations to a word in the topic and then developing one or more of the associations during writing.

When students planned in any of these ways, they began to write with an   44
articulated sense of where they wanted their discourse to go. However, frequently students read the topic and directions a few times and indicated that they had "no idea" what to write. On these occasions, they began writing without any secure sense of where they were heading, acknowledging only that they would "figure it out" as they went along. Often their first sentence was a rephrasing of the question in the topic which, now that it was in their own handwriting and down on paper in front of them, seemed to enable them to plan what ought to come next. In these instances, writing led to planning which led to clarifying which led to more writing. This sequence of planning and writing, clarifying and discarding, was repeated frequently in all of the sessions, even when students began writing with a secure sense of direction.

Although one might be tempted to conclude that these students began writ-   45
ing prematurely and that planning precisely what they were going to write ought to have occurred before they put pen to paper, the data here suggest:

1. that certain strategies, such as creating an association to a key word, focusing in and narrowing down the topic, dichotomizing and classifying, can and do take place in a relatively brief span of time; and
2. that the developing and clarifying of ideas is facilitated once students translate some of those ideas into written form. In other words, seeing ideas on paper enables students to reflect upon, change and develop those ideas further.

Table 4

Overview of All Writing Sessions

	Prewriting time*				Total words / Total composing time				Editing changes		Unresolved problems	Miscues during reading
	S1	S2	S4	S5	S1	S2	S4	S5	Content	Form		
Tony	7.8	3.5	8.0	5.7	302 / 91.2	512 / 76.0	356 / 82.0	550 / 96.0	24	210	89	84
Dee	2.5	2.9	5.0	5.0	409 / 55.5	559 / 65.0	91 / 24.5	212 / 29.0	7	24	40	32
Stan	3.5	4.3	14.8	14.7	419 / 62.0	553 / 73.1	365 / 73.0	303 / 68.0	13	49	45	55
Lueller	2.0	1.5	4.0	13.0	518 / 90.8	588 / 96.8	315 / 93.0	363 / 77.8	2	167	143	147
Beverly	5.5	7.0	32.0	20.0	519 / 79.0	536 / 80.3	348 / 97.4	776 / 120.0	21	100	55	30

*Due to a change in the prewriting directions, only Sessions 1 and 2 are used to calculate the average time spent in prewriting.

Writing

Careful study revealed that students wrote by shuttling from the sense of   46
what they wanted to say forward to the words on the page and back from the
words on the page to their intended meaning. This "back and forth" movement
appeared to be a recursive feature: at one moment students were writing, moving their ideas and their discourse forward; at the next they were backtracking,
rereading, and digesting what had been written.

Recursive movements appeared at many points during the writing process.   47
Occasionally sentences were written in groups and then reread as a "piece" of
discourse; at other times sentences and phrases were written alone, repeated
until the writer was satisfied or worn down, or rehearsed until the act of
rehearsal led to the creation of a new sentence. In the midst of writing, editing occurred as students considered the surface features of language. Often
planning of a global nature took place: in the midst of producing a first draft,
students stopped and began planning how the second draft would differ from
the first. Often in the midst of writing, students stopped and referred to the
topic in order to check if they had remained faithful to the original intent, and
occasionally, though infrequently, they identified a sentence or a phrase that
seemed, to them, to produce a satisfactory ending. In all these behaviors, they
were shuttling back and forth, projecting what would come next and doubling
back to be sure of the ground they had covered.

A number of conclusions can be drawn from the observations of these stu-   48
dents composing and from the comments they made: although they produced
inadequate or flawed products, they nevertheless seemed to understand and
perform some of the crucial operations involved in composing with skill. While
it cannot be stated with certainty that the patterns they displayed are shared by
other writers, some of the operations they performed appear sufficiently sound
to serve as prototypes for constructing two major hypotheses on the nature of
their composing processes. Whether the following hypotheses are borne out in
studies of different types of writers remains an open question:

1. Composing does not occur in a straightforward, linear fashion. The process is one of accumulating discrete bits down on the paper and then working from those bits to reflect upon, structure, and then further develop
   what one means to say. It can be thought of as a kind of "retrospective
   structuring"; movement forward occurs only after one has reached back,
   which in turn occurs only after one has some sense of where one wants
   to go. Both aspects, the reaching back and the sensing forward, have a
   clarifying effect.

2. Composing always involves some measure of both construction and discovery. Writers construct their discourse inasmuch as they begin with a
   sense of what they want to write. This sense, as long as it remains implicit,
   is not equivalent to the explicit form it gives rise to. Thus, a process of constructing meaning is required. Rereading or backward movements become
   a way of assessing whether or not the words on the page adequately capture
   the original sense intended. Constructing simultaneously affords discovery.

Writers know more fully what they mean only after having written it. In this way the explicit written form serves as a window on the implicit sense with which one began.

Editing

Editing played a major role in the composing processes of the students in this study (see Table 5). Soon after students began writing their first drafts, they began to edit, and they continued to do so during the intervals between drafts, during the writing of their second drafts and during the final reading of papers. 49

While editing, the students were concerned with a variety of items: the lexi- 50 con (i.e., spelling, word choice, and the context of words); the syntax (i.e., grammar, punctuation, and sentence structure); and the discourse as a whole (i.e., organization, coherence, and audience). However, despite the students' considered attempts to proofread their work, serious syntactic and stylistic problems remained in their finished drafts. The persistence of these errors may, in part, be understood by looking briefly at some of the problems that arose for these students during editing.

Rule Confusion

(1) All of the students observed asked themselves, "Is this sentence [or feature] correct?" but the simple set of editing rules at their disposal was often inappro- 51 priate for the types of complicated structures they produced. As a result, they misapplied what they knew and either created a hypercorrection or impaired the meaning they had originally intended to clarify; (2) The students observed attempted to write with terms they heard in lectures or class discussions, but since they were not yet familiar with the syntactic or semantic constraints one word placed upon another, their experiments with academic language resulted in what Shaughnessy (1977, p. 49) calls, "lexical transplants" or "syntactic dissonances"; (3) The students tried to rely on their intuitions about language,

Table 5

Editing Changes

	Tony	Dee	Stan	Lueller	Beverly	Totals
Total number of words produced	1720	1271	1640	1754	2179	8564
Total form	210	24	49	167	100	550
Additions	19	2	10	21	11	63
Deletions	44	9	18	41	38	150
Word choice	13	4	1	27	6	51
Verb changes	4	1	2	7	12	26
Spelling	95	4	13	60	19	191
Punctuation	35	4	5	11	14	69
Total content	24	7	13	2	21	67

in particular the sound of words. Often, however, they had been taught to mistrust what "sounded" right to them, and they were unaware of the particular feature in their speech codes that might need to be changed in writing to match the standard code. As a result, when they attempted corrections by sound, they became confused, and they began to have difficulty differentiating between what sounded right in speech and what needed to be marked on the paper.

Selective Perception

These students habitually reread their papers from internal semantic or mean- 52
ing models. They extracted the meaning they wanted from the minimal cues on the page, and they did not recognize that outside readers would find those cues insufficient for meaning.

A study of Table 6 indicates that the number of problems remaining in the 53
students' written products approximates the number of miscues produced during reading. This proximity, itself, suggests that many of these errors persisted because the students were so certain of the words they wanted to have on the page that they "read in" these words even when they were absent; in other words, they reduced uncertainty by operating as though what was in their heads was already on the page. The problem of selective perception, then, cannot be reduced solely to mechanical decoding; the semantic model from which students read needs to be acknowledged and taken into account in any study that attempts to explain how students write and why their completed written products end up looking so incomplete.

Egocentricity

The students in this study wrote from an egocentric point of view. While they 54
occasionally indicated a concern for their readers, they more often took the reader's understanding for granted. They did not see the necessity of making their referents explicit, of making the connections among their ideas apparent, of carefully and explicitly relating one phenomenon to another, or of placing narratives or generalizations within an orienting, conceptual framework.

On the basis of these observations one may be led to conclude that these 55
writers did not know how to edit their work. Such a conclusion must, however, be drawn with care. Efforts to improve their editing need to be based on an informed view of the role that editing already plays in their composing processes. Two conclusions in this regard are appropriate here:

1. Editing intrudes so often and to such a degree that it breaks down the rhythms generated by thinking and writing. When this happens the students are forced to go back and recapture the strands of their thinking once the editing operation has been completed. Thus, editing occurs prematurely, before students have generated enough discourse to approximate the ideas they have, and it often results in their losing track of their ideas.
2. Editing is primarily an exercise in error-hunting. The students are prematurely concerned with the "look" of their writing; thus, as soon as a

Table 6

The Talk-Write Paradigm Miscues — Decoding Behaviors

	TONY	DEE	STAN	LUELLER	BEVERLY	TOTALS
Unresolved problems	89	40	45	143	55	372
"Reading in" missing words or word endings	25	13	11	44	11	104
Deleting words or word endings	6	2	4	14	9	35
"Reading" the desired word rather than the word on the page	5	6	18	15	8	52
"Reading" abbreviations and misspellings as though they were written correctly	48	11	22	74	2	157
	84	32	55	147	30	348

few words are written on the paper, detection and correction of errors replaces writing and revising. Even when they begin writing with a tentative, flexible frame of mind, they soon become locked into whatever is on the page. What they seem to lack as much as any rule is a conception of editing that includes flexibility, suspended judgment, the weighing of possibilities, and the reworking of ideas.

Implications for Teaching and Research

One major implication of this study pertains to teachers' conceptions of 56 unskilled writers. Traditionally, these students have been labeled "remedial," which usually implies that teaching ought to remedy what is "wrong" in their written products. Since the surface features in the writing of unskilled writers seriously interfere with the extraction of meaning from the page, much class time is devoted to examining the rules of the standard code. The pedagogical soundness of this procedure has been questioned frequently,[2] but in spite of the

---

[2] For discussions on the controversy over the effects of grammar instruction on writing ability, see the following: Richard Braddock, Richard Lloyd-Jones, and Lowell Schoer, *Research in Written Composition* (Urbana, Ill.: National Council of Teachers of English, 1963); Frank O'Hare, *Sentence Combining* (NCTE Research Report No. 15, Urbana, Ill.: National Council of Teachers of English, 1973); Elizabeth F. Haynes, "Using Research in Preparing to Teach Writing," *English Journal*, 1978, 67, 82–89.

debate, the practice continues, and it results in a further complication, namely that students begin to conceive of writing as a "cosmetic" process where concern for correct form supersedes development of ideas. As a result, the excitement of composing, of constructing and discovering meaning, is cut off almost before it has begun.

More recently, unskilled writers have been referred to as "beginners," imply- 57 ing that teachers can start anew. They need not "punish" students for making mistakes, and they need not assume that their students have already been taught how to write. Yet this view ignores the highly elaborated, deeply embedded processes the students bring with them. These unskilled college writers are not beginners in a *tabula rasa* sense, and teachers err in assuming they are. The results of this study suggest that teachers may first need to identify which characteristic components of each student's process facilitate writing and which inhibit it before further teaching takes place. If they do not, teachers of unskilled writers may continue to place themselves in a defeating position: imposing another method of writing instruction upon the students' already internalized processes without first helping students to extricate themselves from the knots and tangles in those processes.

A second implication of this study is that the composing process is now 58 amenable to a replicable and graphic mode of representation as a sequence of codable behaviors. The composing style sheets provide researchers and teachers with the first demonstrable way of documenting how individual students write. Such a tool may have diagnostic as well as research benefits. It may be used to record writing behaviors in large groups, prior to and after instruction, as well as in individuals. Certainly it lends itself to the longitudinal study of the writing process and may help to elucidate what it is that changes in the process as writers become more skilled.

A third implication relates to case studies and to the theories derived from 59 them. This study is an illustration of the way in which a theoretical model of the composing process can be grounded in observations of the individual's experience of composing. It is precisely the complexity of this experience that the case study brings to light. However, by viewing a series of cases, the researcher can discern patterns and themes that suggest regularities in composing behavior across individuals. These common features lead to hypotheses and theoretical formulations which have some basis in shared experience. How far this shared experience extends is, of course, a question that can only be answered through further research.

A final implication derives from the preponderance of recursive behaviors in 60 the composing processes studied here, and from the theoretical notion derived from these observations: retrospective structuring, or the going back to the sense of one's meaning in order to go forward and discover more of what one has to say. Seen in this light, composing becomes the carrying forward of an implicit sense into explicit form. Teaching composing, then, means paying attention not only to the forms or products but also to the explicative process through which they arise.

Appendix

Composing Style Sheet

Name: Tony   Mode: Extensive TW₁   Date: October 31, 1975

Session: 1   Topic: Society & Culture   Time: 11:00 AM - 12:30 PM

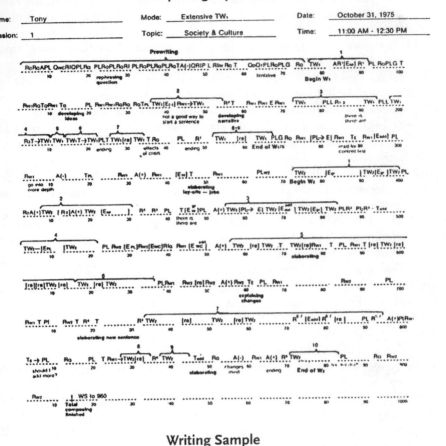

Writing Sample
TONY
Session 1
W1

All men can't be consider equal in a America base on financial situation.[1] Because their are men born in rich families that will never have to worry about any financial difficulties.[2]
 And then theyre / ~~the~~ (are) another type of Americans that is born to a poor family and alway / (may) have some kind of fina—difficulty.[3] Espeicaly nowadays in New York city With the bugdit Crisis / (and all) (If he is able).[4] ~~He may~~ be able To get a job.[5] But are now he lose the job just as easy as he got it.[6] So when he loses his job he'll have to try to get some fina—assistance.[7] ~~A~~ Then he'll probley have even more fin—diffiucuty.[8] So right / (here) you can't see that In Ameriar, all men are not create equal in the fin—sense.[9]

Writing Sample
TONY
Session 1
W2

All men can not be consider equal in America base on financial situations.[1] Because their are men born in rich families that will never have to worry about any financial ~~diffuel~~ diffuliculties.[2] And then they're are / ~~the~~ another type of ameicans that are born to a poor famitly.[3] And This is the type of Americars that ~~will~~ / may alway have some kind of finanical diffuliculty.[4] Espeical today ~~today thein~~ new york The way the city has fallen ~~has fallen~~ into fin—debt.[5] It has become such a big crisis for the ~~people~~ working people, in the [6] If the working man is able to find a job, espeicaly ~~for~~ ~~city~~ with the a city The way ~~the way~~ the city / fin— sitionu is set up now, ~~h~~ He'll probly lose the job a whole lot faster than what he got it.[7] When he loses his job he'll ~~p~~ have even more fin—difficulty.[8] And then he'll be force to ~~got~~ to the city for some fini—assi—.[9] So right here you can see that all men in America are not create equal in the fin—sense.[10]

References

Braddock, R., Lloyd-Jones, R., & Schoer, L. *Research in written composition.* Urbana, Ill.: National Council of Teachers of English, 1963.

Britton, J., Burgess, T., Martin, N., McLeod, A., & Rosen, H. *The development of writing abilities (11–18).* London: Macmillan Education Ltd., 1975.

Burton, D. L. Research in the teaching of English: The troubled dream. *Research in the Teaching of English,* 1973, 1, 160–187.

Cooper, C. R. Doing research/reading research. *English Journal,* 1974, 63, 94–99.

Cooper, C. R., & Odell, L. (Eds.) *Research on composing: Points of departure.* Urbana, Ill.: National Council of Teachers of English, 1978.

Emig, J. A. On teaching composition: Some hypotheses as definitions. *Research in the Teaching of English,* 1967, 1, 127–135.

Emig, J. A. *The composing processes of twelfth graders.* Urbana, Ill.: National Council of Teachers of English, 1971. (Research Report No. 13) [Ed. D. Dissertation, Harvard University, 1969).

Goodman, K. S. (Ed.) *Miscue analysis: Applications to reading instruction.* Urbana, Ill.: NCTE and ERIC, 1973.

Graves, D. H. Children's writing: Research directions and hypotheses based upon an examination of the writing process of seven year old children (Doctoral dissertation, State University of New York at Buffalo, 1973). *Dissertation Abstracts International,* 1974, 34, 6255A.

Haynes, E. F. Using research in preparing to teach writing. *English Journal,* 1978, 67, 82–89.

Mischel, T. A case study of a twelfth-grade writer. *Research in the Teaching of English,* 1974, 8, 303–314.

O'Hare, F. *Sentence-combining: Improving student writing without formal grammar instruction.* Urbana, Ill.: National Council of Teachers of English, 1973. (Research Report No. 15).

Perl, S. *Five writers writing: Case studies of the composing processes of unskilled college writers.* Unpublished doctoral dissertation, New York University, 1978.

Pianko, S. *The composing acts of college freshmen writers.* Unpublished Ed.D. dissertation, Rutgers University, 1977.

Shaughnessy, M. P. *Errors and expectations: A guide for the teacher of basic writing.* New York: Oxford University Press, 1977.

Stallard, C. K. An analysis of the writing behavior of good student writers. *Research in the Teaching of English,* 1974, *8,* 206–218.

Questions for Discussion and Journaling

1. Perl notes that Tony's writing process and resulting text were markedly different when he was writing about his own experience and when he was trying to write less personally. Describe this difference and explain whether it makes sense to you.

2. Why does Perl take it as such a positive sign that Tony and her other research participants' composing processes are "consistent" rather than scattered or random?

3. One of Perl's questions is whether writing processes can be analyzed in a "systematic, replicable" manner (para. 2). What do you think she means by those two terms?

4. Find the section of the article where Perl discusses how she developed her "code" of composing behaviors. What is your sense of how she put it together, and at what point in her research did she do so?

5. Build a list of reasons Perl is critical of previous writing-process research, and explain each of them. How well would you say her research here overcomes or eliminates those problems?

6. Do you think Perl's research methods might have actively shaped the writing her participants produced? That is, if she had changed the design of her study, is it possible she would have gotten different writing from her participants? Explain.

7. Perl appears not to count changes made while drafting sentence-by-sentence as "editing"; instead, she reserves that term for changes made between drafts. Why do you think she makes that distinction?

8. Do you see your own composing as "the carrying forward of an implicit sense into explicit form" (para. 60)? How so, and how not?

Applying and Exploring Ideas

1. Put together a list of the problems Tony had with composing and editing—for example, his tendency to say a sentence one way but write down something

else. As you review the list, do you see problems that you've had trouble with in the past, or any you still have trouble with? If so, how did you solve them—or what have you tried that hasn't worked? Discuss this question with one or more classmates: Have they encountered the problem of selective perception, for example? If so, how have they dealt with it?

2. Perl argues that it's a good thing when people don't wait to write until they know everything they want to say—rather, she wants writers to use the clarifying power of the act of writing itself to help them figure out what they want to say. To what extent does this strategy resemble your own writing process?

3. Perl was researching in a time before camcorders. Today, to do the same research, we would not only set up a camera (thus recording the participant's speech, behaviors, and writing activity simultaneously and in real time) but possibly also capture their keystrokes (assuming they composed at a computer) for a microscopically accurate record of exactly how the participant was writing. If you have a camcorder, try recording yourself or a volunteer while he or she writes, and then use the recording to help you devise a code to explain the processes you recorded. If that's not possible, consider: If you were doing Perl's study today, how would you design it to take advantage of current technology and your own ideas about the writing process? What kind of code would you devise to explain the activity that your technology recorded?

Meta Moment

Name one thing you now understand or will do differently after reading about Tony's process.

Decisions and Revisions:
The Planning Strategies of a Publishing Writer

CAROL BERKENKOTTER

and

Response of a Laboratory Rat—or, Being Protocoled

DONALD M. MURRAY

Berkenkotter, Carol. "Decisions and Revisions: The Planning Strategies of a Publishing Writer." *College Composition and Communication* 34.2 (1983): 156–69. Print.

Murray, Donald M. "Response of a Laboratory Rat—or, Being Protocoled." *College Composition and Communication* 34.2 (1983): 169–72. Print.

Framing the Readings

Sondra Perl, in her 1979 study of "unskilled college writers," used a "think-aloud" or "talk-aloud" protocol, a technique that at the time was very popular. This method solved a very basic problem of research on mental operations—that is, how we know what thoughts people are having that lead them to write certain things—by proposing the following simple solution: Have them talk while they think. Another aspect of Perl's design, a "laboratory" setting where students came to the researcher and wrote in response to specific prompts the researcher provided, was quite common in this time and style of research on writing processes. Most researchers publishing studies on writers' processes, including Carol Berkenkotter, author of one of the pieces you are about to read, used such methods.

But there are real problems with this kind of research, chief among them the artificiality of the setting and the writing tasks. In the following selection, you will read Berkenkotter's account of how she engaged a professional writer, Donald Murray, as a participant for a different kind of research, one that tried to keep the writer in his own context—normal surroundings, real projects—rather than bringing him into a lab.

Like Perl's article, then, Berkenkotter's has two focuses: a test of a particular methodology and a question about a particular aspect of composing—in this case, the revision process of a professional writer.

Berkenkotter and Murray did something else uncharacteristic of research on writing in the era: Murray was given the opportunity to write a reflection on the experience of being a research subject. his thoughts on what Berkenkotter's study found, and observations on the methodology. For this reason, we strongly recommend that you read the pieces back-to-back; the experience of reading Berkenkotter isn't complete without Murray's rejoinder and the interplay between the two pieces.

While you should pay close attention to any researcher's methods and context, the most interesting part of this article for you will likely be what you can learn about how a professional and award-winning writer goes about writing. His processes are odd, and you likely don't go about writing like he does. (Keep in mind that in 1981, when Berkenkotter and Murray undertook the study, cell phones, the Internet, and personal computers were not in widespread use. It was a very different time.) Pay close attention, though to how Murray invents things to say, how he learns from his writing, how he writes for his audience, and how he revises, and ask yourself what his writing gains from his complex planning, drafting, and revising.

Getting Ready to Read

Before you read, do at least one of the following activities:

- Take fifteen minutes and write in response to this prompt: "Explain death to an eleven-year-old." Then consider how it felt to write this. Was it easy? Hard? What did you wonder or think about while you were writing? Set this aside and come back to it after you have read this article.
- Consider whether you have any writing rituals. For example, do you have to have a cup of coffee while you write? Do you need to write on paper before typing? Do you have to take a nap or clean the house?

As you read, consider the following questions

- What discoveries do Berkenkotter and Murray make that contradict their expectations?
- What are strengths and weaknesses of this particular way of studying writing processes?
- What have you learned about writing from reading this article that you didn't know before?

Decisions and Revisions: The Planning Strategies of a Publishing Writer

CAROL BERKENKOTTER

The clearest memory I have of Donald M. Murray is watching him writing at a long white wooden table in his study, which looks out on the New Hampshire woods. Beside his desk is a large framed poster of a small boy sitting on a bed staring at a huge dragon leaning over the railing glowering at him. The poster is captioned, "Donald imagined things." And so he did, as he addressed the problems writers face each time they confront a new assignment. During the summer of 1981, as I listened to him daily recording his thoughts aloud as he worked on two articles, a short story, and an editorial, I came to understand in what ways each writer's processes are unique and why it is important that we pay close attention to the setting in which the writer composes, the kind of task the writer confronts, and what the writer can tell us of his own processes. If we are to understand *how* writers revise, we must pay close attention to the context in which revision occurs.

> If we are to understand *how* writers revise, we must pay close attention to the context in which revision occurs.

Janet Emig, citing Eliot Mishler, has recently described the tendency of writing research toward "context stripping."[1] When researchers remove writers from their natural settings (the study, the classroom, the office, the dormitory room, the library) to examine their thinking processes in the laboratory, they create "a context of a powerful sort, often deeply affecting what is being observed and assessed."[2] Emig's essay points to the need to examine critically the effects of these practices.

The subject of the present study is not anonymous, as are most subjects, nor will he remain silent. I began the investigation with a critical eye regarding what he has said about revision, he with an equally critical attitude toward methods of research on cognitive processes. To some extent our original positions have been confirmed—yet I think each of us, researcher and writer, has been forced to question our assumptions and examine our dogmas. More important, this project stirs the dust a bit and suggests a new direction for research on composing processes.

I met Mr. Murray at the Conference on College Composition and Communication meeting in Dallas, 1981. He appeared at the speaker's rostrum after my session and introduced himself, and we began to talk about the limitations of taking protocols in an experimental situation. On the spur of the moment I asked him if he would be willing to be the subject of a naturalistic study. He hesitated, took a deep breath, then said he was very interested in understanding his own composing processes, and would like to learn more. Out of that brief exchange a unique collaborative research venture was conceived.

To date there are no reported studies of writers composing in natural (as opposed to laboratory) settings that combine thinking-aloud protocols with the writers' own introspective accounts. Recently, researchers have been observing young children as they write in the classroom. In particular, we have seen the promising research of Donald Graves, Lucy Calkins, and Susan Sowers, who have worked intimately with children and their teachers in the Atkinson Schools Project.[3] By using video tapes and by actively working in the classroom as teachers and interviewers, these researchers were able to track the revising processes of individual children over a two-year period. Studies such as these suggest that there may be other ways of looking at writers' composing processes than in conventional research settings.

There remains, however, the question: to what extent can a writer's subjective testimony be trusted? I have shared the common distrust of such accounts.[4] There is considerable cognitive activity that writers cannot report because they are unable to compose and monitor their processes simultaneously. Researchers have responded to this problem by taking retrospective accounts from writers immediately after they have composed,[5] or have studied writers' cognitive activity through the use of thinking-aloud protocols.[6] These protocols have been examined to locate the thoughts verbalized by the subjects while composing, rather than for the subjects' analysis of what they said. Typically, subjects were instructed to "say everything that comes to mind no matter how random or crazy it seems. Do not analyze your thoughts, just say them aloud." The effect of these procedures, however, has been to separate the dancer from the dance, the subject from the process. Introspective accounts made *in medias res* have not been possible thus far because no one has developed techniques that would allow a subject to write and comment on his or her processes between composing episodes. For this reason I had begun to entertain the idea of asking a professional writer to engage in a lengthy naturalistic study. When Donald Murray introduced himself, I knew I wanted him to be the subject.

Methodology

The objectives that I began with are modifications of those Sondra Perl identified in her study of five unskilled writers.[7] I wanted to learn more about the planning and revising strategies of a highly skilled and verbal writer, to discover how these strategies could be most usefully analyzed, and to determine how an understanding of this writer's processes would contribute to what we have already discovered about how skilled writers plan and revise.

The project took place in three stages. From June 15th until August 15th, 1981 (a period of 62 days), Mr. Murray turned on the tape recorder when he entered his study in the morning and left it running during the day wherever he happened to be working: in his car waiting in parking lots, his university office, restaurants, the doctor's office, etc. This kind of thinking-aloud protocol differs from those taken by Linda Flower and John R. Hayes since the subject's composing time is not limited to a single hour; in fact, during the period of time that Mr. Murray was recording his thoughts, I accumulated over one hundred and twenty hours of tape. The writer also submitted photocopies of all text, including notes and drafts made prior to the study. Thus I was able to study a history of each draft.

In the second stage, during a visit to my university, I gave the writer a task 9 which specified audience, subject, and purpose. I asked him to think aloud on tape as he had previously, but this time for only one hour. Between the second and third stages, Mr. Murray and I maintained a dialogue on audiotapes which we mailed back and forth. On these tapes he compared his thoughts on his composing in his own environment over time to those on giving a one-hour protocol in a laboratory setting.

During the third stage of the study, I visited the writer at his home for two 10 days. At this time I observed him thinking aloud as he performed a writing task which involved revising an article for a professional journal. After two sessions of thinking aloud on tape for two and one-half hours, Mr. Murray answered questions concerning the decisions he had made. Over the two-day period we taped an additional four hours of questions and answers regarding the writer's perceptions of his activities.

Another coder and I independently coded the transcripts of the protocols 11 made in the naturalistic and laboratory settings. Using the same procedure I employed in my study of how writers considered their audience (i.e., first classifying and then counting all audience-related activities I could find in each protocol), my coder and I tallied all planning, revising, and editing activities, as well as global and local evaluations of text[8] that we agreed upon. I was particularly interested in Murray's editing activities. Having listened to the tapes I was aware that editing (i.e., reading the text aloud and making word- and sentence-level changes) sometimes led to major planning episodes, and I wanted to keep track of that sequence.

The study was not conducted without problems. The greatest of these arose 12 from how the writer's particular work habits affected the gathering of the data and how he responded to making a one-hour protocol. Unlike most writers who hand draft or type, Mr. Murray spends much time making copious notes in a daybook, then dictates his drafts and partial drafts to his wife, who is an accomplished typist and partner in his work. Later, he reads aloud and edits the drafts. If he determines that copy-editing (i.e., making stylistic changes in the text) is insufficient, he returns to the daybook, makes further notes, and prepares for the next dictation. The revision of one of the articles he was working on went through eight drafts before he sent it off. Two days later he sent the editor an insert.

Murray's distinctive work habits meant that all of the cognitive activity 13 occurring during the dictation that might ordinarily be captured in a protocol was lost since he processed information at a high speed. During these periods

I could not keep track of the content of his thoughts, and became concerned instead with the problem of why he frequently would find himself unable to continue dictating and end the session. There turned out to be considerable value in following the breakdowns of these dictations. I was able to distinguish between those occasions when Murray's composing was, in Janet Emig's terms, "extensive," and when it was "reflexive,"[9] by comparing the relative ease with which he developed an article from well-rehearsed material presented at workshops with the slow evolution of a conceptual piece he had not rehearsed. According to Emig, "The extensive mode . . . focuses upon the writer's conveying a message or communication to another. . . . the style is assured, impersonal, and often reportorial." In contrast, reflexive composing ". . . focuses on the writer's thoughts and feelings. . . . the style is tentative, personal, and exploratory."[10] In the latter case the writer is generating, testing, and evaluating new ideas, rather than reformulating old ones. I could observe the differences between the two modes of composing Emig describes, given Murray's response to the task in which he was engaged. When the writer was thoroughly familiar with his subject, he dictated with great fluency and ease. However, when he was breaking new ground conceptually, his pace slowed and his voice became halting; often the drafts broke down, forcing him to return to his daybook before attempting to dictate again.[11]

A more critical problem arose during the giving of the one-hour protocol.   14 At the time he came to my university, the writer had been working on tasks he had selected, talking into a tape recorder for two months in a familiar setting. Now he found himself in a strange room, with a specific writing task to perform in one short hour. This task was not simple; nor was it familiar. He was asked to "explain the concept of death to the ten- to twelve-year-old readers of *Jack and Jill* magazine." Under these circumstances, Murray clutched, producing two lines of text: "*Dear 11 year old. You're going to die. Sorry. Be seeing you. P. Muglump, Local Funeral Director.*" Both the transcript and later retrospective testimony of the writer indicated that he did not have pets as a child and his memories of death were not of the kind that could be described to an audience of ten- to twelve-year-old children. He also had difficulty forming a picture of his audience, since he suspected the actual audience was grandparents in Florida who send their children subscriptions to *Jack and Jill*. Toward the end of the hour, he was able to imagine a reader when he remembered the daughter of a man he had met the previous evening. The protocol, however, is rich with his efforts to create rhetorical context—he plotted repeated scenarios in which he would be asked to write such an article. Nevertheless, it seems reasonable to conclude that Mr. Murray was constrained by what Lester Faigley and Stephen Witte call "situational variables":[12] the knowledge that he had only one hour in which to complete a draft, his lack of familiarity with the format of *Jack and Jill* (he had never seen the magazine), his doubts that an audience actually existed, and finally, the wash of unhappy memories that the task gave rise to. "So important are these variables," Faigley and Witte contend, "that writing skill might be defined as the ability to respond to them."[13]

One final problem is intrinsic to the case study approach. Although the tapes   15
are rich in data regarding the affective conditions under which the writer composed (he was distracted by university problems, had to contend with numerous interruptions, encountered family difficulties that he had to resolve, not to
mention experiencing his own anxiety about his writing), as Murray reported,
the further away he was in time from what he had done, the less able he was to
reconstruct decisions he had made.

Results

Planning and Revising

In this study I was primarily concerned with the writer's planning, revising, and   16
editing activities. I had to develop a separate code category for the evaluation
of text or content, since the writer frequently stopped to evaluate what he had
written. Figure 1 indicates the percentage of coded activities devoted to planning, revising, and editing for three pieces of discourse.[14] These three pieces
were among the projects Murray worked on over the two-month period when
he was making the protocols.

The coded data (taken from the transcripts of the tapes he made during this   17
time) showed that up to 45%, 56%, and 35% of the writer's activities were
concerned with planning, 28%, 21%, and 18% with either global or local
evaluation, 3.0%, 3.0%, and .0% with revising (a finding which surprised me
greatly, and to which I shall return), and 24%, 20%, and 47% with editing.

Murray's planning activities were of two kinds: the first were the stating of   18
"process goals"—mentioning procedures, that is, that he developed in order to
write (e.g., "I'm going to make a list of titles and see where that gets me," or
"I'm going to try a different lead.").[15] Frequently, these procedures (or "thinking plans" as they are also called)[16] led the writer to generate a series of sub-
plans for carrying out the larger plan. The following excerpt is from the first
draft of an article on revision that Murray was writing for *The Journal of
Basic Writing*. He had been reading the manuscript aloud to himself and was
nearly ready to dictate a second draft. Suddenly he stopped, took his daybook
and began making copious notes for a list of examples he could use to make

	JOURNAL OF BASIC WRITING	COLLEGE COMPOSITION AND COMMUNICATION	EDITORIAL FOR CONCORD MONITOR
Planning	45%	56%	35%
Evaluating	28%	21%	18%
Revising	3.0%	3.0%	.0%
Editing	24%	20%	47%

Figure 1 Percentage of Coded Activities Devoted to Planning, Evaluating, Revising,
and Editing for Three Pieces of Discourse.

the point that the wise editor or teacher should at first ignore sentence-level editing problems to deal with more substantive issues of revision (this excerpt as well as those which follow are taken from the transcript of the tape and the photocopied text of the daybook):

> Let me take another piece of paper here. Questions, ah ... examples, and ah set up ... situation ... *frustration of writer. Cooks a five course dinner and gets response only to the table setting ... or to the way the napkins are folded* or to the ... *order of the forks.* All right. I can see from the material I have how that'll go. I'll weave in. Okay. *Distance in focus. Stand back. Read fast. Question writer.* Then *order doubles advocate. Then voice. Close in. Read aloud.* Okay, I got a number of different things I can see here that I'm getting to. I'm putting different order because that may be, try to emphasize this one. May want to put the techniques of editing and teaching first and the techniques of the writer second. So I got a one and a two to indicate that. [Italics identify words written down.]

In this instance we can see how a writing plan (taking a piece of paper and developing examples) leads to a number of sub-plans: "I'll weave in," "I'm putting in different order because that may be, try to emphasize this one," "May want to put the techniques of editing and teaching first and the techniques of the writer second," etc.

A second kind of planning activity was the stating of rhetorial goals, i.e., [19] planning how to reach an audience: "I'm making a note here, job not to explore the complexities of revision, but simply to show the reader how to do revision." Like many skilled writers, Murray had readers for his longer pieces. These readers were colleagues and friends whose judgment he trusted. Much of his planning activity as he revised his article for *College Composition and Communication* grew out of reading their responses to his initial draft and incorporating his summary of their comments directly onto the text. He then put away the text, and for the next several days made lists of titles, practiced leads, and made many outlines and diagrams in his daybook before dictating a draft. Through subsequent drafts he moved back and forth between the daybook and his edited dictations. He referred back to his readers' comments twice more between the first and last revised drafts, again summarizing their remarks in his notes in the daybook.

To say that Mr. Murray is an extensive planner does not really explain [20] the nature or scope of his revisions. I had initially developed code categories for revising activities; however, my coder and I discovered that we were for the most part double-coding for revising and planning, a sign the two activities were virtually inseparable. When the writer saw that major revision (as opposed to copy-editing) was necessary, he collapsed planning and revising into an activity that is best described as *reconceiving.* To "reconceive" is to scan and rescan one's text from the perspective of an external reader and to continue re-drafting until all rhetorical, formal, and stylistic concerns have been resolved, or until the writer decides to let go of the text. This process, which Nancy Sommers has described as the resolution of the dissonance the writer senses between his intention and the developing text,[17] can be seen in the following episode. The writer had been editing what he thought was a final draft when he saw that more substantive changes were in order. The flurry of editing activity was replaced by reading aloud and scanning the text as the writer realized that his language was inadequate for expressing a goal which he began to formulate as he read:

(reading from pervious page)[18] *It was E. B. While who reminded us, "Don't write about Man. Write about a man."* O.K. I'm going to cut that paragraph there . . . I've already said it. *The conferences when the teacher listens to the student can be short. When the teacher listens to the student in conference . . . when the teacher listens to the student* . . . the conference is, well, *the conference can be short. The student learns to speak first of what is most important to the student at the point.* To mention first what is most *important* . . . what most concerns . . . *the student* about the draft or the process that produced it. *The teacher listens . . . listens, reads the draft through the student's eyes then reads the draft, read or rereads . . . reads or* . . . scans or re-scans the draft to confirm, adjust, or compromise the student's concerns. *The range of student response includes the affective and the cognitive . . . It is the affective that usually controls the cognitive, and the affective responses usually have to be dealt with first* . . . (continues reading down the page) *Once the feelings of inadequacy, overconfidence, despair or elation are dealt with, then the conference teacher will find the other self speaking in more cognitive terms. And usually these comments* . . . O.K. that would now get the monitor into, into the phrase. All right. Put this crisscross cause clearly that page is going to be retyped . . . I'll be dictating so that's just a note. (continues reading on next page) *Listening to students allows the teacher to discover if the student's concerns were appropriate to where the student is in the writing process. The student, for example, is often excessively interested in language at the beginning of the process. Fragmentary language is normal before there is a text.* Make a comment on the text, (writes *intervention*) Now on page ten scanning . . . my God, I don't . . . I don't think I want to make this too much a conference piece. I'm going to echo back to that . . . monitor and also to the things I've said on page two and three. O.K. Let's see what I can do . . . The biggest question that I have is how much detail needs to be on conferences. I don't think they're, I don't think I can afford too much. Maybe some stronger sense of the response that ah . . . students make, how the other self speaks. They've got to get a sense of the other self speaking.

The next draft was totally rewritten following the sentence in the draft: 21 "When the teacher listens to the student, the conference can be short." The revision included previously unmentioned anecdotal reports of comments students had made in conferences, a discussion of the relevant implications of the research of Graves, Calkins, and Sowers, and a section on how the writing workshop can draw out the student's "other self" as other students model the idealized reader. This draft was nearly three pages longer than the preceding one. The only passage that remained was the final paragraph.

Granted that Mr. Murray's dictation frees him from the scribal constraints 22 that most writers face, how can we account for such global (i.e., whole text) revision? One answer lies in the simple, yet elegant, principle formulated by Linda Flower and John R. Hayes.[19] In the act of composing, writers move back and forth between planning, translating (putting thoughts into words), and reviewing their work. And as they do, they frequently "discover" major rhetorical goals.[20] In the episode just cited we have seen the writer shifting gears from editing to planning to reconceiving as he recognized something missing from the text and identified a major rhetorical goal—that he had to make the concept of the other self still more concrete for his audience: "They've got to get a sense of the other self speaking." In this same episode we can also see the cognitive basis for alterations in the macrostructure, or "gist," of a text, alterations Faigley and Witte report having found in examining the revised drafts of advanced student and expert adult writers.[21]

Planning and Incubation

This discussion of planning would be incomplete without some attention to the role of incubation. Michael Polanyi describes incubation as "that persistence of heuristic tension through . . . periods of time in which problems are not consciously entertained."[22] Graham Wallas and Alex Osborn agree that incubation involves unconscious activity that takes place after periods of intensive preparation.[23]   23

Given the chance to observe a writer's processes over time, we can see incubation at work. The flashes of discovery that follow periods of incubation (even brief ones) are unexpected, powerful, and catalytic, as the following episode demonstrates. Mr. Murray was revising an article on revision for the *Journal of Basic Writing*. He had begun to review his work by editing copy, moving to more global issues as he evaluated the draft: 24

> The second paragraph may be . . . Seems to me I've got an awful lot of stuff before I get into it. (Counting paragraphs) 1, 2, 3, 4, 5, 6, 7, 8, 9, 10, ten paragraphs till I really get into the text. Maybe twelve or thirteen. I'm not going to try to hustle it too much. That might be all right.

The writer then reread the first two paragraphs, making small editorial changes and considering stylistic choices. At that point he broke off and noted on the text three questions, "*What is the principle? What are the acts? How can it be taught?*" He reminded himself to keep his audience in mind. "The first audience has got to be the journal, and therefore, teachers." He took a five-minute break and returned to report,

> But, that's when I realized . . . the word hierarchy ah, came to me and that's when I realized that in a sense I was making this too complicated for myself and simply what I have to do is show the reader . . . I'm making a note here . . . *Job not to explore complexities of revision, but simply to show the reader how to do revision.*

From a revision of his goals for his audience, Murray moved quickly into planning activity, noting on his text,   25

Hierarchy of problems. O.K. What I'm dealing with is a hierarchy of problems. *First, focus/content, second, order/structure, third, language/voice* . . . O.K. Now, let's see. I need to ah, need to put that word, hierarchy in here somewhere. Well, that may get into the second paragraph so put an arrow down there (draws arrow from hierarchy to second paragraph), then see what we can do about the title if we need to. Think of things like 'first problems first' (a mini-plan which he immediately rejects). It won't make sense that title, unless you've read the piece. Ah well, come up with a new title.

Here we can observe the anatomy of a planning episode with a number of goals and sub-goals generated, considered, and consolidated at lightning speed: "O.K. What I'm dealing with is a hierarchy of problems." . . . "I need to ah, need to put that word, hierarchy in here somewhere." ". . . so put an arrow down there, then see what we can do about the title . . ." ". . . 'first problems first.' It won't make sense that title . . . Ah well, come up with a hew title." We can also see the writer's process of discovery at work as he left his draft for a brief period and returned having identified a single meaning-laden word. This word gave Murray an inkling of the structure he wanted for the article—a listing of the problems writers face before they can accomplish clear, effective revision. In this case, a short period of incubation was followed by a period of intense and highly concentrated planning when Murray realized the direction he wanted the article to take.

Introspection

One of the most helpful sources in this project was the testimony of the writer as he paused between or during composing episodes. Instead of falling silent, he analyzed his processes, providing information I might have otherwise missed. The following segments from the protocols will demonstrate the kinds of insights subjects can give when not constrained by time. At the time of the first, Mr. Murray had completed the tenth list of titles he had made between June 26th and July 23rd while working on the revision of his article for *College Composition and Communication*. Frequently, these lists were made recursively, the writer flipping back in his daybook to previous lists he had composed:

> I think I have to go back to titles. *Hearing the student's other self.* Hold my place and go back and see if I have any that hit me in the past. *Teaching the reader and the writer. Teaching the reader in the writer. Encouraging the internal dialogue.* I skipped something in my mind that I did not put down. *Make your students talk to themselves. Teaching the writer to read.*

At this point he stopped to evaluate his process:

> All that I'm doing is compressing, ah, compressing is, ah, why I do a title . . . it compresses a draft for the whole thing. Title gives me a point of view, gets the tone, the difference between teaching and teach. A lot of time on that, that's all right.

The following morning the writer reported, "While I was shaving, I thought of another title. *Teaching the other self: the writer's first reader.* I started to think of it as soon as I got up." This became the final title for the article and led to the planning of a new lead.

Later that day, after he had dictated three pages of the fourth of eight drafts, 29 he analyzed what he had accomplished:

> Well, I'm going to comment on what's happened here . . . this is a very complicated text. One of the things I'm considering, of course, is incorporating what I did in Dallas in here . . . ah, the text is breaking down in a constructive way, um, it's complex material and I'm having trouble with it . . . very much aware of pace of proportion; how much can you give to the reader in one part, and still keep them moving on to the next part. I have to give a little bit of head to teaching. . . . As a theatrical thing I am going to have to put some phrases in that indicate that I'm proposing or speculating, speculating as I revise this . . .

This last summation gave us important information on the writer's global 30 and local evaluation of text as well as on his rhetorical and stylistic plans. It is unique because it shows Murray engaged in composing and introspecting at the same time. Generally speaking, subjects giving protocols are not asked to add the demands of introspection to the task of writing. But, in fact, as Murray demonstrated, writers *do* monitor and introspect about their writing simultaneously.

Summary

Some of the more provocative findings of this study concern the sub-processes 31 of planning and revising that have not been observed in conventional protocols (such as those taken by Flower and Hayes) because of the time limitations under which they have been given. When coding the protocols, we noted that Mr. Murray developed intricate style goals:

> It worries me a little bit that the title is too imperative. When I first wrote, most of my articles were like this; they pound on the table, do this, do that. I want this to be a little more reflective.

He also evaluated his thinking plans (i.e., his procedures in planning): "Ah, reading through, ah, hmm . . . I'm just scanning it so I really can't read it. If I read it, it will be an entirely different thing."

Most important, the writer's protocols shed new light on the great and small 32 decisions and revisions that form planning. These decisions and revisions form an elaborate network of steps as the writer moves back and forth between planning, drafting, editing, and reviewing.[24] This recursive process was demonstrated time after time as the writer worked on the two articles and the editorial, often discarding his drafts as he reconceived a major rhetorical goal, and returned to the daybook to plan again. Further, given his characteristic habit of working from daybook to dictation, then back to daybook, we were able to observe that Donald Murray composes at the reflexive and extensive poles described by Janet Emig. When working from material he had "rehearsed" in recent workshops, material with which he was thoroughly familiar, he was able to dictate virtually off the top of his head. At other times he was unable to continue dictating as he attempted to hold too much in suspension in short-term memory. On these occasions the writer returned to the daybook and spent considerable time planning before dictating another draft.

One final observation: although it may be impolitic for the researcher to contradict the writer, Mr. Murray's activity over the summer while he was thinking aloud suggests that he is wrong in his assertion that writers only consider their audiences when doing external revision, i.e., editing and polishing. To the contrary, his most substantive changes, what he calls "internal revision," occurred as he turned his thoughts toward his audience. According to Murray, internal revision includes [33]

> everything writers do to discover and develop what they have to say, beginning with the reading of a completed first draft. They read to discover where their content, form, language, and voice have led them. They use language, structure, and information to find out what they have to say or hope to say. The audience is one person: the writer. [25]

The writer, however, does not speak in a vacuum. Only when he begins to discern what his readers do not yet know can he shape his language, structure, and information to fit the needs of those readers. It is also natural that a writer like Murray would not be aware of how significant a role his sense of audience played in his thoughts. After years of journalistic writing, his consideration of audience had become more automatic than deliberate. The value of thinking-aloud protocols is that they allow the researcher to eavesdrop at the workplace of the writer, catching the flow of thought that would remain otherwise unarticulated.

However, *how* the writer functions when working in the setting to which he or she is accustomed differs considerably from how that writer will function in an unfamiliar setting, given an unfamiliar task, and constrained by a time period over which he or she has no control. For this reason, I sought to combine the methodology of protocol analysis with the techniques of naturalistic inquiry. [34]

This project has been a first venture in what may be a new direction. Research on single subjects is new in our discipline; we need to bear in mind that each writer has his or her own idiosyncrasies. The researcher must make a trade-off, forgoing generalizability for the richness of the data and the qualitative insights to be gained from it. We need to replicate naturalistic studies of skilled and unskilled writers before we can begin to infer patterns that will allow us to understand the writing process in all of its complexity. [35]

Notes

1. Janet Emig, "Inquiry Paradigms and Writing," *College Composition and Communication,* 33 (February, 1982), p. 55.
2. Emig, "Inquiry Paradigms and Writing," p. 67.
3. Donald Graves, "What Children Show Us About Revision," *Language Arts,* 56 (March, 1979), 312–319; Susan Sowers, "A Six Year Old's Writing Process: The First Half of the First Grade,"

Language Arts, 56 (October, 1979), 829-835; Lucy M. Calkins, "Children Learn the Writer's Craft," *Language Arts*, 57 (February, 1980). 207–213.

4. Janet Emig. *The Composing Processes of Twelfth-Graders* (Urbana, IL: National Council of Teachers of English, 1971), pp. 8–11; Linda Flower and John R. Hayes, "A Cognitive Process Theory of Writing," *College Composition and Communication*, 32 (December, 1981), 368.

5. See Janet Emig, *The Composing Processes of Twelfth-Graders*, p. 30; Sondra Perl, "Five Writers Writing: Case Studies of the Composing Processes of Unskilled College Writers," Diss. New York University, 1978, pp. 48, 387–391; "The Composing Processes of Unskilled College Writers," *Research in the Teaching of English*, 13 (December, 1979), 318; Nancy I. Sommers, "Revision Strategies of Student Writers and Experienced Adult Writers," paper delivered at the Annual Meeting of the Modern Language Association, New York, 28 December, 1978. A slightly revised version was published in *College Composition and Communication*, 32 (December, 1980), 378–388.

6. See Linda Flower and John R. Hayes, "Identifying the Organization of Writing Processes," in *Cognitive Processes in Writing*, ed. Lee W. Gregg and Erwin R. Steinberg (Hillsdale, NJ: Lawrence Erlbaum Associates, 1981), p. 4; 'The Cognition of Discovery: Defining a Rhetorical Problem," *College Composition and Communication*, 32 (February, 1980), 23; "The Pregnant Pause: An Inquiry into the Nature of Planning," *Research in the Teaching of English*, 19 (October, 1981), 233; "A Cognitive Process Theory of Writing," p. 363; Carol Berkenkotter, "Understanding a Writer's Awareness of Audience," *College Composition and Communication*, 32 (December, 1981), 389.

7. Perl, "Five Writers Writing: Case Studies of the Composing Processes of Unskilled College Writers," p. 1.

8. Evaluations of text were either global or local. An example of global evaluation is when the writer says, "There's a lack of fullness in the piece." When the writer was evaluating locally he would comment, ". . . and the ending seems weak."

9. Emig, *The Composing Processes of Twelfth-Graders*, p. 4.

10. *Ibid.* See also "Eye, Hand, and Brain," in *Research on Composing: Points of Departure*, ed. Charles R. Cooper and Lee Odell (Urbana, IL: National Council of Teachers of English), p. 70. Emig raises the question, "What if it is the case that classical and contemporary rhetorical terms such as . . . extensive and reflexive may represent centuries old understandings that the mind deals differentially with different speaking and writing tasks. To put the matter declaratively, if hypothetically, modes of discourse may represent measurably different profiles of brain activity."

11. Janet Emig, observing her subject's writing processes, noted that "the *nature of the stimulus*" did not necessarily determine the response. Emig's students gave extensive responses to a reflexive task (*The Composing Processes of Twelfth-Graders*, pp. 30–31, 33). Similarly, Murray gave a reflexive response to an extensive task. Such a response is not unusual when we consider what the writer himself has observed: "The deeper we get into the writing process the more we may discover how affective concerns govern the cognitive, for writing is an intellectual activity carried on in an emotional environment, a precisely engineered sailboat trying to hold course in a vast and stormy Atlantic" ("Teaching the Other Self: The Writer's First Reader," *College Composition and Communication*, 33 [May, 1982], p. 142). For a writer as deeply engaged in his work as Murray, drafting a conceptual piece was as personal and subjective as describing a closely felt experience.

12. Lester Faigley and Stephen Witte, "Analyzing Revision," *College Composition and Communication*, 32 (December, 1981), 410–411.

13. Faigley and Witte, p. 411.

14. These three pieces of discourse were chosen because their results are representative of the writer's activities.

15. Linda Flower and John R, Hayes describe "process goals" as "instructions and plans the writer gives herself for directing her own composing process." See "The Pregnant Pause: An Inquiry Into the Nature of Planning," p. 242. However, this definition is not always agreed upon by cognitive psychologists studying problem-solvers in other fields. On one hand, Allen Newell, Herbert A. Simon, and John R. Hayes distinguish between the goals and plans of a problem-solver, considering a goal as an end to be achieved and a plan as one kind of method for reaching

that end. See John R. Hayes, *Cognitive Psychology* (Homewood, IL: The Dorsey Press, 1978), p. 192; Allen Newell and Herbert A. Simon, *Human Problem Solving* (Englewood Cliffs, NJ: Prentice-Hall, Inc. 1972), pp. 88–92, 428–429. On the other hand, George Miller, Eugene Galanter, and Karl H. Pribram use the term "plan" inclusively, suggesting that a plan is "any hierarchical process in the organism that can control the order in which a sequence of operations is to be performed." See *Plans and the Structure of Human Behavior* (New York: Holt, Rinehart, and Winston, Inc., 1960), p. 16.

16. Flower and Hayes use these terms interchangeably, as have I. "Thinking plans" are plans for text that precede drafting and occur during drafting. Thinking plans occur before the movements of a writer's hand. Because of the complexity of the composing process, it is difficult to separate thinking plans from "process goals." It is possible, however, to distinguish between *rhetorical goals and rhetorical plans.* Murray was setting a goal when he remarked, "The biggest thing is to . . . what I've got to get to satisfy the reader . . . is that point of what do we hear the other self saying and how does it help?" He followed this goal with a plan to "Probe into the other self. What is the other self? How does it function?"

17. Sommers, "Revision Strategies," pp. 385, 387. (See note 5, above.)
18. The material italicized in the excerpts from these transcripts is text the subject is writing. The material italicized and underlined is text the subject is reading that has already been written.
19. Flower and Hayes, "A Cognitive Process Theory of Writing," 365–387.
20. Berkenkotter, "Understanding a Writer's Awareness of Audience," pp. 392, 395.
21. Faigley and Witte, pp. 406–410.
22. Michael Polanyi, *Personal Knowledge: Toward a Post-Critical Philosophy* (Chicago: The University of Chicago Press, 1958), p. 122.
23. Graham Wallas, *The Art of Thought* (New York: Jonathan Cape, 1926), pp. 85–88; Alex Osborn, *Applied Imagination: Principles and Procedures of Creative Problem-Solving,* 3rd rev. ed. (New York: Charles F. Scribner and Sons), pp. 314–325.
24. For a description of the development of a writer's goal structure, see Flower and Hayes, "A Cognitive Process Theory of Writing."
25. Donald M. Murray, "Internal Revision: A Process of Discovery," *Research on Composing: Points of Departure* (See note 10), p. 91.

Response of a Laboratory Rat— or, Being Protocoled

DONALD M. MURRAY

1.

First a note on self-exposure, a misdemeanor in most communities. I have long felt the academic world is too closed. We have an ethical obligation to write and to reveal our writing to our students if we are asking them to share their writing with us. I have felt writers should, instead of public readings, give public workshops in which they write in public, allowing the search for meaning to be seen. I've done this and found the process insightful—and fun.

I have also been fascinated by protocol analysis research. It did seem a fruitful way (a way, there is no one way) to study the writing process. I was, however, critical of the assignments I had seen given, the concentration on inexperienced students as subjects, and the unrealistic laboratory conditions and time limitations.

And, in the absence of more proper academic resources, I have made a career of 3
studying myself while writing. I was already without shame. When Carol Berkenkotter asked me to run in her maze I gulped, but I did not think I could refuse.

2.

The one-hour protocol was far worse than I had expected. If I had done that 4
first there would have been no other protocols. I have rarely felt so completely
trapped and so inadequate. I have gone through other research experiences, but
in this case I felt stronger than I ever had the need to perform. That was nothing that the researcher did. It was a matter of the conditions. I had a desperate
desire to please. I thought of that laboratory experiment where subjects would
push a button to cause pain to other people. I would have blown up Manhattan
to get out of that room. To find equivalent feelings from my past I would have to
go back to combat or to public school. I have developed an enormous compassion and respect for those who have performed for Masters and Johnson.

3.

The process of a naturalistic study we have evolved (Can a rat be a colleague? 5
Since a colleague can be a rat, I don't see why not.) soon became a natural process. I do not assume, and neither did my researcher, that what I said reflected
all that was taking place. It did reflect what I was conscious of doing, and a bit
more. My articulation was an accurate reflection of the kind of talking I do to
myself while planning to write, while writing, and while revising. At no time
did it seem awkward or unnatural. My talking aloud was merely a question of
turning up the volume knob on the muttering I do under my breath as I write.

I feel that if there was any self-consciousness in the process it was helpful. I 6
was, after all, practicing a craft, not performing magic. Writing is an intellectual activity, and I do not agree with the
romantics who feel that the act of writing and the act of thinking are separate.

> Writing is an intellectual activity,
> and I do not agree with the 7
> romantics who feel that the act of
> writing and the act of thinking are
> separate.

Having this researcher, who had
earned my trust, waiting to see what I
wrote was a motivating factor. While
the experiment was going on she was
appropriately chilly and doctoral. But I
still knew someone was listening, and I
suspect that got me to the writing desk
some days.

It is certainly true that debriefing by the researcher at some distance from 8
the time of writing was virtually useless. I could not remember why I had done
what. In fact, the researcher knows the text better than I do. I am concentrating almost entirely on the daily evolving text, and yesterday's page seems like
last year's. I intend to try some teaching experiments in the future that make it
possible for me to be on the scene when my students are writing. I'm a bit more

suspicious now than I had been about the accounts that are reconstructed in a conference days after writing. They are helpful, the best teaching point I know, but I want to find out what happens if we can bring the composing and the teaching closer together.

4.

I certainly agree with what my researcher calls introspection. I am disappointed, however, that she hasn't included the term that I overheard the coders use. Rats aren't all that dumb, and I think there should be further research into those moments when I left the desk and came back with a new insight. They called them: "Bathroom epiphanies."   9

5.

I was surprised by: 10

1. The percentage of my time devoted to planning. I had realized the pendulum was swinging in that direction, but I had no idea how far it had swung. I suspect that when we begin to write in a new genre we have to do a great deal of revision, but that as we become familiar with a genre we can solve more writing problems in advance of a completed text. This varies according to the writer but I have already changed some of my teaching to take this finding into account by allowing my students much more planning time and introducing many more planning techniques.
2. The length of incubation time. I now realize that articles that I thought took a year in fact have taken three, four, or five years.
3. The amount of revision that is essentially planning, what the researcher calls "reconceiving." I was trying to get at that in my chapter, "Internal Revision: A Process of Discovery," published in *Research on Composing: Points of Departure,* edited by Charles R. Cooper and Lee Odell. I now understand this process far better, and much of my revision is certainly a planning or prewriting activity.

6.

I agree with my researcher (what rat wouldn't?) that affective conditions are important in writing. I do think the affective often controls the cognitive, and I feel strongly that much more research has to be done, difficult as it may be, into those conditions, internal and external, that make effective writing possible or impossible.   11

7.

I was far more aware of audience than I thought I was during some of the writing. My sense of audience is so strong that I have to suppress my conscious awareness of audience to hear what the text demands.   12

Related to this is the fact that I do need a few readers. The important role 13
of my pre-publication readers was clear when my revisions were studied. No
surprise here. I think we need more study of the two, or three, or four readers professional writers choose for their work in process. It would be helpful
for us as teachers to know the qualities of these people and what they do for
the writer. I know I choose people who make me want to write when I leave
them.

8.

I worry a bit about the patterns that this research revealed have been laid down 14
in my long-term memory. The more helpful they are the more I worry about
them. I fear that what I discover when I write is what I have discovered before
and forgotten, and that rather than doing the writing that must be done I
merely follow the stereotypes of the past. In other words, I worry that the experienced writer can become too glib, too slick, too professional, too polished—
can, in effect, write too well.

9.

The description of working back and forth from the global to the particular 15
during the subprocesses of planning and revising seems accurate to me.

There is a great deal of interesting research and speculation about this pro- 16
cess, but we need much more. I find it very difficult to make my students aware
of the layers of concern through which the writing writer must oscillate at such
a speed that it appears the concerns are dealt with instantaneously.

Too often in my teaching and my publishing I have given the false impres- 17
sion that we do one thing, then another, when in fact we do many things simultaneously. And the interaction between these things is what we call writing.
This project reaffirmed what I had known, that there are many simultaneous
levels of concern that bear on every line.

10.

I realize how eccentric my work habits appear. I am aware of how fortunate 18
I am to be able to work with my wife. The process of dictation of non-fiction
allows a flow, intensity, and productivity that is quite unusual. It allows me to
spend a great deal of time planning, because I know that once the planning is
done I can produce copy in short bursts. It is not my problem but the researcher's, however, to put my eccentric habits into context.

If I am the first writer to be naked, then it is up to those other writers who 19
do not think they look the same to take off their clothes. I hope they do not
appear as I do; I would be most depressed if I am the model for other writers.
I hope, and I believe, that there must be a glorious diversity among writers.
What I think we have done, as rat and ratee, is to demonstrate that there is
a process through which experienced writers can be studied under normal

working conditions on typical writing projects. I think my contribution is not to reveal my own writing habits but to show a way that we can study writers who are far better writers than I.

11.

Finally, I started this process with a researcher and have ended it with a col-　20
league. I am grateful for the humane way the research was conducted. I have learned a great deal about research and about what we have researched. It has helped me in my thinking, my teaching, and my writing. I am grateful to Dr. Carol Berkenkotter for this opportunity.

Questions for Discussion and Journaling

1. What was your impression of Murray's writing processes as they're described here? How do they compare to yours? What do you do the same or differently?

2. Murray's relationship with his audience seems complicated. Try to describe it, and then compare it to your own sense of audience: How much are *you* thinking about *your* audience while you write?

3. How did this study change Berkenkotter's understanding of writing processes, particularly planning and revision?

4. What problems with existing methods for studying writing process does Berkenkotter identify? If you read Perl, did you notice any of these problems in her methods? What do you think they might mean for Perl's findings? In what ways is Berkenkotter's newer approach to studying writing processes able to solve the weaknesses in other methods? Do any weaknesses remain?

5. Why do you suppose Berkenkotter often refers to Murray as "the writer" and in his response Murray calls Berkenkotter "the researcher"? Why not just use each other's names, since the audience knows them anyway?

6. What do you think of the apparent back-and-forth between the researcher and researched that occurred as Berkenkotter analyzed her data and drew conclusions? Was it good? Bad? Necessary? Irrelevant? Did anything about it surprise you?

Applying and Exploring Ideas

1. Less-experienced writers, especially when writing for school, tend to spend comparatively little time on revision (by which we mean *developing the ideas* in a piece rather than **editing,** which is the sentence-level work that improves the style and correctness of a text). Explore your own writing habits: How do you spend your writing time? How would you characterize your level of writing

experience? How do you think your level of experience relates to the amount of time you spend on various parts of the writing process? In making these estimates, keep the following in mind: Murray, a highly professional and quite reflective writer, had an erroneous impression of how much time he spent on various aspects of his writing process.

2. Begin a writing log in which you list all the writing situations you find yourself in on a day-to-day basis: Every time you write over two weeks, note what you write, the audience for that writing, the genre, the technologies employed, and the skills used. At the end of the period, reflect on what you learned about your writing habits.

3. Try your own brief experiment, re-creating Berkenkotter and Murray's dynamic: Pair with a class partner and designate one of you as researcher and the other as researched. Have the researcher observe the researched's writing process on a short (approximately one-page) piece of writing, and then have the researcher write a brief description of that process while the researched writes a piece of similar length on the experience of doing the writing. Compare these descriptions, and negotiate the findings: What, put together, do the two accounts reveal about the writer's process?

Meta Moment

Name one thing you learned from the Berkenkotter and Murray readings that you could use to help you write more effectively.

Rigid Rules, Inflexible Plans, and the Stifling of Language:
A Cognitivist Analysis of Writer's Block

MIKE ROSE

Rose, Mike. "Rigid Rules, Inflexible Plans, and the Stifling of Language: A Cognitivist Analysis of Writer's Block." *College Composition and Communication* 31.4 (1980): 389–401. Print.

Framing the Reading

All of the readings in this chapter focus on aspects of how writers compose—that is, how they walk through the process of actually producing a text, from coming up with ideas for it to finalizing the piece. Some selections pay more attention to elements or functions of composing (like planning, prewriting, drafting, and revising); others focus on the **constraints** and rules—audiences, situations, grammar rules—that writers must navigate. Mike Rose's study of writer's block brings these elements together by asking what's happening when writers are literally incapable of writing the next sentence.

Rose's career has been one of studying, teaching, and helping writers who have a difficult time writing. At the time Rose wrote this article, the dominant approach to understanding writing problems was to consider them to be *thinking* problems— problems of **cognition**, or mental operation. If we could understand how writers *think*, how their brains process information, the theory was, we would be able to teach writing more effectively because we could understand and teach the mental operations that lead to good writing.

Some proponents of cognitive analysis seemed to want to reduce human thinking to machine processing. They ignored everything going on *outside* a writer's head—that is, the **rhetorical situation** and **context**—and assumed that situation had nothing to do with the rules by which brains process information and thus generate writing. Like other critics of this position, Rose suspected that other rules—cultural rules, school rules—might need more study and critique. Trained in psychological counseling, he applied a different set of cognitivist ideas to this problem of cultural rules and their negative effect on some people's writing. You'll read the results in this article.

It's worth noting that writer's block is a technical term that we tend to overuse. In the same way that anyone who finds focusing for more than ten seconds difficult is likely to claim they have "ADHD" when in fact few people really do, too many writers who can't think of what to say next are likely to claim, jokingly or seriously, that they have "writer's block." Rose is talking about a rarer, more serious problem.

Getting Ready to Read

Before you read, do at least one of the following activities:

- Quickly make a list of rules that seem to always be in your mind when you are writing for school.
- Make a short list of things that make it hard for you to write.
- Write one paragraph about a person or event that negatively impacted your ability to write.

As you read, consider the following questions:

- What kinds of rules seem to keep people from writing, and what kinds of rules seem to enable people to write?
- What are the relationships among **heuristics**, plans, rules, algorithms, set, and perplexity?
- Where do you see yourself, if anywhere, among the various writers Rose describes?

Ruth will labor over the first paragraph of an essay for hours. She'll write a 1 sentence, then erase it. Try another, then scratch part of it out. Finally, as the evening winds on toward ten o'clock and Ruth, anxious about tomorrow's deadline, begins to wind into herself, she'll compose that first paragraph only to sit back and level her favorite exasperated interdiction at herself and her page: "No. You can't say that. You'll bore them to death."

Ruth is one of ten UCLA undergraduates with whom I discussed writer's 2 block, that frustrating, self-defeating inability to generate the next line, the right phrase, the sentence that will release the flow of words once again. These ten people represented a fair cross-section of the UCLA student community: lower-middle-class to upper-middle-class backgrounds and high schools, third-world and Caucasian origins, biology to fine arts majors, C+ to A− grade point averages, enthusiastic to blasé attitudes toward school. They were set off from the community by the twin facts that all ten could write competently, and all were currently enrolled in at least one course that required a significant amount of writing. They were set off among themselves by the fact that five of them wrote with relative to enviable ease while the other five experienced moderate to nearly immobilizing writer's block. This blocking usually resulted in rushed, often late papers and resultant grades that did not truly reflect these students' writing ability. And then, of course, there were other less measurable but probably more serious results: a growing distrust of their abilities and an aversion toward the composing process itself.

What separated the five students who blocked from those who didn't? It 3 wasn't skill; that was held fairly constant. The answer could have rested in the emotional realm—anxiety, fear of evaluation, insecurity, etc. Or perhaps blocking in some way resulted from variation in cognitive style. Perhaps, too, blocking originated in and typified a melding of emotion and cognition not unlike the relationship posited by Shapiro between neurotic feeling and neurotic thinking.[1] Each of these was possible. Extended clinical interviews and testing could have teased out the answer. But there was one answer that surfaced readily in brief explorations of these students' writing processes. It was not profoundly emotional, nor was it embedded in that still unclear construct of cognitive style. It was constant, surprising, almost amusing if its results weren't so troublesome, and, in the final analysis, obvious: the five students who experienced blocking were all operating either with writing rules or with planning strategies that impeded rather than enhanced the composing process. The five students who were not hampered by writer's block also utilized rules, but they were less rigid ones, and thus more appropriate to a complex process like writing. Also, the plans these non-blockers brought to the writing process were more functional, more flexible, more open to information from the outside.

It was constant, surprising, almost amusing if its results weren't so troublesome, and, in the final analysis, obvious: the five students who experienced blocking were all operating either with writing rules or with planning strategies that impeded rather than enhanced the composing process.

These observations are the result of one to three interviews with each stu- 4 dent. I used recent notes, drafts, and finished compositions to direct and hone my questions. This procedure is admittedly non-experimental, certainly more clinical than scientific; still, it did lead to several inferences that lay the foundation for future, more rigorous investigation: (a) composing is a highly complex problem-solving process[2] and (b) certain disruptions of that process can be explained with cognitive psychology's problem-solving framework. Such investigation might include a study using "stimulated recall" techniques to validate or disconfirm these hunches. In such a study, blockers and non-blockers would write essays. Their activity would be videotaped and, immediately after writing, they would be shown their respective tapes and questioned about the rules, plans, and beliefs operating in their writing behavior. This procedure would bring us close to the composing process (the writers' recall is stimulated by their viewing the tape), yet would not interfere with actual composing.

In the next section I will introduce several key concepts in the problem- 5 solving literature. In section three I will let the students speak for themselves.

Fourth, I will offer a cognitivist analysis of blockers' and non-blockers' grace or torpor. I will close with a brief note on treatment.

Selected Concepts in Problem Solving: Rules and Plans

As diverse as theories of problem solving are, they share certain basic assumptions and characteristics. Each posits an *introductory period* during which a problem is presented, and all theorists, from Behaviorist to Gestalt to Information Processing, admit that certain aspects, stimuli, or "functions" of the problem must become or be made salient and attended to in certain ways if successful problem-solving processes are to be engaged. Theorists also believe that some conflict, some stress, some gap in information in these perceived "aspects" seems to trigger problem-solving behavior. Next comes a *processing period*, and for all the variance of opinion about this critical stage, theorists recognize the necessity of its existence—recognize that man, at the least, somehow "weighs" possible solutions as they are stumbled upon and, at the most, goes through an elaborate and sophisticated information-processing routine to achieve problem solution. Furthermore, theorists believe—to varying degrees— that past learning and the particular "set," direction, or orientation that the problem solver takes in dealing with past experience and present stimuli have critical bearing on the efficacy of solution. Finally, all theorists admit to a *solution period*, an end-state of the process where "stress" and "search" terminate, an answer is attained, and a sense of completion or "closure" is experienced. 6

These are the gross similarities, and the framework they offer will be useful in understanding the problem-solving behavior of the students discussed in this paper. But since this paper is primarily concerned with the second stage of problem-solving operations, it would be most useful to focus this introduction on two critical constructs in the processing period: rules and plans. 7

Rules

Robert M. Gagné defines "rule" as "an inferred capability that enables the individual to respond to a class of stimulus situations with a class of performances."[3] Rules can be learned directly[4] or by inference through experience.[5] But, in either case, most problem-solving theorists would affirm Gagné's dictum that "rules are probably the major organizing factor, and quite possibly the primary one, in intellectual functioning."[6] As Gagné implies, we wouldn't be able to function without rules; they guide response to the myriad stimuli that confront us daily, and might even be the central element in complex problem-solving behavior. 8

Dunker, Polya, and Miller, Galanter, and Pribram offer a very useful distinction between two general kinds of rules: algorithms and heuristics.[7] Algorithms are precise rules that will always result in a specific answer if applied to an appropriate problem. Most mathematical rules, for example, are algorithms. Functions are constant (e.g., pi), procedures are routine (squaring the radius), and outcomes are completely predictable. However, few day-to-day 9 situations are mathematically circumscribed enough to warrant the application of algorithms. Most often we function with the aid of fairly general heuristics or "rules of thumb," guidelines that allow varying degrees of flexibility when approaching problems. Rather than operating with algorithmic precision and certainty, we search, critically, through alternatives, using our heuristic as a divining rod—"if a math problem stumps you, try working backwards to solution"; "if the car won't start, check x, y, or z," and so forth. Heuristics won't allow the precision or the certitude afforded by algorithmic operations; heuristics can even be so "loose" as to be vague. But in a world where tasks and problems are rarely mathematically precise, heuristic rules become the most appropriate, the most functional rules available to us: "a heuristic does not guarantee the optimal solution or, indeed, any solution at all; rather, heuristics offer solutions that are good enough most of the time."[8]

Plans

People don't proceed through problem situations, in or out of a laboratory, [10] without some set of internalized instructions to the self, some program, some course of action that, even roughly, takes goals and possible paths to that goal into consideration. Miller, Galanter, and Pribram have referred to this course of action as a plan: "A plan is any hierarchical process in the organism that can control the order in which a sequence of operations is to be performed" (p. 16). They name the fundamental plan in human problem-solving behavior the TOTE, with the initial T representing a *test* that matches a possible solution against the perceived end-goal of problem completion. O represents the clearance to *operate* if the comparison between solution and goal indicates that the solution is a sensible one. The second T represents a further, post-operation, *test* or comparison of solution with goal, and if the two mesh and problem solution is at hand the person *exits* (E) from problem-solving behavior. If the second test presents further discordance between solution and goal, a further solution is attempted in TOTE-fashion. Such plans can be both long-term and global and, as problem solving is underway, short-term and immediate.[9] Though the mechanicality of this information-processing model renders it simplistic and, possibly, unreal, the central notion of a plan and an operating procedure is an important one in problem-solving theory; it at least attempts to metaphorically explain what earlier cognitive psychologists could not—the mental procedures underlying problem-solving behavior.

Before concluding this section, a distinction between heuristic rules and [11] plans should be attempted; it is a distinction often blurred in the literature, blurred because, after all, we are very much in the area of gestating theory and preliminary models. Heuristic rules seem to function with the flexibility of plans. Is, for example, "If the car won't start, try x, y, or z" a heuristic or a plan? It could be either, though two qualifications will mark it as heuristic rather than plan. (A) Plans subsume and sequence heuristic and algorithmic rules. Rules are usually "smaller," more discrete cognitive capabilities; plans can become quite large and complex, composed of a series of ordered algorithms, heuristics, and further planning "sub-routines." (B) Plans, as was mentioned earlier, include criteria to determine successful goal-attainment and, as well, include "feedback" processes—ways to incorporate and use information gained from "tests" of potential solutions against desired goals.

One other distinction should be made: that is, between "set" and plan. Set, also called "determining tendency" or "readiness,"[10] refers to the fact that people often approach problems with habitual ways of reacting, a predisposition, a tendency to perceive or function in one way rather than another. Set, which can be established through instructions or, consciously or unconsciously, through experience, can assist performance if it is appropriate to a specific problem,[11] but much of the literature on set has shown its rigidifying, dysfunctional effects.[12] Set differs from plan in that set represents a limiting and narrowing of response alternatives with no inherent process to shift alternatives. It is a kind of cognitive habit that can limit perception, not a course of action with multiple paths that directs and sequences response possibilities.

The constructs of rules and plans advance the understanding of problem solving beyond that possible with earlier, less developed formulations. Still, critical problems remain. Though mathematical and computer models move one toward more complex (and thus more real) problems than the earlier research, they are still too neat, too rigidly sequenced to approximate the stunning complexity of day-to-day (not to mention highly creative) problem-solving behavior. Also, information-processing models of problem-solving are built on logic theorems, chess strategies, and simple planning tasks. Even Gagné seems to feel more comfortable with illustrations from mathematics and science rather than with social science and humanities problems. So although these complex models and constructs tell us a good deal about problem-solving behavior, they are still laboratory simulations, still invoked from the outside rather than self-generated, and still founded on the mathematico-logical.

Two Carnegie Mellon researchers, however, have recently extended the above into a truly real, amorphous, unmathematical problem-solving process—writing. Relying on protocol analysis (thinking aloud while solving problems), Linda Flower and John Hayes have attempted to tease out the role of heuristic rules and plans in writing behavior.[13] Their research pushes problem-solving investigations to the real and complex and pushes, from the other end, the often mysterious process of writing toward the explainable. The latter is important, for at least since Plotinus many have viewed the composing process as unexplainable, inspired, infused with the transcendent. But Flower and Hayes are beginning, anyway, to show how writing generates from a problem-solving process with rich heuristic rules and plans of its own. They show, as well, how many writing problems arise from a paucity of heuristics and suggest an intervention that provides such rules.

This paper, too, treats writing as a problem-solving process, focusing, however, on what happens when the process dead-ends in writer's block. It will further suggest that, as opposed to Flower and Hayes' students who need more rules and plans, blockers may well be stymied by possessing rigid or inappropriate rules, or inflexible or confused plans. Ironically enough, these are occasionally instilled by the composition teacher or gleaned from the writing textbook.

"Always Grab Your Audience"—The Blockers

In high school, *Ruth* was told and told again that a good essay always grabs 16 a reader's attention immediately. Until you can make your essay do that, her teachers and textbooks putatively declaimed, there is no need to go on. For Ruth, this means that beginning bland and seeing what emerges as one generates prose is unacceptable. The beginning is everything. And what exactly is the audience seeking that reads this beginning? The rule, or Ruth's use of it, doesn't provide for such investigation. She has an edict with no determiners. Ruth operates with another rule that restricts her productions as well: if sentences aren't grammatically "correct," they aren't useful. This keeps Ruth from toying with ideas on paper, from the kind of linguistic play that often frees up the flow of prose. These two rules converge in a way that pretty effectively restricts Ruth's composing process.

The first two papers I received from *Laurel* were weeks overdue. Sections 17 of them were well written; there were even moments of stylistic flair. But the papers were late and, overall, the prose seemed rushed. Furthermore, one paper included a paragraph on an issue that was never mentioned in the topic paragraph. This was the kind of mistake that someone with Laurel's apparent ability doesn't make. I asked her about this irrelevant passage. She knew very well that it didn't fit, but believed she had to include it to round out the paper, "You must always make three or more points in an essay. If the essay has less, then it's not strong." Laurel had been taught this rule both in high school and in her first college English class; no wonder, then, that she accepted its validity.

As opposed to Laurel, *Martha* possesses a whole arsenal of plans and rules 18 with which to approach a humanities writing assignment, and, considering her background in biology, I wonder how many of them were formed out of the assumptions and procedures endemic to the physical sciences.[14] Martha will not put pen to first draft until she has spent up to two days generating an outline of remarkable complexity. I saw one of these outlines and it looked more like a diagram of protein synthesis or DNA structure than the time-worn pattern offered in composition textbooks. I must admit I was intrigued by the aura of process (vs. the static appearance of essay outlines) such diagrams offer, but for Martha these "outlines" only led to self-defeat: the outline would become so complex that all of its elements could never be included in a short essay. In other words, her plan locked her into the first stage of the composing process. Martha would struggle with the conversion of her outline into prose only to scrap the whole venture when deadlines passed and a paper had to be rushed together.

Martha's "rage for order" extends beyond the outlining process. She also 19 believes that elements of a story or poem must evince a fairly linear structure and thematic clarity, or—perhaps bringing us closer to the issue—that analysis of a story or poem must provide the linearity or clarity that seems to be absent in the text. Martha, therefore, will bend the logic of her analysis to reason ambiguity out of existence. When I asked her about a strained paragraph in her paper on Camus' "The Guest," she said, "I didn't want to admit that it [the story's conclusion] was just hanging. I tried to force it into meaning."

Martha uses another rule, one that is not only problematical in itself, but   20
one that often clashes directly with the elaborate plan and obsessive rule above. She believes that humanities papers must scintillate with insight, must present an array of images, ideas, ironies gleaned from the literature under examination. A problem arises, of course, when Martha tries to incorporate her myriad "neat little things," often inherently unrelated, into a tightly structured, carefully sequenced essay. Plans and rules that govern the construction of impressionistic, associational prose would be appropriate to Martha's desire, but her composing process is heavily constrained by the non-impressionistic and non-associational. Put another way, the plans and rules that govern her exploration of text are not at all synchronous with the plans and rules she uses to discuss her exploration. It is interesting to note here, however, that as recently as three years ago Martha was absorbed in creative writing and was publishing poetry in high school magazines. Given what we know about the complex associational, often non-neatly-sequential nature of the poet's creative process, we can infer that Martha was either free of the plans and rules discussed earlier or they were not as intense. One wonders, as well, if the exposure to three years of university physical science either established or intensified Martha's concern with structure. Whatever the case, she now is hamstrung by conflicting rules when composing papers for the humanities.

Mike's difficulties, too, are rooted in a distortion of the problem-solving   21
process. When the time of the week for the assignment of writing topics draws near, Mike begins to prepare material, strategies, and plans that he believes will be appropriate. If the assignment matches his expectations, he has done a good job of analyzing the professor's intentions. If the assignment *doesn't* match his expectations, however, he cannot easily shift approaches. He feels trapped inside his original plans, cannot generate alternatives, and blocks. As the deadline draws near, he will write something, forcing the assignment to fit his conceptual procrustian bed. Since Mike is a smart man, he will offer a good deal of information, but only some of it ends up being appropriate to the assignment. This entire situation is made all the worse when the time between assignment of topic and generation of product is attenuated further, as in an essay examination. Mike believes (correctly) that one must have a plan, a strategy of some sort in order to solve a problem. He further believes, however, that such a plan, once formulated, becomes an exact structural and substantive blueprint that cannot be violated. The plan offers no alternatives, no "subroutines." So, whereas Ruth's, Laurel's, and some of Martha's difficulties seem to be rule-specific ("always catch your audience," "write grammatically"), Mike's troubles are more global. He may have strategies that are appropriate for various writing situations (e.g., "for this kind of political science assignment write a compare/contrast essay"), but his entire approach to formulating plans and carrying them through to problem solution is too mechanical. It is

probable that Mike's behavior is governed by an explicitly learned or inferred rule: "Always try to 'psych out' a professor." But in this case this rule initiates a problem-solving procedure that is clearly dysfunctional.

While Ruth and Laurel use rules that impede their writing process and Mike   22 utilizes a problem-solving procedure that hamstrings him, *Sylvia* has trouble deciding which of the many rules she possesses to use. Her problem can be characterized as cognitive perplexity: some of her rules are inappropriate, others are functional; some mesh nicely with her own definitions of good writing, others don't. She has multiple rules to invoke, multiple paths to follow, and that very complexity of choice virtually paralyzes her. More so than with the previous four students, there is probably a strong emotional dimension to Sylvia's blocking, but the cognitive difficulties are clear and perhaps modifiable.

Sylvia, somewhat like Ruth and Laurel, puts tremendous weight on the   23 crafting of her first paragraph. If it is good, she believes the rest of the essay will be good. Therefore, she will spend up to five hours on the initial paragraph: "I won't go on until I get that first paragraph down." Clearly, this rule—or the strength of it—blocks Sylvia's production. This is one problem. Another is that Sylvia has other equally potent rules that she sees as separate, uncomplementary injunctions: one achieves "flow" in one's writing through the use of adequate transitions; one achieves substance to one's writing through the use of evidence. Sylvia perceives both rules to be "true," but several times followed one to the exclusion of the other. Furthermore, as I talked to Sylvia, many other rules, guidelines, definitions were offered, but none with conviction. While she *is* committed to one rule about initial paragraphs, and that rule is dysfunctional, she seems very uncertain about the weight and hierarchy of the remaining rules in her cognitive repertoire.

"If It Won't Fit My Work, I'll Change It"—The Non-blockers

Dale, Ellen, Debbie, Susan, and Miles all write with the aid of rules. But their   24 rules differ from blockers' rules in significant ways. If similar in content, they are expressed less absolutely—e.g., "*Try* to keep audience in mind." If dissimilar, they are still expressed less absolutely, more heuristically—e.g., "I can use as many ideas in my thesis paragraph as I need and then develop paragraphs for each idea." Our non-blockers do express some rules with firm assurance, but these tend to be simple injunctions that free up rather than restrict the composing process, e.g., "When stuck, write!" or "I'll write what I can." And finally, at least three of the students openly shun the very textbook rules that some blockers adhere to: e.g., "Rules like 'write only what you know about' just aren't true. I ignore those." These three, in effect, have formulated a further rule that expresses something like: "If a rule conflicts with what is sensible or with experience, reject it."

On the broader level of plans and strategies, these five students also differ   25 from at least three of the five blockers in that they all possess problem-solving plans that are quite functional. Interestingly, on first exploration these plans seem to be too broad or fluid to be useful and, in some cases, can barely be expressed with any precision. Ellen, for example, admits that she has a general "outline in [her] head about how a topic paragraph should look" but could not describe much about its structure. Susan also has a general plan to follow, but, if stymied, will quickly attempt to conceptualize the assignment in different ways: "If my original idea won't work, then I need to proceed differently." Whether or not these plans operate in TOTE-fashion, I can't say. But they do operate with the operate-test fluidity of TOTEs.

True, our non-blockers have their religiously adhered-to rules: e.g., "When   26 stuck, write," and plans, "I couldn't imagine writing without this pattern," but as noted above, these are few and functional. Otherwise, these non-blockers operate with fluid, easily modified, even easily discarded rules and plans (Ellen: "I can throw things out") that are sometimes expressed with a vagueness that could almost be interpreted as ignorance. There lies the irony. Students that offer the least precise rules and plans have the least trouble composing. Perhaps this very lack of precision characterizes the functional composing plan. But perhaps this lack of precision simply masks habitually enacted alternatives and sub-routines. This is clearly an area that needs the illumination of further research.

And then there is feedback. At least three of the five non-blockers are an   27 Information-Processor's dream. They get to know their audience, ask professors and T.A.s specific questions about assignments, bring half-finished products in for evaluation, etc. Like Ruth, they realize the importance of audience, but unlike her, they have specific strategies for obtaining and utilizing feedback. And this penchant for testing writing plans against the needs of the audience can lead to modification of rules and plans. Listen to Debbie:

> In high school I was given a formula that stated that you must write a thesis paragraph with *only* three points in it, and then develop each of those points. When I hit college I was given longer assignments. That stuck me for a bit, but then I realized that I could use as many ideas in my thesis paragraph as I needed and then develop paragraphs for each one. I asked someone about this and then tried it. I didn't get any negative feedback, so I figured it was o.k.

Debbie's statement brings one last difference between our blockers and non-   28 blockers into focus; it has been implied above, but needs specific formulation: the goals these people have, and the plans they generate to attain these goals, are quite mutable. Part of the mutability comes from the fluid way the goals and plans are conceived, and part of it arises from the effective impact of feedback on these goals and plans.

Analyzing Writer's Block

Algorithms Rather Than Heuristics

In most cases, the rules our blockers use are not "wrong" or "incorrect"—it is   29 good practice, for example, to "grab your audience with a catchy opening" or "craft a solid first paragraph before going on." The problem is that these rules seem to be followed as though they were algorithms, absolute dicta, rather than the loose heuristics that they were intended to be. Either through instruction, or the power of the textbook, or the predilections of some of our blockers for absolutes, or all three, these useful rules of thumb have been transformed into near-algorithmic urgencies. The result, to paraphrase Karl Dunker, is that these rules do not allow a flexible penetration into the nature of the problem. It is this transformation of heuristic into algorithm that contributes to the writer's block of Ruth and Laurel.

Questionable Heuristics Made Algorithmic

Whereas "grab your audience" could be a useful heuristic, "always make three   30
or more points in an essay" is a pretty questionable one. Any such rule, though probably taught to aid the writer who needs structure, ultimately transforms a highly fluid process like writing into a mechanical lockstep. As heuristics, such rules can be troublesome. As algorithms, they are simply incorrect.

Set

As with any problem-solving task, students approach writing assignments   31
with a variety of orientations or sets. Some are functional, others are not. Martha and Jane (see footnote 14), coming out of the life sciences and social sciences respectively, bring certain methodological orientations with them— certain sets or "directions" that make composing for the humanities a dif- ficult, sometimes confusing, task. In fact, this orientation may cause them to misperceive the task. Martha has formulated a planning strategy from her predisposition to see processes in terms of linear, interrelated steps in a sys- tem. Jane doesn't realize that she can revise the statement that "committed" her to the direction her essay has taken. Both of these students are stymied because of formative experiences associated with their majors—experiences, perhaps, that nicely reinforce our very strong tendency to organize experi- ences temporally.

The Plan That Is Not a Plan

If fluidity and multi-directionality are central to the nature of plans, then the   32
plans that Mike formulates are not true plans at all but, rather, inflexible and static cognitive blueprints.[15] Put another way, Mike's "plans" represent a restricted "closed system" (vs. "open system") kind of thinking, where closed system thinking is defined as focusing on "a limited number of units or items, or members, and those properties of the members which are to be used are known to begin with and do not change as the thinking proceeds," and open system thinking is characterized by an "adventurous exploration of multiple alterna- tives with strategies that allow redirection once 'dead ends' are encountered."[16] Composing calls for open, even adventurous thinking, not for constrained, no- exit cognition.

Feedback

The above difficulties are made all the more problematic by the fact that they   33
seem resistant to or isolated from corrective feedback. One of the most striking things about Dale, Debbie, and Miles is the ease with which they seek
out, interpret, and apply feedback on their rules, plans, and productions. They
"operate" and then they "test," and the testing is not only against some internalized goal, but against the requirements of external audience as well.

Too Many Rules—"Conceptual Conflict"

According to D. E. Berlyne, one of the primary forces that motivate problem-   34
solving behavior is a curiosity that arises from conceptual conflict—the conver-
gence of incompatible beliefs or ideas. In *Structure and Direction in Thinking*,[17]
Berlyne presents six major types of conceptual conflict, the second of which he
terms "perplexity":

> This kind of conflict occurs when there are factors inclining the subject toward
> each of a set of mutually exclusive beliefs, (p. 257)

If one substitutes "rules" for "beliefs" in the above definition, perplexity becomes
a useful notion here. Because perplexity is unpleasant, people are motivated to
reduce it by problem-solving behavior that can result in "disequalization":

> Degree of conflict will be reduced if either the number of competing . . . [rules] or
> their nearness to equality of strength is reduced. (p. 259)

But "disequalization" is not automatic. As I have suggested, Martha and Sylvia
hold to rules that conflict, but their perplexity does *not* lead to curiosity and
resultant problem-solving behavior. Their perplexity, contra Berlyne, leads to
immobilization. Thus "disequalization" will have to be effected from without.
The importance of each of, particularly, Sylvia's rules needs an evaluation that
will aid her in rejecting some rules and balancing and sequencing others.

A Note on Treatment

Rather than get embroiled in a blocker's misery, the teacher or tutor might   35
interview the student in order to build a writing history and profile: How
much and what kind of writing was done in high school? What is the student's
major? What kind of writing does it require? How does the student compose?
Are there rough drafts or outlines available? By what rules does the student
operate? How would he or she define "good" writing? etc. This sort of interview reveals an incredible amount of information about individual composing processes. Furthermore, it ofen reveals the rigid rule or the inflexible plan
that may lie at the base of the student's writing problem. That was precisely
what happened with the five blockers And with Ruth, Laurel, and Martha
(and Jane) what was revealed made virtually immediate remedy possible. Dysfunctional rules are easily replaced with or counter-balanced by functional

ones if there is no emotional reason to hold onto that which simply doesn't work. Furthermore, students can be trained to select, to "know which rules are appropriate for which problems."[18] Mike's difficulties, perhaps because plans are more complex and pervasive than rules, took longer to correct. But inflexible plans, too, can be remedied by pointing out their dysfunctional qualities and by assisting the student in developing appropriate and flexible alternatives. Operating this way, I was successful with Mike. Sylvia's story, however, did not end as smoothly. Though I had three forty-five minute contacts with her, I was not able to appreciably alter her behavior. Berlyne's theory bore results with Martha but not with Sylvia. Her rules were in conflict, and perhaps that conflict was not exclusively cognitive. Her case keeps analyses like these honest; it reminds us that the cognitive often melds with, and can be overpowered by, the affective. So while Ruth, Laurel, Martha, and Mike could profit from tutorials that explore the rules and plans in their writing behavior, students like Sylvia may need more extended, more affectively oriented counseling sessions that blend the instructional with the psychodynamic.

Notes

1. David Shapiro, *Neurotic Styles* (New York: Basic Books, 1965).

2. Barbara Hayes-Ruth, a Rand cognitive psychologist, and I are currently developing an information-processing model of the composing process. A good deal of work has already been done by Linda Flower and John Hayes (see para. 14 of this article). I have just received—and recommend—their "Writing as Problem Solving" (paper presented at American Educational Research Association, April, 1979).

3. *The Conditions of Learning* (New York; Holt, Rinehart and Winston, 1970), p. 193.

4. E. James Archer, "The Psychological Nature of Concepts," in H. J. Klausmeier and C. W. Harris, eds., *Analysis of Concept Learning* (New York: Academic Press, 1966), pp. 37–44; David P. Ausubel, *The Psychology of Meaningful Verbal Behavior* (New York: Grune and Stratton, 1963); Robert M. Gagné, "Problem Solving," in Arthur W. Melton, ed., *Categories of Human Learning* (New York: Academic Press, 1964), pp. 293–317; George A. Miller, *Language and Communication* (New York: McGraw-Hill, 1951).

5. George Katona, *Organizing and Memorizing* (New York: Columbia Univ. Press, 1940); Roger N. Shepard, Carl I. Hovland, and Herbert M. Jenkins, "Learning and Memorization of Classifications," *Psychological Monographs*, 75, No. 13 (1961) (entire No. 517); Robert S. Woodworth, *Dynamics of Behavior* (New York: Henry Holt, 1958), chs. 10–12.

6. *The Conditions of Learning*, pp. 190–91.

7. Karl Dunker, "On Problem Solving," *Psychological Monographs*, 58, No. 5 (1945) (entire No. 270); George A. Polya, *How to Solve It* (Princeton: Princeton University Press, 1945); George A. Miller, Eugene Galanter, and Karl H. Pribram, *Plans and the Structure of Behavior* (New York: Henry Holt, 1960).

8. Lyle E. Bourne, Jr., Bruce R. Ekstrand, and Roger L. Dominowski, *The Psychology of Thinking* (Englewood Cliffs, N.J.: Prentice-Hall, 1971).

9. John R. Hayes, "Problem Topology and the Solution Process," in Carl P. Duncan, ed., *Thinking: Current Experimental Studies* (Philadelphia: Lippincott, 1967), pp. 167–81.

10. Hulda J. Rees and Harold E. Israel, "An Investigation of the Establishment and Operation of Mental Sets," *Psychological Monographs,* 46 (1925) (entire No. 210).

11. Ibid.; Melvin H. Marx, Wilton W. Murphy, and Aaron J. Brownstein, "Recognition of Complex Visual Stimuli as a Function of Training with Abstracted Patterns," *Journal of Experimental Psychology*, 62 (1961), 456–60.

12. James L. Adams, *Conceptual Blockbusting* (San Francisco: W. H. Freeman, 1974); Edward DeBono, *New Think* (New York: Basic Books, 1958); Ronald H. Forgus, *Perception* (New York:

McGraw-Hill, 1966), ch. 13; Abraham Luchins and Edith Hirsch Luchins, *Rigidity of Behavior* (Eugene: Univ. of Oregon Books, 1959); N. R. F. Maier, "Reasoning in Humans. I. On Direction," *Journal of Comparative Psychology,* 10 (1920), 115–43.

13. "Plans and the Cognitive Process of Writing," paper presented at the National Institute of Education Writing Conference, June 1977; "Problem Solving Strategies and the Writing Process," *College English,* 39 (1977), 449–61. See also footnote 2.

14. Jane, a student not discussed in this paper, was surprised to find out that a topic paragraph can be rewritten after a paper's conclusion to make that paragraph reflect what the essay truly contains. She had gotten so indoctrinated with Psychology's (her major) insistence that a hypothesis be formulated and then left untouched before an experiment begins that she thought revision of one's "major premise" was somehow illegal. She had formed a rule out of her exposure to social science methodology, and the rule was totally inappropriate for most writing situations.

15. Cf. "A plan is flexible if the order of execution of its parts can be easily interchanged without affecting the feasibility of the plan . . . the flexible planner might tend to think of lists of things he had to do; the inflexible planner would have his time planned like a sequence of cause-effect relations. The former could rearrange his lists to suit his opportunities, but the latter would be unable to strike while the iron was hot and would generally require considerable 'lead-time' before he could incorporate any alternative sub-plans" (Miller, Galanter, and Pribram, p. 120).

16. Frederic Bartlett, *Thinking* (New York: Basic Books, 1958), pp. 74–76.

17. *Structure and Direction in Thinking* (New York: John Wiley, 1965), p. 255.

18. Flower and Hayes, "Plans and the Cognitive Process of Writing," p. 26.

Questions for Discussion and Journaling

1. Create a list of all the rules that, according to Rose, interfere with "the blockers'" writing. What rules, if any, do you find yourself forced to follow that seem to get in the way of your writing?

2. Describe the difference between the rules that blockers in Rose's study were following and those that non-blockers were following. What accounts for the difference?

3. What's the difference between an *algorithm* and a *heuristic*? Give a couple of examples of each that you use on an everyday basis.

4. Based on Rose's study and descriptions of writers and their rules, write a "rule" explaining what makes a rule good for writers, and what makes a rule bad for writers. You'll get bonus points if you can tell whether your rule is an algorithm or a heuristic.

5. Can you think of mutually exclusive rules that you've tried to follow in your writing? If you can't easily or quickly think of any, comb through the rules that you follow for writing, and see if they're consistent with each other.

6. If you read Tierney and Pearson, you should notice some resonance between *set* as Rose describes it and *alignment* as they describe it. Can you explain the word *set* in terms of alignment?

Applying and Exploring Ideas

1. Find the origins of the rules you follow. Start by listing the ten rules that most powerfully impact your writing, whether good or bad. Now stop and think. Where, and when, did you learn each rule? Did it come from personal experience? Teachers? Parents? Observation of what other people were doing? Are there any rules you follow that you *don't* like? What would happen if you abandoned them?

2. Stop and think: Do you encounter rules in writing that flatly contradict your experience as a writer or reader? (For example: we're aware of a rule against beginning a sentence with "and." And we see good, professional writers do it all the time.) Describe one or two of these rules that you know of.

3. Rose concludes his article with a discussion of the difference between *knowing* a rule is ineffective and *acting* on that knowledge. If you find yourself following a rule that Rose suggests has a negative impact on writing, reflect on these questions: If you had permission to, would you stop following this rule? What is the risk of setting aside one rule and starting to use another? Is it possible that, rather than setting aside a rule completely, you might simply treat it more flexibly and have the best of both worlds?

Meta Moment

Has anyone ever talked to you about *blocking* before? How might understanding this concept and knowing how to actively deal with it be useful to you in your life?

Tuning, Tying, and Training Texts:
Metaphors for Revision

BARBARA TOMLINSON

Tomlinson, Barbara. "Tuning, Tying, and Training Texts: Metaphors for Revision." *Written Communication* 5.1 (1988): 58–81. Print.

Framing the Reading

We've been taught that metaphors are "figurative" language, flowery comparisons that spice up language but are not to be taken literally. And indeed, if one writes, "Amanda glided through the water with the grace of a killer whale," their reader won't take it literally (unless, that is, Amanda *is* a killer whale). But linguists point out that our language is full of metaphors that we don't really register as figurative. For example, we treat *argument* as *war:* "I couldn't defend my position, so he won that battle of wits with an argument that completely disarmed me." Not literal? Perhaps not, but we certainly sometimes *act* as if it's literal.

In this article, Barbara Tomlinson gathers metaphors that professional writers use to describe ways they develop their writing. She argues that the language we use to describe writing reveals our attitudes and assumptions about the nature of writing. We have included this piece in this chapter because we suspect you talk about your writing in some of these ways without really thinking about what it *means* to do so. You should: You might be surprised at what you discover about writing, and about yourself as a writer.

Getting Ready to Read

Before you read, do at least one of the following activities:

- Think of the act of revising a piece of writing and write down how it feels, tastes, sounds, and smells to you. Are these associations negative, positive, or neutral?
- Try to remember how you talk about the acts of writing and revising. Are there any words, phrases, metaphors, or similes that you usually use when you talk about writing? What are they? What do they suggest about how you feel about writing?

As you read, consider the following questions:

- How many of the metaphors mentioned in the article have you heard before? How many have you used yourself? Most interestingly, what metaphors do you use that don't come up here?
- Tomlinson takes a wide range of seemingly unrelated metaphors to describe revision and demonstrates how they come together in an overall story about the nature of writing. What is this story? Is it a compelling one, in your opinion?
- What have you learned about revision—how it works, its place in writing, the importance of it—through reading this piece that you didn't know before?
- What other aspects of writing might we be able to investigate by studying the language we use to describe them?

Rewriting . . . is a slow, grinding business. (Vidal, 1974)

Is rewriting a "slow, grinding business"? Is it a matter of chiseling away at a rock-hard text? or pushing and pulling a text of malleable clay? Is it a job for a smelter? or a surgeon? or a tune-up expert? Literary writers like Vidal frequently tell us so, drawing upon such figurative language to explain their processes of composing. I present and analyze here eight prominent "metaphorical stories" that professional writers use when describing their revising activities in literary interviews. I will argue that such patterns of figurative expressions are an important part of our socially shared knowledge of composing and that, as such, they influence our conceptions of composing—and may well influence our composing behavior. At the same time, these metaphorical stories focus attention on aspects of revising that we may have overlooked, challenging our current ways of classifying revision.

People tend to have two important sources of information about the writing process: metacognitive experiences and culturally shared information. During the process of writing, writers have moments when they become aware of themselves as thinkers and writers, moments when they are, in effect, pausing to observe themselves in the act of writing or to reflect on what they are doing. These moments are "metacognitive experiences," and are a source of information about composing. But because metacognitive experiences are often confusing and unclear, people are likely to use other sources of information to help themselves

Author's Note: I would like to thank Rise Axelrod, Lori Chamberlain, and Charles Cooper for their thoughtful comments on earlier versions of this article. I would also like to thank others who have helped with this project, particularly my superb research assistant, Peter Mortensen, graduate student in literature and composition at the University of California, San Diego.

interpret those experiences, particularly social sources such as teachers, parents, and professional writers. A good deal of what people "know" about composing (perhaps most of what they know) is based not on careful observation of their own activities, but on this culturally shared information about the writing process. (For discussion of culturally shared knowledge as the basis of people's meta-cognitive explanations of their cognitive processes, see Nisbett & Wilson, 1977; Flavell, 1979; for discussion specific to writing, see Tomlinson, 1984.)

Is rewriting a "slow, grinding business"? Is it a matter of chiseling away at a rock-hard text? or pushing and pulling a text of malleable clay?

3

Social scientists Alfred Schutz and W. I. Thomas would contend that such socially distributed information about composing influences our "definition of the [writing] situation"—and consequently our writing behavior (Schutz, 1962; Thomas, 1951). (For evidence that people's theories and assumptions about the world influence their behavior, see, for example, Gentner & Stevens, 1983; for evidence specific to writing, see Boice, 1985; Rose, 1980, 1984, 1985; for evidence specific to metaphor, see Gentner & Gentner, 1983.) With respect to writing, Mike Rose's research has already revealed links between conceptions about composing and composing performance: studying fluent and blocked college writers, Rose (1984) found that blocked writers held dysfunctional assumptions about appropriate composing strategies and tended to operate according to these assumptions; fluent writers envisioned composing as more flexible and operated accordingly.

Since metaphorical expressions about composing that are common in the culture are part of such socially distributed information, it is likely that they too influence our conceptions and our behavior as writers—an assertion certainly supported by the work on metaphor of George Lakoff and Mark Johnson (1980a, 1980b), Michael Reddy (1979), and Donald A. Schon (1979). Lakoff and Johnson, concerned with conceptual metaphors often overlooked in every-day language, assert that we "draw inferences, set goals, make commitments, and execute plans, all on the basis of how we structure our experience, con-sciously and unconsciously, by means of metaphor" (1980a, p. 485). Michael Reddy describes a pervasive and powerful metaphor—the conduit metaphor—that strongly influences our conceptions of communication. Donald A. Schon describes how "stories" told through metaphor influence our thinking. 4

> Each story conveys a different view of reality and represents a special way of seeing. From a situation that is vague, ambiguous, and indeterminate (or rich and complex, depending on one's frame of mind), each story selects . . . for attention a few salient features and relations from what would otherwise be an overwhelmingly complex reality . . . [giving] these elements a coherent organization. (1979, p. 264)

Thus patterns of common figurative expressions can form resonant, coherent narratives that both reflect and influence the ways we conceive of and act on the world. These metaphorical stories enable us to understand and communicate 5 about amorphous, fragmented, complicated experiences like the process of writing; they enable us to bring coherence to our conceptions and communications about composing.

To explore socially shared ways of bringing structure and coherence to revising activities requires a corpus of testimony from writers, which I have selected exclusively from literary interviews. Reviewing over 2,000 published literary interviews (of the type made famous by the *Paris Review*), I have gathered hundreds of instances in which figurative language was used to describe composing from authors of poetry, fiction, nonfiction, plays—authors varying in nationality, ethnicity, and gender. Literary interviews (and other types of interviews as well) suffer from a number of problems when used as evidence about *composing practices* (see Tomlinson, 1984). However, these problems are not relevant when interviews are used instead as a source of *discourse about composing*, as text to be analyzed, my intention here.

I concentrate here on eight metaphorical stories specifically about revising, rather than stories meant to describe the whole process of writing, part of which, of course, involves revision (I do discuss metaphorical stories of that type in Tomlinson, 1986). In the eight stories, authors make reference to revising as refining ore, casting and recasting, sculpting, painting, sewing and tailoring, tying things off, fixing things (particularly mechanical things), or cutting. In the next section, I introduce each story, indicating rather briefly the perspective it offers on revising and some of the applications that may be associated with it. I then go on in the following sections to explore these implications further and to suggest how the varied perspectives of these metaphorical stories, the strength of their internal coherence, and the network of relationships among the stories challenge our common classification of revising.

Metaphorical Stories

Refining Ore

James Dickey, when drawing an analogy between his writing process and refining ore, is actually describing a process of revision-as-reformulation: rather than focusing on the discovery of the "ore," his material, he is concerned with attempts to transform that material into a more valuable commodity.

> I work as a writer—let me see if I can come up with a metaphor or analogy—on the principle of refining low-grade ore. I assume that the first fifty ways that I try it are going to be wrong. I do it by a process of elimination. No matter how back-breaking the shoveling is and running it through the sluices and whatever you have to do to refine low-grade ore, you have the dubious consolation that what you get out of it is just as much real gold as it would be if you were going around picking nuggets up off the ground. It's just that it takes so damn much labor to get it. (1974, p. 133)

Like many writers, Dickey assumes that hidden in the mass of his early drafts are elements that will make the final text valuable; they will be revealed eventually if he tries to get at them in enough different ways and if he separates out and rejects worthless material (what Bernard Malamud [1975] called "dross"— the waste products from molten metal during smelting). But these rough elements must then be transformed into a valuable product, a difficult, even onerous task. Nonetheless Dickey appears to be confident that the hard work of transformation will indeed eventually result in a product just as valuable as those obtained in easier ways. We cannot let Dickey's slightly self-deprecating reference to other, easier methods of composition mislead us; the comments of many other writers suggest that few find their "gold" lying about on the ground.

Casting and Recasting

The possibility of major reformulation during revising is also inherent in   9 analogies to the process of casting material. Jessamyn West says she can only reread her text when it is "molten," when there is the possibility of revising it (1976). And John Fowles appears to think of his material as "fluid," molten, during the time he can revise it, becoming "solid" only with the final casting— publication.

> I love it when a story is still . . . changeable, still fluid, and you can take it any-
> where, do anything with it. Once it's printed, it's set and frozen, like a bronze cast
> of a sculptor. You can't shape it any more. (1977, p. 50)

John Ashbery uses an analogy to casting when he describes how in revision he has eliminated the initiating, generative lines of a poem.

> [The initial phrases] often don't fit into the texture of the poem; it's almost like
> some lost wax or other process where the initial armature or whatever gets
> scrapped in the end. (1974, p. 114)

The "lost wax process" to which Ashbery refers is a procedure for making   10 castings: A mold of particularly heat-resistant metal is built up over a shaped core of wax; the mold is then heated, and the wax melted and drained away, leaving the mold ready for shaping other, less heat-resistant materials. The wax is essential to the process, unnecessary to the product. To compare an aspect of rewriting to a process that eliminates a supporting structure, as Ashbery did, is to suggest that evaluative criteria may lead one to eliminate elements that were vital in the developing of the text. Elements compelling to the process may be unnecessary to the product.

If there are problems in the text, those comparing writing to casting may   11 suggest that the casting can be done again: Jerome Mazzaro (1977) mentions that he had to "recast" an opening; Eudora Welty (1984) and James Michener (1978), their whole texts. To compare rewriting to recasting is to emphasize the possibility of substantial revising through "reheating" the material—returning to a generative state. To envision the text this way implies that the writer can continue to revise during the entire writing of the text: Options for reformulating are not closed early in the process. Furthermore, it implies that subsequent formulations of the text will be easier and more successful because a shape or mold has been developed during prewriting and early drafts.

Sculpting

Analogies to sculpting may allow for or emphasize reformulation of the text.   12
Writers revising may feel like sculptors chiseling. According to William Goyen,

> I generally write just straight ahead . . . If I [look back] I get caught back there revising. . . . It must be like chiseling a sculpture; if the sculptor does too fine a work too soon on what's big, heavy, gross work, then it's out of balance some-where. I should imagine that he has to do all different phases of gross work, and finer and finer and finer detail. (1980, p. 228)

While drawing an analogy to artistic endeavor, Goyen envisions the writer   13
engaged in rather heavy work, "chiseling" and shaping a large block of mate-rial, rather than applying layers of material over a base structure. According to the story, revisers can make major changes in shape through incision and removal, but not through addition, since early in the process the larger shape of the text is blocked out irrevocably. Goyen thus suggests the existence of a real yet unrealized text-as-a-whole, a text that could be irremediably damaged by the indelible strokes of premature detail. The disappointing result would waste not only the author's time and effort but also the potential of the material itself: One could not hope to "resmelt" it or obscure one's errors by painting over them. So Goyen's recommended revising method is cyclical, a repeated work-ing through the text—first large moves, then small—each time cutting a little away in order to reveal "finer and finer" detail.

Other authors may experience their texts, their media, as malleable, pliable,   14
something to push and pull, form and reform. Laura Chester finds the process sensuous.

> I type draft after draft almost obsessively until that first soft clay shapes itself into the poem it has to become. . . . I love the feel of the poem as a malleable substance that I can push and reshape on the page. (1977, p. 75)

Arnold Adoff (1974) says that he has learned to work his material "over and over like . . . a piece of clay." Wallace Stegner (1985) speaks of his manuscript when it is "still malleable." Alice Munro (1973) prefers material that she can "pull." Clarence Major (1985) "reshapes," and Leo Rosten (1964) "reshapes" and "remolds." John Gardner (1979) keeps "pushing" at his text. These proce-dures seem less mediated than casting or chiseling with their respective tools, their chisels and forges. The story emphasizes remolding the *same* material into a *new* shape—often one that has little resemblance to the original form— rather than adding or deleting material. Revising here is reformulation.

Painting

Painting, another delicate process requiring something of art as well as skill,   15
also implies substantial reformulation, though less than occurs with sculpting.

Gore Vidal uses painting imagery when he claims that he has altered his rewriting process over the years, like a painter changing materials.

> I write first drafts with great speed but the older I get (a familiar observation, I know) I rewrite more and more. . . . I'm more an oil painter now. More deliberate. A good deal less certain. (1971, p. 337)

With oils (as opposed to the "egg tempera" of his early years), Vidal has more 16
opportunities for change, more thoughtfulness. Alberto Moravia also compares his writing process to a kind of painting that builds up layer by layer.

> Each book is worked over several times. I like to compare my method with that of painters centuries ago, proceeding, as it were, from layer to layer. The first draft is quite crude, far from being perfect, by no means finished; although even then, even at that point, it has its final structure, the form is visible. After that I rewrite it as many times—apply as many "layers"—as I feel to be necessary. (1957, p. 220)

Moravia highlights the changes and additions of revision, its ability to alter the text subtly or dramatically at any stage, even late in the process of writing. Similarly, Harry Mark Petrakis indicates that with his constant revisions, "Each layer added is a layer that will change the shape and totality of the whole" (1977, p. 99). Helen MacInnes (1964) also makes an analogy to painting: She "retouches" as she goes along. Unlike the refining and casting analogies, the analogy to painting emphasizes a kind of work that is delicate, only mildly physical, guided primarily by aesthetic principles, and focused on developing a product that is valued for its particular uniqueness and significance. The essentials are not necessarily hidden or buried in the rough draft, waiting to be discovered and brought to light, nor are they in potential in the text: They are realized, though "crudely." In effect, the "layering" results in a series of changes and reformulations; the final product may go far beyond the initial sketch in richness and texture because of the enhancements of revision.

Sewing and Tailoring

Joan Didion uses a sewing analogy to describe how she had to insert a substan- 17
tial new section into her draft of *A Book of Common Prayer*:

> Finally, when I got within twenty pages of the end, I realized that I still hadn't delivered this revolution. I had a lot of threads, and I'd overlooked this one. So then I had to go back and lay in the preparation for the revolution. Putting in that revolution was like setting in a sleeve. Do you know what I mean? Do you sew? I mean I had to work that revolution in on the bias, had to ease out the wrinkles with my fingers. (1978, p. 155)

Didion's description of "setting in" her revolution is unlike the other fig- 18
ures we have seen: It suggests not a unitary text, but one that can be divided into elements or components, into which major sections can be inserted even as the text nears completion. Overlooking the ends of an important "thread" merely resulted in an awkward, though manageable construction problem.

The materials were not at fault. And solving a problem of sewing certainly requires craft, skill, but not necessarily the artistry of a painter or sculptor.

Lawrence Durrell also uses an analogy to sewing when he describes his 19 revising. At one point he says: "The construction gave me some trouble, and I let in a hemstitch here, a gusset there" (1963, p. 267). A "hemstitch" is an ornamental stitch that involves pulling out a number of parallel threads, then stitching groups of the cross-threads together. A "gusset" appears to imply a more direct way to solve a "construction" problem, since it consists of a small, triangular piece of material that is inserted in an item of clothing to reinforce it or make a better fit. Durrell represents his revising as essentially strengthening and ensuring the fit of a consciously constructed artifact. I assume that Durrell would describe such revision as "tailoring" (a term also used by Audre Lorde, 1983), since in the same interview he uses the term "retailor" to indicate a kind of revising that he finds himself unable to do: He says, "I know it's a wrong attitude, because some people can, with patience, resurrect and retailor things. But I can't" (1963, p. 271). Metaphorical stories referring to sewing and tailoring place the writer in a practical situation, trying to put together and adjust a simple, serviceable garment, not make valuable metal or unique artwork. They represent revision as a matter of technical skill and cleverness.

Tying Things Off

Didion said she overlooked one thread of many. Like the loose threads that must 20 be taken care of when one sews a garment or weaves fabric, numerous places in the text need small changes. Her story suggests that such small-scale revising is rather limited and undemanding—merely a "tying off" and "clipping" of bits that are loose and unattractive. But the impression that such revisions may be minor is belied by a related image—the image of tying up knots—that Nelson Algren uses to describe what he does during final revisions.

> While I'm finishing a book it's a bit like tying a lot of knots that keep slipping and you're just impatient to get it done. And then you have to go back in, in order to tie it up, and you find you just can't tie it up at the end. You have to go all the way back in to tie it up. (1964, p. 324)

Like Didion, Algren implies that problems of revising are primarily technical 21 difficulties: One must keep finding loose ends, tying off knots, returning when knots have "slipped" (when one's revising is not enough, or when revising in other areas necessitates returning to sections one previously thought finished). But since the strings or ropes or threads that Algren is trying to knot go deep into the texture of the text, their tying seems important: If not adequately tied, they could unravel, leaving the parts of the constructed piece only loosely connected. And, we might conclude, the same danger may attend those who neglect loose threads on a newly sewn garment. Neglecting to take care of such small and last-minute concerns can lead one to produce a text that does not cohere, that "falls apart." So it seems that to compare revising to completing a set of small activities may not be to suggest that it is of little import. Rather, such small activities may be of broad effect—they make the text, necessarily completed by word and phrase, into an integrated whole.

Fixing Things

In some writers' representations, revising is "fixing" the text: "patching" it, like 22 Christopher Isherwood (1976) or "repairing" it, like John A. Williams (1973). There is often a hint of mechanical work involved: Conrad Aiken (1974) speaks of "retooling"; Richard Eberhart (1977), Maxine Kumin (1983), Robert Lowell (1968), Tim O'Brien (1983), and Dennis Schmitz (1977) of "tinkering"; Philip Whalen says that he has "got to bang on it somehow to straighten it out" (1978, p. 37). Marguerite Yourcenar (1984) and Maxine Kumin (1983) both speak of "tightening" and "loosening": "It wasn't a matter of rewriting but simply of tightening up all the bolts, so to speak . . . tightening and loosening are jobs for a mechanic," says Yourcenar (p. 184). Fred Chappell compares a long process of revision to a process in which one gradually finds needed parts and conducts repairs on an old car to get it running.

> You work at it long enough, and it becomes so impersonal and so much an object that you're working on . . . it's like a car you've been trying to get to run, an old Hupmobile, that you've been looking for all the parts for, for the past thirty years, and, one of these days, you know that you're going to take it out on the highway. (1973, p. 43)

Chappell focuses on revision as the process of getting a car to run, getting it 23 out on the road; Robert Creeley uses a similar analogy—in which he compares revision to tuning up a car—to describe how revision can lead to a text that functions harmoniously.

> A poet say like Louis Zuko[f]sky has endless revisions upon his initial writing. It's like tuning up a motor. He really isn't satisfied until all the elements of the statement are for him utterly working in congruence. (1974, p. 208)

Chappell is concerned with obtaining solutions to the problems found in the text; he does not expect to have solutions for all of its problems immediately, but eventually. He expects delay, not because the problems are all inordinately difficult or because he is unskilled at fixing the text, but because new problems continually arise, each special in its own way, problems that must be solved individually, sometimes through tinkering, sometimes through borrowing. His image also suggests, of course, that the text is complicated, requiring the smooth meshing of many different parts, and that fairly small problems can prevent the text from working. Greeley's comment focuses on the difference that attention to those small problems makes: without such attention, the text may "run," it may perform its basic function, but raggedly, requiring more effort from the reader; with the additional revision it runs smoothly. Comments indicating that the text requires mechanical work to fix it suggest that revising writers employ technical or craft skills to solve practical problems. Their attention at this point tends to be on precision rather than energy or design.

Cutting

Many writers report that rewriting involves removing excrescence in order to   24
highlight or clarify important material. The most frequent term in my corpus
for describing an act of revising was *cut*; and *cut*, its synonyms, or comments
that relate to cutting constitute at least a third of the figures about revising that
I found. When a word like *cut* is used to describe revising, it may appear to be
a dead metaphor, a figure that has been used so commonly that neither writer
nor reader may recognize its figurative associations. Certainly this may be true
in many instances; but there are numerous instances in which writers describe
their deleting in such a way as to remind us of these figurative associations.

For example, John Brunner likens his writing process to gardening, his revis-   25
ing to pruning an ornamental plant.

> Organizing [a plot] is akin to pruning an espalier. Given a suitable plant—a
> promising idea—one must display it on the available trellis: the printed page. If
> it tends to wander randomly, it must be disciplined back to the required shape.
> (1978, p. 317)

Other writers also make reference to trimming plants: David Jones (1966),   26
having crawled "out on limbs," then goes ahead and "prunes" them; Penelope
Farmer (1976) "prunes" her stories "radically"; and William Goyen implies
pruning when he says that he will "cut back, and take what is still living there"
(1980, p. 233). Gardening work such as this involves care and delicacy, clearing out bad and dead material, shaping the plant and guiding its tender stems
while fostering its growth. Rather than remaining inert, subject to the writer's
efforts to work on it, the text grows on its own. The essential elements are not
hidden, but in potential. Trained to grow in the right direction, and trimmed
back and shaped when it has not, the plant eventually develops to the point of
optimal value.

Cut assumes special meaning when Henry Miller (1963) tells us that he goes   27
"to work on [his text] with an axe," or when Hugh Leonard tells us that he finds
cutting difficult when he "cannot get a wedge in because each line fits into the
next" (1973, p. 197). Alex Haley (1977) tells us that he "*act*[s] like a surgeon"
when he is writing—focusing on the careful delicate work, even constantly taking showers and washing his hands. "I like to do first drafts at night, when I'm
tired, and then do the surgical work in the morning when I'm sharp" (p. 451).
There are also, of course, surgical associations with Christopher Isherwood's
use of "amputate" in describing his revising (1976). Donald Hall explains
that "the process of peeling away sharpens what's there. It doesn't clarify it,
it sharpens it" (1973, p. 13). Conrad Aiken (1974), B. S. Johnson (1981), and
Alice Munro (1973) "chop"; while Milton Meltzer (1979), James A. Michener
(1978), and Martin Myers (1973) "hack." Hugh MacLennan (1973), Jerome
Mazzaro (1977), Howard Moss (1974), and Chaim Potok (1980) "pare." John
Ciardi (1964), David Jones (1966), and Chaim Potok (1980) "strip" their texts.
James Tate (1977) "brandishes" his "razor," and Herbert Gold (1973) goes
over his first draft to cut out "the loose hairs and revise."

Just as tailoring involves insertion, these uses of *cut* or descriptions of cut- 28
ting away material from the text have in common deletion and diminution.
Henry Miller, with his reference to an axe, gives the impression of bold strokes,
slicing away large chunks of a sturdy, rich text; he seems to assert that bold
strokes cannot damage this text. William Goyen's comment about "taking what
is still living there" focuses on eliminating dead material that will hinder the
growth and strength of the text. Christopher Isherwood, with his "amputate,"
suggests a similar cutting away, necessary to save the text. In "amputating," he
leaves the text healthy but not really whole—cutting away parts of the living
original carries heavy costs. Alex Haley directs our attention to the delicacy of
revising, which must get all of his attention during his "sharpest" period, and
to the importance of revising to the life of the text: Poor cutting may lead to
vital material being removed or the text being scarred—perhaps even to a life-
less text.

Varied Perspectives and Internal Coherence

My review of these stories and their associated implications certainly support 29
Schon's contention that each metaphorical story "conveys a different view of
reality and represents a special way of seeing." The stories themselves and, of
course, the individual expressions of each story function to emphasize and suppress different aspects of the composing process. For example:

Refining ore. Dickey's comparison to refining ore emphasizes that one's first
draft, one's first way of approaching the problem—even one's first 50 ways of
approaching it—may not work, and achieving what one wants will be onerous,
though ultimately rewarding.

Casting and recasting. The casting analogies suggest that one can return to
a generative state during revision, reformulating for a better text, yet taking
advantage of the shape developed in earlier drafts.

Sculpting. Goyen's comparison to sculpture provides clear directions for a workable revising strategy: Start first to shape the whole text, then cycle back to
work at finer levels of revision.

Painting. Vidal's and Moravia's comparisons to painting suggest that the writer
may change either the essence or the effect of the work at any of the numerous
stages in the writing process.

Sewing and tailoring. Didion's and Durrell's comments suggest that one can
insert vital sections into the text even when it is nearly complete and that one
should expect to have to make adjustments, so that the text will fit together and
fit its audience and purpose.

Tying things off. Algren indicates that the last stages of revising are not merely
at the surface; they involve going back into the text to make numerous small
changes and, often, returning again to make more changes in response to what
one has done during revising.

Fixing things. Chappell's image of gradually readying an old car for the road suggests that writers cannot solve all the problems in the text at one time, in one draft; they may need time to discover how to solve other problems.

Cutting. Instances describing cutting often imply the need to separate "dead" material from that which is "alive"; the vitality of the material has to be determined according to the totality of the text rather than merely surface, sentence-level, and word-level symptoms.

To suggest similarities between revising and another process, as these stories 30 do, is to draw our attention to salient features of the process of revision and to highlight those features for a moment while ignoring (or "suppressing") other, momentarily irrelevant features. Focusing on the highlighted features and implications associated with the story, we overlook the ways in which revising is *unlike* those processes: As Kenneth Burke says in *A Grammar of Motives* (1945), "A way of seeing is also a way of not seeing" (p. 49). The result, of course, is both a gain and a loss in understanding.

For it is precisely because each story emphasizes some aspects of revising 31 and suppresses others that it can make the process of revision—which we know to be extraordinarily complex—appear coherent. Each story encourages us to ignore aspects of revising that will not fit into the structure of the story. But in return, the story supplies us with a context for interpreting behaviors and attitudes, a context that we can use to explain unanswered questions about the process, its goals, the nature of the material, the writer's attitudes, the steps one goes through to complete the process, and so forth. This context allows both writer and audience to overcome vagueness, inconsistencies, lacunas in the story's description of revising, and of the associated process. For example, when James Dickey compares his revising to refining ore, he indicates that he has only a vague idea of what is involved in refining (remember, he concludes his series of steps with "and whatever you have to do to refine low-grade ore"). We, members of his audience, may have knowledge of mining or refining no more specific than his. But we nonetheless know, as he does, a relevant "story": Mining is exhausting, back-breaking work with a recalcitrant substance; the substance must be transformed in order to yield valuable—or invaluable—results; the activity is not pleasant, but the results are worthwhile, and so forth. (See Tomlinson, 1986, for further discussion of writing as mining.)

Lakoff and Johnson indicate that a "mere metaphor" can "make coherent a 32 large and diverse range of experiences" because metaphors have entailments. For instance, a metaphor of "revising is mining," or "revising is refining ore," which is how Lakoff and Johnson might formulate Dickey's metaphorical story, would appear to have entailments such as the following:

Revising is hard work on resistant material.

Revising requires reformulating and transforming material.

Revising turns low-grade material into a valuable product.

Revising can be frustrating.

According to Lakoff and Johnson,

> Each of these entailments may itself have other entailments. The result is a large and coherent set of entailments that may, on the whole, either fit or not fit our experiences. . . . When such a coherent network of entailments fits our experiences, those experiences form a coherent whole as instances of the metaphor. What we experience with such a metaphor is a kind of reverberation down through the network of entailments that awakens and connects our memories of our past . . . experiences and serves as a possible guide for future ones. (1980a, p. 482)

Lakoff and Johnson would suggest that a particular metaphorical story about revising might appear appropriate to us, even true, if its entailments are important aspects of our own cultural and personal experiences related to revising. In addition, if the story is coherent and, therefore, memorable, during future writing experiences we may come to recognize those entailments as valid and applicable: We thereby bring structure and coherence to our own writing experiences by means of metaphorical stories we have heard.

A Network of Revising Stories

The first four revising stories—refining, casting, sculpting, and painting—sug- 33
gest that the writer goes back into the text to rework its inorganic substance, to reformulate it. Dickey, refining ore for its gold, breaks apart his drafts into their constituent elements in order to find and transform the most valuable. With their casting and recasting, Ashbery, Fowles, Mazzaro, Michener, Welty, and West return their drafts to the amorphous, liquid state of beginnings and generativity. Goyen returns to chisel away in shaping his text. Adoff, Chester, Gardner, Major, Munro, Rosten, and Stegner may continue to remold their texts many times. And MacInnes, Moravia, Petrakis, and Vidal add layers to alter the texture and form of their texts dramatically. Thus a significant proportion of revising stories indicate that writers see themselves making substantial changes during revising. It also appears that these metaphorical stories about reformulation may form a harmonious group: They all imply a unitary text, rather than one composed of discrete parts that can be handled separately. The intention seems to be primarily to produce an aesthetic object, beautiful and valuable; its potential communicative ability is suppressed. In casting, sculpting, and painting, the objects have considerable aesthetic and communicative value, while the object in the case of refining ore has high value as a commodity. Writers apparently place high value on reformulation as a way to discover, construct, shape, and develop what they have to say. And they demonstrate this in stories that are congruent with one another.

The stories that suggest revising as a process of smaller-scale or late-stage 34
changes—fixing things, sewing, tying things off—offer interpretations of the nature of revising that differ from those suggested by reformulation stories, yet seem in harmony with one another. These stories do not appear to place as much value on either process or text as do stories implying reformulation. The tasks are more those of craft and rule, rather than those of heavy labor or art; they

make fewer demands on physical strength or artistic talent. The products are not so valuable aesthetically or as commodities; and they do not have the kind of communicative function that artistic objects do. These stories stress the superficies of the text; they are stylistic rather than formal, local rather than structural.

Some instances of such metaphorical stories (of fixing things, in particular) 35 even imply that writers are slightly disrespectful of the value of such revising—when the writer is "banging" or "tinkering," for example. And there are other terms used to describe small-scale revising that appear to reflect ambivalence or self-deprecation; writers mention, for example, having to "chew" (William Gass, 1983; Martin Myers, 1973), "diddle away" (Allen Ginsberg, 1967), "niggle" (Lawrence Durrell, 1963), and "pick" (Christopher Isherwood, 1976) at their drafts; needing to "fiddle" (Fred Chappell, 1973; Raymond Federman, 1983; William Gass, 1983; Tom Mallin, 1981; Judith Minty, 1977; Alan Sillitoe, 1981), "fuss" (Ann Sexton, 1974), "mess" (Richard Wilbur, 1974), "monkey" (John Graves, 1980; Leo Rosten, 1964), or "play" (Ralph Ellison, 1974; Anne Sexton, 1974) with them. Stevie Smith and William Gass provide us with the image of a somewhat bedraggled text, dragged about by the writer-as-dog:

> [With a poem] . . . one sort of throws it away and goes and digs it up and tosses it into the air and finishes it off or doesn't finish it off. (Smith, 1966, p. 225)

> Much . . . will have begun . . . earlier . . . and [been] worried and slowly chewed and left for dead many times in the interim. (Gass, 1983, p. 158)

We need not assume that such expressions reflect writers' actual attitudes 36 toward minor, surface, or late-stage revision (they may well represent a rhetorical pose considered appropriate for discussing such revision)—but they do reflect a tendency to discredit revising activities that is not present in reformulation stories.

Taken as a whole, the metaphorical stories about revising in my corpus 37 seem to imply a set of relations among the nature of the material, stage of revision, and how it is revised. The material to be revised may be at one time molten, malleable, flexible; it is possible to reshape it and change it totally. Revising material in such a state tends to be represented by metaphorical stories about hard labor and artistic processes (refining, casting and recasting, painting, sculpting). At another time, the material is still somewhat flexible; alterations can still be made. However, attention is going not to the totality of the text, but to the fit and functioning among parts. Revising material in such a state tends to be represented by stories about draft and mechanical work (fixing things, sewing and tailoring, tying things off). When the text seems to be relatively "solid," writers "cut," focusing either on the material to be saved or that to be eliminated. And when the "surface" of the text seems to have "hardened," at least temporarily, writers engage in craft work again, as they "polish" or "touch up." When we talk about revising as a cyclical, recursive process, we are indicating that these states may occur and reoccur as writers complete their texts, though in general texts move from malleability to solidification, and writers from working on substance and shape to working on surface.

Implications

Rather than attempting to describe, more or less accurately, some "core" experi- 38 ence of revising, these metaphorical stories structure different aspects of revising activities. And in so doing, they challenge our present classification of various activities as "revision." Essentially, we tend to lump together as revision a variety of processes that have little more in common than their timing—they occur *after* some set of initial decisions, statements, efforts at text. To divide revising into two processes, first *revising* or *rewriting* and then *editing*, is still problematic: Depending on definitions, it may further emphasize time as the essential factor in classifying revising activities, may focus only on the broadest of the contrasts that the metaphorical stories suggest (major reformulation versus surface details), and may not be in agreement with emerging research evidence about what writers actually do when they revise. To divide revising activities by the nature of the specific act (addition, deletion, and so on) will likely prove more useful in analyzing revising activities, but such classification does not provide insight into the writer's intent in completing such an act. To divide revising activities, as Donald Murray (1978) does, into "internal" and "external" revision (respectively focused on developing one's own understanding of one's meaning and on conveying that meaning to others) does focus, to some degree, on the writer's intent and understanding of the text, but such classification does not consider the specific acts of revision that may serve the function of internal and external revision. The metaphorical stories that I have discussed here tend to classify revising activities along several dimensions at the same time—dimensions that include the above classifications, but also add to them writers' perceptions' of the text and its needs, their purposes in making a revision, the difficulty required to complete the revising act, their sense of the "feel" of the process, and so forth. As we learn more about revising and how we can describe it, we may find that such metaphorical stories suggest fruitful ways both to complicate and to make coherent our classification of revising activities.

References

Adoff, A. (1974). Arnold Adoff (L. B. Hopkins, Interv.). In L. B. Hopkins (Ed.), *More books by more people: Interviews with sixty-five authors of books for children* (pp. 1–9). New York: Citation Press.

Aiken, C. (1974). Conrad Aiken (R. H. Wilbur, Interv.). In G. Plimpton (Ed.), *Writers at work: The Paris Review interviews* (4th ser., pp. 21–24). New York: Penguin Books.

Algren, N. (1964). (H. E. F. Donohue, Interv.). In H. E. F. Donohue (Ed.), *Conversations with Nelson Algren*. New York: Hill & Wang.

Ashbery, J. (1974). Craft interview with John Ashbery (J. Bloom & R. Losada, Interv.). In W. Packard (Ed.), *The craft of poetry: Interviews from the New York Quarterly* (pp. 111–132). Garden City, NY: Doubleday.

Boice, R. (1985). Cognitive components of blocking. *Written Communication, 2*, 91–104.

Brunner, J. (1978). John Brunner (P. Walker, Interv.). In P. Walker (Ed.), *Speaking of science fiction: The Paul Walker interviews* (pp. 315–324). Oradell, NJ: Luna Publications.

Burke, K. (1945). *A grammar of motives*. Englewood Cliffs, NJ: Prentice-Hall.

Chappell, F. (1973). Fred Chappell (J. Graham, Interv.). In G. Garrett (Ed.), *The writer's voice: Conversations with contemporary writers* (pp. 31–50). New York: Morrow.

Chester, L. (1977). Laura Chester: Pavane for the passing of a child (A. T. Turner, Interv.). In A. T. Turner (Ed.), *Fifty contemporary poets: The creative process* (pp. 70–78). New York: David McKay.

Ciardi, J. (1964). John Ciardi (R. Newquist, Interv.). In R. Newquist (Ed.), *Counterpoint* (pp. 113–126). New York: Simon & Schuster.

Creeley, R. (1974). Craft interview with Robert Creeley (C. P. Davies & M. J. Fortunato, Interv.). In W. Packard (Ed.). *The craft of poetry: Interviews from the* New York Quarterly (pp. 195–223). Garden City, NY: Doubleday.

Dickey, J. (1974). Craft interview with James Dickey (W. Packard, Interv.). In W. Packard (Ed.), *The craft of poetry: Interviews from the* New York Quarterly (pp. 133–151). Garden City, NY: Doubleday.

Didion, J. (1978). Joan Didion: The art of fiction 71 (L. Kuehl, Interv.). *Paris Review*, No. 74, 142–163.

Durrell, L. (1963). Lawrence Durrell (J. Mitchell & G. Andrewski, Interv.). In G. Plimpton (Ed.), *Writers at work: The* Paris Review *interviews* (2nd ser., pp. 257–282). New York: Penguin Books.

Eberhart, R. (1977). Richard Eberhart: "A snowfall" (A. T. Turner, Interv.). In A. T. Turner (Ed.), *Fifty contemporary poets: The creative process* (pp. 85–89). New York: David McKay.

Ellison, R. (1974). A completion of personality (J. Hersey, Interv.) In J. Hersey, *The writer's craft* (pp. 267–282). New York: Alfred A. Knopf.

Farmer, P. (1976). Penelope Farmer (C. Jones & O. R. Way, Interv.). In C. Jones & O. R. Way (Eds.), *British children's authors: Interviews at home* (pp. 77–84). Chicago: American Library Association.

Federman, R. (1983). Raymond Federman (L. McCaffery, Interv.). In T. LeClair & L. McCaffery (Eds.), *Anything can happen: Interviews with contemporary American novelists* (pp. 126–151). Urbana: University of Illinois Press.

Flavell, J. H. (1979). Metacognition and cognitive monitoring: A new area of cognitive–developmental inquiry. *American Psychologist, 34,* 906–911.

Fowles, J. (1977). John Fowles (J. F. Baker Interv.). In Publishers Weekly Editors & Contributors (Eds.), *The author speaks* (pp. 50–53). New York: R. R. Bowker.

Gardner, J. (1979). John Gardner: The art of fiction 73 (P. F. Ferguson, J. R. Maier, F. McConnell, & S. Matthiessen, Interv.). *Paris Review,* No. 75, 36–74.

Gass, W. (1983). William Gass (T. LeClair, Interv.). In T. LeClair & L. McCaffery (Eds.), *Anything can happen: Interviews with contemporary American novelists* (pp. 152–176). Urbana: University of Illinois Press.

Gentner, D., & Gentner, D. R. (1983). Flowing waters or teeming crowds: Mental models of electricity. In D. Gentner & A. L. Stevens (Eds.), *Mental models* (pp. 99–129). Hillsdale, NJ: Lawrence Erlbaum.

Gentner, D., & Stevens, A. L. (Eds.). (1983). *Mental models.* Hillsdale, NJ: Lawrence Erlbaum.

Ginsberg, A. (1967). Allen Ginsberg (T. Clark, Interv.). In G. Plimpton (Ed.), *Writers at work: The* Paris Review *interviews* (3rd ser., pp. 279–320). New York: Penguin Books.

Gold, H. (1973). Interview: Herbert Gold (S. J. Thorpe, Interv.). *California Quarterly,* No. 5, 65–76.

Goyen, W. (1980). William Goyen: A poet telling stories (P. Bennett, Interv.). In P. Bennett (Ed.), *Talking with Texas writers: Twelve interviews* (pp. 227–247). College Station, TX: Texas A&M University Press.

Graves, J. (1980). John Graves: A hard scrabble world (P. Bennett, Interv.). In P. Bennett (Ed.), *Talking with Texas writers: Twelve interviews* (pp. 63–88). College Station, TX: Texas A&M University Press.

Haley, A. (1977). Alex Haley (J. F. Baker, Interv.). In Publishers Weekly Editors & Contributors (Eds.). *The author speaks* (pp. 448–451). New York: R. R. Bowker.

Hall, D. (1973). Here where no one has ever been: An interview with Donald Hall (G. FitzGerald & R. Parshall, Interv.). *Falcon, 4,* 5–16.

Isherwood, C. (1976). Christopher Isherwood (W. I. Scobie, Interv.). In G. Plimpton (Ed.) *Writers, at work: The* Paris Review *interviews* (4th ser., pp. 211–242). New York: Penguin Books.

Johnson, B. S. (1981). B. S. Johnson (A. Burns, Interv.). In A. Burns & C. Sugnet (Eds.), *The imagination on trial: British and American writers discuss their working methods* (pp. 83–94). London: Allison & Busby.

Jones, D. (1966). David Jones (P. Orr, Interv.). *The poet speaks* (pp. 97–104). In P. Orr (Ed.), New York: Barnes & Noble.

Kumin, M. (1983). Settling in another field (R. Jackson, Interv.). In R. Jackson (Ed.), *Acts of mind* (pp. 107–112). University: University of Alabama Press.

Lakoff, G., & Johnson, M. (1980a). Conceptual metaphor in everyday language. *Journal of Philosophy, 77,* 453–484.

Lakoff, G., & Johnson, M. (1980b). *Metaphors we live by.* Chicago: University of Chicago Press.

Leonard, H. (1973). Leonard: Difficult to say "No" (D. Hickey & G. Smith, Interv.). In D. Hickey & G. Smith (Eds.), *Flight from the Celtic twilight* (pp. 191–201). Indianapolis, IN: Bobbs–Merrill.

Lorde, A. (1983). Audre Lorde (C. Tate, Interv.). In C. Tate (Ed.), *Black women writers at work* (pp. 100–116). New York: Continuum.

Lowell, R. (1968). Robert Lowell (F. Seidel, Interv.). In Thomas Parkinson (Ed.), *Robert Lowell: A collection of critical essays* (pp. 12–35). Englewood Cliffs, NJ: Prentice-Hall.

MacInnes, H. (1964). Helen MacInnes (R. Newquist, Interv.). In R. Newquist (Ed.), *Counterpoint* (pp. 457–464). New York: Simon & Schuster

MacLennan, H. (1973). Hugh MacLennan: The tennis racket is an antelope bone (G. Gibson, Interv.). In G. Gibson (Ed.), *Eleven Canadian novelists* (pp. 130–148). Toronto: House of Anansi Press.

Major, C. (1985). Clarence Major (N. L. Bunge Interv.). In N. L. Bunge (Ed.), *Finding the words: Conversations with writers who teach* (pp. 53–67). London: Ohio University Press.

Malamud, B. (1975) Bernard Malamud: The art of fiction 52 (D. Stern, Interv.). *Paris Review,* No. 61, 40–64.

Mallin, T. (1981). Tom Mallin (A. Burns, Interv.). In A. Burns & C. Sugnet (Eds.), *The imagination on trial: British and American writers discuss their working methods* (pp. 95–103). London: Allison & Busby.

Mazzaro, J. (1977). Jerome Mazzaro: "At Torrey Pines State Park" (A. T. Turner, Interv.). In A. T. Turner (Ed.), *Fifty contemporary poets: The creative process* (pp. 228–238). New York: David McKay.

Meltzer, M. (1979). Milton Meltzer (P. Janeczko, Interv.). In M. J. Weiss (Ed.), *From writers to students: The pleasures and pains of writing* (pp. 67–74). Newark, DE: International Reading Association.

Michener, J. A. (1978). James A. Michener (J. Hayes, Interv.). In M. J. Bruccoli (Ed.), *Conversations with writers II* (pp. 142–180). Detroit: Gale Research.

Miller, H. (1963). Henry Miller (G. Wickes, Interv.). In G. Plimpton (Ed.), *Writers at work: The* Paris Review *interviews* (2nd ser., pp. 165–191). New York: Penguin Books.

Minty, J. (1977). Judith Minty: "The end of summer" (A. T. Turner, Interv.). In A. T. Turner (Ed.), *Fifty contemporary poets: The creative process* (pp. 242–248). New York: David McKay.

Moravia, A. (1957). Alberto Moravia (A. M. de Dominicis & B. Johnson, Interv.). In M. Cowley (Ed.), *Writers at work: The* Paris Review *interviews* (1st ser., pp. 209–229). New York: Penguin Books.

Moss, H. (1974). Craft interview with Howard Moss (M. J. Fortunato & L. Silbert, Interv.). In W. Packard (Ed.), *The craft of poetry: Interviews from the* New York Quarterly (pp. 265–293). Garden City, NY: Doubleday.

Munro, A. (1973). Alice Munro (G. Gibson, Interv.). In G. Gibson (Ed.), *Eleven Canadian novelists* (pp. 237–264). Toronto: House of Anansi Press.

Murray, D. M. (1978). Internal revision: A process of discovery. In C. R. Cooper & L. Odell (Eds.), *Research on composing: Points of departure* (pp. 85–103). Urbana, IL: National Council of Teachers of English.

Myers, M. (1973). Martin Myers: A wobble in the lens (G. Gibson, Interv.). In G. Gibson (Ed.), *Eleven Canadian novelists* (pp. 86–98). Toronto: House of Anansi Press.

Nisbett, R. E., & Wilson, T. D. (1977). Telling more than we can know: Verbal reports on mental processes. *Psychological Review, 84,* 231–259.

O'Brien, T. (1983). Tim O'Brien (L. McCaffery, Interv.). In T. LeClair & L. McCaffery (Eds.), *Anything can happen: Interviews with contemporary American novelists* (pp. 262–278). Urbana: University of Illinois Press.

Petrakis, H. M. (1977). The song of the thrush: An interview with Harry Mark Petrakis (B. F. Rodgers, Jr., Interv.). *Chicago Review, 28*(3), 97–119.

Potok, C. (1980). Chaim Potok (H. U. Ribalow, Interv.). In H. U. Ribalow (Ed.), *The tie that binds: Conversations with Jewish writers* (pp. 111–137). San Diego, CA: A. S. Barnes.

Reddy, M. (1979). The conduit metaphor: A case of frame conflict in our language about language. In A. Ortony (Ed.), *Metaphor and thought* (pp. 284–324). Cambridge: Cambridge University Press.

Rose, M. (1980). Rigid rules, inflexible plans, and the stifling of language. *College Composition and Communication, 31,* 389–401.

Rose, M. (1984). *Writer's block: The cognitive dimension.* Carbondale: Southern Illinois University Press.

Rose, M. (1985). Complexity, rigor, evolving method, and the puzzle of writer's block: Thoughts on composing-process research. In M. Rose (Ed.). *When a writer can't write: Studies in writer's block and other composing-process problems* (pp. 227–260). New York: Guilford.

Rosten, L. (1964). Leo Rosten (R. Newquist, Interv.). In R. Newquist (Ed.), *Counterpoint* (pp. 521–536). New York: Simon & Schuster.

Schmitz, D. (1977). Dennis Schmitz: "Rabbits" (A. T. Turner, Interv.). In A. T. Turner (Ed.), *Fifty contemporary poets: The creative process* (pp. 268–272). New York: David McKay.

Schon, D. A. (1979). Generative metaphor: A perspective on problem-setting in social policy. In A. Ortony (Ed.), *Metaphor and thought* (pp. 254–283). Cambridge: Cambridge University Press.

Schutz, A. (1962). M. Natanson (Ed.). *Collected papers I: The problem of social reality.* The Hague: Martinus Nijhoff.

Sexton, A. (1974). Craft interview with Anne Sexton (W. Packard & T. Victor, Interv.). In W. Packard (Ed.), *The craft of poetry; Interviews from the* New York Quarterly (pp. 19–23). Garden City, NY: Doubleday.

Sillitoe, A. (1981). Alan Sillitoe (A. Burns, Interv.). In A. Burns & C. Sugnet (Eds.), *The imagination on trial: British and American writers discuss their working methods* (pp. 149–160). London: Allison & Busby.

Smith, S. (1966). Stevie Smith (P. Orr, Interv.). In P. Orr (Ed.), *The poet speaks* (pp. 225–231). New York: Barnes & Noble.

Stegner, W. (1985). Wallace Stegner (N. L. Bunge, Interv.). In N. L. Bunge (Ed.), *Finding the words: Conversations with writers who teach* (pp. 118–127). London: Ohio University Press.

Tate, J. (1977). James Tate: "A box for Tom" (A. T. Turner, Interv.). In A. T. Turner (Ed.), *Fifty contemporary poets: The creative process* (pp. 315–321). New York: David McKay.

Thomas, W. I. (1951). E. H. Volkert (Ed.), *Social behavior and personality: Contributions of W. I. Thomas to theory and social research.* New York: Social Science Research Council.

Tomlinson, B. (1984). Talking about the composing process: The limitations of retrospective accounts. *Written Communication, 1,* 206–218.

Tomlinson, B. (1986). Cooking, mining, gardening, hunting: Metaphorical stories writers tell about their writing processes. *Metaphor and Symbolic Activity, 1,* 57–79.

Vidal, G. (1971). Gore Vidal (E. Walter, Interv.. In J. F. McCrindle (Ed.), *Behind the scenes: Theater and film interviews from the* Transatlantic Review (pp. 327–341). New York: Holt, Rinehart & Winston.

Vidal, G. (1974). Gore Vidal: The art of fiction (L. G. Clarke, Interv.). *Paris Review,* No. 59, 130–165.

Welty, E. (1984). Eudora Welty (C. Ruas, Interv.). In C. Ruas (Ed.), *Conversations with American writers* (pp. 3–17). New York: Knopf.

West, J. (1976). Jessamyn West (D. Tooker & R. Hofheins, Interv.). In D. Tooker & R. Hofheins (Eds.), *Fiction: Interviews with northern California novelists* (pp. 181–191). New York: Harcourt Brace Jovanovich/William Kaufmann.

Whalen, P. (1978). Tiger whiskers (A. Waldman, Interv.). In D. Allen (Ed.), *Off the wall: Interviews with Philip Whalen* (pp. 5–37). Bolinas, CA: Four Seasons Foundation.

Wilbur, R. (1974). Craft interview with Richard Wilbur (J. Briggs & M. Newman, Interv.). In W. Packard (Ed.), *The craft of poetry: Interviews from the* New York Quarterly (pp. 177–194). Garden City, NY: Doubleday.

Williams, J. A. (1973). John A. Williams (J. O'Brien, Interv.). In J. O'Brien (Ed.), *Interviews with Black writers* (pp. 225–243). New York: Liveright.

Yourcenar, M. (1984). (Matthieu Galey, Interv.). *With open eyes: Conversations with Matthieu Galey* (A. Goldhammer, Trans.). Boston: Beacon Press.

Questions for Discussion and Journaling

1. Notice the distinction Tomlinson makes between using interviews with writers as evidence of their "*composing practices*" and as evidence of "*discourse* [talk] *about composing*" (see para. 6). Why does Tomlinson think the latter is sound research while the former may not be trustworthy?

2. Explain why focusing on a metaphor as a way of seeing writing is also a way of *not* seeing writing. How can we get around that problem?

3. Do any of the metaphors that Tomlinson describes for revision seem true to your experience? Would you use any of them? Are there others you use?

4. Is it possible that Tomlinson is going a step too far in concluding that different metaphors might come into play at different times in the development of a text (first "*molten or malleable*," later "*less flexible*," ultimately "*a hardened surface that can only be polished*") (para. 37)? How could you argue against this interpretation based on the data she offers?

5. Do the metaphors you use to describe revision shape the ways that you revise, or do they have little or no effect?

Applying and Exploring Ideas

1. Tomlinson focuses specifically on revision. Select some other aspect of composing (like planning or monitoring) and build a list of metaphors for it.

Interview your classmates if you have difficulty thinking of metaphors that are commonly used. How do your metaphors compare to Tomlinson's? What can you conclude from the similarities and differences?

2. Tomlinson argues that "a good deal of what people 'know' about composing . . . is based not on careful observation of their own activities, but on . . . culturally shared information about the writing process" (para. 2). What do you think she means by this? Can you give examples of such "cultural knowledge" of writing—things you believe about writing or that shape your experience of it that you haven't personally experienced?

Meta Moment

Brainstorm some specific ways that your writing can benefit from what you learned here about metaphors.

Letter to West Port High School's English Department

MARIA P. REY

Framing the Paper

Maria P. Rey, a student at the University of Central Florida, wrote this letter as an assignment for her English Composition 1101 course in Fall 2009. The assignment asked her to reflect on the selections she read from this chapter (including, as you will see, the selections by Anne Lamott and Mike Rose) and to convey her new knowledge to an audience. Rey had to choose her own claims, purpose, audience, and genre, and then write appropriately, given her choices. She chose to share some of what she had learned in 1101 with her former English teachers at West Port High School in an attempt to convince them to change some of their teaching strategies. In particular, Rey echoes some of Mike Rose's claims that rigid rules can cause students to "block."

Rey worked on this letter for several weeks. The draft you see here is what Rey turned in with her end-of-semester portfolio.

October 20, 2009

West Port High School
Department of English
2160 Widener Terrace
Wellington, FL
33414

Dear West Port High School English Teachers:

You have unleashed me from a classroom enclosed by walls, and now I sit in a discussion room lit by windows. You have released me from a place that hovered over me with ceilings of rules and laws I had to stay within to a roof-less oasis that gives me limitless methods of expression. I am not comparing high school and college classrooms, but rather the different states of mind I obtained due to differences in teaching and expectations.

One of the writing rules Rey is concerned about is the requirement to have a catchy opening. Do you think she is trying too hard here, or do you think this opening is effective?

I am not writing you today to criticize or undermine your skills or qualifications, for it is people like you that I thank everyday for how much knowledge has been passed on to me. My purpose in writing you this letter is to persuade you to re-evaluate not only the method of teaching but more importantly the substance of what is taught. High school teachers place a lot of constraints on students that complicate the writing process and also slow them from becoming good writers.

What is the impact of the first two sentences in this paragraph? How well do they help you understand her concerns and claims?

The bodies you lecture to every day are not just students. Regardless of how good or bad they may be, every one of them is a living, breathing, capable writer who can be molded and shaped into a GREAT writer. In fact, students are some of the most active writers you can find. I recently logged all of the writing I did in a seven-day period; from text messages to my shopping lists, everything I remembered I had written was logged. I was surprised when I realized that I spend 25% of my waking day writing. In a week that was relatively low on written homework and reading, a quarter of my day was dedicated solely to writing. Like me, most students spend a substantial portion of their time writing. This demonstrates the importance of using us as primary sources to attain feedback so that your teaching will mold weak writers into strong ones, and good writers to great ones.

What's the "this" Rey refers to here ("This demonstrates")? How could she strengthen the link between her example and her claim?

Unfortunately, my high school education consisted of countless professors, each with different and contradicting sets of rules. Each teacher would give me different guidelines that I had to follow to achieve my two goals: my short-term goal, which was to get a good grade in their class, and my long-term goal, which was to become a good writer. Mike Rose, a lecturer in English at the University of California, found in research he conducted that "students who experienced blocking were all operating either with writing rules or . . . strategies that impeded rather than enhanced

If this were a research paper, Rey would need to add page numbers for this quote and add a Works Cited entry. Given her audience and genre, does she make the "right" choice in omitting them?

the composing process." A perfect description of the problem I faced. I know that you provide these rules in an attempt to ease the writing process, not to make it more difficult. The problem lies in how these rules are explained to us. Perhaps if the guidelines were given along with an explanation of why it is proper to use that rule in that particular case and why it may not be effective in others, students would see it as an option, not an obligation. This would enable students to choose the most effective strategy from the knowledge given to them by all of their teachers, and prevent confusion of what seem to be contradicting laws of writing.

All of my professors had different rules on what made good writing "good." There were four main "rules" that have blocked me from becoming a good writer.

The first of the four is a structural rule that every student is taught in the state of Florida due to the F-CAT testing. I realize it may be the best structure to follow to pass the test, since it is what they look for when grading, but a lot of teachers present it as the best structure to use for any kind of essay or assignment. The rule is that an essay is not complete without one introductory paragraph, three main body paragraphs that support each of the main points and lastly the conclusion paragraph. Notice that they specify the exact number of paragraphs that are acceptable for each of the components of the piece, a total of five paragraphs maximum.

To complicate it further, there were also exact guidelines of the components necessary for writing a paragraph correctly. A good paragraph had to contain no less than three sentences but no more than five. The outcomes of these "easy to follow" guidelines were one of two:

#1. CAUSE: The student's writing would be so limited that they felt no need to elaborate on their thoughts or produce well-thought-out pieces.

This fragment ("A perfect description...") seems intentional. Do you think it works, given Rey's audience and purpose?

In a number of places, Rey moves from active to passive voice. Why? Are the shifts effective?

Rey seems to have trouble linking ideas here. How could she make a smoother transition?

Here Rey gets to the "meat" of her letter—the four "rules" that have troubled her. Can you find and understand then easily? How might she reorganize to make them clearer to readers?

Rey seems to struggle with how to explain and organize her important claims here. What do you think she is getting at in dividing "outcomes" into "causes" and "results"? How could she have better labeled and organized her points here?

RESULT: They focused on staying within their writing limits instead of the content, this prevented them from thinking critically and kept them at a very elementary level of writing.

Or #2. CAUSE: The student's writing was so limited that in order to express themselves accurately they tried to bend the rules.

RESULT: The five paragraphs were enormous chunks of five extremely long run-on sentences.

As you can see by the outcomes, this method of writing left no hope for me and countless others to develop our skills and only hindered us from successfully progressing into higher levels. Although most of the students resorted to elementary writing where they didn't have to make much of an effort, I became the rule bending student. As a result, I received a lot of criticism, and to this day I have trouble forming multiple sentences that support each other, rather than one never ending statement. I support the importance of having an introduction and conclusion with a solid body to hold it all together, but I suggest that further elaboration of ideas should be encouraged when writing, not limited by strict quantities of components.

The second guideline I was given created a lot of problems for me. I was told, "The first thing you must complete when writing an essay is the introduction and your introduction MUST create instant impact for reader." This led to hours of staring at my blank Word document, leading to another hour or so to come up with a decent introduction. Once I had written my introduction I had to check for the impact effect, this led me to realize I didn't have one and consequently increased the time I spent on my introduction an additional hour. Although it is important to create a strong introduction that creates impact, it should be up to the writer to decide when to work on it. If someone is given strict limits at the beginning of their piece, they are not only going to dread writing the rest, but they are going to suffer from severe writer's block every time they attempt completing any assignment. In contrast, if they have the option of deciding when to create the beginning, they are able to work on the rest in the meantime and potentially be inspired in the process.

Were you ever taught to . . . ? Have you ever been taught . . . ? Were you ever taught that good writing should only take three tries to be good? I was taught that it should only take three drafts to create a well-written essay, a rough draft, a peer-reviewed draft and the final draft. I always asked myself what I could have found if I could have gone over it just one more time. I might realize that I missed an entire point that was crucial to my main idea, or I might find several unnecessary parts that actually weaken my piece. My point is that good writing is hard to produce with limited trials and is even harder to be made good if you are always thinking that it's your last chance to make it final. Anne Lamott, a professional writer, supports my point in her piece "Shitty First Drafts" when she states, "Almost all good writing begins with terrible first efforts." Everyone makes mistakes, from professional writers to high school and college students. So what if it takes us ten tries to make the paper good, as long as it is in your hands on the due date? Wouldn't teachers prefer reading a good tenth draft than a third not so good draft?

> What is Rey attempting to convey in the first two sentences of this paragraph? Is this rhetorical strategy effective?

> Rey is working hard to incorporate some of the writers she has read, but she doesn't always do so very elegantly. How could she incorporate Lamott, for example, differently?

Despite the harm that constraints have on the process of writing, the last of the four rules was not as detrimental to my methods as it was to the quality and overall efficiency of what I wrote. Most teachers offer to review and correct their students' drafts before the due date, and I was one of the students who took full advantage of the opportunity. Unfortunately, every time I got my paper back (or even when I went over the paper with my teachers), all I received were spelling and grammar corrections.

These comments were greatly appreciated, but I wanted to know what my teachers thought about my writing. Was the piece I worked so hard on only for a way to practice my spelling skills? After my teachers finished reading my papers, I would always ask what they thought of what I wrote. What did they think of my ideas, my opinions? Nine out of ten times I would receive a blank stare, and the short, unhelpful statement, "Good. Make sure you check your spelling and grammar mistakes." Fixing those little mistakes was important to me, but the teachers' responses always made me feel like the teachers never really read the content of what I wrote, since they were never willing to discuss it with me. I can bet that by now you have picked out several—maybe even countless— grammatical errors in what you have been reading, but did that impact the effectiveness of what I am saying to you?

Rey ends this paragraph with a good question. Do you think her structure, grammar, transitions, etc., will affect how her former high school teachers receive her letter?

As a freshman college student, I cannot over emphasize the importance of setting revising and editing priorities when grading your student's work. The first and most important component that must be looked at is the content of the piece. If the content isn't effective or even adequate for the purpose of the assignment, it cannot be considered skilled writing, regardless of how perfect the grammar and spelling is. The assignments I am given in my composition class rely on content. I am only given a question that my piece must answer, and everything else is up to me. I have to choose a genre, an audience, and a format that is only effective if the content of my piece makes it work. Spelling and grammar corrections come in at the end, once my content is established. As teachers, I understand you are trained to catch mistakes, but the teachers that help make the good writers are able to look at the whole picture and judge the overall effectiveness of the writing.

None of the teachers I have had were bad. Even though I was negatively affected by some of the methods they used, and some of the rigid rules they taught me, my teachers hoped the methods would help me become a better writer. This is why I write to you today, to make a suggestion from my experience as a student. Consider the four rules that have blocked me, and how prevalent they are in your teaching. What impact could they have on your students' development as writers? When guidelines become laws and suggestions become rules, the natural flow of writing is destroyed. Good writing lies within everyone. Students have millions of unique ideas and opinions just waiting to be shared. The key is for teachers to provide the support to aid expression and not hinder it.

Sincerely,

Maria P. Rey

Some Other Questions to Consider

- What rules have you been taught that have "blocked" you? Who taught them to you? Would you be willing to write to the people who taught them to you, in the same way that Rey writes to her teachers?
- Where does Rey most clearly make her claim(s)? Where else could she place her claims?
- How effectively does Rey integrate the ideas from this chapter? Are there other ideas from the chapter that you might suggest to strengthen Rey's claims?
- Does Rey's letter read like a letter to you? She does seem to waver at times from talking directly to her audience to talking *about* them. Why do you think that talking directly to her former teachers about their impact on her is difficult for her?

The Average Writer:
A Self-Analysis

CLAYTON STARK

Framing the Paper

Clayton Stark wrote this paper for an Honors English Composition course in Spring 2009. The autoethnography was the first major paper assigned in the course, but he continued to revise it all semester for his end-of-semester portfolio. The version you see here is the "final" draft submitted in his portfolio.

Stark 1

Clayton Stark
ENC1102H
Dr. Wardle
April 15, 2009

The Average Writer: A Self-Analysis

For more than thirty years, researchers have been studying writing in order to understand how people undertake the task of writing. It all started with Sondra Perl, a researcher who asked the question, how do we write? Since then, the field has exploded with studies trying to explain what the mind actually does when people write. We have seen James Britton's idea that writing is a linear process, to a more amorphous shape. Now, thanks to Nancy Sommers, we know that writing is more of a winding river or complex web than it is just a single line. Sondra Perl has found a code for analyzing writing systematically. Research has explored the minds of unskilled writers. And entered the world of experienced professionals, who are very good at what they do.

Why do you think Stark uses the phrase "It all started . . ."? What's the "it" he refers to?

Stark 2

Yet, there are still more questions to be answered. Each of the researchers above has had a gap in their work that I intend to fill with this paper. We have studied the experienced, the poor, the children, but what of the average writer? A student in school who is not anything special, who was never very good at the writing portion of his SAT's. What are the patterns of this type of writer? I will also attempt to show that the best person that you can research for writing is yourself, not someone else. And that Perl's code, while complex and thorough, needs to be added to. 'Periods of silence' are the writing process from her code that is in question. I call them pauses, and I will attempt to show that silence can be powerful.

The rest of this article will be divided into the methods which I used in order to obtain my data, a review of my principle findings about my writing style and the gaps mentioned above, and finally a discussion of what these results actually mean in accordance to my research questions. After the end of that I will include the paper that I analyzed, the transcripts of my study, and the code that I got from my transcript.

In order to obtain my data, I first had to have a prompt for writing. I chose to study myself responding to a prompt for my English class that asked me to read a research article by Christina Haas and Linda Flower called "Rhetorical Reading Strategies and the Construction of Meaning" and then, in our own words, describe what rhetorical reading was and then explain whether we read rhetorically. This prompt was a good one to use for such a study because it asks a very direct question, hopefully narrowing my thought processes to just writing and not jumping all over the place.

For the actual composition, I sat down when I felt I was in my best writing mood. That's how I chose my time to write; just like I normally

---

Here Stark is attempting to establish a niche that his own research can address. What do you make of the language he uses to do this? What other phrasing might he have used?

In saying that "Perl's code . . . needs to be added to," Stark suggests another interesting "niche."

Do you appreciate Stark's direct statement of his paper's content and organization? Does his directness conflict with any writing "rules" that your previous teachers have imposed?

What do you think would have been the pros and cons of studying another kind of assignment, one that was more open-ended?

do. I was in my room when I wrote it, sitting at my desk and typing it up on my computer. As I typed, I had everything open that I normally would, AIM (AOL Instant Messenger) and Skype going in the background. Some music, but only loud enough to be just barely audible. While I typed, I talked every thought that crossed my mind, no matter what it was. I recorded this on my computer as I was typing with a program called Sound Recorder Mac, a freeware program that I downloaded online specifically for this paper. The writing process took me two days to complete. On the first day I planned out and wrote the paper and then went to bed. The next morning, in the same surroundings, I edited the paper. A copy of the paper can be found in *Appendix A*.

After the actual writing of the paper, I began typing up the actual recordings of my transcript. There is only one problem with these recordings—I did not speak loudly enough at all times and I began to mumble during some portions, so the transcript is not fully complete. When coding the transcript, I marked these parts as unknown. The complete transcript is available in *Appendix B*. My complete code can be found in *Appendix C*, and will be referred to when I discuss what I have learned about my own writing. After the coding, I went through and searched for patterns and frequency of what I did while I was writing in order to form my results of this paper.

From conducting this study, a lot of knowledge about the way which I write, and quite possibly the way that other people write, has been gained. For starters, there is the writer's environment. As a writer, I function best when there is a deadline set for me. If there is, the writing has more motivation and thus is of higher quality sooner than something that I just write for the sake of writing. On

Are you surprised by all the external factors present during Stark's drafting, or is your process similar?

(We've included Stark's appendices after his paper so that you can learn more about how he conducted his research and what his final product looked like.)

Do you also feel more motivated to write when faced with a deadline?

Stark 4

the computer screen there were two distractions that served for nine of the total eleven distractions that I had while writing. They were AIM and Skype. While working on a paper, I find that it is nice to have a friendly face that you can glance up at while you collect your thoughts. Sometimes, however, this can lead to stray thoughts and conversations. These stray conversations usually end up not adding anything to the paper, and can often take away from it.

Music is another important factor in my writing. More than half the time I write, I have one kind of music playing or another. Unlike most other student writers, I just have my music at a volume where it is just barely audible. It almost turns into elevator music, only quieter and with words. Because of this, I am able to fall into patterns of well thought-out writing that follow the rhythm of the music that is playing. This is clearly visible in the portions of my transcript shown below.

$... - P_L - W_P - P_L - L - W_P - W - P_L - W_P - ... - D - W_P - L - W_P - [] - W_P - P_G - ...$

> How do you think that Stark initially figured out that his writing follows the rhythm of the music he is listening to?

For ease of seeing a pattern, the writing elements have been highlighted. A clearly identifiable pattern has formed here. Write for a sentence or two and then rest. Much of the resting time was used to plan the next phase that would be written. This pattern remains present throughout the transcript for the most part. The only part where the transcript deviates from this is after a long burst of writing. After a long burst of writing there were on average three other things before the next writing was done. This number varied greatly though, from as many as five to as few as one. By far, music is more helpful than harmful as long as it is at a reasonable volume.

This study has also taught me that my writing is often recursive. Even though I know that I'm going to come back to a paper to edit it

Stark 5

later, I couldn't help going back to fix things that didn't sound right to me. Of my whole writing process, 16% was spent on revisions. Most of the revisions that I did while writing though were simple changes, correcting errors that I made while typing or going back and changing the wording of a single sentence because it sounded odd. Once I made an organizational change during my writing but I never made a conceptual change during this time.

What do you think Stark means by "conceptual change"? Do you wish he had said more here about the kinds of changes he made?

All this information can be seen in Table 1 found below. The total breakdown of my writing is shown by each different writing process that could have occurred during my writing. The data also shows how often I used each process during the editing session of my paper.

Table 1

The different writing processes I coded for, their symbol, and their frequency of occurrence

As you can see, Stark's coding system is similar to Perl's, but perhaps even more complicated. Are the percentages helpful to you? How do you think he coded his data in order to calculate them? Would it have been helpful for you to hear more about his coding system?

Writing Process	Symbol	Frequency (writing)	Percentage (writing)	Frequency (editing)	Percentage (editing)
Planning (general)	P	5	03.13%	0	00.00%
Planning (global)	P_G	11	05.88%	1	01.64%
Planning (local)	P_L	17	10.63%	9	14.75%
Writing (general)	W	13	08.13%	0	00.00%
Writing (with planning)	W_P	24	15.00%	7	11.48%
Writing (burst)	W_B	6	03.75%	0	00.00%
Revision (lexical)	R_L	12	07.50%	15	24.59%
Revision (organizational)	R_O	1	00.63%	3	04.92%
Revision (conceptual)	R_C	0	00.00%	3	04.92%
Formatting	F	3	0.188%	0	00.00%
Distraction	D	11	05.88%	0	00.00%
Pause	[]	18	11.25%	1	01.64%
Stray Thought	{}	10	06.25%	0	00.00%
Rereading	π	17	10.63%	18	29.51%
Research	L	7	04.38%	4	06.56%
Losing Place	?	1	00.63%	0	00.00%
Unknown	UNK	4	02.50%	0	00.00%
Total		**160**	**100.00%**	**61**	**100.00%**

Stark 6

In total I marked 121 different processes over an hour of planning, writing, and editing.

I also found out something interesting about stray thoughts. I would have thought that stray thought would have come most often after distractions. From my research I was proven incredibly wrong. Stray thoughts were most commonly preceded by some form of writing. This occurred 70% of the time, where as distractions only accounted for 10% of my own stray thoughts. Over my time writing the paper, I estimate that roughly two minutes and forty five seconds of my total writing time was occupied with stray thoughts. How would an outside researcher be able to know about these stray thoughts? The answer to this is simply that an outside researcher cannot know these things.

Another thing that I have learned about the way that I write has to do with pauses. Before conducting my research, if you asked why someone was pausing I would say that it was because he or she is not concentrating on the work at hand. Looking through my transcript I can see that pauses can have a wide variety of uses. A pause after planning or writing often meant that my brain was considering what I was writing and processing the vast amounts of information that was flowing through my head. In other words, I was planning without actually thinking about it. Below is a piece of my transcript that exemplifies this.

We think that this is a pretty interesting finding ("A pause after planning or writing . . ."). Is this finding clear enough to you, or could it use more explanation?

$$... - P - [] - P_G - P - [] - D... - D - [] - L - ... - W_B ([] - [] - [] - [] - []) - ...$$

From this we get all three types of pauses that I have. The first one, as seen in the first segment, is a pause after planning. This signifies that my brain is processing the plan that I have formed. It is trying to catch up with itself and make sure that everything so far makes sense and works. This type of pause occurred 16.67%

of the time. The next type, shown in the second part, comes after a distraction. This is me actually not concentrating on my work. This was the original reason I thought that most people pause when writing; however, this only accounts for 11.11% of my pauses. The rest of my pauses occurred after writing. In the last piece of the transcript, you can see a burst of writing that I had that most clearly shows this. This also shows the most common time that the breaks after writings came. 72.22% of my pauses came after writing, and nearly 85% of them were during bursts of writing that lasted long enough to catch up with myself before moving on to my next sentence. This shows that pauses are more than just pauses, they are the writer attempting to keep up with themselves and not get too far ahead or behind themselves at any given time.

> *Do you understand and/or relate to Stark's experience of trying to "keep up with" himself while he writes?*

> *How else might Stark transition to his conclusion?*

To tie up any loose ends, it seems to me that the best way to study a writer is to study one's self. How else would you know why patterns of writing occur? You would just be able to say that there was a clear pattern while writing, but because I was both the writer and the researcher, I could give you more. I could tell you that that pattern occurred when there was music present, and that the pattern occurred at the beat of the present music when my brain listened to it at a subconscious level. Detail and accuracy are much greater when studying yourself because you know your own thoughts. You know what is going on when you aren't speaking. When you have a burst of writing. Outside research can only speculate as to why these things happen. You, on the other hand, have lived with yourself, and studied yourself to find what works, for your whole life. You know you own habits and tendencies.

As for pauses, I think that it's clear now that a "period of silence" is not that at all. Rather they should be called periods of enlightenment. Pauses

Stark 8

are crucial so that your train of thought does not get drastically far ahead of your writing. Without these pauses I believe that both sentence and paragraph structure would falter. More often than not a pause is used for constructive purposes rather than destructive ones.

Appendix A

Reading Notebook 5

In the research paper "Rhetorical Reading Strategies and Construction of Meaning," three clearly identifiable forms of reading have been distinguished. Christina Haas and Linda Flower, the authors of the article, have studied ten readers. Four of post-college level, and six freshmen; three of average reading level and three of above average reading level. From this they have discovered, or rather identified, three types of reading strategies: content based strategies, function or feature based strategies, and finally rhetorical strategies. These women have also given definitions to these different reading strategies and outlined how students use them.

The strategies that they identified are as follows. Content reading, they've decided, is concerned with information regarding interpretation, summarization, or paraphrasing the text of what they have read. More informally, this has been called "information getting." It is the most basic level of reading. One step above that is function and feature reading. Function and feature strategies are defined as readers trying to take a piece of text and decide what that piece is. For example they will say that a sentence is the introduction, the main point, or a supporting detail. Function and feature is focused on what the text was doing rather than what it actually said. The final level of reading and also the most advanced is rhetorical reading. Rhetorical reading was defined as trying to find a purpose, context or effect of the given text. In other words, the reader is figuring out why a certain text was written.

Rhetorical reading, in my opinion, is reading on a much deeper level than is normally expected of teachers. In high school, rhetorical reading is not a part of the curriculum. When used correctly, this kind of reading intertwines with the others in order to form a broader picture of the the topic that is being read about as well as a deeper understanding of both meaning and purpose. When reading about things with which they are not familiar, rhetorical readers will try to figure out who the work was written for and why it was written. By doing this the rhetorical reader grasps the main ideas and concepts, both stated and implied, that the paper is trying to covey. By doing this they can more readily understand what they are reading. Also rhetorical readers have an improved ability to find the points of an article, both expressed and implied.

In my own experience, I have been a rhetorical reader, but not as often as the more experienced readers whom this study describes. For example, if I know nothing about an article, I will try to figure out why the article was written but seldom think about the intended audience or the effect of the article has on the audience. In other texts where I know the target audience. I tend to think more about the impact that a text has had on that audience, and less about author and purpose. I question why they wrote what they have, and use that information to derive a deeper meaning from the text. Seldom do I ever think about the context in which something is written. Maybe its because I have always been given the context in which something was written or maybe it's because I have never really valued this part of a reading. Now that I understand the importance of rhetorical reading, that may change because I have seen that doing this helps people to better understand what they read. Indeed it did as I was reading "Rhetorical Reading Strategies and the Construction of Meaning." While reading this article I thought about it being written for research purposes. I understood the context, and the audience, and by taking them into account, I could form a better understanding of the article.

For the future, I will try to better use and develop rhetorical reading strategies of my own because it has been proven to make understanding of reading much greater. This is both by Haas and Flower, as well as in my own experience reading their article. I have have discovered the importance of trying to figure out who wrote an article, why they wrote the article, who the article was written for, and other questions of purpose. It has made my comprehension of difficult text, in my own opinion, better. And hopefully I have learned from it and can use it more often when I read.

Appendix B

I'm starting my auto-ethnography. Lets see, assignment, (pause) What is rhetorical reading? Do you think you read rhetorically? Alright, rhetorical reading let me go through and see what that paper has to say about rhetorical reading. Where did I mark that? Rhetorical reading is an active attempt at constructing a rhetorical context as a way of making sense of it, in other words that means that rhetorical reading is trying to find out why something was written, and who wrote it (banging, pauses) in order to make more sense out of a reading. Hmm. (pause) So right now I'm writhing down rhetorical reading (pauses) and thinking about what that actually means to me. Why it was written, for whom and by whom (pauses). Distracted by Krystina, (typing) Ok, going back to my rhetorical reading. (typing), umm. (pauses and mumbling) ONE! (laughing) Alright, rhetorical reading also reefers to . . . (pauses) Lets see where are rhetorical reading strategies in here I know I put a big star by it. Context strategies, function strategies, it should be right after this rhetorical situation, trying to account for the writer's, ah purpose of writing, context of the writing, effect of the writing, ummm . . . To do it readers use cues and their own knowledge of situations. Ummm . . ., Basically you try to find out why the writer has written it and who audience is. For example with this piece the audience that Haas and Flower are writing to are other rhetoric and composition teachers in their field. And they're writing to see if more experienced readers do this and the answer that they've come up with is definitely yes. And they definitely do read better as a result of it. So, now. That's one, that's the first part of the question. Do you think that you read rhetorically. Well that's a yes and a no and, uh, it depends on the situation. Sometimes I do and sometimes I don't. Hmm . . . (pauses) I'm getting a drink. S*** where's my glass? Alright, I lost my cup so this is going to be a long pause. Alright I found it. Alright File. Open. Reading notebook 4. Open, (pauses) Today is the 28th Reading Notebook 5. Alright lets start with the introduction. (pauses) I wanna start off by . . ., I wanna start off by . . . umm . . . how do I wanna start? I want to start by summarizing the different kinds of reading, including rhetorical, then I wanna go to defining rhetorical reading, (pauses) and finally I want to talk about my own rhetorical reading experiences. After that I'll see what I come up with and go through and edit it. Ok, how to start? Lets start with something simple. The title of their paper. *In the research paper by Christina,* wow that's a weird spelling, *Haas and Linda Flower* (shoot I can't spell) *these two clearly identifiable,* (hold on, aim distraction) yes. Two clearly identifiable, oh no it's not two it's three, go back and change that. *Forms of reading have been* discovered? unearthed? what's the word that I want to use? I'll just use, I don't know, distinguished! (typing) Now I'm going to change by Christina Haas and Linda Flower to the title of the article (typing) I believe this is good because . . . I don't know why I'm doing it. (typing and mumbling) put the comma inside the quote. Alright, oh I know why I'm doing it, so I can use their names in the next part *Christina Haas and Linda Flower have studied* (pauses) how many did they study? They studied ten, three and three and four. Yep ten. *Studied ten readers, four of post college level, and six freshmen, three of average level and three above average,* (typing) Now I'm trying to figure out what I want to say next. Something about what they've discovered from this (typing) *or rather identified* (typing) *types* (mumbling) ty not ti. *Discovered three types of strategies.* Oh crap that's repetitive. Three types of reading strategies, (pauses) I'll now list them (typing) semicolon. Trying to find them, trying to find them. *Content based strategies, function or feature based strategies,* why do I keep spelling based like that, that's dumb, *and finally, rhetorical based strategies.* Now I want to define what each one of these is and then where will I go? I'll go into, more in-depth into the rhetorical strategies. That works, (typing) *These women define contact strategies as,* hold on, *these women have also given definitions to.* Have also given definitions to (pauses) also given definitions to, *these different reading strategies. Content reading, they've decided, is concerned with information* (pauses) concerned with information *regarding interpretation, summarization,* How do you you spell that? Who knows. That's not how, Oh I need an a instead of an e *or paraphrasing text of what they have read,* (pauses) *More informally, this has been called information getting,* ummm. *Function and feature,* where am I, feature *strategies.* (pauses) *are defined as* (pauses) *readers trying to take a piece of text and decide what that piece is. For example they will say that a sentence is the introduction, the main point, or a supporting detail.* (pauses) *they try, function and feature is focused on what the text was doing rather than it what it actually said.* I think that's one I do a lot. (pauses) Changing that to a new paragraph, where I begin "content reading." You listened to me!? You must think I'm crazy. OH. Aim distraction, she listened to me. Am I mad? No. I'm not mad I just think that's kinda weird. Ok. Ba-Back to writing. Wow I almost ha- Is this on your recording? Yeah. It is. (laughing) What? Answer me. Oh, you're not talking to me. Ok. Alright. Oh, right, on to rhetorical. *Rhetorical reading is defined as* find the page. Ummm . . . *trying to find a purpose, context, or effect of the given text.* (pauses) *Basically it is the act of trying to distinguish one text from another.* Now I'm going to move into the body about what rhetorical reading actually is, oh, I can branch out into what it does. What it does, Alright. (typing) *In my opinion, is reading on a much deeper than is normally expected by teachers. This kind of reading intertwines with the others in order to form* (pauses) *a broader picture of the topic that is being written about as well as a deeper understanding of both meaning and purpose.* (pauses) (typing) Hold on I used the wrong word there, that's a miscue. This kind of reading intertwines with the others in order to from a broader picture of the topic that is being, oh no that's right. I thought I put beginning there. Oh crap am I double spacing this? Yeah, ok, now it is. M&M's OOO. I want some. Aww. I can't have any, dam. (pauses) Alright. *In order to be a rhetorical reader, one must try to make sense of the purpose of on article, book, etc. he or she is reading,* ummm. I'm looking through the passage for more information, (senseless gibberish) (typing) *things which are not familiar, rhetorical reader will,* whoops. I spelled too many words wrong there *will go, will go, will try to figure out.* will try to figure out how. I totally lost my train of thought. This is what happenes when I talk and type, it doesn't work. When reading, about things, *with which. They* Rhetorical readers will try to figure out *who the work.* Hi Krystina, *was written for. By doing this the rhetorical reader* (pauses) *grasps what the paper is trying to,* grasps, *the main ideas and concepts, both stated and implied,* wow that (indistinguishable) is really trippy, *that the paper is trying to convey.* (pauses) Whoops I didn't mean to put a period there. That's a grammatical error. Fixed! *They can more readily* how do you spell that, not like that, readily readily, that's close, they can more readily *understand what they are reading and pull out things that they need to know faster,* hmm. I think I. (pauses) *In my own experience, I have used rhetorical reading, but not as often as the more experienced writers,* writers? *readers who this survey studied.* (pauses) *For example, if I know nothing an article I will try to figure out why the article was written, but seldom think about the intended audience or the effect of the article on this audience,* (typing for minutes) (pauses) Alright, 9:05 I'm out of ideas. (2 minute pause) Now where shall I go? In the complete opposite direction. (typing) *In a text where I know,* where I know, where I know *the target audience I tend to think more about the effect that this text will have on that audience. I question why they wrote what they wrote.* (mumbling) (pauses) I think I'm going to have to close it up pretty soon because i don't know what else to say. Ummmm . . . (typing) hmm . . . (pauses) (begins singing Sugar Ray–Under the Sun) I'm going to go get another drink. Rereading what I wrote. Already. From the fourth paragraph down. Reading through the reading again. Ah, context. *Seldom do I ever think about context in which . . .* maybe it's never not nope, can't use double negative *always been given the context something is written.* or maybe it's because I never really valued this part of rhetorical reading, (pauses) (typing and mumbling) indeed *it is . . . as I was reading. Rhetorical reading* oops, *strategies in the construction of meaning. indeed,* i-n-d-e-a-d-e? (typing) *I got,* I got, I donno because I didn't write it down, darn it. (pauses) *This article is written for re, for research purposes,* no that's not even close. *For the future, I will try to* whoops, wa-wa? wo-wo? wu-wu? *try to . . .* I will try to . . . *better,* no to better isn't one word, *use and develop rhetorical* whoops *reading strategies of my own, because it has been proven to make reading understanding much greater.* (pauses) *This is both by Haas and Flower as well as in my own experience reading their article. I have discovered* what? *the importance of trying to figure out who wrote an article, why they wrote it, who they wrote the article for and many other such things. It has made my reading ability in my own opinion, much better and hopefully I have learned from it, I feel like rhetorical reading will help me in the future, especially when I have to read something that I don't necessarily* that's spelled wrong *understand very well.* Alright I'm done for now I'm going to take a break. And I need tea.

Alright starting my auto-ethnography part two. First I'm going to read through and see if everything that I have makes sense. and then I'm going to edit it, (silence as I read through paper) (typing) *of the average* (pauses) *Three types of reading strategies. Content based strategies, function and feature strategies, and rhetorical reading strategies,* (pages turning) (typing) *and outline how students use them. The strategies that they identify are as follows.* (pauses) Ah. *Inserting that context reading is the most basic reading level. One step above that is function and feature reading. Function and feature strategies are defined as readers trying to take a piece of text and decide what the piece is. For example they will say that a sentence is the introduction, the main point, or a supporting detail Function and feature is focused on what the text is doing rather than what it actually said,* Inert after that *the final level of reading, and also the most advanced, is rhetorical reading,* (clicking) *Rhetorical reading was defined as trying to find purpose, context, or effect of a given text. Basically they're trying* no that's wrong. In the wrong spot maybe? No just completely the wrong point, take that out. *In other words the reader is* what's the reader do, the reader is . . . Making each specific text . . . No, The rander is . . . The reader is . . . what are they doing? I know what it is (just don't know how to express it. Let me check through here. Identifying with the purpose of the text? (pauses) I already said that. Figuring out why the text was written. That's what I want to say. *Why a certain text was written. It is reading on a much deeper level than is normally expected,* or teachers that's a miscue, of teachers. *In high school, rhetorical reading is not normally taught.* (pauses) Rhetorical reading is not part of the curriculum, Curriculum. *This kind of reading intertwines with the others in order to form a broader picture.* When done correctly. *When used correctly this kind of reading intertwines with the others in order to form a broader picture of the topic that is being read as well as a deeper understanding of both meaning and purpose,* (pauses) That needs to be moved. Somewhere. The question is where? (pauses) Here? In the first paragraph? (pauses) No. Maybe just taken out completely. *When reading about things with which they are unfamiliar, rhetorical readers will try to figure out who the work was written for, and why it was written* Inserted. *By doing this the rhetorical reader grasps the main ideas and concepts both stated and implied that the paper.* Miscue right there That, *the paper is trying to convert. They can more readily understand what they are reading and pull out points.* Alright, that whole sentence is completely terrible. The last sentence of the fourth paragraph-third paragraph I'm sorry. Is completely terrible I am going to say. *They can more readily understand what the* what'd they say in this article? (pages turning) claims of the article? Nah *Understand what they are reading. Also they have an improved ability to find the points of an article and to* (typing) *figure out unexpressed claims.* And to figure out, and to figure out unexpressed claims, *with rhetorical reading they are also able to do this faster than other readers.* Period. I can take out the last sentence of paragraph three. Make sure that sounds good. *They can more readily understand what they are reading.* By doing this that's what it needs. *By doing this.* There. *Also rhetorical readers* (pauses) *both expressed and and implied for unexpressed claims.* I'm going to take out the whole faster thing, (sighs) *In my own experience, I have been a rhetorical reader but not as often as those whom the study describes. For example if I know nothing about an article I will try to figure out why it was written, hut seldom think about the the intended audience or effect the article . . . the article on this audience.* Insert has, miscue. On *this audience.* On the audience. *I believe that doing this will help me better understand what I read.* That needs to be taken out right now. (pauses) And moved somewhere else, but where? *In other texts where I know the target audience I lend to think more about the impact the text has had on that audience and less about author and purpose.* (clicking) (pauses) I need to find somewhere for that last sentence, unless I just completely take it out again. (pauses) I'll put it in right after change. *I believe that doing this will help me better understand . . .* (pauses) *because I have seen that doing this will . . .* (pauses) *helps people to better understand what they read.* (pauses) *rhetorical reading* (pauses) *This article,* insert article, miscue. *it being written for research purposes. I understood context and the audience and by taking them Into account, could form a better understanding of the article,* Hmm . . . (mumbling) *For the future* (pauses) *As well as in my own experience reading their article I have discovered the importance of trying to figure out who wrote the article, why they wrote the article,* (pauses) *who the article was written for and many other, and other questions of purpose. Which have made my reading abilities, in my own opinion, not much better yet . . .* (pauses) reading, *my comprehension of difficult text. I feel like rhetorical reading,* (pauses) *Learn from it and can use it more often when I read.* Done at 10:56AM

Appendix C

Writing Code:

P_G – L – P – D – P – [] – P_G – P – [] – D – {} – D – UNK – D – [] – L – P_G – P_L – P – P_L – P_G – L – P_G

– P – P_G – D – F – P_L – P_G – P_L – W_P – {} – W_P – {} – W_P – D – π – R_L – W_P – P_L – W – R_L – W – {}

– W – {} – P_L – W_P – P_L – L – W_P – W – P_L – W_P – UNK – {} – W – π – P_L – W_P – π – R_L – W_P – P_L

– P_G – W – W_P – π – P_L – π – W_P – P_L – π – W_P – {} – W_B ([] – [] – [] – [] – []) – {} – R_O – F – P_L –

D – W_P – L – W_P – [] – W_P – P_G – P_L – W_B ([] – []) – W – R_L – π – F – D – [] – W – L – UNK – W_P

– π – W_P – π – ? – {} – π – R_L – π – W_P – D – W_P – π – R_L – D – W – R_L – W – R_L – π – W_P – P_L –

W_B – ([]) – W_B – [] – P_L – W – π – W_P – UNK – P_G – [] – W – [] – D – π – P_L – W_B ([] – W_P – R_L –

R_L) – π – P_L – W_P – P_G – W_P – π – P_L – R_L – R_L – W_B([]) – R_L

Editing Code:

$P_G - \pi - R_L - \pi - - P_L - R_L - L - R_L - \pi - R_L - \tau - R_C - W_P - P_L - L - P_L - W_P - R_L - \pi - R_L - \pi$

$- R_L - \pi - R_C - \pi - R_L - W_P - R_L - \pi - P_L - P_L - L - P_L - W_P - P_L - W_P - R_O - \pi - R_L - [] - \pi - P_L$

$- R_L - R_C - \pi - R_L - \pi - R_O - \pi - P_L - R_O - \pi - R_L - \pi - P_L - \pi - P_L - R_L - \pi$

Key

Symbol	Meaning	Symbol	Meaning	Symbol	Meaning

Some Questions to Consider

- In his opening paragraphs, Stark tries to establish his territory (the first "move" in John Swales's **CARS model**—see pp. 6–8) by giving an overview of research on the writing process. How well does he achieve his goal? Would you do anything differently if you were to write this section?
- As teachers, we have never had another student (even a graduate student) who attempted to expand Perl's code, as Stark does here. Why do you think this might be? What allowed Stark to attempt it?
- Take a look at the "processes" Stark coded for. What role do these play in your own writing? If you were replicating Stark's investigation, which processes would you code for?
- We were intrigued by Stark's saying that he likes to keep AIM and Skype open while he drafts ("I find that it is nice to have a friendly face . . ."). The two of us often work together on writing, but it has never occurred to us to use Skype while we were drafting. Is this something you do? Why or why not? In Stark's case, did Skype turn out to be a good thing?
- Stark notes that his writing is often recursive. Does the same apply to you? Consider exploring this question in your own autoethnography.

How Do I Write?

DOMINIEQ RANSOM

Framing the Paper

Dominieq Ransom wrote this autoethnography for her English Composition 1101 course in Fall 2009 at the University of Central Florida. This was the draft included in her end-of-semester portfolio. You will see that she chose to study herself in a natural environment, but doing a sort of "timed" writing (though the time limit was self-imposed). Ransom created her own method for analyzing herself, which involved writing down her thoughts instead of speaking them aloud. As you read her paper, take note of how she makes the three "moves" that John Swales outlines in his **CARS model** (establishing a territory, establishing a niche, and filling that niche—see pp. 6–8). In particular, notice what she chose as her territory. As you read her paper, consider what other territory she might have chosen to stake out.

Ransom 1

Dominieq Ransom
ENC 1101
Mr. Bryan
Dec. 1, 2009

How Do I Write?

To become good at something takes practice. Mozart didn't just wake up and become a great musician. Emeril didn't walk into a kitchen and all of a sudden become a master chef. This belief applies to every aspect of life, even in the world of writing. Every writer, from Shakespeare to Mark Twain, started as an unskilled writer and worked their way up to being seen as a professional writer.

Over the years, researchers have studied both professional and unskilled writers to understand their writing process. One researcher, Sondra Perl, studied unskilled writers in a laboratory setting. Perl's study analyzed

> *Could Ransom make a stronger connection between the catchy opening and her focus on process research? What might that transition look like?*

Ransom 2

subjects to understand the different flaws in their writing process, and how these affect their writing (184). Another researcher, Carol Berkenkotter, studied the writing of a professional writer, Donald Murray, in his natural environment. Berkenkotter analyzed how a skilled writer's process affected their writing (201). Both Perl and Berkenkotter used the think aloud protocol. The think aloud protocol is when a researcher studies a subject while they're writing, and has them say everything they're thinking as they write. Perl and Berkenkotter's studies created an understanding of the processes of writing of unskilled and skilled writers. However, these researchers were unable to get into the mind of their subject and truly understand their thoughts. Being unable to do so, their research had gaps in terms of how well they could understand how these writers truly wrote. Their research left a question to be answered. What does a person know about their own writing process?

My research picked up where Perl and Berkenkotter left off. My study involved me analyzing myself under a time constraint of an hour, and instead of using the think aloud protocol. I will wrote down my thoughts on paper. My research suggests that studying one's own process of writing can be more beneficial than the use of studying other subjects. My research also demonstrates how a person can come to better understand their own writing process and how it affects their writing.

Methodology

To obtain the data for this study, I studied myself using an English journal assignment. I was responding to a topic that I wasn't familiar with. It was a direct question that didn't require me to personally address it. For this study I chose to do a naturalistic experiment. My natural environment involved me being in my room with the door closed and locked, rocking to

---

Do you think it is accurate to say that Perl was looking for "flaws"?

Ransom focuses on "research methods" as her "territory." What would her study have looked like if she had focused on research findings instead?

Why do you think Ransom uses the word "truly" here?

What do you think Ransom means by "It was a direct question that didn't require me personally to address it"?

the music playing loudly in the background. I typed my response on my laptop, and kept out a separate piece of paper to record my thoughts. I used a time constraint of an hour. This is the amount of time I normally take to do my English homework before class. Every five minutes or so while I was responding to the prompt I stopped and wrote down my thoughts.

> Would it be helpful for you as a reader if Ransom had explained why she chose to write down her thoughts instead of thinking aloud?

Afterward, I transcribed the notes I made while writing and coded them. Since I didn't use the think aloud protocol and opted to write down my thoughts and actions, the notes were already there, I just had to code them, unlike Perl and Berkenkotter. They had to listen to recordings and watch videos very carefully, and in some cases they still were unable to make out some of the words their subjects were saying. While coding my transcripts, I realized that my writing process possessed a pattern.

> What do you think Ransom means by suggesting that her writing process "possessed a pattern"?

Findings

My research suggested that writing under a time constraint has both positive and negative effects on my writing. Timed writing causes me to write faster. I noticed that I spent much of my time having writing bursts which lasted for five minute intervals. These writing bursts were filled with information that I obtained from the text. I was trying to get as much information out of my head towards the prompt as I could, because I knew I had to finish the journal and get to class on time. With the use of a time constraint I responded to the text more precisely, because I felt the need to "get to the point." In the setting of a timed writing, I had a better understanding of the text since it was fresh in my mind. Although I did go back and reread parts of the text, I didn't spend much time dwelling on simple facets of it.

Although writing under a time constraint helps me stay focused on my writing, it also hinders my performance and writing process. While writing

Ransom 4

under a time constraint I do make many simple mistakes such as word choice, omitting information, and misspelling words. This causes me to spend more time editing. I spent almost fifteen percent of my time editing and almost nine percent formatting my paper to what I felt was acceptable. Writing under a time constraint also hinders my writing because I don't plan before I write, due to a lack of time. This makes my thoughts unorganized and sometimes causes me to feel as though the journals I submit are inadequate.

Do you wonder where Ransom came up with these percentages? How/where could she have explained this?

Although I normally use the hour before class to write my response to the journal prompts, this study somehow was different, due to the extent of the prompt. Even though I was in my natural environment with few distractions, I found that the time I had was the biggest distraction of all. During the study I kept checking the time (8 times to be exact). This caused me to feel rushed because I couldn't take my time and complete the journal the way I wanted to. This also happened to Mr. Murray, the subject of Berkenkotter's study. While Berkenkotter studied him in his natural environment he was able to compose with ease, but when he was put into a setting that involved a time constraint, he was unable to write properly. During that time he produced little over two sentences.

What is Ransom suggesting that her study was different from ("this study somehow was different")?

Why was Ransom checking the time so much?

When I analyzed my study, I realized that writing down my thoughts while responding to the prompt had both negative and positive impacts on my research. Writing down my thoughts caused me to be unable to devote my time completely to responding to the prompt. I also wrote clear and concise notes so that I would be able to transcribe them thoroughly, because I wouldn't be able to review my study. Perl and Berkenkotter were able to analyze findings and review their subjects repeatedly with data they recorded using video and tape recorders.

Ransom writes a lot about the acts of researching and analyzing. Try revising some of her sentences so that they focus primarily on her findings instead.

Ransom 5

Writing down my thoughts did prove to be an advantage because I had evidence of what I was thinking while I was writing. Perl and Berkenkotter didn't know everything their subjects were thinking, because you don't always talk as fast as you think. I found myself writing things down on paper that I wouldn't have said out loud due to fear of criticism. Perl and Berkenkotter's subjects might have felt this way, too. Writing down my thoughts also helped with writer's block, because it allowed me to analyze my thoughts while writing them and think about the prompt. This led to thinking, which led to writing, which led to thinking while writing.

These last two sentences present one of Ransom's most interesting findings. What do you think are the implications of this finding?

Conclusion

In conducting this study I identified strengths and weaknesses in my writing. It has shown me that I write best under a time constraint. It also has shown me that my writing process could be better if I gave myself more time to write. With the use of an extended time I would still be focused on the journal. This would allow me to incorporate time for planning. By adding in extra time to plan my journals my thoughts would be more organized before writing. I found that when I don't plan I spend more time editing because my thoughts aren't organized or formatted properly. With the use of the extra time I wouldn't feel as rushed, and the mistakes I make while writing would decrease.

Do these two sentences ("It has shown me . . . if I gave myself more time to write.") contradict each other? How could you reconcile them?

Perl and Berkenkotter's experiments increased understanding of the process of writing with the use of the think aloud protocol. My study allowed the use of liberal thought with the use of writing down my ideas instead of using the think aloud protocol. If I had tried to use the think aloud protocol instead of writing I would probably not have said much because I don't talk very quickly. I also get so into my writing that I would eventually have stopped talking.

What do you think Ransom means by "liberal thought"?

Ransom 6

My study has shown that there are different ways to analyze a writing process, and the think aloud protocol is not the only way one can go about doing so. Although writing down your thoughts instead of using the think aloud protocol has some flaws, it allows writers to analyze their thoughts more. After conducting my research, I realized that everyone writes in a way that makes them comfortable, and the best way to understand the process of writing is to study your own.

Note how Ransom comes back here to her paper's "niche."

Do you feel that this is a strong concluding claim? Are there other findings that you would have been interested in seeing her highlight here?

Ransom 7

Works Cited

Berkenkotter, Carol. "Decisions and Revisions: The Planning Strategies of a Publishing Writer." Wardle and Downs 199–216.

Perl, Sondra. "The Composing Process of Unskilled College Writers." Wardle and Downs 182–197.

Wardle, Elizabeth, and Doug Downs, eds. *I Am a Writer in the World: Researching Personal and Academic Literacies.* Acton, MA: Copley-Xanedu Custom, 2009. Print.

Some Other Questions to Consider

- Quickly make a list of findings from the readings in this chapter that most interested you. If you consider this to be the "territory" for your own auto-ethnography introduction, what might be a niche that you could fill? What have researchers still not learned that you could learn by doing your own study?
- Ransom found that taking notes led to writing, which led to thinking. Do you think this happens to you? Have you tried writing for exploration—that is, in order to come up with ideas?

Interlude:

WHAT WRITERS SAY

The article that stood out the most, to me, and one that gave me confidence as a developing writer, was Anne Lamott's 'Shitty First Drafts." Before college, I thought published authors were born with a gift, which allowed them to write with fluency and ease. After reading "Shitty First Drafts" I realized that even professional writers go through their own struggling processes and multiple drafts before reaching that perfect paper. It made me realize that even I could become a good writer if I worked at it.

—Jillian Loisel, Student

We do not frame the short essays here in the way that we framed the scholarly essays. Rather than giving you background about each author and discussion questions for each essay, we frame the group of essays and then leave you in peace to read them. They are not dense or difficult texts, for the most part, and if you are interested in the authors we encourage you to look them up and read some of their other work.

These are professional writers talking about how they write—their understanding of writing "rules" and conventions, their motivations and hurdles, their rituals, their mental blocks, and their sense of themselves as writers. In the introduction to this chapter we noted that these writers are discussing many of the same concepts considered in the research articles—but they are not conducting research: They are commenting on their own experiences. As you read what these authors have to say, ask yourself how their claims relate to the research claims and what these authors are saying about writing that affirms or contradicts commonly understood conceptions of writing.

Right away you should notice that none of these writers thinks that writing is easy or quick. They all struggle, take breaks, search for better words, throw away what they've written, learn from their drafts, revise, and complain. None of them would be likely to argue that good writers are just "born." As you read their essays, ask what you can learn from these writers that can help you. Does their attitude about what writing *is* have an impact on what they *do*? If you adopt some of their attitudes and practices, what might happen to you as a writer? What do these writers know that you don't? What do these writers know and do that Tony (from Sondra Perl's article, found on pp. 191–214) or the blockers (from Mike Rose's article, found on pp. 236–249) *don't* know or do?

There is one other concept I wish I had known more about during my time in high school. Although tedious, it is always a clever idea to write a first draft. Anne Lamott, a writer and creative writing professor, wrote an article about the significance of it and how initial first drafts are always "shitty." The great majority of writers cannot just spit out a book, an article, or any writing task they might be working on in just one single draft. Writing a "shitty" first draft is far more helpful than it sounds and is something that all writers can benefit from. Lamott makes a good point by saying, "Very few writers really know what they are doing until they've done it" (Lamott para. 2). She is saying that as a writer, you can't get a strong idea of what you want to write until you've already started. Many people think that when experienced writers start their piece, they "spit out" a sole draft that expresses everything they should be communicating. This is clearly a common misconception because even great writers make first, second, even third drafts, and the first is always a mess.

—Sam Greenberg, Student

Shitty First Drafts

ANNE LAMOTT

Lamott, Anne. "Shitty First Drafts." *Bird by Bird: Some Instructions on Writing and Life.* New York: Anchor, 1994. 21–27. Print.

Now, practically even better news than that of short assignments is the idea of shitty first drafts. All good writers write them. This is how they end up with good second drafts and terrific third drafts. People tend to look at successful writers, writers who are getting their books published and maybe even doing well financially, and think that they sit down at their desks every morning feeling like a million dollars, feeling great about who they are and how much talent they have and what a great story they have to tell; that they take in a few deep breaths, push back their sleeves, roll their necks a few times to get all the cricks out, and dive in, typing fully formed passages as fast as a court reporter. But this is just the fantasy of the uninitiated. I know some very great writers, writers you love who write beautifully and have made a great deal of money, and not *one* of them sits down routinely feeling wildly enthusiastic and confident. Not one of them writes elegant first drafts. All right, one of them does, but we do not like her very much. We do not think that she has a rich inner life or that God likes her or can even stand her. (Although when I mentioned this to my priest friend Tom, he said you can safely assume you've created God in your own image when it turns out that God hates all the same people you do.)

> I know some very great writers, writers you love who write beautifully and have made a great deal of money, and not *one* of them sits down routinely feeling wildly enthusiastic and confident.

Very few writers really know what they are doing until they've done it. Nor do they go about their business feeling dewy and thrilled. They do not type a few stiff warm-up sentences and then find themselves bounding along like huskies across the snow. One writer I know tells me that he sits down every morning and says to himself nicely, "It's not like you don't have a choice, because you do—you can either type or kill yourself." We all often feel like we are pulling teeth, even those writers whose prose ends up being the most natural and fluid. The right words and sentences just do not come pouring out like ticker tape most of the time. Now,

Muriel Spark is said to have felt that she was taking dictation from God every morning—sitting there, one supposes, plugged into a Dictaphone, typing away, humming. But this is a very hostile and aggressive position. One might hope for bad things to rain down on a person like this.

For me and most of the other writers I know, writing is not rapturous. In fact, the only way I can get anything written at all is to write really, really shitty first drafts. 3

The first draft is the child's draft, where you let it all pour out and then let it romp all over the place, knowing that no one is going to see it and that you can shape it later. You just let this childlike part of you channel whatever voices and visions come through and onto the page. If one of the characters wants to say, "Well, so what, Mr. Poopy Pants?" you let her. No one is going to see it. If the kid wants to get into really sentimental, weepy, emotional territory, you let him. Just get it all down on paper, because there may be something great in those six crazy pages that you would never have gotten to by more rational, grown-up means. There may be something in the very last line of the very last paragraph on page six that you just love, that is so beautiful or wild that you now know what you're supposed to be writing about, more or less, or in what direction you might go—but there was no way to get to this without first getting through the first five and a half pages. 4

I used to write food reviews for *California* magazine before it folded. (My writing food reviews had nothing to do with the magazine folding, although every single review did cause a couple of canceled subscriptions. Some readers took umbrage at my comparing mounds of vegetable puree with various ex-presidents' brains.) These reviews always took two days to write. First I'd go to a restaurant several times with a few opinionated, articulate friends in tow. I'd sit there writing down everything anyone said that was at all interesting or funny. Then on the following Monday I'd sit down at my desk with my notes, and try to write the review. Even after I'd been doing this for years, panic would set in. I'd try to write a lead, but instead I'd write a couple of dreadful sentences, xx them out, try again, xx everything out, and then feel despair and worry settle on my chest like an x-ray apron. It's over, I'd think, calmly. I'm not going to be able to get the magic to work this time. I'm ruined. I'm through. I'm toast. Maybe, I'd think, I can get my old job back as a clerk-typist. But probably not. I'd get up and study my teeth in the mirror for a while. Then I'd stop, remember to breathe, make a few phone calls, hit the kitchen and chow down. Eventually I'd go back and sit down at my desk, and sigh for the next ten minutes. Finally I would pick up my one-inch picture frame, stare into it as if for the answer, and every time the answer would come: All I had to do was to write a really shitty first draft of, say, the opening paragraph. And no one was going to see it. 5

So I'd start writing without reining myself in. It was almost just typing, just making my fingers move. And the writing would be *terrible*. I'd write a lead paragraph that was a whole page, even though the entire review could only be three pages long, and then I'd start writing up descriptions of the food, one dish at a time, bird by bird, and the critics would be sitting on my shoulders, commenting like cartoon characters. They'd be pretending to snore, or rolling 6 their eyes at my overwrought descriptions, no matter how hard I tried to tone those descriptions down, no matter how conscious I was of what a friend said to me gently in my early days of restaurant reviewing. "Annie," she said, "it is just a piece of *chicken*. It is just a bit of *cake*."

But because by then I had been writing for so long, I would eventually   7
let myself trust the process—sort of, more or less. I'd write a first draft that was maybe twice as long as it should be, with a self-indulgent and boring beginning, stupefying descriptions of the meal, lots of quotes from my black-humored friends that made them sound more like the Manson girls than food lovers, and no ending to speak of. The whole thing would be so long and incoherent and hideous that for the rest of the day I'd obsess about getting creamed by a car before I could write a decent second draft. I'd worry that people would read what I'd written and believe that the accident had really been a suicide, that I had panicked because my talent was waning and my mind was shot.

The next day, though, I'd sit down, go through it all with a colored pen,   8
take out everything I possibly could, find a new lead somewhere on the second page, figure out a kicky place to end it. and then write a second draft. It always turned out fine, sometimes even funny and weird and helpful. I'd go over it one more time and mail it in.

Then, a month later, when it was time for another review, the whole process   9
would start again, complete with the fears that people would find my first draft before I could rewrite it.

Almost all good writing begins with terrible first efforts. You need to start   10
somewhere. Start by getting something—anything—down on paper. A friend of mine says that the first draft is the down draft—you just get it down. The second draft is the up draft—you fix it up. You try to say what you have to say more accurately. And the third draft is the dental draft, where you check every tooth, to see if it's loose or cramped or decayed, or even, God help us, healthy.

What I've learned to do when I sit down to work on a shitty first draft is   11
to quiet the voices in my head. First there's the vinegar-lipped Reader Lady, who says primly, "Well, *that's* not very interesting, is it?" And there's the emaciated German male who writes these Orwellian memos detailing your thought crimes. And there are your parents, agonizing over your lack of loyalty and discretion; and there's William Burroughs, dozing off or shooting up because he finds you as bold and articulate as a houseplant; and so on. And there are also the dogs: let's not forget the dogs, the dogs in their pen who will surely hurtle and snarl their way out if you *ever stop* writing, because writing is, for some of us, the latch that keeps the door of the pen closed, keeps those crazy ravenous dogs contained.

Quieting these voices is at least half the battle I fight daily. But this is better   12
than it used to be. It used to be 87 percent. Left to its own devices, my mind spends much of its time having conversations with people who aren't there. I walk along defending myself to people, or exchanging repartee with them, or rationalizing my behavior, or seducing them with gossip, or pretending I'm on their TV talk show or whatever. I speed or run an aging yellow light or don't

come to a full stop, and one nanosecond later am explaining to imaginary cops exactly why I had to do what I did, or insisting that I did not in fact do it.

I happened to mention this to a hypnotist I saw many years ago, and he 13 looked at me very nicely. At first I thought he was feeling around on the floor for the silent alarm button, but then he gave me the following exercise, which I still use to this day.

Close your eyes and get quiet for a minute, until the chatter starts up. Then 14 isolate one of the voices and imagine the person speaking as a mouse. Pick it up by the tail and drop it into a mason jar. Then isolate another voice, pick it up by the tail, drop it in the jar. And so on. Drop in any high-maintenance parental units, drop in any contractors, lawyers, colleagues, children, anyone who is whining in your head. Then put the lid on, and watch all these mouse people clawing at the glass, jabbering away, trying to make you feel like shit because you won't do what they want—won't give them more money, won't be more successful, won't see them more often. Then imagine that there is a volume-control button on the bottle. Turn it all the way up for a minute, and listen to the stream of angry, neglected, guilt-mongering voices. Then turn it all the way down and watch the frantic mice lunge at the glass, trying to get to you. Leave it down, and get back to your shitty first draft.

A writer friend of mine suggests opening the jar and shooting them all in the 15 head. But I think he's a little angry, and I'm sure nothing like this would ever occur to you.

What Writing Is

STEPHEN KING

King, Stephen. "What Writing Is." *On Writing: A Memoir of the Craft*. New York: Pocket Books, 2000. 95–99. Print.

Telepathy, of course. It's amusing when you stop to think about it—for years 1 people have argued about whether or not such a thing exists, folks like J. B. Rhine have busted their brains trying to create a valid testing process to isolate it, and all the time it's been right there, lying out in the open like Mr. Poe's Purloined Letter. All the arts depend upon telepathy to some degree, but I believe that writing offers the purest distillation. Perhaps I'm prejudiced, but even if I am we may as well stick with writing, since it's what we came here to think and talk about.

My name is Stephen King. I'm writing the first draft of this part at my desk 2 (the one under the eave) on a snowy morning in December of 1997. There are things on my mind. Some are worries (bad eyes, Christmas shopping not even started, wife under the weather with a virus), some are good things (our younger son made a surprise visit home from college, I got to play Vince Taylor's "Brand New Cadillac" with The Wallflowers at a concert), but right

> Books are a uniquely portable magic.

now all that stuff is up top. I'm in another place, a basement place where there are lots of bright lights and clear images. This is a place I've built for myself over the years. It's a far-seeing place. I know it's a little strange, a little bit of a contradiction, that a far-seeing place should also be a basement place, but that's how it is with me. If you construct your own far-seeing place, you might put it in a treetop or on the roof of the World Trade Center or on the edge of the Grand Canyon. That's your little red wagon, as Robert McCammon says in one of his novels.

This book is scheduled to be published in the late sum- 3 mer or early fall of 2000. If that's how things work out, then you are somewhere downstream on the timeline from me ... but you're quite likely in your own far-seeing place, the one where you go to receive telepathic messages. Not that you *have* to be there; books are a uniquely portable magic. I usually listen to one in the car (always unabridged; I think abridged audio-books are the pits), and carry another wherever I go. You just never know when you'll want an

escape hatch: mile-long lines at tollbooth plazas, the fifteen minutes you have to spend in the hall of some boring college building waiting for your advisor (who's got some yank-off in there threatening to commit suicide because he/she is flunking Custom Kurmfurling 101) to come out so you can get his signature on a drop-card, airport boarding lounges, laundromats on rainy afternoons, and the absolute worst, which is the doctor's office when the guy is running late and you have to wait half an hour in order to have something sensitive mauled. At such times I find a book vital. If I have to spend time in purgatory before going to one place or the other, I guess I'll be all right as long as there's a lending library (if there is it's probably stocked with nothing but novels by Danielle Steel and *Chicken Soup* books, ha-ha, joke's on you, Steve).

So I read where I can, but I have a favorite place and probably you do, 4 too—a place where the light is good and the vibe is usually strong. For me it's the blue chair in my study. For you it might be the couch on the sunporch, the rocker in the kitchen, or maybe it's propped up in your bed—reading in bed can be heaven, assuming you can get just the right amount of light on the page and aren't prone to spilling your coffee or cognac on the sheets.

So let's assume that you're in your favorite receiving place just as I am in 5 the place where I do my best transmitting. We'll have to perform our mentalist routine not just over distance but over time as well, yet that presents no real problem; if we can still read Dickens, Shakespeare, and (with the help of a footnote or two) Herodotus, I think we can manage the gap between 1997 and 2000. And here we go—actual telepathy in action. You'll notice I have nothing up my sleeves and that my lips never move. Neither, most likely, do yours.

Look—here's a table covered with a red cloth. On it is a cage the size of a 6 small fish aquarium. In the cage is a white rabbit with a pink nose and pink-rimmed eyes. In its front paws is a carrot-stub upon which it is contentedly munching. On its back, clearly marked in blue ink, is the numeral 8.

Do we see the same thing? We'd have to get together and compare notes to 7 make absolutely sure, but I think we do. There will be necessary variations, of course: some receivers will see a cloth which is turkey red, some will see one that's scarlet, while others may see still other shades. (To colorblind receivers, the red tablecloth is the dark gray of cigar ashes.) Some may see scalloped edges, some may see straight ones. Decorative souls may add a little lace, and welcome—my tablecloth is your tablecloth, knock yourself out.

Likewise, the matter of the cage leaves quite a lot of room for individual 8 interpretation. For one thing, it is described in terms of *rough comparison*, which is useful only if you and I see the world and measure the things in it with similar eyes. It's easy to become careless when making rough comparisons, but the alternative is a prissy attention to detail that takes all the fun out of writing. What am I going to say, "on the table is a cage three feet, six inches in length, two feet in width, and fourteen inches high"? That's not prose, that's an instruction manual. The paragraph also doesn't tell us what sort of material the cage is made of—wire mesh? steel rods? glass?—but does it really matter? We all understand the cage is a see-through medium; beyond that, we don't care. The most interesting thing here isn't even the carrot-munching rabbit in the cage, but the number on its back. Not a six, not a four, not nineteen-point-five. It's an eight. This is what we're looking at, and we all see it. I didn't tell you. You didn't ask me. I never opened my mouth and you never opened yours. We're not even in the same *year* together, let alone the same room . . . except we *are* together. We're close.

We're having a meeting of the minds.   9

I sent you a table with a red cloth on it, a cage, a rabbit, and the number   10
eight in blue ink. You got them all, especially that blue eight. We've engaged in an act of telepathy. No mythy-mountain shit; real telepathy. I'm not going to belabor the point, but before we go any further you have to understand that I'm not trying to be cute; there *is* a point to be made.

You can approach the act of writing with nervousness, excitement, hope-   11
fulness, or even despair—the sense that you can never completely put on the page what's in your mind and heart. You can come to the act with your fists clenched and your eyes narrowed, ready to kick ass and take down names. You can come to it because you want a girl to marry you or because you want to change the world. Come to it any way but lightly. Let me say it again: *you must not come lightly to the blank page.*

I'm not asking you to come reverently or unquestioningly; I'm not asking   12
you to be politically correct or cast aside your sense of humor (please God you have one). This isn't a popularity contest, it's not the moral Olympics, and it's not church. But it's *writing*, damn it, not washing the car or putting on eyeliner. If you can take it seriously, we can do business. If you can't or won't, it's time for you to close the book and do something else.

Wash the car, maybe.   13

Calming the Inner Critic and Getting to Work

ALLEGRA GOODMAN

Goodman, Allegra. "Calming the Inner Critic and Getting to Work." *New York Times,* 12 Mar. 2001. Web. 30 Nov. 2009.

They say writing is lonely work. But that's an exaggeration. Even alone at their desks, writers entertain visitors: characters of a novel, famous and not so famous figures from the past. On good days, all these come to the table. On bad days, however, only unwelcome visitors appear: the specter of the third-grade teacher who despaired of your penmanship. The ghost of the first person who told you that spelling counts. The voice of reason pointing out that what you are about to attempt has already been done—and done far better than you might even hope. 1

So why bother? Why even begin? It is, after all, abundantly clear that you are not Henry James. Your themes are hackneyed, your style imitative. As for your emotions, memories, insights and invented characters, what makes you think anyone will care? These are the perfectly logical questions of the famous, petty and implacable inner critic. 2

> What should a writer do when the inner critic comes to call?

What should a writer do when the inner critic comes to call? How to silence these disparaging whispers? I have no magic cure, but here, from my own experience, is a modest proposal to combat the fiend. 3

Forget the past. Nothing stops the creative juices like thoughts of the literary tradition. "You'll never be John Donne!" your inner critic shrieks. Or: "*Middlemarch*! Now that was a book!" These thoughts used to fill me with gloom. Then I went to graduate school at Stanford, and I steeped myself in Shakespeare, Wordsworth and Defoe. The experience set me free. 4

It happened like this. I was sitting in Green Library trying to write a story, and I looked at all the shelves of books around me, and suddenly the obvious occurred to me. All the great Romantic poets and Elizabethan playwrights and Victorian novelists that tower over me—they're dead! Oh, they still cast their shadow, but I'm alive, and they are irrefutably dead. Their language is exquisite, their scenes divine, but what have these writers done lately? Not a damn thing. Think about it. The idea should give you hope. Past masters are done. Their achievements are finite, known, measurable. Present writers, 5 on the other hand, live in possibility. Your masterpiece could be just around the corner. Genius could befall you at any moment.

"Well," your inner critic counters gloomily, "just remember that when you're gone, your books will suffer the same fate as all the rest. They'll be relics at best. More likely, they'll just languish in obscurity." To which I have to say: So what? I won't be around to care. 6

Carpe diem. Know your literary tradition, savor it, steal from it, but when you sit down to write, forget about worshiping greatness and fetishizing masterpieces. If your inner critic continues to plague you with invidious comparisons, scream, "Ancestor worship!" and leave the building. 7

Treat writing as a sacred act. Just as the inner critic loves to dwell on the past, she delights in worrying about the future. "Who would want to read this?" she demands. "Nobody is going to publish a book like that!" Such nagging can incapacitate unpublished writers. Published writers, on the other hand, know that terrible books come out all the time. They anguish: "The reviewers are going to crucify me, and nobody will want to publish me after that." 8

But take a step back. What are you really afraid of here? When you come down to it, this is just a case of the inner critic masquerading as public opinion, and playing on your vanity. 9

I know only one way out of this trap, which is to concentrate on your writing itself, for itself. Figuring out what the public wants, or even what the public is: that's the job of pollsters and publicists and advertisers. All those people study the marketplace. But the creative artist can change the world. A true writer opens people's ears and eyes, not merely playing to the public, but changing minds and lives. This is sacred work. 10

Love your material. Nothing frightens the inner critic more than the writer who loves her work. The writer who is enamored of her material forgets all about censoring herself. She doesn't stop to wonder if her book is any good, or who will publish it, or what people will think. She writes in a trance, losing track of time, hearing only her characters in her head. 11

This is a state of grace possible only when you are truly desperate to tell a story. Suddenly you are so full of voices, ideas and events that it is as if you were rushing from the scene of the crime. How you arrange your sentences or whether a similar tale has been told before: these could not be farther from your mind. It never occurs to you to question whether your characters are well drawn or whether their dialogue is realistic because all these people are pushing and shoving and talking at once, and to your mind they are real, so realism is not much of a problem. 12

There is nothing better than listening to your characters regale you. I laughed and shook my head at the things Sharon Spiegelman said and did in *Paradise Park*. I was surprised sometimes, as I wrote *Kaaterskill Falls*, by the sweetness of Isaac Shulman and the determination of his wife, Elizabeth, and by the calculating, grieving, uncompromising voice of the old Rav Kirshner. They were all fictional characters, and yet in the writing they were real. 13

Now you may ask, what if my characters won't talk to me? What if they won't even visit? The only answer is to think and think some more, and then go out and read and look and listen some more. Do not sit and mope. Do not sigh. Do not 14 throw up your hands and give up on the whole project. Do not go back to the drawing board. There is nothing more depressing than an empty drawing board. No, go back to the world, which is where all characters originally come from.

Go back to your library, your forest, your newspapers, your family, your day 15 job, your photos, your music, your maps and jottings of old dreams. All these are teeming with life, and life is the stuff of fiction. There are no guarantees, but if you go out where stories congregate, it's far more likely that characters will come.

Recognize that deep down you love your inner critic. How sad, how sordid. 16 How cheap. Secretly writers do love the censor within. We say we hate that sanctimonious inner voice, but there is no better excuse for procrastination, lethargy and despair. There is no better excuse for getting nothing done than to lock yourself in battle with the famous inner demons of self-criticism and doubt.

External obstacles have such obvious, prosaic remedies: time can be found, 17 paper purchased. But when it comes to inner obstacles, the difficulty is spiritual, and thus infinite. "I'm blocked!" you moan. Or, "I'm such a perfectionist, I can never finish." Which is to say your inner critic is blocking the way and too busy pointing out mistakes to let you finish. It's terribly depressing but, admit it, also comforting, to hear that you'll never perfect your work, and thus never finish. If you know you'll never finish, then there is no point in trying any longer. And if you don't try, then you can't fail.

This is a safe situation, but not conducive to creative work. If you want 18 to write, or really to create anything, you have to risk falling on your face. How much easier to sit back and snipe at the efforts of yourself and others. How sophisticated you can become, your own contribution unimpeachable, because it does not exist. Sometimes insightful, always acute, the inner critic can become your closest literary friend, the one who tells you the truth, the one who makes you laugh at yourself and punctures your delusions.

This is all to the good. The danger is in identifying so much with your 19 inner critic that you enjoy self-deprecation more than your work itself. Writer, beware! The inner critic is insidious, subversive, always available for depressive episodes. Stay alert. Know the enemy. Know yourself.

Ultimately every writer must choose between safety and invention; between 20 life as a literary couch potato and imaginative exercise. You must decide which you like better, the perfectionist within or the flawed pages at hand.

Perhaps you'd rather hold yourself to the impossibly high standards of writ- 21 ers long dead. Or perhaps you'd rather not waste time writing something that will go unpublished, unnoticed and unread. You have received no encouragement from anyone else, and so you would never think of encouraging yourself. Or you choose to be a realist. You're smart enough to see your talent is limited, your gift too small to pursue. You can convince yourself of all this, or you can listen to your imagination instead. You can fire yourself up with words and voices. You can look out into the world teeming with stories and cast your net.

To See Your Story Clearly, Start by Pulling the Wool over Your Own Eyes

KENT HARUF

Haruf, Kent. "To See Your Story Clearly, Start by Pulling the Wool over Your Own Eyes." *New York Times*. 20 Nov. 2000. Web. 30 Nov. 2009.

The habits and methods of writers are sometimes peculiar enough to be 1 interesting.

John Cheever wrote some of his early stories in his underwear. Hemingway 2 is said to have written some of his fiction while standing up. Thomas Wolfe reportedly wrote parts of his voluminous novels while leaning over the top of a refrigerator. Flannery O'Connor sat for two hours every day at a typewriter facing the back of a clothes dresser, so that in those last painful years, when she was dying of lupus, she'd have as close to nothing as possible to look at while she wrote her stories about sin.

Eudora Welty has said that she straight-pinned pieces of her stories together 3 on the dining room table, as though she were pinning together parts of a dress. Maya Angelou secreted herself in a hotel room for days and weeks of concentrated isolation while she worked on her autobiographical tales. Richard Russo wrote his first novels in the secluded corners of cafes.

As for me, I prefer a coal room in the basement of our house in southern 4 Illinois, and I write my first drafts blind on an old manual typewriter.

When we bought the house six years ago, my wife and I swept out the coal 5 room, put in a table and shelves and laid down a piece of carpet. The room is about 6 feet by 9 and has a single ground-level window through which coal once was shoveled. Hanging from a nail above my desk is the skull of a Hereford bull, complete with horns and dark gaping eye sockets. The skull came from Cherry County, Nebraska, which is beautiful big grassy sand-hill country; and if you shake the skull, you can still produce a sprinkling of sand from its calcified insides. I keep this skull hanging over my desk both for itself and because I want to think it prevents me from writing baloney.

I have a plat on the wall of the county in northeastern 6 Colorado that is the prototype for the invented Holt County that I write about and where all of my invented people live and die and commit their acts of sudden kindness and unexpected cruelty. I have brown wrapping paper taped up on the wall, on which I make notes about whatever novel I'm working on, and I have several pictures on the wall drawn by my youngest daughter, who's an artist, and also four photographs of western landscape paintings by Keith Jacobshagen and Ben Darling, and—not least—I have on the wall a black-and-white photograph of a High Plains barbed wire fence choked with tumbleweeds.

On my desk I keep a sapling chewed by a beaver. I also keep on my desk a bird's   7
nest, a piece of black turf from Northern Ireland, a plastic bag of red sand from the stage at the new Globe Theater (taken after the production of Shakespeare's *Winter's Tale*), a piece of brick and some paddock dirt from Faulkner's home at Rowan Oaks, an old-fashioned hand warmer in a velvet sack, a blue bandana, a jackknife that once belonged to my maternal grandfather, Roy Shaver, who was a sheep rancher in South Dakota, and an obsidian arrowhead my father found in the North Dakota Badlands, where he was born almost 100 years ago.

I do not pay much attention to these   8
things, but having them there makes a difference. I suppose it is in some way totemic. The things on my desk and on the walls above it connect me emotionally to memories, ways of living, people and geographical areas that are important to me. It's an emotional attachment to all these things that connects me up with the impulse to write. I don't feel

> The things on my desk and on the walls above it connect me emotionally to memories, ways of living, people and geographical areas that are important to me.

sentimental about these things in any sloppy way, but I do feel a strong emotion remembering things, remembering people, remembering places and sights. Every time I go down to work, I feel as if I'm descending into a sacred place.

As for the work, once I get to my office, it's done in a ritualistic, habitual   9
way. First of all, I admit that I have a special attachment to the old pulpy yellow paper that was once used by newspaper reporters. You can't buy it anymore. Or at least I can't. But I was very lucky about seven years ago when the secretary at the university where I'd been teaching discovered six reams of it while cleaning out old cabinets, and she gave them to me. It was a great gift to me, like manna, like a propitious omen.

I'm very frugal with this old yellow paper: I type on both sides. I believe I   10
have enough to last me the rest of my writing career. I use it only for first drafts of the scenes in novels. And then I use a manual typewriter, a Royal, with a wide carriage, and write the first draft of a scene on this yellow paper and, as I say, I write the first draft blindly.

This is not new with me. It's the old notion of blinding yourself so you can   11
see. So you can see differently, I mean. I remove my glasses, pull a stocking cap down over my eyes, and type the first draft single-spaced on the yellow paper in the actual and metaphorical darkness behind my closed eyes, trying to avoid being distracted by syntax or diction or punctuation or grammar or spelling

or word choice or anything else that would block the immediate delivery of the story.

I write an entire scene or section on one side of one page, in a very concen- 12 trated and incomplete way. I'm trying to avoid allowing the analytical part of my mind into the process too soon. Instead, I'm trying to stay in touch with subliminal, subconscious impulses and to get the story down in some spontane- ous way.

I haven't always written in this peculiar manner. Formerly, like anyone else 13 would, I wrote on a manual typewriter on yellow paper (which was still avail- able 25 years ago) with my eyes wide open. I wrote my first novel, *The Tie That Binds*, in this way. Then computers became affordable, and I wrote my second novel, *Where You Once Belonged*, on a computer, but I never did like the way that felt.

I missed the tactile sensation of working with paper, the visceral rightness of 14 it and the familiar clacking of typewriter keys. Also, it was too easy to rewrite each sentence on a computer, and I tend to rewrite endlessly, anyway. Further- more, unless you print out constantly, you lose parts of drafts, certain phrases and sentences, that you may wish later you had saved.

So when I began to write *Plainsong*, my third novel, I knew I wanted to go 15 back to using a typewriter, at least for the first draft, and I knew I had to find a way to curb my tendency to rewrite each sentence so often that no sentence ever sounded good enough. That's when the notion of writing blind occurred to me.

It helps that I'm a decent typist. (I took a full year of typing in high school; 16 I was the only male student in the second semester, a circumstance that was not altogether unpleasant.) Only once have I typed past the bottom of the page onto the platen, and I took that mistake as a healthy reminder to be concise. And there was only one time in my blindness that I got off the home row of my typewriter and wrote nonsense. That served as a healthy correc- tive, too. It's not hard to write nonsense, not much harder than it is to write slack prose.

After finishing the first draft, I work for as long as it takes (for two or 17 three weeks, most often) to rework that first draft on a computer. Usually that involves expansion: filling in and adding to, but trying not to lose the spontaneous, direct sound. I use that first draft as a touchstone to make sure everything else in that section has the same sound, the same tone and impres- sion of spontaneity. I revise until I feel I'm done, and then I am done with that section or scene. I don't often go back and change much after that. So when I finish the last chapter, having redrafted the last page sufficiently, I'm done with the book.

But it's important to me to maintain this impression of spontaneity. By 18 spontaneity I mean a sense of freshness and vividness. Perhaps at times even a suggestion of awkwardness. Otherwise, to me prose sounds stilted and too polished, as if the life of it were perfected out of it. It's very difficult to arrive at this sense of freshness and spontaneity in prose—in my experience, it takes a great deal of effort and practice and years of concentrated apprenticeship—but I believe it is one of the most important attributes to achieve. That, and simplicity. And clarity. Those would be the holy trinity in the art of fiction writing.

Still, I have to say, writing is all messier and more a matter of dead ends and 19 fits and starts than a recitation like this one makes it out to be. And perhaps because writing fiction—this weird practice of telling artful lies, this peculiar habit of inventing imaginary people who talk and move and sleep and dream and wake up and kick and kiss one another—is so bizarre in itself is the reason why writers have to find bizarre ways to make it possible even to consider doing it.

So of course they have to write in their underwear and face the backs of 20 dressers. Of course they have to pull stocking caps down over their faces. Otherwise they might as well do something practical and ordinary, become doctors and lawyers and ditch diggers like everyone else.

Directions: Write, Read, Rewrite. Repeat Steps 2 and 3 as Needed.

SUSAN SONTAG

Sontag, Susan. "Directions: Write, Read, Rewrite. Repeat Steps 2 and 3 as Needed." *New York Times*. 18 Dec. 2000. Web. 30 Nov. 2009.

Reading novels seems to me such a normal activity, while writing them is 1 such an odd thing to do. . . . At least so I think until I remind myself how firmly the two are related. (No armored generalities here. Just a few remarks.)

First, because to write is to practice, with particular intensity and attentive- 2 ness, the art of reading. You write in order to read what you've written and see if it's O.K. and, since of course it never is, to rewrite it—once, twice, as many times as it takes to get it to be something you can bear to reread. You are your own first, maybe severest, reader. "To write is to sit in judgment on oneself," Ibsen inscribed on the flyleaf of one of his books. Hard to imagine writing without rereading.

But is what you've written straight off never all right? Yes, sometimes even 3 better than all right. And that only suggests, to this novelist at any rate, that with a closer look, or voicing aloud—that is, another reading—it might be better still. I'm not saying that the writer has to fret and sweat to produce something good.

"What is written without effort is in general read without pleasure," said Dr. 4 Johnson, and the maxim seems as remote from contemporary taste as its author. Surely, much that is written without effort gives a great deal of pleasure.

No, the question is not the judgment of readers, who may well prefer a 5 writer's more spontaneous, less elaborated work, but a sentiment of writers, those professionals of dissatisfaction. You think, "If I can get it to this point the first go around, without too much struggle, couldn't it be better still?"

And though the rewriting—and the rereading—sound like effort, they are actually the most pleasurable parts of writing. Sometimes the only pleasurable parts. Setting out to write, if you have the idea of "literature" in your head, is formidable, intimidating. A plunge in an icy lake. Then comes the warm part: when you already have something to work with, upgrade, edit.

Let's say it's a mess. But you have a chance to fix it. You 7 try to be clearer. Or deeper. Or more eloquent. Or more eccentric. You try to be true to a world. You want the book to be more spa-cious, more authoritative. You want to winch yourself up from yourself. You want to winch the book out of your balky mind. As the statue is entombed in the block of marble, the novel is inside your head. You try to liberate it. You try to get this wretched stuff on the page closer to what you think your book should be—what you know, in your spasms of elation, it can be. You read the sentences over and over. Is this the book I'm writing? Is this all?

Or let's say it's going well; for it does go well, sometimes. (If it didn't, some   8 of the time, you'd go crazy.) There you are, and even if you are the slowest of scribes and the worst of touch typists, a trail of words is getting laid down, and you want to keep going; and then you reread it. Perhaps you don't dare to be satisfied, but at the same time you like what you've written. You find yourself taking pleasure—a reader's pleasure—in what's there on the page.

Writing is finally a series of permissions you give yourself to be expressive in   9 certain ways. To invent. To leap. To fly. To fall. To find your own characteristic way of narrating and insisting; that is, to find your own inner freedom. To be strict without being too self-excoriating. Not stopping too often to reread. Allowing yourself, when you dare to think it's going well (or not too badly), simply to keep rowing along. No waiting for inspiration's shove.

Blind writers can never reread what they dictate. Perhaps this matters less   10 for poets, who often do most of their writing in their head before setting any-thing down on paper. (Poets live by the ear much more than prose writers do.) And not being able to see doesn't mean that one doesn't make revisions. Don't we imagine that Milton's daughters, at the end of each day of the dictation of "Paradise Lost," read it all back to their father aloud and then took down his corrections?

But prose writers, who work in a lumberyard of words, can't hold it all in   11 their heads. They need to see what they've written. Even those writers who seem most forthcoming, prolific, must feel this. (Thus Sartre announced, when he went blind, that his writing days were over.) Think of portly, venerable Henry James pacing up and down in a room in Lamb House composing *The Golden Bowl* aloud to a secretary. Leaving aside the difficulty of imagining how James's late prose could have been dictated at all, much less to the racket made by a Remington typewriter circa 1900, don't we assume that James reread what had been typed and was lavish with his corrections?

When I became, again, a cancer patient two years ago and had to break off   12 work on the nearly finished *In America*, a kind friend in Los Angeles, knowing my despair and fear that now I'd never finish it, offered to take a leave from his job and come to New York and stay with me as long as needed, to take down my dictation of the rest of the novel. True, the first eight chapters were done (that is, rewritten and reread many times), and I'd begun the next-to-last chap-ter, and I did feel I had the arc of those last two chapters entirely in my head. And yet, and yet, I had to refuse his touching, generous offer.

It wasn't just that I was already too befuddled by a drastic chemo cocktail   13 and lots of painkillers to remember what I was planning to write. I had to be able to see what I wrote, not just hear it. I had to be able to reread.

Reading usually precedes writing. And the impulse to write is almost always   14
fired by reading. Reading, the love of reading, is what makes you dream of
becoming a writer. And long after you've become a writer, reading books others write—and rereading the beloved books of the past—constitutes an irre-
sistible distraction from writing. Distraction. Consolation. Torment. And, yes,
inspiration.

Of course, not all writers will admit this. I remember once saying something   15
to V. S. Naipaul about a nineteenth-century English novel I loved, a very well-
known novel that I assumed he, like everyone I knew who cared for literature,
admired as I did. But no, he'd not read it, he said, and seeing the shadow of
surprise on my face, added sternly, "Susan, I'm a writer, not a reader."

Many writers who are no longer young claim, for various reasons, to read   16
very little, indeed, to find reading and writing in some sense incompatible.
Perhaps, for some writers, they are. It's not for me to judge. If the reason is
anxiety about being influenced, then this seems to me a vain, shallow worry.
If the reason is lack of time—there are only so many hours in the day, and
those spent reading are evidently subtracted from those in which one could be
writing—then this is an asceticism to which I don't aspire.

Losing yourself in a book, the old phrase, is not an idle fantasy but an addic-   17
tive, model reality. Virginia Woolf famously said in a letter, "Sometimes I think
heaven must be one continuous unexhausted reading." Surely the heavenly part
is that—again, Woolf's words—"the state of reading consists in the complete
elimination of the ego." Unfortunately, we never do lose the ego, any more
than we can step over our own feet. But that disembodied rapture, reading, is
trancelike enough to make us feel ego-less.

Like reading, rapturous reading, writing fiction—inhabiting other selves—   18
feels like losing yourself, too.

Everybody likes to think now that writing is just a form of self-regard. Also   19
called self-expression. As we're no longer supposed to be capable of authen-
tically altruistic feelings, we're not supposed to be capable of writing about
anyone but ourselves.

But that's not true. William Trevor speaks of the boldness of the nonauto-   20
biographical imagination. Why wouldn't you write to escape yourself as much
as you might write to express yourself? It's far more interesting to write about
others.

Needless to say, I lend bits of myself to all my characters. When, in *In Amer-*   21
ica, my immigrants from Poland reach Southern California—they're just outside the village of Anaheim—in 1876, stroll out into the desert and succumb to
a terrifying, transforming vision of emptiness, I was surely drawing on my own
memory of childhood walks into the desert of southern Arizona—outside what
was then a small town, Tucson—in the 1940s. In the first draft of that chapter,
there were saguaros in the Southern California desert. By the third draft I had
taken the saguaros out, reluctantly. (Alas, there aren't any saguaros west of the
Colorado River.)

What I write about is other than me. As what I write is smarter than I am.   22
Because I can rewrite it. My books know what I once knew, fitfully, intermittently.

And getting the best words on the page does not seem any easier, even after so many years of writing. On the contrary.

Here is the great difference between reading and writing. Reading is a voca- 23 tion, a skill, at which, with practice, you are bound to become more expert. What you accumulate as a writer are mostly uncertainties and anxieties.

All these feelings of inadequacy on the part of the writer—this writer, 24 anyway—are predicated on the conviction that literature matters. Matters is surely too pale a word. That there are books that are "necessary," that is, books that, while reading them, you know you'll reread. Maybe more than once. Is there a greater privilege than to have a consciousness expanded by, filled with, pointed to literature?

Book of wisdom, exemplar of mental playfulness, dilator of sympathies, 25 faithful recorder of a real world (not just the commotion inside one head), servant of history, advocate of contrary and defiant emotions . . . a novel that feels necessary can be, should be, most of these things.

As for whether there will continue to be readers who share this high notion 26 of fiction, well, "there's no future to that question," as Duke Ellington replied when asked why he was to be found playing morning programs at the Apollo. Best just to keep rowing along.

Becoming a Writer

JUNOT DÍAZ

Díaz, Junot. "Becoming a Writer." *O, The Oprah Magazine*. Oprah.com, 13 Oct. 2009. Web. 16 Feb. 2010.

It wasn't that I couldn't write. I wrote every day. I actually worked really 1 hard at writing. At my desk by 7 a.m., would work a full eight and more. Scribbled at the dinner table, in bed, on the toilet, on the No. 6 train, at Shea Stadium. I did everything I could. But none of it worked. My novel, which I had started with such hope shortly after publishing my first book of stories, wouldn't budge past the 75-page mark. Nothing I wrote past page 75 made any kind of sense. Nothing. Which would have been fine if the first 75 pages hadn't been pretty damn cool. But they were cool, showed a lot of promise. Would also have been fine if I could have just jumped to something else. But I couldn't. All the other novels I tried sucked worse than the stalled one, and even more disturbing, I seemed to have lost the ability to write short stories. It was like I had somehow slipped into a No-Writing Twilight Zone and I couldn't find an exit. Like I'd been chained to the sinking ship of those 75 pages and there was no key and no patching the hole in the hull. I wrote and I wrote and I wrote, but nothing I produced was worth a damn.

> I wrote and I wrote and I wrote, but nothing I produced was worth a damn.

Want to talk about stubborn? I kept at it for five straight years. Five damn 2 years. Every day failing for five years? I'm a pretty stubborn, pretty hard-hearted character, but those five years of fail did a number on my psyche. On me. Five years, 60 months? It just about wiped me out. By the end of that fifth year, perhaps in an attempt to save myself, to escape my despair, I started becoming convinced that I had written all I had to write, that I was a minor league Ralph Ellison, a Pop Warner Edward Rivera, that maybe it was time, for the sake of my mental health, for me to move on to another profession, and if the inspiration struck again some time in the future . . . well, great. But I knew I couldn't go on much more the way I was going. I just couldn't. I was living with my fiancée at the time (over now, another terrible story) and was so depressed and self-loathing I could barely function. I finally broached the topic with her of, maybe, you know, doing something else. My fiancée was so desperate to see me happy (and perhaps more than a little convinced by my fear that maybe the thread had run out on my talent) that she told me to make a list of what else I could do besides writing. I'm not a list person like she was, but I wrote one. It took a month to pencil down three things. (I really don't have many other skills.) I stared at that list for about another month. Waiting, hoping, praying for the book, for my writing, for my talent to catch fire. A last-second reprieve. But nada. So I put the manuscript away. All the hundreds of failed pages, boxed and hidden in a closet. I think I cried as I did it. Five years of my life and the dream that I had of myself, all down the tubes because I couldn't pull off something other people seemed to pull off with relative ease: a novel. By then I wasn't even interested in a Great American Novel. I would have been elated with the eminently forgettable NJ novel.

So I became a normal. A square. I didn't go to bookstores or read the Sunday 3 book section of the *Times*. I stopped hanging out with my writer friends. The bouts of rage and despair, the fights with my fiancée ended. I slipped into my new morose half-life. Started preparing for my next stage, back to school in September. (I won't even tell you what I was thinking of doing, too embarrassing.) While I waited for September to come around, I spent long hours in my writing room, sprawled on the floor, with the list on my chest, waiting for the promise of those words to leak through the paper into me.

Maybe I would have gone through with it. Hard to know. But if the world is 4 what it is so are our hearts. One night in August, unable to sleep, sickened that I was giving up, but even more frightened by the thought of having to return to the writing, I dug out the manuscript. I figured if I could find one good thing in the pages I would go back to it. Just one good thing. Like flipping a coin, I'd let the pages decide. Spent the whole night reading everything I had written, and guess what? It was still terrible. In fact with the new distance the lameness was even worse than I'd thought. That's when I should have put everything in the box. When I should have turned my back and trudged into my new life. I didn't have the heart to go on. But I guess I did. While my fiancée slept, I separated the 75 pages that were worthy from the mountain of loss, sat at my desk, and despite every part of me shrieking no no no no, I jumped back down the rabbit hole again. There were no sudden miracles. It took two more years of heartbreak, of being utterly, dismayingly lost before the novel I had dreamed about for all those years finally started revealing itself. And another three years after that before I could look up from my desk and say the word I'd wanted to say for more than a decade: done.

That's my tale in a nutshell. Not the tale of how I came to write my novel 5 but rather of how I became a writer. Because, in truth, I didn't become a writer the first time I put pen to paper or when I finished my first book (easy) or my second one (hard). You see, in my view a writer is a writer not because she writes well and easily, because she has amazing talent, because everything she does is golden. In my view a writer is a writer because even when there is no hope, even when nothing you do shows any sign of promise, you keep writing anyway. Wasn't until that night when I was faced with all those lousy pages that I realized, really realized, what it was exactly that I am.

Using These Essays

Focus on two or three of the writers who discuss their own processes here. Read what they have to say about what they do as writers. Then, using the research material you have read in this chapter, analyze what they say. For example, do you see common metaphors about writing? Do you see writers grappling with rules they've been taught that don't work for them? Do any of these "skilled" writers have problems like Tony, the unskilled writer in Perl's study? Do you think Tony could have benefited from hearing these authors' stories?

Meta Moment
- What do you have to gain by reading both research about writing processes and writers' reflections on their own processes? Find at least three things you learned that were useful by doing this
- Freewrite for ten minutes about your conceptions of good writing and writers before reading this chapter, and now after reading it. What has changed?

Writing about Writing Processes: Assignments and Advice

I learned the most from the Autoethnography assignment; I never thought studying my own writing process could be so useful. During the assignment, I got the chance to compare my own writing process with that of another college student, as well as a professional writer. I learned that, like many other writers (both unskilled and skilled), I revise my work compulsively. I rarely get through two sentences without going back to reread what I wrote. By bringing this problem to my attention, I was able to find ways to solve the dilemma.

—**Jillian Loisel, Student**

To help you learn and explore the ideas in this chapter, we are suggesting three Assignment Options for larger writing projects: Autoethnography, Portrait of a Writer, and a Combination Assignment.

Assignment Option 1. Autoethnography

For this assignment, you will conduct a study similar to those conducted by Perl and Berkenkotter, but instead of looking at someone else, you will examine yourself and your own writing processes and write an **autoethnography** in which you describe them. Your method will be to record (preferably with video and audio) your total writing process as you complete a writing assignment for a class. Your purpose is to try to learn some things about your actual writing practices that you might not be aware of and to reflect on what you learn using the terms and concepts you've read about in this chapter.

Brainstorming   To make this assignment as useful as possible, you need to plan ahead, so figure out what you will be writing for this or other classes in the next few weeks, and make a decision about what you will study. Consider the following:

- What kinds of assignments are easiest or most difficult for you to write?
- What kinds of assignments would be the most useful to examine yourself writing?

Make sure that you know how to use your computer's recording device, if it has one; if you have a camera and video recording capabilities in your computer, make plans to capture yourself on video, too. (If your computer has none of these capabilities, discuss alternate means of recording your process with your instructor.)

Researching   As you write the assignment that you will study, record yourself every time that you work on it—this even includes times when you are thinking and planning for it, or when you are revising. Keep the following in mind:

- You may not be near your recording device(s) when you are planning; if that is the case, then keep a log in which you note your thoughts about the assignment.
- When you sit down to type the paper, think out loud the entire time. This will feel strange, and it will take some effort. Do your best.
- Try to externalize everything you are thinking. If you have trouble knowing what to say, go back to Perl and Berkenkotter and look at the kinds of things that Tony and Donald Murray said aloud when they were being studied.

When you have completely finished writing the paper, listen to the recording of yourself and transcribe it. This means typing everything that you said on the tape, even the "ums" and "ahs." Type up this transcription to use for your analysis. It will be helpful to double space (or even triple space) the transcript so that you can make notes on it.

Analyzing   Alone or with your class, as your teacher directs, come up with a code to help you look at your transcription. To help you generate the code, return to Berkenkotter, Perl, and Stark. What did they look at when they analyzed their transcriptions? Some suggestions for things you might include would be notes about context (where and when you wrote, what distractions you faced, your attitude, any deadlines, and so on), and codes for planning, brainstorming, large-scale revision, small-scale revision, pausing, and so on.

What you want is a code that will help you understand what is happening when you write. Beware the following potential pitfalls:

- If the code is too vague, you won't learn anything at all.
- If the code is too detailed (for example, if you try to do what Perl did and record the exact amount of time you took for each action), you might never get done coding.

We recommend coming up with a code with the rest of your class, and then trying to use that code on a practice transcript that your teacher provides. This will help you see if the code is useful.

Once you have settled on a code, use it to analyze your transcript. Try one or more of the following methods:

- Get a box of highlighters of different colors, and use each color to highlight the parts of the text that correspond to parts of the code (for example, pink is for planning).
- Simply underline parts of the transcript and label them in shorthand (e.g., P for planning).
- Use your word processing program's highlighting or "track changes" feature to insert comments in the margin.

Once you have coded the transcript, go back and look at what you did, and consider the following:

- What is interesting about what you found?
- What immediately jumps out at you? Did you do some things a lot, and other things rarely or never?
- How does your analysis suggest you compare to Tony and Donald Murray?

Like some of the authors in this chapter, you might make some charts or tables for yourself, in order to visually explore what percentage of time you spent on various activities.

Planning   What are you going to write about? You don't need to go into excruciating detail about everything you coded. Instead, you should decide what you want to claim about what you found:

- How would you describe your writing process?
- What are the most important take-home points from your analysis?
- Are there aspects of your process that are definitively impacted by technologies like instant messaging, social networking, Skype, or even word processing?

Decide what your claims will be and then look back at your analysis and decide what bits of data you would like to use in your paper to help support your claims.

At this point you and your teacher will also need to discuss what genre you are going to write. Who is your audience? What is your purpose? You might write about your findings in an informal reflective essay in which you discuss your process and compare yourself to some of the writers in the chapter. Or your teacher might want you to write a more formal, researched argument. In this case, you should use Perl and Berkenkotter as models. Note that they open their articles by discussing other research on their subject (also called "establishing the territory"), then noting one or more gaps or niches or questions in the existing research (for example, no one has studied a "normal" college writer, or no writer has studied herself using these research methods), then explaining their research methods, and finally discussing their findings.

Drafting   Your drafting processes will vary depending on the **genre** (text type) and purpose that you and your teacher agree upon:

- If you are writing the reflective essay, you are most likely writing for yourself (writing to learn) and to share what you learn with your teacher, who wants to encourage you in your efforts to become a better writer. Consider what claims you want to make in this reflective essay, and begin drafting. As you revise the essay, consider the appropriate **tone** and length, given your purpose(s).
- If you are writing a more scholarly research article, you might begin by outlining the various sections of your paper: In your introduction, what other research will you cite? Whose work provides important background information for your study? What is the gap or niche that your study fills? How will you describe your research methods? What are the main claims you want to make in the findings?

    One trick that some writers use is to write headings for each section, with main claims underneath. Then the writer can go back and write one section at a time in order to break up the writing.

Once you have a "shitty first draft," revise it to make it a little more coherent. Then share it with a classmate, being sure to tell him or her what genre you wrote and what kinds of help you would like him or her to give you.

What Makes It Good?   The purpose of this assignment was for you to try to learn some things about your actual writing practices that you might not have been aware of, and to reflect on what you learned using the terms and concepts you've read about in this chapter. Does your paper demonstrate that this purpose was achieved?

In addition, your readers will want to learn something from having read your paper. Does your finished text clearly convey your insights and findings?

A Caveat   We have found that some students just "go through the motions" when they complete this assignment, and don't make an attempt to learn something about themselves as writers. When those students write their papers, they have very little to say about results or insights. They tend to say pretty clichéd things like "I am distracted when I write. I should try to write with fewer distractions." In general, if the insights of the paper were obvious to you before you ever conducted the autoethnography, then you have not fully engaged in the project and are unlikely to receive a good grade on it.

Alternative Autoethnography Assignment   Instead of studying yourself writing one assignment, compare yourself writing two very different kinds of texts (maybe in-school and out-of-school, or humanities and science) and analyze them to see whether—or how—your process changes depending on what you write.

Assignment Option 2. Portrait of a Writer

The authors in this chapter clearly believe that good writing takes hard work and multiple drafts and that many of us are hampered from being better writers by the "rules" and misconceptions we have been taught about writing.

This is true even of very famous people who write a lot every day. Sonia Soto-mayor, who at the time this book went to press had recently joined the United States Supreme Court, has been widely criticized for her writing. She even criticizes herself, saying, "Writing remains a challenge for me even today—everything I write goes through multiple drafts—I am not a natural writer" (http://www.politico .com/blogs/joshgerstein/0609/Sotomayor_writing_a_challenge_even_today.html). Here she conflates being a "good" writer with being a "natural" writer; she seems to believe that some people are born good writers and some people aren't. Her conception is that a "good" writer only has to write one draft; anyone who has to write multiple drafts must be a "bad" writer. Even from this one short quotation, you can see that Sonia Sotomayor's conceptions of writing are limiting and would not hold up if closely examined by the researchers and professional writers in this chapter.

Use what you have read in this unit to consider the story you have to tell about yourself as a writer. How do you see yourself as a writer? Is that self-perception helping you be the best writer you can be? The purpose of this assignment is for you to apply what you have learned in this chapter to help you better understand why and how you write—and how you might write differently.

Brainstorming   Try the following to generate material for your assignment:

- Go back to the discussion and activity questions you completed as you read the articles in this chapter. What did you learn about yourself and your writing processes there?

- Consider what you write and don't write currently.
- Consider how you prepare—or don't prepare—to write a paper.
- Think of any kinds of writing that you enjoy, and any kinds of writing that you dread.
- Freewrite about the writing rules that block you, and the writing rules that aid you.
- Make a list of all the metaphors or similes about writing and revision that you and your friends use.

You should spend a substantial amount of time reflecting on yourself as a writer using the concepts and ideas that you learned in this chapter. Even if some or most of your brainstorming doesn't end up in your paper, the act of reflecting should be useful to you as a writer.

Planning   Look at all the notes and freewriting that you did during the brainstorming, and consider:

- What's interesting here?
- What catches your interest the most?
- What is new or surprising to you?

Settle on a few of these surprises or "aha!" moments as the core of what you will write for this assignment. For each of these core elements of your essay, brainstorm examples, details, and explanations that would help your reader understand what you are trying to explain about yourself.

Drafting   Write a three- to five-page essay in which you describe your view of yourself as a writer, using examples and explanations to strengthen your description. As appropriate, you might refer to the authors of texts in this chapter to help explain your experiences, processes, or feelings. Conclude the essay by considering how or whether the things you have learned in this chapter might change your conception of yourself as a writer or your writing behaviors. You and your teacher should discuss potential audiences for this essay:

- Are you writing to the teacher, to demonstrate what you've learned in this chapter?
- Are you writing for yourself, to help solidify what you've learned?
- Would you like to adapt your essay to write for someone else—maybe your parents, to demonstrate who you are as a writer and what influences you can identify? Maybe to a teacher who had an impact, positive or negative, on who you are as a writer?

Of course, this choice of audience and purpose will have a significant impact on your essay—its form, content, tone, language, level of formality, and so on.

As an alternative, you might talk with your teacher about more creative ways to paint your self-portrait:

- Try writing a play outlining your writing process.
- Transform a metaphor about writing into a visual description—for example, a collage—of who you are as a writer or what you think "good writing" is.

- Create a hypertext essay where readers can look at pictures, watch video, listen to songs, even listen to your own voice, as you describe yourself and your conceptions of writers, the writing process, and "good writing."

What Makes It Good?   The purpose of this assignment was for you to step back and consider yourself as a writer, applying what you learned in this chapter to help you better understand why and how you write—and how you might write differently, or perhaps even understand yourself differently as a writer. When you've finished it, ask yourself:

- Were you able to apply what you learned in this chapter to understand yourself better as writer? (If not, that will likely show up in the depth of your writing.)
- Did you successfully identify an audience for your piece and write appropriately for that audience?

Assignment Option 3. Combination Assignment

Write a short essay in response to the "Portrait of a Writer" prompt, and study yourself writing that essay in order to conduct the autoethnography.

Suggested Additional Readings and Resources

Bowden, Darsie. "Who Is a Writer: What Writers Tell Us." *National Conversation on Writing.* NCoW, 2009. Web. 18 Feb. 2010.

Charney, Davida, John J. Newman, and Mike Palmquist. "'I'm Just No Good at Writing': Epistemological Style and Attitudes toward Writing." *Written Communication* 12.3 (1995): 298–329. Print.

Didion, Joan. "On Keeping a Notebook." *Slouching towards Bethlehem.* New York: Farrar, 1990. 131–41. Print.

Eliot, T. S. "East Coker." *Four Quartets. 1943.* London: Faber, 2001. 13–20. Print.

Goldberg, Natalie. *Writing Down the Bones.* Boston: Shambhala, 1986. Print.

Harris, Muriel. "Don't Believe Everything You're Taught." *The Subject Is Writing.* Ed. Wendy Bishop. Portsmouth, NH: Boynton/Cook, 1993. 189–201. Print.

Orwell, George. "Why I Write." *Gangrel* (Summer 1946): 5–10. *Why I Write.* New York: Penguin, 2005. 1–10. Print.

Pipher, Mary. *Writing to Change the World.* New York: Riverhead, 2006. Print.

Rushdie, Salman, John Grisham, Ian McEwan, Margaret Atwood, and David Foster Wallace. Interviews by Charlie Rose. *Collection: Writers on Writing. The Charlie Rose Show.* WNET, New York, 2008. CharlieRose.com. Web. 18 Feb. 2010.

Sommers, Nancy, and Laura Saltz. "The Novice as Expert: Writing the Freshman Year." *College Composition and Communication* 56 (2004): 124–49. Print.

Titlepage.tv. Host Daniel Menaker. Titlepage, 2008. Web. 18 Feb. 2010.

3 | Literacies: How Have You Become the Reader and Writer You Are Today?

If you are reading this textbook right now, you are a literate person. You went to school, learned to read and write, and made it into college, where you are now being asked to write new and different kinds of texts. When experts in the field refer to **literacy**, though, they're typically referring to more than just the ability to read and write: They're referring more broadly to fluency or expertise in communicating and interacting with other people. Accordingly, it's more accurate to speak about **literacies** than about *literacy* when evaluating your own competence in communication.

In your daily life, for example, you read and write all kinds of things that you probably rarely talk about in school—you check your Facebook account, you text friends, you Skype. You interpret thousands of visual images every time you turn on

If your literacies include MMORPGs, you might recognize the screen capture above as being from *World of Warcraft*. Otherwise, it might just look like a random computer-generated nightmare to you. *Image used by permission. ©2010 Blizzard Entertainment, Inc.*

the television, read a magazine, or go to the mall. You also have literacies particular to your interests—you may know everything there is to know about a particular baseball player's RBIs, for example, or you may have advanced to an impressively high level in a complex, massively mult player online role-playing game like *World of Warcraft*. And, of course, you have home literacies that may be very different from school or hobby-related literacies. You may come from a family where languages other than English are spoken, or you may live in a community that values collaborative literacy practices (such as storytelling) that school does not.

Researchers in Writing Studies are particularly interested in these more complex ideas about literacy because they want to understand how people acquire literacies and what literacies a society should assist people in acquiring. For example, in contemporary United States culture, schools don't educate people in highly specialized literacies—for example, those related to most hobbies, like radio-controlled vehicles or gaming. Computer literacy was once in this category; as the use of computers went mainstream in the 1980s and 1990s, however—and particularly as it grew in importance in the workplace—the school system realized it needed to commit significant resources toward educating students in computer and information literacy. (How well it has achieved this goal is an open question.)

This chapter's readings focus particularly on questions of what counts as "literacy," how we become literate, and how cultures support various literacies. Deborah Brandt's piece, "Sponsors of Literacy," poses some definitions of literacy and some questions about how we acquire the literacies that we do. An excerpt from Malcolm X's autobiography and a brief memoir by Sherman Alexie follow; both serve as examples of the principles Brandt discusses and raise questions about motivations for literacy, access to literacy, and the power literacy can provide. In "Protean Shapes in Literacy Events," ethnographer Shirley Brice Heath discusses what counts as literacy and what kinds of literacies have traditionally been valued by people who make sharp distinctions between "oral" and "literate" cultures. "The Future of Literacy," the fifth article in this chapter, was collaboratively composed by six researchers specializing in electronic literacies, as "Web 2.0" self-publishing technologies were becoming a major force in writing. These researchers pose the question of how teachers are preparing to educate students for whom "literacy" means not only their command over words on paper but over "digitized bits of video, sound, photographs, still images, words, and animations" that communicate "across conventional linguistic, cultural, and geopolitical borders" (p. 397). Finally, we end the chapter with Dennis Baron's historical discussion of various writing "technologies," including the pencil. As he considers the literacy impact of computer technology, he notes that we cannot foresee whether recent technological changes "will result in a massive change in world literacy rates and practices" (see p. 439).

Before you begin reading, take a few minutes to consider how you became the literate person you are today. No two people have exactly the same literacies, and yours are peculiar to your own personal history—your family, your geographic location, your culture, your hobbies, your religious training, your schooling, and so on. Consider, for example, the following questions:

- When and how did you learn to read?
- What did you read?
- Were there things you were not allowed to read?
- Where did you first or most memorably encounter texts as a child—for example, at home, at school, at a place of worship, at daycare, at a friend's or relative's house?

Your experiences have shaped your literacy practices—both what they are, and what they are not—so your answers will not be the same as other people's. All of us were shaped by what Deborah Brandt, whose work you'll read shortly, calls **literacy sponsors**—people, ideas, or institutions that helped us become literate, but literate in specific ways. If you attended private school instead of public school, for example, what were you exposed to and what literate experiences did you not have that public school kids might have had?

As you reflect on your own experiences, consider both the texts you were exposed to and those you were not exposed to, or the ones that you were explicitly denied. When you learned to write, what motivated you to want to write? Who helped you—or didn't? What kinds of things did you write and for whom? As you grew older, did your interest in writing change? What factors impacted those changes—friends? Teachers? Parents? New hobbies?

This brief reflection on your literacy history should illustrate the point we are trying to make: you are a literate person, and you are an expert on your own literacy practices and history. You come to this chapter knowing a lot, and through the readings and activities you'll find here, we hope to help you uncover more of what you know, in addition to learning some things that you did not know before.

Chapter Goals

- To understand the concepts of *literacy* and *multiple literacies*
- To understand ways of conducting contributive research and writing about literacy that can be shared with an audience
- To understand research and writing as processes that require planning, incubation, revision, and collaboration
- To acquire additional vocabulary for talking about yourself as a writer and reader
- To come to greater awareness of the forces that have shaped you as a writer and reader
- To strengthen your ability to read complex, research-based texts more confidently
- To gain more expertise in writing from readings and citing sources

Sponsors of Literacy

DEBORAH BRANDT

Brandt, Deborah. "Sponsors of Literacy." *College Composition and Communication* 49.2 (1998): 165–85. Print.

Framing the Reading

Deborah Brandt is a professor in the Department of English at the University of Wisconsin–Madison. She has written several books about literacy, including *Literacy as Involvement: The Acts of Writers, Readers and Texts* (Southern Illinois University Press, 1990); *Literacy in American Lives* (Cambridge University Press, 2001); and *Literacy and Learning: Reading, Writing, Society* (Jossey-Bass, 2009). She has also written a number of scholarly research articles about literacy, including the one you are about to read here, "Sponsors of Literacy," which describes some of the data she collected when writing *Literacy in American Lives*. In that book, Brandt examined the way literacy learning changed between 1895 and 1985, noting that literacy standards have risen dramatically. In "Sponsors of Literacy" she discusses the forces that shape our literacy learning and practices.

Brandt's breakthrough idea in this piece is that people don't become literate on their own; rather, literacy is *sponsored* by people, institutions, and circumstances that both make it possible for a person to become literate and shape the way the person actually acquires literacy. In interviewing a stunningly large number of people from all ages and walks of life, Brandt began recognizing these literacy sponsors everywhere, and thus her article here (and the book that the same research led to) is crammed with examples of them, ranging from older siblings to auto manufacturers and World War II.

While we think of the term *sponsor* as suggesting support or assistance, Brandt doesn't confine her discussion to the supportive aspects of literacy sponsors. Her research shows ways in which, while opening some doors, literacy sponsors may close others. Literacy sponsors are not always (or even, perhaps, usually) altruistic—they have self-interested reasons for sponsoring literacy, and very often only some kinds of literacy will support their goals. (If you've ever wondered why schools encourage you to read, but seem less than thrilled if you'd rather read Harlequin romances than Ernest Hemingway, Brandt's explanation of literacy sponsorship may provide an answer.) Brandt also discusses cases where people "misappropriate" a literacy sponsor's intentions by using a particular literacy for their own ends rather than for the sponsor's.

Brandt's portrayal of the tension between people and their literacy sponsors illustrates one more important point in thinking about literacy acquisition and how each of us has become literate. We claim in the chapter introduction that you have a combination of literacies that make you unique. While this is true, people also share many of the *same* literacy experiences. Brandt can help us understand this, too. Some literacy sponsors are organizations or institutions, like a public school system or a major corporation, whose sponsorship affects large numbers of people. In the Middle Ages prior to the invention of the printing press, the biggest literacy sponsor in Western civilization was the Roman Catholic Church, which shaped the literacies of virtually every person in feudal Europe as well as vast native populations around the world. Remember, literacy sponsors are not necessarily empowering; they can also disempower and *prevent* people from becoming literate in some ways while fostering other literacies. "Big" literacy sponsors like these have likely influenced your literacy narrative in the same way they've influenced many others, giving you something in common with others around you even as your particular literacies are unique to you.

Getting Ready to Read

Before you read, do at least one of the following activities:

- Compare notes with a roommate or friend about what your school literacy experience was like. What books did the school encourage you to read and discourage you from reading? What events and activities supported reading?
- Make a list of the ways you've seen U.S. culture and your own local community encourage and emphasize reading. What are the reasons usually given for being a good reader and writer, and who gives those reasons?

As you read, consider the following questions:

- What are Brandt's primary terms, in addition to *literacy sponsor*, and how do they apply to you?
- Where do you see yourself in the examples Brandt gives, and where do you not? Keep your early literacy experiences in mind as you read.
- What are implications of Brandt's idea of literacy sponsors for your education *right now* as a college student?

In his sweeping history of adult learning in the United States, Joseph Kett 1 describes the intellectual atmosphere available to young apprentices who worked in the small, decentralized print shops of antebellum America. Because printers also were the solicitors and editors of what they published, their workshops served as lively incubators for literacy and political discourse. By the mid-nineteenth century, however, this learning space was disrupted when the invention of the steam press reorganized the economy of the print industry. Steam presses were so expensive that they required capital outlays beyond the means of many printers. As a result, print jobs were outsourced, the processes of editing and printing were split, and, in tight competition, print apprentices became low-paid mechanics with no more access to the multi-skilled environment of the craft-shop (Kett 67–70). While this shift in working conditions may be evidence of the deskilling of workers induced by the Industrial Revolution (Nicholas and Nicholas), it also offers a site for reflecting upon the dynamic sources of literacy and literacy learning. The reading and writing skills of print apprentices in this period were the achievements not simply of teachers and learners nor of the discourse practices of the printer community. Rather, these skills existed fragilely, contingently within an economic moment. The pre-steam press economy enabled some of the most basic aspects of the apprentices' literacy, especially their access to material production and the public meaning or worth of their skills. Paradoxically, even as the steam-powered penny press made print more accessible (by making publishing more profitable), it brought an end to a particular form of literacy sponsorship and a drop in literate potential.

The apprentices' experience invites rumination upon literacy learning and teaching today. Literacy looms as one of the great engines of profit and competitive advantage in the 20th century: a lubricant for consumer desire; a means for integrating corporate markets; a foundation for the deployment of weapons and other technology; a raw material in the mass production of information. As ordinary citizens have been compelled into these economies, their reading and writing skills have grown sharply more central to the everyday trade of information and goods as well as to the pursuit of education, employment, civil rights, status. At the same time, people's literate skills have grown vulnerable to unprecedented turbulence in their economic value, as conditions, forms, and standards of literacy achievement seem to shift with almost every new generation of learners. How are we to understand the vicissitudes of individual literacy development in relationship to the large-scale economic forces that set the routes and determine the wordly worth of that literacy?

The field of writing studies has had much to say about individual literacy development. Especially in the last quarter of the 20th century, we have theorized, researched, critiqued, debated, and sometimes even managed to enhance the literate potentials of ordinary citizens as they have tried to cope with life as they find it. Less easily and certainly less steadily have we been able to relate what we see, study, and do to these larger contexts of profit making and competition. This even as we recognize that the most pressing issues we deal with—tightening associations between literate skill and social viability, the breakneck pace of change in communications technology, persistent inequities in access and reward—all relate to structural conditions in literacy's bigger picture. When economic forces are addressed in our work, they appear primarily as generalities: contexts, determinants, motivators, barriers, touchstones. But rarely are they systematically related to the local conditions and embodied moments of literacy learning that occupy so many of us on a daily basis.[1]

This essay does not presume to overcome the analytical failure completely. 4 But it does offer a conceptual approach that begins to connect literacy as an individual development to literacy as an economic development, at least as the two have played out over the last ninety years or so. The approach is through what I call sponsors of literacy. Sponsors, as I have come to think of them, are any agents, local or distant, concrete or abstract, who enable, support, teach, model, as well as recruit, regulate, suppress, or withhold literacy—and gain advantage by it in some way. Just as the ages of radio and television accustom us to having programs *brought* to us by various commercial sponsors, it is useful to think about who or what underwrites occasions of literacy learning and use. Although the interests of the sponsor and the sponsored do not have to converge (and, in fact, may conflict) sponsors nevertheless set the terms for access to literacy and wield powerful incentives for compliance and loyalty. Sponsors are a tangible reminder that literacy learning throughout history has always required permission, sanction, assistance, coercion, or, at minimum, contact with existing trade routes. Sponsors are delivery systems for the economies of literacy, the means by which these forces present themselves to—and through—individual learners. They also represent the causes into which people's literacy usually gets recruited.[2]

For the last five years I have been tracing sponsors of literacy across the 20th 5 century as they appear in the accounts of ordinary Americans recalling how they learned to write and read. The investigation is grounded in more than 100 in-depth interviews that I collected from a diverse group of people born roughly between 1900 and 1980. In the interviews, people explored in great detail their memories of learning to read and write across their lifetimes, focusing especially on the people, institutions, materials, and motivations involved in the process. The more I worked with these accounts, the more I came to realize that they were filled with references to sponsors, both explicit and latent, who appeared in formative roles at the scenes of literacy learning. Patterns of sponsorship became an illuminating site through which to track the different cultural attitudes people developed toward writing vs. reading as well as the ideological congestion faced by late-century literacy learners as their sponsors proliferated and diversified (see my essays on "Remembering Reading" and "Accumulating Literacy"). In this essay I set out a case for why the concept of sponsorship is so richly suggestive for exploring economies of literacy and their effects. Then, through use of extended case examples, I demonstrate the practical application of this approach for interpreting current conditions of literacy teaching and learning, including persistent stratification of opportunity and escalating standards for literacy achievement. A final section addresses implications for the teaching of writing.

Sponsorship

Intuitively, *sponsors* seemed a fitting term for the figures who turned up most
typically in people's memories of literacy learning: older relatives, teachers,
priests, supervisors, military officers, editors, influential authors. Sponsors,
as we ordinarily think of them, are powerful figures who bankroll events or
smooth the way for initiates. Usually richer, more knowledgeable, and more
entrenched than the sponsored, sponsors nevertheless enter a reciprocal relationship with those they underwrite. They lend their resources or credibility to
the sponsored but also stand to gain benefits from their success, whether by
direct repayment or, indirectly, by credit of association. *Sponsors* also proved
an appealing term in my analysis because of all the commercial references that
appeared in these 20th-century accounts—the magazines, peddled encyclopedias, essay contests, radio and television programs, toys, fan clubs, writing
tools, and so on, from which so much experience with literacy was derived. As
the 20th century turned the abilities to read and write into widely exploitable
resources, commercial sponsorship abounded.

   In whatever form, sponsors deliver the ideological freight that must be borne
for access to what they have. Of course, the sponsored can be oblivious to or
innovative with this ideological burden. Like Little Leaguers who wear the logo
of a local insurance agency on their uniforms, not out of a concern for enhancing the agency's image but as a means for getting to play ball, people throughout
history have acquired literacy pragmatically under the banner of others' causes.
In the days before free, public schooling in England, Protestant Sunday Schools
warily offered basic reading instruction to working-class families as part of evangelical duty. To the horror of many in the church sponsorship, these families insis-
tently, sometimes riotously demanded of their Sunday Schools more instruction,
including in writing and math, because it provided means for upward mobility.[3]
Through the sponsorship of Baptist and Methodist ministries, African Americans
in slavery taught each other to understand the Bible in subversively liberatory
ways. Under a conservative regime, they developed forms of critical literacy that
sustained religious, educational, and political movements both before and after
emancipation (Cornelius). Most of the time, however, literacy takes its shape
from the interests of its sponsors. And, as we will see below, obligations toward
one's sponsors run deep, affecting what, why, and how people write and read.

   The concept of sponsors helps to explain, then, a range of human relationships and ideological pressures that turn up at the scenes of literacy learning—
from benign sharing between adults and youths, to euphemized coercions in
schools and workplaces, to the most notorious impositions and deprivations
by church or state. It also is a concept useful for tracking literacy's material:
the things that accompany writing and reading and the ways they are manufactured and distributed. Sponsorship as a sociological term is even more broadly
suggestive for thinking about economies of literacy development. Studies of
patronage in Europe and *compradrazgo* in the Americas show how patron-
client relationships in the past grew up around the need to manage scarce
resources and promote political stability (Bourne; Lynch; Horstman and Kurtz).

Pragmatic, instrumental, ambivalent, patron-client relationships integrated otherwise antagonistic social classes into relationships of mutual, albeit unequal dependencies. Loaning land, money, protection, and other favors allowed the politically powerful to extend their influence and justify their exploitation of clients. Clients traded their labor and deference for access to opportunities for themselves or their children and for leverage needed to improve their social standing. Especially under conquest in Latin America, *compradrazgo* reintegrated native societies badly fragmented by the diseases and other disruptions that followed foreign invasions. At the same time, this system was susceptible to its own stresses, especially when patrons became clients themselves of still more centralized or distant overlords, with all the shifts in loyalty and perspective that entailed (Horstman and Kurtz 13–14).

In raising this association with formal systems of patronage, I do not wish   9
to overlook the very different economic, political, and educational systems within which U.S. literacy has developed. But where we find the sponsoring of literacy, it will be useful to look for its function within larger political and economic arenas. Literacy, like land, is a valued commodity in this economy, a key resource in gaining profit and edge. This value helps to explain, of course, the lengths people will go to secure literacy for themselves or their children. But it also explains why the powerful work so persistently to conscript and ration the powers of literacy. The competition to harness literacy, to manage, measure, teach, and exploit it, has intensified throughout the century. It is vital to pay attention to this development because it largely sets the terms for individuals' encounters with literacy. This competition shapes the incentives and barriers (including uneven distributions of opportunity) that greet literacy learners in any particular time and place. It is this competition that has made access to the right kinds of literacy sponsors so crucial for political and economic well-being. And it also has spurred the rapid, complex changes that now make the pursuit of literacy feel so turbulent and precarious for so many.

In the next three sections, I trace the dynamics of literacy sponsorship   10
through the life experiences of several individuals, showing how their opportunities for literacy learning emerge out of the jockeying and skirmishing for economic and political advantage going on among sponsors of literacy. Along the way, the analysis addresses three key issues: (1) how, despite ostensible democracy in educational chances, stratification of opportunity continues to organize access and reward in literacy learning; (2) how sponsors contribute to what is called "the literacy crisis," that is, the perceived gap between rising standards for achievement and people's ability to meet them; and (3) how encounters with literacy sponsors, especially as they are configured at the end of the 20th century, can be sites for the innovative rerouting of resources into projects of self-development and social change.

Sponsorship and Access

A focus on sponsorship can force a more explicit and substantive link between   11
literacy learning and systems of opportunity and access. A statistical correlation

between high literacy achievement and high socioeconomic, majority-race status routinely shows up in results of national tests of reading and writing performance.[4] These findings capture yet, in their shorthand way, obscure the unequal conditions of literacy sponsorship that lie behind differential outcomes in academic performance. Throughout their lives, affluent people from high-caste racial groups have multiple and redundant contacts with powerful literacy sponsors as a routine part of their economic and political privileges. Poor people and those from low-caste racial groups have less consistent, less politically secured access to literacy sponsors—especially to the ones that can grease their way to academic and economic success. Differences in their performances are often attributed to family background (namely education and income of parents) or to particular norms and values operating within different ethnic groups or social classes. But in either case, much more is usually at work.

As a study in contrasts in sponsorship patterns and access to literacy, consider the parallel experiences of Raymond Branch and Dora Lopez, both of whom were born in 1969 and, as young children, moved with their parents to the same, mid-sized university town in the midwest.[5] Both were still residing in this town at the time of our interviews in 1995. Raymond Branch, a European American, had been born in southern California, the son of a professor father and a real estate executive mother. He recalled that his first-grade classroom in 1975 was hooked up to a mainframe computer at Stanford University and that, as a youngster, he enjoyed fooling around with computer programming in the company of "real users" at his father's science lab. This process was not interrupted much when, in the late 1970s, his family moved to the midwest. Raymond received his first personal computer as a Christmas present from his parents when he was twelve years old, and a modem the year after that. In the 1980s, computer hardware and software stores began popping up within a bicycle-ride's distance from where he lived. The stores were serving the university community and, increasingly, the high-tech industries that were becoming established in that vicinity. As an adolescent, Raymond spent his summers roaming these stores, sampling new computer games, making contact with founders of some of the first electronic bulletin boards in the nation, and continuing, through reading and other informal means, to develop his programming techniques. At the time of our interview he had graduated from the local university and was a successful freelance writer of software and software documentation, with clients in both the private sector and the university community.

Dora Lopez, a Mexican American, was born in the same year as Raymond Branch, 1969, in a Texas border town, where her grandparents, who worked as farm laborers, lived most of the year. When Dora was still a baby her family moved to the same midwest university town as had the family of Raymond Branch. Her father pursued an accounting degree at a local technical college and found work as a shipping and receiving clerk at the university. Her mother, who also attended technical college briefly, worked part-time in a bookstore. In the early 1970s, when the Lopez family made its move to the midwest, the Mexican-American population in the university town was barely one per cent. Dora recalled that the family had to drive seventy miles to a big city to find not

12

13

only suitable groceries but also Spanish-language newspapers and magazines that carried information of concern and interest to them. (Only when reception was good could they catch Spanish-language radio programs coming from Chicago, 150 miles away.) During her adolescence, Dora Lopez undertook to teach herself how to read and write in Spanish, something, she said, that neither her brother nor her U.S.-born cousins knew how to do. Sometimes, with the help of her mother's employee discount at the bookstore, she sought out novels by South American and Mexican writers, and she practiced her written Spanish by corresponding with relatives in Colombia. She was exposed to computers for the first time at the age of thirteen when she worked as a teacher's aide in a federally-funded summer school program for the children of migrant workers. The computers were being used to help the children to be brought up to grade level in their reading and writing skills. When Dora was admitted to the same university that Raymond Branch attended, her father bought her a used word processing machine that a student had advertised for sale on a bulletin board in the building where Mr. Lopez worked. At the time of our interview, Dora Lopez had transferred from the university to a technical college. She was working for a cleaning company, where she performed extra duties as a translator, communicating on her supervisor's behalf with the largely Latina cleaning staff. "I write in Spanish for him, what he needs to be translated, like job duties, what he expects them to do, and I write lists for him in English and Spanish," she explained.

In Raymond Branch's account of his early literacy learning we are able to see 14 behind the scenes of his majority-race membership, male gender, and high-end socioeconomic family profile. There lies a thick and, to him, relatively accessible economy of institutional and commercial supports that cultivated and subsidized his acquisition of a powerful form of literacy. One might be tempted to say that Raymond Branch was born at the right time and lived in the right place— except that the experience of Dora Lopez troubles that thought. For Raymond Branch, a university town in the 1970s and 1980s provided an information-rich, resource-rich learning environment in which to pursue his literacy development, but for Dora Lopez, a female member of a culturally unsubsidized ethnic minority, the same town at the same time was information- and resource-poor. Interestingly, both young people were pursuing projects of self-initiated learning, Raymond Branch in computer programming and Dora Lopez in biliteracy. But she had to reach much further afield for the material and communicative systems needed to support her learning. Also, while Raymond Branch, as the son of an academic, was sponsored by some of the most powerful agents of the university (its laboratories, newest technologies, and most educated personnel), Dora Lopez was being sponsored by what her parents could pull from the peripheral service systems of the university (the mail room, the bookstore, the second-hand technology market). In these accounts we also can see how the development and eventual economic worth of Raymond Branch's literacy skills were underwritten by late-century transformations in communication technology that created a boomtown need for programmers and software writers. Dora Lopez's biliterate skills developed and paid off much further down the economic-reward ladder, in government-sponsored youth programs and commercial enterprises, that, in the 1990s, were absorbing surplus migrant workers into a low-wage, urban service economy.[6] Tracking patterns of literacy sponsorship, then, gets beyond SES shorthand to expose more fully how unequal literacy chances relate to systems of unequal subsidy and reward for literacy. These are the systems that deliver large-scale economic, historical, and political conditions to the scenes of small-scale literacy use and development.

This analysis of sponsorship forces us to consider not merely how one social group's literacy practices may differ from another's, but how everybody's literacy practices are operating in differential economies, which supply different access routes, different degrees of sponsoring power, and different scales of monetary worth to the practices in use. In fact, the interviews I conducted are filled with examples of how economic and political forces, some of them originating in quite distant corporate and government policies, affect people's day-to-day ability to seek out and practice literacy. As a telephone company employee, Janelle Hampton enjoyed a brief period in the early 1980s as a fraud investigator, pursuing inquiries and writing up reports of her efforts. But when the breakup of the telephone utility reorganized its workforce, the fraud division was moved two states away and she was returned to less interesting work as a data processor. When, as a seven-year-old in the mid-1970s, Yi Vong made his way with his family from Laos to rural Wisconsin as part of the first resettlement group of Hmong refugees after the Vietnam War, his school district—which had no ESL programming—placed him in a school for the blind and deaf, where he learned English on audio and visual language machines. When a meager retirement pension forced Peter Hardaway and his wife out of their house and into a trailer, the couple stopped receiving newspapers and magazines in order to avoid cluttering up the small space they had to share. An analysis of sponsorship systems of literacy would help educators everywhere to think through the effects that economic and political changes in their regions are having on various people's ability to write and read, their chances to sustain that ability, and their capacities to pass it along to others. Recession, relocation, immigration, technological change, government retreat all can—and do—condition the course by which literate potential develops.

Sponsorship and the Rise in Literacy Standards

As I have been attempting to argue, literacy as a resource becomes available to ordinary people largely through the mediations of more powerful sponsors. These sponsors are engaged in ceaseless processes of positioning and repositioning, seizing and relinquishing control over meanings and materials of literacy as part of their participation in economic and political competition. In the give and take of these struggles, forms of literacy and literacy learning take shape. This section examines more closely how forms of literacy are created out of competitions between institutions. It especially considers how this process relates to the rapid rise in literacy standards since World War II. Resnick and Resnick lay out the process by which the demand for literacy achievement has been escalating, from basic, largely rote competence to more complex analytical and interpretive skills. More and more people are now being expected to accomplish more and more things with reading and writing. As print and its spinoffs have entered virtually every sphere of life, people have grown increasingly dependent on their literacy skills for earning a living and exercising and protecting their civil rights. This section uses one extended case example to trace the role of institutional sponsorship in raising the literacy stakes. It also considers how one man used available forms of sponsorship to cope with this escalation in literacy demands.

The focus is on Dwayne Lowery, whose transition in the early 1970s from   17
line worker in an automobile manufacturing plant to field representative for a major public employees union exemplified the major transition of the post-World War II economy—from a thing-making, thing-swapping society to an information-making, service-swapping society. In the process, Dwayne Lowery had to learn to read and write in ways that he had never done before. How his experiences with writing developed and how they were sponsored—and distressed—by institutional struggle will unfold in the following narrative.

A man of Eastern European ancestry, Dwayne Lowery was born in 1938   18
and raised in a semi-rural area in the upper midwest, the third of five children of a rubber worker father and a homemaker mother. Lowery recalled how, in his childhood home, his father's feisty union publications and left-leaning newspapers and radio shows helped to create a political climate in his household. "I was sixteen years old before I knew that goddamn Republicans was two words," he said. Despite this influence, Lowery said he shunned politics and newspaper reading as a young person, except to read the sports page. A diffident student, he graduated near the bottom of his class from a small high school in 1956 and, after a stint in the Army, went to work on the assembly line of a major automobile manufacturer. In the late 1960s, bored with the repetition of spraying primer paint on the right door checks of 57 cars an hour, Lowery traded in his night shift at the auto plant for a day job reading water meters in a municipal utility department. It was at that time, Lowery recalled, that he rediscovered newspapers, reading them in the early morning in his department's break room. He said:

> At the time I guess I got a little more interested in the state of things within the state. I started to get a little political at that time and got a little more information about local people. So I would buy [a metropolitan paper] and I would read that paper in the morning. It was a pretty conservative paper but I got some information.

At about the same time Lowery became active in a rapidly growing pub-   19
lic employees union, and, in the early 1970s, he applied for and received a union-sponsored grant that allowed him to take off four months of work and travel to Washington, D.C., for training in union activity. Here is his extended account of that experience:

> When I got to school, then there was a lot of reading. I often felt bad. If I had read more [as a high-school student] it wouldn't have been so tough. But they pumped a lot of stuff at us to read. We lived in a hotel and we had to some extent

homework we had to do and reading we had to do and not make written reports but make some presentation on our part of it. What they were trying to teach us, I believe, was regulations, systems, laws. In case anything in court came up along the way, we would know that. We did a lot of work on organizing, you know, learning how to negotiate contracts, contractual language, how to write it. Gross National Product, how that affected the Consumer Price Index. It was pretty much a crash course. It was pretty much crammed in. And I'm not sure we were all that well prepared when we got done, but it was interesting.

After a hands-on experience organizing sanitation workers in the west, Lowery returned home and was offered a full-time job as a field staff representative for the union, handling worker grievances and contract negotiations for a large, active local near his state capital. His initial writing and rhetorical activities corresponded with the heady days of the early 1970s when the union was growing in strength and influence, reflecting in part the exponential expansion in information workers and service providers within all branches of government. With practice, Lowery said he became "good at talking," "good at presenting the union side," "good at slicing chunks off the employer's case." Lowery observed that, in those years, the elected officials with whom he was negotiating often lacked the sophistication of their Washington-trained union counterparts. "They were part-time people," he said. "And they didn't know how to calculate. We got things in contracts that didn't cost them much at the time but were going to cost them a ton down the road." In time, though, even small municipal and county governments responded to the public employees' growing power by hiring specialized attorneys to represent them in grievance and contract negotiations. "Pretty soon," Lowery observed, "ninety percent of the people I was dealing with across the table were attorneys."

This move brought dramatic changes in the writing practices of union reps, 20 and, in Lowery's estimation, a simultaneous waning of the power of workers and the power of his own literacy. "It used to be we got our way through muscle or through political connections," he said. "Now we had to get it through legalistic stuff. It was no longer just sit down and talk about it. Can we make a deal?" Instead, all activity became rendered in writing: the exhibit, the brief, the transcript, the letter, the appeal. Because briefs took longer to write, the wheels of justice took longer to turn. Delays in grievance hearings became routine, as lawyers and union reps alike asked hearing judges for extensions on their briefs. Things went, in Lowery's words, "from quick, competent justice to expensive and long term justice."

In the meantime, Lowery began spending up to 70 hours a week at work, 21 sweating over the writing of briefs, which are typically fifteen to thirty-page documents laying out precedents, arguments, and evidence for a grievant's case. These documents were being forced by the new political economy in which Lowery's union was operating. He explained:

When employers were represented by an attorney, you were going to have a written brief because the attorney needs to get paid. Well, what do you think if you were a union grievant and the attorney says, well, I'm going to write a brief and

Dwayne Lowery says, well, I'm not going to. Does the worker somehow feel that their representation is less now?

To keep up with the new demands, Lowery occasionally traveled to major cities for two or three-day union-sponsored workshops on arbitration, new legislation, and communication skills. He also took short courses at a historic School for Workers at a nearby university. His writing instruction consisted mainly of reading the briefs of other field reps, especially those done by the college graduates who increasingly were being assigned to his district from union headquarters. Lowery said he kept a file drawer filled with other people's briefs from which he would borrow formats and phrasings. At the time of our interview in 1995, Dwayne Lowery had just taken an early and somewhat bitter retirement from the union, replaced by a recent graduate from a master's degree program in Industrial Relations. As a retiree, he was engaged in local Democratic party politics and was getting informal lessons in word processing at home from his wife.

Over a 20-year period, Lowery's adult writing took its character from a   22
particular juncture in labor relations, when even small units of government began wielding (and, as a consequence, began spreading) a "legalistic" form of literacy in order to restore political dominance over public workers. This struggle for dominance shaped the kinds of literacy skills required of Lowery, the kinds of genres he learned and used, and the kinds of literate identity he developed. Lowery's rank-and-file experience and his talent for representing that experience around a bargaining table became increasingly peripheral to his ability to prepare documents that could compete in kind with those written by his formally-educated, professional adversaries. Face-to-face meetings became occasions mostly for a ritualistic exchange of texts, as arbitrators generally deferred decisions, reaching them in private, after solitary deliberation over complex sets of documents. What Dwayne Lowery was up against as a working adult in the second half of the 20th century was more than just living through a rising standard in literacy expectations or a generalized growth in professionalization, specialization, or documentary power—although certainly all of those things are, generically, true. Rather, these developments should be seen more specifically, as outcomes of ongoing transformations in the history of literacy as it has been wielded as part of economic and political conflict. These transformations become the arenas in which new standards of literacy develop. And for Dwayne Lowery—as well as many like him over the last 25 years—these are the arenas in which the worth of existing literate skills become degraded. A consummate debater and deal maker, Lowery saw his value to the union bureaucracy subside, as power shifted to younger, university-trained staffers whose literacy credentials better matched the specialized forms of escalating pressure coming from the other side.

In the broadest sense, the sponsorship of Dwayne Lowery's literacy experi-   23
ences lies deep within the historical conditions of industrial relations in the 20th century and, more particularly, within the changing nature of work and labor struggle over the last several decades. Edward Stevens Jr. has observed the rise in this century of an "advanced contractarian society" (25) by which

formal relationships of all kinds have come to rely on "a jungle of rules and regulations" (139). For labor, these conditions only intensified in the 1960s and 1970s when a flurry of federal and state civil rights legislation curtailed the previously unregulated hiring and firing power of management. These developments made the appeal to law as central as collective bargaining for extending employee rights (Heckscher 9). I mention this broader picture, first, because it relates to the forms of employer backlash that Lowery began experiencing by the early 1980s and, more important, because a history of unionism serves as a guide for a closer look at the sponsors of Lowery's literacy.

These resources begin with the influence of his father, whose membership in   24 the United Rubber Workers during the ideologically potent 1930s and 1940s grounded Lowery in class-conscious progressivism and its favorite literate form: the newspaper. On top of that, though, was a pragmatic philosophy of worker education that developed in the U.S. after the Depression as an anti-communist antidote to left-wing intellectual influences in unions. Lowery's parent union, in fact, had been a central force in refocusing worker education away from an earlier emphasis on broad critical study and toward discrete techniques for organizing and bargaining. Workers began to be trained in the discrete bodies of knowledge, written formats, and idioms associated with those strategies. Characteristic of this legacy, Lowery's crash course at the Washington-based training center in the early 1970s emphasized technical information, problem solving, and union-building skills and methods. The transformation in worker education from critical, humanistic study to problem-solving skills was also lived out at the school for workers where Lowery took short courses in the 1980s. Once a place where factory workers came to write and read about economics, sociology, and labor history, the school is now part of a university extension service offering workshops—often requested by management—on such topics as work restructuring, new technology health and safety regulations, and joint labor-management cooperation.[7] Finally, in this inventory of Dwayne Lowery's literacy sponsors, we must add the latest incarnations shaping union practices: the attorneys and college-educated co-workers who carried into Lowery's workplace forms of legal discourse and "essayist literacy."[8]

What should we notice about this pattern of sponsorship? First, we can   25 see from yet another angle how the course of an ordinary person's literacy learning—its occasions, materials, applications, potentials—follows the transformations going on within sponsoring institutions as those institutions fight for economic and ideological position. As a result of wins, losses, or compromises, institutions undergo change, affecting the kinds of literacy they promulgate and the status that such literacy has in the larger society. So where, how, why, and what Lowery practiced as a writer—and what he didn't practice—took shape as part of the post-industrial jockeying going on over the last thirty years by labor, government, and industry. Yet there is more to be seen in this inventory of literacy sponsors. It exposes the deeply textured history that lies within the literacy practices of institutions and within any individual's literacy experiences. Accumulated layers of sponsoring influences—in families, workplaces, schools, memory—carry forms of literacy that have been shaped out of ideological and economic struggles of the past. This history, on the one hand, is a sustaining resource in the quest for literacy. It enables an older generation to pass its literacy resources onto another. Lowery's exposure to his father's newspaper-reading and supper-table political talk kindled his adult passion for news, debate, and for language that rendered relief and justice. This history also helps to create infrastructures of opportunity. Lowery found crucial supports for extending his adult literacy in the educational networks that unions established during the first half of the 20th century as they were consolidating into national powers. On the other hand, this layered history of sponsorship is also deeply conservative and can be maladaptive because it teaches forms of literacy that oftentimes are in the process of being overtaken by new political realities and by ascendent forms of literacy. The decision to focus worker education on practical strategies of recruiting and bargaining—devised in the thick of Cold War patriotism and galloping expansion in union memberships—became, by the Reagan years, a fertile ground for new forms of management aggression and cooptation.

It is actually this lag or gap in sponsoring forms that we call the rising 26 standard of literacy. The pace of change and the place of literacy in economic competition have both intensified enormously in the last half of the 20th century. It is as if the history of literacy is in fast forward. Where once the same sponsoring arrangements could maintain value across a generation or more, forms of literacy and their sponsors can now rise and recede many times within a single life span. Dwayne Lowery experienced profound changes in forms of union-based literacy not only between his father's time and his but between the time he joined the union and the time he left it, twenty-odd years later. This phenomenon is what makes today's literacy feel so advanced and, at the same time, so destabilized.

Sponsorship and Appropriation in Literacy Learning

We have seen how literacy sponsors affect literacy learning in two powerful 27 ways. They help to organize and administer stratified systems of opportunity and access, and they raise the literacy stakes in struggles for competitive advantage. Sponsors enable and hinder literacy activity, often forcing the formation of new literacy requirements while decertifying older ones. A somewhat different dynamic of literacy sponsorship is treated here. It pertains to the potential of the sponsored to divert sponsors' resources toward ulterior projects, often projects of self-interest or self-development. Earlier I mentioned how Sunday School parishioners in England and African Americans in slavery appropriated church-sponsored literacy for economic and psychic survival. "Misappropriation" is always possible at the scene of literacy transmission, a reason for the tight ideological control that usually surrounds reading and writing instruction. The accounts that appear below are meant to shed light on the dynamics of appropriation, including the role of sponsoring agents in that process. They are also meant to suggest that diversionary tactics in literacy learning may be invited now by the sheer proliferation of literacy activity in contemporary life.

The uses and networks of literacy crisscross through many domains, exposing people to multiple, often amalgamated sources of sponsoring powers, secular, religious, bureaucratic, commercial, technological. In other words, what is so destabilized about contemporary literacy today also makes it so available and potentially innovative, ripe for picking, one might say, for people suitably positioned. The rising level of schooling in the general population is also an inviting factor in this process. Almost everyone now has some sort of contact, for instance, with college-educated people, whose movements through workplaces, justice systems, social service organizations, houses of worship, local government, extended families, or circles of friends spread dominant forms of literacy (whether wanted or not, helpful or not) into public and private spheres. Another condition favorable for appropriation is the deep hybridity of literacy practices extant in many settings. As we saw in Dwayne Lowery's case, workplaces, schools, families bring together multiple strands of the history of literacy in complex and influential forms. We need models of literacy that more astutely account for these kinds of multiple contacts, both in and out of school and across a lifetime. Such models could begin to grasp the significance of re-appropriation, which, for a number of reasons, is becoming a key requirement for literacy learning at the end of the 20th century.

The following discussion will consider two brief cases of literacy diversion. 28 Both involve women working in subordinate positions as secretaries, in print-rich settings where better-educated male supervisors were teaching them to read and write in certain ways to perform their clerical duties. However, as we will see shortly, strong loyalties outside the workplace prompted these two secretaries to lift these literate resources for use in other spheres. For one, Carol White, it was on behalf of her work as a Jehovah's Witness. For the other, Sarah Steele, it was on behalf of upward mobility for her lower-middle-class family.

Before turning to their narratives, though, it will be wise to pay some atten- 29 tion to the economic moment in which they occur. Clerical work was the largest and fastest-growing occupation for women in the 20th century. Like so much employment for women, it offered a mix of gender-defined constraints as well as avenues for economic independence and mobility. As a new information economy created an acute need for typists, stenographers, bookkeepers, and other office workers, white, American-born women and, later, immigrant and minority women saw reason to pursue high school and business-college educations. Unlike male clerks of the 19th century, female secretaries in this century had little chance for advancement. However, office work represented a step up from the farm or the factory for women of the working class and served as a respectable occupation from which educated, middle-class women could await or avoid marriage (Anderson, Strom). In a study of clerical work through the first half of the 20th century, Mary Christine Anderson estimated that secretaries might encounter up to 97 different genres in the course of doing dictation or transcription. They routinely had contact with an array of professionals, including lawyers, auditors, tax examiners, and other government overseers (52–53). By 1930, 30% of women office workers used machines other than typewriters (Anderson 76) and, in contemporary offices, clerical workers have often been the first employees to learn to operate CRTs and personal computers and to teach others how to use them. Overall, the daily duties of 20th-century secretaries could serve handily as an index to the rise of complex administrative and accounting procedures, standardization of information, expanding communication, and developments in technological systems.

With that background, consider the experiences of Carol White and Sarah 30 Steele. An Oneida, Carol White was born into a poor, single-parent household in 1940. She graduated from high school in 1960 and, between five maternity leaves and a divorce, worked continuously in a series of clerical positions in both the private and public sectors. One of her first secretarial jobs was with an urban firm that produced and disseminated Catholic missionary films. The vice-president with whom she worked most closely also spent much of his time producing a magazine for a national civic organization that he headed. She discussed how typing letters and magazine articles and occasionally proofreading for this man taught her rhetorical strategies in which she was keenly interested. She described the scene of transfer this way:

> [My boss] didn't just write to write. He wrote in a way to make his letters appealing. I would have to write what he was writing in this magazine too. I was completely enthralled. He would write about the people who were in this [organization] and the different works they were undertaking and people that died and people who were sick and about their personalities. And he wrote little anecdotes. Once in a while I made some suggestions too. He was a man who would listen to you.

The appealing and persuasive power of the anecdote became especially important to Carol White when she began doing door-to-door missionary work for the Jehovah's Witnesses, a pan-racial, millenialist religious faith. She now uses colorful anecdotes to prepare demonstrations that she performs with other women at weekly service meetings at their Kingdom Hall. These demonstrations, done in front of the congregation, take the form of skits designed to explore daily problems through Bible principles. Further, at the time of our interview, Carol White was working as a municipal revenue clerk and had recently enrolled in an on-the-job training seminar called Persuasive Communication, a two-day class offered free to public employees. Her motivation for taking the course stemmed from her desire to improve her evangelical work. She said she wanted to continue to develop speaking and writing skills that would be "appealing," "motivating," and "encouraging" to people she hoped to convert.

Sarah Steele, a woman of Welsh and German descent, was born in 1920 into 31 a large, working-class family in a coal mining community in eastern Pennsylvania. In 1940, she graduated from a two-year commercial college. Married soon after, she worked as a secretary in a glass factory until becoming pregnant with the first of four children. In the 1960s, in part to help pay for her children's college educations, she returned to the labor force as a receptionist and bookkeeper in a law firm, where she stayed until her retirement in the late 1970s.

Sarah Steele described how, after joining the law firm, she began to model her 32 household management on principles of budgeting that she was picking up from one of the attorneys with whom she worked most closely. "I learned cash flow from Mr. B____," she said. "I would get all the bills and put a tape in the adding machine and he and I would sit down together to be sure there was going to be money ahead." She said that she began to replicate that process at home with household bills. "Before that," she observed, "I would just cook beans when I had to instead of meat." Sarah Steele also said she encountered the genre of the credit report during routine reading and typing on the job. She figured out what constituted a top rating, making sure her husband followed these steps in preparation for their financing a new car. She also remembered typing up documents connected to civil suits being brought against local businesses, teaching her, she said, which firms never to hire for home repairs. "It just changes the way you think," she observed about the reading and writing she did on her job. "You're not a pushover after you learn how business operates."

The dynamics of sponsorship alive in these narratives expose important ele- 33 ments of literacy appropriation, at least as it is practiced at the end of the 20th century. In a pattern now familiar from the earlier sections, we see how opportunities for literacy learning—this time for diversions of resources—open up in the clash between long-standing, residual forms of sponsorship and the new: between the lingering presence of literacy's conservative history and its pressure for change. So, here, two women—one Native American and both working-class— filch contemporary literacy resources (public relations techniques and accounting practices) from more-educated, higher-status men. The women are emboldened in these acts by ulterior identities beyond the workplace: Carol White with faith and Sarah Steele with family. These affiliations hark back to the first sponsoring arrangements through which American women were gradually allowed to acquire literacy and education. Duties associated with religious faith and child rearing helped literacy to become, in Gloria Main's words, "a permissable feminine activity" (579). Interestingly, these roles, deeply sanctioned within the history of women's literacy—and operating beneath the newer permissible feminine activity of clerical work—become grounds for covert, innovative appropriation even as they reinforce traditional female identities.

Just as multiple identities contribute to the ideologically hybrid charac- 34 ter of these literacy formations, so do institutional and material conditions. Carol White's account speaks to such hybridity. The missionary film company with the civic club vice president is a residual site for two of literacy's oldest campaigns—Christian conversion and civic participation—enhanced here by 20th-century advances in film and public relations techniques. This ideological reservoir proved a pleasing instructional site for Carol White, whose interests in literacy, throughout her life, have been primarily spiritual. So literacy appropriation draws upon, perhaps even depends upon, conservative forces in the history of literacy sponsorship that are always hovering at the scene of acts of learning. This history serves as both a sanctioning force and a reserve of ideological and material support.

At the same time, however, we see in these accounts how individual acts 35 of appropriation can divert and subvert the course of literacy's history, how changes in individual literacy experiences relate to larger-scale transformations.

Carol White's redirection of personnel management techniques to the cause of the Jehovah's Witnesses is an almost ironic transformation in this regard. Once a principal sponsor in the initial spread of mass literacy, evangelism is here rejuvenated through late-literate corporate sciences of secular persuasion, fund-raising, and bureaucratic management that Carol White finds circulating in her contemporary workplaces. By the same token, through Sarah Steele, accounting practices associated with corporations are, in a sense, tracked into the house, rationalizing and standardizing even domestic practices. (Even though Sarah Steele did not own an adding machine, she penciled her budget figures onto adding-machine tape that she kept for that purpose.) Sarah Steele's act of appropriation in some sense explains how dominant forms of literacy migrate and penetrate into private spheres, including private consciousness. At the same time, though, she accomplishes a subversive diversion of literate power. Her efforts to move her family up in the middle class involved not merely contributing a second income but also, from her desk as a bookkeeper, reading her way into an understanding of middle-class economic power.

Teaching and the Dynamics of Sponsorship

It hardly seems necessary to point out to the readers of CCC that we haul a 36 lot of freight for the opportunity to teach writing. Neither rich nor powerful enough to sponsor literacy on our own terms, we serve instead as conflicted brokers between literacy's buyers and sellers. At our most worthy, perhaps, we show the sellers how to beware and try to make sure these exchanges will be a little fairer, maybe, potentially, a little more mutually rewarding. This essay has offered a few working case studies that link patterns of sponsorship to processes of stratification, competition, and reappropriation. How much these dynamics can be generalized to classrooms is an ongoing empirical question.

I am sure that sponsors play even more influential roles at the scenes of lit- 37 eracy learning and use than this essay has explored. I have focused on some of the most tangible aspects—material supply, explicit teaching, institutional aegis. But the ideological pressure of sponsors affects many private aspects of writing processes as well as public aspects of finished texts. Where one's sponsors are multiple or even at odds, they can make writing maddening. Where they are absent, they make writing unlikely. Many of the cultural formations we associate with writing development—community practices, disciplinary traditions, technological potentials—can be appreciated as make-do responses to the economics of literacy, past and present. The history of literacy is a catalogue of obligatory relations. That this catalogue is so deeply conservative and, at the same time, so ruthlessly demanding of change is what fills contemporary literacy learning and teaching with their most paradoxical choices and outcomes.[9]

In bringing attention to economies of literacy learning I am not advocating 38 that we prepare students more efficiently for the job markets they must enter. What I have tried to suggest is that as we assist and study individuals in pursuit of literacy, we also recognize how literacy is in pursuit of them. When this process stirs ambivalence, on their part or on ours, we need to be understanding.

Acknowledgments

This research was sponsored by the NCTE Research Foundation and the Center on English Learning and Achievement. The Center is supported by the U.S. Department of Education's Office of Educational Research and Improvement, whose views do not necessarily coincide with the author's. A version of this essay was given as a lecture in the Department of English, University of Louisville, in April 1997. Thanks to Anna Syvertsen and Julie Nelson for their help with archival research. Thanks too to colleagues who lent an ear along the way: Nelson Graff, Jonna Gjevre, Anne Gere, Kurt Spellmeyer, Tom Fox, and Bob Gundlach.

Notes

1. Three of the keenest and most eloquent observers of economic impacts on writing, teaching, and learning have been Lester Faigley, Susan Miller, and Kurt Spellmeyer.
2. My debt to the writings of Pierre Bourdieu will be evident throughout this essay. Here and throughout I invoke his expansive notion of "economy," which is not restricted to literal and ostensible systems of money making but to the many spheres where people labor, invest, and exploit energies—their own and others'—to maximize advantage, see Bourdieu and Wacquant, especially 117–120 and Bourdieu, Chapter 7.
3. Thomas Laqueur (124) provides a vivid account of a street demonstration in Bolton, England, in 1834 by a "pro-writing" faction of Sunday School students and their teachers. This faction demanded that writing instruction continue to be provided on Sundays, something that opponents of secular instruction on the Sabbath were trying to reverse.
4. See, for instance, National Assessments of Educational Progress in reading and writing (Applebee et al.; and "Looking").
5. All names used in this essay are pseudonyms.
6. I am not suggesting that literacy that does not "pay off" in terms of prestige or monetary reward is less valuable. Dora Lopez's ability to read and write in Spanish was a source of great strength and pride, especially when she was able to teach it to her young child. The resource of Spanish literacy carried much of what Bourdieu calls cultural capital in her social and family circles. But I want to point out here how people who labor equally to acquire literacy do so under systems of unequal subsidy and unequal reward.
7. For useful accounts of this period in union history, see Heckscher; Nelson.
8. Marcia Farr associates "essayist literacy" with written genres esteemed in the academy and noted for their explictness, exactness, reliance on reasons and evidence, and impersonal voice.
9. Lawrence Cremin makes similar points about education in general in his essay "The Cacophony of Teaching." He suggests that complex economic and social changes since World War Two, including the popularization of schooling and the penetration of mass media, have created "a far greater range and diversity of languages, competencies, values, personalities, and approaches to the world and to its educational opportunities" than at one time existed. The diversity most of interest to him (and me) resides not so much in the range of different ethnic groups there are in society but in the different cultural formulas by which people assemble their educational—or, I would say, literate—experience.

Works Cited

Anderson, Mary Christine. "Gender, Class, and Culture: Women Secretarial and Clerical Workers in the United States, 1925–1955." Diss. Ohio State U, 1986.

Applebee, Arthur N., Judith A. Langer, and Ida V. S. Mullis. *The Writing Report Card: Writing Achievement in American Schools.* Princeton: ETS, 1986.

Bourdieu, Pierre. *The Logic of Practice.* Trans. Richard Nice. Cambridge: Polity, 1990.

Bourdieu, Pierre and Loic J. D. Wacquant. *An Invitation to Reflexive Sociology*. Chicago: Chicago UP, 1992.

Bourne, J. M. *Patronage and Society in Nineteenth-Century England*. London: Edward Arnold, 1986.

Brandt, Deborah. "Remembering Reading, Remembering Writing." *CCC* 45 (1994): 459–79.

_____. "Accumulating Literacy: Writing and Learning to Write in the 20th Century." *College English* 57 (1995): 649–68.

Cornelius, Janet Duitsman. '*When I Can Ready My Title Clear*': *Literacy, Slavery, and Religion in the Antebellum South*. Columbia: U of South Carolina, 1991.

Cremin, Lawrence. "The Cacophony of Teaching." *Popular Education and Its Discontents*. New York: Harper, 1990.

Faigley, Lester. "Veterans' Stories on the Porch." *History, Reflection and Narrative: The Professionalization of Composition, 1963–1983*. Eds. Beth Boehm, Debra Journet, and Mary Rosner. Norwood: Ablex, 1999. 23–38.

Farr, Marcia. "Essayist Literacy and Other Verbal Performances." *Written Communication* 8 (1993): 4–38.

Heckscher, Charles C. *The New Unionism: Employee Involvement in the Changing Corporation*. New York: Basic, 1988.

Horstman, Connie, and Donald V. Kurtz. *Compradrazgo in Post-Conquest Middle America*. Milwaukee: Milwaukee-UW Center for Latin America, 1978.

Kett, Joseph F. *The Pursuit of Knowledge Under Difficulties: From Self Improvement to Adult Education in America 1750–1990*. Stanford: Stanford UP, 1994.

Laqueur, Thomas. *Religion and Respectability: Sunday Schools and Working Class Culture 1780–1850*. New Haven: Yale UP, 1976.

Looking at How Well Our Students Read: The 1992 National Assessment of Educational Progress in Reading. Washington: US Dept. of Education, Office of Educational Research and Improvement, Educational Resources Information Center, 1992.

Lynch, Joseph H. *Godparents and Kinship in Early Medieval Europe*. Princeton: Princeton UP, 1986.

Main, Gloria L. "An Inquiry Into When and Why Women Learned to Write in Colonial New England." *Journal of Social History* 24 (1991): 579–89.

Miller, Susan. *Textual Carnivals: The Politics of Composition*. Carbondale: Southern Illinois UP, 1991.

Nelson, Daniel. *American Rubber Workers & Organized Labor, 1900–1941*. Princeton: Princeton UP, 1988.

Nicholas, Stephen J., and Jacqueline M. Nicholas. "Male Literacy, 'Deskilling,' and the Industrial Revolution." *Journal of Interdisciplinary History* 23 (1992): 1–18.

Resnick, Daniel P., and Lauren B. Resnick. "The Nature of Literacy: A Historical Explanation." *Harvard Educational Review* 47 (1977): 370–85.

Spellmeyer, Kurt. "After Theory: From Textuality to Attunement With the World." *College English* 58 (1996): 893–913.

Stevens, Jr., Edward. *Literacy, Law, and Social Order*. DeKalb: Northern Illinois UP, 1987.

Strom, Sharon Hartman. *Beyond the Typewriter: Gender, Class, and the Origins of Modern American Office Work, 1900–1930*. Urbana: U of Illinois P, 1992.

Questions for Discussion and Journaling

1. How does Brandt define *literacy sponsor*? What are the characteristics of a literacy sponsor?
2. How does Brandt support her claim that sponsors always have something to gain from their sponsorship? Can you provide any examples from your own experience?
3. How do the sponsored sometimes "misappropriate" their literacy lessons?
4. Consider Brandt's claim that literacy sponsors "help to organize and administer stratified systems of opportunity and access, and they raise the literacy stakes in struggles for competitive advantage" (para. 27). What does Brandt mean by the term *stratified*? What "stakes" is she referring to?
5. Giving the examples of Branch and Lopez as support, Brandt argues that race and class impact how much access people have to literacy sponsorship. Summarize the kinds of access Branch and Lopez had—for example, in their early education, access to books and computers, parental support, and so on—and decide whether you agree with Brandt's claim.

Applying and Exploring Ideas

1. Compare your own literacy history to those of Branch and Lopez, using categories like those in discussion question number 5 above. Then consider who your primary literacy sponsors were (people, as well as institutions like churches or clubs or school systems) and what literacies they taught you (academic, civic, religious, and so on). Would you consider the access provided by these sponsors adequate? What literacies have you not had access to that you wish you had?
2. Have you ever had literacy sponsors who withheld (or tried to withhold) certain kinds of literacies from you? For example, did your school ban certain books? Have sponsors forced certain kinds of literacies on you (for example, approved reading lists in school) or held up some literacies as better than others (for example, saying that certain kinds of books didn't "count" as reading)? Were you able to find alternative sponsors for different kinds of literacy?
3. Interview a classmate about a significant literacy sponsor in their lives, and then discuss the interview in an entry on a class wiki or blog, a brief presentation, or a one-page report. Try to cover these questions in your interview:
   a. Who or what was your literacy sponsor?
   b. What did you gain from the sponsorship?
   c. Did you "misappropriate" the literacy in any way?
   d. What materials, technologies, and so forth were involved?
      In reflecting on the interview, ask yourself the following:
   a. Did the sponsorship connect to larger cultural or material developments?

b. Does the sponsorship let you make any hypotheses about the culture of your interviewee? How would you test that hypothesis?

c. Does your classmate's account have a "So what?"—a point that might make others care about it?

Meta Moment

Review the goals for this chapter: For which ones is Brandt's article relevant? Are there experiences you're currently having that Brandt's thinking seems to explain or predict?

Library of Congress

Learning to Read

MALCOLM X

X, Malcolm. *The Autobiography of Malcolm X.* Ed. Alex Haley. New York: Ballantine, 1965. Print.

Framing the Reading

Malcolm X was born Malcolm Little in Omaha, Nebraska, in 1925. Essentially orphaned as a child, he lived in a series of foster homes, became involved in criminal activity, and dropped out of school in eighth grade after a teacher told him his race would prevent him from being a lawyer. In 1945, he was sentenced to prison, where he read voraciously. After joining the Nation of Islam, he changed his last name to "X," explaining in his autobiography that "my 'X' replaced the white slave-master name of 'Little.'" A strong advocate for the rights of African Americans, Malcolm X became an influential leader in the Nation of Islam but left the organization in 1964, becoming a Sunni Muslim and founding an organization dedicated to African American unity. Less than a year later, he was assassinated.

In this chapter we excerpt a piece from *The Autobiography of Malcolm X*, which he narrated to Alex Haley shortly before his death. We see Malcolm X's account as exemplifying many of the principles that Deborah Brandt introduces in "Sponsors of Literacy" (pp. 331–350). For example, Malcolm X's account of how he came to reading is remarkable for how clearly it shows the role of motivation in **literacy** and learning: when he had a *reason* to read, he read, and reading fed his motivation to read further. His account also demonstrates the extent to which literacies shape the worlds available to people and the experiences they can have, as well as how **literacy sponsors** affect the kinds of literacy we eventually master.

We expect that reading Malcolm X's experiences in coming to reading will bring up your own memories of this stage in your life, which should set you thinking about what worlds your literacies give you access to and whether there are worlds in which you would be considered "illiterate." We think you'll find a comparison of your experiences and Malcolm X's provocative and telling.

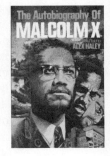

Getting Ready to Read

Before you read, do at least one of the following activities:

- Do some reading online about Malcolm X and his biography.

- Start a discussion with friends, roommates, family, or classmates about whether, and how, "knowledge is power."

As you read, consider the following questions:

- How would Malcolm X's life have been different if his literacy experiences had been different?
- How was Malcolm X's literacy inextricably entangled with his life experiences, his race, and the religion he chose?
- How do Malcolm X's early literacy experiences and literacy sponsors compare to your own?

It was because of my letters that I happened to stumble upon starting to   1
acquire some kind of a homemade education.

I became increasingly frustrated at   2
not being able to express what I wanted to convey in letters that I wrote, especially those to Mr. Elijah Muhammad. In the street, I had been the most articulate hustler out there—I had commanded attention when I said something. But now, trying to write simple English, I not only wasn't articulate, I wasn't even functional. How would I sound writing in slang, the way I would *say* it, something such as "Look, daddy, let me pull your coat about a cat, Elijah Muhammad—"

> In the street, I had been the most articulate hustler out there—I had commanded attention when I said something. But now, trying to write simple English, I not only wasn't articulate, I wasn't even functional.

Many who today hear me somewhere in person, or on television, or those   3
who read something I've said, will think I went to school far beyond the eighth grade. This impression is due entirely to my prison studies.

It had really begun back in the Charlestown Prison, when Bimbi first made   4
me feel envy of his stock of knowledge. Bimbi had always taken charge of any conversation he was in, and I had tried to emulate him. But every book I picked up had few sentences which didn't contain anywhere from one to nearly all of the words that might as well have been in Chinese. When I just skipped those words, of course, I really ended up with little idea of what the book said. So I had come to the Norfolk Prison Colony still going through only book-reading motions. Pretty soon, I would have quit even these motions, unless I had received the motivation that I did.

I saw that the best thing I could do was get hold of a dictionary—to study,   5
to learn some words. I was lucky enough to reason also that I should try to improve my penmanship. It was sad. I couldn't even write in a straight line.

It was both ideas together that moved me to request a dictionary along with some tablets and pencils from the Norfolk Prison Colony school.

I spent two days just riffling uncertainly through the dictionary's pages. I'd never realized so many words existed! I didn't know *which* words I needed to learn. Finally, just to start some kind of action, I began copying.

In my slow, painstaking, ragged handwriting, I copied into my tablet everything printed on that first page, down to the punctuation marks.

I believe it took me a day. Then, aloud, I read back, to myself, everything I'd written on the tablet. Over and over, aloud, to myself, I read my own handwriting.

I woke up the next morning, thinking about those words—immensely proud to realize that not only had I written so much at one time, but I'd written words that I never knew were in the world. Moreover, with a little effort, I also could remember what many of these words meant. I reviewed the words whose meanings I didn't remember. Funny thing, from the dictionary first page right now, that "aardvark" springs to my mind. The dictionary had a picture of it, a long-tailed, long-eared, burrowing African mammal, which lives off termites caught by sticking out its tongue as an anteater does for ants.

I was so fascinated that I went on—I copied the dictionary's next page. And the same experience came when I studied that. With every succeeding page, I also learned of people and places and events from history. Actually the dictionary is like a miniature encyclopedia. Finally the dictionary's A section had filled a whole tablet—and I went on into the B's. That was the way I started copying what eventually became the entire dictionary. It went a lot faster after so much practice helped me to pick up handwriting speed. Between what I wrote in my tablet, and writing letters, during the rest of my time in prison I would guess I wrote a million words.

I suppose it was inevitable that as my word-base broadened, I could for the first time pick up a book and read and now begin to understand what the book was saying. Anyone who has read a great deal can imagine the new world that opened. Let me tell you something: from then until I left that prison, in every free moment I had, if I was not reading in the library, I was reading on my bunk. You couldn't have gotten me out of books with a wedge. Between Mr. Muhammad's teachings, my correspondence, my visitors—usually Ella and Reginald—and my reading of books, months passed without my even thinking about being imprisoned. In fact, up to then, I never had been so truly free in my life.

The Norfolk Prison Colony's library was in the school building. A variety of classes was taught there by instructors who came from such places as Harvard and Boston universities. The weekly debates between inmate teams were also held in the school building. You would be astonished to know how worked up convict debaters and audiences would get over subjects like "Should Babies Be Fed Milk?"

Available on the prison library's shelves were books on just about every general subject. Much of the big private collection that Parkhurst had willed to the prison was still in crates and boxes in the back of the library—thousands of old books. Some of them looked ancient: covers faded, old-time parchment-looking binding. Parkhurst, I've mentioned, seemed to have been principally interested in history and religion. He had the money and the special interest to have a lot of books that you wouldn't have in general circulation. Any college library would have been lucky to get that collection.

As you can imagine, especially in a prison where there was heavy emphasis 14 on rehabilitation, an inmate was smiled upon if he demonstrated an unusually intense interest in books. There was a sizable number of well-read inmates, especially the popular debaters. Some were said by many to be practically walking encyclopedias. They were almost celebrities. No university would ask any student to devour literature as I did when this new world opened to me, of being able to read and *understand*.

I read more in my room than in the library itself. An inmate who was known 15 to read a lot could check out more than the permitted maximum number of books. I preferred reading in the total isolation of my own room.

When I had progressed to really serious reading, every night at about ten 16 P.M. I would be outraged with the "lights out." It always seemed to catch me right in the middle of something engrossing.

Fortunately, right outside my door was a corridor light that cast a glow into 17 my room. The glow was enough to read by, once my eyes adjusted to it. So when "lights out" came, I would sit on the floor where I could continue reading in that glow.

At one-hour intervals the night guards paced past every room. Each time 18 I heard the approaching footsteps, I jumped into bed and feigned sleep. And as soon as the guard passed, I got back out of bed onto the floor area of that light-glow, where I would read for another fifty-eight minutes—until the guard approached again. That went on until three or four every morning. Three or four hours of sleep a night was enough for me. Often in the years in the streets I had slept less than that.

The teachings of Mr. Muhammad stressed how history had been "whitened"— 19 when white men had written history books, the black man simply had been left out. Mr. Muhammad couldn't have said anything that would have struck me much harder. I had never forgotten how when my class, me and all of those whites, had studied seventh-grade United States history back in Mason, the history of the Negro had been covered in one paragraph, and the teacher had gotten a big laugh with his joke, "Negroes' feet are so big that when they walk, they leave a hole in the ground."

This is one reason why Mr. Muhammad's teachings spread so swiftly all 20 over the United States, among *all* Negroes, whether or not they became fol-lowers of Mr. Muhammad. The teachings ring true—to every Negro. You can hardly show me a black adult in America—or a white one, for that matter—who knows from the history books anything like the truth about the black man's role. In my own case, once I heard of the "glorious history of the black man," I took special pains to hunt in the library for books that would inform me on details about black history.

I can remember accurately the very first set of books that really impressed   21
me. I have since bought that set of books and have it at home for my children
to read as they grow up. It's called *Wonders of the World*. It's full of pictures of
archeological finds, statues that depict, usually, non-European people.

I found books like Will Durant's *Story of Civilization*. I read H. G. Wells'   22
Outline of History. *Souls of Black Folk* by W. E. B. Du Bois gave me a glimpse
into the black people's history before they came to this country. Carter G. Wood-
son's *Negro History* opened my eyes about black empires before the black slave
was brought to the United States, and the early Negro struggles for freedom.

J. A. Rogers' three volumes of *Sex and Race* told about race-mixing before   23
Christ's time; about Aesop being a black man who told fables; about Egypt's Pha-
raohs; about the great Coptic Christian Empires; about Ethiopia, the earth's oldest continuous black civilization, as China is the oldest continuous civilization.

Mr. Muhammad's teaching about how the white man had been created led   24
me to *Findings in Genetics* by Gregor Mendel. (The dictionary's G section was
where I had learned what "genetics" meant.) I really studied this book by the
Austrian monk. Reading it over and over, especially certain sections, helped
me to understand that if you started with a black man, a white man could be
produced; but starting with a white man, you never could produce a black
man—because the white gene is recessive. And since no one disputes that there
was but one Original Man, the conclusion is clear.

During the last year or so, in the *New York Times*, Arnold Toynbee used   25
the word "bleached" in describing the white man. (His words were: "White
(i.e., bleached) human beings of North European origin. . . .") Toynbee also
referred to the European geographic area as only a peninsula of Asia. He said
there is no such thing as Europe. And if you look at the globe, you will see
for yourself that America is only an extension of Asia. (But at the same time
Toynbee is among those who have helped to bleach history. He has written that
Africa was the only continent that produced no history. He won't write that
again. Every day now, the truth is coming to light.)

I never will forget how shocked I was when I began reading about slavery's   26
total horror. It made such an impact upon me that it later became one of my
favorite subjects when I became a minister of Mr. Muhammad's. The world's
most monstrous crime, the sin and the blood on the white man's hands, are
almost impossible to believe. Books like the one by Frederick Olmstead opened
my eyes to the horrors suffered when the slave was landed in the United States.
The European woman, Fannie Kimball, who had married a Southern white slave-
owner, described how human beings were degraded. Of course I read *Uncle
Tom's Cabin*. In fact, I believe that's the only novel I have ever read since I
started serious reading.

Parkhurst's collection also contained some bound pamphlets of the Aboli-   27
tionist Anti-Slavery Society of New England. I read descriptions of atrocities,
saw those illustrations of black slave women tied up and flogged with whips;
of black mothers watching their babies being dragged off, never to be seen by
their mothers again; of dogs after slaves, and of the fugitive slave catchers, evil
white men with whips and clubs and chains and guns. I read about the slave

preacher Nat Turner, who put the fear of God into the white slavemaster. Nat Turner wasn't going around preaching pie-in-the-sky and "non-violent" freedom for the black man. There in Virginia one night in 1831, Nat and seven other slaves started out at his master's home and through the night they went from one plantation "big house" to the next, killing, until by the next morning 57 white people were dead and Nat had about 70 slaves following him. White people, terrified for their lives, fled from their homes, locked themselves up in public buildings, hid in the woods, and some even left the state. A small army of soldiers took two months to catch and hang Nat Turner. Somewhere I have read where Nat Turner's example is said to have inspired John Brown to invade Virginia and attack Harper's Ferry nearly thirty years later, with thirteen white men and five Negroes.

I read Herodotus, "the father of History," or, rather, I read about him. 28 And I read the histories of various nations, which opened my eyes gradually, then wider and wider, to how the whole world's white men had indeed acted like devils, pillaging and raping and bleeding and draining the whole world's non-white people. I remember, for instance, books such as Will Durant's story of Oriental civilization, and Mahatma Gandhi's accounts of the struggle to drive the British out of India.

Book after book showed me how the white man had brought upon the 29 world's black, brown, red, and yellow peoples every variety of the sufferings of exploitation. I saw how since the sixteenth century, the so-called "Christian trader" white man began to ply the seas in his lust for Asian and African empires, and plunder, and power. I read, I saw, how the white man never has gone among the non-white peoples bearing the Cross in the true manner and spirit of Christ's teachings—meek, humble, and Christ-like.

I perceived, as I read, how the collective white man had been actually nothing 30 but a piratical opportunist who used Faustian machinations to make his own Christianity his initial wedge in criminal conquests. First, always "religiously," he branded "heathen" and "pagan" labels upon ancient non-white cultures and civilizations. The stage thus set, he then turned upon his non-white victims his weapons of war.

I read how, entering India—half a *billion* deeply religious brown people— 31 the British white man, by 1759, through promises, trickery and manipulations, controlled much of India through Great Britain's East India Company. The parasitical British administration kept tentacling out to half of the subcontinent. In 1857, some of the desperate people of India finally mutinied—and, excepting the African slave trade, nowhere has history recorded any more unnecessary bestial and ruthless human carnage than the British suppression of the non-white Indian people.

Over 115 million African blacks—close to the 1930s population of the 32 United States—were murdered or enslaved during the slave trade. And I read how when the slave market was glutted, the cannibalistic white powers of Europe next carved up, as their colonies, the richest areas of the black continent. And Europe's chancelleries for the next century played a chess game of naked exploitation and power from Cape Horn to Cairo.

Ten guards and the warden couldn't have torn me out of those books. Not 33
even Elijah Muhammad could have been more eloquent than those books were
in providing indisputable proof that the collective white man had acted like a
devil in virtually every contact he had with the world's collective non-white
man. I listen today to the radio, and watch television, and read the headlines
about the collective white man's fear and tension concerning China. When the
white man professes ignorance about why the Chinese hate him so, my mind
can't help flashing back to what I read, there in prison, about how the blood
forebears of this same white man raped China at a time when China was trust-
ing and helpless. Those original white "Christian traders" sent into China millions of pounds of opium. By 1839, so many of the Chinese were addicts that
China's desperate government destroyed twenty thousand chests of opium. The
first Opium War was promptly declared by the white man. Imagine! Declaring
war upon someone who objects to being narcotized! The Chinese were severely
beaten, with Chinese-invented gunpowder.

The Treaty of Nanking made China pay the British white man for the 34
destroyed opium; forced open China's major ports to British trade; forced
China to abandon Hong Kong; fixed China's import tariffs so low that cheap
British articles soon flooded in, maiming China's industrial development.

After a second Opium War, the Tientsin Treaties legalized the ravaging 35
opium trade, legalized a British-French-American control of China's customs. China tried delaying that Treaty's ratification; Peking was looted and
burned.

"Kill the foreign white devils!" was the 1901 Chinese war cry in the Boxer 36
Rebellion. Losing again, this time the Chinese were driven from Peking's choic-
est areas. The vicious, arrogant white man put up the famous signs, "Chinese
and dogs not allowed."

Red China after World War II closed its doors to the Western white world. 37
Massive Chinese agricultural, scientific, and industrial efforts are described in a
book that *Life* magazine recently published. Some observers inside Red China
have reported that the world never has known such a hate-white campaign as
is now going on in this non-white country where, present birth-rates continuing, in fifty more years Chinese will be half the earth's population. And it seems
that some Chinese chickens will soon come home to roost, with China's recent
successful nuclear tests.

Let us face reality. We can see in the United Nations a new world order being 38
shaped, along color lines—an alliance among the non-white nations. America's
U.N. Ambassador Adlai Stevenson complained not long ago that in the United
Nations "a skin game" was being played. He was right. He was facing reality.
A "skin game" *is* being played. But Ambassador Stevenson sounded like Jesse
James accusing the marshal of carrying a gun. Because who in the world's his-
tory ever has played a worse "skin game" than the white man?

Mr. Muhammad, to whom I was writing daily, had no idea of what a new 39
world had opened up to me through my efforts to document his teachings
in books.

When I discovered philosophy, I tried to touch all the landmarks of philo- 40
sophical development. Gradually, I read most of the old philosophers, Occidental
and Oriental. The Oriental philosophers were the ones I came to prefer; finally,
my impression was that most Occidental philosophy had largely been borrowed
from the Oriental thinkers. Socrates, for instance, traveled in Egypt. Some sources
even say that Socrates was initiated into some of the Egyptian mysteries. Obviously Socrates got some of his wisdom among the East's wise men.

I have often reflected upon the new vistas that reading opened to me. I knew 41
right there in prison that reading had changed forever the course of my life. As
I see it today, the ability to read awoke inside me some long dormant craving
to be mentally alive. I certainly wasn't seeking any degree, the way a college
confers a status symbol upon its students. My homemade education gave me,
with every additional book that I read, a little bit more sensitivity to the deaf-
ness, dumbness, and blindness that was afflicting the black race in America.
Not long ago, an English writer telephoned me from London, asking questions.
One was, "What's your alma mater?" I told him, "Books." You will never catch
me with a free fifteen minutes in which I'm not studying something I feel might
be able to help the black man.

Yesterday I spoke in London, and both ways on the plane across the Atlantic 42
I was studying a document about how the United Nations proposes to insure the
human rights of the oppressed minorities of the world. The American black man
is the world's most shameful case of minority oppression. What makes the black
man think of himself as only an internal United States issue is just a catch-phrase,
two words, "civil rights." How is the black man going to get "civil rights" before
first he wins his *human* rights? If the American black man will start thinking
about his *human* rights, and then start thinking of himself as part of one of the
world's great peoples, he will see he has a case for the United Nations.

I can't think of a better case! Four hundred years of black blood and sweat 43
invested here in America, and the white man still has the black man begging
for what every immigrant fresh off the ship can take for granted the minute he
walks down the gangplank.

But I'm digressing. I told the Englishman that my alma mater was books, a 44
good library. Every time I catch a plane, I have with me a book that I want to
read—and that's a lot of books these days. If I weren't out here every day bat-
tling the white man, I could spend the rest of my life reading, just satisfying my
curiosity—because you can hardly mention anything I'm not curious about. I
don't think anybody ever got more out of going to prison than I did. In fact,
prison enabled me to study far more intensively than I would have if my life
had gone differently and I had attended some college. I imagine that one of
the biggest troubles with colleges is there are too many distractions, too much
panty-raiding, fraternities, and boola-boola and all of that. Where else but in
a prison could I have attacked my ignorance by being able to study intensely
sometimes as much as fifteen hours a day?

Questions for Discussion and Journaling

1. Who seems to be Malcolm X's intended audience? How do you know?

2. How does Malcolm X define *literacy*? How does this definition compare to school-based literacy?

3. Drawing on Deborah Brandt's definition of *literacy sponsor*, list as many of Malcolm X's literacy sponsors as you can find. (Remember that sponsors don't have to be people, but can also be ideas or institutions, which can withhold literacy as well as provide it.) Which sponsors were most influential? What were their motivations?

4. Brandt explains that people often subvert or misappropriate the intentions of their sponsors (see pp. 335, 344–345, paras. 7 and 27). Was this ever the case with Malcolm X? If so, how?

5. Like Malcolm X, many readers have memories in which a reference work like a dictionary or an encyclopedia figures significantly. Did his account bring back any such memories for you? If so, what were they?

6. Malcolm X asserts that his motivation for reading—his desire to understand his own experiences—led him to read far more than any college student. Respond to his claim. Has a particular motivation helped you decide what, or how much, to read?

7. What was the particular role for *writing* that Malcolm X describes in his account of his literacy education? How do you think it helped him read? Can you think of ways that writing helped *you* become a better reader?

Applying and Exploring Ideas

1. Both Deborah Brandt and Malcolm X wrote before much of the technology that you take for granted was invented. How do you think technologies such as the World Wide Web, text messaging, Skype, and the like shape what it means to be "literate" in the United States today?

2. Write a one-page narrative about the impact of an early literacy sponsor on your life. Recount as many details as you can and try to assess the difference that sponsor made in your literate life.

3. Malcolm X turned to the dictionary to get his start in acquiring basic literacy. If you met a person learning to read today, what primary resource would you suggest to them? Would it be print (paper) or electronic? How would you tell them to use it, and how do you think it would help them?

Meta Moment

What do you think your teacher might say is the most important idea in the Malcolm X text? Do you agree, or do you have a different opinion on what the most important idea is? Explain.

The Joy of Reading and Writing:
Superman and Me

SHERMAN ALEXIE

Alexie, Sherman. "The Joy of Reading and Writing: Superman and Me." *The Most Wonderful Books: Writers on Discovering the Pleasures of Reading*. Minneapolis: Milkweed Editions, 1997. 3–6. Print.

Framing the Reading

Sherman Alexie was born in 1966 and grew up on the Spokane Indian Reservation in Wellpinit, Washington. Although he was born with water on the brain and not expected to survive, he learned to read by the time he was three and became a voracious reader at an exceptionally young age. His classmates ridiculed him for this, but he nonetheless made reading and education a priority, attending college on a scholarship and finding a poetry teacher who encouraged him to write. Since then, he has published over twenty books, including novels, short story and poetry collections, and screenplays. He has written screenplays for three movies, including *Smoke Signals*, for which he won numerous awards. Among his other numerous awards, Alexie won the World Heavyweight Poetry Bout title in 1998 and kept the title for four years. On top of all that, Alexie also frequently performs stand-up at comedy festivals.

Clearly, Alexie's life story has been an unusual one. Coming from a world of poverty, he managed to become successful and critically acclaimed. In the short essay included here, Alexie discusses how he came to literacy, through what Deborah Brandt would call the "sponsorship" of Superman comics and his father's love of books. He notes that if he had been "anything but an Indian boy living on the reservation, he might have been called a prodigy." Instead, he was considered "an oddity" (para. 5).

Getting Ready to Read

Before you read, do at least one of the following activities:

- Research the Spokane Indian Reservation where Alexie grew up: Learn what you can about its location, culture, and history.
- Alexie mentions in his essay that most Native Americans now would not willingly attend Catholic school: Try to find out why this is the case by researching the history of Catholic education of Native American groups. For

help, you might look at the *Journal of American Indian Education*, which is online.

- Consider when you learned to read. What texts and events were central to your learning?

As you read, consider the following questions:

- What claims and assumptions does Alexie make that you don't understand? (Take notes as you read. If, for example, you don't know why he would claim that "a smart Indian is a dangerous person," make a note about this to bring up in class.)
- Why does Alexie repeatedly assert that he was "lucky"?

I learned to read with a Superman comic book. Simple enough, I suppose. 1 I cannot recall which particular Superman comic book I read, nor can I remember which villain he fought in that issue. I cannot remember the plot, nor the means by which I obtained the comic book. What I can remember is this: I was 3 years old, a Spokane Indian boy living with his family on the Spokane Indian Reservation in eastern Washington state. We were poor by most standards, but one of my parents usually managed to find some minimum-wage job or another, which made us middle-class by reservation standards. I had a brother and three sisters. We lived on a combination of irregular paychecks, hope, fear, and government surplus food.

My father, who is one of the few Indians who went to Catholic school on 2 purpose, was an avid reader of westerns, spy thrillers, murder mysteries, gangster epics, basketball player biographies, and anything else he could find. He bought his books by the pound at Dutch's Pawn Shop, Goodwill, Salvation Army, and Value Village. When he had extra money, he bought new novels at supermarkets, convenience stores, and hospital gift shops. Our house was filled with books. They were stacked in crazy piles in the bathroom, bedrooms, and living room. In a fit of unemployment-inspired creative energy, my father built a set of bookshelves and soon filled them with a random assortment of books about the Kennedy assassination, Watergate, the Vietnam War, and the entire 23-book series of the Apache westerns. My father loved books, and since I loved my father with an aching devotion, I decided to love books as well.

> I still remember the exact moment when I first understood, with a sudden clarity, the purpose of a paragraph. I didn't have the vocabulary to say "paragraph," but I realized that a paragraph was a fence that held words.

I can remember picking up my father's books before I could read. The words 3 themselves were mostly foreign, but I still remember the exact moment when

I first understood, with a sudden clarity, the purpose of a paragraph. I didn't have the vocabulary to say "paragraph," but I realized that a paragraph was a fence that held words. The words inside a paragraph worked together for a common purpose. They had some specific reason for being inside the same fence. This knowledge delighted me. I began to think of everything in terms of paragraphs. Our reservation was a small paragraph within the United States. My family's house was a paragraph, distinct from the other paragraphs of the LeBrets to the north, the Fords to our South, and the Tribal School to the west. Inside our house, each family member existed as a separate paragraph but still had genetics and common experiences to link us. Now, using this logic, I can see my changed family as an essay of seven paragraphs: mother, father, older brother, the deceased sister, my younger twin sisters, and our adopted little brother.

At the same time I was seeing the world in paragraphs, I also picked up 4 that Superman comic book. Each panel, complete with picture, dialogue, and narrative was a three-dimensional paragraph. In one panel, Superman breaks through a door. His suit is red, blue, and yellow. The brown door shatters into many pieces. I look at the narrative above the picture. I cannot read the words, but I assume it tells me that "Superman is breaking down the door." Aloud, I pretend to read the words and say, "Superman is breaking down the door." Words, dialogue, also float out of Superman's mouth. Because he is breaking down the door, I assume he says, "I am breaking down the door." Once again, I pretend to read the words and say aloud, "I am breaking down the door." In this way, I learned to read.

This might be an interesting story all by itself. A little Indian boy teaches 5 himself to read at an early age and advances quickly. He reads "Grapes of Wrath" in kindergarten when other children are struggling through "Dick and Jane." If he'd been anything but an Indian boy living on the reservation, he might have been called a prodigy. But he is an Indian boy living on the reservation and is simply an oddity. He grows into a man who often speaks of his childhood in the third person, as if it will somehow dull the pain and make him sound more modest about his talents.

A smart Indian is a dangerous person, widely feared and ridiculed by Indi- 6 ans and non-Indians alike. I fought with my classmates on a daily basis. They wanted me to stay quiet when the non-Indian teacher asked for answers, for volunteers, for help. We were Indian children who were expected to be stupid. Most lived up to those expectations inside the classroom but subverted them on the outside. They struggled with basic reading in school but could remember how to sing a few dozen powwow songs. They were monosyllabic in front of their non-Indian teachers but could tell complicated stories and jokes at the dinner table. They submissively ducked their heads when confronted by a non-Indian adult but would slug it out with the Indian bully who was 10 years older. As Indian children, we were expected to fail in the non-Indian world. Those who failed were ceremonially accepted by other Indians and appropriately pitied by non-Indians.

I refused to fail. I was smart. I was arrogant. I was lucky. I read books late 7
into the night, until I could barely keep my eyes open. I read books at recess,
then during lunch, and in the few minutes left after I had finished my classroom
assignments. I read books in the car when my family traveled to powwows or
basketball games. In shopping malls, I ran to the bookstores and read bits and
pieces of as many books as I could. I read the books my father brought home
from the pawnshops and secondhand. I read the books I borrowed from the
library. I read the backs of cereal boxes. I read the newspaper. I read the bulletins posted on the walls of the school, the clinic, the tribal offices, the post
office. I read junk mail. I read auto-repair manuals. I read magazines. I read
anything that had words and paragraphs. I read with equal parts joy and desperation. I loved those books, but I also knew that love had only one purpose.
I was trying to save my life.

Despite all the books I read, I am still surprised I became a writer. I was 8
going to be a pediatrician. These days, I write novels, short stories, and poems.
I visit schools and teach creative writing to Indian kids. In all my years in the
reservation school system, I was never taught how to write poetry, short stories, or novels. I was certainly never taught that Indians wrote poetry, short
stories, and novels. Writing was something beyond Indians. I cannot recall a
single time that a guest teacher visited the reservation. There must have been
visiting teachers. Who were they? Where are they now? Do they exist? I visit
the schools as often as possible. The Indian kids crowd the classroom. Many
are writing their own poems, short stories, and novels. They have read my
books. They have read many other books. They look at me with bright eyes
and arrogant wonder. They are trying to save their lives. Then there are the
sullen and already defeated Indian kids who sit in the back rows and ignore
me with theatrical precision. The pages of their notebooks are empty. They
carry neither pencil nor pen. They stare out the window. They refuse and resist.
"Books," I say to them. "Books," I say. I throw my weight against their locked
doors. The door holds. I am smart. I am arrogant. I am lucky. I am trying to
save our lives.

Questions for Discussion and Journaling

1. Alexie claims that Indian children were "expected to be stupid" (para. 6).
   Explain in a paragraph or two how expectations can impact children's literacy
   learning. Can you think of examples from your own childhood where expectations of you—positive or negative—shaped what you did or didn't do?

2. Alexie lists a variety of ways that Indian children failed inside of school but
   excelled outside of school. Using this list, consider what it meant to be "literate" on the Indian reservation where Alexie grew up. What literacy skills did
   the Indian children have that were not valued or seen inside school?

3. Who and what do you consider to be Alexie's most important literacy sponsors? What do you think his life might have been like if he had had access to more powerful literacy sponsors when he was growing up, or if he had grown up in a different setting?

4. Alexie claims that he "read with equal parts joy and desperation." He tells us that he "loved those books," but that this love "had only one purpose. I was trying to save my life" (para. 7). What does he mean? What would it mean to read with desperation? Why did he feel that reading books could save his life? Do you think that he was right?

Applying and Exploring Ideas

1. The stories of Malcolm X and Sherman Alexie might lead you to believe that anyone can overcome poverty and discrimination if they just have enough determination to read and write. Do you think that this is, in fact, the case? How can you use Deborah Brandt's research to help you think through this question? You might also look to history, or even to your own experiences, to help you consider this question.

2. Informally interview a couple of your classmates about their early literacy experiences. How frequently, if at all, do comic books and drawing show up in their early literacy experiences? In what ways did such texts impact them? If you are interested in exploring this topic further, you might look at Thomas Newkirk's studies of young children's writing (including *More than Stories* and *Misreading Masculinity: Boys, Literacy, and Popular Culture*).

Protean Shapes in Literacy Events: Ever-Shifting Oral and Literate Traditions

SHIRLEY BRICE HEATH

Heath, Shirley Brice. "Protean Shapes in Literacy Events: Ever-Shifting Oral and Literate Traditions." *Spoken and Written Language: Exploring Orality and Literacy*. Ed. Deborah Tannen. Norwood: Ablex, 1982. 91–117. Print.

Framing the Reading

Shirley Brice Heath is a professor of linguistics and English at Stanford University. According to her Web site, her "research has centered on the out-of-school lives of young people in subordinated communities." Heath is a past recipient of a Mac-Arthur prize, has written six books on language, and is an international authority on literacy. Heath is well-known for her use of a research method called **ethnography**. Ethnographic studies describe cultures or groups using data-gathering means such as observations, interviews and participation with the group being studied. Her books include the prize-winning ethnographic studies *Ways with Words: Language, Life, and Work in Communities and Classrooms* (1983) and *Identity and Inner-City Youth: Beyond Ethnicity and Gender* (1993). In 1999 she released a documentary video, *ArtShow*, that describes four youth-based arts organizations in the United States.

The selection here is a chapter from an edited scholarly collection focusing on some of the data Heath collected during a ten-year study in which she examined literacy practices in two towns in the Piedmont Carolinas. Heath's goal for the study, which she eventually published as *Ways with Words*, was to understand and highlight the early literacy practices of students from "nonmainstream" backgrounds. In this selection, Heath reports on **literacy events** in Trackton, an African American community.

As you begin reading, pay special attention to Heath's introduction and to the way she creates a space for her own research by first discussing the research and theorizing of others. For example, Heath starts with some assumptions that were common in the "state-of-the-art" literacy research at the time she began her study. One was that there is a clear division between **orality** and literacy, and that cultures are either entirely one or the other. Another was that a culture transitioning from orality to literacy might have a "restricted" literacy: people could read, but limited reading skills kept them from successfully participating in the literate world around them. Yet another fundamental assumption at the time Heath was conducting her research was that literacy was *better* than orality; it made a culture smarter, freer, more advanced, more powerful, and better able to cope with the world. Taken together, these assumptions form what Heath calls in her opening paragraph "a dichotomous view of oral and literate societies" (see para. 1), which in turn creates the **exigence** for Heath's research and resulting argument—that is, the need for her to speak.

It's important to know that Heath's work helped precipitate a major change in the way that literacy researchers define literacy. While it was very common in the 1960s and 1970s for literacy researchers to talk about "orality *versus* literacy," work such as Heath's has made such thinking seem oversimplified and outmoded. Today, literacy researchers are likely to talk about oral, print, and electronic literacies ("electracies"?) of various sorts.

Before you begin reading Heath, it might be useful for you to look at the summary of John Swales's **CARS model** of research introductions in the Introduction to this book (pp. 6–8). See if you can identify Swales's three "moves" in Heath's introduction.

Getting Ready to Read

Before you read, do at least one of the following activities:

- Consider in what ways the community you grew up in was "oral" and in what ways it relied on print texts. Make a list of the different ways that people used talk and the ways they used print texts. Was one generally preferred over another? If so, how? Why?
- Start a discussion with friends, roommates, or family members about the nature of communication technologies like instant-messaging (chat) and text-messaging (SMS via cell phones and other devices): Do these technologies more closely resemble *oral* or *literate* (print-based) practices? Why? After the discussion, consider: Did people argue strongly for one position over the other, or did they tend to want to say "both" or "neither"?
- Look up some definitions of the word *protean* and make some guesses as to what Heath will be talking about with a title like "Protean Shapes in Literacy Events."

As you read, consider the following questions, keeping in mind that an ethnographic study is not *generalizable*—that is, you cannot make claims about *all* African American communities based on the experiences of the residents of Trackton:

- How does Heath define *literacy*?
- What is a *literacy event*?
- How does Heath suggest we should understand the relationship between *orality* and (textual) *literacy*?
- How might the home literacy environment of Trackton residents impact the schooling experiences of its young people?

- How did Heath's findings call into question ideas about literacy that existed before her research?

'the Proteus-nature . . . of ever-shifting language'
JOHN UPTON, *Critical Observations on Shakespeare*, 1747

Since the mid-1970s, anthropologists, linguists, historians, and psychologists have turned with new tools of analysis to the study of oral and literate societies. They have used discourse analysis, econometrics, theories of schemata and frames, and proposals of developmental performance to consider the possible links between oral and written language, and between literacy and its individual and societal consequences. Much of this research is predicated on a dichotomous view of oral and literate traditions, usually attributed to researchers active in the 1960s. Repeatedly, Goody & Watt (1963), Ong (1967), Goody (1968), and Havelock (1963) are cited as having suggested a dichotomous view of oral and literate societies and as having asserted certain cognitive, social, and linguistic effects of literacy on both the society and the individual. Survey research tracing the invention and diffusion of writing systems across numerous societies (Kroeber, 1948) and positing the effects of the spread of literacy on social and individual memory (Goody & Watt, 1963; Havelock, 1963, 1976) is cited as supporting a contrastive view of oral and literate social groups. Research which examined oral performance in particular groups is said to support the notion that as members of a society increasingly participate in literacy, they lose habits associated with the oral tradition (Lord, 1965).

The language of the oral tradition is held to suggest meaning without explicitly stating information (Lord, 1965). Certain discourse forms, such as the parable or proverb (Dodd, 1961), are formulaic uses of language which convey meanings without direct explication. Thus, truth lies in experience and is verified by the experience of listeners. Story plots are said to be interwoven with routine formulas, and fixed sayings to make up much of the content of the story (Rosenberg, 1970). In contrast, language associated with the literate tradition is portrayed as making meaning explicit in the text and as not relying on the experiences of readers for verification of truth value. The epitome of this type of language is said to be the formal expository essay (Olson, 1977). The setting for learning this language and associated literate habits is the school. Formal schooling at all levels is said to prescribe certain features of sentence structure, lexical choice, text cohesion, and topic organization for formal language—both spoken and written (Bourdieu, 1967). An array of abilities, ranging from metalinguistic awareness (Baron, 1979) to predictable critical skills (reported in Heath, 1980) are held to derive from cultural experiences with writing.

In short, existing scholarship makes it easy to interpret a picture which 3
depicts societies existing along a continuum of development from an oral tradition to a literate one, with some societies having a restricted literacy, and others
having reached a full development of literacy (Goody, 1968:11). One also finds
in this research specific characterizations of oral and written language associated with these traditions.

But a close reading of these scholars, especially Goody (1968) and Goody 4
and Watt (1963), leaves some room for questioning such a picture of consistent
and universal processes or products—individual or societal—of literacy. Goody
pointed out that in any traditional society, factors such as secrecy, religious
ideology, limited social mobility, lack of access to writing materials and alphabetic scripts could lead to restricted literacy. Furthermore, Goody warned that
the advent of a writing system did not amount to technological determinism
or to sufficient cause of certain changes in either the individual or the society.

Goody went on to propose exploring
the concrete context of written communication (1968:4) to determine how
the potentialities of literacy developed
in traditional societies. He brought
together a collection of essays based
on the ethnography of literacy in traditional societies to illustrate the wide
variety of ways in which TRADITIONAL,
i.e. pre-industrial but not necessarily
pre-literate, societies played out their
uses of oral and literate traditions.

> The public media today give much
> attention to the decline of literacy
> skills. . . . However, the media pay
> little attention . . . to the actual
> uses of literacy in work settings,
> daily interactions in religious,
> economic, and legal institutions,
> and family habits of socializing the
> young into uses of literacy.   5

Few researchers in the 1970's have,
however, heeded Goody's warning
about the possible wide-ranging effects
of societal and cultural factors on literacy and its uses. In particular, little attention has been given in MODERN complex industrial societies to the social and
cultural correlates of literacy or to the work experiences adults have which
may affect the maintenance and retention of literacy skills acquired in formal schooling. The public media today give much attention to the decline of
literacy skills as measured in school settings and to the failure of students to
acquire certain levels of literacy. However, the media pay little attention to
occasions for literacy retention—to the actual uses of literacy in work settings,
daily interactions in religious, economic, and legal institutions, and family habits of socializing the young into uses of literacy. In the clamor over the need to
increase the teachings of basic skills, there is much emphasis on the positive
effects extensive and critical reading can have on improving oral language. Yet
there are scarcely any data comparing the forms and functions of oral language
with those of written language produced and used by members of social groups
within a complex society. One of the most appropriate sources of data for
informing discussions of these issues is that which Goody proposed for traditional societies: the concrete context of written communication. Where, when,

how, for whom, and with what results are individuals in different social groups of today's highly industrialized society using reading and writing skills? How have the potentialities of the literacy skills learned in school developed in the lives of today's adults? Does modern society contain certain conditions which restrict literacy just as some traditional societies do? If so, what are these factors, and are groups with restricted literacy denied benefits widely attributed to full literacy, such as upward socioeconomic mobility, the development of logical reasoning, and access to the information necessary to make well-informed political judgments?

The Literacy Event

The LITERACY EVENT is a conceptual tool useful in examining within particular communities of modern society the actual forms and functions of oral and literate traditions and co-existing relationships between spoken and written language. A literacy event is any occasion in which a piece of writing is integral to the nature of participants' interactions and their interpretive processes (Heath, 1978).

In studying the literacy environment, researchers describe: print materials available in the environment, the individuals and activities which surround print, and ways in which people include print in their ongoing activities. A literacy event can then be viewed as any action sequence, involving one or more persons, in which the production and/or comprehension of print plays a role (Anderson, Teale, & Estrada 1980:59). There are rules for the occurrence of literacy events, just as there are for speech events (Hymes, 1972). Characteristics of the structures and uses of literacy events vary from situation to situation. In addition to having an appropriate structure, a literacy event has certain interactional rules and demands particular interpretive competencies on the part of participants. Some aspects of reading and/or writing are required by at least one party, and certain types of speech events are appropriate within certain literacy events. Speech events may describe, repeat, reinforce, expand, frame, or contradict written materials, and participants must learn whether the oral or written mode takes precedence in literacy events. For example, in filling out an application form, should applicants listen to oral instructions or complete the form? On many occasions, an interview consists of participating orally with someone who fills out a form based on the oral performance, and access to the written report is never available to the applicant in the course of the interview. Oral comments often contradict the usual assumption that written materials are to be read: You don't have to read this, but you should have it.

The having of something in writing is often a ritualistic practice, and more often than not, those who hold the written piece are not expected to read what they have. In other cases, the actual reading of the piece of written material may be possible, but not sufficient, because some oral attestation is necessary. A church congregational meeting may be an occasion in which all must read the regulations of applying for a loan or a grant for church support (this is usually done by having the minister read them aloud). But the entire congregation must orally attest that they have read and approved the regulations. On other occasions, the written material must be present, but the speech event takes precedence. A Girl Scout comes to sell cookies at the door; she passes out a folder asserting who she is, to which troop she belongs, and to which project her fund will go. After handing over this piece of paper, the Girl Scout talks about the cookies and the project which the sale will benefit. Few individuals read the folder instead of listening to the Girl Scout. Here, the speech event takes precedence at the critical moments of the interaction. It is important to know what the framing situations for literacy events are in a variety of contexts, for situations may differ markedly from each other and may, in fact, contradict such traditional expectations of literacy as those taught in school or in job training programs. For example, ways of asking clarification of the USES of written materials are often far more important in daily out-of-school life than are questions about the content. What will be done with forms submitted to the Department of Motor Vehicles after an accident is of as much consequence as, if not more consequence than, the actual content of the forms. Thus it may be hypothesized that examination of the contexts and uses of literacy in communities today may show that THERE ARE MORE LITERACY EVENTS WHICH CALL FOR APPROPRIATE KNOWLEDGE OF FORMS AND USES OF SPEECH EVENTS THAN THERE ARE ACTUAL OCCASIONS FOR EXTENDED READING OR WRITING.

Furthermore, the traditional distinctions between the habits of those characterized as having either oral or literate traditions may not actually exist in many communities of the United States, which are neither non-literate nor fully literate. Their members can read and write at least at basic levels, but they have little occasion to use these skills as taught in school. Instead, much of their daily life is filled with literacy events in which they must know how to use and how to respond in the oral mode to written materials. In short, descriptions of the concrete context of written communication which give attention to social and cultural features of the community as well as to the oral language surrounding written communications may discredit any reliance on characterizing particular communities as having reached either restricted or full development of literacy or as having language forms and functions associated more with the literate tradition than with the oral, or vice versa.

The Community Context

Some testing of these ideas is possible from data collected in a Piedmont community of the Carolinas between 1969 and 1979. The community, Trackton, is a working-class all-Black community, whose adults work in the local textile mills and earn incomes which exceed those of many public school teachers in the state. All adults in this community can read and write, and all talk enthusiastically about the need for their children to do well in school. Ethnographic work in the primary networks within the community, the religious institutions, and work settings documented the forms and functions written and spoken language took for individual members of Trackton. The literacy event was the focus of descriptions of written language uses in these contexts.

At Home in Trackton

In the daily life of the neighborhood, there were numerous occasions when 11
print from beyond the primary network intruded; there were fewer occasions
when adults or children themselves produced written materials. Adults did not
read to children, and there were few pieces of writing produced especially for
children. Sunday School books, and single-page handouts from Sunday School
which portrayed a Biblical scene with a brief caption, were the only exceptions.
Adults, however, responded to children of all ages, if they inquired about messages provided in writing: they would read a house number, a stop sign, a name
brand of a product, or a slogan on a T-shirt, if asked to do so by a child. In
September, children preparing to go to school often preferred book bags, pencil boxes, and purses which bore labels or slogans. Adults did not consciously
model, demonstrate, or tutor reading and writing behaviors for the young.
Children, however, went to school with certain expectancies of print and a
keen sense that reading is something one does to learn something one needs to
know. In other words, before going to school, preschoolers were able to read
many types of information available in their environment. They knew how
to distinguish brand names from product descriptions on boxes or bags; they
knew how to find the price on a label which contained numerous other pieces
of written information. They knew how to recognize the names of cars, motor-
cycles, and bicycles not only on the products themselves, but also on brochures
about these products. In these ways they read to learn information judged
necessary in their daily lives, and they had grown accustomed to participating
in literacy events in ways appropriate to their community's norms (see Heath,
1980 for a fuller description). They had frequently observed their community's
social activities surrounding a piece of writing: negotiation over how to put a
toy together, what a gas bill notice meant, how to fill out a voter registration
form, and where to go to apply for entrance to daycare programs.

There were no bedtime stories, children's books, special times for reading, or 12
routine sets of questions from adults to children in connection with reading.[1]
Thus, Trackton children's early spontaneous stories were not molded on written materials. They were derived from oral models given by adults, and they
developed in accordance with praise and varying degrees of enthusiasm for
particular story styles from the audience. In these stories, children rendered a
context, or set the stage for the story, and called on listeners to create jointly
an imagined background for stories. In the later preschool years, the children,
in a monologue-like fashion, told stories about things in their lives, events they
saw and heard, and situations in which they had been involved. They produced
these stories, many of which can be described as story-poems, during play with
other children or in the presence of adults. Their stories contained emotional

---

[1]Preschool literacy socialization is a growing field of research heavily influenced by studies of social
interactions surrounding language input to children learning to talk. For a review of this literature and
especially its characterizations of how mainstream school-oriented families prepare their children for
taking meaning from print, see Heath, 1982. The most thorough study of literacy socialization in a comparative perspective is Scollon and Scollon, 1981.

evaluation of others and their actions; dialogue was prevalent; style shifting in verbal and nonverbal means accompanied all stories.

All of these features of story-telling by children call attention to the story 13 and distinguish it as a speech event which is an occasion for audience and storyteller to interact pleasantly to a creative tale, not simply a recounting of daily events. Story-telling is very competitive, especially as children get older, and new tricks must be devised if one is to remain a successful story-teller. Content ranges widely, and there is truth only in the universals of human experience which are found in every story. Fact as related to what really happened is often hard to find, though it may be the seed of the story. Trackton stories often have no obvious beginning in the form of a routine; similarly, there is no marked ending; they simply go on as long as the audience will tolerate the story (see Heath, 1980 and chapter 5 of Heath, 1983, for a fuller description).

In response to these stories, Trackton adults do not separate out bits and 14 pieces of the story and question the children about them. Similarly, they do not pick out pieces of the daily environment and ask children to name these or describe their features. Children live in an on-going multiple-channeled stream of stimuli, from which they select, practice, and determine the rules of speaking and interacting with written materials. Children have to learn at a very early age to perceive situations, determine how units of these situations are related to each other, recognize these relations in other situations, and reason through what it will take to show their correlation of one situation with another. The specifics of labels, features, and rules of behaving are not laid out for them by adults. The familiar routines described in the research literature on mainstream school-oriented parents are not heard in Trackton. They do not ask or tell their children: What is that? What color is it? Is that the way to listen? Turn the book this way. Let's listen and find out. Instead, parents talk about items and events of their environment. They detail the responses of personalities to events; they praise, deride, and question the reasons for events and compare new items and events to those with which they are familiar. They do not simplify their talk about the world for the benefit of their young. Preschoolers do not learn to name or list the features of items in either the daily environment or as depicted through illustration in printed materials. Questions addressed to them with the greatest frequency are of the type What's that like? Where'd that come from? What are you gonna do with that? They develop connections between situations or items not by specification of labels and features in these situations, but by configuration links.

Recognition of similar general shapes or patterns of links seen in one situ- 15 ation and connected to another pervade their stories and their conversations, as illustrated in the following story. Lem, playing off the edge of the porch, when he was about two and a half years of age, heard a bell in the distance. He stopped, looked at his older siblings nearby, and said:

Way
Far
Now

It a church bell
Ringin'
Dey singin'
Ringin'
You hear it?
I hear it
Far
Now.

Lem here recalls being taken to church the previous Sunday and hearing a   16
bell. His story is in response to the current stimulus of a distant bell. He reca-
pitulates the sequence of events: at church, the bell rang while the people sang
the opening hymn. He gives the story's topic in the line It a church bell, but he
does not orient the listeners to the setting or the time of the story. He seems to
try to recreate the situation both verbally and non-verbally so it will be recognized and responded to by listeners. Lem poetically balances the opening and
closing in an INCLUSIO, beginning Way, Far, Now, and ending Far, Now. The
effect is one of closure, though he doesn't announce the ending of his story.
He invites others to respond to his story: You hear it? I hear it. All of these
methods call attention to the story, and distinguish it as a story. The children
recall scenes and events through nonverbal and verbal manipulation. They use
few formulaic invitations to recall, such as You know, You see, etc. Instead,
they themselves try to give the setting and the mood as they weave the tale to
keep the audience's attention. The recall of a setting may depend on asking
the listener to remember a smell, a sound, a place, a feeling, and to associate
these in the same way the storyteller does. A smiliar type of recall of relevant
context or set of circumstances marks children's memories or reassociations
with print. When they see a brandname, number, etc., they often recall where
and with whom they first saw it, or call attention to parts now missing which
were there previously. Slight shifts in print styles, decorations of mascots used
to advertise cereals, or alterations of television advertising mottos are noticed
by children.

Trackton children's preschool experiences with print, stories, and talk about   17
the environment differ greatly from those usually depicted in the literature for
children of mainstream school-oriented parents. Similarly, adults in Trackton
used written materials in different ways and for different purposes than those
represented in the traditional literature on adult reading habits and motivations (cf. Staiger, 1979; Hall & Carlton, 1977). Among Trackton adults, reading was a social activity which did not focus on a single individual. Solitary
reading without oral explanation was viewed as unacceptable, strange, and
indicative of a particular kind of failure, which kept individuals from being
social. Narratives, jokes, sidetracking talk, and negotiation of the meaning of
written texts kept social relations alive. When several members of the community jointly focused on and interpreted written materials, authority did not rest
in the materials themselves, but in the meanings which would be negotiated by
the participants.

New instructions on obtaining medical reports for children about to enter 18
school provoked stories of what other individuals did when they were confronted with a similar task; all joined in talk of particular nurses or doctors
who were helpful in the process. Some told of reactions to vaccinations and
troubles they had had getting to and from the doctor's office. In the following conversation, several neighbors negotiate the meaning of a letter about a
daycare program. Several neighbors were sitting on porches, working on cars
nearby, or sweeping their front yards when a young mother of four children
came out on her porch with a letter she had received that day.

Lillie Mae: You hear this, it says Lem [her two-year-old son] might can get into
               Ridgeway [a local neighborhood center daycare program], but I
               hafta have the papers ready and apply by next Friday.

First female neighbor (mother of three children who are already in school): You
               ever been to Kent to get his birth certificate?

Second female neighbor (with preschool children): But what hours that program
               gonna be? You may not can get him there.

Lillie Mae: They want the birth certificate? I got his vaccination papers.

Third female neighbor: Sometimes they take that, 'cause they can 'about tell the
               age from those early shots.

First female neighbor: But you better get it, 'cause you gotta have it when he go
               to school anyway.

Lillie Mae: But it says here they don't know what hours yet. How am I gonna
               get over to Kent? How much does it cost? Lemme see if the pro-
               gram costs anything [she reads aloud part of the letter].

Conversation on various parts of the letter continued for nearly an hour, while 19
neighbors and Lillie Mae pooled their knowledge of the pros and cons of such
programs. They discussed ways of getting rides to Kent, the county seat thirty
miles away, to which all mothers had to go to get their children's birth certificates to prove their age at school entrance. The discussion covered the possibility
of visiting Lillie Mae's doctor and getting papers from him to verify Lem's age,
teachers now at the neighborhood center, and health benefits which came from
the daycare programs' outreach work. A question What does this mean? asked
of a piece of writing was addressed to any and all who would listen; specific
attention to the text itself was at times minimal in the answers which followed.

Adults read and wrote for numerous purposes, almost all of them social. 20
These were:

1. Instrumental—to provide information about practical problems of daily
   life (bills, checks, price tags, street signs, house numbers)
2. Interactional—to give information pertinent to social relations with
   individuals not in the primary group (cartoons, bumper stickers, letters,
   newspaper features, greeting cards)
3. News-related—to provide information about secondary contacts or distant events (newspaper items, political flyers, directives from city offices)

4. Confirmation—to provide support for attitudes or ideas already held (reference to the Bible, brochures advertising products, etc.)
5. Provision of permanent records—to record information required by external agencies (birth certificates, loan notes, tax forms). Trackton residents wrote most frequently for the following reasons:
6. Memory-supportive—to serve as a memory aid (addresses, telephone numbers, notes on calendars)
7. Substitutes for oral messages—to substitute for oral communication on those occasions when face-to-face or telephone contact was not possible or would prove embarrassing (thank-you letters to people in distant cities, notes about tardiness to school or absence at school or work, a request to local merchants for credit to be extended to a child needing to buy coal, milk, or bread for the family).

On all of these occasions for reading and writing, individuals saw literacy 21 as an occasion for social activities: women shopped together, discussed local credit opportunities and products, and sales; men negotiated the meaning of tax forms, brochures on new cars, and political flyers. The evening newspaper was read on the front porch, and talk about the news drifted from porch to porch. Inside, during the winter months, talk about news items interrupted on-going conversations on other topics or television viewing. The only occasions for solitary reading by individuals were those in which elderly men and women read their Bible or Sunday School materials alone, or school-age children sat alone to read a library book or a school assignment. In short, written information almost never stood alone in Trackton; it was reshaped and reworded into an oral mode. In so doing, adults and children incorporated chunks of the written text into their talk. They also sometimes reflected an awareness of a different type of organization of written materials from that of their usual oral productions. Yet their literacy habits do not fit those usually attributed to fully literate groups: they do not read to their children, encouraging conversational dialogue on books; they do not write or read extended prose passages; reading is not an individual pursuit nor is it considered to have intellectual, aesthetic, or critical rewards. But Trackton homes do not conform to habits associated with the oral tradition either. Literacy is a resource; stories do not fit the parable model; children develop very early wide-ranging language skills; and neither their language nor their parents' is marked by a preponderance of routine formulaic expressions.

At Church

Trackton is a literate community in the sense that its members read and write 22 when occasions within their community demand such skills. Outside the community, there are numerous occasions established by individuals and institutions in which Trackton residents must show their literacy skills. One of these situations is in the church life of the Trackton people. Most residents go to country churches for Sunday services, which are usually held twice a month. In these churches, the pastor serves not one, but several churches, and he also holds another job as well during the week. A pastor or reverend is always a man, usually a man who in his younger days was known as wild and had come to the Lord after recognizing the sins of his youth. Many pastors had been musicians entertaining in clubs before their conversion to religion. Few had formal theological training; instead they had gone to Black colleges in the South and majored in religion. Most had at least a four-year college education, and many had taken additional training at special summer programs, through correspondence courses, or in graduate programs at nearby integrated state schools. In their jobs outside the church, they were businessmen, school administrators, land-owning farmers, or city personnel.

The country churches brought together not only residents of Trackton, a 23 majority of whom worked in textile mills, but also school-teachers, domestic workers, hospital staff, clerks in local retail businesses, and farmers. Levels of formal education were mixed in these churches, and ranged from the elderly men and women who had had only a few years of grammar school in their youth, to the minister and some school administrators who had graduate-level education. Yet, in the church, all these types and levels of literacy skills came together in a pattern which reflected a strong reliance on the written word in both substance and style. Everyone wanted others to know he could read the Bible and church materials (even if he did not do so regularly). Church was an occasion to announce knowledge of how to handle the style of written language as well as its substance. Numerous evidences of formal writing marked every church service, and on special occasions, such as celebration of the accomplishments of a church member, formal writing was very much in evidence. For these celebration services, there were brochures which contained a picture of the individual, an account of his or her life, lists of members of the family, and details of the order of service. Funeral services included similar brochures. All churches had hymn books, and a placard on either side of the front of the church announced the numbers of the hymns. Choir leaders invited the congregation to turn to the hymn and read the words with him; he announced the number of the verses of the hymn to be sung. The minister expected adults to bring their Bibles to church along with their Sunday School materials and to read along with him or the Sunday School director. Mimeographed church bulletins dictated the order of the service from the opening hymn to the benediction. The front and back covers of the bulletin contained drawings and scripture verses which illustrated either the sermon topic or the season of the year. Announcements of upcoming events in the recreational life of the church or political activities of the Black community filled one page of the bulletin. Reports of building funds and missionary funds were brief and were supplemented by the pastor's announcements in church service.

Yet many parts of the service move away from the formality of these written 24 sources. The congregation often begins singing the hymn written in the book, but they quickly move away from the written form to 'raise' the hymn. In this performance, the choir leader begins the hymn with the written words and the congregation follows briefly; however, another song leader will break in with new words for a portion of the hymn; the audience waits to hear these, then picks up the words and follows. The hymn continues in this way, with different members of the congregation serving as song leader at various points. Some of the words may be those which are written in the hymnbook, others may not be. A member of the congregation may begin a prayer at a particular juncture of the hymn, and the congregation will hum until the prayer is completed. The ending of the hymn is to an outsider entirely unpredictable, yet all members of the congregation end at the same time. Hymns may be raised on the occasion of the announcement of a hymn by the choir leader, spontaneously during a story or testimonial by a church member, or near the end of a sermon. In the raising of a hymn, written formulas are the basis of the hymn, but these are subject to change, and it is indeed that change which makes the congregation at once creator and performer. The formulas are changed and new formulas produced to expand the theme, to illustrate points, or to pull back from a particular theme to pick up another which has been introduced in a prayer or in the sermon. Every performance of a particular hymn is different, and such performances bear the mark of the choir leader and his interactional style with the congregation.

A similar phenomenon is illustrated in oral prayers in church. These are often written out ahead of time by those who have been asked by the minister to offer a prayer at next Sunday's service. The prayer as follows was given orally by a 45-year old female school teacher. 25

1   We thank thee for watchin' over us, kind heavenly Father
2   Through the night.
3   We thank thee, oh Lord.
4   For leadin' 'n guidin' us
5   We thank thee, kind heavenly Father
6   For your strong-arm protection around us.
7   Oh Lord, don't leave us alone.
8   We feel this evenin', kind heavenly Father, if you leave us
9   We are the least ones of all.
10   Now Lord, I ask thee, kind heavenly Father.
11   to go 'long with my family,
12   I ask thee, kind heavenly Father, to throw your strong-arm protectors around
13   Oh Lord, I ask thee, oh Lord,
14   to take care of my childrens, Lord, wherever they may be.
15   Oh Lord, don't leave us, Jesus.
16   I feel this morning, kind heavenly Father, if you leave me.
17   Oh, Lord, please, Lord, don't leave me
18   in the hands of the wicked man.
19   Oh Lord, I thank thee kind heavenly Father
20   for what you have done for me.
21   Oh Lord, I thank thee, kind heavenly Father
22   Where you have brought me from.
23   Oh Lord, I wonder sometime if I didn't have Jesus on my side,

24   Lord, have mercy now.

25   what would I do, oh Lord?

26   Have mercy, Jesus.

27   I can call on 'im in the midnight hour,

28   I can call on 'im, Lord, in the noontime, oh Lord,

29   I can call on 'im anytime o' day, oh Lord.

30   He'p me, Jesus,

31   Oh Lord, make me strong

32   Oh Lord, have mercy on us, Father

33   When we have done all that you have 'signed our hands to do. Lord,

34   Have mercy, Lord,

35   I want you to give me a home beyond the shinin' river, oh Lord.

36   Where won't be no sorrowness.

37   Won't be no shame and tears, oh Lord.

38   It won't be nothing, Lord, but glory, alleluia.

39   When we have done all that you 'signed our hands to do, kind heavenly Father,

40   And we cain't do no mo',

41   We want you to give us a home in thy kingdom, oh Lord.

42   For thy Christ's sake. Amen.

After the service, when I asked the schoolteacher about her prayer, she gave me the following text she had composed and written on a card she held in her hand during the prayer:

> Kind heavenly Father, we thank thee for watching over us through the night.
> We thank thee for thy guidance, kind heavenly Father, for your strong protection.
> We pray that you will be with us, Lord, be with our families, young and old, near and far.
> Lead us not into temptation, Lord. Make us strong and ever mindful of your gifts to us all. Amen.

A comparison of the oral and the written prayer indicates numerous differences, but the major ones are of four types.

Use of formulaic vocatives. Oh Lord, kind heavenly Father, and *Jesus* appear again and again in the prayer once the woman has left the printed text. In the written text, all but the final sentence contains such a vocative, but in the oral text, there are often two per sentence. In descriptions of folk sermons, such vocatives are said to be pauses in which the preacher collects his thoughts for the next passage (Rosenberg, 1970). Here, however, the thoughts have been collected, in that the entire text was written out before delivery, but the speaker continues to use these vocatives and to pause after these before moving on to another plea.

Expression of personal involvement. Throughout the written version, the woman uses *we,* but in the expanded oral version, she shifts from *we* to *I,* and uses *my* and *me* where the plural might have been used had she continued the pattern from the written version. She shifts in line 10 to a singular plea, speaking as the weak sinner, the easily tempted, and praying for continued strength and readiness to being helped by her Lord. The written prayer simply asks for guidance (orally stated as *'leadin'' and 'guidin''*) and strong protection ('strong-arm protection' and 'protector' in the oral version). The plea that the sinner not be faced with temptation is expressed in the written version in a familiar phrase from the Lord's Prayer, and is followed by a formulaic expression often used in ministers' prayers Make us ever mindful of. . At line 22, she stops using *thee*, *thy*, and *thou*, archaic personal pronouns; thereafter she uses second person singular *you*.

Expression in a wide variety of sentence structures. The written version uses   30
simple sentences throughout, varying the style with insertion of vocatives, and repetitions of paired adjectives ('young and old', 'near and far'). The spoken version includes compound-complex sentences with subordination, and repetition of simple sentences with variation (e.g., 'I can call on 'im'. . .). There are several incomplete sentences in the spoken version (line 16–18), which if completed would have been complex in structure.

Use of informal style and Black English vernacular forms. The opening of the   31
spoken version and the written version uses standard English forms, and the first suggestion of informality comes with the dropping of the g in line 4. As the prayer progresses, however, several informal forms and features associated with the Black English vernacular are used: *'long*(= along), childrens, *'im*(= him), anytime o'day, he'p(= help), *'signed*(= assigned), omission of *there* (in lines 36, 37) and use of *it* for standard English in line 38, double negative (lines 36, 37, 38, 40), *cain't*(= can't), and *mo'*(= more).

There is no way to render the shifts of prosody, the melodic strains, and the   32
changes in pace which accompany the spoken version. The intonation pattern is highly marked, lilting, and the speaker breaks into actual melody at the end of line 10, and the remainder of the prayer is chanted. (Note that at this point she also shifted to the singular first person pronoun.) Sharp pitch modulations mark the prayer, and on one occasion (end of line 35), a member of the congregation broke in with a supporting bar of the melody, lasting only 3.5 seconds). All vocatives after line 6 are marked by a lilting high rise–mid fall contour.

It is possible to find in numerous studies of the religious life of Afro-Amer-   33
icans lengthy discussions of the historical role of the spoken word (see, for example, Levine, 1977:155ff for a discussion of literacy and its effects on Black religion). Current research with preachers (e.g. Mitchell, 1970; Rosenberg, 1970) and gospel songwriters (e.g. Jackson, 1966; Heilbut, 1971) in Black communities underscore and pick up numerous themes from historical studies. Repeatedly these sources emphasize the power of words as action and the substantiating effect a dynamic creative oral rendering of a message has on an audience. Preachers and musicians claim they cannot stick to a stable rendering of written words; thoughts which were once shaped into words on paper become recomposed in each time and space; written words limit a performance which must be created anew with each audience and setting. Though some of

the meaning in written words remains stable, bound in the text, the meaning of words people will carry with them depends on the integration of those words into personal experience. Thus the performance of words demands the calling in of the personal experience of each listener and the extension by that listener of the meanings of those words to achieve the ultimate possibility of any message.

In terms of the usual expectations of distinctions between the oral and liter-   34 ate mode, practices in the church life of Trackton residents provide evidence that neither mode is in control here. Members have access to both and use both. Oral spontaneous adjustments from the written material result in longer, more complex sentences, with some accompanying shifts in style from the formal to the more informal. Clearly in the oral mode, the highly personalized first person singular dominates over the more formal collective first person. Pacing, rate of speech, intonation, pitch, use of melodic phrases, and finally a chant, have much fluctuation and range from high to low when written materials are recomposed spontaneously. Spoken versions of hymns, prayers, and sermons show the speaker's attempt to identify with the audience, but this identification makes use of only some features usually associated with the oral tradition (e.g., high degree of involvement of speaker, extensive use of first person). Other features associated with oral performance (e.g., simple sentences linked together by simple compounds, and highly redundant formulaic passages which hold chunks of information together) are not found here. The use of literate sources, and even literate bases, for oral performances does not lead to a demise of many features traditionally associated with a pure oral tradition. In other words, the language forms and uses on such occasions bear the mark of both oral and literate traditions, not one or the other.

At Work

In their daily lives at home and in church, Trackton adults and children have   35 worked out ways of integrating features of both oral and written language in their language uses. But what of work settings and contacts with banks, credit offices, and the employment office—institutions typical of modernized, industrial societies?

Most of the adults in Trackton worked in the local textile mills. To obtain   36 these jobs, they went directly to the employment office of the individual mills. There, an employment officer read to them from an application form and wrote down their answers. They were not asked if they wanted to complete their own form. They were given no written information at the time of their application, but the windows and walls of the room in which they waited for personal interviews were plastered with posters about the credit union policy of the plant and the required information for filling out an application (names of previous employers, Social Security number, etc.). But all of this information was known to Trackton residents before they went to apply for a job. Such information and news about jobs usually passed by word of mouth. Some of the smaller mills put advertisements in the local paper and indicated they would accept applications during certain hours on particular days. Interviewers either told individuals at the time of application they had obtained jobs, or the employment officer agreed to telephone in a few days. If applicants did not have telephones, they gave a neighbor's number, or the mill sent a postcard.

Once accepted for the job, totally inexperienced workers would be put in 37 the particular section of the mill in which they were to work, and were told to watch experienced workers. The foreman would occasionally check by to see if the observer had questions and understood what was going on. Usually before the end of the first few hours on the shift, the new worker was put under the guidance of certain other workers and told to share work on a particular machine. Thus in an apprentice-like way new workers came on for new jobs, and they worked in this way for only several days, since all parties were anxious for this arrangement to end as soon as possible. Mills paid in part on a piece-work basis, and each machine operator was anxious to be freed to work at his or her own rapid pace as soon as possible. Similarly, the new worker was anxious to begin to be able to work rapidly enough to qualify for extra pay.

Within each section of the mill, little written material was in evidence. Safety 38 records, warnings, and, occasionally, reports about new products, or clippings from local newspapers about individual workers or events at the mill's recreational complex, would be put up on the bulletin board. Foremen and quality control personnel came through the mill on each shift, asking questions, noting output, checking machines, and recording this information. They often asked the workers questions, and the information would be recorded on a form carried by the foreman or quality control engineer. Paychecks were issued each Friday, and the stub carried information on Federal and state taxes withheld, as well as payments for health plans or automatic payments made for credit loans from the credit bureau. Mill workers generally kept these stubs in their wallets, or in a special box (often a shoe box, sometimes a small metal filebox) at home. They were rarely referred to at the time of issuance of the paycheck, unless a recent loan had been taken out or paid off at the credit bureau. Then workers would check the accuracy of the amounts withheld. In both the application stage and on the job, workers had to respond to a report or a form being filled out by someone else. This passive performance with respect to any actual reading or writing did not occur because the workers were unable to read and write. Instead, these procedures were the results of the mill's efforts to standardize the recording and processing of information. When asked why they did not let applicants fill out their own employment form, employment officers responded:

> It is easier if we do it. This way, we get to talk to the client, ask questions not on the form, clarify immediately any questions they have, and, for our purposes, the whole thing is just cleaner. When we used to have them fill out the forms, some did it in pencil, others had terrible handwriting, others gave us too much or too little information. This way, our records are neat, and we know what we've got when someone has finished an application form.

In the past, job training at some of the mills had not been done 'on the floor', 39 but through a short session with manuals, an instructor, and instruction 'by the book'. Executives of the mills found this process too costly and inefficient, and those who could do the best job of handling the written materials were not necessarily the best workers on the line.

Beyond the mill, Trackton adults found in banks, credit union offices, and loan offices the same type of literacy events. The oral performance surrounding a written piece of material to which they had little or no access was what counted or made a difference in a transaction. When individuals applied for credit at the credit union, the interviewer held the folder, asked questions derived from information within the folder, and offered little or no explanation of the information from which he derived questions. At the end of interviews, workers did not know whether or not they would receive the loan or what would be done with the information given to the person who interviewed them. In the following interview (see figure 1), the credit union official directs questions to the client primarily on the basis of what is in the written documents in the client's folder.[2] She attempts to reconcile the written information with the current oral request. However, the client is repeatedly asked to supply information as though she knows the contents of the written document. Referents for pronouns (*it* in 4, *this* in 7, *this* in 10, and *they* in 16) are not clearly identified, and the client must guess at their referents without any visual or verbal clues. Throughout this literacy event, only one person has access to the written information, but the entire oral exchange centers around that information. In (4) the credit union employee introduces new information; *it* refers to the amount of the current loan. The record now shows that the client has a loan which is being repaid by having a certain amount deducted from her weekly paycheck; for those in her salary range, there is an upper limit of $1700 for a loan.

But this information is not clear from the oral exchange, and it is known only to the credit union employee and indicated on documents in the client's folder. The calculation of a payment of $50 per month (10) is based on this information, and the way in which this figure was derived is never explained to the client. In (10) the official continues to read from the folder, but she does not ask for either confirmation or denial of this information. Her ambiguous statement, 'We're gonna combine this', can only be assumed to mean the current amount of the loan with the amount of the new loan, the two figures which will now equal the total of the new principal $1700. The statement of gross weekly salary as $146.66 is corrected by the client (11), but the official does not verbally acknowledge the correction; she continues writing. Whether she records the new figure and takes it into account in her calculations is not clear. The official continues reading (12) and is once again corrected by the client. She notes the new information and shortly closes off the interview.

In this literacy event, written materials have determined the outcome of the request, yet the client has not been able to see those documents or frame questions which would clarify their contents. This pattern occurred frequently for Trackton residents, who argued that neighborhood center programs and other

40

41

42

---

[2] This transcript was first included in Heath, 1979, a report on several types of literacy events in the work settings of Trackton residents. In these events, neither customarily expected literacy behaviors nor general conversational roles were followed.

Total units of discourse: 16
4 elicitations directed to CI, 4 responses by CI
4 utterances directed to folder by Off
2 responses by CI to folder information
2 announcements of exits by Off

A-CU5 Heath 1979
CI : Client
Off: Credit Union Official
    (enters office where client is seated)

(1) Off: okay, hh, what kind of a loan did you ⌐hh wanna see about now?
                                                 (pause)
(2) CI: ⌐ well, hh, I wanna   wanted it for my hhh personal reserve.
                              (exits)
(3) Off: let me get your folder, I'll be right back.
    (reenters)   (looking at folder)
(4)   and you want to increase it to seventeen.
    (looking toward client)
(5)   and your purpose?
                 (pause)
(6) CI: I hhh need a personal   uh, I got some small bills.
                                           (looking at folder)
(7) Off: because when I did this, I, hhh, didn't know, but you were telling me both had to sign.
    (looking at client)
(8)   what kind of bills?
(9) CI: water, gas, clothes, hhh, water department.
                                ⌐flips through folder, writing figures on pad)
(10) Off: okay, now you're paying fifty a month, and you want, you, hhh, ummmmm
    you want your payments to stay at that, okay, you live at 847 J. O. Connell,
                           (pause)
    and you've been there three years, okay   um. let's see, we're gonna combine this,
    gross weekly salary is $146 ⌐46, forty-hour week
(11) CI: └no, about $170
    (looking at folder)   (pause)
(12) Off: you don't have a car and your rent is $120, and you still owe Sears, hhh   it's twenty=
(13) CI: =no, it's more than that=
    (looking at client)
(14) Off: =what is it now?
(15) CI: I think it's about $180 ⌐some
(16) Off: └is that everything, yea. all we've got to do is apply to the credit bureau,
    they decide, you can come back tomorrow.

Figure 1

adult education programs should be aimed not at teaching higher level reading skills or other subjects, but at ways of getting through such interviews or other situations (such as visits to dentists and doctors), when someone else held the information which they needed to know in order to ask questions about the contents of that written material in ways which would be acceptable to institution officials.

Conclusions

Trackton is a literate community in the sense that the residents are able to read 43 printed and written materials in their daily lives, and on occasion they produce written messages as part of the total pattern of communication in the community. Residents turn from written to spoken uses of language and vice versa as the occasion demands, and the two modes of expression seem to supplement and reinforce each other in a unique pattern. However, the conventions appropriate for literacy events within the community, in their worship life, and in their workaday world call for different uses of speech to interpret written materials. In a majority of cases, Trackton adults show their knowledge of written materials only through oral means. On many occasions, they have no opportunity to attend directly to the written materials through any active use of their own literacy skills; instead, they must respond in appropriate speech events which are expected to surround interpretation of these written materials.

It is impossible to characterize Trackton through existing descriptions of either the oral or the literate traditions; seemingly, it is neither, and it is both. Literacy events which bring the written word into a central focus in interactions and interpretations have their rules of occurrence and appropriateness according to setting and participants. The joint social activity of reading the newspaper across porches, getting to the heart of meaning of a brochure on a new product, and negotiating rules for putting an antenna on a car produce more speaking than reading, more group than individual effort, repeated analogies and generalizations, and fast-paced, overlapping syntactically complex language. The spontaneous recomposing of written hymns, sermons, and prayers produces not parables, proverbs, and formulas, but re-creations of written texts which are more complex in syntactic structure, performance rules, and more demanding of close attention to lexical and semantic cues, than are their written counterparts. For these recomposing creations are, like community literacy events, group-focused, and members of the group show their understanding and acceptance of the meaning of the words by picking up phrases, single words, or meanings, and creating their own contribution to a raised hymn or a prayer.

In work settings, when others control access to and restrict types of written information, Trackton residents have to learn to respond to inadequate meaning clues, partial sentences, and pronouns without specified referents. In these latter situations, especially those in financial and legal institutions, Trackton residents recognize their deficiency of skills, but the skills which are missing are not literacy skills, but knowledge about oral language uses which would enable them to obtain information about the content and uses of written documents, and to ask questions to clarify their meanings. Learning how to do this appropriately, so as not to seem to challenge a person in power, is often critical to obtaining a desired outcome and maintaining a job or reputation as a 'satisfactory' applicant, or worker.[3]

Descriptions of these literacy events and their patterns of uses in Trackton do not enable us to place the community somewhere on a continuum from full literacy to restricted literacy or non-literacy. Instead, it seems more appropriate to think of two continua, the oral and the written. Their points and extent of

---

[3] Current work by linguists, sociologists, and anthropologists in medical, legal, and business settings repeatedly emphasizes the hazards of inappropriate behavior in these situations. See, for example, Cicourel, 1981, for a survey of research in medical settings; O'Barr, 1981, for a similar overview of legal studies. Gumperz, 1976, 1977, and to appear, and Gumperz and Cook-Gumperz, 1981, provide numerous theoretical and methodological perspectives on interethnic communication in professional contexts.

overlap, and similarities in structure and function, follow one pattern for Trackton, but follow others for communities with different cultural features. And it is perhaps disquieting to think that many of these cultural features seem totally unrelated to features usually thought to help account for the relative degree of literacy in any social group. For example, such seemingly unrelated phenomena as the use of space in the community and the ways in which adults relate to preschool children may be as important for instilling literacy habits as aspirations for upward mobility or curiosity about the world. In Trackton, given the uses of space and the ways in which adults interacted with preschool children, no amount of books suddenly poured into the community, or public service programs teaching parents how to help their children learn to read, would have made an appreciable difference. The linkage between houses by open porches, the preference of young and old to be outdoors rather than inside, the incorporation of all the community in the communication network of each household, and the negative value placed on individual reading, reinforced the social group's negotiation of written language. Formal writing always had to be renegotiated into an informal style, one which led to discussion and debate among several people. Written messages gave residents something to talk about; after they talked, they might or might not follow up on the message of the written information, but what they had come to know had come to them from the text through the joint oral negotiation of meaning.

Trackton children do not learn to talk by being introduced to labels for either 47 everyday objects or pictures and words in books. Instead, without adjusted, simplified input from adults, they become early talkers, modeling their ways of entering discourse and creating story texts on the oral language they hear about them. They tell creative story-poems which attempt to recapture the settings of actions as well as the portrayal of actions. They achieve their meaning as communicators and their sense of their own worth as communicators through the responses they obtain to their oral language, not in terms of responses in a one-to-one situation of reading a book with an adult. Words indeed must be as 'behavioral' as any other form of action (Carothers, 1959). They carry personal qualities, have a dynamic nature, and cannot become static things always retaining their same sense. As one mother said of her ways of teaching her two-year old son to talk: 'Ain't no use me tellin' 'im: "learn this, learn that, what's this, what's that?" He just gotta learn, gotta know; he see one thing one place one time, he know how it go, see sump'n like it again, maybe it be the same, maybe it won't.' In each new situation, learning must be reevaluated, reassessed for both the essence of meaning that occurs across contexts and for the particular meaning obtained in each new and different context.

What does this mean for the individual readers in Trackton? How different 48 is their way of comprehending literate materials from that more commonly ascribed to literate individuals? For example, current research in reading suggests three ways or levels of extracting meaning from print: attending to the text itself, bringing in experiences or knowledge related to the text, and interpreting beyond the text into a creative/imaginative realm or to achieve a new synthesis of information from the text and reader experience (see Rumelhart,

1976; Rumelhart & Ortony, 1977; Adams, 1980 for technical discussions of these processes). Trackton residents as a group do use these methods of getting information from print. One person, reading aloud, decodes the written text of the newspaper, brochure, set of instructions, etc. This level of extracting meaning from the text is taken as the basis for the move to the next level, that of relating the text's meaning to the experience of members of the group. The experience of any one individual has to become common to the group, however, and that is done through the recounting of members' experiences. Such recountings attempt to re-create the scenes, to establish the character of the individuals involved, and, to the greatest extent possible, to bring the audience into the experience itself. At the third level, there is an extension beyond the common experience to a reintegration. For example, what do both the text and the common relating of text's meaning to experience say to the mother trying to decide how best to register her child for a daycare program? Together again, the group negotiates this third level. The process is time-consuming, perhaps less efficient than one individual reading the information for himself and making an individual decision. But the end result has been the sharing of information (next year's mother receiving a similar form will hear this discussion re-created in part). Furthermore, the set of experiences related to the task at hand is greater than a single individual would have: the mother has been led to consider whether or not to enlist the doctor's help, which information to take for registration, and a host of other courses of action she might not have considered on her own. Thus Trackton residents in groups, young and old, are familiar with processes for comprehending text similar to those delineated for individual readers by reading teachers and researchers. Major differences between their experiences with literacy and those generally depicted in the mainstream literature are in the degree of focus on specific decoding skills (such as letter-sound relationships), the amount of practice at each level of extracting meaning available for each individual in the community, and the assignment of interpretive responsibility to the group rather than to any one individual.

There are still other questions which could be asked of the uses of oral 49 and literate skills in Trackton. What of the social consequences of their uses of literacy? Because they do not frequently and intensively engage in reading and writing extended prose, is their literacy 'restricted', and what has this meant for them in socioeconomic terms? Work in the textile mills provided an income equal to or better than that of several types of professionals in the region: schoolteachers, salesmen, and secretaries. Successful completion of composition and advanced grammar classes in high school would not have secured better paying jobs for Trackton residents, unless very exceptional circumstances had come into play in individual cases. Improved scores on tests of reading comprehension or the Scholastic Aptitude Tests would not necessarily have given them access to more information for political decision-making than they had through the oral medium of several evening and morning television and radio news broadcasts. They tended to make their political judgments for local elections on the basis of personal knowledge of candidates or the word of someone else who knew the candidates. In national and state elections, almost all voted the party, and they said no amount of information on the individual candidates would cause them to change that pattern.

These behaviors and responses to what Goody might term 'restricted lit- 50 eracy' echo similar findings in the work of social historians asking hard questions about the impact of literacy on pre-industrial groups. For such diverse groups as the masses of seventeenth-century France (Davis, 1975), sixteenth and seventeenth-century England (Cressy, 1980), and colonial New England (Lockridge, 1974), social historians have examined the functions, uses, degrees, and effects of literacy. All agree that the contexts and uses of literacy in each society determined its values, forms, and functions. The societal changes which came with the advent of literacy across societies were neither consistent nor universal. Cressy (1980) perhaps best summarizes the conclusions of social historians about the universal potentialities of literacy:

1. People could be rational, acquire and comprehend information, and make well-founded political, social, and religious decisions without being able to read or write.
2. Literate people were no wiser or better able to control their universe than were those who were illiterate.

In short, in a variety of times and places, 'Literacy unlocked a variety of 51 doors, but it did not necessarily secure admission' (Cressy, 1980:189).

Cressy and other social historians underscore the fact that, in some societies, 52 literacy did not have the beneficial effects often ascribed to it. Davis found that, for the unlettered masses of seventeenth century France, printing made possible new kinds of control from the top segments of the society. Before the printing press, oral culture and popular community-based social organizations seemed strong enough to resist standardization and thrusts for uniformity. With literacy, however, people began to measure themselves against a widespread norm and to doubt their own worth. In some cases, this attitude made people less politically active than they had been without print or opportunities for literacy. Lockridge (1974), in his study of colonial New England, concluded that literacy did not bring new attitudes or move people away from the traditional views held in their illiterate days. Eisenstein (1979) suggested that shifts in religious traditions enabled print to contribute to the creation of new notions of a collective morality and to an increased reliance on rhetoric in the verbal discourse of sermons and homiletics.

But these are studies of pre-industrial societies; what of literacy in industrial 53 societies? Stone (1969) proposed the need to examine in industrial groups the FUNCTIONS of literacy in a variety of senses ranging from the conferring of technical skills to an association with self-discipline. Stone further suggested that each society may well have its own weighted checklist of factors (e.g. social stratification, job opportunities, Protestantism, and sectarian competition) which causes literacy to serve one or another function. Sanderson (1972), building on Stone's work, showed that the economic development of the English industrial revolution made low literacy demands of the educational system.

His argument points out the need to examine closely job demands for literacy; changes in mechanization may call for shifts of types of literacy skills. Indeed, in the English industrial revolution, the increased use of machinery enabled employers to hire workers who were less literate than were those who had previously done the hand work. Successful performance in cottage industries, for example, required a higher level of literacy for a larger proportion of workers than did mechanized textile work.

Research by economic and educational historians of the late nineteenth century United States has examined the effects of literacy not only on the economic laws of supply and demand of job opportunities, but also on the values society placed on a correct oral reading style and acceptable performance on standardized tests. Reading for comprehension and an expansion of creative thinking were less frequently assessed in the late nineteenth century than they had been earlier (Calhoun, 1973). Soltow and Stevens (1977) point out the extent to which standardized measures of performance were lauded by parents, and they suggest that acceptable performance on these tests convinced parents their children would be able to achieve occupational and social mobility. Whether or not the schools taught children to read at skill levels that might make a real difference in their chances for upward occupational mobility is not at all clear. Nevertheless, if students acquired the social and moral values and generalized 'rational' and 'cultured' behaviors associated with literate citizens, occupational mobility often resulted. 54

This social historical research raises some critical questions for the study of communities in today's complex society. A majority of communities in the modern world are neither preliterate, i.e., without access to print or writing of some kind, nor fully literate (Goody, 1968). They are somewhere in between. Some individuals may have access to literacy and choose to use it for some purposes and not for others. Some communities may restrict access to literacy to some portions of the population (Walker, 1981); others may provide a climate in which individuals choose the extent to which they will adopt habits associated with literacy (Heath, 1980). As Resnick and Resnick (1977) have shown, the goal of a high level of literacy for a large proportion of the population is a relatively recent phenomenon, and new methods and materials in reading instruction, as well as particular societal and economic supports, may be needed to achieve such a goal. 55

Furthermore, in large complex societies such as the United States, the national state of technological development and the extent of intrusion of governmental agencies in the daily lives of citizens may have combined to set up conditions in which literacy no longer has many of the traditional uses associated with it. Understanding and responding to the myriad of applications, reporting forms, and accounting procedures which daily affect the lives of nearly every family in the United States bears little resemblance to the decoding of extended prose passages or production of expository writing, the two literacy achievements most associated with school success. Furthermore, television and other media have removed the need to rely on reading to learn the basics of news and sports events, how to dress properly for the weather, and 56 what to buy and where to find it. Increasingly industry is turning to on-the-job training programs which depend on observation of tasks or audio-visual instruction rather than literate preparation for job performance; specialists handle reports related to production, quality control, inventory, and safety. In industry, the specialized demands of reporting forms, regulations and agency reports, and programming requirements call for a communications expert, not simply a 'literate' manager. In a recent survey of employer attitudes toward potential employees, employers called not for the literacy skills generally associated with school tasks, but instead for an integration of mathematical and linguistic skills, and displays of the capability of learning 'on one's own', and listening and speaking skills required to understand and give instructions and describe problems (RBS, 1978).

These shifts in larger societal contexts for literacy are easily and frequently 57 talked about, but their specific effects on communities such as Trackton, though occasionally inferred, are very rarely examined. It is clear that, in what may be referred to as the post-industrial age, members of each community have different and varying patterns of influence and control over forms and uses of literacy in their lives. They exercise considerable control within their own primary networks. In institutions, such as their churches, they may have some control. In other institutions, such as in their places of employment, banks, legal offices, etc., they may have no control over literacy demands. The shape of literacy events in each of these is different. The nature of oral and written language and the interplay between them is ever-shifting, and these changes both respond to and create shifts in the individual and societal meanings of literacy. The information to be gained from any prolonged look at oral and written uses of language through literacy events may enable us to accept the protean shapes of oral and literate traditions and language, and move us away from current tendencies to classify communities as being at one or another point along a hypothetical continuum which has no societal reality.

References

Adams, M. J. 1980 Failures to Comprehend and Levels of Processing in Reading, *in* Theoretical issues in Reading Comprehension, R. J. Spiro, B. C. Bruce, and W. F. Brewer, eds. Hillsdale, N.J.: Erlbaum.

Anderson, Alonzo B., William B. Teale, and Elette Estrada 1980 Low-income Children's Preschool Literacy Experiences: Some naturalistic observations. The Quarterly Newsletter of the Laboratory of Comparative Human Cognition 2.3:59–65.

Baron, Naomi 1979 Independence and Interdependence in Spoken and Written Language. Visible Language, I.I.

Bourdieu, Pierre 1967 Systems of Education and Systems of Thought. International Social Science Journal 19.3:338–58.

Calhoun, Daniel 1973 The Intelligence of a People. Princeton, N.J.: Princeton University Press.

Carothers, J. C. 1959 Culture, Psychiatry, and the Written Word. Psychiatry 307–20.

Cicourel, Aaron V. 1981 Language and Medicine. *In* Language in the USA. Charles A. Ferguson and Shirley Brice Heath, eds. Cambridge: Cambridge University Press.

Cressy, David 1980 Literacy and the Social Order: Reading and writing in Tudor and Stuart England. Cambridge: Cambridge University Press.

Davis, Natalie 1975 Printing and the People. *In* Society and Culture in Early Modern France. Stanford, CA: Stanford University Press.

Dodd, C. H. 1961 The Parables of the Kingdom. New York: Charles Scribner's Sons.

Eisenstein, Elizabeth L. 1979 The Printing Press as an Agent of Change, 2 Vols. Cambridge: Cambridge University Press.

Goody, Jack, ed. 1968 Literacy in Traditional Societies. Cambridge: Cambridge University Press.

Goody, Jack and Ian Watt 1963 The Consequences of Literacy. Comparative Studies in Society and History 5:304–45.

Gumperz, John J. 1976 Language, Communication, and Public Negotiation. *In* Anthropology and the Public Interest: Fieldwork and theory. P. Sanday, ed. New York: Academic Press.

_____1977 Sociocultural Knowledge in Conversational Inference. *In* Georgetown Round Table on Languages and Linguistics 1977. M. Saville-Troike, ed. Washington, D.C., Georgetown University. Press.

_____To appear Conversational Strategies.

Gumperz, John J. and Jenny Cook-Gumperz 1981 Ethnic Differences in Communicative Style. *In* Language in the USA. Charles A. Ferguson and Shirley Brice Heath, eds. Cambridge: Cambridge University Press.

Hall, Oswalo and Richard Carlton 1977 Basic Skills at School and Work: The study of Albertown, an Ontario community. Toronto, Ontario: Ontario Economic Council.

Havelock, Eric 1963 Preface to Plato. Cambridge, MA: Harvard University Press.

_____1976 Origins of Western Literacy. Toronto: Ontario Institute for Studies in Education.

Heath, Shirley Brice 1978 Outline Guide for the Ethnographic Study of Literacy and Oral Language from Schools to Communities. Philadelphia: Graduate School of Education.

_____1979 Language Beyond the Classroom. Paper prepared for the Delaware Symposium on Language Studies. University of Delaware.

_____1980 The Functions and Uses of Literacy. Journal of Communication 29.2:125–33.

_____1982 What No Bedtime Story Means: Narrative skills at home and school. Language in Society 11.1.

_____Ways with Words: Ethnography of Communication in Communities and Classrooms. New York: Cambridge UP, 1983.

Hymes, Dell H. 1972 Models of the Interaction of Language and Social Life. *In* Directions in Sociolinguistics. John J. Gumperz and Dell Hymes, eds. New York: Holt, Rinehart and Winston.

Jackson, Mahalia 1966 Movin' On Up. New York: Random House.

Kroeber, Alfred 1948 Anthropology. New York: Harcourt, Brace.

Levine, Lawrence W. 1977 Black Culture and Black Consciousness: Afro-American folk thought from slavery to freedom. New York: Oxford University Press.

Lockridge, Kenneth A. 1974 Literacy in Colonial New England. New York: Norton.

Lord, Albert B. 1965 The Singer of Tales. Cambridge, MA: Harvard University Press.

Mitchell, Henry H. 1970 Black Preaching. Philadelphia: Lippincott.

O'Barr, William M. 1981 The Language of the Law. *In* Language in the USA. Charles A. Ferguson and Shirley Brice Heath, eds. Cambridge: Cambridge University Press.

Olson, David 1977 From Utterance to Text: The bias of language in speech and writing. Harvard Educational Review 47.3:257–81.

Ong, Walter 1967 The Presence of the Word. New Haven: Yale University Press.

Research for Better Schools 1978 Employer Attitudes toward the Preparation of Youth for Work. Philadelphia: Research for Better Schools.

Resnick, Daniel P. and Laurean B. Resnick 1977 The Nature of Literacy: A historical exploration. Harvard Educational Review 43:370–85.

Rosenberg, Bruce A. 1970 The Art of the American Folk Preacher. New York: Oxford University Press.

Rumelhart, D. E. 1976 Toward an Interactive Model of Reading (Technical Report; 56) Center of Human Information Processing, University of California, San Diego.

Rumelhart, D. and A. Ortony 1977 The Representation of Knowledge in Memory, in Schooling and the Acquisition of Knowledge. R. C. Anderson, R. J. Spiro and W. E. Montague, eds. Hillsdale, N.J.: Erlbaum Associates.

Sanderson, Michael 1972 Literacy and Social Mobility in the Industrial Revolution in England. Past and Present 56:75–103.

Scollon, Ron and Suzanne B. K. Scollon 1981 Narrative, Literacy, and Face in Interethnic Communication. Norwood, N.J.: Ablex.

Soltow, Lee and Edward Stevens 1977 Economic Aspects of School Participation in Mid-nineteenth-century United States. Journal of Interdisciplinary History 7:221–43.

Staiger, Ralph C. 1979 Motivation for Reading: An international bibliography. In Roads to Reading, Ralph C. Staiger, ed. Paris: UNESCO.

Stone, Lawrence 1969 Literacy and Education in England, 1640–1900. Past and Present 42:70–139.

Walker, Willard 1981 Native Writing Systems. In Language to the USA. Charles A. Ferguson and Shirley Brice Heath, eds. Cambridge: Cambridge University Press.

Questions for Discussion and Journaling

1. Refer to John Swales's **CARS model** of research introductions (on pp. 6–8) to help you analyze Heath's introduction. Label the places where she establishes the territory, the niche, and her **contribution**. Analyze how Heath draws on sources to create and occupy a research niche. Which sources does she use for which functions?

2. How does Heath define a *literacy event*? What are some of the literacy events she identifies in Trackton? Do you think that her definition of a literacy event is still accurate in today's world, when so much about literacy has changed?

3. From Heath's description of Trackton residents' storytelling and singing and praying in church, what values (such as creativity) seem important to those attending the church? How do both orality and literacy support or express those values?

4. Heath repeatedly demonstrates that Trackton residents do not see "the word" as the ultimate authority; instead, they interpret it together and challenge and change the written word as needed for a given context. What then seems to be the ultimate authority for this group of people, if it is not the written word?

5. How do Trackton residents' literacies compare to prevailing assumptions about what literacy was supposed to be at the time Heath was writing?

6. Heath says that Trackton parents usually did not ask their children straightforward questions or just ask for recitation of information; rather, they expected their children to make connections and judgments based on the context. If we

accept this observation, how do you think it might relate to Trackton residents' experiences when applying for jobs or loans? What sorts of questions did adults in your life ask you when you were a child? How do these compare with the experiences of Trackton children?

7. Heath cites Cressy as writing that "Literacy unlocked a variety of doors, but it did not necessarily secure admission" (see para. 51). What would you say Heath is trying to stress by using this quotation? What "doors" did literacy unlock for the residents of Trackton? What doors were they unable to walk through, even though they were literate? Have you seen the same distinction made in other readings in this chapter (for example, in writings by Malcolm X or Deborah Brandt)?

Applying and Exploring Ideas

1. Build a list of how "being literate" is different for you than it was for the residents of Trackton in the 1970s. Write down all the differences you can think of. Then write a brief (half-page) introduction to your list summarizing what has changed in the intervening thirty years. Consider technology, certainly, but also perhaps habits, attitudes, and so on.

2. Interview your parents about your own literacy learning, comparing your recollections with theirs. Briefly summarize the interview, noting in particular any artifacts that were either discussed or presented (books they read to you, pictures you drew, your first writings, or the first storybook you read, for example). Compare your summary with those of classmates and list similarities and differences. What do you make of the comparison? Also, consider: Did you hold anything back (that is, *not* share it with your class)? If so, what, and why?

3. Briefly describe five literacy events in your everyday life and compare them to those of the residents of Trackton.

Meta Moment

How might reading this article help you achieve the goals of this chapter? From the range of ideas in this article, can you tell which might be most useful to you in your learning in this course?

The Future of Literacy

DÀNIELLE DEVOSS

GAIL E. HAWISHER

CHARLES JACKSON

JOSEPH JOHANSEN

BRITTNEY MORASKI

CYNTHIA L. SELFE

DeVoss, Dànielle, Gail E. Hawisher, Charles Jackson, Joseph Johansen, Brittney Moraski, and Cynthia L. Selfe. "The Future of Literacy." *Literate Lives in the Information Age: Narratives of Literacy from the United States.* Ed. Cynthia Selfe and Gail Hawisher. Mahwah: Lawrence Erlbaum, 2004. 183–210. Print.

Framing the Reading

As you read selections in this book, we want you to keep paying attention to **authorship**—who is speaking, and how what they say might connect with who they are and what they're doing. We also want you to keep thinking about **conventions** in scholarly writing and publication. For example, take a look at the MLA citation for "The Future of Literacy" (above). From this entry, you can see that the selection has six authors and that it originally appeared in *Literate Lives in the Information Age: Narratives of Literacy from the United States,* a text edited by Selfe and Hawisher. If you were to Google Selfe or Hawisher, you'd pretty quickly find that they are two of the main authorities in the field of Writing Studies on what we know now as digital literacies and electronic technologies in writing. DeVoss, Jackson, Johansen, and Moraski are the subjects of case studies in the article; DeVoss and Johansen were working professionals with advanced degrees at the time the article was written, and Jackson and Moraski (who graduated from Harvard in 2009 and is now working as an educational consultant in China) were high school students.

Pictured above are, in order, Gail Hawisher, Joseph Johansen, Brittney Moraski, and Cynthia Selfe.

You might also notice that the authors are listed in alphabetical order by last name. Multiple authors frequently do this when they want to emphasize the fact that they made equal contributions to the piece.

The piece is easy enough to read, as it walks through each of four case studies of literate learners, drawing from them that the authors argue are important for literacy educators and advocates to consider as the definitions of **literacy** change with new writing technologies. We will leave it to you as readers to decide what the main point of the argument is and, therefore, what these writers want their piece to *do*, to accomplish, with its readers.

Getting Ready to Read

Before you read, do at least one of the following activities:

- Write a one-sentence definition of *literacy*: "Literacy is _____ ."
- Make a list with a classmate, roommate, or friend of the ways you write electronically in ordinary life (word processing, blogging, Facebooking, tagging, and so on). How many items are on the list? How many of them include, at least sometimes, images as well as alphabetic text?

As you read, consider the following questions:

- What research methods have the writers used to develop the perspectives they present in this piece?
- How does the piece sound and feel? Is it a dispassionate, "just-the-facts" account, or does it *advocate* for a position or a point of view? (Could it do both?)
- How do elements of texts that aren't alphabetic (e.g., audio or visual elements) change the way we encounter the texts? What kinds of new literacies might reading them require?

In the next decade, what will the term *literacy* mean, especially within online 1
environments? What new kinds of literacy practices will characterize those students now preparing to enter and graduate from our nation's schools? How will these graduates communicate over the globally extended computer networks now distinguishing 21st century workplaces? And how will these networks continue to transform, or not, these graduates' ordinary everyday literacy practices?

Grounded by their education and values in what Jay David Bolter (1991) has 2
called the "late age of print," teachers and schools today face many challenges. They must be prepared not only to work with students and their new literacies in productive ways, but also to modify current curricula to account for students

who spend as much time reading the texts of coded simulations or visual arguments as they do the pages of novels. In other words, the U.S. educational system and its teachers must be ready to meet the needs of students who compose meaning not only with words, but also with digitized bits of video, sound, photographs, still images, words, and animations and to support communications across conventional linguistic, cultural, and geopolitical borders.

> The U.S. educational system and its teachers must be ready to meet the needs of students who compose meaning not only with words, but also with digitized bits of video, sound, photographs, still images, words, and animations and to support communications across conventional linguistic, cultural, and geopolitical borders.

This chapter offers case studies of four people: two young professionals, a woman and man, both 28 when interviewed in 2001 and who recently completed advanced degrees; and two students, a young woman and man, aged 15 and 16, respectively, who are currently making their way through public high school in two different states. These individuals, along with many others like them, form a vector for literacy in the coming decades. Tracing this vector, considering its direction and pace, can help us glimpse the future and speculate on some answers to pressing questions about the future of 21st century literacies.

As we participate in the early years of this 21st century, parents, educators, and policymakers will find it increasingly important to understand literacy as it has changed, and continues to change, in the digital age, to formulate new insights about what it means to read, compose, and exchange text in electronic environments. The four individuals in this chapter, typical, in some important ways, of students now entering and graduating from U.S. public schools and university classrooms, can help us engage in this task. Their stories, furthermore, challenge us to explore the multiple literacies that now characterize online environments.

The Case Study of Dànielle DeVoss

Dànielle DeVoss, born on August 8, 1973, was the first of two children in her White, middle class, midwestern family. Dànielle's parents pursued their own advanced educations early in their marriage and were committed to the literacy development of their children. As Dànielle noted:

> They encouraged my brother and I to read. I was involved in summer reading programs as young as I can remember. . . . [Around the house, there were] daily newspapers, all sorts of magazines (sports, home improvement, news, politics), books, and novels. My mother preferred historical, cultural, and religious . . . books. My father preferred fiction paperbacks. . . . My mother took us regularly to the library and to used bookstores when we got older.

Dànielle's parents were also responsible, at least indirectly, for the computer-based literacies she began to acquire relatively early in life. As she tells the story:

> I first came in contact with computers when my parents bought a computer . . . when my brother and I were fairly young. I think I was maybe 10. The computer quickly became his domain, but I eventually learned how to use it by looking over his shoulder, and as we got older, we fought for time on the computer. I used the computer as a social space, accessing computer bulletin board systems by phone. . . .
>
>   I learned pretty much by looking over my brother's shoulder and then jumping on the computer when he and his friends were gone. He did eventually teach me a few things, but most of my initial learning was on my own. . . . My brother primarily used the computer for the same reason I did—games and bulletin board systems. . . .
>
>   Between all the bulletin board systems we called, my brother and I wound up logging about 250 calls a month (I know this thanks to the per-call fees from the local phone company when I was growing up).

As Dànielle progressed through secondary school, her mother made every effort to direct her daughter's interest in computers toward more conventional academic pursuits, but Dànielle continued to enjoy gaming and bulletin board/ chat room exchanges. In these gaming environments, she became adept at reading and interpreting imaginary scenarios and composing the exchanges between characters of various types and abilities. She learned, as well, to create elaborate descriptions of her own characters and to respond to the complex situations that other players' characters generated. Her literacy in these electronic environments, Dànielle remembers, had a great deal to do with her increasing confidence as a reader and writer off-line, as well: The exchanges in games and chat rooms, for instance, were especially instructive to her growing sense of rhetorical awareness because they so often resulted in social consequences that she felt keenly: 6

> Chat rooms and bulletin board systems are complicated spaces where missteps or inappropriate talk can pretty much exclude you from a conversation, or make you the target of venomous textual assaults.

Dànielle also learned other literacy skills and values in the online gaming environments she frequented, those based as much in the visual, kinesthetic, and interactive components of gaming, as in the alphabetic. These practices, moreover, diverged dramatically from the conventional literacy instruction she received in school, where, as she got older, writing instruction was increasingly limited to the alphabetic and to the two-dimensional representational space of the page. Although she certainly did well on such conventional tasks, Dànielle's real attention remained focused on composing the interactive scenarios and exchanges of gaming situations; learning to read and predict the rule-based movements of characters in time and space; visualizing, mapping, and navigating her own way through the multidimensional compositional space of games:

> [T]rying to create mental maps of the text-only games I played taught me a lot about mapping out textual spaces and trying to think of them in terms of "real"

space. The text-only games required a heck of a lot of imagination, too—often, the games weren't that well written, and it was your interaction with the games that really made the difference. . . .

[Y]ou had to create complex mental maps. I remember when I first started playing games in these realms and being lost. I'd wander in circles, and wasn't able to return to particular areas within the game. It was frustrating, so I became much more adept at creating mental maps of where I was and where I wanted to go. I started by paying attention to short distances, mapping how I was moving during one stint of playing. As I did this, I was able to create larger maps and form a stronger sense of the realm in which I was playing in.

Most of these new-media literacy skills and understandings, we should add, Dànielle acquired on her own, without a great deal of systematic help or guidance from others. Few of her teachers, their own understanding of literacy tuned into the relatively narrow bandwidth of the alphabetic, knew enough about computers to take her literacy development in electronic contexts seriously; none were likely to consider the games and chat rooms in which she participated to be an appropriate context for the instruction of literacy.

For the next decade, Dànielle continued her online gaming and, as computers offered increasingly sophisticated environments for both gaming and composing, she developed considerable skill in designing Web sites using HTML code. She also became familiar with Adobe Photoshop; Macromedia Dreamweaver and a variety of other HTML editors; Microsoft Word, PowerPoint, and Excel; Corel WordPerfect and Presentations; QuarkXpress; Aldus PageMaker; and several kinds of bibliographic software. Dànielle enjoyed composing web texts, in part, because these activities resonated with the earlier literacies she practiced in gaming environments. Both kinds of composition allowed her to combine alphabetic and visual elements; to organize texts along temporal and spatial axes; and to explore the structure of large bodies of complicated material. To compose both kinds of texts, Dànielle relied on her ability to predict the movements of readers, to organize and arrange materials according to these predictions, and to navigate space-time creations.

Dànielle's web literacy abilities are especially evident in the main organizational interface of a site she created while working on her PhD at Michigan Technological University (see Figure 1). The site opens with a retro-style collage crafted from pictures and texts that Dànielle scanned from popular magazines of the 1930s and 1940s. With these pictures, and borrowing from the layout and design of the historical two-dimensional, print-based texts, Dànielle composed a three-dimensional text in a new-media environment. On top of these images, she superimposed banner headlines—to remind readers of an older style of the magazine cover—and made these alphabetic bits into electronic links that led to other areas of her new-media text. Rather than flipping through pages on which the full text of an article appears, readers click instead on a headline to access additional new-media compositions: hypertextual syllabi, an online photography exhibit, an e-mail connection. In this activity, readers are encouraged to rethink their magazine literacy in terms of the new-media literacies structuring the site itself. Through this design, unlike

Figure 1

many of her composition instructors, Dànielle sought to connect online litera-cies with print-based literacies. As she explains:

> Part of what I want readers to feel when they navigate the site is that hypertext isn't a new concept. The ability to read a magazine requires a sophisticated sense of navigation, flipping, moving, and browsing. Creating a collage of images from old magazines and linking them was a move I wanted to make toward disrupting the belief that hypertext is an entirely new technology.

The Case Study of Joseph Johansen

Joseph Johansen, born on July 14, 1973, in Provo, Utah, was the second of 11 children in his White, middle class family. His parents, members of the Church of Jesus Christ of Latter-Day Saints, fostered a strong, intergenerational tradi-tion of literacy. As Joseph described his family's history: 9

> I think a good place to begin would be with my grandfather. I attribute a great deal of my parents' emphasis on education to him. My grandpa grew up on a farm. As a young man all he wanted to be was a sheepherder. He loved to write poetry, read religious and historical books, and to experience nature. Sheepherd-ing gave him ample opportunity to do this. Well, a few years after he got married, I believe he had either four or five children at the time, he was injured to the extent that he couldn't continue working on the farm and tending the sheep. So he decided to go back to school with a family and no job. He worked his way through school and ended up with a doctorate in microbiology. I believe he was the first in his family with any college education. He spent the rest of his career teaching microbiology in various universities. As a result of my grandfather's

legacy, each of his seven sons went on to get advanced degrees in engineering, medicine, or computer-related fields.

Although Joseph carried his parents' love of education and reading into formal schooling contexts, his relationship with writing was not always positive:

> Writing . . . [was] a little different. I know that my parents valued communication and understood that writing was important for good communication, but honestly I didn't enjoy writing until my senior year in high school or later. I never did well in English courses as a younger child. I would pull a C, maybe an occasional B, but usually nothing more.

It was through writing, however, that Joseph first encountered computers. He was involved in a course where students were encouraged to learn and then write about a variety of topics including computers. Joseph then began programming with Basic and learned how to create banners and graphics files on computers, getting his first glimpse of the machine's potential as an emerging medium for visual composition. Such a focus fit well with Joseph's longstanding interest in art, a focus encouraged by his parents, if not by his teachers: 10

> My father is an art teacher. He exposed me to visual literacy at a very young age through art lessons and insights into the way he saw things. He has always encouraged me to develop visual literacies. . . .
>
> For a while I was into comic book art, so I would collect comic books and the character cards that went with them. I would try to recreate the characters I saw and make my own. I became interested in airbrush art in high school. I used to make tee shirts and even painted a mural on my bedroom wall (I am sure my mom hated that but she never said anything).
>
> My teachers . . . convinced me that there was no money in [the love of art]. My dad certainly wasn't making a lot of money and he was a great artist. [And so] I decided to become a computer engineer. That way I could make money and continue doing art work as a hobby.

When Joseph finished high school and completed his missionary work in France, however, he discovered graphic design, a field highly dependent on computer-based communications and networked environments, and one that valued, in addition, his interest in visual arts. Thus, by the time Joseph had finished his bachelor's degree, worked as a graphic designer, and enrolled in a master's-level program in professional communication, much of his composition work took place in new-media environments that involved computer-based graphic design, web design, photo editing, word processing, and multimedia design. In his words, Joseph loved: 11

> . . . designing visual media . . . Web sites, chat rooms (ironic since I don't really use them), multimedia movies, animations, 3-D imagery and animations, streaming video, flash movies, and CD-ROMs.

In undertaking these new-media projects, Joseph taught himself how to use Office, Photoshop, Illustrator, Image Ready, Freehand, Fireworks, Dreamweaver, Director, Flash, Bryce, Poser, QuarkXpress, and Streamline, with the help of books and CDs he purchased and by engaging in discussions with expert users in chat rooms, discussion boards, and listservs. Although he was enrolled in a graduate-level communications program at a well-regarded university, his teachers, like Dànielle's, had been able to provide Joseph relatively little systematic help in pursuing his visual literacy interests:

> Unfortunately, [neither] of the schools that I have been to are very strong in the visual-computer area. . . . Both schools have great art programs and great computer programs, but neither of them integrated the two very well. I know some schools do but I can't afford them.
>
> So I have had to tailor what the schools do offer to meet my needs. This has meant a lot of work outside of class researching topics that dealt with the merging of art and computers.

Despite these challenges, Joseph continued to focus on visual literacy, recog- 12 nizing the culture's increasing dependence on reading, understanding, and composing texts in which meaning is communicated through the visual elements of still photographs, video, animated images, graphics, and charts—a move Gunther Kress (1999) describes as the "turn to the visual" (p. 66). Like Dànielle, Joseph also appreciated the intertextual applications of the new-media literacies:

> Working in a variety of media from text to illustration to video has given me a fairly deep arsenal that I can pull from in composing. It allows me to create "textured" works, which I find interesting.

The visual essay *Robojoe* represents an example of Joseph's new-media compositions (see Figure 2). Joseph created this Flash movie in a graduate seminar at Clemson University in the spring of 2001, responding to an assignment that

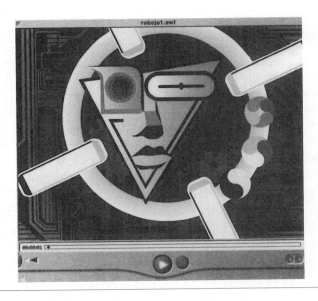

Figure 2

asked him to explore the relationship between humans and technology. His goal was to create a totally visual argument that would make a meaningful comment on this topic. *Robojoe* opens on a foregrounded representation of a triangular cybernetic face glowing blue against a pale gray background of whirling gears and pulsing circuit boards. Superimposed over this representation is a dynamic grid calibrated along x and y axes. The grid follows any mouse movements made by readers as they explore this page. With this interface, Joseph argues that technology—represented by the dynamic grid calibrated along x and y axes, the turning gears, and the pulsing circuit board—has come to both under- and over-write the human body, here portrayed as a triangular cybernetic face. This technological revision, Joseph maintains in an accompanying alphabetic commentary on this visual essay, has turned our muscles, the actuators of motion, into moving gears; our heart and nervous system, the body's energy sources, into pulsing circuits; and the human brain into central processing units, represented by the disk input slot in the cybernetic face.

Links from the main screen of this visual essay, three yin-yang symbols 13
of varying complexity, lead to three more perspectives on and stories about technology, each of which was explored in the seminar Joseph took. The first and simplest link takes readers from the splash page to a sequence of moving images that depict the common, reductive, binary perspective that many humans adopt in relation to technology: Technology is either a great good or it is a terrible evil. This story, appropriately, Joseph has composed using shapes that recall only the most primitive of machines: the wedge, the pulley, the lever, and the screw. The second, more complicated, link off the splash page leads to a further complication of the earlier perspective. In this second series of moving images, Joseph indicates that technology's effects may be both good and bad in varying degrees, as represented by the juxtaposition of various images in different combinations: a symbol of atomic energy, an artificial heart, and an airplane come together; a caduceus and a death's head converge; a light bulb, a sailing vessel, and an airship designed by DaVinci move across the screens. In the third and final story, Joseph maintains that computers, represented here by strings of binary code, introduce an increasingly complex instantiation of technology into our culture and suggests the complex ways in which these machines have shaped the human experience: increasing the global reach of communication efforts, as indicated by the transmitting tower; changing our understanding of time, represented by the clock; supporting the spread of multinational capitalism, symbolized by the hand grasping money; and altering our understanding of artificial intelligence, as suggested by the robot. In this argument, Joseph suggests that the imaginary line separating good and bad technologies has disappeared as the boundaries separating the human and the technological have similarly blurred.

The Case Study of Brittney Moraski

Brittney Moraski, born August 28, 1986, into a White, middle class Catholic 14
family living in the rural Upper Peninsula of Michigan, grew up as the youngest

of three sisters and three brothers. She attended the elementary school in the same mid-size town where she was born, and went on to attend the local high school. Brittney's mother attended several years of college and her father, a sixth-grade teacher, holds a master's degree in Education.

Both parents place a high value on literacy. Brittney's mother has "always 15 enjoyed reading" and her father "constantly reads magazines on ultralight and powered parachute flying," in addition to daily newspapers. As Brittney notes, her parents

> . . . never stressed the importance of education—it . . . [was] unnecessary. Even in childhood, my brothers, sisters, and I . . . instinctively understood the importance of education.

Brittney, unusually poised for a 15 year old when interviewed, reported that she always had her "nose in a book," and she attributed her love of reading and learning to her family:

> [They were] . . . fantastic about reading to me. I was read to constantly, especially during car rides. Such diligence and attention from my family members has no doubt played a major role in the development of my intellectual facilities. . . .
>
> [Now,] I enjoy history, and I found *Robert Kennedy: His Life* by Evan Thomas to be a fantastic book, I've read many books on the Holocaust, including *Night* by Elie Wiesel and *The Diary of Anne Frank.* I'm beginning to become interested in classical literature (I loathed it before) and recently read *The Pearl* by John Steinbeck. I read the news articles on Yahoo! to stay current in world and national affairs and subscribe to *Time* magazine. I enjoy writing essays and research papers and love creating Web sites.

The first computer that Brittney remembers in the house was her brother's, and it was on this machine that Brittney began her digital literacy practices when she was five:

> My brother Garrett got a computer when I was young, and I remember that I had a dinosaur (my passion at the time) program in which I made a printout that read:
>
>> brittney ligh moraski is 5 years old. her sisters and brothers names are courtney and leslye and brittney garrett brett brandon dad [bob] mom [beth] mitzi is are best friend in the world.

Brittney also used a computer when she visited the home of her best friend, Mitzi. As a result, by the time Brittney got to school she already associated computers with literacy, self-expression, and fun:

> I became comfortable with computers before I started school, so I already had exposure to technology. We had a computerized reading program at school called Accelerated Reader, where students read books that were assigned a point value. After reading the book, we would take a test on the computer. Depending on how the student did on the test, points would be awarded. Being the voracious reader that I was at the time, I acquired over 700 points during my elementary years.

As Brittney progressed in school, she became increasingly adept at using and navigating in computer-supported literacy environments, often working and learning in Mitzi's company: 16

> I just dove into computers as a young child, and I used it, especially in word processing, often before many of my peers. I used Microsoft Works in fourth grade to create my graphs and papers for my science fair project. A huge amount of credit goes to the Barras (Mitzi and her father) for my technological progression—they taught me everything.
>
> I would go over to Mitzi's house and together we would try (and try) to create the things necessary for my homework. It took us hours to learn how to create a graph in Works.
>
> I didn't have a computer of my own until I was a sixth grader, so the only time I used the computer was when I was at her house. Needless to say, I spent an extraordinary (and worthwhile) amount of time there throughout my childhood. Her (and her family's) help and support has been tremendous.

In her own home, Brittney rapidly became the technology expert. And like many children coming of age in a technological world, she passed her growing expertise upstream to her parents, teaching them how to send e-mail, connect to the Internet, and use Microsoft Money.

Computers became a major part of Brittney's social life as well. As a sophisticated 15 year old, she observed that computer-based literacy had become a means of extending the personal relationships of her friends: 17

> My friends embrace technology because it allows them to communicate with their friends, makes homework assignments easier, and allows them to create cards and posters. . . . When my friends have crushes with certain guys . . . the computer becomes an important flirting tool. Getting that guy on your instant-messenger list can result in conversations that may lead to "going out."

By the time Brittney got to high school, she was reading books on web design, HTML coding, and programs like Photoshop; and enrolling in online distance education classes to supplement her education. As she noted, a great deal of her day was spent in online literacy activities, although she believed her outdated computer had cramped her style to some extent: 18

> I have a moderately slow, nondescript PC computer. It has been jazzed up recently; however, one of Mitzi's brothers helped me to install a CD burner, more memory, and an additional hard drive.
>
> . . . I spend a tremendous amount of time using a computer! . . . I have the Internet at home, and I use it for a multitude of functions. I access my Spanish course online, send and receive e-mails, use Yahoo! Messenger to check news headlines and see how my stocks are doing, purchase stocks through ShareBuilder, buy books and CDs at Half.com or Amazon.com, use M-W.com to look up the definitions of words, chat with friends on ICQ, update the school's Web site, look up topics that interest me, download songs, search for scholarships or contests, learn more about the college admissions process and visit the sites of my preferred

universities, look for upcoming camps or workshops, research for homework, and more, and more, and more! One recent example of how I use my computer: We were asked at CCD to chose a patron saint and report on it the next week. Well, I used Yahoo! and Google to find sites that list patron saints, and pretty soon I was at catholic-focum.com, trying to find my "personal" saint. I eventually settled on St. Catherine of Alexandria, the patroness of wisdom, philosophers, scholars, and students, but I was tempted to choose St. Vitus, who guards against oversleeping! :)

Given the extent of her online activities, Brittney's computer skills quickly 19 outstripped those of many of her teachers. And, although Brittney was appreciative of those instructors who took the trouble to enter her digital world and was tolerant of their initial efforts, she was also realistic about the time it would take for adults to catch on to the dynamic technologies that were already a part of her life and brutally frank about the instruction she felt her school could offer students like her:

> I appreciate [it] when my teachers embrace technology—I understand that it can be a scary thing. However, very few teachers use technology in the classroom. While my algebra teacher has a Web site that he uses to post homework, the art teacher at school gives PowerPoint presentations, and my health teacher had us take a computerized test to see if we were right- or left-brained, there is little use of dynamic technology in school, but I'm certain that this will change as the years progress.
>
> I think my personal initiative in understanding and utilizing computers will serve me better than what my school has taught me. But that's really life in a nutshell. We do best at things we have a genuine interest in, not those that are spoon-fed to us.

Brittney's assessment of the educational system she inhabited was both accurate and incisive. Although Brittney's teachers were supportive of her computer-based learning activities and had even chosen her to attend a summer institute computer-based communication class, many of her online literacy practices remained invisible to the instructors with whom she worked on a daily basis. This was true, at least in part, because many of these online literacy activities fell outside the relatively narrow bandwidth of the conventional practices her teachers recognized as literate behavior.

None of Brittney's teachers, for instance, realized that her extensive exchanges 20 in chat rooms helped to define her attitude toward face-to-face conversations and her sophisticated ear for nuance in verbal exchanges. Similarly, Brittney's developing understanding of visual literacy was generally invisible to her high school teachers, as were her digital composing efforts that combined both alphabetic and visual elements. As a result, only Brittney herself knew how much her online activities—for instance, her growing understanding of visual design—had begun to contribute to the success of her conventional alphabetic assignments. As she explained:

> [L]ately . . . I've realized that the aesthetic quality and layout of a Web site greatly determines its credibility and effectiveness . . . I think cleanliness, readable fonts,

and professional-looking graphics are very important. . . . It is important to "read" graphics and understand the relationship between text and how it is displayed (i.e., bold text = main idea, small text = footnote). . . .

When I write conventional texts, I . . . use visual layouts to contribute to the true message of my writing.

Given her situation, by the time she entered high school, Brittney became 21 quite adept at leading a double life in terms of her literacy practices and values. For most of her academic classes, to please her teachers, she composed what she called "conventional" texts like the following essay entitled "Schindler's List." But to challenge herself and to engage in the literacy practices she knew would matter most to her when she graduated, she designed her school's Web site and created visual PowerPoint texts like "Honduras 2001," about a social action project she undertook with members of her church (see Figs. 3 and 4).

The Case Study of Charles Jackson

Born on October 23, 1985, to a White mother and a Black father, Charles 22 Jackson lived in Salt Lake City, Utah, until his family moved to Georgia, and later came to settle in Greenwood, South Carolina. The oldest of five children, Charles lives at home with his four younger sisters and his parents.

Charles' mother and father, both of whom left college to care for their chil- 23 dren, have always valued reading and writing within their home. His mother, Charles noted, likes

. . . to write stories and stuff like that. . . . My mom reads all the time. In fact my dad gets mad at her sometimes because she reads so much. . . . Whenever I have a book report for school my mom makes me read the book to her. She doesn't trust me to read it by myself so she does that to make sure that I get my readings done.

His father, explained Charles,

. . . likes to read science fiction and stuff . . . [but] my dad does . . . everything on the computer. He reads on the computer. He watches TV on the computer. He looks up stuff on the Internet. He likes to read books and stuff about his games on the computer. . . . His favorite game is "Home World"; you might have heard of it. He likes that game a lot. He buys books and books on that game. He really likes it.

. . . I think he uses computers for his job . . . I think he orders parts or something like that for Lockheed Martin. He uses computers . . . to order parts and look up prices and stuff like that.

Raised in a home environment where his mother and father valued and practiced multiple forms of literacy, and in multiple environments, Charles learned how to read and write online about the same time he learned to read and write in print:

I think I was like four or five years old. I couldn't write well, but I could read. I remember reading Mercer Meyer. . . . My parents helped me learn to read, and my teachers helped me learn to write.

Brittney Moraski
February 13, 2002
Schindler's List   English, Book Report

Schindler's List, a novel by Thomas Keneally, prevails in its account of the Holocaust and Oskar Schindler's uncanny heroism. The novel fails, however, to convey the very human and personal suffering of European Jewry at the hands of the Nazis. *Schindler's List* presents a cut-and-dry recitation of the tragedies of the Holocaust and does not leave the reader with a strong sense of personal loss at its conclusion. The author's use of complex and, at times, incorrect sentences detracts from the story and makes it difficult to read. The faults of the novel, however, disappear in Steven Spielberg's film adaptation of *Schindler's List*. The movie presents the horrors of the Holocaust visually, and most importantly, poignantly. While Spielberg's film captures an essence of the Holocaust that Keneally's words do not express, it is only when the movie and novel are used in concert that the history of the Holocaust is appropriately depicted.

While *Schindler's List* has considerable faults, it does present an amazing story. Keneally's cantankerous sentences may discredit the flow of the novel, but the lives of Oskar Schindler and the *Schindlerjuden* are so intriguing that the story itself remains captivating. Schindler, a Nazi Party member, used his clout and authority within the Reich to protect over a thousand Jews during the Holocaust. An important industrialist, Schindler contracted Jews, otherwise imprisoned in labor and death camps, to work in his factories under the guise that they were essential workers and that their efforts were necessary to keep up the production of German Army supplies. In his concentration camps, prisoners were cared for and fed. Schindler forbade SS guard beatings and executions of prisoners. While life in Schindler's camps was not easy, the *Schindlerjuden* (Schindler's Jews) considered them a paradise. People on Schindler's list had hope, and better yet a guarantee of a future beyond the war.

While Keneally does an impressive job telling the *Schindlerjuden's* story, his book lacks the emotional impact that most Holocaust literature possesses. Keneally's style of writing fails in describing the enormous tragedies of the Holocaust. Since a majority of the characters in *Schindler's List* survive the Nazi's Final Solution, their stories lack a certain amount of tragedy and devastation. Readers of the novel are not adequately exposed to the brutality and atrocities present throughout the Holocaust, and, consequently, are not left with a sense of personal grief or loss at the novel's end.

The film version of *Schindler's List*, directed by Steven Spielberg, debuted in 1993. The three-hour video was a winner of seven Academy Awards, including Best Picture and Best Director, and was considered by many to be one of the greatest films of all time. Spielberg's video succeeds in its portrayal of the Holocaust because it uses imagery to make its impact. Spielberg's *Schindler's List* brings the chilling anti-Semitic jeers of village children and the brutality and sheer iniquity of SS guards to the screen. The palpable horror and grief in Jewish families becomes heart-wrenchingly real in the video, and history, however distant, supercedes time and exposes the physical agony of those affected by the Holocaust.

The whole of *Schindler's List* is more than the sum of a moving novel or a cinematic piece of art. Together, the novel and video complement each other, preserving a wide breadth of the Holocaust for future generations to learn and grow from. With the gravity of its subject matter. *Schindler's List*, as a novel and a movie, stands as a testimony, a written and visual witness, to what cannot be forgotten.

Figure 3 **"Schindler's List."**

Created by Brittney Moraski
brittney_moraski@yahoo.com

Honduras 2001
The Experience for a
Lifetime

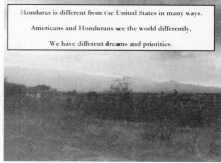

Honduras is different from the United States in many ways.

Americans and Hondurans see the world differently.

We have different dreams and priorities.

We may be very different, but we are also very much alike.

Wealthy or struggling, American or Honduran, I believe everyone experiences the same joys and sorrows that make us all human.

Although this Honduran school is primitive and rundown, the students are lucky to attend.

30% of Honduran children do not go beyond the 6th grade.

Many Honduran children never attend school.

Without education, mothers raise their children in plastic shacks, and without education, their children are just as likely to raise their children the same way.

We are so lucky and that seems horribly unfair.

Why should I be able to throw my lunch away when a little girl in Honduras is always hungry?

It wasn't easy being a volunteer in Honduras.

Most of the time, I just wanted to go home.

Now that I'm back in America, I realize my time in Honduras was very special.

It showed me that *I* could do something to improve the world.

Figure 4 **"Honduras 2001."**

. . . the first time I remember using computers [was] when I was four years old.
. . . I went to this dude's house. I think he was a friend of my dad. We went down
in his basement, and he had computer stuff everywhere, on the walls and everywhere. We took some parts home and set them up. We had this little bitty screen
with two colors. You know, green and black. You could type stuff in it. That was
about it. Couldn't run games on it.

I took a book from the library and I would try to type it. I tried to learn the
shift key and the caps lock key. I remember I wrote like one sentence and it took
me an hour. I was about five. My dad told me how to use the shift key. And for a
while all my letters were capitalized because I didn't know how not to.

Charles continued to practice literacy in both computer-based and print- 24
based environments as he grew up. In print environments, he developed a taste
for comic books—*Ghost Rider, The Incredible Hulk,* and *Captain America*—
and a strong preference for historical books and biographies rather than novels.
In electronic environments, Charles developed an early love of gaming, spending hours with early games like *PacMan, Asteroids,* and *Superman.* Charles
also tried out other gaming systems and became especially fond of role-playing
environments. As he remembered his initial gaming experiences:

I had the first *Ultima* game and it was tight. There was a little itty bitty dude wan-
dering around with a little horse and tiny dots on the screen for the village. Later
I got into flight simulators like the Red *Baron.* Then as games got more advanced
I moved on to new games like *Tomb Raider* and all those games.

Then we went on to the 32 to 64 bit era . . . I played *Crash Bandicoot* and
Final Fantasy. I have the original *Final Fantasy* . . . it's rated M but I don't care.
It's about this dude who has two guns and a sword. The sword is huge; it looks
like a buster sword. It is so cool.

Charles' father encouraged his son's interest in online environments and
worked with him to build computers out of the spare parts that littered the
family's basement. The pair then shared the machines with the rest of the family through a trickle-down system. "Now I have my own computer," Charles
noted. "It is actually my dad's old computer. The one in my sisters' room is my
old computer. When my dad gets an upgrade, I get his old one and my sisters
get mine."

In academic settings, however, particularly in elementary school, Charles 25
had considerably less access to computers. Although his school did acquire
a computer lab when he was in the second grade, Charles had only minimal
access to these machines and limited help from teachers in learning to use
them. When his instructors did integrate computers into their classroom work,
they focused on conventional, alphabetic literacy:

I had about an hour a week [on the computers]. [And], if I was lucky I could
[also] use them for 10 minutes before recess. . . .

The teachers helped me learn about computers, but I don't think they really
knew what they were doing. They were new to computers like we were. They
helped us out by encouraging us to use them and to help us learn to read and

write with them. . . .They taught us to use word processors and encyclopedias on computers.

Confronted by such limitations at school, Charles continued to develop an increasingly broad range of online literacies at home. In this effort, he was particularly motivated by his continued interest in computer gaming:

> If you don't know how to read and write then you are going to have trouble using computers, but they can help you read and write better. Say you want to play games. You are going to have to learn how to read in order to play the games. You have to read on the screen what the menus say.

Charles' gaming activities not only encouraged his reading but his composing skills, as well:

> I do a lot of computer coding. Mostly C++ stuff. I do a lot of writing for my games. I try to come up with ideas. I just sit down and try to come up with ideas. Often I will write down a plot or [try] different methods of coding to get a camera angle to work or a certain character to move, stuff like that.

In the gaming environments he frequented, Charles, like Dànielle, also became adept at reading and interpreting imaginary scenarios, composing the exchanges of characters and gamers within such environments, and responding to the complex situations that games depicted. As he explained:

26

> [Y]ou need to learn to read between the lines. You need to know the right things to say to people and how to communicate with them. You need to know how to develop friendships. It is important to read between the lines so that you can know what people want you to do and how to go about doing it.

As Charles became increasingly adept at both gaming and game design, he also learned to read the texts of the games themselves—figuring out the grammars, or rule sets, that shaped his interaction with these dynamic environments and acquiring the kinesthetic, intercultural, and problem-solving literacies that the games demanded:

> I think with playing games there is a grammar. Games have different genres just like books do. So when you pick up a game of a certain genre you kind of expect to know how to play that game. Say you pick up an action game you kind of expect, say you expect Mario to move around in certain ways. You expect certain controls to be there and when they are not there then you get confused, because the grammar is not complete in that game or is not what you are expecting. The way controls are used, the menus that are used, the terms, the buttons that are used. You see—like for example the Final Fantasy series—in *Final Fantasy VII,* the button that you use is X. Well in *Final Fantasy VIII* it is O. . . . The Japanese games use the O button and the American games use X for everything.
>
> I think that the main skill that I've learned is puzzle solving. Take *Tomb Raider.* Despite the pretty girl, it is a puzzle-solving game. So you have to figure how to move the blocks to fit a certain square, how to swing across the rope a certain way, and how to make all the pieces fit just right. What I eventually learned to do,

is after about level three I learned how to put the puzzles together and learned what to expect in the game—especially in *Tomb Raider 2.*

In the gaming chat rooms that he frequented online, Charles, like Dànielle, 27 honed his rhetorical skills, not only with people from the United States, but with gamers from other countries as well:

> You have to be courteous. You have to know how to read and write well because people get really annoyed if you are like, "I want to learn how to make a game. How do I do this?" . . . Like some guy from Yugoslavia comes on, and you can hardly tell what he is saying. But I don't feel so bad trying to help them . . . because they can't really help it. English isn't their language. A lot of the people I speak with don't know English that well. You have to be understanding of that. Half the people on there speak German. . . .
>
> I learned to be considerate of people to make sure that I get the respect that I get as well as being respectful to others. You know the old Golden Rule thing. Make sure that you don't put people down. Like if someone thinks they have a great idea and it really isn't you should tell them that it is and then give them constructive criticism on how to make it better. Like some people on there are like, "Oh man that sucks! You shouldn't be out here!" And that just isn't right because everybody is learning how to do new things. Everyone was like that at one point. Calm down a little bit, and let them do it. If you like turn away everybody when they are just learning how to do something, then no one will want to do it again.

If his teachers didn't always recognize that the literacy skills he acquired in the problem-solving environments of online games transferred productively to the more conventional literacy tasks he was assigned in school, Charles certainly appreciated this fact himself:

> Well, playing games has taught me about writing because a lot of games are like problem solving. . . . When you are making a computer game you have to think about everything and what can go wrong, what you are forgetting. And that has helped me in writing because it's the same thing when I am composing a paper for a teacher. I have to think of everything that I am writing, and everything that I can do to make it better and everything that I have done that might make it wrong. Might make it not work or flow correctly. . . .
>
> Games have taught me how to use menus. Lots of games make you apply patches. That forces you to use your computer, set up things and install programs. Video games are good with new technologies anyway, so when I look at a game I can look at how it was made and use the same technologies in my own games.

Charles' online experiences also helped him develop an increasingly keen set of visual literacy skills. As he noted:

> [On my Web site] I have to make sure that the images express what I want them to. I have to make sure that it is accessible, and that it will work on other computers. You have to make sure that you don't just use text. Like if you go to a Web site it is nothing but text then you are like text, text, text, text. If you have an

image then you are like, Oh, that's what that means. This is especially true with video. Video tutorials are great to teach you how to like make models or something. They show you like what button to push and how to do things.

. . . I visualize what I am writing. Like in a story. You have to be able to visualize or write things down so that you can make sure you have all your thoughts straight; then you will know that your story won't be messed up. You won't say that he was born in like 1965 and that he is 70 years old. Because I have done that before.

As a result of his own literacy work online, Charles had definite ideas of what coming generations of students, like his younger sisters, should be learning in school. The literacy curriculum he imagined for the future was focused around problem solving in online environments and developing visual as well as alphabetic literacy. As he explained: 28

> Children watch cable right? They watch Nickelodeon right? Well next thing they see is a commercial for Nick.com and the next thing you know your sisters are all in your room playing games from Nick.com
>
> The Internet is just like everywhere. Students are going to have to know how to do it. It is going to be required. They will have to do a lot of projects using stuff from the Internet. They will have to get pictures off the Internet and stuff like that. Read maps on the Internet and stuff like that.
>
> I would include like the history of icons. How they went back to the Byzantine Empire, the Roman Catholics when the church split. How to look at icons and know what they mean without words Like that Nike symbol. I betcha every kid in South Carolina knows what that Nike symbol means because it is on all their shoes and clothes. Which icons are more recognizable? Which icons [do] teens recognize the most? And which [do] they recognize the least? And how [do] advertisers use this to create their slogans and stuff? I d probably teach them how to create symbols for emotions, new symbols, not the smiley face. And then [we'd] see how easily other students could identify the symbols. That would be interesting.

We've included here a screen shot of the splash page of Charles's Web site, but the image alone doesn't begin to do justice to the expertise he demonstrates in online game-design.[1] At this site, which opens on a splash page dominated by a menacing warrior in black, a character of his own creation, Charles introduces *The Quest of the Golden Fleece*, a game that he began designing after encountering the story of Jason and the Argonauts in his English class at Berea High School. Charles describes his game with some pride in the site's introduction: 29

> *The Quest of the Golden Fleece* is a real-time, 3-D, action FPG that is set in ancient mythological time: It has been in development for almost a year, and it is looking promising. The game is run on the Genesis3d engine, which rivals that of Half-Life and Quake engines.

---

[1]An example of Charles' expertise in online game-design environments can be experienced at http://www.geocities.com/charliensane in which he presents "The Quest of the Golden Fleece: Live the Myth" (Jackson, 2002).

Figure 5

The Quest of the Golden Fleece is absolutely immersing. You can travel about the known world seeking out treasures or discovering new peoples. You can move through vast ancient cities communicating with townspeople, buying and selling goods, or being a gladiator in the many coliseums. You are Jason who must find the Golden Fleece so he can take the town of Thebes back from his evil Uncle Pelias. The gods play a major part in the journey as they may help or hurt you. The game allows you to choose which path you wish to take while maintaining a . . . flowing story line.

The Web site that Charles has constructed around this complex and intriguing game includes extensive sections entitled "screenshots," "game-play," "characters," and "tutorials," all composed by Charles. These sections, richly illustrated with colorful computer-based images and animations that Charles has created, are rife with allusions, both to the classical text of the *Odyssey* and to the classical texts of the online gaming world—the *Legacy of Kain* series, for example, with *Soul Reaver 2* among them.[2] With his creation of *The Quest of the Golden Fleece*, Charles has transformed the conventional literacy instruction that he was provided in his high school English class into the kind of digital literacy practices that he values outside of school and that he sees as integral to his success in the future.

The Future of Literacy Studies in a Changing World

The four people in this chapter have all been, and in the cases of Brittney and 30
Charles continue to be, not only insightful students of the new media but also excellent students in general. With a great deal of support from their parents and teachers, they have all developed considerable skill and success in conventional

---

[2] These games can be accessed on the Web. See http://www.legacyofkain.com/ for *The Legacy of Kain* and http://www.eidosinteractive.com/gss/legacy/legacyofkain/main.html for *Soul Reaver*.

educational settings and literacy environments. They make good grades, they write and read conventional materials with facility, and they have graduated, or will graduate, without difficulty, from the institutions they attended. If these students themselves have been successful, however, the formal literacy instruction they received may have been less so. Their teachers prepared them well for a world of print-based, alphabetic literacy, but these instructors provided very little official instruction or systematic guidance in those literacies that lay outside this very narrow bandwidth. In contrast, it is clear that Dànielle and Joseph, along with Brittney and Charles, consider the reading and composing skills they acquired informally in electronic environments—literacies marked by the kinesthetic, the visual, the navigational, the intercultural; by a robust combination of code, image, sound, animation, and words—to be far more compelling, far more germane to their future success than the more traditional literacy instruction they have received in school.

This response should not surprise us. More than 30 years ago, in her book 31 *Culture and Commitment,* Margaret Mead (1970) argued that the kind of educational efforts children found most valuable in preparing them to function successfully as adults depended, to a great extent, on the changes happening in the culture around them.[3] In stable cultures that changed slowly, Mead explained, students valued an education that passed along traditionally based knowledge from an adult-teacher who knew, from experience, how to handle many of the challenges that students would encounter later in life. In less stable cultures, however, cultures characterized by rapid change and disruption, by the "development of new forms of technology in which the old are not expert"

---

[3] In her 1970 book, *Culture and Commitment,* Mead describes three different cultural styles, distinguished by the ways in which children are prepared for adulthood. The first, the "postfigurative," characterizes societies in which change is largely imperceptible and the "future repeats the past." In such cultures, adults are able to pass along the necessary knowledge to children. "The essential characteristic of post-figurative cultures," Mead maintained, "is the assumption, expressed by members of the older generation in their every act, that their way of life (however many changes may, in fact, be embodied in it) is unchanging, eternally the same" (p. 14). Education within such cultures privileges the passing down of traditional values and knowledge through an adult teacher.

The second of Mead's styles, that characterizing "configurative" cultures, arises when some form of disruption is experienced by a society. In this kind of culture, young people look to their contemporaries for guidance in making choices rather than relying on their elders for expertise and role models in a changing world.

A third, and final, cultural style—which Mead terms the "prefigurative"—is symptomatic of a world changing so fast that it exists "without models and without precedent" (p. xx). In prefigurative cultures, change is so rapid that "neither parents nor teachers, lawyers, doctors, skilled workers, inventors, preachers, or prophets" (p. xx) can teach children what they need to know about the world. The prefigurative cultural style, Mead argues, prevails in a world where the "past, the culture that had shaped [young adults'] understanding—their thoughts, their feelings, and their conceptions of the world—was no sure guide to the present. And the elders among them, bound to the past, [can] provide no models for the future" (p. 70).

In the prefigurative culture of the 21st century, then, it is little wonder that most adults have limited success in predicting the changes happening around them, in anticipating and coping with the world as it morphs through successive and confusing new forms. Similarly, it is little wonder that English composition instructors, and most writing programs, have had limited success in predicting and understanding the importance of visual, spatial, and multimodal literacies.

(p. 39), young people no longer have the luxury of relying solely on the information provided by their elders to equip them for a changing world. Instead, they depended on the help of their peers and on their own efforts to figure out the skills they needed in the coming years.

Within this context, it is useful to think about the kind of world, and the 32 pace of change, that confronts Dànielle, Joseph, Brittney, and Charles. When Dànielle and Joseph were born, in 1973, for instance, personal computers had not been invented, nor had any modern computer networks been established. By the time they turned 10, however, Queen Elizabeth had sent her first e-mail message, and France had deployed the Minitel network to millions of its citizens. This rapid pace of change was to continue. By the time Dànielle and Joseph turned 20, and Brittney and Charles had begun attending first grade, both the Internet and the World Wide Web had been invented, and the World Bank and the United Nations had already established their own Web sites. Within another seven years, as Dànielle and Joseph were thinking about their graduate careers, and Brittney and Charles were making their way through secondary school in the year 2000, more than 93 million Internet host systems had been registered and the World Wide Web had reached a size of more than 1 billion indexible pages.[4]

By 2003, as Brittney and Charles were well into their high school careers, 33 and Dànielle and Joseph were embarking on their professional careers, over half a billion people across the world had access to the Internet. A global snapshot at this time would show that among the countries of Europe, Germany, the United Kingdom, and Italy had the largest populations of people who access the Internet at home, and that the United States constitutes 29% of the global Internet, with Europe reporting 23%, Asia-Pacific 13%, and South America 2% ("Global Net Population Increases," 2003). It's also interesting to note that a recent Harris survey (HarrisInteractive, 2002) found that 93% of college students in the United States regularly use the Internet, making them the most connected segment of the U.S. population (92% of them say they own computers).[5]

None of these facts would surprise the four participants we have profiled 34 in this chapter. Nor would they be surprised to learn that the United States Army had already designed and built a multimillion dollar simulation facility in which to hold virtual war games or that the Bankers Trust Corporation in New

---

[4] These markers of Internet development and many others can be found in *Hobbes' Internet Timeline,* compiled by Robert H. Zakon (1993–2003). Hobbes' timeline chronicles the growth of the Internet from 1993 to 2003, focusing primarily on the development of hardware, software, and networking systems. This timeline and others can be accessed from the Web site of the Internet Society at http://info.isoc .org/internet/history/.

[5] Here's the information Harris Interactive gives about the study:

The 360 Youth/Harris Interactive College Explorer™ Outlook Study is an online college survey from 360 Youth, Inc. and Harris Interactive. The study covers a variety of topics about the 18–30-year-old college market, from market power and influence, technology adoption and attitudes, to category penetration and spending.

York City had designed and used an online fantasy game, much like *Doom* or *Myst*, to provide corporate training on sexual harassment to its employees in the 1990s (Dillon, 1998). Indeed, it can be argued that Dànielle and Joseph, Brittney and Charles already know a great deal about the world for which they were preparing themselves and a great deal about the specific skills they would need in order to function as literate citizens and productive employees in this changing online world.

These four cases document in very personal terms the dynamic culture of 21st century life in the United States. Dànielle and Joseph, Brittney and Charles live in a very different world from the one inhabited by their parents and teachers. In this environment, the literacy education that teachers and parents provided to students a decade or a century ago will no longer do to equip people for success; too many major changes have altered our world in unexpected ways. Nation states previously isolated by impermeable borders have entered into geopolitical, monetary, trade, and environmental alliances that function regionally and globally. As the influence of nation states gives way, faster transportation, extended computer networks, and almost instantaneous communications systems support the exchange of information and people on a global scale. These transnational patterns, in addition, support the establishment of multiple and overlapping global authorities—The World Trade Organization, the World Bank, the United Nations—that extend people's understanding of political, economic, and social roles beyond the physical borders of their home countries.

These postmodern changes can be disorienting. As Manuel Castells (1997) points out, when power is "diffused in global networks of power, information, and images" (p. 359), disassociated with conventional centralized authorities like geographically determined nation states, social roles, political alliances, and traditional systems of authoritative values, people often feel alienated, fragmented, confronted with a disturbing loss of traditional authorities or conventional certainties.[6] But even as people are confronted by unstable and contradictory postmodern contexts, as Castells (1997) points out, they are also coping strategically with them as social and political agents. Increasingly, these groups and individuals assemble and communicate online, within the very computer networks that contributed to the unstable conditions in the first place. In such environments, for example, people like to participate in a new kind of identity politics anchored by the powerful connections of race, gender, history, and common interests, forming interest groups; political action groups; and groups focused on feminist, environmental, religious, or race issues. They also participate in social groups online, groups formed around

---

[6] In his outstanding series of three volumes, entitled *The Information Age: Economy, Society, and Culture* (1996, 1997, 1998), sociologist Manuel Castells charted the world-order transformations associated with the rise of the information age on a global level. Among the effects of these transformations are the decline of conventional centralized authorities like geographically determined nation states, political alliances, and traditional systems of authoritative values; and the increase of online criminal and terrorist activities. Castells also traced the emergence of identity politics online, especially groups focused on race, gender, history, and language issues.

gaming, dating, chatting about genealogy, films, or music. More important, Castells (1997) noted, as people exchange ideas in such groups—and often take action collectively—they are also involved in contesting, negotiating, and rewriting the new "social codes" under which societies will be "rethought, and re-established" in the coming decades (p. 360).

Literacy practices, it is clear, change dramatically within such online environ- 37 ments; texts must be able to cross national borders, time zones, language groups, and geographic distances; to resist the limitations of a single symbolic system and its attendant conventions.[7] They must communicate on multiple channels, using visual, aural, and kinesthetic elements as well as alphabetic components. To increase their effectiveness, such compositions may also become highly inter-textual in terms of their resonance across media boundaries, as Diana George and Diane Shoos (1999) point out. Frequently, for instance, such texts bring communicative elements from television and movies to bear on the related texts of advertisements or games, thus establishing a network of meanings that play off of one another and gain strength from their cumulative allusions, much like what Charles described happening with Nickelodeon or the Nike icon. In such a world, it is of little wonder that Dànielle and Joseph, Brittney and Charles found their formal English composition instruction to be of limited interest. As with most contemporary writing instruction now offered in schools, their work in these classes focused on informative, technical, or creative writing, and it fell almost exclusively within the narrow bandwidth of the alphabetic. The skills they developed in these classes, although useful in some arenas, are not fully capable of preparing young people for a world that will depend on visual lit-eracy, web literacy, gaming/simulation literacy, in short, multimodal literacies.

At the same time, within this dynamic environment, the self-sponsored lit- 38 eracy skills that Dànielle and Joseph, Brittney and Charles have developed online assume new currency and new importance. In a world dominated by computer networks that extend across language and cultural borders, busi-ness and industry, governments and organizations, individuals and groups have already begun to understand and value the visual literacy skills that Joseph has developed. Similarly, the coding and web-design literacy that Dànielle has acquired; the online language studies in which Brittney participates; and the collaborative problem-solving and gaming literacy that Charles has pursued have become increasingly valuable skills within new online environments.

These abilities represent the new literacy practices and values that educa- 39 tors must begin to recognize and integrate into formal classroom instruction if the United States and other countries hope to prepare citizens who can func-tion effectively in the online communication environments that characterize

---

[7] The excellent work of The New London Group makes an eloquent case for multiliteracies in a world characterized by online communications that must cut across traditional geopolitical, linguistic, and cultural borders. We recommend the 1996 *Harvard Educational Review* article entitled "A Pedagogy of Multiliteracies" and the 2000 volume, *Multiliteracies,* edited by Bill Cope and Mary Kalantzis for The New London Group. Additionally, the valuable work of Gunther Kress (1999), " 'English' at the Cross-roads," made a closely related case for teachers of English composition.

the 21st century. To accomplish this task, educators, certainly those who teach English composition only in its more conventional forms, will need to change their attitudes about literacy in general, and they will need additional technology resources so that they can work more closely with students to learn about the new, self-sponsored media literacies these youngsters are developing and practicing online. Among these resources will be regularly updated computers and software, adequately wired school and university buildings with connections to the Internet, help from knowledgeable technical staff members, and additional professional development aimed at new-media education.

Teachers armed with these resources can then work collaboratively with   40
students to develop meaningful assignments that will bring new literacies into composition classrooms in ways that both engage and challenge contemporary learners. For example, although students like Brittney and Charles have a great deal of situated practice with new-media literacies, they both need more overt instruction to be able to articulate the various rules and conventions adhering to specific kinds of communications within different cultural contexts. These young people also need help in framing their understandings critically so that they can question their own judgment and look at their work from the perspectives of audiences increasingly different from themselves. Finally, these students need a teacher's help in learning how to transform their practices—to transfer their knowledge of new-media literacies into other contexts, cultures, or areas of endeavor.[8]

Within such an environment, teachers could pay increased attention to the   41
new-media literacies students bring to the classroom, comparing these literacies to more conventional literacies and seeking to learn from this comparison more about the worlds that students inhabit and believe they will face in the coming years. Students would be able to take advantage or their teachers' perspectives, enhancing their new-media practices in ways that they might not accomplish on their own. With a range of emerging, competing, and conventional literacies in play, and with both teachers and students focused on how to meet the needs of different audiences, how to communicate information in a variety of formats, and how to accomplish their communicative purposes most effectively within a full range of media contexts, classrooms might become more like the places we all wish they would be: vigorous teaching and learning environments, characterized, as educator Paulo Freire (1990) suggested, by a kind of reciprocal learning in which

> . . . the teacher-of-the-students and the students-of-the-teacher cease to exist and a new term emerges: teacher-students with students-teachers . . . They become jointly responsible for a process in which all grow. (p. 67)

---

[8] The pedagogical framework we outline here, and the terms we employ, are those of The New London Group. In the groundbreaking book *Multiliteracies*, edited by Bill Cope and Mary Kalantzis (2000), these scholars lay out a multiliteracies pedagogy that relies on four broad approaches to instruction: situated practice, overt instruction, critical framing, and transformed practice (pp. 239–248).

References

Bolter, Jay David. (1991). *Writing space: The computer, hypertext and the history of writing*. Hillsdale, NJ: Lawrence Erlbaum Associates.

Castells, Manuel. (1996). *The rise of the network society* (Vol. 1 in *The information age: Economy, society, and culture*). Malden, MA: Blackwell.

Castells, Manuel. (1997). *The power of identity* (Vol. 2 in *The information age: Economy, society, and culture*). Malden, MA: Blackwell.

Castells, Manuel. (1998). *End of the millennium* (Vol. 3 in *The information age: Economy, society, and culture*). Malden, MA: Blackwell.

Cope, Bill, & Kalantzis, Mary. (Eds.). (2000). *Multiliteracies: Literacy learning and the design of social futures*. London: Routledge.

Dillon, Nancy. (1998, September 25). *Games make training child's play*. Computer World site. Retrieved May 2, 2003, from http://www.computerworld.com/news/1998/story/511280, 26370,00.html

Freire, Paulo. (1990), *Pedagogy of the oppressed* (Myra Bergman Ramos, Trans.). New York: The Continuum Publishing Company.

George, Diana, & Shoos, Diane. (1999). Dropping bread crumbs in the intertextual forest: Critical literacy in a postmodern age. In Gail E. Hawisher & Cynthia L. Selfe (Eds.), *Passions, pedagogies, and 21st century technologies* (pp. 115–126). Logan: Utah State University Press.

Global Net population increases. (2003, February 25). Retrieved May 2, 2003, from http:// www .nua.ie/surveys/?f=VS&art_id=905358729&rel=true

HarrisInteractive. (2002, July 29). College students spend $200 billion per year. Retrieved May 1, 2003, from http://www.harrisinteractive.com/news/allnewsbydate.asp? NewsID=480

Jackson, Charles. (2002). The quest of the Golden Fleece: Live the myth. Retrieved May 1, 2003, from http://www.geocities.com/charliensane

Kress, Gunther. (1999). 'English' at the crossroads: Rethinking curricula of communication in the context of the turn to the visual. In Gail E. Hawisher & Cynthia L. Selfe (Eds.), *Passions, pedagogies, and 21st century technologies* (pp. 66–88). Logan: Utah State University Press.

Mead, Margaret. (1970). *Culture and commitment: The new relationships between the generations in the 1970s*. Garden City, NY: Doubleday.

Zakon, Robert H. (1993–2003). *Hobbes' Internet timeline, v6.0*. Retrieved April 21, 2003, at the Web site of the Internet Society at http://info.asoc.org/internet/history/

Questions for Discussion and Journaling

1. Compare your own literacy influences to the literacy influences of each of the four case studies. Which case study do you most relate to? Why?

2. What do the writers mean when they argue that we "compose meaning not only with words, but also with digitized bits of video, sound, photographs, still images, words, and animations" (see para. 2)?

3. How do we "compose" meaning? List all the kinds of composing you do that includes more than words. Which do you find most satisfying? Why?

4. The authors argue that Dànielle DeVoss learned literacy skills such as "visual, kinesthetic, and interactive components of gaming" (see para. 6) through her participation in computer games. Do you agree that these skills are, in fact, literacy skills? Why or why not?

5. Joseph Johansen's and Brittney Moraski's schools did not integrate the kinds of visual and computer literacies that interested them, forcing them to work on art and computers outside of class. Do you think schools should integrate more visual and technical literacies? If so, how might they do this? If not, why not?

6. Consider how visual and technical literacies have been integrated into your own schooling, if in fact they have been. How do your in-school experiences compare to your experiences with technical and visual literacies outside of school?

Applying and Exploring Ideas

1. Write a letter to your college or university president arguing for what you think should be the place of visual and technical literacies in your curriculum. Be sure to make clear claims and back them with evidence and examples.

2. Consider the strengths and weaknesses of conventional print texts as compared with texts that utilize new media. What would this article (or this textbook) be like as a DVD or an interactive hypertext? How might it have been structured? What might have been included or left out?

Meta Moment

Which of the learning goals for this chapter would you *not* have accomplished if you had not read this piece?

From Pencils to Pixels:
The Stages of Literacy Technologies

DENNIS BARON

Baron, Dennis. "From Pencils to Pixels: The Stages of Literacy Technologies." *Passions, Pedagogies, and 21st Century Technologies*. Ed. Gail Hawisher and Cynthia Selfe. Logan: Utah State UP, 1999. 15–33. Print.

Framing the Reading

Dennis Baron is a linguist who has studied **literacy**, communication technologies, and the laws countries make about language use (like making English the "official" language of the United States). In this essay, which developed material he later used in his 2009 book *A Better Pencil: Readers, Writers, and the Digital Revolution*, Baron examines the history of a few writing technologies that we are unlikely to even recognize *as* "technology" anymore. In thinking, for example, about how pencils were once state-of-the-art technology, Baron suggests that writing was never *not* technological, that every writing technology has taken time to become established, and that writing technologies must be learned.

Baron's work raises more questions than it answers, but in doing so it shows us how comparatively limited the research is at the intersection of technology and literacy. According to Baron, literacy researchers have largely failed to understand writing *as a technology*; as a result, he argues, they haven't really understood what we're actually doing when we write. In using historical explanations and discussion of writing tools that many of us no longer recognize as technological to begin with, Baron raises interesting questions about the future of writing. What will happen when the computers we use now are no longer really recognized as "unnatural" technologies? How will that altered perception influence how we write?

Getting Ready to Read

Before you read, do at least one of the following activities:

- Write your own definition of "technology," and provide some examples. What kinds of things count as technology, and what don't?
- Make a quick list of all the technologies you use for writing.

- Talk with a parent or grandparent about what writing technologies were dominant when they were in school. How do those technologies compare with the ones you use today?

As you read, consider the following questions:

- For Baron, what counts as a technology?
- How do literacy technologies empower some people and disempower others?
- What does Baron seem to want us to learn from his work?
- How does the authenticity Baron talks about relate to literacy?

The computer, the latest development in writing technology, promises, or threatens, to change literacy practices for better or worse, depending on your point of view. For many of us, the computer revolution came long ago, and it has left its mark on the way we do things with words. We take word processing as a given. We don't have typewriters in our offices anymore, or pencil sharpeners, or even printers with resolutions less than 300 dpi. We scour *MacUser* and *PC World* for the next software upgrade, cheaper RAM, faster chips, and the latest in connectivity. We can't wait for the next paradigm shift. Computerspeak enters ordinary English at a rapid pace. In 1993, "the information superhighway" was voted the word—actually the phrase—of the year. In 1995, the word of the year was "the World Wide Web," with "morph" a close runner-up. The computer is also touted as a gateway to literacy. The Speaker of the House of Representatives suggested that inner-city school children should try laptops to improve their performance. The Governor of Illinois thinks that hooking up every school classroom to the Web will eliminate illiteracy. In his second-term victory speech, President Clinton promised to have every eight-year-old reading, and to connect every twelve-year-old to the National Information Infrastructure. Futurologists write books predicting that computers will replace books. Newspapers rush to hook online subscribers. The *New York Times* will download the Sunday crossword puzzle, time me as I fill in the answers from my keyboard, even score my results. They'll worry later about how to get me to pay for this service.

I will not join in the hyperbole of predictions about what the computer will or will not do for literacy, though I will be the first to praise computers, to acknowledge the importance of the computer in the last fifteen years of my own career as a writer, and to predict that in the future the computer will be put to communication uses we cannot now even begin to imagine, something quite beyond the word processing I'm now using to produce a fairly conventional text, a book chapter.

I readily admit my dependence on the new technology of writing. Once, called away to a meeting whose substance did not command my unalloyed attention, I began drafting on my conference pad a memo I needed to get out to my staff by lunchtime. I found that I had become so used to composing virtual prose at the keyboard I could no longer draft anything coherent directly onto a piece of paper. It wasn't so much that I couldn't think of the words, but the physical effort of handwriting, crossing out, revising, cutting and pasting (which I couldn't very well do at a meeting without giving away my inattention), in short, the writing practices I had been engaged in regularly since the age of four, now seemed to overwhelm and constrict me, and I longed for the flexibility of digitized text.

When we write with cutting-edge tools, it is easy to forget that whether it consists of energized particles on a screen or ink embedded in paper or lines gouged into clay tablets, writing itself is always first and foremost a technology, a way of engineering materials in order to accomplish an end. Tied up as it is with value-laden notions of literacy, art, and science, of history and psychology, of education, of theory, and of practicality, we often lose sight of writing as technology, until, that is, a new technology like the computer comes along and we are thrown into excitement and confusion as we try it on, try it out, reject it, and then adapt it to our lives—and of course, adapt our lives to it.

> Whether it consists of energized particles on a screen or ink embedded in paper or lines gouged into clay tablets, writing itself is always first and foremost a technology, a way of engineering materials in order to accomplish an end.

4

New communications technologies, if they catch on, go through a number of strikingly similar stages. After their invention, their spread depends on accessibility, function, and authentication. Let me first summarize what I mean, and then I'll present some more detailed examples from the history of writing or literacy technologies to illustrate. 5

The Stages of Literacy Technologies

Each new literacy technology begins with a restricted communication function and is available only to a small number of initiates. Because of the high cost of the technology and general ignorance about it, practitioners keep it to themselves at first—either on purpose or because nobody else has any use for it—and then, gradually, they begin to mediate the technology for the general public. The technology expands beyond this "priestly" class when it is adapted to familiar functions often associated with an older, accepted form of communication. As costs decrease and the technology becomes better able to mimic more ordinary or familiar communications, a new literacy spreads across a population. Only then does the technology come into its own, no longer imitating the previous forms given us by the earlier communication technology, but creating new forms and new possibilities for communication. Moreover, in a kind of backward wave, the new technology begins to affect older technologies as well. 6

While brave new literacy technologies offer new opportunities for produc-   7
ing and manipulating text, they also present new opportunities for fraud. And
as the technology spreads, so do reactions against it from supporters of what
are purported to be older, simpler, better, or more honest ways of writing. Not
only must the new technology be accessible and useful, it must demonstrate
its trustworthiness as well. So procedures for authentication and reliability
must be developed before the new technology becomes fully accepted. One
of the greatest concerns about computer communications today involves their
authentication and their potential for fraud.

My contention in this essay is a modest one: the computer is simply the lat-   8
est step in a long line of writing technologies. In many ways its development
parallels that of the pencil—hence my title—though the computer seems more
complex and is undoubtedly more expensive. The authenticity of pencil writing
is still frequently questioned: we prefer that signatures and other permanent
or validating documents be in ink. Although I'm not aware that anyone actually opposed the use of pencils when they began to be used for writing, other
literacy technologies, including writing itself, were initially met with suspicion
as well as enthusiasm.

Humanists and Technology

In attacking society's growing dependence on communication technology, the   9
Unabomber (1996) targeted computer scientists for elimination. But to my
chagrin he excluded humanists from his list of sinister technocrats because he
found them to be harmless. While I was glad not to be a direct target of this
mad bomber, I admit that I felt left out. I asked myself, if humanists aren't
harmful, then what's the point of being one? But I was afraid to say anything
out loud, at least until a plausible suspect was in custody.

Humanists have long been considered out of the technology loop. They use   10
technology, to be sure, but they are not generally seen as pushing the envelope.
Most people think of writers as rejecting technological innovations like the
computer and the information superhighway, preferring instead to bang away
at manual typewriters when they are not busy whittling new points on their
no. 2 quill pens.

And it is true that some well-known writers have rejected new-fangleness.   11
Writing in the *New York Times,* Bill Henderson (1994) reminds us that in 1849
Henry David Thoreau disparaged the information superhighway of his day,
a telegraph connection from Maine to Texas. As Thoreau put it, "Maine and
Texas, it may be, have nothing important to communicate." Henderson, who
is a director of the Lead Pencil Club, a group opposed to computers and con-
vinced that the old ways are better, further boasts that Thoreau wrote his anti-
technology remarks with a pencil that he made himself. Apparently Samuel
Morse, the developer of the telegraph, was lucky that the only letter bombs
Thoreau made were literary ones.

In any case, Thoreau was not the complete Luddite that Henderson would   12
have us believe. He was, in fact, an engineer, and he didn't make pencils for the

same reason he went to live at Walden Pond, to get back to basics. Rather, he designed them for a living. Instead of waxing nostalgic about the good old days of hand-made pencils, Thoreau sought to improve the process by developing a cutting-edge manufacturing technology of his own.

The pencil may be old, but like the computer today and the telegraph in 13 1849, it is an indisputable example of a communication technology. Henderson, unwittingly concedes as much when he adds that Thoreau's father founded "the first quality pencil [factory] in America." In Thoreau's day, a good pencil was hard to find, and until Thoreau's father and uncle began making pencils in the New World, the best ones were imported from Europe. The family fortune was built on the earnings of the Thoreau Pencil Company, and Henry Thoreau not only supported his sojourn at Walden Pond and his trip to the Maine woods with pencil profits, he himself perfected some of the techniques of pencil-making that made Thoreau pencils so desirable.

The pencil may seem a simple device in contrast to the computer, but 14 although it has fewer parts, it too is an advanced technology. The engineer Henry Petroski (1990) portrays the development of the wood-cased pencil as a paradigm of the engineering process, hinging on the solution of two essential problems: finding the correct blend of graphite and clay so that the "lead" is not too soft or too brittle; and getting the lead into the cedar wood case so that it doesn't break when the point is sharpened or when pressure is applied during use. Pencil technologies involve advanced design techniques, the preparation and purification of graphite, the mixing of graphite with various clays, the baking and curing of the lead mixture, its extrusion into leads, and the preparation and finishing of the wood casings. Petroski observes that pencil making also involves a knowledge of dyes, shellacs, resins, clamps, solvents, paints, woods, rubber, glue, printing ink, waxes, lacquer, cotton, drying equipment, impregnating processes, high-temperature furnaces, abrasives, and mixing (Petroski 12). These are no simple matters. A hobbyist cannot decide to make a wood-cased pencil at home and go out to the craft shop for a set of instructions. Pencil-making processes were from the outset proprietary secrets as closely guarded as any Macintosh code.

The development of the pencil is also a paradigm of the development of lit- 15 eracy. In the two hundred fifty years between its invention, in the 1560s, and its perfection at John Thoreau and Company, as well as in the factories of Conté in France, and Staedtler and Faber in Germany, the humble wood pencil underwent several changes in form, greatly expanded its functions, and developed from a curiosity of use to cabinet-makers, artists and note-takers into a tool so universally employed for writing that we seldom give it any thought.

The Technology of Writing

Of course the first writing technology was writing itself. Just like the telegraph 16 and the computer, writing itself was once an innovation strongly resisted by traditionalists because it was unnatural and untrustworthy. Plato was one leading thinker who spoke out strongly against writing, fearing that it would weaken our memories. Pessimistic complaints about new literacy technologies, like those made by Plato, by Bill Henderson, and by Henderson's idol, Henry David Thoreau, are balanced by inflated predictions of how technologies will change our lives for the better. According to one school of anthropology, the invention of writing triggered a cognitive revolution in human development (for a critique of this so-called Great Divide theory of writing, see Street 1984). Historians of print are fond of pointing to the invention of the printing press in Europe as the second great cognitive revolution (Eisenstein 1979). The spread of electric power, the invention of radio, and later television, all promised similar bio-cultural progress. Now, the influence of computers on more and more aspects of our existence has led futurologists to proclaim that another technological threshold is at hand. Computer gurus offer us a brave new world of communications where we will experience cognitive changes of a magnitude never before known. Of course, the Unabomber and the Lead Pencil Club think otherwise.

Both the supporters and the critics of new communication technologies like to compare them to the good, or bad, old days. Jay Bolter disparages the typewriter as nothing more than a machine for duplicating texts—and as such, he argues, it has not changed writing at all. In contrast, Bolter characterizes the computer as offering a paradigm shift not seen since the invention of the printing press, or for that matter, since the invention of writing itself. But when the typewriter first began to sweep across America's offices, it too promised to change writing radically, in ways never before imagined. So threatening was the typewriter to the traditional literates that in 1938 the *New York Times* editorialized against the machine that depersonalized writing, usurping the place of "writing with one's own hand." 17

The development of writing itself illustrates the stages of technological spread. We normally assume that writing was invented to transcribe speech, but that is not strictly correct. The earliest Sumerian inscriptions, dating from ca. 3500 BCE, record not conversations, incantations, or other sorts of oral utterances, but land sales, business transactions, and tax accounts (Crystal 1987). Clay tokens bearing similar marks appear for several thousand years before these first inscriptions. It is often difficult to tell when we are dealing with writing and when with art (the recent discovery of 10,000-year-old stone carvings in Syria has been touted as a possible missing link in the art-to-writing chain), but the tokens seem to have been used as a system of accounting from at least the 9th millennium BCE. They are often regarded as the first examples of writing, and it is clear that they are only distantly related to actual speech (see figure 1). 18

We cannot be exactly sure why writing was invented, but just as the gurus of today's technology are called computer geeks, it's possible that the first writers also seemed like a bunch of oddballs to the early Sumerians, who might have called them cuneiform geeks. Surely they walked around all day with a bunch of sharp styluses sticking out of their pocket protectors, and talked of nothing but new ways of making marks on stones. Anyway, so far as we know, writing itself begins not as speech transcription but as a relatively restricted and obscure record-keeping shorthand. 19

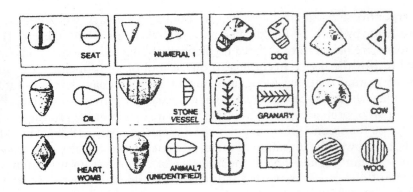

Figure 1 Clay Tokens and Sumerian Inscriptions Some of the commonest shapes are here compared with the incised characters in the earliest Sumerian incriptions (only some of which have been interpreted) (Crystal 1987, 196).

As innovative uses for the literacy technology are tried out, practitioners may 20
also adapt it to older, more familiar forms in order to gain acceptance from a wider group. Although writing began as a tool of the bean counters, it eventually added a second, magical/religious function, also restricted and obscure as a tool of priests. For writing to spread into a more general population in the ancient world, it had first to gain acceptance by approximating spoken language. Once writers—in a more "modern" sense of the word—discovered what writing could do, there was no turning back. But even today, most written text does not transcribe spoken language: the comparison of script and transcript in figure 2 makes this abundantly clear.

Of course writing never spread very greatly in the ancient world. William 21
Harris (1989) argues convincingly that no more than ten percent of the classical Greek or Roman populations could have been literate. One reason for this must be that writing technology remained both cumbersome and expensive: writing instruments, paints, and inks had to be hand made, and writing surfaces like clay tablets, wax tablets, and papyrus had to be laboriously prepared. Writing therefore remained exclusive, until cheap paper became available, and the printing press made mass production of written texts more affordable and less labor-intensive.

What Writing Does Differently

As a literacy technology like writing begins to become established, it also goes 22
beyond the previous technology in innovative, often compelling ways. For example, while writing cannot replace many speech functions, it allows us to communicate in ways that speech does not. Writing lacks such tonal cues of the human voice as pitch and stress, not to mention the physical cues that accompany face to face communication, but it also permits new ways of bridging time and space. Conversations become letters. Sagas become novels. Customs

Scripted dialogue:

Thersites: The common curse of mankind, folly and ignorance, be thine in great revenuel heaven bless thee from a tutor, and discipline come not near thee! Let thy blood be thy direction till thy death! then, if she that lays thee out says thou art a fair corpse, I'll be sworn and sworn upon't she never shrouded any but lazars. Amen.

Shakespeare, *Troilus and Cressida,* II, iii, 30.

Unscripted dialogue (ostensibly):

Lt. Col North: I do not recall a specific discussion. But, I mean. It was widely known within the CIA. I mean we were tracking that sensitive intelligence. I—I honestly don't recall, Mr. Van Cleve. I mean it—it didn't seem to me, at the time, that it was something that I was trying to hide from anybody. I was not engaged in it. And one of the purposes that I thought we had that finding for was to go back and ratify that earlier action, and to get on with replenishing. I mean, that was one—what I understood one of the purposes of the draft to be.

from *Taking the Stand: The Testimony of Lt. Col. Oliver North,* 15

Figure 2 Script and Transcript

---

become legal codes. The written language takes on a life of its own, and it even begins to influence how the spoken language is used. To cite an obvious example, people begin to reject traditional pronunciations in favor of those that reflect a word's spelling: the pronunciation of the "l" in falcon (compare the l-less pronunciation of the cognate name Faulkner) and the "h" in such "th" combinations as *Anthony* and *Elizabeth* (compare the nicknames *Tony* and *Betty,* which reflect the earlier, h-less pronunciation).

In order to gain acceptance, a new literacy technology must also develop   23
a means of authenticating itself. Michael Clanchy (1993) reports that when writing was introduced as a means of recording land transfer in 11th-century England, it was initially perceived (and often rightly so) as a nasty Norman trick for stealing Saxon land.

As Clanchy notes, spoken language was easily corroborated: human wit-   24
nesses were interactive. They could be called to attest whether or not a property transfer had taken place. Doubters could question witnesses, watch their eyes, see whether witnesses sank when thrown bound into a lake. Written documents did not respond to questions—they were not interactive. So the writers and users of documents had to develop their own means of authentication. At first, seals, knives, and other symbolic bits of property were attached to documents in an attempt to give them credibility. Medieval English land transfers also adopted the format of texts already established as trustworthy, the Bible or the prayer book, complete with illuminations, in order to convince readers of their validity.

Questions of validity came up because writing was indeed being used to   25
perpetrate fraud. Monks, who controlled writing technology in England at the time, were also responsible for some notorious forgeries used to snatch

land from private owners. As writing technology developed over the centuries, additional ways of authenticating text came into use. Individualistic signatures eventually replaced seals to the extent that today, many people's signatures differ significantly from the rest of their handwriting. Watermarks identified the provenance of paper; dates and serial numbers further certify documents, and in the absence of other authenticators, stylistic analysis may allow us to guess at authorship on the basis of comparative and internal textual evidence. In the digital age, we are faced with the interesting task of reinventing appropriate ways to validate cybertext.

The Pencil as Technology

Just as writing was not designed initially as a way of recording speech, the 26 pencil was not invented to be a writing device. The ancient lead-pointed stylus was used to scribe lines—the lead made a faint pencil-like mark on a surface, suitable for marking off measurements but not for writing. The modern pencil, which holds not lead but a piece of graphite encased in a wooden handle, doesn't come on the scene until the 1560s.

The 16th-century pencil consists of a piece of graphite snapped or shaved 27 from a larger block, then fastened to a handle for ease of use. The first pencils were made by joiners, woodworkers specializing in making furniture, to scribe measurements in wood. Unlike the traditional metal-pointed scribing tools, pencils didn't leave a permanent dent in the wood. By the time Gesner observed the pencil, it had been adopted as a tool by note-takers, natural scientists, or others who needed to write, sketch, or take measurements in the field. Carrying pens and ink pots outdoors was cumbersome. Early pencils had knobs at one end so that they could be fastened with string or chain to a notebook, creating the precursor to the laptop computer.

Pencils were also of use to artists. In fact the word pencil means "little tail," 28 and refers not only to the modern wood-cased pencil but to the artist's brush. Ink and paint are difficult to erase: they must be scraped off a surface with a knife, or painted over. But graphite pencil marks were more easily erased by using bread crumbs, and of course later by erasers made of rubber—in fact the eraser substance (caoutchouc, the milky juice of tropical plants such as ficus) was called rubber because it was used to rub out pencil marks.

Thoreau and Pencil Technology

It is true that Thoreau rejected modern improvements like the telegraph as 29 worthless illusions. In *Walden* he says, "They are but improved means to an unimproved end." Thoreau did not write much of pencils. He even omitted the pencil in his list of items to take into the Maine woods, though like naturalists before him, he certainly carried one on his twelve-day excursion in order to record his thoughts. Despite this silence, Thoreau devoted ten years of his life to improving pencil technology at his family's pencil factory.

De figuris lapidum, &c.

&titij puto, quod aliquos Stimmi An-
glicum voca-
re audio) ge-
nere, in mu-
cronem dera-
fi, in manubri
um ligneum
inferto.

L. Lateres
è luto finguntur & coquunt, ad ædi-
ficiorum parietes, pauimenta, cami-
nos: item ad furnos, aliosq̃ vfus.

Lithoftrota dicuntur loca lapidi-
bus ftrata: vt apud Varronem pauimenta nobilia lithoftrota, fiebant au-
tem è cruftis paruis, marmoreis præ-
cipuè, quibus folum pauiméti incru-
ftabatur. Vide Agricolam libro 7. de
nat. fofsilium.

M. Menfæ fiunt nó folùm è ligno:
fed etiam lapicibus & marmore, fiue
folidæ: fiue marmore aut lapide fifsili
incruftatæ dur taxat.

Molaris lapidis icon pofita eft Ca-
pite

Figure 3 De Figuris Lapidum Translation: "The stylus. . . is made . . . from a sort of
lead (which I have heard some call English antimony), shaved to a point and inserted
in a wooden handle." From *De rerum fossilum lapidum et gemmarum maxime, figuris
et similitudinibus liber,* a book on the shapes and images of fossils, esp. those in stone
and rock. Gesner wrote a Greek-Latin dictionary, was a doctor, lectured on physics,
and, obviously, was a rock hound.

It was this pencil technology, not inherited wealth or publication royalties,
that provided the income for one of the greatest writers of the American
renaissance.

As Petroski tells it, the pencil industry in the eighteenth century was buf-   30
feted by such vagaries as the unpredictable supply of graphite, dwindling
cedar forests, protective tariffs, and, for much of its history, an international
consumer preference for British-made pencils. All of this affected John Thoreau and Co., manufacturers of pencils. Until the nineteenth century, the best

pencil graphite (or plumbago, as it was often called), came from Borrowdale, in England. There were other graphite deposits around the world, but their ore was not particularly pure. Impure ore crumbled or produced a scratchy line. In the later eighteenth century, the Borrowdale deposits began to run low, and exports were curtailed. After the French Revolution, with his supply of English graphite permanently embargoed, the French pencil-maker Nicholas-Jacques Conté learned to produce a workable writing medium by grinding the local graphite, mixing it with clay and water, and forcing the mixture into wooden casings.

This process allowed the French to produce their own pencils, and it also 31 permitted manufacturers to control the hardness of the lead, which in turn controlled the darkness of the mark made by the pencil. (The more clay, the harder the lead, and the lighter and crisper the mark; less clay gives a darker, grainier mark). So successful was Conté's process that Conté became synonymous with pencil, and Conté crayons are still valued by artists. In Nuremberg, Staedtler teamed to mix ground graphite with sulfur. He and his rival, Faber, founded German pencil dynasties that also survive to this day.

The superiority of Borrowdale English graphite was evident to American 32 consumers as well, and they regularly preferred imports to domestic brands. American pencil manufacturers had a hard time convincing the public that they could make a good native pencil. In 1821 Charles Dunbar discovered a deposit of plumbago in Bristol, New Hampshire, and he and his brother-in-law, John Thoreau, went into the pencil business. By 1824 Thoreau pencils were winning recognition. Their graphite, however, was not as pure as Borrowdale, and since the Conté process was unknown in the United States, American pencils, though cheaper than imports, remained inferior.

Henry Thoreau set about to improve his father's pencil. According to Pet- 33 roski, Thoreau began his research in the Harvard Library. But then, as now, there was little written on pencil manufacture. Somehow, Thoreau learned to grind graphite more finely than had been done before and to mix it with clay in just the right proportion, for his improvements on the pencil-making process, combined with the high import duty imposed on British pencils after the War of 1812, led to great demand for Thoreau pencils.

Thoreau did not ascribe transcendent value to pencils. As Petroski sees it, 34 Thoreau's purpose was simply to make money. Once he developed the best pencil of the day, Thoreau saw no sense in trying to improve on his design. His pencils sold for seventy-five cents a dozen, higher than other brands, a fact which Emerson remarked on, though he still recommended Thoreau pencils to his friends. It is easy for us to think of Thoreau only as a romantic who lived deliberately, disobeyed civil authority, and turned Walden Pond into a national historic site. But to do these things, he was also an engineer and marketing expert. When pencil competition grew, shaving his profit margin, Thoreau stopped pushing pencils and sold his graphite wholesale to electrotypers because this proved more lucrative (Petroski 122).

Perhaps, then, Thoreau, despite his technological expertise, opposed Morse's 35 telegraph just to protect the family business. It is more likely, though, from the absence of references to pencil-making in any of his writings, that Thoreau honestly thought pencils were better for writing than electrical impulses, and he simply kept his business life and his intellectual life in separate compartments. In any case, Thoreau's resistance to the telegraph didn't stop the project.

The Telephone

The introduction of the telephone shows us once again how the pattern of communications technology takes shape. The telephone was initially received as an interesting but impractical device for communicating across distance. Although as Thoreau feared, the telegraph eventually did permit Maine and Texas and just about everywhere else to say nothing to one another, Samuel F. B. Morse, who patented the telegraph and invented its code, saw no use for Alexander Graham Bell's even newer device, the telephone. Morse refused Bell's offer to sell him the rights to the telephone patent. He was convinced that no one would want the telephone because it was unable to provide any permanent record of a conversation. 36

Indeed, although we now consider it indispensable, like writing, the uses of the telephone were not immediately apparent to many people. Telephone communication combined aspects of speaking and writing situations in new ways, and it took a while to figure out what the telephone could and couldn't do. Once they became established, telephones were sometimes viewed as replacements for earlier technologies. In some cities, news and sports broadcasts were delivered over the telephone, competing with the radio (Marvin 1988). Futurologists predicted that the telephone would replace the school or library as a transmitter of knowledge and information, that medical therapy (including hypnosis) could be delivered and criminals punished over the phone through the use of electrical impulses. The telephone even competed with the clock and the thermometer: when I was growing up in New York in the 1950s, my family regularly called MEridian 6-1212 to find out the time, and WEather 7-1212 for the temperature and forecast. 37

Of course the telephone was not only a source of information. It also threatened our privacy. One early fear of putting telephones in people's homes was that strangers could call up uninvited; people could talk to us on the phone whom we would never wish to converse with in person—and no one predicted then that people selling useless products would invariably call at dinner time. Today, as our email addresses circulate through the ether, we find in our electronic mailboxes not just surprise communications from long-lost acquaintances who have tracked us down using Gopher and other Web browsers, but also unwelcome communiqués from intruders offering get-rich-quick schemes, questionable deals, and shoddy merchandise. Even unsolicited religious messages are now circulating freely on net news groups. 38

The introduction of the telephone for social communication also required considerable adaptation of the ways we talk, a fact we tend to forget because we think of the modern telephone as a reliable and flexible instrument. People had to learn how to converse on the telephone: its sound reproduction was 39 poor; callers had to speak loudly and repeat themselves to be understood, a situation hardly conducive to natural conversation. Telephones were located centrally and publicly in houses, which meant that conversations were never private. Telephones emulated face-to-face communication, but they could not transmit the visible cues and physical gestures that allow face-to-face conversation to proceed smoothly, and this deficiency had to be overcome. Many people still accompany phone conversations with hand and facial gestures; very young children often nod into the phone instead of saying "Yes" or "No," as if their interlocutor could see them.

Initially, people were unsure of the appropriate ways to begin or end phone   40 conversations, and lively debates ensued. The terms "hello" and "good-bye" quickly became standard, despite objections from purists who maintained that "hello" was not a greeting but an expression of surprise, and that "good-bye," coming from "God be with you," was too high-toned and serious a phrase to be used for something so trivial as telephone talk. As people discovered that telephones could further romantic liaisons, guardians of the public morality voiced concern or disgust that sweethearts were actually making kissing noises over the phone. Appropriate language during conversation was also an issue, and phone companies would cut off customers for swearing (like today's computer Systems Operators, or Sysops, the telephone operators, or "hello girls" as they were called in the early days, frequently listened in on conversations and had the authority to interrupt or disconnect calls).

While the telephone company routinely monitored the contents of telephone   41 calls, when transcripts of telephone conversations were first introduced as evidence in trials, phone companies argued that these communications were just as private and privileged as doctor-patient exchanges (Marvin 68). Phone companies also tried to limit telephone access solely to the subscriber, threatening hotels and other businesses with loss of phone service if they allowed guests or customers to make calls. Telephone companies backed down from their demand that phones only be used by their registered owners once another technological development, the pay telephone, was introduced, and their continued profits were assured (this situation is analogous to the discussions of copy protection and site licensing for computer software today).

The Computer and the Pattern of Literacy Technology

Writing was not initially speech transcription, and pencils were first made for   42 woodworkers, not writers. Similarly, the mainframe computer when it was introduced was intended to perform numerical calculations too tedious or complex to do by hand. Personal computers were not initially meant for word processing either, though that has since become one of their primary functions.

Mainframe line editors were so cumbersome that even computer program-   43 mers preferred to write their code with pencil and paper. Computer operators actually scorned the thought of using their powerful number-crunchers to process mere words. Those who braved the clumsy technology to type text were condemned to using a system that seemed diabolically designed to slow a writer down well below anything that could be done on an IBM Selectric, or even with a pencil. (Interestingly, when the typewriter was developed, the keyboard was designed to slow down writers, whose typing was faster than the machine could handle; initially computers too were slow to respond to keystrokes, and until type-ahead capability was developed, typists were frustrated by loud beeps indicating they had exceeded the machine's capacity to remember what to do.)

Early word-processing software for personal computers did little to improve the situation. At last, in the early 1980s, programs like Wordstar began to produce text that looked more like the typing that many writers had become used to. Even so, writers had to put up with screens cluttered with formatting characters. Word wrap was not automatic, so paragraphs had to be reformatted every time they were revised. Furthermore, printed versions of text seldom matched what was on the computer screen, turning page design into a laborious trial-and-error session. Adding to the writer's problems was the fact that the screen itself looked nothing like the piece of paper the text would ultimately be printed on. The first PC screens were grayish-black with green phosphor letters, displaying considerably less than a full page of text. When it came along, the amber screen offered what was seen as a major improvement, reducing eye strain for many people. Today we expect displays not only with black on white, just like real paper, and high resolution text characters, but also with color, which takes us a step beyond what we could do with ordinary typing paper. 44

If the initial technical obstacles to word processing on a PC weren't enough to keep writers away from the new technology, they still had to come up with the requisite $5,000 or more in start-up funds for an entry-level personal computer. Only die-hards and visionaries considered computer word processing worth pursuing, and even they held on to their Selectrics and their Bics just in case. 45

If you type this:

^BCombining Special Effects^B. To combine special effects, simply insert one control character after another. For example, your ^BWordstar^B^VTM^V cursor may look like this: H^HI^HN^HZ

I^Ba^BI = /(a^Vx^V^T2^T + a^Vy^V^T2^T + a^Vz^V^T2^T)

You (might) get this:

Combining Special Effects. To combine special effects, simply insert one control character after another. For example, your Wordstar™ cursor may look like this: ■

|a| = / $(a_x^2 + a_y^2 + a_z^2)$

Figure 4 Instructions from a Wordstar manual

The next generation of word-processing computers gave us WYSIWYG: 46
"what you see is what you get," and that helped less-adventurous writers make
the jump to computers. Only when Macintosh and Windows operating systems
allowed users to create on-screen documents that looked and felt like the old,
familiar documents they were used to creating on electric typewriters did word
processing really become popular. At the same time, start-up costs decreased
significantly and, with new, affordable hardware, computer writing technology
quickly moved from the imitation of typing to the inclusion of graphics.

Of course that, too, was not an innovation in text production. We'd been 47
pasting up text and graphics for ages. The decorated medieval charters of
eleventh-century England are a perfect parallel to our computerized graphics
a millennium later. But just as writing in the middle ages was able to move
beyond earlier limitations, computer word processing has now moved beyond
the texts made possible by earlier technologies by adding not just graphics,
but animation, video, and sound to documents. In addition, Hypertext and
HTML allow us to create links between documents or paths within them,
both of which offer restructured alternatives to linear reading.

The new technology also raises the specter of digital fraud, and the latest 48
literacy technology is now faced with the task of developing new methods of
authentication to ensure confidence and trust in its audience (see figure 5).

Over the years, we have developed a number of safeguards for preventing or 49
detecting fraud in conventionally produced texts. The fact that counterfeit currency still gets passed, and that document forgeries such as the *Hitler Diaries*
or hoaxes like the physicist Alan Sokal's spoof of deconstruction, "Transgressing the Boundaries Toward a Transformational Hermeneutics of Quantum
Gravity," come to light from time to time shows that the safeguards, while
strong, are not necessarily foolproof. The average reader is not equipped to
detect many kinds of document falsification, and a lot of text is still accepted
on trust. A writer's reputation, or that of a publisher, predisposes readers to
accept certain texts as authoritative, and to reject others. Provenance, in the
world of conventional documents, is everything. We have learned to trust writing that leaves a paper trail.

Things are not so black and white in the world of digital text. Of course, 50
as more and more people do business on the Internet, the security of transactions, of passwords, credit card numbers, and bank accounts becomes vital.
But the security and authenticity of "ordinary" texts is a major concern as
well. Anyone with a computer and a modem can put information into cyberspace. As we see from figure 5, digitized graphics are easy to alter. Someone
intent on committing more serious deception can with not too much trouble
alter text, sound, graphics, and video files. Recently several former Columbia
University students were arrested for passing fake twenty-dollar bills that
they had duplicated on one of Columbia's high-end color printers. The
Treasury Department reported that while these counterfeits were easy for
a non-expert to spot, some $8,000 to $9,000 of the bad money had been
spent before the counterfeiters attracted any attention. Security experts, well
aware of the problems of digital fraud, are developing scramblers, electronic

Figure 5 Example of Digital Fraud From Feb. 1954 *Scientific American,* William J. Mitchell, "When is seeing believing?" (68–73). Mitchell explains the process used to create this photograph of Marilyn Monroe and Abraham Lincoln that never existed in the original. The final result can be so seamless that the forgery is undetectable. Examples of the intrusion of such false images include an ABC News broadcast in which correspondent Nina Totenberg was shown on camera with the White House in the background. In actuality, she was miles away in a studio and the montage gave the impression she was reporting from the field. Needless to say, fraudulent computer text is even easier to compose and promulgate across the bandwidth.

watermarks and invisible tagging devices to protect the integrity of digital files, and hackers are probably working just as hard to defeat the new safeguards. Nonetheless, once a file has been converted to hard copy, it is not clear how it could be authenticated.

Digitized text is even easier to corrupt accidentally, or to fiddle with on purpose. Errors can be inadvertently introduced when print documents are scanned. With electronic text, it may be difficult to recover other indicators that we expect easy access to when we deal with print: the date of publication, the edition (sometimes critical when dealing with newspapers or literary texts), editorial changes or formatting introduced during the digitization process, changes in accompanying graphics (for example, online versions of the *Washington Post* and the *New York Times* use color illustrations not found in the paper editions). And of course digital text can be corrupted on purpose in ways that will not be apparent to unsuspecting readers.

Electronic texts also present some challenges to the ways we attribute expertise to authors. When I read newsgroups and electronic discussion lists, I must develop new means for establishing the expertise or authority of a poster. I recently tried following a technical discussion on a bicycle newsgroup about the relative advantages of butyl and latex innertubes. I can accept the advice of a bicycle mechanic I know, because we have a history, but posters to a newsgroup are all strangers to me. They may be experts, novices, cranks, or some combination of the three, and in the case of the two kinds of tire tubes, I had difficulty evaluating the often conflicting recommendations I received. After reading the newsgroup for a while, becoming familiar with those who post regularly, and getting a sense of the kinds of advice they gave and their attitudes toward the subject, I began to develop a nose for what was credible. My difficulty was compounded, though, because the most authoritative-sounding poster, in the conventional sense of authoritative—someone who evoked principles of physics and engineering to demonstrate that flats were no more common or disastrous with latex than butyl tubes, and who claimed to have written books on bicycle repair—was clearly outshouted by posters attesting the frequency and danger of rupturing latex inner tubes. In the end I chose to stay with butyl, since everyone seemed to agree that, though heavier than latex, it was certainly not the worst thing in the world to ride on.

My example may seem trivial, but as more and more people turn to the 53 World Wide Web for information, and as students begin relying on it for their research papers, verifying the reliability and authenticity of that information becomes increasingly important, as does revisiting it later to check quotations or gather more information. As anyone knows who's lost a file or tried to revisit a website, electronic texts have a greater tendency to disappear than conventional print resources.

Conclusion

As the old technologies become automatic and invisible, we find ourselves more 54 concerned with fighting or embracing what's new. Ten years ago, math teachers worried that if students were allowed to use calculators, they wouldn't learn their arithmetic tables. Regardless of the value parents and teachers still place on knowing math facts, calculators are now indispensable in math class. When we began to use computers in university writing classes, instructors didn't tell students about the spell-check programs on their word processors, fearing the students would forget how to spell. The hackers found the spelling checkers anyway, and now teachers complain if their students don't run the spell check before they turn their papers in.

Even the pencil itself didn't escape the wrath of educators. One of the major 55 technological advances in pencil-making occurred in the early twentieth century, when manufacturers learned to attach rubber tips to inexpensive wood pencils by means of a brass clamp. But American schools allowed no crossing out. Teachers preferred pencils without erasers, arguing that students would do better, more premeditated work if they didn't have the option of revising. The students won this one, too: eraserless pencils are now extremely rare. Artists use them, because artists need special erasers in their work; golfers too use pencils without erasers, perhaps to keep themselves honest. As for the no-crossing-out rule, writing teachers now routinely warn students that writers never get it right the first time, and we expect them to revise their work endlessly until it is polished to perfection.

The computer has indeed changed the ways some of us do things with words, 56 and the rapid changes in technological development suggest that it will continue to do so in ways we cannot yet foresee. Whether this will result in a massive change in world literacy rates and practices is a question even more difficult to answer. Although the cost of computers has come down significantly enough for them to have made strong inroads into the American office and education environment, as well as in the American middle class home, it is still the case that not every office or every school can afford to computerize, let alone connect to the World Wide Web. And it is likely that many newly-computerized environments will not have sufficient control over the technology to do more than use it to replicate the old ways.

After more than a decade of study, we still know relatively little about 57 how people are using computers to read and write, and the number of people online, when viewed in the perspective of the total population of the United States, or of the world—the majority of whose residents are still illiterate—is still quite small. Literacy has always functioned to divide haves from have nots, and the problem of access to computers will not be easy to solve (see Moran, this volume)

In addition, researchers tend to look at the cutting edge when they examine 58 how technology affects literacy. But technology has a trailing edge as well as a down side, and studying how computers are put to use raises serious issues in the politics of work and mechanisms of social control. Andrew Sledd (1988) pessimistically views the computer as actually reducing the amount of literacy needed for the low end of the workplace: "As for ordinary kids, they will get jobs at Jewel, dragging computerized Cheerios boxes across computerized check-out counters."

Despite Sledd's legitimate fear that in the information age computers will 59 increase the gap between active text production and routine, alienating, assembly-line text processing, in the United States we live in an environment that is increasingly surrounded by text. Our cereal boxes and our soft drink cans are covered with the printed word. Our televisions, films, and computer screens also abound with text. We wear clothing designed to be read. The new computer communications technology does have ability to increase text exposure even more than it already has in positive, productive ways. The simplest one-word Web search returns pages of documents which themselves link to the expanding universe of text in cyberspace.

Computer communications are not going to go away. How the computer 60 will eventually alter literacy practices remains to be seen. The effects of writing took thousands of years to spread; the printing press took several hundred years to change how we do things with words. Although the rate of change of computer development is significantly faster, it is still too early to do significant speculating.

In the brave new world virtual text, if you chain an infinite number of monkeys to an infinite number of computers, you will eventually get, not Hamlet, but Hamlet BASIC.

We have a way of getting so used to writing technologies that we come to 61 think of them as natural rather than technological. We assume that pencils are a natural way to write because they are old—or at least because we have come to think of them as being old. We form Lead Pencil Clubs and romanticize do-it-yourselfers who make their own writing equipment, because home-made has come to mean "superior to store-bought."

But pencil technology has advanced to the point where the ubiquitous no. 2 62 wood-cased pencil can be manufactured for a unit cost of a few pennies. One pencil historian has estimated that a pencil made at home in 1950 by a hobby-ist or an eccentric would have cost about $50. It would cost significantly more nowadays. There's clearly no percentage in home pencil-making. Whether the computer will one day be as taken-for-granted as the pencil is an intriguing question. One thing is clear: were Thoreau alive today he would not be writing with a pencil of his own manufacture. He had better business sense than that. More likely, he would be keyboarding his complaints about the information superhighway on a personal computer that he assembled from spare parts in his garage.

Questions for Discussion and Journaling

1. Who was the Unabomber? How did he use writing? What technologies did he use for writing?

2. Sometimes Baron seems to shrug at technology and suggest that it's hard to imagine new technologies as fundamentally changing the shape or nature of writing. Do you agree that this seems to be one of his messages? If so, do you agree with it?

3. Why might the first class of people to have access to a technology be called "priestly," as Baron describes them near the beginning of his piece (para. 6)?

4. What are some other literacy technologies you can think of that, like the pencil, were once high technology but are now barely recognized as technology at all? What do these technologies have in common?

5. Why does Baron focus so much on *fraud* and *authenticity* in discussing writing technologies?

6. Look back over the illustrations and images in Baron's text. What do they contribute to it? Do you understand the illustrations and images as *writing*? Would considering them *writing* require adding to the list of technologies commonly associated with writing and literacy?

Applying and Exploring Ideas

1. Select a writing technology Baron talks about and write a brief history of how it has spread to its current number of users since it was invented. Does Baron's account of how new literacy technologies spread seem to fit the technology you're studying?

2. Baron devotes some time to discussing the "Thoreau pencil," an improvement on previous pencils. What writing technology do you wish someone would improve? What kinds of improvement does it need?

3. Think about communication technologies that keep a record of a conversation and those that don't. What are the advantages of keeping, and not keeping, such records? Can you think of any communication technologies that *don't* keep a record that we would still recognize as writing?

4. Poll your classmates to build a list of knowledge that people need to gain about a particular new writing technology (for example, texting). What do people report needing to learn about how to use the technology, and how to be socially acceptable with it (for example, avoiding cell-yell)?

Meta Moment

Does it help you to think of writing as a technology? What, if anything, changes in how you understand writing if you think of it in these terms?

Motivation in Literacy Development

TYLER CECCHINI

HUGO PEREZ

Framing the Paper

Tyler Cecchini and Hugo Perez, students at the University of Central Florida, wrote this essay in their English Composition 1101 Honors course in Fall 2008. It responds to the "Group Analysis of Literacy History" assignment (the second at the end of this chapter), and as those instructions note, it multiplies the value of any single literacy narrative by combining and comparing many narratives in search of the trends, patterns, and common features among them. Cecchini and Perez used the assignment to ask whether there was a pattern of similarity in the literacy histories of successful college students: specifically, they asked whether these students were especially motivated in early childhood to become literate. The version of their paper found here is a revision of their portfolio draft; they submitted this piece to the Writing Studies undergraduate research journal *Young Scholars in Writing* and received a request for limited changes, some of which appear in this version.

Cecchini and Perez 1

Tyler Cecchini and Hugo Perez
ENC 1101 Honors
Dr. Wardle
Dec. 3, 2008

Motivation in Literacy Development

In "Sponsors of Literacy," Deborah Brandt describes how a person's

surroundings and circumstances can motivate him or her to become literate

or to change his or her literacy practices. Brandt describes the situation of

Dwayne Lowery, a man raised in the upper Midwest in the late 1930s and

1940s. Lowery was uninterested in school, and graduated near the bottom

of his high school class. He went on to work in an automobile assembly

line for almost twenty years before he became a field staff representative for

Cecchini and Perez 2

unions. Lowery had never been highly interested in politics or even reading. However, due to his interest in union affairs, he was motivated to learn how to deal with contracts and negotiations. Lowery was even motivated to attend several workshops that would teach him union regulations, laws, and how to write negotiations. When negotiations went from being mainly oral to textual and presented in briefs, Lowery continued to attend workshops, motivated to continue representing his union members. Lowery's case shows how motivation can change a person's attitude toward literacy, and even cause him or her to change his or her literacy practices.

Can you describe how this introduction follows the CARS model (pp. 6–8)? Where do each of the CARS steps happen?

What distinction do Cecchini and Perez make between what Brandt discusses and what they wish to study? How important is it?

While Brandt does show how motivation helps a person change his or her literacy practices, she does not discuss to any degree how motivation may help develop early literacy skills. This led us to wonder, what were the main motivating factors for early literacy development in students who turn out to be highly successful?

Methods

To begin researching the possible effects of motivation on early literacy skills, we interviewed eight first-year honor students at the University of Central Florida. We chose to interview these students because they have shown academic success, not only in literacy, but all school subjects. We interviewed:

- Jim, an eighteen-year-old freshman from Orlando, Florida majoring in Sports and Fitness

- Robert, a nineteen-year-old freshman from Jacksonville, Florida majoring in Elementary Education

- Steve, a nineteen-year-old freshman from Casselberry, Florida majoring in Social Science Education

- Anne, an eighteen-year-old freshman from Pompano Beach, Florida majoring in Finance and Marketing

Cecchini and Perez have changed the names of participants but provide other personal information about them. Have they done enough to protect participants' privacy? How much does privacy matter in research like this?

- Neil, an eighteen-year-old from Satellite Beach, Florida majoring in Computer Science
- Mickey, a nineteen-year-old from Saint Cloud, Minnesota, who is currently undecided about his major
- Seth, an eighteen-year-old from Palm Harbor, Florida majoring in Micro- and Molecular Biology
- Cheryl, an eighteen-year-old from Jacksonville, North Carolina majoring in Chemistry.

The authors' discussion of their research methods is extremely brief. Do you know what you need to about how they researched? Do you have any questions about their methods? Do you have any opinions about the research strategy of conducting written rather than oral interviews?

These interviews consisted of written responses to several interview questions, as well as responses to follow-up interview questions sent through email (see Appendices A and B). We read these interviews and coded them as themes emerged regarding student motivation.

Results

In the following report, we will present the results of our study on the role of motivation in early literacy skills. Not only will we describe its role, but we will also address several sources that provided the students with this motivation. From the interviews, we found that there are five main motivating factors: family role models, reading and writing for pleasure, technology, special programs, and self-motivation. We believe that all of these sources played a role, either positive or negative, in helping to motivate the students to improve their literacy. We will move from the earliest sources of motivation to the ones found later in the literary histories of the students.

Here the writers preview their findings and explain the rationale for the order in which they discuss them. Do you think readers benefit from this?

The Positive Effects of Curiosity and Freedom

One of the earliest forms of literacy motivation that we found in several of the students was self-motivation. Many students explain reading as being a source to satisfy their curiosity, as well as a form of independence.

Cecchini and Perez 4

Several of the students stated that they read because they were curious, like Neil. Neil remarked, "I saw other people reading and I wanted to figure out how these symbols meant something, and what they were saying." Even after Neil learned the secret of books, he felt a natural curiosity towards them, always wanting to know what would happen next in the story. Anne also felt the lure of books at a young age. She remembered seeing the books in her house and wondering what they were. She often would take these same books and try to read them, even though they were years beyond her knowledge.

Many students also claimed that they wanted to read and write so that they could have independence from their parents and teachers. Steve responded, "I was motivated because I wanted to be able to read my picture books by myself and not have to rely on my parents." Mickey also shared these sentiments, feeling that learning how to read and write would help him to "function more independently." Neil and Robert both expressed that as they grew older and their literacy skills matured, they were allowed to pick their own books and to read at the level they thought would challenge them. While the challenge incorporated in reading harder books may have been a motivating factor, both students had to learn how to read and write independently, without their parents, before they could independently decide which books they would like to read. However, despite their desire for freedom, we found that many of the students' families played motivational roles in their literacy developments.

The Positive Effects of Family Interaction

Family is known to play an important role in aspects of child development. Families help to teach fundamental lessons and to help keep a child on

Notice that in this draft the writers don't discuss the findings in the same order as they list them here, and they have not used headings in the following subsections that match their list of findings. Do you think discrepancies like this matter? If so, how much? If not, why not?

Do you think the writers provide sufficient evidence in this section for the central assertion that they make?

track while exploring literacy. Several of the students we interviewed said that not only did their family play a part in their literacy development; their family also acted as their role models.

Several students revealed that their older siblings motivated them to learn how to read and write. Neil stated that his brother took on the title of role model, and that seeing his older brother (only his senior by a few years) and several of his brother's friends inspired him to learn how to read. Neil commented, "He [Neil's older brother] couldn't show me the proper ways for everything, but I was given a glimpse into knowledge beyond my age by learning from him." Mickey also said that his brother played a motivational role in his learning how to read. Although Mickey does not describe whether his brother specifically taught him how to read, he does say that reading was one way of being "grown-up," like his older brother.

Robert's and Anne's siblings took on slightly different roles in helping them develop their literacy skills. Robert said that his older brother would tease him for not being able to read. Rather than letting these negative comments discourage him, Robert actually took his brother's comments and used them, allowing them to give him the motivation and drive to learn how to read. Anne was raised by parents who spoke fluent Creole, but virtually no English. Because of this, if Anne had any questions about what a word meant or how to say something, she would turn to her two older sisters. Today, Anne is unsure whether her sisters knew the answers to many of her questions, but they regularly told her to find the answer on her own. This helped Anne learn to depend on herself and read independently at a fairly young age.

Several students also claimed that their parents played a significant role in their literacy development. While all of the students emphasized

Cecchini and Perez 6

how important their parents were in helping them read and write, only a few saw their parents as actual inspiration. Anne claimed that her parents were very strong motivators in her literacy development, even though they spoke little English and were unable to help her with her schoolwork. Anne remembers seeing the hardships her parents experienced from the language barrier and believes that this was a strong motivator for her to become literate in English. She also remembered her mother telling her, "If you go to school, no one can stop you from being what you want to be." These words stayed with her and prompted her to do well in school.

Unlike Anne's parents, who were unable to help with her literacy learning, Seth remembers his parents taking a large role in his literacy. Seth remembered having a hard time reading and writing until he was twelve. He said that his parents would spend hours trying to teach him how to read and write, even though both worked every day. He remembers practicing every day on his own, trying to make his parents proud of his reading achievements. He and his parents continued this for several years, and eventually employed the help of his teacher, Mrs. C. He believes that seeing his parents trying so hard to teach him how to read and write helped motivate him to be a better reader and writer.

Cheryl's parents also played an important motivational role in her reading and writing. Cheryl's mother would volunteer at the school, often in the library, and her father created a "reading loft" for her first-grade class. Even though the loft did not stay at home and her father had little to do with it after building it, she still felt that it motivated her to read. "It had a ladder that you could climb to the top on, and during our silent reading, you were allowed to sit in it and read if you had been good for

What do you think of the authors' strategy of devoting most of their paper to recounting data (stories) offered by their research participants? Is it effective? Why or why not?

the day or week. It was covered with pillows and blankets that the teacher had brought in." Even though this is technically a material motivator, Cheryl felt that being able to say "my dad built that" and being able to enjoy something her father made just for her classroom provided some motivation for her literacy.

At this point, many students knew how to read and write, but did not experience the motivation necessary to enjoy these activities outside of school. This motivation was quickly found through different pastimes.

Hobbies as Motivation for Literacy

Hobbies help people to pursue interests outside their regular occupation and engage in some form of pleasure. This is a relief from the busy world to something more relaxing. Along with relief, many of the students admitted that hobbies also provided the motivation needed to enjoy reading and writing.

Robert had a hobby that supplied the motivation needed to develop and enhance his literacy skills. Robert's hobby was playing the piano, which stemmed from his love of music. But in order to perform music, he needed to learn to read and write. Robert did not read the average beginner books; he read music theory books. While Robert did not necessarily like reading, he read the music theory books constantly in order to perfect his piano playing. These books helped him to understand music, but they also taught him the fundamentals of reading, allowing him to develop better reading skills. Eventually, the young "Mr. Piano Man" transitioned from reading music theory to reading novels.

A few of the students, like Anne, Neil, Cheryl, and Robert, found that reading was their passion, and certain books served as motivation to read

Cecchini and Perez 8

outside of the classroom. Cheryl's motivation came from J.K. Rowling's *Harry Potter* series and her inspirational writing techniques. Cheryl quickly became hooked on these magical books that took her into a whole new world. Cheryl is sad that the series is over, but continues to read because of her love of J.K. Rowling's writing style. Although she read other books, such as *Freddie the Frog* and any book about Amelia Bedelia, Cheryl feels that *Harry Potter* was the first book to help motivate her to read novels rather than short stories.

Like Cheryl, Neil received the passion to read from a unique series of books. Neil liked to read fantasy books while he was in the gifted program. Neil liked the magic and spells within these books that sent him into their world. Anne also gets taken away in her own world while reading novels. Anne said, "It let me tap into a different world each time. I loved the feeling of being attached to a certain character or plot." Her favorite series of books was *The Boxcar Children*, which she read for pleasure. Robert also read for pleasure. He would read the *Lord of the Rings* series for fun and loved the author, J. R. R. Tolkien, saying "the world the author created made me very curious to read more of his books." Authors like J.K. Rowling and others had a significant impact on several of the students, causing them to enjoy reading as a hobby, which in turn, gave them the motivation to develop their literacy skills outside of school.

At the beginning of this century, the only tools that could help students to read and write outside of school were their hobbies. However, over the past few decades, we find that students have begun using technology to help with literacy. Technology has become a prevalent tool in almost all aspects of our life. Different types of

The authors seem to say that one motivation to become literate was to be able to read for fun—in other words, participants wanted to learn to read because they wanted to read. Do you think there's a logical flaw in this argument, or do the authors simply need to make their point more clearly?

This paragraph makes a transition to a discussion of technology as a motivator—before the new heading, rather than after it. Does this work? What would happen if the writers combined this paragraph with the one that opens the next section?

Cecchini and Perez 9

technology help to relay information, provide us with power, and even play a role in literacy development.

Technology as a Motivation for Literacy

Technologies such as television and computer games have become major components in the teaching of reading and writing during the last few decades. Readers are getting involved with the new ways of reading and writing by using computers and special programs. Today, technology is rapidly becoming a main motivating tool for literacy.

Many of the students remember playing computer games, such as "Reading Rabbit," "Math Blaster," and "Mavis Beacon Teaches Typing," to help them with reading and writing. For many of the students, these games provided a fun way to learn how to read, write, or type. Robert stated, "Those games helped me learn to read and recognize colors and shapes. It also made learning fun, so I was more willing to learn and practice."

Along with computer games, Cheryl also used a computer reading program, called "Accelerated Reading," to help with her reading skills. This program required the students to read a certain number of books and pass tests on them, while making sure that they read books within a certain reading level. This program motivated Cheryl to read because she always wanted to have a high reading level, which allowed her to read higher level books.

This section focuses on technologies that teach math, reading, and vocabulary. What about writing technologies? What do you make of the fact that there's no data provided on this question?

Anne learned from technology, but not in the same way as the other students. While she did play computer games occasionally, Anne loved watching TV shows. She would watch "Sesame Street" and "Barney" and then try to imitate some of the words. She remembers how she would often use these words in the wrong context, but would learn the proper

Cecchini and Perez 10

usage from her sisters. This helped her to expand her vocabulary and learn the proper usage of words, similar to the way several of the computer games did for the other students.

While family, books, and technology all provide students the motivation to begin reading and writing, some students need help with certain problems before they can be fully motivated to read and write.

Programs as Literacy Motivators

For some students, reading and writing comes with great difficulty. Until they are able to stand on their own, they may have problems feeling motivated to read and write. Certain programs, even those with material rewards, often help students so that they receive the necessary help and motivation to develop their literacy skills.

Seth and Jim had the use of special programs when learning how to read and write. Jim was diagnosed with dyslexia early in life while Seth had problems grasping the concepts of reading and writing. Jim attended the Kurtz Center in the Orlando area to improve his literacy skills. This center taught Jim how to specifically deal with his dyslexia and allowed him to excel academically. After the Kurtz Center, Jim attended Markham Woods Academy, which further helped him to overcome his dyslexia and develop his composition skills. Like Jim, Seth received help from his school by being placed into a special program, which helped him to improve his reading and writing. However, Seth experienced the most improvement when he worked with Mrs. C. Mrs. C taught him about creative writing, which Seth enjoyed very much Seth loved it so much, that when he was in high school, three of his poems were published in his school's poem book.

Other special programs that encourage children to read often offer treats and goodies as rewards. Steve's elementary school participated in "Book it," a program which offered free Pizza Hut pizza after the student read a certain number of books. Like the program "Book it," Neil was involved in a gifted program for kids with bright futures. They would offer free books and materials to help the children to learn literacy. He was offered fantasy books, which he got addicted to very quickly. Neil took full advantage of this opportunity, receiving new materials quite often.

Conclusion

Overall, we found that motivation plays a role in the literacy development of honors students. The main motivating factors that we found were family role models, reading or writing for pleasure, technology, special programs, and self-motivation. All of the students experienced at least one of these motivating factors; several experienced two or three. Without these motivating factors, the students we interviewed would not have become the literate successes that they are today.

Through our interviews, we found that most students had an inner drive to learn how to read and write. Whether they were learning literacy skills because they were curious, or wanted independence from their parents, without some sort of self-motivation, the students would not have wanted to learn how to read and write, leading to severe problems later on in life.

We also found that families were catalysts in most of the students' development of literacy skills. Many of the students felt that their parents were a source of motivation, not just because they constantly told them to read and write, but by showing their own experiences, volunteering, and

The authors' research participants were all honors students. Here, they say "most students" have an inner drive to become literate. Whom do you think they mean? Do you think discussing their limited sample more directly would allow readers to make more of their findings?

Cecchini and Perez 12

getting help for their children whenever possible. Siblings were also a great
source of motivation; some motivated their younger siblings by helping
them learn while others helped by teasing. Despite the methods used,
family was a very influential factor in whether the students were motivated
to read and write.

Our study also found that many students were motivated to read and
write because of a hobby. The student's hobbies would interest them so
much that they often turned to books to find new information about their
specific hobby. Some students even found that other books or forms of
writing could serve as their hobby, leading them to find more books and
pieces of literature like the one they just read. Whatever the hobby, many
of the students claimed that the pleasure they found from their hobbies
helped them to develop and continue their literacy skills.

> How helpful do you find the writers' review of their findings here? Is the summary too long, too short, just right? Did the writers leave anything out?

We found that technology and special programs were motivators, for
they allowed reading and writing to be fun Not only were the computer
games fun, but they also helped to keep the morale and spirit of the students
from falling in times when reading and writing were difficult. These games
showed the students that reading and writing can be fun, and that if you
practice enough, you will improve and become a better reader or writer.

Finally, for those students who had difficulties with reading and
writing or needed extra motivation to read, we found that programs
helped motivate these students. These programs gave the students ways
of dealing with their struggles in a specialized manner. Without the help
of these programs, the students would have fallen behind, always to be
discouraged. Therefore, by helping the students overcome these problems,
and by offering awards for doing so, the students received the confidence,
as well as the motivation to continue reading and writing.

How well do the researchers' recommendations follow from their findings? What else might they have to take into account in order for these recommendations to have the greatest chance of working?

The results from this study can be used to help students who are less successful at reading and writing. While not all students benefit from having a functional family, schools can help in many ways to help the students become successful readers and writers. Schools could incorporate specialized computer games into their normal curriculum to help students read and learn. This would provide an interesting and fun way in which students could learn literacy skills, making reading and writing less of a chore and something to be looked forward to. Schools could also have special-interest books in their classroom and encourage the students to read them. This may help students to find a hobby or interest that they would like to learn more about, leading them to read more of these special interest books, therefore further improving their reading skills. Finally, schools should have some means of testing students so that those with reading or writing disabilities can receive the proper attention, rather than being placed in a special needs class. These simple changes in schools would help to motivate the students, creating a want to read and write, and therefore, would help improve their literacy skills.

Reference

Brandt, Deborah. (1998). Sponsors of literacy. *College Composition and Communication, 49*(2), 165–185.

Appendix A: Interview Questions

1. In Brandt's study, she defines "literacy sponsor." Re-read the definition and then make a list of your most influential literacy sponsors.

2. In Heath's study, she defines a "literacy event." Re-read the definition and then briefly describe some of the literacy events that stand out most from your early childhood.

3. In Trackton, children were not explicitly taught to read. Rather, they picked up reading through asking questions of adults. How does this compare with how you learned to read?

4. In Trackton, children were not asked easy questions directed at them (like "what color is that?" or "what letter is that?"). Rather, they were asked more complicated questions requiring them to infer and make connections ("what kind of thing is that?" or "what is that like?"). Do you remember the kinds of questions your family members asked you when you were very young?

5. In Trackton, reading was a social event. Groups of people read and discussed what they read together. When you remember your early reading experiences, do you remember them as social or solitary?

6. In Trackton, oral stories were common. As a child, did you read or tell or hear stories more commonly?

7. How did you learn to read? What motivated you to read?

8. How did you learn to write? What motivated you to write?

9. Think of one problem that you had with reading and writing as a child. What was the problem and what resources did you draw on to help you with that problem?

10. How much parental involvement was there in your reading and writing? What kind of involvement was it—for example, did they tell

you to do your homework? Help you do your homework? Tell you to read? Read to you on a daily basis?

11. What other people besides your parents were most involved in your early reading and writing? What kind of involvement did they have?

12. Consider the ways that different technologies impacted your early reading and writing. What were they and did they impact your motivation to read or write?

13. What social and economic factors do you think influenced the context in which you learned to read and write? Think about Brandt here—for example, did you speak the dominant language at home? Was your school well funded or poorly funded? Did most of the students in your school have involved or uninvolved parents? Did you have access to resources and technologies for writing? And how might your life have been different if the social and economic factors had been different?

Appendix B: Follow-Up Interview Questions

1. What were your main reasons for writing? Do you write for fun or from parental motivation? Has it always been this way?

2. Was there any subject that you guys cared about that encouraged you to expand your reading and writing?

3. Robert, Neil, and Jim: Can you please elaborate on how piano, computers, and fitness made you want to read?

4. Jim and Seth: Would you say that your storytellers motivated you to try and find more stories like the ones they told?

5. Would you consider computer games a great motivator in how you learned to read and write? Please explain.

Cecchini and Perez 16

6. Did independent reading make you motivated to read and write? Did you like independent reading and writing?

7. Were you ever motivated to do well because of rewards? Explain some of these rewards.

8. What role did curiosity play in your learning how to read and write? Did you read because you were curious?

Some Other Questions to Consider

- If you were reviewing submissions for a journal on writing research, what would be your three main recommendations to Cecchini and Perez for revision? What would you tell them are the three greatest strengths of their piece?
- Suppose you were to take Cecchini and Perez's research as a jumping-off point for your own research, just like they use Brandt's as a point of departure for their own. What do you suspect these writers *haven't* commented on about motivations for literacy that further research should investigate?
- What other methods (besides interviewing) can you imagine for investigating the question that Cecchini and Perez are pursuing?

Writing about Literacies: Assignments and Advice

The best strategy I used when composing my papers this semester would be constructing an outline. Before I begin drafting my paper, I plan ahead what my thesis is and organize my ideas into separate paragraphs. Then I provide valuable evidence for each idea from a variety of sources such as quotes from the textbook and academic databases. Planning and organizing my thoughts in advance gives me an idea of how my paper will appear in structure and in content.

—Natasha Gumtie, Student

To help you learn and explore the ideas in this chapter, we are suggesting two Assignment Options for larger writing projects: Literacy Narrative and Group Analysis of Literacy History.

Assignment Option 1. Literacy Narrative

Drawing on what you have read in this chapter, examine your own literacy history, habits, and processes. The purpose of this inquiry is to get to know yourself better as a reader and writer. As Malcolm X argued, awareness gives power and purpose: the more you know about yourself as a reader and writer, the more control you are likely to have over these processes.

Invention, Research, and Analysis   Start your literacy narrative by considering your history as a reader and writer. Try to get at what your memories and feelings about writing/reading are and how you actually write/read now. Do not make bland generalizations ("I really love to write") but go into detail about how you learned to write/read. Mine your memory, thinking carefully about where you've been and where you are as a reader and writer. You might ask yourself questions such as:

- How did you learn to write and/or read?
- What kinds of writing/reading have you done in the past?
- How much have you enjoyed the various kinds of writing/reading you've done?
- What are particularly vivid memories that you have of reading, writing, or activities that involved them?
- What is your earliest memory of reading and your earliest memory of writing?
- What sense did you get, as you were learning to read and write, of the *value* of reading and writing, and where did that sense come from?
- What frustrated you about reading and writing as you progressed through school? By the same token, what pleased you about them?
- What kind of writing/reading do you do most commonly?

- What is your favorite kind of writing/reading?
- What are your current attitudes or feelings toward reading and writing?
- Where do you think your feelings about and habits of writing and reading come from? What in your past has made you the kind of writer/reader you are today?
- Who are some people in your life who have acted as literacy sponsors?
- What are some institutions and experiences in your life that have acted as literacy sponsors?
- What have any of the readings in this chapter reminded you about from your past or present as a reader and writer?

Questions like these help you start thinking deeply about your literate past. You should try to come up with some answers for all of them, but it's unlikely that you'll actually include all of these answers in your literacy narrative itself. Right now you're just thinking and writing about what reading and writing was like for you. When you plan the narrative, you'll select from among all the material you've been remembering and thinking about. The question then becomes, how will you decide what to talk about out of everything you *could* talk about? This depends in part on your analysis of what you're remembering.

As you consider what all these memories and experiences suggest, you should be looking for an overall "So what?"—a main theme, a central "finding," an overall conclusion that your consideration leads you to draw. It might, for example, be one of the following:

- An insight about why you read and write as you do today based on past experience
- An argument about what works or what doesn't work in literacy education, on the basis of your experience
- A resolution to do something differently. or to *keep* doing something that's been working
- A description of an ongoing conflict or tension you experience when you read and write
- The story of how you resolved such a conflict earlier in your literacy history

Planning and Drafting   Your consideration and analysis of your previous experience, one way or another, will lead you to a *main point* that you'll use your literacy narrative to demonstrate and support.

Because your literacy narrative tells the particular story of a particular person—you—its shape will depend on the particular experiences you've had and the importance you attach to them. Therefore, it's difficult to suggest a single structure for the literacy narrative that will work for all writers. The structure that you use should support your particular intention and content. Nevertheless, you should consider the following as you begin to draft:

- Headings or sections (like Part I or Act I or "Early Literacy Memories") might be helpful, but your content may better lend itself to write one coherent, unbroken essay. Do what works for you, given the material you want to include. Just be sure to organize and make some sort of point (or points).

- Because your literacy narrative is about you, you may find it difficult to write it without talking about yourself in the first person. Using "I" when you need to will make the piece feel somewhat informal, which is appropriate to this kind of writing.
- If you wish, include pictures or artifacts with your narrative. You could bring in your first spelling test or the award you won for the essay contest or the article in the school newspaper about your poem.
- If your circumstances make it appropriate, write this narrative in some mode other than paper-alphabetic: For example, write it as a blog entry on your Web site and incorporate multimedia, or write it as a performed or acted presentation, or make it a PowerPoint presentation, a YouTube video, a poster, or whatever else works to reach the audience you want to and help you make your point.

What Makes It Good?   This assignment asks you to carefully think about your history as a reader and writer, to tell a clear story that helps make a point, and to write a readable piece. So, be sure your piece:

- tells a story or stories about your literacy history,
- talks about where you are now as a writer and reader and how your past has shaped your present, and
- makes some overall point about your literacy experiences.

Of course, this essay should also be clear, organized, interesting, and well edited. In addition, the strongest literacy narratives will incorporate ideas and concepts from the readings in this unit to help frame and explain your experiences.

Assignment Option 2. Group Analysis of Literacy History

Collaborate with a group of classmates on a formal research study of some theme that emerges when everyone's literacy experiences are compared. You can use the following instructions to guide the writing of this kind of study, which lends itself to answering "bigger" questions or making larger points than a single literacy narrative can.

Conduct a Self-Study   All students in the group should post answers to the following questions on the class blog, wiki, or Web site:

- How did you learn to write and/or read?
- What kinds of writing/reading have you done in the past?
- How much have you enjoyed the various kinds of writing/reading you've done?
- What are particularly vivid memories that you have of reading, writing, or activities that involved them?
- What is your earliest memory of reading and your earliest memory of writing?
- What sense did you get, as you were learning to read and write, of the *value* of reading and writing, and where did that sense come from?
- What frustrated you about reading and writing as you progressed through school? By the same token, what pleased you about them?
- What kind of writing/reading do you do most commonly?

- What is your favorite kind of writing/reading?
- What are your current attitudes or feelings toward reading and writing?
- Where do you think your feelings about and habits of writing and reading come from? What in your past has made you the kind of writer/reader you are today?
- Who are some people in your life who have acted as literacy sponsors?
- What are some institutions and experiences in your life that have acted as literacy sponsors?
- What have any of the readings in this chapter reminded you about from your past or present as a reader and writer?

Discuss and Code the Self-Study   In your group, read the answers to the self-interviews. Look together for common themes, recurring trends, or unique experiences, and determine which of these might be most interesting to further research and write about. Be sure to consider what data you will need to collect to explore these themes. (For example, do you need to interview some classmates further—or people outside the class?) Common themes that emerge from this sort of study include the role of technology in literacy, hobbies as literacy sponsors, motivations for literacy learning, privilege and access, and help overcoming literacy struggles.

Collaborate to Write about Emergent Themes   Pair up with another student and choose an emergent theme to write a paper about. As a pair, pinpoint a specific research question related to your theme and gather whatever further data are necessary. Drawing on terms and ideas from this chapter's readings, you can then write your analysis of and findings on this theme.

Planning and Drafting   Before beginning to write, the group as a whole should consider audience and genre appropriate for this paper. Discuss the following questions together:

- Who should be the audience for what you write? How can you best reach them?
- How would you like to write about your findings? In a somewhat formal, scholarly way? In a more storytelling narrative way?
- What content/format would make this narrative most effective? Paper, text-only? Paper, text, and images? Online text and images? Online text, images, video?

As you analyze and begin to write with your partner, you should consider the following questions:

- What is your research question?
- What answers to this question do your research and analysis suggest?
- What data support each of these answers?
- What have you learned from your paper, and what does it mean for the rest of us?

Those questions will actually help you arrange your paper, too, in most cases. That is, an introduction poses your research question and explains the value of it.

The following section explains how you attempted to answer the question—what methods you used to gather the data you used to try to reach answers. The next section discusses the data and what answers it led you to. Finally, the conclusion answers "So what?"—the implications that your findings seem to suggest.

If you haven't written collaboratively before, you may find it a bit of a challenge to coordinate schedules with your co-writer, to decide how to break up the work of writing the piece, and to make sure you share ideas and information efficiently. You'll also most likely need to rewrite each other's material a bit—this will help it sound like the piece was written in a single voice.

What Makes It Good?   A good analysis of an issue emerging from your group's literacy history may take a number of different shapes but will tend to have these traits in common:

- A clear, directly stated research question
- A detailed description of what methods you used to try to answer the question
- A clear explanation of what you found in your research and what conclusions it leads you to
- An explanation of "so what?"—why your findings might matter
- The usual: readable, fluent prose; transitions that make the paper easy to follow; and editing and proofreading that keep the paper from distracting readers with typographical errors and mistakes

Suggested Additional Readings and Resources

Evans, Rick. "Learning 'Schooled Literacy': The Literate Life Histories of Mainstream Student Readers and Writers." *Discourse Processes* 16.3 (1993): 317–40. Print.

Newkirk, Thomas. *Misreading Masculinity: Boys, Literacy, and Popular Culture*. Portsmouth: Heineman, 2002. Print.

Porter, Roy. "Reading Is Bad for Your Health: European Notions through the 19th Century." *History Today* 48.3 (1998): 11–16. Print.

Robbins, Sarah. *Managing Literacy, Mothering America*. Pittsburgh: U of Pittsburgh P, 2006. Print.

Schaafsma, David. *Eating on the Street: Teaching Literacy in a Multicultural Society*. Pittsburgh: U of Pittsburgh P, 1994. Print.

Skilton-Sylvester, Ellen. "Literate at Home but Not at School: A Cambodian Girl's Journey from Playwright to Struggling Writer." *School's Out!: Bridging Out-of-School Literacies with Classroom Practices*. Ed. Glenda Hull and Katherine Schultz. New York: Teacher's College P, 2002. 61–90. Print.

Smith, Michael, and Jeffrey Wilhelm. *Reading Don't Fix No Chevys*. Portsmouth: Heinemann, 2002. Print.

4 | Discourses: How Do Communities Shape Writing?

Work sucks.

A comedy from Mike Judge, creator of 'Beavis and Butt-head' and co-creator of 'King of the Hill'

Office Space

In this chapter we ask you to consider the idea that literacy learning is never over. Rather, the writers gathered in this chapter argue that we constantly evolve and acquire new literacies as we move among what James Gee calls **Discourses** (with a capital "D") and John Swales calls **discourse communities**.

Gee, Swales, and the other authors whose work appears in this chapter are describing something you do every day: When you go to your dorm and interact with your roommates, for example, you are in one Discourse; when you go to biology class, you are in another. *Discourses* are group members' shared "ways of being in the world" (that's from Gee, p. 484). And most of us are amazingly efficient at navigating multiple Discourses: What you learn in biology class about evolution might conflict with what you are taught in your Bible study course, for example, but you manage to engage in both.

The movie *Office Space* portrays both a specific discourse community (Initech, a computer software company) and a broader "office" or workplace discourse community.

When a group of people shares goals or purposes and uses communication to achieve them, we can call that group a *discourse community* (that's from Swales, p. 471). As we constantly move among different discourse communities and engage in different Discourses, we readjust our use of language, our interpretation of texts, and our ways of seeing and "being in the world." For example, if you watched the movie *Twilight* in a class called "The Monster in Contemporary Culture," you would almost certainly talk about it very differently from the way you would talk about it after seeing it in the theater with friends. You would likely even *watch* it differently—with a different kind of attention—and notice different things about it.

This chapter begins with reading selections that try to explain what is happening when people move among these various communities, and the authors define terms that make the phenomenon clearer. The first selection, John Swales's "The Concept of Discourse Community," argues that six distinct characteristics help define discourse communities. You can use his argument to begin identifying the discourse communities of which you're a part. That understanding will deepen as you encounter James Gee's "Literacy, Discourse, and Linguistics: Introduction." In this selection, Gee approaches the same phenomenon from another angle, exploring what members of discourse communities must have in common in order to "recognize" each other and arguing about how people usually go about acquiring these Discourses. Like many of the other writers in this chapter, Gee asks how people new to a discourse community learn (or don't learn) to use language in the ways new communities find appropriate.

In addition to asking how people read the *texts* in a discourse community, the authors represented in this chapter ask how people read the other *people* and *activities* in it. They wonder, for example, what happens when members of a discourse community don't interact appropriately? Again, these are questions you should easily be able to relate to your own experiences: Have you ever tried to join a group where you just never seemed to fit in? Have you ever been required to take a class where everyone seemed to be speaking a language you just didn't "get"? In "Discourse Communities and Communities of Practice: Membership, Conflict, and Diversity," Ann Johns addresses some of these questions of "belonging." Johns uses the term **communities of practice** as another name for discourse communities, and she raises the intriguing question of how communities of practice change and evolve by adding new members who do things a little differently from the way existing members do them.

In "Identity, Authority, and Learning to Write in New Workplaces," Elizabeth Wardle (who coedited this book) examines what happens as a writer enters a new workplace and tries to become **enculturated,** or adept at the culture, of a new community. Wardle uses the case study of a computer support specialist newly installed in a university humanities department to illustrate the struggle of one writer to master the language that would earn him the respect and cooperation of the other department members. Rather than *communities of practice*, Wardle talks about discourse communities like the department as **activity systems** that center on a common project or goal. This perspective lets her analyze the relationship between the language the activity system seems to demand and the strangeness of that language to the writer being enculturated. In "Learning to Serve: The Language and Literacy of Food Service Workers," Tony Mirabelli studies workers in food service and introduces the term **multiliteracies** to explain how people read not only texts but also other people and activities.

One inescapable conclusion from the readings in this chapter is that people keep learning to write and use language in new ways as long as they continue to interact with new kinds of people and groups. The terms and ideas you encounter in this chapter should improve your ability to navigate a new community in which you are required to use language in new ways. When you find yourself having to "relearn" how to write in a new situation, the readings in this chapter should help you understand that there's nothing wrong with your need to do so. While this chapter focuses mostly on nonacademic discourse communities, in Chapter 5 you'll see how the concepts you learn here also apply to writing in courses across the university—because, broadly speaking, each department or major is made up of at least one distinct discourse community.

Chapter Goals

- To understand how language practices mediate group activities
- To gain tools for examining the discourses and texts of various communities
- To gain tools for conducting ethnographic research
- To conduct research and write about it for an audience
- To understand writing and research as processes
- To improve as a reader of complex, research-based texts

The Concept of Discourse Community

JOHN SWALES

Swales, John. "The Concept of Discourse Community." *Genre Analysis: English in Academic and Research Settings*. Boston: Cambridge UP, 1990. 21–32. Print.

Framing the Reading

John Swales is a professor of linguistics and codirector of the Michigan Corpus of Academic Spoken English at the University of Michigan. He received his Ph.D. from Cambridge University and has spent most of his career in linguistics working with nonnative speakers of English on strategies to help them succeed as readers and writers in the university. His publications include *English in Today's Research World* (2000) and *Academic Writing for Graduate Students* (2004) (both coauthored with Christine Feak), *Research Genres* (2004), and *Episodes in ESP* (1985; **ESP** stands for English for Specific Purposes, a research area devoted to the teaching and learning of English for specific communities).

This excerpt is a chapter of a book Swales wrote called *Genre Analysis*. In it, he refers to concepts discussed previously in the book, which will be somewhat confusing since you have not read his book's preceding chapters. In the beginning of this chapter, Swales also refers to an ongoing academic argument over the social (**constructed**) nature of language use and to arguments about what a **discourse community** is and how it is different from a **speech community**. You likely will not fully understand this discussion, since you may not be familiar with the academic debates to which he refers. What's important for you to understand is simply that a lot of people think that *discourse community* is an important enough concept to argue about. Once Swales gets through this background/framing material, he goes on to define the term himself in section 2.3, since he thinks other people's definitions have not been clear and specific enough. This is where you should really start paying attention. As Swales defines his six characteristics of a discourse community, you should try to imagine groups you belong to that exhibit all six of these characteristics.

Be aware that Swales's style of writing is a little dry and formal, and he may use specialized linguistic terms that you don't understand. He is good, however, at highlighting his main claims and defining his terms, so if you pay close attention, he should clear up most of your confusion. If he uses terms that he does not define, and with which you are not familiar (for example, **lexis**), be sure to take a moment to look them up in a dictionary. You need to use the six characteristics he

describes to analyze communities you are familiar with, so it is important that you understand his definition.

One of the most important—and complex—of Swales's characteristics is **genre**. Unfortunately, Swales does not spend much time defining this term because he assumes that his readers are familiar with it. *Genres* are types of texts that are recognizable to readers and writers, and that meet the needs of the **rhetorical situations** in which they function. So, for example, we recognize wedding invitations and understand them as very different from horoscopes. We know that, when we are asked to write a paper for school, our teacher probably does not want us to turn in a poem instead.

Genres develop over time in response to recurring **rhetorical** needs. We have wedding invitations because people keep getting married and we need an efficient way to let people know and to ask them to attend. Rather than making up a new rhetorical solution every time the same situation occurs, we generally turn to the genre that has developed—in this case, the genre of the wedding invitation.

Swales demonstrates that discourse communities all use genres, many of which are recognizable to people outside the group (for example, memos or reports), but he notes that groups develop their own **conventions** for those genres in light of their desired goals. So memos written within AT&T, for example, might look very different from memos written by the members of the local school board.

It might be helpful to think of genres as textual tools used by groups of people as they work toward their desired ends; genres and the conventions that guide them change as the community discovers more efficient adaptations, as group membership changes, or as the group's desired ends change. For example, consider a team of biologists studying the effect of industrial pollutants on the cell structure of microorganisms in a particular body of water. In doing their research and reporting on it, the team of biologists will use many genres that are recognized outside of their discourse community, including research logs, notebooks, lab reports, conference presentations, and published scholarly papers; in many cases, however, they will have developed discourse-specific conventions guiding the production of these genres (for example, the Council of Science Editors' rules for documentation in published papers). As is the case in every discourse community, the genres and conventions that biologists use continue to change, in part as a result of new technologies (the Internet, computerized data analysis tools) that help them analyze and disseminate information in ever more efficient ways.

Getting Ready to Read

Before you read, do at least one of the following activities:

- Look up Swales's book *Genre Analysis* on a book-buying Web site or Wikipedia and read at least two reviews of it. See if you can find a listing of its table of contents. How much do you think you're missing by reading only a single chapter? (Do you feel inspired to find the book and read the rest?)
- Write a brief description of a time you've felt "out of place." What made you feel that way?

As you read, consider the following questions:

- How does what Swales describes relate to your own experience moving among different groups or communities?
- What are potential problems with Swales's explanations—places they *don't* line up with your own experiences?
- How would you describe the audience Swales seems to imagine himself writing to?

2.1 A Need for Clarification

Discourse community, the first of three terms to be examined in Part II, has so   1
far been principally appropriated by instructors and researchers adopting a 'Social View' (Faigley, 1986) of the writing process. Although I am not aware of the original provenance of the term itself, formative influences can be traced to several of the leading 'relativist' or 'social constructionist' thinkers of our time. Herzberg (1986) instances Perelman and Olbrechts-Tyteca's *The New Rhetoric* (1969), Kuhn's *The Structure of Scientific Revolutions* (1970) and Fish's *Is There a Text in this Class?* (1980). Porter (1988) discusses the significance of Foucault's analysis of 'discursive formations' in *The Archaeology of Knowledge* (1972); other contributors are Rorty (*Philosophy and the Mirror of Nature*, 1979) and Geertz (*Local Knowledge*, 1983), with Wittgenstein's *Philosophical Investigations* (1958) as an earlier antecedent (Bruffee, 1986), particularly perhaps for the commentary therein on 'language games' (3.5).

Whatever the genealogy of the term discourse community, the relevant point   2
in the present context is that it has been appropriated by the 'social perspectivists' for their variously applied purposes in writing research. It is this use that I wish to explore and in turn appropriate. Herzberg (1986) sets the scene as follows:

> Use of the term 'discourse community' testifies to the increasingly common assumption that discourse operates within conventions defined by communities, be they academic disciplines or social groups. The pedagogies associated with writing across the curriculum and academic English now use the notion of 'discourse communities' to signify a cluster of ideas: that language use in a group is a form of social behavior, that discourse is a means of maintaining and extending the group's knowledge and of initiating new members into the group, and that discourse is epistemic or constitutive of the group's knowledge.
>
> (Herzberg, 1986:1)

Irrespective of the merits of this 'cluster of ideas', the cluster is, I suggest, *consequential* of the assumption that there are indeed entities identifiable as discourse communities, not *criterial* for establishing or identifying them. They point us towards asking *how* a particular discourse community uses its discoursal conventions to initiate new members or *how* the discourse of another reifies particular values or beliefs. While such questions are well worth asking, they do not directly assist with the logically prior ones of how we recognize such communities in the first place.

Herzberg in fact concedes that there may be a definitional problem: 'The idea of "discourse community" is not well defined as yet, but like many imperfectly defined terms, it is suggestive, the center of a set of ideas rather than the sign of a settled notion' (1986:1). However, if discourse community is to be 'the center of a set of ideas'—as it is in this book—then it becomes reasonable to expect it to be, if not a settled notion, at least one that is sufficiently explicit for others to be able to accept, modify or reject on the basis of the criteria proposed.

Several other proponents of the 'social view', while believing that discourse community is a powerful and useful concept, recognize it currently raises as many questions as it answers. Porter (1988:2), for instance, puts one set of problems with exemplary conciseness: 'Should discourse communities be determined by shared objects of study, by common research methodology, by opportunity and frequency of communication, or by genre and stylistic conventions?' Fennell et al. (1987) note that current definitions have considerable vagueness and in consequence offer little guidance in identifying discourse communities. They further point out that definitions which emphasize the reciprocity of 'discourse' and 'community' (community involves discourse and discourse involves community) suffer the uncomfortable fate of ending up circular.

We need then to clarify, for procedural purposes, what is to be understood by discourse community and, perhaps in the present circumstances, it is better to offer a set of criteria sufficiently narrow that it will eliminate many of the marginal, blurred and controversial contenders. A 'strong' list of criteria will also avoid the circularity problem, because in consequence it will certainly follow that not all communities—as defined on other criteria—will be discourse communities, just as it will follow that not all discourse activity is relevant to discourse community consolidation. An exclusionary list will also presumably show that the kind of disjunctive question raised by Porter is misplaced. It is likely to show that neither shared object of study nor common procedure nor interaction nor agreed discoursal convention will themselves individually be necessary and sufficient conditions for the emergence of a discourse community, although a combination of some or all might. Conversely, the absence of any one (different subject areas, conflicting procedures, no interaction, and multiple discourse conventions) may be enough to prevent discourse community formation—as international politics frequently reminds us.

> We need then to clarify, for procedural purposes, what is to be understood by discourse community and, perhaps in the present circumstances, it is better to offer a set of criteria sufficiently narrow that it will eliminate many of the marginal, blurred and controversial contenders.

It is possible, of course, that there is no pressing need to clarify the concept 6
of *discourse community* because, at the end of the account, it will turn out to
be nothing more than composition specialists' convenient translation of the
long-established concept of *speech community* common to sociolinguistics and
central to the ethnography of communication. This view, for example, would
seem to be the position of Freed and Broadhead (1987). After a couple of
opening paragraphs on *speech community* in linguistics and on audience analysis, they observe, 'only recently have compositional studies begun to investigate communities of writers and readers, though the terminology seems to be
changing to "discourse communities" in order to signal the focus on the written rather than the spoken' (1987:154). Whether it is appropriate to identify
discourse community with a subset of *speech community* is the topic of the
next section.

2.2 Speech Communities and Discourse Communities

Speech community has been an evolving concept in sociolinguistics and the con- 7
sequent variety of definitional criteria has been discussed—among others—by
Hudson (1980), Saville-Troike (1982) and especially by Braithwaite (1984).
At the outset, a speech community was seen as being composed of those who
share similar *linguistic rules* (Bloomfield, 1933), and in those terms we could
legitimately refer to, say, the speech community of the English-speaking world.
Later, Labov will emphasize 'shared norms' rather than shared performance
characteristics but still conclude that 'New York City is a single speech community, and not a collection of speakers living side by side, borrowing occasionally from each other's dialects' (Labov, 1966:7). Others, such as Fishman
(1971), have taken as criterial patterned regularities in the *use* of language.
In consequence, a speech community is seen as being composed of those who
share functional rules that determine the appropriacy of utterances. Finally,
there are those such as Hymes who argue for multiple criteria:

> A speech community is defined, then, tautologically but radically, as a community
> sharing knowledge of rules for the conduct and interpretation of speech. Such
> sharing comprises knowledge of at least one form of speech, and knowledge also
> of its patterns of use. Both conditions are necessary.
>
> (Hymes, 1974:51)

There are a number of reasons why I believe even a tight definition of speech
community (shared linguistic forms, shared regulative rules and shared cultural
concepts) will not result in making an alternative definition of discourse community unnecessary. The first is concerned with medium; not so much in the trivial
sense that 'speech' just will not do as an exclusive modifier of communities that
are often heavily engaged in writing, but rather in terms of what that literary
activity implies. Literacy takes away locality and parochiality, for members are
more likely to communicate with other members in distant places, and are more
likely to react and respond to writings rather than speech from the past.

A second reason for separating the two concepts derives from the need to distinguish a *sociolinguistic* grouping from a *sociorhetorical* one. In a sociolinguistic speech community, the communicative needs of the *group,* such as socialization or group solidarity, tend to predominate in the development and maintenance of its discoursal characteristics. The primary determinants of linguistic behavior are social. However, in a sociorhetorical discourse community, the primary determinants of linguistic behavior are functional, since a discourse community consists of a group of people who link up in order to pursue objectives that are prior to those of socialization and solidarity, even if these latter should consequently occur. In a discourse community, the communicative needs of the *goals* tend to predominate in the development and maintenance of its discoursal characteristics.

Thirdly, in terms of the fabric of society, speech communities are centripetal (they tend to absorb people into that general fabric), whereas discourse communities are centrifugal (they tend to separate people into occupational or speciality-interest groups). A speech community typically inherits its membership by birth, accident or adoption; a discourse community recruits its members by persuasion, training or relevant qualification. To borrow a term from the kind of association readers of this book are likely to belong to, an archetypal discourse community tends to be a *Specific Interest Group.*

2.3 A Conceptualization of Discourse Community

I would now like to propose six defining characteristics that will be necessary and sufficient for identifying a group of individuals as a discourse community.

1. *A discourse community has a broadly agreed set of common public goals.* These public goals may be formally inscribed in documents (as is often the case with associations and clubs), or they may be more tacit. The goals are *public,* because spies may join speech and discourse communities for hidden purposes of subversion, while more ordinary people may join organizations with private hopes of commercial or romantic advancement. In some instances, but not in many, the goals may be high level or abstract. In a Senate or Parliament there may well exist overtly adversarial groups of members, but these adversaries may broadly share some common objective as striving for improved government. In the much more typical non-adversarial discourse communities, reduction in the broad level of agreement may fall to a point where communication breaks down and the discourse community splits. It is commonality of goal, not shared object of study that is criterial, even if the former often subsumes the latter. But not always. The fact that the shared object of study is, say, the Vatican, does not imply that students of the Vatican in history departments, the Kremlin, dioceses, birth control agencies and liberation theology seminaries form a discourse community.
2. *A discourse community has mechanisms of intercommunication among its members.*

8

9

10

11

12

The participatory mechanisms will vary according to the community: meetings, telecommunications, correspondence, newsletters, conversations and so forth. This criterion is quite stringent because it produces a negative answer to the case of 'The Café Owner Problem' (Najjar, personal communication). In generalized form, the problem goes as follows: individuals A, B, C and so on occupy the same professional roles in life. They interact (in speech and writing) with the same clienteles; they originate, receive and respond to the same kind of messages for the same purposes; they have an approximately similar range of genre skills. And yet, as Café owners working long hours in their own establishments, and not being members of the Local Chamber of Commerce, A, B and C never interact with one another. Do they form a discourse community? We can notice first that 'The Café Owner Problem' is not quite like those situations where A, B and C operate as 'point'. A, B and C may be lighthouse keepers on their lonely rocks, or missionaries in their separate jungles, or neglected consular officials in their rotting outposts. In all these cases, although A, B and C may never interact, they all have lines of communication back to base, and presumably acquired discourse community membership as a key element in their initial training.

Bizzell (1987) argues that the café owner kind of social group will be 13 a discourse community because 'its members may share the social-class-based or ethnically-based discursive practices of people who are likely to become café owners in their neighborhood' (1987:5). However, even if this sharing of discursive practice occurs, it does not resolve the logical problem of assigning membership of a community to individuals who neither admit nor recognize that such a community exists.

3. *A discourse community uses its participatory mechanisms primarily to* 14 *provide information and feedback.*
Thus, membership implies uptake of the informational opportunities. Individuals might pay an annual subscription to the *Acoustical Society of America* but if they never open any of its communications they cannot be said to belong to the discourse community, even though they are formally members of the society. The secondary purposes of the information exchange will vary according to the common goals: to improve performance in a football squad or in an orchestra, to make money in a brokerage house, to grow better roses in a gardening club, or to dent the research front in an academic department.

4. *A discourse community utilizes and hence possesses one or more genres* 15 *in the communicative furtherance of its aims.*
A discourse community has developed and continues to develop discoursal expectations. These may involve appropriacy of topics, the form, function and positioning of discoursal elements, and the roles texts play in the operation of the discourse community. In so far as 'genres are how things get done, when language is used to accomplish them' (Martin, 1985:250), these discoursal expectations are created by the *genres* that articulate the operations of the discourse community. One of the purposes of this criterion is

to question discourse community status for new or newly-emergent group-ings. Such groupings need, as it were, to settle down and work out their communicative proceedings and practices before they can be recognized as discourse communities. If a new grouping 'borrows' genres from other discourse communities, such borrowings have to be assimilated.

5. *In addition to owning genres, a discourse community has acquired some specific lexis.* 16

This specialization may involve using lexical items known to the wider speech communities in special and technical ways, as in information tech-nology discourse communities, or using highly technical terminology as in medical communities. Most commonly, however, the inbuilt dynamic towards an increasingly shared and specialized terminology is realized through the development of community-specific abbreviations and acro-nyms. The use of these (ESL, EAP, WAC, NCTE, TOEFL, etc.) is, of course, driven by the requirements for efficient communication exchange between experts. It is hard to conceive, at least in the contemporary English-speak-ing world, of a group of well-established members of a discourse commu-nity communicating among themselves on topics relevant to the goals of the community and not using lexical items puzzling to outsiders. It is hard to imagine attending perchance the convention of some group of which one is an outsider and understanding every word. If it were to happen—as might occur in the inaugural meeting of some quite new grouping—then that grouping would not yet constitute a discourse community.

6. *A discourse community has a threshold level of members with a suitable degree of relevant content and discoursal expertise.* 17

Discourse communities have changing memberships; individuals enter as apprentices and leave by death or in other less involuntary ways. How-ever, survival of the community depends on a reasonable ratio between novices and experts.

2.4 An Example of a Discourse Community

As we have seen, those interested in discourse communities have typically sited their discussions within academic contexts, thus possibly creating a false impression that such communities are only to be associated with intellectual paradigms or scholarly cliques. Therefore, for my principal example of a dis-course community, I have deliberately chosen one that is not academic, but which nevertheless is probably typical enough of many others. The discourse community is a hobby group and has an 'umbrella organization' called the Hong Kong Study Circle, of which I happen to be a member. The aims of the HKSC (note the abbreviation) are to foster interest in and knowledge of the stamps of Hong Kong (the various printings, etc.) and of their uses (postal rates, cancellations, etc.). Currently there are about 320 members scattered across the world, but with major concentrations in Great Britain, the USA and Hong Kong itself and minor ones in Holland and Japan. Based on the membership list, my guess is that about a third of the members are non-native speakers of 18

English and about a fifth women. The membership varies in other ways: a few are rich and have acquired world-class collections of classic rarities, but many are not and pursue their hobby interest with material that costs very little to acquire. Some are full-time specialist dealers, auctioneers and catalogue publishers, but most are collectors. From what little I know, the collectors vary greatly in occupation. One standard reference work was co-authored by a stamp dealer and a Dean at Yale; another was written by a retired Lieutenant-Colonel. The greatest authority on the nineteenth century carriage of Hong Kong mail, with three books to his credit, has recently retired from a lifetime of service as a signalman with British Rail. I mention these brief facts to show that the members of the discourse community have, superficially at least, nothing in common except their shared hobby interest, although Bizzell (1992) is probably correct in pointing out that there may be psychological predispositions that attract particular people to collecting and make them 'kindred spirits'.

The main mechanism, or 'forum' (Herrington, 1985) for intercommunication 19 is a bi-monthly Journal and Newsletter, the latest to arrive being No. 265. There are scheduled meetings, including an Annual General Meeting, that takes place in London, but rarely more than a dozen members attend. There is a certain amount of correspondence and some phoning, but without the Journal/Newsletter I doubt the discourse community would survive. The combined periodical often has a highly interactive content as the following extracts show:

2. Hong Kong, Type 12, with Index
No one has yet produced another example of this c.d.s. that I mentioned on J.256/7 as having been found with an index letter 'C' with its opening facing downwards, but Mr. Scamp reports that he has seen one illustrated in an auction catalogue having a normal 'C' and dated MY 9/59 (Type 12 is the 20 mm single-circle broken in upper half by HONG KONG). It must be in someone's collection!

3. The B.P.O.'s in Kobe and Nagasaki
Mr. Pullan disputes the statement at the top of J.257/3 that 'If the postal clerk had not violated regulations by affixing the MR 17/79 (HIOGO) datestamp on the front, we might have no example of this c.d.s. at all." He states that 'By 1879 it was normal practice for the sorter's datestamp to be struck on the front, the change from the back of the cover occurring generally in 1877, though there are isolated earlier examples'; thus there was no violation of regulations.

My own early attempts to be a full member of the community were not marked by success. Early on I published an article in the journal which used a fairly complex frequency analysis of occurrence—derived from Applied Linguistics—in order to offer an alternative explanation of a puzzle well known to members of the HKSC. The only comments that this effort to establish credibility elicited were 'too clever by half and 'Mr Swales, we won't change our minds without a chemical analysis'. I have also had to learn over time the particular terms of approval and disapproval for a philatelic item (cf. Becher, 1981) such as 'significant', 'useful', 'normal', and not to comment directly on the monetary value of such items.

Apart from the conventions governing articles, queries and replies in the 20
Journal/Newsletter, the discourse community has developed a genre-specific
set of conventions for describing items of Hong Kong postal history. These
occur in members' collections, whether for display or not, and are found in
somewhat more abbreviated forms in specialized auction catalogues, as in the
following example:

> 1176   1899 Combination PPC to Europe franked CIP 4 C canc large CANTON
> dollar chop, pair HK 2 C carmine added & Hong Kong index B cds. Arr
> cds. (1) (Photo) HK $1500.

Even if luck and skill were to combine to interpret PPC as 'picture postcard',
CIP as 'Chinese Imperial Post', a 'combination' as a postal item legitimately
combining the stamps of two or more nations and so on, an outsider would
still not be in a position to estimate whether 1500 Hong Kong dollars would
be an appropriate sum to bid. However, the distinction between insider and
outsider is not absolute but consists of gradations. A professional stamp dealer
not dealing in Hong Kong material would have a useful general schema,
while a member of a very similar discourse community, say the China Postal
History Society, may do as well as a member of the HKSC because of overlapping goals.

The discourse community I have discussed meets all six of the proposed 21
defining criteria: there are common goals, participatory mechanisms, information exchange, community specific genres, a highly specialized terminology and
a high general level of expertise. On the other hand, distance between members
geographically, ethnically and socially presumably means that they do not form
a speech community.

2.5 Remaining Issues

If we now return to Herzberg's 'cluster of ideas' quoted near the beginning 22
of this section, we can see that the first two (language use is a form of social
behaviour, and discourse maintains and extends a group's knowledge) accord
with the conceptualization of discourse community proposed here. The third is
the claim that 'discourse is epistemic or constitutive of the group's knowledge'
(Herzberg, 1986:1). This claim is also advanced, although in slightly different
form, in a paper by Bizzell:

> In the absence of consensus, let me offer a tentative definition: a 'discourse com-
> munity' is a group of people who share certain language-using practices. These
> practices can be seen as conventionalized in two ways. Stylistic conventions regu-
> late social interactions both within the group and in its dealings with outsiders:
> to this extent 'discourse community' borrows from the sociolinguistic concept
> of 'speech community'. Also, canonical knowledge regulates the world-views of
> group members, how they interpret experience; to this extent 'discourse commu-
> nity' borrows from the literary-critical concept of 'interpretive community'.
>
> (Bizzell, 1992: 1)

The issue of whether a community's discourse and its discoursal expectations are constitutive or regulative of world-view is a contemporary reworking of the Whorfian hypothesis that each language possesses a structure which must at some level influence the way its users view the world (Carroll, 1956). The issue is an important one, because as Bizzell later observes 'If we acknowledge that participating in a discourse community entails some assimilation of its world view, then it becomes difficult to maintain the position that discourse conventions can be employed in a detached, instrumental way' (Bizzell, 1992: 9).

However, this is precisely the position I wish to maintain, especially if *can be* 23 *employed* is interpreted as *may sometimes be employed*. There are several reasons for this. First, it is possible to deny the premise that participation entails assimilation. There are enough spies, undercover agents and fifth columnists in the world to suggest that non-assimilation is at least possible. Spies are only successful if they participate successfully in the relevant speech and discourse communities of the domain which they have infiltrated; however, if they also *assimilate* they cease to be single spies but become double agents. On a less dramatic level, there is enough pretense, deception and face-work around to suggest that the acting out of roles is not that uncommon; and to take a relatively innocuous context, a prospective son-in-law may pretend to be an active and participating member of a bridge-playing community in order to make a favorable impression on his prospective parents-in-law.

Secondly, sketching the boundaries of discourse communities in ways that 24 I have attempted implies (a) that individuals may belong to several discourse communities and (b) that individuals will vary in the number of discourse communities they belong to and hence in the number of genres they command. At one extreme there may be a sense of discourse community deprivation— 'Cooped up in the house with the children all day'. At the other extreme, there stand the skilled professional journalists with their chameleon-like ability to assume temporary membership of a wide range of discourse communities. These observations suggest discourse communities will vary, both intrinsically and in terms of the member's perspective, in the degree to which they impose a world-view. Belonging to the Hong Kong Study Circle is not likely to be as constitutive as abandoning the world for the seclusion of a closed religious order.

Thirdly, to deny the instrumental employment of discourse conventions is to 25 threaten one common type of apprenticeship and to cast a hegemonical shadow over international education. Students taking a range of different courses often operate successfully as 'ethnographers' of these various academic milieux (Johns, 1988a) and do so with sufficient detachment and instrumentality to avoid developing multiple personalities, even if, with more senior and specialized students, the epistemic nature of the discourse may be more apparent, as the interesting case study by Berkenkotter et al. (1988) shows. I would also like to avoid taking a position whereby a foreign student is seen, via participation, to assimilate inevitably the world-view of the host discourse community. While this may happen, I would not want to accept that discourse conventions cannot be successfully deployed in an instrumental manner (see James, 1980 for further discussion of variability in foreign student roles). Overall, the extent to which discourse is constitutive of world-view would seem to be a matter of investigation rather than assumption.

Just as, for my applied purposes, I do not want to accept assimilation of world-view as criterial, so neither do I want to accept a threshold level of personal involvement as criterial. While it may be high in a small business, a class or a department, and may be notoriously high among members of amateur dramatic discourse communities, the fact remains that the active members of the Hong Kong Study Circle—to use an example already discussed—form a successful discourse community despite a very low level of personal involvement. Nor is centrality to the main affairs of life, family, work, money, education, and so on, criterial. Memberships of hobby groups may be quite peripheral, while memberships of professional associations may be closely connected to the business of a career (shockingly so as when a member is *debarred*), but both may equally constitute discourse communities. Finally, discourse communities will vary in the extent to which they are norm-developed, or have their set and settled ways. Some, at a particular moment in time, will be highly conservative ('these are things that have been and remain'), while others may be norm-developing and in a state of flux (Kuhn, 1970; Huckin, 1987).

The delineation of these variable features throws interesting light on the fine study of contexts for writing in two senior college Chemical Engineering classes by Herrington (1985). Herrington concluded the Lab course and Design Process course 'represented distinct communities where different issues were addressed, different lines of reasoning used, different writer and audience roles assumed, and different social purposes served by writing' (1985:331). (If we also note that the two courses were taught in the same department at the same institution by the same staff to largely the same students, then the Herrington study suggests additionally that there may be more of invention than we would like to see in our models of disciplinary culture.) The disparities between the two courses can be interpreted in the following way. Writing in the Lab course was central to the 'display familiarity' macro-act of college assignments (Horowitz, 1986a)—which the students were accustomed to. Writing in the Design course was central to the persuasive reporting macro-act of the looming professional world, which the students were not accustomed to. The Lab course was *norm-developed,* while the Design course was *norm-developing.* As Herrington observes, in Lab both students and faculty were all too aware that the conceptual issue in the assignments was *not* an issue for the audience—the professor knew the answers. But it was an issue in Design. As a part consequence, the level of *personal involvement* was much higher in the Design course where professor and student interacted together in a joint problem-solving environment.

The next issue to be addressed in this section is whether certain groupings, including academic classes, constitute *discourse* communities. Given the six criteria, it would seem clear that shareholders of General Motors, members of the Book of the Month Club, voters for a particular political party, clienteles of restaurants and bars (except perhaps in soap-operas), employees of a university, and inhabitants of an apartment block all fail to qualify.

But what about academic classes? Except in exceptional cases of well-knit groups of advanced students already familiar with much of the material, an academic class is unlikely to be a discourse community at the outset. However, the hoped-for outcome is that it will form a discourse community (McKenna, 1987). Somewhere down the line, broad agreement on goals will be established, a full range of participatory mechanisms will be created, information exchange and feedback will flourish by peer-review and instructor commentary, understanding the rationale of and facility with appropriate genres will develop, control of the technical vocabulary in both oral and written contexts will emerge, and a level of expertise that permits critical thinking be made manifest. Thus it turns out that providing a relatively constrained operational set of criteria for defining discourse communities also provides a coign of vantage, if from the applied linguist's corner, for assessing educational processes and for reviewing what needs to be done to assist non-native speakers and others to engage fully in them.

Finally, it is necessary to concede that the account I have provided of dis- 29 course community, for all its attempts to offer a set of pragmatic and operational criteria, remains in at least one sense somewhat removed from reality. It is utopian and 'oddly free of many of the tensions, discontinuities and conflicts in the sorts of talk and writing that go on everyday in the classrooms and departments of an actual university' (Harris, 1989:14). Bizzell (1987) too has claimed that discourse communities can be healthy and yet contain contradictions; and Herrington (1989) continues to describe composition researchers as a 'community' while unveiling the tensions and divisions within the group. The precise status of conflictive discourse communities is doubtless a matter for future study, but here it can at least be accepted that discourse communities can, over a period of time, lose as well as gain consensus, and at some critical juncture, be so divided as to be on the point of splintering.

References

Becher, Tony. 1981. Towards a definition of disciplinary cultures. *Studies in Higher Education* 6:109–22.

Berkenkotter, Carol, Thomas N. Huckin, and John Ackerman. 1988. Conventions, conversations and the writer: case study of a student in a rhetoric Ph.D. program. *Research in the Teaching of English* 22:9–44.

Bizzell, Patricia. 1987. Some uses of the concept of 'discourse community.' Paper presented at the Penn State Conference on Composition, July, 1987.

Bizzell, Patricia. 1992. "What is a Discourse Community?" *Academic Discourse and Critical Consciousness.* U Pittsburgh P. 222–237.

Bloomfield, L. 1933, *Language.* New York: Holt & Company.

Braithwaite, Charles A. 1984. Towards a conceptualization of 'speech community'. In *Papers from the Minnesota Regional Conference on Language and Linguistics:* 13–29.

Bruffee, K. A. 1986. Social construction, language, and the authority of knowledge: a bibliography. *College English* 48:773–90.

Carroll, John B. (ed.) 1956. *Language, thought and reality: selected writings of Benjamin Lee Whorf.* New York: John Wiley.

Faigley, Lester. 1986. Competing theories of process: a critique and a proposal. *College English* 48:527–42.

Fennell, Barbara, Carl Herndl, and Carolyn-Miller. 1987. Mapping discourse communities. Paper presented at the CCC Convention, Atlanta, Ga, March, 1987.

Fish, Stanley. 1980. *Is there a text in this class?* Harvard, Mass: Harvard University Press.

Fishman, Joshua (ed.) 1971. *Sociolinguistics: a brief introduction*. Rowley, Mass: Newbury House.

Foucault, Michel. 1972. *The archaeology of knowledge*. New York: Harper & Row.

Freed, Richard C. and Glenn J. Broadhead. 1987. Discourse communities, sacred texts, and institutional norms. *College Composition and Communication* 38:154–65.

Geertz, Clifford. 1983. *Local knowledge: further essays in interpretive anthropology*. New York Basic Books.

Harris, Joseph. 1989. The idea of community in the study of writing. *College Composition and Communication* 40:11–22.

Herrington, Anne. 1985. Writing in academic settings a study of the context for writing in two college chemical engineering courses. *Research in the Teaching of English* 19:331–61.

Herrington, Anne. 1989. The first twenty years of *Research in the Teaching of English* and the growth of a research community in composition studies. *Research in the Teaching of English* 23:117–38.

Herzberg, Bruce. 1986. The politics of discourse communities. Paper presented at the CCC Convention, New Orleans, La, March, 1986.

Horowitz, Daniel M. 1986a. What professors actually require: academic tasks for the ESL classroom. *TESOL Quarterly* 20:445–62.

Huckin, Thomas N. 1987. Surprise value in scientific discourse. Paper presented at the CCC Convention. Atlanta, Ga, March, 1987.

Hudson, R.A. 1980. *Sociolinguistics*. Cambridge: Cambridge University Press.

Hymes, Dell. 1974. Foundations in *sociolinguistics: ethnographic approach*. Philadelphia: University of Pennsylvania Press.

James, Kenneth. 1980. Seminar overview. In Greenall and Price (eds.):7–21.

Johns, Ann M. 1988a. The discourse communities dilemma: identifying transferable skills for the academic milieu. *English for Specific Purposes*. 7:55–60.

Kuhn, Thomas S. 1970. *The structure of scientific revolutions* (second edition). Chicago University of Chicago Press.

Labov, William. 1966. *The social stratification of English in New York City*. Washington, D.C.: Center for Applied Linguistics.

Martin, J. R. 1985. Process and text: two aspects of human semiosis. In Benson and Greaves (eds.): 248–74.

McKenna, Eleanor. 1987. Preparing foreign students to enter discourse communities in the US. *English for Specific Purposes* 6:187–202.

Perelman, Chaim and L. Olbrechts-Tyteca. 1969, *The new rhetoric; a treatise on argumentation*. Notre Dame, IN: Notre Dame University Press.

Porter, James E. 1988. The problem of defining discourse communities. Paper presented at the CCC Convention, St. Louis, March, 1988.

Rorty, Richard. 1979. *Philosophy and the mirror of nature*. Princeton, NJ: Princeton University Press.

Saville-Troike, Muriel. 1982. *The ethnography of communication*. Oxford: Basil Blackwell.

Wittgenstein, Ludwig. 1958. *Philosophical investigations*. Oxford: Basil Blackwell.

Questions for Discussion and Journaling

1. Use your own words to describe each of the six characteristics of a discourse community according to Swales. Can you find examples of each from your own experience?
2. Swales discusses his own attempt to join the Hong Kong Study Circle. What went wrong? Which of the six characteristics did he have trouble with?
3. According to Swales, would a first-year college classroom count as a discourse community? What about a graduate class? Why or why not?
4. Swales argues that it is possible to participate in a discourse community without being assimilated in it. What does this mean?
5. Consider a discourse community you belong to, and describe how it meets the six characteristics of a discourse community. For example, what are its shared goals? What is its lexis? What are its genres?
6. Consider a time when you participated in a discourse community but resisted it or were not assimilated into it. What happened?

Applying and Exploring Ideas

1. Write a short narrative in which you dramatize Swales's problems joining the HKSC or in which you imagine the problems a newcomer has in learning the ropes in any new discourse community you can imagine, from *World of Warcraft* to medical school to a sorority.
2. Write a one-page letter to an incoming student in which you explain what discourse communities are and how knowing about them will be helpful to that student in college.
3. Spend a few hours hanging out with or near a discourse community of your choice—dorm, store, gaming community, and so forth. Write down every use of specialized language that you hear—whether it is an unusual word or phrase, or simply an unusual use of a fairly common word or phrase. And note on your "lexis list" when a term you were familiar with was being used with a new meaning or in a new way.

Meta Moment
Do you understand anything differently about your own writing experiences after reading Swales's description of how discourse communities work? If so, consider a way that this understanding can help you navigate discourse communities in the future.

Literacy, Discourse, and Linguistics:
Introduction

JAMES PAUL GEE

Gee, James P. "Literacy, Discourse, and Linguistics: Introduction." *Journal of Education* 171.1 (1989): 5–17. Print.

Framing the Reading

James Paul Gee (his last name is pronounced like the "gee" in "gee whiz") is the Tashia Morgridge Professor of Reading at the University of Wisconsin at Madison. Gee has taught linguistics at Stanford, Northeastern University, Boston University, and the University of Southern California. His book *Sociolinguistics and Literacies* (1990) was important in the formation of the interdisciplinary field known as "New Literacy Studies," and he's published a number of other works on literacy as well, including *Why Video Games Are Good for Your Soul* (2005). Based on his research, he's a widely respected voice on literacy among his peers.

In this article, Gee introduces his term **Discourses**, which he explains as "saying (writing)-doing-being-valuing-believing combinations" that are "ways of being in the world" (para. 5). (The capital D is important for Gee, to make a *Discourse* distinct from *discourse*, or "connected stretches of language" that we use every day to communicate with each other.) Gee spends a lot of time working to make these definitions clear, using a variety of examples. A number of other terms crop up as well in his work: *dominant* and *nondominant* Discourses, *primary* and *secondary* Discourses, **literacy**, **apprenticeship**, **metaknowledge**, and **mushfake**, among others. Probably the most useful way to read this article for the first time is to try to (1) define terms and (2) apply what Gee is saying to your own experience by thinking of related examples from your own life.

There is one particularly controversial argument in the article. Gee insists that you can't "more or less" embody a Discourse—you're either recognized by others as a full member of it or you're not. Many readers can't make this argument line up with their perceptions of their own experiences in acquiring new Discourses; they haven't experienced this "all-or-nothing" effect. It's also possible to read Gee's article as undermining itself: He explains that we are never "purely" members of a single Discourse but, rather, that a given Discourse is influenced by other Discourses of which we're also members. By this reasoning, there may be no such thing as embodying a Discourse fully or perfectly.

The important thing is this: When you encounter that subargument, or others you might have trouble accepting, your job as a reader is to stay engaged in the *overall* argument while "setting aside" the particular argument you're not sure about. As you know from your own experience, people can be wrong about smaller points while still being right about bigger ones. Further, scholarly arguments are made very precisely with very careful language; Gee's argument might work if you read it exactly as he intended it to be understood, without trying to apply it too broadly. But you should also read critically and test his claims against your experiences.

If you are interested in seeing and hearing from Gee directly, you can watch a short MacArthur Foundation video of him talking about games and learning by searching YouTube for "James Gee games learning."

Getting Ready to Read

Before you read, do at least one of the following activities:

- Google the term *mushfake.* What comes up?
- Consider two or three activities you take part in that are very different from each other, having different languages and purposes (for example, college, volunteering, and a hobby like gaming). Does one activity influence the way you participate in the others, or do they remain distinctly separate in your life? Explain.

As you read, consider the following questions:

- Why is Gee so concerned with how people learn Discourses? What does this have to do with education?
- Are there alternative explanations for the knowledge Gee describes? Could we have similar knowledge for some reason *other than* that there are Discourses?
- Does Gee's discussion of *Discourses* sound similar to ideas you've encountered in other chapters in this book? If so, which ones?

What I propose in the following papers, in the main, is *a way of talking* 1 *about* literacy and linguistics. I believe that a new field of study, integrating "psycho" and "socio" approaches to language from a variety of disciplines, is emerging, a field which we might call *literacy studies.* Much of this work, I think (and hope), shares at least some of the assumptions of the following papers. These papers, though written at different times, and for different purposes, are, nonetheless, based on the claim that the focus of literacy studies or applied linguistics should *not* be language, or literacy, but *social practices.* This claim, I believe, has a number of socially important and cognitively interesting consequences.

"Language" is a misleading term; it too often suggests "grammar." It is a 2 truism that a person can know perfectly the grammar of a language and not know how to use that language. It is not just *what* you say, but *how* you say it. If I enter my neighborhood bar and say to my tattooed drinking buddy, as I sit down, "May I have a match please?" my grammar is perfect, but what I have said is wrong nonetheless. It is less often remarked that a person could be able to use a language perfectly and *still* not make sense. It is not just *how* you say it, but what you *are* and *do* when you say it. If I enter my neighborhood bar and say to my drinking buddy, as I sit down, "Gime a match, wouldya?," while placing a napkin on the bar stool to avoid getting my newly pressed designer jeans dirty, I have said the right thing, but my "saying-doing" combination is nonetheless all wrong.

F. Niyi Akinnaso and Cheryl A iroturu (1982) present "simulated job 3 interviews" from two welfare mothers in a CETA job training program. The first woman, asked whether she has ever shown initiative in a previous job, responds: "Well, yes, there's this Walgreen's Agency, I worked as a microfilm operator, OK. And it was a snow storm, OK. And it was usually six people workin' in a group . . ." and so forth (p. 34). This woman is simply using the wrong grammar (the wrong "dialect") for this type of (middle-class) interview. It's a perfectly good grammar (dialect), it just won't get you this type of job in this type of society.

> "Language" is a misleading term;
> it too often suggests "grammar."
> It is a truism that a person can
> know perfectly the grammar of a
> language and not know how to   4
> use that language.

The second woman (the authors' "success" case) responds to a similar question by saying ". . . I was left alone to handle the office. I didn't really have a lot of experience. But I had enough experience to deal with any situations that came up . . . and those that I couldn't handle at the time, if there was someone who had more experience than myself, I asked questions to find out what procedure I would use. If something came up and if I didn't know who to really go to, I would jot it down . . . on a piece of paper, so that I wouldn't forget that if anyone that was more qualified than myself, I could ask them about it and how I would go about solving it. So I feel I'm capable of handling just

I am deeply indebted to Candy Mitchell for editing this collection of papers, and to Jim O'Brien for copy-editing the papers appearing here for the first time. The following people are responsible (they may be aghast to hear) for having helped to lead me to the views I hold. First, a set of people whose writings have inspired me: Wallace Chafe, Michael Cole, John Gumperz, Shirley Brice Heath, Dell Hymes, William Labov, Roger and Suzanne Scollon, Brian Street, Cordon Wells, and Jim Wertsch. Second, a group of people not only whose writings have inspired me, but whose discussion of the issues in these papers with me, as well as whose friendship, has left me always in their debt: Elaine Andersen, Maria Brisk, Chip Bruce, Courtney Cazden, David Dickenson, Steve Krashen, Steve Cordon, Steve Griffin, Henry Giroux, Donaldo Macedo, Sarah Michaels, Bea Mikulecky, Elliot Mishler, Car cy Mitchell, Catherine Snow, and Dennie Wolt. These papers ultimately all have their origin in the kindness that Sarah Michaels and Courtney Cazden extended to me when I first arrived in Boston by inviting me to take an interest in their concerns.

about any situation, whether it's on my own or under supervision" (p. 34). This woman hasn't got a real problem with her grammar (remember this is *speech*, not *writing*), nor is there any real problem with the *use* to which she puts that grammar, but she is expressing the *wrong values*. She views being left in charge as just another form of supervision, namely, supervision by "other people's" knowledge and expertise. And she fails to characterize her own expertise in the overly optimistic form called for by such interviews. Using this response as an example of "successful training" is only possible because the authors, aware that language is more than grammar (namely, "use"), are unaware that communication is more than language use.

At any moment we are using language we must say or write the right thing in the right way while playing the right social role and (appearing) to hold the right values, beliefs, and attitudes. Thus, what is important is not language, and surely not grammar, but *saying (writing)-doing-being-valuing-believing combinations*. These combinations I call "Discourses," with a capital "D" ("discourse" with a little "d," to me, means connected stretches of language that make sense, so "discourse" is part of "Discourse"). Discourses are ways of being in the world; they are forms of life which integrate words, acts, values, beliefs, attitudes, and social identities as well as gestures, glances, body positions, and clothes. 5

A Discourse is a sort of "identity kit" which comes complete with the appropriate costume and instructions on how to act, talk, and often write, so as to take on a particular role that others will recognize. Being "trained" as a linguist meant that I learned to speak, think, and act like a linguist, and to recognize others when they do so. Some other examples of Discourses: (enacting) being an American or a Russian, a man or a woman, a member of a certain socioeconomic class, a factory worker or a boardroom executive, a doctor or a hospital patient, a teacher, an administrator, or a student, a student of physics or a student of literature, a member of a sewing circle, a club, a street gang, a lunchtime social gathering, or a regular at a local bar. We all have many Discourses. 6

How does one acquire a Discourse? It turns out that much that is claimed, controversially, to be true of second language acquisition or socially situated cognition (Beebe, 1988; Dulay, Burt, & Krashen, 1982; Grosjean, 1982; Krashen, 1982, 1985a, 1985b, Krashen & Terrell, 1983; Lave, 1988; Rogoff & Lave, 1984) is, in fact, more obviously true of the acquisition of Discourses. Discourses are not mastered by overt instruction (even less so than languages, and hardly anyone ever fluently acquired a second language sitting in a classroom), but by enculturation ("apprenticeship") into social practices through scaffolded and supported interaction with people who have already mastered the Discourse (Cazden, 1988; Heath, 1983). This is how we all acquired our native language and our home-based Discourse. It is how we acquire all later, more public-oriented Discourses. If you have no access to the social practice, you don't get in the Discourse, you don't have it. You cannot overtly teach anyone a Discourse, in a classroom or anywhere else. Discourses are not bodies of knowledge like physics or archeology or linguistics. Therefore, ironically, while you can overtly teach someone *linguistics*, a body of knowledge, you can't 7

teach them *to be a linguist*, that is, to use a Discourse. The most you can do is
to let them practice being a linguist with you.

The various Discourses which constitute each of us as persons are chang-   8
ing and often are not fully consistent with each other; there is often conflict
and tension between the values, beliefs, attitudes, interactional styles, uses of
language, and ways of being in the world which two or more Discourses represent. Thus, there is no real sense in which we humans are consistent or well
integrated creatures from a cognitive or social viewpoint, though, in fact, most
Discourses assume that we are (and thus we do too, while we are in them).

All of us, through our *primary socialization* early in life in the home and   9
peer group, acquire (at least) one initial Discourse. This initial Discourse,
which I call our *primary Discourse,* is the one we first use to make sense of the
world and interact with others. Our primary Discourse constitutes our original
and home-based sense of identity, and, I believe, it can be seen whenever we
are interacting with "intimates" in totally casual (unmonitored) social interaction. We acquire this primary Discourse, not by overt instruction, but by being
a member of a primary socializing group (family, clan, peer group). Further,
aspects and pieces of the primary Discourse become a "carrier" or "foundation" for Discourses acquired later in life. Primary Discourses differ significantly across various social (cultural, ethnic, regional, and economic) groups
in the United States.

After our initial socialization in our home community, each of us interacts   10
with various non-home-based social institutions—institutions in the public
sphere, beyond the family and immediate kin and peer group. These may be
local stores and churches, schools, community groups, state and national businesses, agencies and organizations, and so forth. Each of these social institutions
commands and demands one or more Discourses and we acquire these fluently
to the extent that we are given access to these institutions and are allowed
apprenticeships within them. Such Discourses I call *secondary Discourses.*

We can also make an important distinction between *dominant Discourses*   11
and *nondominant Discourses.* Dominant Discourses are secondary Discourses
the mastery of which, at a particular place and time, brings with it the (potential) acquisition of social "goods" (money, prestige, status, etc.). Non-dominant
Discourses are secondary Discourses the mastery of which often brings solidarity with a particular social network, but not wider status and social goods in
the society at large.

Finally, and yet more importantly, we can always ask about how much *ten-*   12
sion or conflict is present between any two of a person's Discourses (Rosaldo,
1989). We have argued above that some degree of conflict and tension (if only
because of the discrete historical origins of particular Discourses) will almost
always be present. However, some people experience more overt and direct
conflicts between two or more of their Discourses than do others (for example,
many women academics feel conflict between certain feminist Discourses and
certain standard academic Discourses such as traditional literary criticism). I
argue that when such conflict or tension exists, it can deter acquisition of one
or the other or both of the conflicting Discourses, or, at least, affect the fluency

of a mastered Discourse on certain occasions of use (e.g., in stressful situations such as interviews).

Very often dominant groups in a society apply rather constant "tests" of the 13 fluency of the dominant Discourses in which their power is symbolized. These tests take on two functions: they are tests of "natives" or, at least, "fluent users" of the Discourse, and they are *gates* to exclude "non-natives" (people whose very conflicts with dominant Discourses show they were not, in fact, "born" to them). The sorts of tension and conflict we have mentioned here are particularly acute when they involve tension and conflict between one's primary Discourse and a dominant secondary Discourse.

Discourses, primary and secondary, can be studied, in some ways, like lan- 14 guages. And, in fact, some of what we know about second language acquisition is relevant to them, if only in a metaphorical way. Two Discourses can *interfere* with one another, like two languages; aspects of one Discourse can be *transferred* to another Discourse, as one can transfer a grammatical feature from one language to another. For instance, the primary Discourse of many middle-class homes has been influenced by secondary Discourses like those used in schools and business. This is much less true of the primary Discourse in many lower socio-economic black homes, though this primary Discourse has influenced the secondary Discourse used in black churches.

Furthermore, if one has not mastered a particular secondary Discourse 15 which nonetheless one must try to use, several things can happen, things which rather resemble what can happen when one has failed to fluently master a second language. One can fall back on one's primary Discourse, adjusting it in various ways to try to fit it to the needed functions; this response is very common, but almost always socially disastrous. Or one can use another, perhaps related, secondary Discourse. Or one can use a simplified, or stereotyped version of the required secondary Discourse. These processes are similar to those linguists study under the rubrics *of language contact, pidginization,* and *creolization.*

I believe that any socially useful definition of "literacy" must be couched in 16 terms of the notion of Discourse. Thus, I define *"literacy"* as *the mastery of or fluent control over a secondary Discourse.* Therefore, literacy is always plural: *literacies* (there are many of them, since there are many secondary Discourses, and we all have some and fail to have others). If we wanted to be rather pedantic and literalistic, then we could define "literacy" as "mastery of or fluent control over secondary Discourses *involving print*" (which is almost all of them in a modern society). But I see no gain from the addition of the phrase "involving print," other than to assuage the feelings of people committed (as I am not) to reading and writing as decontextualized and isolable skills. We can talk about *dominant literacies* and *nondominant literacies* in terms of whether they involve mastery of dominant or nondominant secondary Discourses. We can also talk about a literacy being *liberating* ("powerful") if it can be used as a "meta-language" (a set of meta-words, meta-values, meta-beliefs) for the critique of other literacies and the way they constitute us as persons and situate us in society. Liberating literacies can reconstitute and resituate us.

My definition of "literacy" may seem innocuous, at least to someone already 17 convinced that decontextualized views of print are meaningless. Nonetheless, several "theorems" follow from it, theorems that have rather direct and unsettling consequences.

First theorem: Discourses (and therefore literacies) are not like languages in 18 one very important regard. Someone can speak English, but not fluently. However, someone cannot engage in a Discourse in a less than fully fluent manner. You are either in it or you're not. Discourses are connected with displays of an identity; failing to fully display an identity is tantamount to announcing you don't have that identity, that at best you're a pretender or a beginner. Very often, learners of second languages "fossilize" at a stage of development significantly short of fluency. This can't happen with Discourses. If you've fossilized in the acquisition of a Discourse prior to full "fluency" (and are no longer in the process of apprenticeship), then your very lack of fluency marks you as a *non*-member of the group that controls this Discourse. That is, you don't have the identity or social role which is the basis for the existence of the Discourse in the first place. In fact, the lack of fluency may very well mark you as a *pretender* to the social role instantiated in the Discourse (an *outsider* with pretensions to being an *insider*).

There is, thus, no workable "affirmative action" for Discourses: you can't 19 be let into the game after missing the apprenticeship and be expected to have a fair shot at playing it. Social groups will not, usually, give their social goods—whether these are status or solidarity or both—to those who are not "natives" or "fluent users" (though "mushfake," discussed below, may sometimes provide a way for non-initiates to gain access). While this is an *empirical* claim, I believe it is one vastly supported by the sociolinguistic literature (Milroy, 1980, 1987; Milroy & Milroy, 1985).

This theorem (that there are no people who are partially literate or semi- 20 literate, or, in any other way, literate but not fluently so) has one practical consequence: notions like "functional literacy" and "competency-based literacy" are simply incoherent. As far as literacy goes, there are only "fluent speakers" and "apprentices" (metaphorically speaking, because remember, Discourses are not just ways of talking, but ways of talking, acting, thinking, valuing, etc.).

Second theorem: Primary Discourses, no matter whose they are, can never 21 really be liberating literacies. For a literacy to be liberating it must contain both the Discourse it is going to critique and a set of meta-elements (language, words, attitudes, values) in terms of which an analysis and criticism can be carried out. Primary Discourses are initial and contain only themselves. They can be embedded in later Discourses and critiqued, but they can never serve as a meta-language in terms of which a critique of secondary Discourses can be carried out. Our second theorem is not likely to be very popular. Theorem 2 says that all primary Discourses are limited. "Liberation" ("power"), in the sense I am using the term here, resides in acquiring at least one more Discourse in terms of which our own primary Discourse can be analyzed and critiqued.

This is not to say that primary Discourses do not contain critical attitudes 22 and critical language (indeed, many of them contain implicit and explicit

Meta-language — unexamined?

racism and classism). It is to say that they cannot carry out an *authentic* criticism, because they cannot verbalize the words, acts, values, and attitudes they *use,* and they cannot mobilize explicit meta-knowledge. Theorem 2 is quite traditional and conservative—it is the analogue of Socrates's theorem that the unexamined life is not worth living. Interestingly enough, Vygotsky (1987, chapter 6) comes very closely to stating this theorem explicitly.

Other theorems can be deduced from the theory of literacy here developed, 23 but these two should make clear what sorts of consequences the theory has. It should also make it quite clear that the theory is *not* a neutral meta-language in terms of which one can argue for *just any* conclusions about literacy.

✗ Not all Discourses involve writing or reading, though many do. However, all 24 writing and reading is embedded in some Discourse, and that Discourse always involves more than writing and reading (e.g., ways of talking, acting, valuing, and so forth). You cannot teach anyone to write or read outside any Discourse (there is no such thing, unless it is called "moving a pen" or "typing" in the case of writing, or "moving one's lips" or "mouthing words" in the case of reading). Within a Discourse you are always teaching more than writing or reading. When I say "teach" here, I mean "apprentice someone in a master-apprentice relationship in a social practice (Discourse) wherein you scaffold their growing ability to say, do, value, believe, and so forth, within that Discourse, through demonstrating your mastery and supporting theirs even when it barely exists (i.e., you make it look as if they can do what they really can't do)." That is, you do much the same thing middle-class, "super baby" producing parents do when they "do books" with their children.

Now, there are many Discourses connected to schools (different ones for 25 different types of school activities and different parts of the curriculum) and other public institutions. These "middle-class mainstream" sorts of Discourses often carry with them power and prestige. It is often felt that good listeners and good readers ought to pay attention to *meaning* and not focus on the petty details of mechanics, "correctness," the superficial features of language. Unfortunately, many middle-class mainstream status-giving Discourses often *do* stress superficial features of language. Why? Precisely because such superficial features are the *best* test as to whether one was apprenticed in the "right" place, at the "right" time, with the "right" people. Such superficial features are exactly the parts of Discourses most impervious to overt instruction and are only fully mastered when everything else in the Discourse is mastered. Since these Discourses are used as "gates" to ensure that the "right" people get to the "right" places in our society, such superficial features are ideal. A person who writes in a petition or office memo: "If you cancel the show, all the performers would have did all that hard work for nothing" has signaled that he or she isn't the "right sort of person" (was not fully acculturated to the Discourse that supports this identity). That signal stays meaningful long after the content of the memo is forgotten, or even when the content was of no interest in the first place.

Now, one can certainly encourage students to simply "resist" such "superfi- 26 cial features of language." And, indeed, they will get to do so from the bottom of society, where their lack of mastery of such superficialities was meant to place them anyway. But, of course, the problem is that such "superficialities" cannot be taught in a regular classroom in any case; they can't be "picked up" later, outside the full context of an early apprenticeship (at home and at school) in "middle-class-like" school-based ways of doing and being. That is precisely why they work so well as "gates." This is also precisely the tragedy of E. D. Hirsch, Jr.'s much-talked-about book *Cultural Literacy* (1987), which points out that without having mastered an extensive list of trivialities people can be (and often are) excluded from "goods" controlled by dominant groups in the society. Hirsch is wrong in thinking that this can be taught (in a classroom of all places!) apart from the socially situated practices that these groups have incorporated into their homes and daily lives. There is a real contradiction here, and we ignore it at the peril of our students and our own "good faith" (no middle-class "super baby" producing parents ignore it).

Beyond changing the social structure, is there much hope? No, there is not. So we better get on about the process of changing the social structure. Now, whose job is that? I would say, people who have been allotted the job of teaching Discourses, for example, English teachers, language teachers, composition teachers, TESOL teachers, studies-skills teachers. We can pause, also, to remark on the paradox that even though Discourses cannot be overtly taught, and cannot readily be mastered late in the game, the University wants teachers to overtly teach and wants students to demonstrate mastery. Teachers of Discourses take on an impossible job, allow themselves to be evaluated on how well they do it, and accept fairly low status all the while for doing it. 27

So what can teachers of Discourses do? Well, there happens to be an advantage to failing to master mainstream Discourses, that is, there is an advantage to being socially "maladapted." When we have really mastered anything (e.g., a Discourse), we have little or no conscious awareness of it (indeed, like dancing, Discourses wouldn't work if people were consciously aware of what they were doing while doing it). However, when we come across a situation where we are unable to accommodate or adapt (as many minority students do on being faced, late in the game, with having to acquire mainstream Discourses), we become consciously aware of what we are trying to do or are being called upon to do. Let me give an example that works similarly, that is, the case of classroom second language learning. Almost no one really acquires a second language in a classroom. However, it can happen that exposure to another language, having to translate it into and otherwise relate it to your own language, can cause you to become consciously aware of how your first language works (how it means). This "metaknowledge" can actually make you better able to manipulate your first language. 28

Vygotsky (1987) says that learning a foreign language "allows the child to understand his native language as a single instantiation of a linguistic system" (p. 222). And here we have a clue. Classroom instruction (in language, composition, study skills, writing, critical thinking, content-based literacy, or whatever) can lead to metaknowledge, to seeing how the Discourses you have already got relate to those you are attempting to acquire, and how the ones you are trying 29 to acquire relate to self and society. Metaknowledge is liberation and power, because it leads to the ability to manipulate, to analyze, to resist while advancing. Such metaknowledge can make "maladapted" students smarter than "adapted" ones. Thus, the liberal classroom that avoids overt talk of form and superficialities, of how things work, as well as of their socio-cultural-political basis, is no help. Such talk can be powerful so long as one never thinks that in talking about grammar, form, or superficialities one is getting people to actually acquire Discourses (or languages, for that matter). Such talk is always political talk.

But, the big question: If one cannot acquire Discourses save through active 30 social practice, and it is difficult to compete with the mastery of those admitted early to the game when one has entered it as late as high school or college, what can be done to see to it that metaknowledge and resistance are coupled with Discourse development? The problem is deepened by the fact that true acquisition of many mainstream Discourses involves, at least while being in them, active complicity with values that conflict with one's home- and community-based Discourses, especially for many women and minorities.

The question is too big for me, but I have two views to push nonetheless. 31 First, true acquisition (which is always full fluency) will rarely if ever happen. Even for anything close to acquisition to occur, classrooms must be active apprenticeships in "academic" social practices, and, in most cases, must connect with these social practices as they are also carried on outside the "composition" or "language" class, elsewhere in the University.

Second, though true acquisition is probably not possible, "mushfake" Dis- 32 course is possible. Mack (1989) defines "mushfake," a term from prison culture, as making "do with something less when the real thing is not available. So when prison inmates make hats from underwear to protect their hair from lice, the hats are mushfake. Elaborate craft items made from used wooden match sticks are another example of mushfake." "Mushfake Discourse" means partial acquisition coupled with metaknowledge and strategies to "make do" (strategies ranging from always having a memo edited to ensure no plural, possessive, and third-person "s" agreement errors to active use of black culture skills at ''psyching out" interviewers, or to strategies of "rising to the meta-level" in an interview so the interviewer is thrown off stride by having the rules of the game implicitly referred to in the act of carrying them out).

"Mushfake," resistance, and metaknowledge: this seems to me like a good 33 combination for successful students and successful social change. So I propose that we ought to produce "mushfaking," resisting students, full of metaknowledge. But isn't that to politicize teaching? A Discourse is an integration of saying, doing, and *valuing*, and all socially based valuing is political. All successful teaching, that is, teaching that inculcates Discourse and not just content, is political. That too is a truism.

As a linguist I am primarily interested in the functioning of language in Dis- 34 courses and literacies. And a key question in this sort of linguistics is how language-within-Discourses is acquired (in socially situated apprenticeships) and how the languages from different Discourses transfer into, interfere with, and otherwise influence each other to form the linguistic texture of whole societies and to interrelate various groups in society. To see what is at stake here, I will briefly discuss one text, one which clearly brings out a host of important issues in this domain. The text, with an explanation of its context, is printed below. The text is demarcated in terms of "lines" and "stanzas," units which I believe are the basis of speech:

> CONTEXT OF TEXT A young middle-class mother regularly reads storybooks to both her 5- and 7-year-old daughters. Her 5-year-old had had a birthday party, which had had some problems. In the next few days the 5-year-old has told several relatives about the birthday party, reporting the events in the language of her primary Discourse system. A few days later, when the mother was reading a storybook to her 7-year-old, the 5-year-old said she wanted to "read" (she could not decode), and *pretended* to be reading a book, while telling what had happened at her birthday party. Her original attempt at this was not very good, but eventually after a few tries, interspersed with the mother reading to the other girl, the 5 year-old produced the following story, which is not (just) in the language of her primary Discourse system:

STANZA ONE (Introduction)

1. This is a story
2. About some kids who were once friends
3. But got into a big fight
4. And were not

STANZA TWO (Frame: Signalling of Genre)

5. You can read along in your storybook
6. I'm gonna read aloud

[story-reading prosody from now on]

STANZA THREE (Title)

7. "How the Friends Got Unfriend"

STANZA FOUR (Setting: Introduction of Characters)

8. Once upon a time there was three boys 'n three girls
9. They were named Betty Lou, Pallis, and Parshin, were the girls
10. And Michael, Jason, and Aaron were the boys
11. They were friends

STANZA FIVE (Problem: Sex Differences)

12. The boys would play Transformers
13. And the girls would play Cabbage Patches

STANZA SIX (Crisis: Fight)

14. But then one day they got into a fight on who would be which team
15. It was a very bad fight

16. They were punching
17. And they were pulling
18. And they were ?banging

STANZA SEVEN (Resolution 1: Storm)

19. Then all of a sudden the sky turned dark
20. The rain began to fall
21. There was lightning going on
22. And they were not friends

STANZA EIGHT (Resolution 2: Mothers punish)

23. Then um the mothers came shooting out 'n saying
24. "What are you punching for?
25. You are going to be punished for a whole year"

STANZA NINE (Frame)

26. The end
27. Wasn't it fun reading together?
28. Let's do it again
29. Real soon!

This text and context display an event, which I call *filtering,* "in the act" of 35 actually taking place. "Filtering" is a process whereby aspects of the language, attitudes, values, and other elements of certain types of secondary Discourses (e.g., dominant ones represented in the world of school and trans-local government and business institutions) are *filtered* into primary Discourse (and, thus, the process whereby a literacy can influence home-based practices). Filtering represents *transfer* of features from secondary Discourses into primary Discourses. This transfer process allows the child to practice aspects of dominant secondary Discourses in the very act of acquiring a primary Discourse. It is a key device in the creation of a group of elites who appear to demonstrate quick and effortless mastery of dominant secondary Discourses, by "talent" or "native ability," when, in fact, they have simply *practiced* aspects of them longer.

The books that are part of the storybook reading episodes surrounding this 36 child's oral text encode language that is part of several specific secondary Discourses. These include, of course, "children's literature," but also "literature" proper. Such books use linguistic devices that are simplified analogues of "literary" devices used in traditional, canonical "high literature." These devices are often thought to be natural and universal to literary art, though they are not. Many of them have quite specific origins in quite specific historical circumstances (though, indeed, some of them are rooted in universals of sense making and are devices that occur in nonliterary talk and writing).

One device with a specific historical reference is the so-called "sympathetic 37 fallacy." This is where a poem or story treats natural events (e.g., sunshine or storms) as if they reflected or were "in harmony" or "in step" with (sympathetic with) human events and emotions. This device was a hallmark of 19th-century Romantic poetry, though it is common in more recent poetry as well.

Notice how in the 5-year-old's story the sympathetic fallacy is not only used, but is, in fact, the central organizing device in the construction of the story. The fight between the girls and boys in stanza 6 is immediately followed in stanza 7 by the sky turning dark, with lightning flashing, and thence in line 22: "and they were not friends." Finally, in stanza 8, the mothers come on the scene to punish the children for their transgression. The sky is "in tune" or "step" with human happenings. **38**

The function of the sympathetic fallacy in "high literature" is to equate the world of nature (the macrocosm) with the world of human affairs (the microcosm) as it is depicted in a particular work of art. It also suggests that these human affairs, as they are depicted in the work of literary art, are "natural," part of the logic of the universe, rather than conventional, historical, cultural, or class-based. **39**

In the 5-year-old's story, the sympathetic fallacy functions in much the same way as it does in "high literature." In particular, the story suggests that gender differences (stanza 4: boy versus girl) are associated with different interests (stanza 5: Transformers versus Cabbage Patches), and that these different interests inevitably lead to conflict when male and female try to be "equal" or "one" or sort themselves on other grounds than gender (stanza 6: "a fight on who would be which team"). **40**

The children are punished for transgressing gender lines (stanza 8), but *only after* the use of the sympathetic fallacy (in stanza 7) has suggested that *division by gender*, and the conflicts which transgressing this division lead to, are sanctioned by nature—are "natural" and "inevitable" not merely conventional or constructed in the very act of play itself. **41**

Notice, then, how the very form and structure of the language, and the linguistic devices used, carry an *ideological message*. In mastering this aspect of this Discourse, the little girl has unconsciously "swallowed whole," ingested, a whole system of thought, embedded in the very linguistic devices she uses. This, by the way, is another example of how linguistic aspects of Discourses can never be isolated from nonlinguistic aspects like values, assumptions, and beliefs. **42**

Let's consider how this text relates to our theory of Discourse and literacy. The child had started by telling a story about her birthday to various relatives, over a couple of days, presumably in her primary Discourse. Then, on a given day, in the course of repeated book reading episodes, she reshapes this story into another genre. She incorporates aspects of the book reading episode into her story. Note, for example, the introduction in stanza 1, the frame in stanza 2, the title in stanza 3, and then the start of the story proper in stanza 4. She closes the frame in stanza 9. This overall structure shapes the text into "storybook reading," though, in fact, there is no book and the child can't read. I cannot help but put in an aside here: note that this girl is engaged in an apprenticeship in the Discourse of "storybook reading," a mastery of which I count as a literacy, though in this case there is no book and no reading. Traditional accounts of **43** literacy are going to have deep conceptual problems here, because they trouble themselves too much over things like books and reading.

Supported by her mother and older sister, our 5-year-old is mastering the 44 secondary Discourse of "storybook reading." But this Discourse is itself an aspect of apprenticeship in another, more mature Discourse, namely "literature" (as well as, in other respects, "essayist Discourse," but that is *another story*). This child, when she goes to school to begin her more public apprenticeship into the Discourse of literature, will look like a "quick study" indeed. It will appear that her success was inevitable given her native intelligence and verbal abilities. Her success was inevitable, indeed, but because of her earlier apprenticeship. Note too how her mastery of this "storybook reading" Discourse leads to the incorporation of a set of values and attitudes (about gender and the naturalness of middle-class ways of behaving) that are shared by many other dominant Discourses in our society. This will facilitate the acquisition of other dominant Discourses, ones that may, at first, appear quite disparate from "literature" or "storybook reading."

It is also clear that the way in which this girl's home experience interpo- 45 lates primary Discourse (the original tellings of the story to various relatives) and secondary Discourses will cause *transfer* of features from the secondary Discourse to the primary one (thanks to the fact, for instance, that this is all going on at home in the midst of primary socialization). Indeed, it is *just such episodes* that are the *locus* of the process by which dominant secondary Discourses filter from public life into private life.

The 5-year-old's story exemplifies two other points as well. First, it is rather 46 pointless to ask, "Did she really intend, or does she really know about such meanings?" The Discourses to which she is apprenticed "speak" *through her* (to other Discourses, in fact). So, she can, in fact, "speak" quite beyond herself (much like "speaking in tongues," I suppose). Second, the little girl ingests an ideology whole here, so to speak, and not in any way in which she could analyze it, verbalize it, or critique it. This is why this is not an experience of learning a liberating literacy.

To speak to the educational implications of the view of Discourse and literacy 47 herein, and to close these introductory remarks, I will leave you to meditate on the words of Oscar Wilde's Lady Bracknell in *The Importance of Being Earnest*. "Fortunately, in England, at any rate, education produces no effect whatsoever. If it did, it would prove a serious danger to the upper classes, and probably lead to acts of violence in Grosvenor Square" (quoted in Ellman, 1988, p. 561).

References

Akinnaso, F. N., & Ajirotutu, C. S. (1982). Performance and ethnic style in job intervews. In J. J. Gumperz (Ed.), *Language and social identity* (pp. 119–144). Cambridge: Cambridge University Press.

Beebe, L. M. (Ed.) (1988). *Issues in second language acquisition: Multiple perspectives.* New York: Newbury House.

Cazden, C. (1988). *Classroom discourse: The language, of teaching and learning.* Portsmouth, NH: Heinemann.

Dulay, H., Burt, M., & Krashen, S. (1982). *Language two.* New York: Oxford University Press.

Ellman, R. (1988). *Oscar Wilde.* New York: Vintage Books.

Grosjean, F. (1986). *Life with two languages.* Cambridge: Harvard University Press.

Heath, S. B. (1983). *Ways with words: Language, life, and work in communities and classrooms.* Cambridge: Cambridge University Press.

Hirsch, E. D. (1987). *Cultural literacy: What every American needs to know.* Boston: Houghton Mifflin.

Krashen, S. (1982). *Principles and practice in second language acquisition.* Hayward, CA: Alemany Press.

Krashen, S. (1985a). *The input hypothesis: Issues and implications.* Harlow, U.K.: Longman.

Krashen, S. (1985b). *Inquiries and insights.* Hayward, CA: Alemany Press.

Krashen, S., &. Terrell, T. (1983). *The natural approach: Language acquisition in the classroom.* Hayward, CA: Alemany Press.

Lave, J. (1988). *Cognition in practice.* Cambridge: Cambridge University Press.

Mack, N. (1989). The social nature of words: Voices, dialogues, quarrels. *The Writing Instructor,* 8, 157–165.

Milroy, J., & Milroy, L. (1985). *Authority in language: Investigating language prescription and standardisation.* London: Routledge & Kegan Paul.

Milroy, L. (1980). *Language and social networks.* Oxford: Basil Blackwell.

Milroy, L. (1987). *Observing and analysing natural language.* Oxford: Basil Blackwell.

Rogoff, B., & Lave, J. (Eds.). (1984). *Everyday cognition: Its development in a social context.* Cambridge: Harvard University Press.

Rosaldo, R. (1989). *Culture and truth: The remaking of social analysis.* Boston: Beacon Press.

Vygotsky, L. S. (1987). *The collected works of L. S. Vygotsky, Volume 1: Problems of general psychology. Including the volume thinking and speech* (R. W. Rieber & A. S. Carton, Eds.). New York: Plenum.

Questions for Discussion and Journaling

1. What does Gee mean when he says that you can speak with perfect grammar and yet be "wrong nonetheless" (para. 2)? Does this conflict with what you've been taught in school about grammar?

2. Gee argues that you can say something in the right way but do the wrong thing, which he calls the "'saying-doing combination'" (para. 2). What does this mean?

3. Explain Gee's distinction between *Discourse* with a capital *D* and *discourse* with a lowercase *d*. Does it make sense to you? Why or why not?

4. What does Gee means by the terms *primary Discourse, secondary Discourse, dominant Discourse,* and *nondominant Discourse?*

5. What does it mean to say that "Discourses are connected with displays of an **identity**" (para. 18)? What are the implications of this claim, if it is true?

6. Gee argues that reading and writing never happen, and thus can't be taught, apart from some Discourse. Further, he argues, teaching someone to read or

write also means teaching them to "'say, do, value, believe'" as members of that Discourse do (para. 24). How is this connected to his claims about the relationship between Discourse and identity?

7. In paragraph 13, Gee argues that members of dominant Discourses apply "constant 'tests'" to people whose primary Discourse is not the dominant one. Later, he explains that members of dominant Discourses often pay close attention to how mechanically "correct" others' language is because these features are the "*best* test as to whether one was apprenticed in the 'right' place, at the 'right' time, with the 'right' people" (para. 25). What is Gee talking about here? Can you think of an example you have seen or experienced that illustrates what Gee is describing?

8. Why do you think dominant Discourse "tests" happen? What is the benefit to members of the dominant Discourse?

9. How does Gee define *literacy*? What is his attitude toward print-based literacy, specifically?

10. How does Gee define *enculturation*?

11. What is *metaknowledge* and what is its value, according to Gee?

12. Consider a Discourse that you consider yourself to be already a part of. How do you *know* you are a part of it?

13. Consider a Discourse to which you do not belong but want to belong—a group in which you are or would like to be what Gee calls an *apprentice*. What is hardest about learning to belong to that Discourse? Who or what aids you the most in becoming a part? Do you ever feel like a "pretender"? If so, what marks you as a pretender?

Applying and Exploring Ideas

1. Write a dialogue between John Swales and James Gee in which they discuss their concepts of *discourse communities* and *Discourse*. In the work represented in this chapter, Gee pessimistically argues that it is not possible to join a dominant Discourse once you've been enculturated into a nondominant one, whereas Swales seems to believe that people not only join new discourse communities all the time, but can even successfully pretend to be part of a discourse community that they really do not want to join. Imagine what Swales and Gee might say to one another about this topic. Do you think it would be possible for them to establish common ground? If so, how?

2. Write a description of the "saying (writing)-doing-being-valuing-believing" of your own primary Discourse (the one you were enculturated into at birth). Be sure to note things like grammatical usage, common phrases, tone of voice, formality of speech, and values related to that Discourse. Once you have done this, write a description of the "saying (writing)-doing-being-valuing-believing" of *academic* Discourse as you have encountered it so far. Finally, discuss sources of **transfer** (overlap) and sources of conflict between these two Discourses.

3. Gee argues that English teachers are the ones who have to do something about the fact that people from noncominant Discourses can't join dominant Discourses late in life. Write a letter to one of your high school or college English teachers in which you explain what Discourses are, describe the difference between dominant and nondominant Discourses, and ask the teacher to take some specific action of your choosing to better help students from nondominant Discourses.

4. Gee notes that there are often conflicts and tensions between Discourses. Consider different Discourses you belong to that have different values, beliefs, attitudes, language use, and so on. How do you navigate between or among these Discourses?

Meta Moment

Do Gee's claims help you understand any of your own or other people's experiences differently? How could you use some knowledge gained from Gee in another setting?

Discourse Communities and Communities of Practice:
Membership, Conflict, and Diversity

ANN M. JOHNS

Johns, Ann M. "Discourse Communities and Communities of Practice: Membership, Conflict, and Diversity." *Text, Role, and Context: Developing Academic Literacies.* Cambridge, New York: Cambridge UP, 1997. 51–70. Print.

Framing the Reading

Ann Johns, like the other scholars whose work you have read so far in this chapter, is a well-known linguist—in fact, she coedited a journal with John Swales from 1985 to 1993. While she was at San Diego State University, Johns directed the American Language Institute, the Writing across the Curriculum Program, the Freshman Success Program, and the Center for Teaching and Learning, and she still found time to research and write twenty-three articles, twenty-two book chapters, and four books (including *Genre in the Classroom* [2001] and *Text, Role, and Context*, from which the following reading is taken). Since retiring from San Diego State, Johns continues to write articles and consult around the world.

Think of Johns's text as the extension of an ongoing conversation in this chapter. When John Swales defined **discourse community**, he noted in passing that participating in a discourse community did not necessarily require joining it, but he did not pursue the idea of **conflict** within communities any further. James Gee does not help much with this problem because he argues that people from *nondominant* home **Discourses** can only join *dominant* Discourses through **mushfake**. This is where Ann Johns steps in. She published well after both Swales and Gee, so she had time to think through some of the issues they were considering and then extend the conversation by really delving into the problem of conflict within discourse communities.

When talking about conflicts related to discourse communities, Johns focuses primarily on *academic* discourse communities. She talks about some of the "expected" **conventions** of discourse in the academy (what she calls "uniting forces") and then describes sources of contention. Johns brings up issues of **rebellion** against discourse community conventions, change

within conventions of communities, the relationship of **identity** to discourse community membership, and the problems of **authority** and control over acceptable community discourse. As always, the reading will be easier for you if you can try to relate what the author describes to your own experiences or to things you have witnessed or read about elsewhere.

Getting Ready to Read

Before you read, do at least one of the following activities:

- If you've read other articles in this chapter already, make a list of the difficulties or problems you've had with the concept of *discourse communities* so far. What have you not understood, what has not made sense, or what questions have you been left with?
- Write a note to yourself on this question What does the idea of *membership* mean to you? When you hear that word, what do you associate it with? What memories of it do you have? Do you often use it or hear it?

As you read, consider the following questions:

- What does it mean to have *authority* in relation to texts and discourse communities?
- How does trying to become a member of a discourse community impact your sense of self—do you feel your "self" being compressed or pressured, or expanding?
- How are discourse communities related to *identity*?

If there is one thing that most of [the discourse community definitions] have in common, it is an idea of language [and genres] as a basis for sharing and holding in common: shared expectations, shared participation, commonly (or communicably) held ways of expressing. Like audience, discourse community entails assumptions about conformity and convention (Rafoth, 1990, p. 140).

What is needed for descriptive adequacy may not be so much a search for the conventions of language use in a particular group, but a search for the varieties of language use that work both with and against conformity, and accurately reflect the interplay of identity and power relationships (Rafoth, 1990, p. 144).

A second important concept in the discussion of socioliteracies is *discourse community.* Because this term is abstract, complex, and contested,[1] I will approach it by attempting to answer a few of the questions that are raised in the literature, those that seem most appropriate to teaching and learning in academic contexts.

---

[1] Some of the contested issues and questions are: "How are communities defined?" (Rufoth, 1990); "Do discourse communities even exist?" (Prior, 1994); "Are they global or local? Or both?" (Killingsworth, 1992); "What is the relationship between discourse communities and genres?" (Swales, 1988b, 1990).

1. Why do individuals join social and professional communities? What appear to be the relationships between communities and their genres?
2. Are there levels of community? In particular, can we hypothesize a general academic community or language?
3. What are some of the forces that make communities complex and varied? What forces work against "shared participation and shared ways of expressing?" (Rafoth, 1990, p. 140).

I have used the term discourse communities because this appears to be the 2 most common term in the literature. However, *communities of practice*, a related concept, is becoming increasingly popular, particularly for academic contexts (see Brown & Duguid, 1995; Lave & Wenger, 1991). In the term *discourse communities*, the focus is on texts and language, the genres and lexis that enable members throughout the world to maintain their goals, regulate their membership, and communicate efficiently with one another. Swales (1990, pp. 24–27) lists six defining characteristics of a discourse community:

1. [It has] a broadly agreed set of common public goals.
2. [It has] mechanisms of intercommunication among its members (such as newsletters or journals).
3. [It] utilizes and hence possesses one or more genres in the communicative furtherance of its aims.
4. [It] uses its participatory mechanisms primarily to provide information and feedback.
5. In addition to owning genres, [it] has acquired some specific lexis.
6. [It has] a threshold level of members with a suitable degree of relevant content and discoursal expertise.

The term communities of practice refers to genres and lexis, but especially 3 to many practices and values that hold communities together or separate them from one another. Lave and Wenger, in discussing students' enculturation into academic communities, have this to say about communities of practice:

> As students begin to engage with the discipline, as they move from exposure to experience, they begin to understand that the different communities on campus are quite distinct, that apparently common terms have different meanings, apparently shared tools have different uses, apparently related objects have different interpretations. . . . As they work in a particular community, they start to understand both its particularities and what joining takes, how these involve language, practice, culture and a conceptual universe, not just mountains of facts (1991, p. 13).

Thus, communities of practice are seen as complex collections of individuals who share genres, language, values, concepts, and "ways of being" (Geertz, 1983), often distinct from those held by other communities.

In order to introduce students to these visions of community, it is useful to 4 take them outside the academic realm to something more familiar, the recreational and avocational communities to which they, or their families, belong. Thus I begin with a discussion of nonacademic communities before proceeding to issues of academic communities and membership.

Communities and Membership

Social, Political, and Recreational Communities

People are born, or taken involuntarily by their families and cultures, into some   5
communities of practice. These first culture communities may be religious, tribal, social, or economic, and they may be central to an individual's daily life experiences. Academic communities, on the other hand, are selected and voluntary, at least after compulsory education. Therefore, this chapter will concentrate on communities that are chosen, the groups with which people maintain ties because of their interests, their politics, or their professions. Individuals are often members of a variety of communities outside academic life: social and interest groups with which they have chosen to affiliate. These community affiliations vary in terms of individual depth of interest, belief, and commitment. Individual involvement may become stronger or weaker over time as circumstances and interests change.

Nonacademic communities of interest, like "homely" genres, can provide   6
a useful starting point for student discussion. In presenting communities of this type, Swales uses the example of the Hong Kong Study Circle (HKSC),[2] of which he is a paying member, whose purposes are to "foster interest in and knowledge of the stamps of Hong Kong" (1990, p. 27). He was once quite active in this community, dialoging frequently with other members through HKSC publications.[3] However, at this point in his life, he has other interests (birds and butterflies), and so he is now an inactive member of HKSC. His commitments of time and energy have been diverted elsewhere.

> Why do individuals join social and professional communities? Are there levels of community? What are some of the forces that make communities complex and varied?

Members of my family are also affiliated with several types of communities.   7
We are members of cultural organizations, such as the local art museum and the theater companies. We receive these communities' publications, and we attend some of their functions, but we do not consider ourselves to be active. We also belong to a variety of communities with political aims. My mother, for example, is a member of the powerful lobbying group, the American Association of Retired Persons (AARP). The several million members pay their dues because of their interests in maintaining government-sponsored retirement (Social Security) and health benefits (Medicare), both of which are promoted by AARP lobbyists in the U.S. Congress. The AARP magazine, *Modern Maturity,* is a powerful organ of the association, carefully crafted to forward the group's aims. Through this publication, members are urged to write to their elected representatives

---

[2] Note that most communities use abbreviations for their names and often for their publications. All community members recognize these abbreviations, of course.

[3] These written interactions are impossible for the noninitiated to understand, I might point out.

about legislation, and they are also informed about which members of Congress are "friends of the retired." However, members are offered more than politics: Articles in the magazine discuss keeping healthy while aging, remaining beautiful, traveling cheaply, and using the Internet. AARP members also receive discounts on prescription drugs, tours, and other benefits.[4]

Recently, my husband has become very active in a recreational discourse community, the international community of cyclists.[5] He reads publications such as *Bicycling* ("World's No. 1 Road and Mountain Bike Magazine") each month for advice about better cyclist health ("Instead of Pasta, Eat This!"),[6] equipment to buy, and international cycling tours. Like most other communities, cycling has experts, some of whom write articles for the magazines to which he subscribes, using a register that is mysterious to the uninitiated: "unified gear triangle"; "metal matrix composite." Cyclists share values (good health, travel interests), special knowledge, vocabulary, and genres, but they do not necessarily share political or social views, as my husband discovered when conversing with other cyclists on a group trip. In publications for cyclists, we can find genres that we recognize by name but with community-related content: editorials, letters to the editor, short articles on new products, articles of interest to readers (on health and safety, for example), advertisements appealing to readers, and essay/commentaries. If we examine magazines published for other interest groups, we can find texts from many of the same genres.

As this discussion indicates, individuals often affiliate with several communities at the same time, with varying levels of involvement and interest. People may join a group because they agree politically, because they want to socialize, or because they are interested in a particular sport or pastime. The depth of an individual's commitment can, and often does, change over time. As members come and go, the genres and practices continue to evolve, reflecting and promoting the active members' aims, interests, and controversies.

Studying the genres of nonacademic communities, particularly those with which students are familiar, helps them to grasp the complexity of text production and processing and the importance of understanding the group practices, lexis, values, and controversies that influence the construction of texts.

Professional Communities

Discourse communities can also be professional; every major profession has its organizations, its practices, its textual conventions, and its genres. Active community members also carry on informal exchanges: at conferences, through e-mail interest groups, in memos, in hallway discussions at the office, in laboratories and elsewhere, the results of which may be woven intertextually into

---

[4] When I asked my mother to drop her AARP membership because of a political stand the organization took, she said, "I can't, Ann. I get too good a deal on my medicines through my membership."

[5] Those of us who are outsiders call them "gearheads." Often, terms are applied to insiders by community outsiders.

[6] Brill, D. (1994, November). What's free of fat and cholesterol, costs 4 cents per serving, and has more carbo than pasta? Rice! *Bicycling*, pp. 86–87.

public, published texts. However, it is the written genres of communities that are accessible to outsiders for analysis. We need only to ask professionals about their texts in order to collect an array of interesting examples. One of the most thoroughly studied professional communities is the law. In his *Analysing Genre: Language Use in Professional Settings* (1993), Bhatia discusses at some length his continuing research into legal communities that use English and other languages (pp. 101–143). He identifies the various genres of the legal profession: their purposes, contexts, and the form and content that appear to be conventional. He also contrasts these genres as they are realized in texts from various cultures.

However, there are many other professional discourse communities whose 12 genres can be investigated, particularly when students are interested in enculturation. For example, students might study musicians who devote their lives to pursuing their art but who also use written texts to dialogue with others in their profession. To learn more about these communities, I interviewed a bassoonist in our city orchestra.[7] Along with those who play oboe, English horn, and contrabassoon, this musician subscribes to the major publication of the double-reed community, *The International Double Reed Society Journal*. Though he has specialized, double-reed interests, he reports that he and many other musicians also have general professional aims and values that link them to musicians in a much broader community. He argues that all practicing musicians within the Western tradition[8] share knowledge; there is a common core of language and values within this larger community. Whether they are guitarists, pianists, rock musicians, or bassconists, musicians in the West seem to agree, for example, that the strongest and most basic musical intervals are 5–1 and 4–1, and that other chord intervals are weaker. They share a basic linguistic register and an understanding of chords and notation. Without this sharing, considerable negotiation would have to take place before they could play music together. As in other professions, these musicians have a base of expertise, values, and expectations that they use to facilitate communication. Thus, though a musician's first allegiance may be to his or her own musical tradition (jazz) or instrument (the bassoon), he or she will still share a great deal with other expert musicians—and much of this sharing is accomplished through specialized texts.

What can we conclude from this section about individual affiliations with 13 discourse communities? First, many people have chosen to be members of one or a variety of communities, groups with whom they share social, political, professional, or recreational interests. These communities use written discourses that enable members to keep in touch with each other, carry on discussions, explore controversies, and advance their aims; the genres are their vehicles for communication. These genres are not, in all cases, sophisticated or intellectual, literary or high-browed. They are, instead, representative of the values, needs,

---

[7] I would like to thank Arlan Fast of the San Diego Symphony for these community insights.

[8] Knowledge is also shared with musicians from other parts of the world, of course. However, some of the specific examples used here apply to the Western musical tradition.

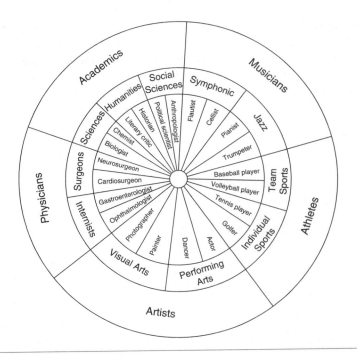

Figure 1 Levels of Community.

and practices of the community that produces them. Community membership may be concentrated or diluted; it may be central to a person's life or peripheral. Important for the discussion that follows is the juxtaposition of generalized and specialized languages and practices among these groups. Musicians, lawyers, athletes, and physicians, for example, may share certain values, language, and texts with others within their larger community, though their first allegiance is to their specializations. Figure 1 illustrates this general/specific relationship in communities.

In the case of physicians, for example, there is a general community and a   14 set of values and concepts with which most may identify because they have all had a shared basic education before beginning their specializations. There are publications, documents, concepts, language, and values that all physicians can, and often do, share. The same can be said of academics, as is shown in the figure. There may be some general academic discourses,[9] language, values, and concepts that most academics share. Thus faculty often identify themselves with a college or university and its language and values, as well as with the more specialized areas of interest for which they have been prepared.

This broad academic identification presents major problems for scholars   15 and literacy practitioners, for although it is argued that disciplines are different

---

[9] For example, *The Chronicle of Higher Education* and several pedagogical publications are directed to a general academic audience.

(see Bartholomae, 1985; Belcher & Braine, 1995; Berkenkotter & Huckin, 1995; Carson et al., 1992; Lave & Wenger, 1991, among others), many faculty believe that there is a general academic English as well as a general set of critical thinking skills and strategies for approaching texts.

Because this belief in a general, shared academic language is strong and universal, the next section of this chapter is devoted to this topic. [16]

Academic Communities

What motivates this section more than anything else is its usefulness as a starting point in the exploration of academic literacies and its accessibility to students at various levels of instruction who need to become more aware of the interaction of roles, texts, and contexts in academic communities. Many literacy faculty have mixed classes of students from a number of disciplines or students just beginning to consider what it means to be an academic reader and writer. For these students, and even for some of the more advanced, a discussion of what are considered to be general academic languages and textual practices is a good place to start their analyses—although not a good place to finish. [17]

In the previous section it was noted that professionals may affiliate at various levels of specificity within their discourse communities. They often share language, knowledge, and values with a large, fairly heterogeneous group, though their first allegiances may be with a specialized group within this broader "club." This comment can apply to individuals in academic communities as well. Faculty have their own discipline-specific allegiances (to biology, chemistry, sociology, engineering); nonetheless, many believe that there are basic, generalizable linguistic, textual, and rhetorical rules for the entire academic community that can apply. [18]

Discipline-specific faculty who teach novices at the undergraduate level, and some who teach graduate students as well, sometimes complain that their students "do not write like academics" or "cannot comprehend" academic prose, arguing that these are general abilities that we should be teaching. The discussion that follows acknowledges their complaints and sets the stage for discussions of more specific academic issues and pedagogies in later chapters. [19]

Language, Texts, and Values

This section on academic textual practices draws principally from three sources: "Reflections on Academic Discourse" (Elbow, 1991); *Words and Lives: The Anthropologist as Author* (Geertz, 1988); and *The Scribal Society: An Essay on Literacy and Schooling in the Information Age* (Purves, 1990) (see also Dudley-Evans, 1995). Elbow and Purves are well-known composition theorists from different theoretical camps who were cited in Chapter I. Geertz, an anthropologist, has studied academic communities and their genres for many years. All three of these experts live in the United States, and this may affect their views; however, in many universities in the world in which English is employed, these beliefs about general text features are also shared, except perhaps in literature and some of the humanities disciplines. Following is a composite of the arguments made by [20] the three academics about the nature, values, and practices in general expository academic prose, including some commentary on each topic.

1. *Texts must be explicit.* Writers should select their vocabulary carefully 21 and use it wisely. In some cases, such as with certain noun compounds, paraphrase is impossible because specialized academic vocabulary must be used. Citation must be constructed carefully. Data analysis should be described and discussed explicitly. The methodology should be stated so clearly that it is replicable. Ambiguity in argumentation should be avoided.

Comment. Faculty often complain that students are "careless" in their use 22 of vocabulary, in their citation practices, and in their argumentation and use of data. Because many literacy classes value the personal essay and because many readings in literacy classes are in story form or are adapted or specially written for these classes, students are not exposed to the exactness of some academic prose. One of our responsibilities in developing socioliterate practices is to expose students to authentic academic texts and to analyze these texts for their specificity.

2. *Topic and argument should be prerevealed in the introduction.* Purves 23 says that experienced academics, particularly when writing certain kinds of texts, should "select a single aspect of [a] subject and announce [their] theses and purposes as soon as possible" (1990, p. 12).

Comment. Finding the argument in a reading and noticing how data, exam- 24 ples, or narration are used to support this argument are essential academic abilities that are praised by faculty from many disciplines. In like manner, understanding and presenting a clear argument that is appropriate to a genre are writing skills that appear high on faculty wish lists for students, particularly for those who come from diverse rhetorical traditions (see Connor, 1987). Most faculty require that arguments and purposes appear early, generally in an introduction. One of the discipline-specific faculty with whom I work tells her students not to "spend much time clearing their throats." She wants them to "get right down to the argument."

We must be aware, however, that the pressure to reveal topic, purposes, and 25 argumentation early in a written text may be a culture-specific value and apply only to certain kinds of texts within specific communities. There is considerable discussion in the contrastive rhetoric and World Englishes literature about the motivations for text organization and content and the necessity (or lack thereof) for prerevealing information. Local cultures and first languages, as well as academic disciplines, can influence how and where arguments appear.

3. *Writers should provide "maps" or "signposts" for the readers throughout* 26 *the texts, telling the readers where they have been in the text and where they are going.* By using a variety of tactics, writers can assist readers in predicting and summarizing texts and in understanding the relationships among topics and arguments. Most of these tactics fall under the metadiscourse rubric.

Comment. Metadiscourse is defined in the following way: 27

It is writing about reading and writing. When we communicate, we use metadiscourse to name rhetorical actions: *explain, show, argue, claim, deny, suggest, add, expand, summarize;* to name the part of our discourse, *first, second . . . in conclusion;* to reveal logical connections, *therefore . . . if so . . .* to guide our readers, *Consider the matter of* (Williams, 1989, p. 28).

Literacy textbooks for both reading and writing often emphasize the understanding and use of metadiscourse in texts. However, it is important to note that language and culture can have considerable influence on the ways in which metadiscourse is used. For example, in countries with homogeneous cultures, academic written English may have fewer metadiscoursal features (Mauranen, 1993) than in heterogeneous, "writer-responsible" cultures (see Hinds, 1987) such as the United States, Great Britain, or Australia. As in the case of all texts, academic discourses are influenced by the cultures and communities in which they are found, often in very complicated ways.

4. *The language of texts should create a distance between the writer and the* 28 *text to give the appearance of objectivity.* Geertz (1988) speaks of academic, expository prose as "author-evacuated"; the author's personal voice is not clearly in evidence, because the first person pronoun is absent and arguments are muted. He compares author-evacuated prose with the "author-saturated" prose of many literary works, in which individual voice pervades. As mentioned earlier, this "author-evacuation" is particularly evident in pedagogical genres, such as the textbook. One way to create the evacuated style is to use the passive, a common rhetorical choice for the sciences, but there are other ways as well.

Comment. Discipline-specific faculty sometimes tell us that students are 29 unable to write "objectively" or to comprehend "objective" prose.[10] These students have not mastered the ability to clothe their argumentation in a particular register, to give it the kind of objective overlay that is valued in academic circles. When I asked one of my first-year university students to tell the class what he had learned about academic English, he said: "We can't use 'I' anymore. We have to pretend that we're not there in the text." In many cases, he is right. Literacy teachers need to help students to analyze texts for their author-evacuated style, and to discuss the particular grammatical and lexical choices that are made to achieve the appearance of objectivity and distance.

5. *Texts should maintain a "rubber-gloved" quality of voice and register.* 30 They must show a kind of reluctance to touch one's meanings with one's naked fingers (Elbow, 1991, p. 145).

Comment. For some academic contexts, writers appear to remove themselves emotionally and personally from the texts, to hold their texts at arms' 31 length (metaphorically). The examination of texts in which this "rubber-gloved quality" is evident will provide for students some of the language to achieve these ends. What can students discover? Many academic writers abjure the use of emotional words, such as *wonderful* and *disgusting;* they hide behind syntax and "objective" academic vocabulary.

---

[10] "Objective" appears in quotation marks because, though academic writing may have the appearance of being objective, all texts are biased.

6. *Writers should take a guarded stance, especially when presenting argu-*   32
mentation and results. Hedging through the use of modals (*may, might*) and
other forms (*It is possible that* . . .) is perhaps the most common way to be
guarded.

Comment. Hedging appears to be central to some academic discourses, par-   33
ticularly those that report research. In a study of two science articles on the
same topic published for two different audiences, Fahenstock (1986) found
that the article written for experts in the field was replete with hedges ("*appear
to* hydrolyze," "*suggesting* that animal food"), as scientists carefully reported
their findings to their peers. However, the article written for laypersons was
filled with "facts," much like those in the textbooks described in Chapter 3. For
these and other reasons, we need to introduce students to expert and nonexpert
texts; we need to expose them at every level to the ways in which genre, context, readers, writers, and communities affect linguistic choices.

7. *Texts should display a vision of reality shared by members of the par-*   34
*ticular discourse community to which the text is addressed (or the particular
faculty member who made the assignment).*

Comment. This may be the most difficult of the general academic require-   35
ments, for views of reality are often implicit, unacknowledged by the faculty
themselves and are not revealed to students. Perhaps I can show how this "reality vision" is so difficult to uncover by discussing my research on course syllabi. I have been interviewing faculty for several years about the goals for their
classes, goals that are generally stated in what is called a syllabus in the United
States, but might be called a class framework or schedule of assignments in
other countries. These studies indicated that most faculty tend to list as goals
for the course the various topics that will be studied. The focus is exclusively
on content. They do not list the particular views of the world that they want
students to embrace, or the understandings that they want to encourage. In a
class on "Women in the Humanities," for example, the instructor listed topics
to be covered in her syllabus, but she did not tell the students that she wanted
them to analyze images of women in cultures in order to see how these images
shape various cultural contexts. In a geography class, the instructor listed topics to be covered, but he did not tell his students about his goals for analysis and synthesis of texts. Why are the critical-thinking goals and disciplinary
values hidden by most faculty? I don't know. Perhaps instructors believe that
students should intuit the values, practices, and genres required in the course;
or the faculty have difficulty explicitly stating goals that are not related to
content. Certainly content is the most commonly discussed issue at discipline-
specific (DS) curriculum meetings, and this may influence faculty choices. In a
later chapter I will discuss one of the questionnaires that I use to elicit from
faculty the "views of reality" or "ways of being" that my students and I would
like to see stated explicitly in the syllabi.

In contrast to DS faculty, we literacy faculty are often most interested   36
in processes and understandings, in developing students metacognition
and metalanguages—and these interests are often reflected in our syllabi.

[Following,] for example, are the student goals for a first-year University writing class developed by a committee from my university's Department of Rhetoric and Writing Studies:[11]

a. To use writing to clarify and improve your understanding of issues and texts

b. To respond in writing to the thinking of others and to explore and account for your own responses

c. To read analytically and critically, making active use of what you read in your writing

d. To understand the relationships between discourse structure and the question at issue in a piece of writing, and to select appropriate structures at the sentence and discourse levels

e. To monitor your writing for the grammar and usage conventions appropriate to each writing situation

f. To use textual material as a framework for understanding and writing about other texts, data or experiences

No matter what kind of class is being taught, faculty need to discuss critical-thinking and reading and writing goals frequently with students. They need to review why students are given assignments, showing how these tasks relate to course concepts and student literacy growth. 37

8. *Academic texts should display a set of social and authority relations; they should show the writer's understanding of the roles they play within the text or context.*[12] 38

Comment. Most students have had very little practice in recognizing the language of social roles within academic contexts, although their experience with language and social roles outside the classroom is often quite rich. Some students cannot recognize when they are being talked down to in textbooks, and they cannot write in a language that shows their roles vis-à-vis the topics studied or the faculty they are addressing. These difficulties are particularly evident among ESL/EFL students; however, they are also found among many other students whose exposure to academic language has been minimal. One reason for discussing social roles as they relate to texts from a genre, whether they be "homely" discourses or professional texts, is to heighten students' awareness of the interaction of language, roles, and contexts so that they can read and write with more sophistication. 39

9. *Academic texts should acknowledge the complex and important nature of intertextuality, the exploitation of other texts without resorting to plagiarism.* 40

---

[11] Quandahl, E. (1995). Rhetoric and writing studies 100: A list of goals. Unpublished paper, San Diego State University, San Diego, CA.

[12] When I showed this point to Virginia Guleff, a graduate student, she said, "So students have to know their place!" Perhaps we should put it this way: They need to know different registers in order to play different rules. The more people use these registers, the more effective they can become and, not incidentally, the more power they can have over the situation in which they are reading or writing.

Students need to practice reformulation and reconstruction of information so that they do not just repeat other texts by "knowledge telling" (Bereiter & Scardamalia, 1989) but rather use these texts inventively for their purposes (called "knowledge transforming"; Bereiter & Scardamalia, 1989).

Comment. Carson (1993), in a large study of the intellectual demands on 41 undergraduate students, found that drawing from and integrating textual sources were two of the major challenges students face in attaining academic literacy. And no wonder. Widdowson (1993, p. 27) notes that

> When people make excessive and unacknowledged use of [another's text], and are found out, we call it plagiarism. When people are astute in their stitching of textual patchwork, we call it creativity. It is not easy to tell the difference. . . . If a text is always in some degree a conglomerate of others, how independent can its meaning be?

Drawing from sources and citing them appropriately is the most obvious 42 and most commonly discussed aspect of intertextuality. As a result, Swales and Feak (1994) claim that citation may be the defining feature of academic discourses. However, there are other, more subtle and varied borrowings from past discourses, for, as Widdowson notes, "Any particular text is produced or interpreted in reference to a previous knowledge of other texts" (1993, p. 27).

10. *Texts should comply with the genre requirements of the community or* 43 *classroom.*

Comment. This, of course, is another difficult challenge for students. As 44 mentioned earlier, pedagogical genres are often loosely named and casually described by DS faculty. It is difficult to identify the conventions of a student research paper, an essay examination response, or other pedagogical genres because, in fact, these vary considerably from class to class. Yet DS faculty expect students to understand these distinctions and to read and write appropriately for their own classes. My students and I often ask faculty: "What is a good critique for your class?" or "What is a good term paper?" We request several student-written models and, if possible, interview the faculty member about their assigned texts and tasks.

This section has outlined what may be some general rules for academic 45 literacy, most of which are refined within each discipline and classroom. Although it would be difficult to defend several of these beliefs because of the wide range of academic discourses and practices, listing and discussing these factors can prepare students for an examination of how texts are socially constructed and whether some of the points made here are applicable to specific texts.

Of course, we also need to expose students to texts that contradict these 46 rules for academic discourse. We should examine literary genres, which break most of the rules listed. We should look at specialized texts that have alternative requirements for register. In any of our pedagogical conversations, the objective should not be to discover truths but to explore how social and cultural forces may influence texts in various contexts.

Community Conflicts and Diversity

So far, the discussion of communities and their genres has focused on the unit- 47
ing forces, particularly the language, practices, values, and genres that groups
may share. It has been suggested that people can join communities at will and
remain affiliated at levels of their own choosing. For a number of reasons, this
is not entirely accurate. In some cases people are excluded from communities
because they lack social standing, talent, or money, or because they live in the
wrong part of town. In other cases, community membership requires a long
initiatory process, and even then there is no guarantee of success. Many students work for years toward their doctoral degrees, for example, only to find
that there are no faculty positions available to them or that their approach to
research will not lead to advancement.

Even after individuals are fully initiated, many factors can separate them. 48
Members of communities rebel, opposing community leaders or attempting
to change the rules of the game and, by extension, the content and argumentation in the texts from shared genres. If the rebellion is successful, the rules
may be changed or a new group may be formed with a different set of values
and aims. There may even be a theoretical paradigm shift in the discipline. In
academic communities, rebellion may result in the creation of a new unit or
department, separate from the old community, as has been the case recently in
my own university.[13] Even without open rebellion, there is constant dialogue
and argument within communities as members thrash out their differences and
juggle for power and identity, promoting their own content, argumentation,
and approaches to research.

Although much could be said about factors that affect communities outside 49
the academic realm, the following discussion will focus on a few of the rich and
complex factors that give academic communities their character.

The Cost of Affiliation

If students want to become affiliated with academic discourse communities, or 50
even if they want to succeed in school, they may have to make considerable
sacrifices. To become active academic participants, they sometimes must make
major trade-offs that: can create personal and social distance between them
and their families and communities. Students are asked to modify their language to fit that of the academic classroom or discipline. They often must drop,
or at least diminish in importance, their affiliations to their home cultures in
order to take on the values, language, and genres of their disciplinary culture.
The literature is full of stories of the students who must make choices between
their communities and academic lives (see, for example, Rose's *Lives on the*

---

[13] San Diego State's new Department of Rhetoric and Writing Studies is composed of composition instructors who asked to leave the Department of English, as well as of faculty from the previously independent Academic Skills Center.

Boundary, 1989). In an account of his experiences, Richard Rodriguez (1982, p. 56), a child of Mexican immigrant parents, wrote the following:

> What I am about to say to you has taken me more than twenty years to admit: a primary reason for my success in the classroom was that I couldn't forget that schooling was changing me and separating me from the life I had enjoyed before becoming a student. . . . If because of my schooling, I had grown culturally separated from my parents, my education has finally given me ways of speaking and caring about that fact.

Here Rodriguez is discussing his entire schooling experience; however, as   51
students advance in schools and universities, they may be confronted with even more wrenching conflicts between their home and academic cultures and languages. In her story of a Hispanic graduate student in a Ph.D. sociology program in the United States, Casanave (1992) tells how the tension between this student's personal values and language and her chosen department's insistence on its own scientific language and genres finally drove her from her new academic community. When she could no longer explain her work in sociology in everyday language to the people of her primary communities (her family and her clients), the student decided to leave the graduate program. The faculty viewed her stance as rebellious, an open refusal to take on academic community values. By the time she left, it had become obvious to all concerned that the faculty were unable, or unwilling, to bend or to adapt some of their disciplinary rules to accommodate this student's interests, vocation, and language.

A graduate student from Japan faced other kinds of affiliation conflicts when   52
attempting to become a successful student in a North American linguistics program (Benson, 1996). This student brought from her home university certain social expectations: about faculty roles, about her role as a student, and about what is involved in the production of texts. She believed, for example, that the faculty should provide her with models of what was expected in her papers; she felt that they should determine her research topics and hypotheses. This had been the case in her university in Japan, and she had considerable difficulty understanding why the American faculty did not conform to the practices of her home country. She tried to follow her professors' instructions with great care, but they chastised her for "lacking ideas." In her view, the faculty were being irresponsible; however, some faculty viewed her as passive, unimaginative, and dependent. What she and many other students have found is that gaining affiliation in graduate education means much more than understanding the registers of academic language.

These examples are intended to show that full involvement or affiliation in   53
academic discourse communities requires major cultural and linguistic trade-offs from many students. Faculty expect them to accept the texts, roles, and contexts of the discipline, but acceptance requires much more sacrifice and change than the faculty may imagine. In our literacy classes, we can assist academic students in discussing the kinds of problems they encounter when attempting to resolve these conflicts. However, we can also assist our faculty colleagues, who often are unaware of their students' plight, through workshops, student presentations, and suggestions for reading.

Issues of Authority

What happens after a person has become an academic initiate, after he or she has completed the degree, published, and been advanced? There are still community issues to contend with, one of which relates to authority, Bakhtin (1986, p. 88) noted that "in each epoch, in each social circle, in each small world of family, friends, acquaintances and comrades in which a human being grows and lives, there are always authoritative utterances that set the tone."

In academic circles, these "authoritative utterances" are made by journal or e-mail interest-group editors, by conference program planners, and by others. At the local level, this authority can be held by department chairs or by chairs of important committees. Prior (1994, p. 522) speaks of these academically powerful people as "an elite group that imposes its language, beliefs and values on others through control of journals, academic appointments, curricula, student examinations, research findings and so on." It is important to note that Prior extends his discussion beyond authority over colleagues to broad authority over students through curricula and examinations. This type of pedagogical authority is very important, as all students know, so it will be discussed further.

In many countries, provincial and national examinations drive the curricula, and theoretical and practical control over these examinations means authority over what students are taught. In the People's Republic of China, for example, important general English language examinations have been based for years on word frequency counts developed in several language centers throughout the country. Each "band," or proficiency level on the examination, is determined by "the most common 1,000 words," "the most common 2,000 words," and so on.[14] Although features of language such as grammar are tested in these examinations, it is a theory about vocabulary, based on word frequency, that is central. It is not surprising, then, that most Chinese students believe that vocabulary is the key to literacy, particularly the understanding of "exact" meanings of words. When I have worked with teachers in China, I have frequently been asked questions such as "What is the exact meaning of the term 'discourse'? What does 'theory' mean?" These teachers requested a single definition, something I was often unable to provide.

The centralized power over important examinations in China, over the TOEFL and graduate entrance examinations in the United States, and over the British Council Examinations in other parts of the world gives considerable authority within communities to certain test developers and examiners. This

---

[14] "Most common" appears in quotation marks because what is most common (other than function words) is very difficult to determine. These lists are influenced by the type of language data that is entered into the computer for the word count: whether it is written or spoken, its register etc. If data are varied, other vocabulary become common.

At one point in my career, I attempted to develop low-proficiency English for Business textbooks for adults using a famous publisher's list of most common words. I failed because the data used to establish the frequency lists were taken from children's books. The common words in children's language and those most common in business language are considerably different (Johns, 1985).

authority permits little pedagogical latitude to teachers preparing students for these "gate-keeping" examinations. As practitioners, we can use test preparation pedagogies, or we can critique these examinations (Raimes, 1990), as we should; but we cannot institute large-scale change until we gain control and authority over the examination system.

With students at all academic levels, we practitioners should raise the issues 58
of authority, status, and control over community utterances in literacy classes. About their own social groups, we can ask: "Who has status in your clubs and why? Who has status in your ethnic or geographical communities and why? How do they exert control over people, over utterances, and over publications?" When referring to academic situations and authority, we can ask: "Who wrote this textbook? What are the authors' affiliations? Are they prestigious? How does the language of the textbook demonstrate the author's authority over the material and over the students who read the volume?" We can also ask: "Who writes your important examinations? What are their values?" Or we can ask: "Who has status in your academic classrooms? Which students have authority and why?" And finally, we might ask: "How can you gain authority in the classroom or over texts?"

Throughout a discussion of authority relationships, we need to talk about 59
communities, language, and genres: how texts and spoken discourses are used to gain and perpetuate authority. We can assist students to analyze authoritative texts, including those of other students, and to critique authority relationships. Our students need to become more aware of these factors affecting their academic lives before they can hope to produce and comprehend texts that command authority within academic contexts.

Conventions and Anticonventionalism

There are many other push and pull factors in academic communities, fac- 60
tors that create dialogue, conflict, and change. Communities evolve constantly, though established community members may attempt to maintain their power and keep the new initiates in line through control over language and genres. A student or a young faculty member can be punished for major transgressions from the norm, for attempting to move away from what the more established, initiated members expect. In order to receive a good grade (or be published), writers often must work within the rules. Understanding these rules, even if they are to be broken, appears to be essential.

As individuals within an academic community become more established 61
and famous, they can become more anticonventional, in both their texts and their lives. Three famous rule breakers come to mind, though there are others. Stephen J. Gould, a biologist, has written a series of literate essays for the general public, principally about evolution, that look considerably different from the scientific journal article. Gould has broken his generic traditions to "go public" because he already has tenure at Harvard, he likes to write essays, and he enjoys addressing a public audience (see Gould, 1985). Deborah Tannen, an applied linguist, has also "gone public," publishing "pop books" about communication

between men and women that are best-sellers in the United States (see Tannen, 1986, 1994). She continues to write relatively conventional articles in journals, but she also writes often for the layperson. Clifford Geertz, the anthropologist, refuses to be pigeon-holed in terms of topic, argumentation, or genre. Using his own disciplinary approaches, he writes texts on academic cultures as well as the "exotic" ones that are typical to anthropologists (see Geertz, 1988). Gould, Tannen, and Geertz have established themselves within their disciplines. Now famous, they can afford to defy community conventions as they write in their individual ways.

Rule breaking is a minefield for many students, however. They first need to understand some of the basic conventions, concepts, and values of a community's genres. Learning and using academic conventions is not easy, for many students receive little or no instruction. To compound the problems, students need constantly to revise their theories of genres and genre conventions (see Bartholomae, 1985). Some graduate students, for example, often express confusion about conventions, anticonventions, and the breaking of rules, for faculty advice appears to be idiosyncratic, based not on community conventions but on personal taste. Some faculty thesis advisers, particularly in the humanities, require a careful review of the literature and accept nothing else; others may insist on "original"[15] work without a literature review. For some advisers there is a "cookie cutter" macrostructure that all papers must follow; others may prefer a more free-flowing, experimental text. Graduate students complain that discovering or breaking these implicit rules requires much research and many visits to faculty offices, as well as many drafts of their thesis chapters (see Schneider & Fujishima, 1995).

It should be clear from this discussion that we cannot tell students "truths" about texts or community practices. However, we can heighten student awareness of generic conventions, and we can assist students in formulating questions that can be addressed to faculty. In our literacy classes, we are developing researchers, not dogmatists, students who explore ideas and literacies rather than seek simple answers.

Dialogue and Critique

In any thriving academic community, there is constant dialogue: disagreements among members about approaches to research, about argumentation, about topics for study, and about theory. The journal *Science* acknowledges this and accepts two types of letters to the editor to enable writers to carry out informal dialogues. In other journals, sections are set aside for short interchanges between two writers who hold opposing views (see the *Journal of Second Language Writing*, for example). Most journals carry critiques of new volumes in book review sections, and many published articles are in dialogue with other texts. Academic communities encourage variety and critique (within limits), because that is how they evolve and grow.

---

[15] Since I am arguing here that all texts rely on other texts, I put "original" in quotation marks.

Most professional academics know the rules for dialogue: what topics are cur- 65
rently "hot," how to discuss these topics in ways appropriate for the readers of
their genres, how far they can go from the current norms, and what they can use
(data, narratives, nonlinear texts) to support their arguments. Some professionals
who understand the rules can also break them with impunity. They can push the
boundaries because they know where the discipline has been and where it may be
going, and how to use their authority, and the authority of others, to make their
arguments. In a volume on academic expertise, Geisler (1994) comments that
there are three "worlds" with which expert academics must be familiar before
they can join, or contravene, a disciplinary dialogue: the "domain content world"
of logically related concepts and content; the "narrated world" of everyday experience; and the "abstract world" of authorial conversation. Academic experts
must manipulate these worlds in order to produce texts that can be in dialogue or
conflict with, yet appropriate to, the communities they are addressing.

This discussion has suggested that communities and their genres are useful 66
to study not only because they can share conventions, values, and histories
but because they are evolving: through affiliation of new, different members;
through changes in authority; through anticonventionalism, dialogue, and critique. Students know these things about their own communities; we need to
draw from this knowledge to begin to explore unfamiliar academic communities and their genres.

This chapter has addressed some of the social and cultural factors that influ- 67
ence texts, factors that are closely related to community membership. Although
there is much debate in the literature about the nature of discourse communities and communities of practice, it can be said with some certainty that community affiliations are very real to individual academic faculty. Faculty refer to
themselves as "chemists," "engineers." "historians," or "applied linguists"; they
read texts from community genres with great interest or join in heated debates
with their peers over the Internet. They sometimes recognize that the language,
values, and genres of their communities (or specializations) may differ from
those of another academic community, though this is not always the case. At a
promotions committee made up of faculty from sixteen departments in which
I took part, a member of the quantitative group in the Geography Department
said of a humanities text, "We shouldn't accept an article for promotion without statistics." And we all laughed, nervously.

Academics, and others, may belong to several communities and have in com- 68
mon certain interests within each. Thus, faculty may have nothing in common
with other faculty in their disciplines but the discipline itself; their social, political, and other interests can, and often do, vary widely. In one department, for
example, musical interests can be diverse. There may be country-western fans,
opera fans, jazz enthusiasts, and those whose only musical experiences consist
of listening to the national anthem at baseball games. Recreational interests
may also differ. Among faculty, there are motorcyclists and bicyclists, hikers
and "couch potatoes," football fans and those who actually play the sport.

A complex of social, community-related factors influences the socioliteracies 69
of faculty and the students who are in their classes. As literacy practitioners, we

need to help our students examine these factors by bringing other faculty and students, and their genres, into our classrooms, as well as drawing from our own students' rich resources.

References

Bakhtin, M. M. (1986). *Speech genres and other late essays*. (V. W. Mc Gee, Trans.). C. Emerson & M. Holquist (Eds.). Austin: University of Texas Press.

Bartholomae, D. (1985). Inventing the university. In M. Rose (Ed.), *When a writer can't write: Studies in writer's block and other composing process problems* (pp. 134–165). New York: Guilford Press.

Belcher, D., & Braine, G. (Eds.). (1995). *Academic writing in a second language: Essays on research and pedagogy.* Norwood, NJ: Ablex.

Benson, K. (1996). *How do students and faculty perceive graduate writing tasks? A case study of a Japanese student in a graduate program in linguistics.* Unpublished manuscript, San Diego State University.

Bereiter, C., & Scardamalia, M. (1989). Intentional learning as a goal of instruction. In J. Resnick (Ed.), *Knowing, learning* (pp. 361–392). Hillsdale, NJ: Lawrence Erlbaum.

Berkenkotter, C., & Huckin, T. (1995). *Genre knowledge in disciplinary communities.* Hillsdale, NJ: Lawrence Erlbaum.

Bhatia, V. J. (1993). *Analyzing genre: Language use in professional settings.* London & New York: Longman.

Brill, D. (1994, November). What's free of fat and cholesterol, costs 4 cents per serving, and has more carbo than pasta? Rice! *Bicycling, 86–87.*

Brown, J. S., & Duguid, P. (1995, July 26). Universities in the digital age. *Xerox Palo Alto Paper.* Palo Alto, CA: Xerox Corporation.

Carson, J. G. (1993, April). *Academic literacy demands of the undergraduate curriculum: Literacy activities integrating skills.* Paper presented at the International TESOL Conference, Atlanta, GA.

Carson, J. G., Chase, N., Gibson, S., & Hargrove, M. (1992). Literacy demands of the undergraduate curriculum. *Reading Research and Instruction, 31, 25–50.*

Casanave, C. P. (1992). Cultural diversity and socialization: A case study of a Hispanic woman in a doctoral program in Sociology. In D. Murray (Ed.), *Diversity as a resource: Redefining cultural literacy* (pp. 148–182). Arlington, VA: TESOL.

Connor, U. (1987). Argumentative patterns in student essays: Cross-cultural differences. In U. Connor & R. B. Kaplan (Eds.), *Writing across languages: Analysis of L2 text* (pp. 57–71). Reading, MA: Addison-Wesley.

Dudley-Evans, T. (1995). Common-core and specific approaches to teaching academic writing. In D. Belcher & G. Braine (Eds.), *Academic writing in a second language: Essays on research and pedagogy* (pp. 293–312). Norwood, NJ: Ablex.

Elbow, P. (1991). Reflections on academic discourse. *College English, 53(2), 135–115.*

Fahenstock, J. (1986). Accommodating science. *Written Communication, 3, 275–296.*

Geertz, C. (1983). *Local knowledge: Further essays in interpretive anthropology.* New York: Basic Books.

Geertz, C. (1988). *Words and lives: The anthropologist as author.* Palo Alto, CA: Stanford University Press.

Geisler, C. (1994). Literacy and expertise in the academy. *Language and Learning Across the Disciplines, 1, 35–57.*

Gould, S. J. (1985). *The flamingo's smile.* New York: Norton.

Hinds, J. (1987). Reader versus writer responsibility: A new typology. In U. Connor & R. B. Kaplan (Eds.), *Writing across languages: An analysis of L2 texts* (pp. 141–152). Reading, MA: Addison-Wesley.

Johns, A. M. (1985). The new authenticity and the preparation of commercial reading texts for lower-level ESP students. *CATESOL Occasional Papers, 11,* 103–107.

Killingsworth, M. J. (1992). Discourse communities—local and global. *Rhetoric Review, 11,* 110–122.

Lave, J., & Wenger, E. (1991). *Situated learning: Legitimate peripheral participation.* New York: Cambridge University Press.

Mauranen, A. (1993). Contrastive ESP rhetoric Metatext in Finnish-English economic texts. *English for Specific Purposes, 12,* 3–22.

Prior, P. (1994). Response, revision and disciplinarity: A microhistory of a dissertation prospectus in sociology. *Written Communication, 11,* 483–533.

Purves, A. C. (1990). *The scribal society: An essay on literacy and schooling in the information age.* New York: Longman.

Rafoth, B. A. (1990). The concept of discourse community: Descriptive and explanatory adequacy. In G. Kirsch & D. H. Roen (Eds.), *A sense of audience in written communication* (pp. 140–152). *Written Communication Annual, Vol. 5.* Newbury Park, CA: Sage.

Raimes, A. (1990). The TOEFL Test of Written English: Some causes for concern. *TESOL Quarterly, 24,* 427–442.

Rodriguez, R. (1982). *Hunger of memory: The education of Richard Rodriguez.* New York: Bantam Books.

Rose, M. (1989). *Lives on the boundary: The struggles and achievements of America's underprepared.* New York: Free Press.

Schneider, M., & Fujishima, N. K. (1995). When practice doesn't make perfect: The case of a graduate ESL student. In D. Belcher & G. Braine (Eds.), *Academic writing in a second language: Essays on research & pedagogy* (pp. 3–22). Norwood, NJ: Ablex.

Swales, J. M. (1988b). Discourse communities, genres and English as an international language. *World Englishes, 7,* 211–220.

Swales, J. M. (1990). *Genre analysis: English in academic and research settings.* New York: Cambridge University Press.

Swales, J. M., & Feak, C. B. (1994). *Academic writing for graduate students: Essential tasks and skills.* Ann Arbor: University of Michigan Press.

Tannen, D. (1986). *That's not what I meant: How conversational style makes or breaks your relations with others.* New York: W. Morrow.

Tannen, D. (1994). *Talking from 9–5: How women's and men's conversational styles affect who gets heard, who gets credit, and what gets done at work.* New York: W. Morrow.

Widdowson, H. G. (1993). The relevant conditions of language use and learning. In M. Krueger & F. Ryan (Eds.), *Language and content: Discipline- and content-based approaches to language study* (pp. 27–36). Lexington, MA: D. C. Heath.

Williams, J. (1989). *Style: Ten lessons in clarity and grace.* (3rd. ed.). Glenview, IL: Scott Foresman.

Questions for Discussion and Journaling

1. What are some of the complications Johns outlines that are related to joining a discourse community?

2. Johns notes that people joining a new discourse community can rebel against some of its conventions and in so doing actually change the discourse community. Explain what this means and try to think of some historical examples

in which this has happened. If you read Gee, compare Johns's view of *change* in discourse communities with Gee's view.

3. Have you ever felt that learning to write or speak in a new discourse community conflicted with your sense of self, your values, your beliefs? If so, what happened? If not, why do you think you have been exempt from this sort of conflict?

4. Johns cites a number of examples to argue that learning to write and speak in new ways is not just a **cognitive** matter but also impacts values and identity. She says, "full involvement or affiliation . . . requires major cultural and linguistic trade-offs" (para. 53). Draw on some examples of your own to explain what you think this means. Do you agree or disagree with her claim here? Why?

5. How do you feel about your *authority* over the kinds of texts you have been asked to write so far in college?

6. Why is rule breaking a "minefield" for students but not for the more famous or established academic writers Johns cites? Have you ever been punished or rewarded for rule breaking related to texts? What happened?

Applying and Exploring Ideas

1. In paragraph 58, Johns outlines a number of questions that teachers should discuss with their students regarding authority and control of language in their classrooms. Go through and answer her list of questions in as much detail as you can. When you are finished, reread your answers and use them to help you write a letter to an incoming student in which you explain the concepts of *discourse communities*, *authority*, and *control* and explain the relationships among them. Then, explain why having an explicit understanding of these concepts is useful and give specific examples from your own experiences to illustrate what you are saying.

2. Plan an insurrection in your writing classroom. What are some writing rules you'd like to break? Do these rules represent the values or authority of a particular discourse community? How would breaking these rules impact your membership in the discourse community and your own identity? Try writing a Declaration of Independence from the particular rule or rules in question, and then see if your classmates are persuaded by it to vote in favor of revolution.

Meta Moment

How would understanding what Johns is writing about help you in becoming a member of new discourse communities? Or, conversely, how can the ideas here help you understand why you might not *want* to abide by the rules of a new discourse community?

Identity, Authority, and Learning to Write in New Workplaces

ELIZABETH WARDLE

Wardle, Elizabeth. "Identity, Authority, and Learning to Write in New Workplaces." *Enculturation* 5.2 (2004): n. pag. Web. 18 Feb. 2010.

Framing the Reading

Elizabeth Wardle is an associate professor at the University of Central Florida, where she directs the Writing Program. She was finishing her Ph.D. at about the time that Ann Johns was retiring; thus, you can think of her work as growing from the work of the scholars you have read so far. She had, for example, the benefit of being exposed to the entire Gee/Swales/Johns conversation as it was happening and was able to identify what else seemed to need saying.

Wardle is interested in how people learn to write, not as children but as adults moving among different **discourse communities**. The following article is one that she researched as a Ph.D. student. While in graduate school, Wardle experienced many of the conflicts that Johns described in the selection reprinted in this chapter— she was asked to use language in ways that did not feel "right" or "natural" to her, she struggled with finding the right **register** and **lexis** for her writing, and writing in "academic" ways seemed to stifle her creative voice. It makes sense, then, that she would research someone else struggling to **enculturate** in a new discourse community.

This article is the result of that study. It describes a new employee, fresh out of college, trying to communicate with a new workplace community and failing— miserably. His failure stems from many of the issues Johns and Gee discussed earlier in this chapter—**authority** (or lack of it), **rebellion** (a specific kind that Wardle calls **nonparticipation**), and a sense of **identity** that conflicts with the new discourse community. Wardle introduces some new theoretical terms here—she talks about **activity systems** rather than discourse communities, for example—but she defines these terms in her article. You should be able to use her definitions plus your understanding of discourse communities to help you understand what she's saying and why she thinks it matters.

Getting Ready to Read

Before you read, do at least one of these activities:

- Think over your time in college so far and write a few paragraphs about whether your identity has been changed by your college experiences to date, and, if it has, *how* it has changed. How can you explain the changes (or lack of change)?

- Make a list of terms or phrases you're using now that you weren't at the beginning of your college experience. Do you associate any of this new language with new discourse communities?

As you read, consider the following questions:

- How does Wardle describe being a "newcomer" to an activity system? Is there anything familiar about her description that you recognize from your own experience?
- If you read Johns's article, consider how Johns's way of talking about *authority* differs from Wardle's way of talking about it. What do you think accounts for the difference?
- How are Wardle's *activity systems* different from *discourse communities, communities of practice*, and *Discourses*?

Despite the media's continued representation of communication as "utilitarian and objective" (Bolin), and the acceptance of this view by much of the public and even by many academics, research in rhetoric and composition over the past twenty years has moved toward a much more complex view of communication. Of particular interest to professional communication specialists is research suggesting that learning to write in and for new situations and workplaces is complex in ways that go far beyond texts and cognitive abilities. This research posits that for workers to be successfully enculturated into new communities of practice[1] (Lave and Wenger) or activity systems (Engeström; Russell, "Rethinking" and "Activity Theory"), including learning to write in ways that are appropriate to those new communities, neophytes must learn and conform to the conventions, codes, and genres of those communities (Bazerman; Berkenkotter, Huckin, and Ackerman; Berkenkotter and Huckin; Bizzell). However, *when and how much* each neophyte must conform largely depends on how much authority and cultural capital[2] the neophyte possesses or cultivates to accomplish work effectively. Additionally, issues of identity and values are important factors in neophytes' abilities and willingness to learn to write in and for new workplaces, as they must choose between ways of thinking and writing with which they are comfortable and new ways that seem foreign or at odds with their identities and values (Doheny-Farina; Doheny-Farina and Odell). Researchers who examine issues of identity and

> Learning to write in and for new situations and workplaces is complex in ways that go far beyond texts and cognitive abilities.

authority as important aspects of communicating in workplace settings find that workers' identities are bound up in myriad ways with the genres they are asked to appropriate (Dias et al.; Dias and Paré; Paré). According to Anis Bawarshi, "a certain genre replaces or . . . adds to the range of possible selves that writers have available to them" (105).

As composition widens its focus beyond academic writing, it is increasingly 2 important to consider what it means to write in the workplace. Not only will such knowledge help us prepare students for the writing beyond the classroom, but, as Bolin points out, those of us working in rhetoric and composition must continue to respond to complaints by the media and general public that we have not fulfilled our responsibilities and "polished" students' language use so that they can convey information "clearly." We can respond to these complaints more effectively when we better understand the ways in which writing is bound up with issues of identity and authority. While we recognize the importance of identity and authority issues in the process of enculturating new workers, we do not always fully understand how these issues influence their writing.

Here I first outline theories of identity and authority that are useful in under- 3 standing how newcomers learn to write in and for new situations. The socio-historic theoretical perspective I offer draws on research from two groups: compositionists who focus on cultural-historical activity theory[3] (Russell, "Rethinking" and "Activity Theory"; Prior; Dias et al.) and sociologists who study apprenticeship (Lave and Wenger; Wenger). Combined, these lines of research expand genre theory (Bawarshi; Russell, "Rethinking") and describe the complexities of learning to write, both in school and the workplace (Dias, et al.; Dias and Paré; Prior). The socio-historic view usefully illuminates the construction of subject positions and subjectivities specifically within institutions and disciplines.

Second, I illustrate some of the difficulties inherent in writing and identity 4 formation by telling the story of one new worker who struggled with written conventions and codes in his new workplace largely because of issues of identity and authority: how he saw himself versus how other members of this workplace community saw him. Most importantly, I argue that rather than assisting in the new worker's enculturation, members of the community expected a type of servitude: they perceived him not as a community member but as a tool, an identity that he fought strongly against.

Identity

To tease out relationships between identity and writing in the workplace, we 5 need theories that consider the workplace as a legitimate and important influence on subject formation. Socio-historic theories provide one such perspective and describe identity construction within institutions. Like other postmodern theories, socio-historic theories see identity—the "subject"—as a complex "construction of the various signifying practices . . . formed by the various discourses, sign systems, that surround her" (Berlin 18). However, socio-historic theories view the subject as not only *constructed* by signifying practices but also as *constructing* signifying practices: "writers' desires are [not] completely determined, as evidenced by the fact that textual instantiations of a genre are rarely if ever exactly the same" (Bawarshi 91). Socio-historic theories also provide specific tools for analyzing the "levers" within institutions, allowing for a detailed examination of power and the formation of subject positions. Activity theory (Cole; Cole and Engeström; Cole and Scribner; Engeström; Russell, "Rethinking" and "Activity Theory"), for example, which focuses on the relationships among shared activities within communities and individual participants' sometimes competing understandings of motives, conventions, and divisions of labor for carrying out the activities, provides a framework for understanding the interactions of individuals, groups, and texts that enables researchers to illustrate the complex interactions among various aspects of an activity system (see Figure 1).

Activity theorists such as David Russell have also argued the importance of 6 the relationship between writing and identity: as we encounter genres mediating new activity systems, we must determine whether we can and/or must appropriate those genres, thus expanding our involvement within those systems. We must also consider whether expanding involvement in one system forces us away from other activity systems we value—away from "activity systems of family, neighborhood, and friends that construct ethnic, racial, gender, and class identit(ies)" ("Rethinking" 532). Writers can sometimes "challenge the genre positions and relations available to them," thus changing genres rather than choosing between the genres and their various activity systems (Bawarshi 97). However, socio-historic theories do not view such resistance as the result of self-will or "inherent forces within each human being that love liberty, seek to enhance their own powers or capacities, or strive for emancipation" (Rose 35), but rather suggest that "resistance arises from the contradictions individuals experience in their multiple subject positions" (Bawarshi 100). As

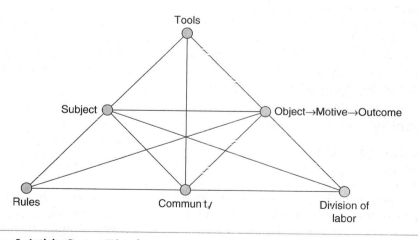

Figure 1 Activity System Triangle
(*Based on Engeström: Learning by Expanding*)

writers shape and change genres, the power of those genres also shapes and enables writers' identities (Bawarshi 97).

Sociologist Etienne Wenger's theory of communities of practice (shaped, ini- 7 tially, with Jean Lave) is particularly useful for describing workplace encultura- tion as it is affected by and as it affects written practices. Wenger specifically focuses on matters of identity within *workplace* groups and activities, describ- ing identity as a "negotiated experience . . . a layering of events of participation and reification by which our experience and its social interpretation inform each other" (149). According to Wenger, "layers build upon each other to pro- duce our identity as a very complex interweaving of participative experience and reificative projections" (151). To "find their own unique identities" within new organizations (Wenger 156), newcomers must choose levels and types of engagement; they must find modes of belonging. Wenger describes three inter- related modes of belonging: engagement, imagination, and alignment.

- *Engagement* entails defining a "common enterprise" that newcomers and old-timers pursue together to develop "interpersonal relationships" and "a sense of interacting trajectories that shape identities in relation to one another" (184). While engagement can be positive, "a lack of mutuality in the course of engagement creates relations of marginality that can reach deeply into [newcomers'] identities" (193).
- *Imagination*, "a process of expanding . . . self by transcending . . . time and space and creating new images of the world and [self]" (176), entails newcomers "locating [their] engagement in a broader system . . . defining a trajectory that connects what [they] are doing to an extended identity . . . [and] assuming the meaning of foreign artifacts and actions" (185). While imagination can lead to a positive mode of belonging, it can also "be dis- connected and ineffective . . . it can be so removed from any lived form of membership that it detaches [newcomers'] identit[ies] and leaves [them] in a state of uprootedness." Newcomers can lose "touch with the sense of social efficacy by which [their] experience of the world can be interpreted as competence" (178).
- *Alignment* entails "negotiating perspectives, finding common ground . . . defining broad visions and aspirations . . . [and] walking boundaries . . . reconciling diverging perspectives" (186–87). Alignment "requires share- able artifacts/boundary objects able to create fixed points around which to coordinate activities. It can also require the creation and adoption of broader discourses that help reify the enterprise and by which local ac- tions can be interpreted as fitting within a broader framework" (187). However, alignment "can be a violation of [a person's] sense of self that crushes [their] identity" (181).

To fully participate, according to Wenger, new workers must find ways to 8 engage in the work that other community members do, including the writing they do; newcomers must be able to imagine their own work—and writing—as being an important part of a larger enterprise. And they must be comfortable that the larger enterprise and its smaller components—down to the writing conventions of that community—are compatible with the identities they envision for themselves. Joining new workplace communities, then, is not simply a matter of learning new skills but also of fielding new calls for identity construction. This understanding of identity suggests that people *enact* and *negotiate* identities in the world over time: "Identity is dynamic (Hecht, 1993), and it is something that is presented and re-presented, constructed and reconstructed in interaction (including written communication)" (Rubin 9).

At times, however, participation in new communities requires accepting for oneself identities that are at odds with the values of other communities to which one belongs (Lave and Wenger. Russell, "Rethinking"). One way newcomers reconcile the competing demands of various communities is to choose to participate in some aspects of a new community and not others. Such choices are a source of power in that "power derives from belonging as well as from exercising control over what we belong to" (Wenger 207). In addition, choices about participation impact newcomers' emerging identities within communities of practice. For example, the choice of non-participation can lead to marginalization within the workplace (Wenger 167). Identity formation in any new community, then, is a negotiation in which newcomers have some measure of "control over the meanings in which [they] are invested" and can "assert [their] identities as productive of meaning" (Wenger 188, 208)—even if they do so by refusing to participate in some workplace activities.

Achieving enculturation in workplace communities requires neophytes to engage in new practices—including new *written* practices. Some new written practices may be opposed to newcomers' values and ethics; others may simply be foreign to them; still others may ask them to give up some measure of authority to which they believe they are entitled. The resultant struggles will often be visible in their written practices. If new workers fail to write in ways that a workplace community of practice recognizes as effective and appropriate, the reasons may be related to identity rather than ability: "Stylistic options 'leak' clues about writers' social identities. Rhetorical choices help writers construct the social identities they wish to project in given writing episodes" (Rubin 4). Thus, failing to write in ways communities establish as appropriate can be a form of resistance that "does not arise from ignorance of standard forms [but rather] entails considerable language awareness" (Rubin 7). On the other hand, new workers may not be consciously aware that their writing choices are matters of identification: "marking social identity in writing is . . . oftentimes quite below the focal awareness of the writer" (8). Because each individual "is heterogeneously made up of various competing discourses, conflicted and contradictory scripts . . . our consciousness [is] anything but unified" (Berlin 18).

Authority

As Wenger's theory implies, authority (like identity) is continually negotiated within communities of practice. Authority is bestowed by institutions, can be just as easily withdrawn by those same institutions or its members, and must be maintained through appropriate expressions of authority (Bourdieu). Bruce Lincoln argues that authority is best understood in relational terms "as the effect of a posited, perceived, or institutionally ascribed asymmetry between speaker and audience that permits certain speakers to command not just the attention but the confidence, respect, and trust of their audience, or . . . to make audiences act *as if* this were so" (4). When speakers possess authority, exercising that authority "need not involve argumentation and may rest on the naked assertion that the identity of the speaker warrants acceptance of the speech" (5). Those listening accept the speaker's pronouncement because the speaker *is who she is*. At any given time, however, faith in a speaker's authority can be suspended (either momentarily or forever) if "an explanation is requested . . ." because "the relation of trust and acceptance characteristic of authority is suspended, at least temporarily, in that moment" (6). Authority, then, is an intangible quality granted to persons through institutions, which renders their pronouncements as accepted by those in that institution's communities of practice, but which must be maintained through individuals' speech and actions.

Conversely, a person can understand clearly how to speak in ways that are   12
acceptable in particular circumstances, but if not endowed with some recognized institutional authority, all the relevant and appropriate words in the world will not command it: "authority comes to language from outside . . . Language at most represents this authority, manifests and symbolizes it" (Bourdieu 109). Bourdieu, while not specifically explaining enculturation, suggests that authority may be a kind of "social magic," dependent upon the "social position of the speaker," and reinforced by her ability to appropriately adjust her speech acts:

> Most of the conditions that have to be fulfilled in order for a performative utterance to succeed come down to the question of the appropriateness of the speaker—or, better still, his social function—and of the discourse he utters . . . it must be uttered by the person legitimately licensed to so do . . . it must be uttered in a legitimate situation . . . in front of legitimate receivers . . . [and] it must be enunciated according to the legitimate forms (syntactic, phonetic, etc.). (Bourdieu 111–12)

Thus, if the neophyte is granted some measure of authority by an institu-   13
tion but does not quickly learn the appropriate speech conventions of her new community of practice, she may soon lose the authority with which she began. While newcomers to a community normally experience a "grace period" for adopting community practices, it does not last forever and soon the neophyte must express her authority in her new community appropriately: "[L]earning to become a legitimate participant in a community involves learning how to talk (and be silent) in the manner of full participants" (Lave and Wenger 105).

If we understand writing as one tool among many through which knowledge,   14
identity, and authority are continually negotiated, then we must view learning to write in new ways as a complex and often messy network of tool-mediated human relationships best explored in terms of the social and cultural practices that people bring to their shared uses of tools. If we accept these assumptions, we find ourselves faced with several questions: What happens when new workers

find that to "get along" in a new workplace they must accept basic assumptions about what is valuable and appropriate that are contrary to their own—or that, in fact, degrade them to the status of an object or tool? What happens when a new worker's assumptions are frequently made obvious to the community, and those assumptions fly in the face of accepted ways of doing things?

Learning to Write in a New Workplace: Alan's Story

My story of "Alan"—a computer support specialist who did not learn/choose   15
to write in ways his humanities department colleagues (primarily professors and graduate students) found appropriate and legitimate—illustrates answers to some of the questions about identity and authority as they intersect with writing in the workplace. For seven months, I observed and interviewed Alan, a new computer specialist in a humanities department at a large Midwestern university. I also collected 140 email messages he wrote and many others that were written to him and spent time in public computer labs listening as people discussed their computer problems with Alan. Finally, near the end of the study, I conducted a written survey with all members of the humanities department regarding their use of computers and technology and their awareness of various initiatives Alan had discussed with them via email.

Alan and the other members of the humanities department were constantly   16
at cross purposes—he did not write in ways the community members saw as appropriate, and he did not view their conventions as ones he should adopt, given his position in the community. Most importantly, the community of practice did not appear to view him as a fledging member but rather as an object—a tool enabling them to get work done. His discursive choices can be viewed as an attempt to reject the identity of tool and to appropriate authority for himself. Thus, Alan's story serves to illustrate some of the complexities associated with learning to write in new workplaces.

Who Is Alan and What Is His Place in the Humanities Department?

Alan was a 23-year-old white male who received a B.A. in art and design from   17
a large Midwestern university. He became interested in computers as an undergraduate and as his interest in computers grew, he performed two computer-related work-study jobs on campus. He decided he liked working with computers and looked for a computer job when he graduated. Alan's first professional position was as computer support specialist responsible for several thousand "users" in various locations at the same university from which he graduated. He was unhappy in this position, primarily because he felt his supervisor did not give him enough responsibility, instead assigning the most difficult tasks to student workers who had been in the department for a long time. He left this job for another in an academic humanities department within the same university, again as a computer support specialist.

In the academic department, Alan was the sole computer support special-   18
ist, surrounded by faculty members with varying computer abilities. While no

one else performed a job similar to his, the department included other support staff—all women, primarily administrative assistants—and Alan supervised one student worker several hours per week. Alan's supervisor, the department chair (a white male in his early fifties with a Ph.D. and numerous publications and awards), initially left most computer-related decisions to Alan, though the chair's collaborative administrative style made the division of labor unclear to newcomers. A Computer Resources Committee also interacted regularly with Alan, but whether they had authority over him was unclear. The mentoring he received was fairly hands-off, resembling what Lave and Wenger call "benign community neglect" (93), a situation that left Alan to find his own way, which he saw as a vote of confidence.

What Was Alan's View of Himself and His Authority?

Alan's sense of what it meant to fill a support staff position was very different 19 from the faculty's sense. He left his previous position because it had not allowed him much responsibility, his supervisors "relied on students' work more than" his, and he felt he "was getting no respect." This previous experience strongly informed his understanding of his current job. Because Alan had some measure of institutional authority by way of the cultural capital associated with technical knowledge, Alan did not initially have to prove himself knowledgeable or competent in the ways many new workers do. He was immediately ascribed authority and respect due to his assumed technical expertise in a place where such expertise was rare. When I asked Alan to name and describe his position he replied: "I am basically a systems administrator, which means I am God here. Anywhere in this department. Except for with the department chair." This continued to be Alan's attitude during his tenure in the department. He often indicated that there was no one "above him" but the department chair. During his fourth week in the position, Alan told me he "couldn't believe how much authority" he had, "how high up in the computer world responsibility-wise" he was. He stressed that his title put "only one other person above" him in the university or the department.

Alan's sense of his level of authority was evident in the way he talked about 20 the faculty members in the department. He described the faculty members as "just users; nobodies [who] use the computers I set up." He indicated they were beneath him: "I put myself down on their level." To Alan, the faculty were simply "users" of his tools. He did not seem to understand—or care about—the faculty members' work or how his tools enabled them to do that work. His focus was on what *he* did: making machines work. His comments illustrate his attempt to find a mode of belonging through imagination; unfortunately, he imagined an identity for himself fairly removed from the reality of the situation.

In reality, he was hired in a support staff position, as a "tool" to fix things 21 the faculty needed. The faculty clearly viewed Alan as support personnel. They were happiest when things worked smoothly and when Alan's work hummed along invisibly and successfully behind the scenes. When his assistance was required, they expected him to appear immediately; some faculty even went so far as to copy email messages to the chair and computer resources committee to ensure that Alan knew there would be repercussions if he did not appear when called upon. Alan's view of everyone else as "just users" came across clearly in his writing (which primarily took place via email) and eventually called his competence into question such that department members often failed to respond to him, were ignorant of his initiatives to help them, and laughed at him and his emails. This misalignment between Alan's imagined role for himself and the role imagined for him by others led to a lack of the positive engagement Wenger argues may help newcomers enculturate; Alan and the other members of the humanities department were not actively engaging or mutually negotiating their work together.

How Did Alan Relate to the Department in Writing?

A number of discourse conventions existed in the department that could have   22 afforded Alan further authority. Had he adopted these conventions, Alan could have achieved alignment with the department, for example using emails as "boundary objects able to create fixed points around which to coordinate activities" (Wenger 187). Alan did not adopt the conventions of the department, however. Although it is possible for writers "to enact slightly different intentions" and "resist the ideological pull of genres in certain circumstances," their resistance will only be "recognized and valued as resistance and not misinterpretation, or worse, ignorance" if it is "predicated on one's knowledge of a genre" (Bawarshi 92). Alan's written interactions with the department were seen not as resistance but as ignorance, and identified him as an outsider without authority.

One of the conventions Alan did not follow when he wrote involved the   23 department's approximately 15 or 20 listservs, each reaching a specific audience. Tailoring emails to a particular audience was an accepted writing convention in the activity system. During the beginning of each fall semester, listserv addresses were sent out and department members were encouraged to use the list that most directly reached their message's audience. Alan chose to use the list that reached all department members for nearly every email he wrote—despite the fact that he administered all the lists and knew lists more tailored to his messages existed. His email activity did not "fit within [the] broader structures," demonstrating his lack of alignment with the department (Wenger 173).

A survey of the department I conducted indicated that Alan's lack of audi-   24 ence awareness and tailoring had negative consequences for his identity in the department: most people were unaware of his efforts to better their computer system because they either did not read or did not remember reading the information he sent out via email. In other words, the members of the department did not see Alan as engaged in work with and for them. For example, much of his time was spent setting up a new departmental computer network that would benefit all department members by providing them private, disk-free storage space. He discussed this in emails many times, but usually in emails that mentioned a number of other items directed at more specialized audiences.

As a result, over half the survey respondents did not know he was setting up a new network. People indicated on the survey that they stopped reading an email if the first item of business did not relate to them.

Other accepted departmental conventions governed the content and style of emails. The community members were highly literate, hyper-aware language users, in the traditional sense of the terms, who valued professional, grammatically correct, Standard English in written communication. The unspoken convention that email within the department be grammatically correct was pervasive and widely practiced in the community. Abiding by this convention was difficult for Alan, who explicitly said on several occasions that he felt his writing abilities were not good. His emails show a number of grammatical errors including sentence fragments, double negatives, and misplaced punctuation. In addition, Alan's emails often contained directives about the use of computers and labs; he frequently implied that people should respect his authority and position in the department by doing what he asked. His utterances were intended to be "*signs of authority* . . . to be believed and obeyed" (Bourdieu 66). However, he sent these emails to many irrelevant audiences and his grammar, punctuation, and sentence structure often undermined his authority as understood by audience members. 25

Although Alan was institutionally authorized to speak about technology, and recognized as a technical authority, he was not able to "speak in a way that others . . . regard[ed] as acceptable in the circumstances" (Thompson 9). Survey respondents' comments suggested that people dismissed Alan's legitimacy because of his writing choices. While he appeared to feel this dismissal, he did not change his writing behavior and his institutional authority began to erode. 26

What Was the Outcome?

The fact that Alan, a newcomer, used email in ways that old-timers saw as inappropriate—and that this use of email caused conflict—is not surprising; after all, newcomers are expected to make missteps. But rather than adapting and changing to communicate more effectively in his new workplace, Alan resisted and clung to his own ways of writing, causing conflict and breakdowns in the community of practice. Members of the department were similarly unwilling to change their view of what they found acceptable in email. They insisted on what Bourdieu calls "the dominant competence" and imposed their idea of linguistic competence as "the only legitimate one" (56). The community didn't negotiate or compromise its idea of linguistic competence for Alan; the only real possibility for negotiation had to come from Alan—and it did not. 27

Because our identities are shaped to some extent by the communities in which we choose to participate—as well as by those settings we inhabit and in which we choose *not* to participate (Wenger 164)—workers such as Alan may also be demonstrating their desire to identify with communities of practice other than the primary ones in which they work by refusing to appropriate new ways of writing. By refusing to participate in communication conventions adopted by the majority of members of the community, Alan attempted to 28 assert the identity he imagined for himself (powerful network administrator) and to resist the one imposed on him by the workplace. Pushing past resistance to work effectively with others requires people to relinquish aspects of their desired primary identities: "[L]egitimate participation entails the loss of certain identities even as it enables the construction of others" (Hodges 289). Clearly, Alan did not feel this was an acceptable proposition. The result for Alan, as Wenger might predict, was increasing marginalization. His emails were not only the butt of cruel and constant jokes in the department, but they also failed to garner support and convey necessary information. People ignored his emails or laughed at them, and neither response was conducive to getting work done. Ultimately, Alan's choice of non-participation resulted in "disturbances and breakdowns in work processes" (Hasu and Engeström 65).

Socio-historic activity theory argues that such situations can lead to posi- 29 tive developments because breakdowns can potentially serve as catalysts for change: "Discoordination and breakdown often lead to re-mediation of the performance and perspectives, sometimes even to re-mediation of the overall activity system in order to resolve its pressing inner contradictions" (Hasu and Engeström 65). However, for a breakdown to lead to positive change, those involved must be willing to consider and negotiate various perspectives and everyone must be willing to appropriate some new ways of seeing and doing. This did not happen in Alan's case. He clung to his own ways of writing and communicating, which demonstrated that he was not engaging, aligning, and imagining a role for himself as a member of the humanities department. Other members of the humanities department no more changed to accommodate Alan than Alan did to fit in with them.

After a year and a half, Alan left and found employment elsewhere. 30

Discussion

Clearly, Alan's enculturation into the humanities department was not success- 31 ful. He was an outsider, a worker unlike the other community members in age, education, occupation, linguistic abilities, and concern for conventions. Since new workers are often different in these ways and still manage to negotiate communication strategies that are effective and acceptable enough so that work can be done, what might account for Alan's resistance to writing in ways that his new community saw as legitimate and appropriate?

One reason for his resistance was that Alan and other members of his depart- 32 ment had a different understanding of the division of labor in the department and, thus, a different view of Alan's authority. Alan might have viewed changing his writing habits as an admission that he did not play the role he imagined for himself within the department. Despite his vocal assertions to the contrary, he was not "God" in the department. While he entered the department with some measure of authority by virtue of his technical expertise, he had to prove himself and create his *ethos* continually through language—perhaps even more than through action for this particular workplace. This was something he could not or would not do.

However, a socio-linguistic analysis I conducted of Alan's writing suggests 33 that he did not feel as much authority as he claimed to have, even from the beginning of his time in the department when he had the most cooperation and respect because of his technical capital. Of 150 sentences I studied for the analysis, only 39 were directives. While all of Alan's emails were usually sent to department-wide listservs, the overwhelming majority of his directives (28 of the 39) were addressed to graduate students alone. Only 3 were written to faculty or staff members, and 6 were written to the department as a whole. Alan's use of directives suggests that while he claimed to have authority and see the faculty as simply "users," he did not, in fact, feel much authority over them, so he confined most of his directives to graduate students. Even then, Alan used hedges over two-thirds of the time, suggesting that his felt sense of authority was shaky. This understanding best matched the department's understanding. He could make technical changes and monitor and limit operations; however, he could not force people to act in the ways he wanted them to or prohibit them from using equipment, as he threatened in more than one email.

Given the limitations of his actual authority—which conflicted with his 34 desired authority—Alan's refusal to change his writing might have been one way of claiming an identity he wanted, one that included the authority and autonomy to which he felt entitled. However, his refusal to write in ways seen as acceptable by the department had the opposite effect: his method of writing stripped him of the institutional authority originally invested in him. Although Alan's words could be understood, they were not "likely to be listened to [or] recognized as acceptable." He lacked "the competence necessary in order to speak the legitimate language," which could have granted him "linguistic capital . . . a profit of distinction" (Bourdieu 55). Since authoritative language is useless "without the collaboration of those it governs," Alan's initial authority was lessened with each utterance seen by the department as illegitimate (Bourdieu 113). We should keep in mind that Alan's choices are unlikely to have been conscious; quite often linguistic action is not "the outcome of conscious calculation" (Thompson 17).

A second reason for Alan's failure to adopt community writing conventions 35 might have been his resistance to being used as a tool. As a support person, Alan joined this activity system as one of its tools, not as a community member. As a technical worker with a B.A. in a university humanities department filled with people who had M.A.s and Ph.D.s, he and the other members of the workplace were not mutually engaged. Rather, the community members used him as a tool to help achieve goals Alan did not share or value. Computer system administrators (like many other workers) are used as tools to do work that others cannot. As a result of his position, Alan was not part of the community of practice; rather, his ability to maintain computer networks figured in as one of many pieces of the humanities community: the community members needed him and his activity to use their computers.

Though Alan was hired to function as a tool, he did not sit quietly like a 36 hammer or wrench until he was needed, he did not perform exactly the same way each time he was needed, and he did not remain silent when his work was complete. As a person, Alan didn't always choose to perform his tasks when and how community members wanted. In addition, he initiated and responded to dialogue, and (most frustrating for members of the humanities department) chose to do so in ways contrary to the community expectations. Alan's refusal to write in ways that the faculty felt he should was, perhaps, one means of flouting their linguistic authority, demonstrating that he was not a servant or tool to be used at will. Rather than quietly performing the tasks asked of him, and writing about them in the ways the community members saw as legitimate, Alan resisted the department by seeing *them* as *his* tools and by choosing non-participation over acquiescence to their written conventions. Alan's method of resistance did bring him to the conscious attention of department members; they quickly came to see him as a human being who did not silently serve them in response to their every need or desire. However, his method of resistance did not enable Alan to complete his own work successfully, nor did it lead the humanities department to include him as a human member of their community. Thus, Alan's method of resistance in this case was successful on one level, but detrimental to both himself and the workplace on other levels.

Alan's example illustrates that learning to write in new communities entails   37
more than learning discrete sets of skills or improving cognitive abilities. It is a process of involvement in communities, of identifying with certain groups, of choosing certain practices over others; a process strongly influenced by power relationships—a process, in effect, bound up tightly with identity, authority, and experience. Alan's case also suggests that enculturation theories have overlooked an important point: not all new workers are expected, or themselves expect, to enculturate into a community. Some, perhaps many in our service-oriented society, are present in communities of practice not as members but as tools. Given these points, those of us interested in how people learn to write in new environments, in school and beyond, and those of us struggling to teach new ways of writing to students who resist what we ask of them, must continue to study and consider the importance of factors beyond texts and cognitive ability.

Acknowledgments

Thanks to Rebecca Burnett (Iowa State University) and Charie Thralls (Utah State University) for encouraging this study and responding to early drafts; to David Russell (Iowa State University) and Donna Kain (Clarkson University) for responding to later drafts; and to Lisa Coleman and Judy Isaksen, *Enculturation* guest editor and board member respectively, for their helpful reviews.

Notes

1. "A community of practice is a set of relations among persons, activity, and world, over time and in relation with other tangential and overlapping communities of practice" (Lave and Wenger 98).
2. "Knowledge, skills, and other cultural acquisitions, as exemplified by educational or technical qualifications" (Thompson 14).

3. Though relatively new to many in our field, activity theory is used more and more widely within composition studies; see, for example, Bazerman and Russell; Berkenkotter and Ravotas; Dias, et al.; Dias and Paré; Grossman, Smagorinsky and Valencia; Harms; Hovde; Kain; Russell, "Rethinking" and "Activity Theory"; Smart; Spinuzzi; Wardle; Winsor. Activity theory's implications for composition instruction are outlined in Russell's "Activity Theory and Its Implications for Writing Instruction" and in Wardle's *Contradiction, Constraint, and Re-Mediation: An Activity Analysis of FYC* and "Can Cross-Disciplinary Links Help Us Teach 'Academic Discourse' in FYC?"

Works Cited

Bawarshi, Anis. *Genre and the Invention of the Writer: Reconsidering the Place of Invention in Composition*. Logan: Utah State UP, 2003. Print.

Bazerman, Charles. *Shaping Written Knowledge: The Genre and Activity of the Experimental Article in Sciences*. Madison: U of Wisconsin P, 1988. Print.

Bazerman, Charles, and David Russell. *Writing Selves/Writing Societies: Research from Activity Perspectives*. Fort Collins: The WAC Clearinghouse and *Mind, Culture, and Activity*, 2002. Print.

Berkenkotter, Carol, Thomas Huckin, and Jon Ackerman. "Conversations, Conventions, and the Writer." *Research in the Teaching of English* 22 (1988): 9–44. Print.

Berkenkotter, Carol, and Thomas Huckin. "Rethinking Genre from a Sociocognitive Perspective." *Written Communication* 10 (1993): 475–509. Print.

Berkenkotter, Carol, and Doris Ravotas. "Genre as a Tool in the Transmission of Practice and across Professional Boundaries." *Mind, Culture, and Activity* 4.4 (1997): 256–74. Print.

Berlin, James. "Poststructuralism, Cultural Studies, and the Composition Classroom: Postmodern Theory in Practice." *Rhetoric Review* 11 (1992): 16–33. Print.

Bizzell, Patricia. "Cognition, Convention, and Certainty: What We Need to Know about Writing." *Pre/Text* 3 (1982): 213–43. Print.

Bolin, Bill. "The Role of the Media in Distinguishing Composition from Rhetoric." *Enculturation* 5.1 (Fall 2003): n. pag. Web. 1 July 2004.

Bourdieu, Pierre. *Language and Symbolic Power*. Ed. John B. Thompson. Trans. Gino Raymond and Matthew Adamson. Cambridge: Harvard UP, 1991. Print.

Cole, Michael. *Cultural Psychology*. Cambridge: Harvard UP, 1996. Print.

Cole, Michael, and Yrgo Engeström. "A Cultural-Historical Approach to Distributed Cognition." Ed. Gavriel Salomon. *Distributed Cognitions: Psychological and Educational Considerations*. Cambridge: Cambridge UP, 1993. 1–46. Print.

Cole, Michael, and Sylvia Scribner. *The Psychology of Literacy*. Cambridge: Harvard UP, 1981. Print.

Dias, Patrick, and Anthony Paré, eds. *Transitions: Writing in Academic and Workplace Settings*. Cresskill: Hampton, 2000. Print.

Dias, Patrick, Aviva Freedman, Peter Medway, and Anthony Paré. *Worlds Apart: Acting and Writing in Academic and Workplace Contexts*. Mahwah: Lawrence Erlbaum, 1999. Print.

Doheny-Farina, Stephen. "A Case Study of an Adult Writing in Academic and Non-Academic Settings." *Worlds of Writing: Teaching and Learning in Discourse Communities at Work*. Ed. Carolyn B. Matalene. New York: Random, 1989. 17–42. Print.

Doheny-Farina, Stephen, and Lee Odell. "Ethnographic Research on Writing: Assumptions and Methodology." *Writing in Nonacademic Settings*. Eds. Lee Odell and Dixie Goswami. New York: Guilford, 1985. 503–35. Print.

Engeström, Yrgo. *Learning by Expanding: An Activity-Theoretical Approach to Developmental Research*. Helsinki: Orienta-Konsultit, 1987. Print.

Grossman, Pamela L., Peter Smagorinsky, and Sheila Valencia. "Appropriating Tools for Teaching English: A Theoretical Framework for Research on Learning to Teach." *American Journal of Education* 108 (1999): 1–29. Print.

Harms, Patricia. *Writing-across-the-Curriculum in a Linked Course Model for First-Year Students: An Activity Theory Analysis*. Ames: Iowa State UP, 2003. Print.

Hasu, Mervi, and Yrgo Engeström. "Measurement in Action: An Activity-Theoretical Perspective on Producer-User Interaction." *International Journal of Human-Computer Studies* 53 (2000): 61–89. Print.

Hodges, Diane. "Participation as Dis-Identification With/In a Community of Practice." *Mind, Culture, and Activity* 5 (1998): 272–90. Print.

Hovde, Marjorie. "Tactics for Building Images of Audience in Organizational Contexts: An Ethnographic Study of Technical Communicators." *Journal of Business and Technical Communication* 14.4 (2000): 395–444. Print.

Kain, Donna J. *Negotiated Spaces: Constructing Genre and Social Practice in a Cross-Community Writing Project*. Ames: Iowa State UP, 2005. Print.

Lave, Jean, and Etienne Wenger. *Situated Learning: Legitimate Peripheral Participation*. New York: Cambridge UP, 1991. Print.

Lincoln, Bruce. *Authority: Construction and Corrosion*. Chicago: U of Chicago P, 1994. Print.

Paré, Anthony. "Genre and Identity: Individuals, Institutions, and Ideology." *The Rhetoric and Ideology of Genre*. Eds. Richard Coe, Lorelei Lingard, and Tatiana Teslenko. Cresskill: Hampton, 2002. Print.

Prior, Paul. *Writing/Disciplinarity: A Sociohistoric Account of Literate Activity in the Academy*. Mahwah: Lawrence Erlbaum, 1998. Print.

Rose, Nikolas. *Inventing Ourselves: Psychology, Power, and Personhood*. Cambridge: Cambridge UP, 1996. Print.

Rubin, Donald L. "Introduction: Composing Social Identity." *Composing Social Identity in Written Language*. Ed. Donald Rubin. Hillsdale: Lawrence Erlbaum, 1995. 1–30. Print.

Russell, David. "Rethinking Genre in School and Society: An Activity Theory Analysis." *Written Communication* 14 (1997): 504–39. Print.

———. "Activity Theory and Its Implications for Writing Instruction." *Reconceiving Writing, Rethinking Writing Instruction*. Ed. Joseph Petraglia. Mahwah: Lawrence Erlbaum, 1995. 51–77. Print.

Smart, Graham. "Genre as Community Invention: A Central Bank's Response to Its Executives' Expectations as Readers." *Writing in the Workplace: New Research Perspectives*. Ed. Rachel Spilka. Carbondale: Southern Illinois UP, 1993. 124–40. Print.

Spinuzzi, Clay. "Pseudotransactionality, Activity Theory, and Professional Writing Instruction." *Technical Communication Quarterly* 5.3 (1996): 295–308. Print.

Thompson, John B. "Editor's Introduction." *Language and Symbolic Power*. By Pierrie Bourdieu. Cambridge: Harvard UP, 1999. 1–31. Print.

Wardle, Elizabeth. *Contradiction, Constraint, and Re-Mediation: An Activity Analysis of FYC*. Ames: Iowa State UP, 2003. Print.

———. "Can Cross-Disciplinary Links Help Us Teach 'Academic Discourse' in FYC?" *Across the Disciplines* 1 (2004): n. pag. Web. 1 July 2004.

Wenger, Etienne. *Communities of Practice: Learning, Meaning, and Identity*. New York: Cambridge UP, 1998. Print.

Winsor, Dorothy. "Genre and Activity Systems: The Role of Documentation in Maintaining and Changing Engineering Activity Systems." *Written Communication* 16.2 (1999): 200–24. Print.

Questions for Discussion and Journaling

1. According to Wardle (citing Wenger), what are the three ways that newcomers try to belong in a new community? Give a specific example to illustrate each "mode of belonging." Then consider why a newcomer might choose *not* to participate in some aspect of a new community.

2. Wardle quotes Rubin as saying that "stylistic options 'leak' clues about writers' social identities" (para. 10). If you've read Gee, you might remember some of his examples for this kind of "clue-leaking." Do you have examples from your own experience?

3. Wardle quotes Hasu and Engeström, well-known activity theory scholars, as saying that conflict and breakdown can actually be positive (para. 29), helping to reshape how a community does things in ways that are more productive. However, the conflicts between Alan and his work community did not have positive results. Why do you think this is? How could his conflicts have been handled so that they *did* result in positive change?

4. Toward the end of the article, Wardle quotes Thompson as saying that the choices we make with language are very often unconscious (para. 34); that is, we might be using language in resistant ways unintentionally. Do you agree that this is possible, or do you think that people are usually making conscious choices when they use language?

5. Wardle seems to be arguing that Alan did not successfully join his new work-place community because he was resisting it: He did not want to adopt the identity that people in that community imagined for him. James Gee would probably have a very different opinion about this; he would most likely argue that Alan's primary Discourse was very different from the dominant Discourse he encountered in the Humanities Department and that Alan would not have been able to join that Discourse even if he had wanted to. Do you agree more with Wardle or Gee? Why?

6. When Wardle was drafting this article, several readers objected to her claim that people like Alan are used as tools, not seen as community members. What do you think?

7. Think of all the people you know who have some sort of institutionally ascribed authority. (Hint: One of them probably assigned this reading!) Can you think of a time when one or more of them lost their authority through their linguistic actions or behaviors? If so, what happened?

Applying and Exploring Ideas

1. Write a reflective essay in which you (first) define what it means to have authority over texts and within discourse communities, and (second) discuss your feelings about your own authority (or lack of it) within any discourse community you would like to focus on. Consider, for example, how you know whether you have authority there and how you gained text and discourse

authority there (if you did); alternatively, consider how it feels to be at the mercy of someone else's authority in a discourse community.

2. Drawing on Wardle and Johns, conduct a brief analysis of U.S. presidential rhetoric in order to consider how presidents use language to convey authority. Go to PresidentialRhetoric.com and read and listen to one of the speeches made by U.S. presidents. Determine how they convey authority through words, phrases, tone, and delivery. Bring your results to class and compare your findings with those of other students.

Meta Moment

Why do you think the readings in this chapter seem to refer to *authority* so much? How might thinking about sources of authority help you as a writer on the job, in college, or in your personal writing?

Learning to Serve:
The Language and Literacy of Food Service Workers

TONY MIRABELLI

Mirabelli, Tony. "Learning to Serve: The Language and Literacy of Food Service Workers." *What They Don't Learn in School.* Ed. Jabari Mahiri. New York: Peter Lang, 2004. 143–62. Print.

Framing the Reading

Tony Mirabelli earned a Ph.D. in Education in Language, Literacy and Culture from the University of California–Berkeley in 2001 and is currently the coordinator of the Athletic Center's Tutorial Program at that same school. He is also a lecturer in the Graduate School of Education there.

Mirabelli's essay, much like Wardle's article, employs theories about language use in communities to examine how workers in a diner interact through language and texts. While Wardle looks at a white-collar worker, Mirabelli is interested in the language and literacy practices of blue-collar service workers. In fact, he introduces the concept of **multiliteracies** to argue that these workers do not just read texts: They also read people and situations.

If you read James Gee at the beginning of this chapter, this argument should be familiar to you. Gee, you will remember, argues that there is too much focus on textual literacies and that print-based literacies cannot be separated from what he calls the "saying (writing)-doing-being-valuing-believing" within **Discourses**. The connection between Gee and Mirabelli is not accidental. Mirabelli relies on assumptions from an academic area called New Literacy Studies, which Gee was instrumental in establishing. As you might expect, knowing this, Mirabelli cites Gee when defining his theoretical terms. (And if you look at the publication information for the book in which Mirabelli's article originally appeared, you'll find that Gee reviewed that book for the publisher.)

We recommend that, if you've read other pieces in this chapter, you treat Mirabelli as an opportunity to "gather up" the concepts you've already encountered in those writings; a lot of them seem to come together in Mirabelli's analysis. For example, his work draws quite directly on Swales's definitions of **discourse community**, and you can see how his ideas work (at various times) with and against what you have read in Gee, Johns, and Wardle. As such, Mirabelli's very rich analysis of a particular

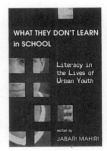

WHAT THEY DON'T LEARN
in SCHOOL

Literacy in
the Lives of
Urban Youth

edited by
JABARI MAHIRI

activity system is an opportunity for you to test the ideas you've been working on throughout the chapter.

Getting Ready to Read

Before you read, do at least one of these activities:

- Think back to your first job. What was it like learning to do it? What did you have to learn? How difficult did you find it? Why?
- Find some friends who have worked in food service, and have them compare notes: Are there different Discourses for different kinds of food service?

As you read, consider the following questions:

- How do you understand the notion of Discourses differently depending on which (or what kind of) Discourse is being studied and analyzed?
- How many kinds of literacies do you imagine there are? Is there a "literacy" for *every* kind of reading? (How many kinds of reading are there?)
- How do discourse communities, Discourses, communities of practice, and activity systems avoid stereotyping—or is this impossible? As analysts and researchers of discourse, how do *we* avoid abusive stereotyping?

Bitterwaitress.com is one of the newest among a burgeoning number of worker-produced websites associated with the service industry.[1] The menu on the first page of this website offers links to gossip about celebrity behavior in restaurants, gossip about chefs and restaurant owners, accounts from famous people who were once waitresses,[2] and customer-related horror stories. There is also a forum that includes a "hate mail" page that posts email criticisms of the website itself, as well as general criticisms of waitressing, but the criticisms are followed by rebuttals usually from past or present waitresses. Predictably, most of the criticisms either implicitly or explicitly portray waitresses as ignorant and stupid. One email respondent didn't like what he read on the customer horror story page and sent in this response:

> If you find your job [as a waitress] so despicable, then go get an education and get a REAL job. You are whining about something that you can fix. Stop being such a weakling, go out and learn something, anything, and go make a real contribution to society. . . . Wait, let me guess: you do not have any marketable skills or useful knowledge, so you do what any bumbling fool can do, wait on tables. This is your own fault.

This response inspired a number of rebuttals of which the following two best summarize the overall sentiment expressed in response to the rant above. The first is from the webmaster of bitterwaitress.com:

Is it possible that I have an education, maybe I went to, oh say, Duke, and I just waitressed for some free time? Or that there are very many people in the industry who do this so that they CAN get an education? Not all of us were born with a trust fund.—There is, I might add, considerably more or less to a job than a "clear cut" salary. If you . . . live in New York, . . . you'll know that empty stores and uncrowded subways are half the reason to work at night. By the way, what are the three Leovilles? What are the two kinds of tripe? Who was Cesar Ritz' partner? What is the JavaScript for a rollover? I guess I would have to ask a bumbling fool those questions. So, tell me then.

The second is from a mother of four: 3

I might not have a college education, but I would love to see those so called intelligent people get a big tip out of a bad meal, or from a person who is rude and cocky just because that's the way they are—that takes talent and its not a talent you can learn at any university. So, think about it before you say, "poor girl—to dumb to get a real job. . . ."

Assumptions that waitresses (and waiters) are ignorant and stupid and that waiting on tables contributes little to society are not new. The rebuttals to commonplace, pejorative understandings of the food service industry suggest, however, that there is complexity and skill that may go unrecognized by the general public or institutions such as universities. Indeed institutions, particularly government and corporate entities in the United States, like the Bureau of Labor Statistics or the National Skills Labor Board, define waiting on tables as a low skilled profession. By defining this kind of work as low skilled, there is a concomitant implication that the more than one-third of America's workforce who do it are low skilled.   4

> Assumptions that waitresses (and waiters) are ignorant and stupid and that waiting on tables contributes little to society are not new. The rebuttals to commonplace, pejorative understandings of the food service industry suggest, however, that there is complexity and skill that may go unrecognized by the general public or institutions such as universities.

Service occupations, otherwise known as "in-person" services (Reich, 1992)   5
or "interactive services" (Leidner, 1993; MacDonald and Sirianni, 1996), include any kind of work which fundamentally involves face-to-face or voice-to-voice interactions and conscious manipulation of self-presentation. As distinguished from white-collar service work, this category of "emotional proletariat" (MacDonald and Sirianni, 1996) is comprised primarily of retail sales workers, hotel workers, cashiers, house cleaners, flight attendants, taxi drivers, package delivery drivers, and waiters, among others. According to the U.S. Bureau of Labor Statistics (1996), one-fifth of the jobs in eating, drinking, and grocery store establishments are held by youth workers between the ages of 16 and 24.

While this kind of work is traditionally assumed to be primarily a stop-gap for young workers who will later move up and on to other careers, it also involves youths who will later end up in both middle- and working-class careers. It should not be forgotten that more than two thirds of the workers involved in food service are mature adults—many or most who began their careers in the same or similar industries. Interactive service work is a significant part of the economy in the U.S. today, and the Bureau of Labor Statistics predicts that jobs will be "abundant" in this category through 2006.

Economists such as Peter Drucker (1993) suggest that interactive service 6 workers lack the necessary education to be "knowledge" workers. These economists support general conceptions that service work is "mindless," involving routine and repetitive tasks that require little education. This orientation further suggests that these supposedly low skilled workers lack the problem identifying, problem solving, and other high level abilities needed to work in other occupations. However, relatively little specific attention and analysis have been given to the literacy skills and language abilities needed to do this work. My research investigates these issues with a focus on waiters and waitresses who work in diners. Diner restaurants are somewhat distinct from fast food or fine-dining restaurants, and they also epitomize many of the assumptions held about low skilled workplaces that require interactive services. The National Skills Standard Board, for instance, has determined that a ninth-grade level of spoken and written language use is needed to be a waiter or a waitress. Yet, how language is spoken, read, or written in a restaurant may be vastly different from how it is used in a classroom. A seemingly simple event such as taking a customer's food order can become significantly more complex, for example, when a customer has a special request. How the waitress or waiter understands and uses texts such as the menu and how she or he "reads" and verbally interacts with the customer reflect carefully constructed uses of language and literacy.

This chapter explores these constructed ways of "reading" texts (and cus- 7 tomers) along with the verbal, "performances" and other manipulations of self-presentation that characterize interactive service work. In line with MacDonald and Sirianni (1996), I hope this work will contribute to the development of understandings and policies that build more respect and recognition for service work to help ensure it does not become equated with servitude.

Literacy and Contemporary Theory

In contrast to institutional assessments such as the National Skills Standards 8 Board (1995), current thinking in key areas of education, sociology, anthropology and linguistics views language, literacy, and learning as embedded in social practice rather than entirely in the minds of individuals (Street, 1984; Gee, 1991; Lave and Wenger, 1991; Kress, 1993; Mahiri and Sablo, 1996; New London Group, 1996; Gee, Hull, and Lankshear, 1996). As earlier chapters in this book have noted, Gee (1991: 5)—a key proponent of this conception of literacy—explains that to be literate means to have control of "a socially accepted association among ways of using language, of thinking, and of acting that can be used to identify oneself as a member of a socially meaningful group or 'social network.'" In a similar fashion, research work located explicitly within workplace studies proposes that literacy is "a range of practices specific to groups and individuals of different cultures, races, classes and genders" (Hull et al., 1996: 5).

   In most societal institutions, however, literacy continues to be defined by con-   9
siderations of achievement and by abstract, standardized tests of individual students. Also, there is a decided focus on printed texts over other mediums of communication like visual and audio. Such a focus limits our understanding of literacy in terms of its use in specific situations in multiple modes of communication. The New Literacy Studies orientation that shapes the work reported in this book argues that literacy extends beyond individual experiences of reading and writing to include the various modes of communication and situations of any socially meaningful group or network where language is used in multiple ways. The New London Group (1996), for example, claims that due to changes in the social and economic environment, schools too must begin to consider language and literacy education in terms of "multiliteracies." The concept of multiliteracies supplements traditional literacy pedagogy by addressing the multiplicity of communications channels and the increasing saliency of cultural and linguistic diversity in the world today. Central to this study is the understanding that literate acts are embedded in specific situations and that they also extend beyond the printed text involving other modes of communication including both verbal and nonverbal. In this chapter, I illustrate something of the character of literacies specific to the "social network" of waiting on tables and show how they are distinct from the conceptions of literacy commonly associated with formal education. This is not simply to suggest that there is a jargon specific to the work, which of course there is, but that there is something unique and complex about the ways waiters and waitresses in diners use language and literacy in doing their work.

Methodology

Taken together, extant New Literacies Studies research makes a formidable argu-   10
ment for the need to re-evaluate how we understand literacy in the workplace—
particularly from the perspective of interactive service workers. The research reported here is modeled after Hull and her colleagues' groundbreaking ethnographic study of skill requirements in the factories of two different Silicon Valley computer manufacturing plants (1996). Instead of studying manufacturing plants, the larger research study I conducted and that underpins the study reported here involves two diner restaurants—one that is corporately owned and one that is privately owned. In this chapter, however, I focus only on the one that is privately owned to begin addressing the specific ways that language use and literacy practices function in this kind of workplace.

   To analyze the data, I relied on some of the methodological tools from   11
the work of Hull and her colleagues (1996). In short, I looked at patterns of thought and behavior in the setting; I identified key events taking place; I did

conversational analysis of verbal interactions; and I conducted sociocultural analyses of key work events.

The data used in this chapter came from direct participation, observa- 12 tion, field notes, documents, interviews, tape recordings, and transcriptions, as well as from historical and bibliographic literature. I myself have been a waiter (both part-time and full-time over a ten-year period), and I was actually employed at the privately owned restaurant during my data collection period. In addition to providing important insights into worker skills, attitudes, and behaviors, my experience and positioning in this setting also enabled access to unique aspects of the work that might have otherwise gone unnoticed. The primary data considered in this chapter were collected during eight-hour periods of participant observation on Friday and/or Saturday nights in the restaurant. I chose weekend nights because they were usually the busiest times in the diner and were therefore the most challenging for the workers. Weekend shifts are also the most lucrative for the restaurant and the workers.

Lou's Restaurant

Lou's Restaurant[3] is a modest, privately owned diner restaurant patterned in 13 a style that is popular in the local region. It has an open kitchen layout with a counter where individual customers can come and sit directly in front of the cooks' line and watch the "drama" of food service unfold while enjoying their meals. The food served at Lou's is Italian-American and it includes pastas, seafood, and a variety of sautéed or broiled poultry, beef, and veal. As is often the case with diner restaurants, Lou's has over ninety main course items, including several kinds of appetizers and salads, as well as a number of side dishes. The primary participants focused on in this chapter are three waiters at Lou's: John, Harvey, and myself.

After finishing my master's degree in English literature and deciding to move 14 out of the state where I taught English as a Second Language at a community college, I ended up working as a waiter for two years at Lou's. This work allowed me to survive financially while further advancing my academic career. At the time I began my study at this site, the only waiter to have worked longer than two years at Lou's was John. Like myself, John began working in the restaurant business to earn extra money while in school after he had been discharged from the Marines, where he had been trained as a radio operator, telephone wireman, and Arabic translator. Two days after his honorable discharge, he started working in the restaurant that four years later would become Lou's. He subsequently has worked there for ten years. John also is the most experienced waiter at Lou's, and although the restaurant does not have an official "head" waiter, John is considered by his peers to be the expert. In an interview, he noted that it took almost ten years before he felt that he had really begun to master his craft.

Harvey might also be considered a master waiter, having been in the profes- 15 sion for over thirty years. However, at the beginning of the study he had been with Lou's for only two weeks. He was initially reticent to participate in the study because he said he lacked experience at this restaurant, and "didn't know the menu." Having left home when he was 14 years old to come "out West," over the years he had done a stint in the Air Force, held a position as a postal clerk, worked as a bellhop and bartender, and even had the opportunity to manage a local cafe. He decided that he did not like managerial work because he missed the freedom, autonomy, and customer interaction he had as a waiter and took a position at Lou's.

The Menu

Harvey's concern over not knowing the menu was not surprising. The menu is 16
the most important printed text used by waiters and waitresses, and not knowing it can dramatically affect how they are able to do their work. The menu is
the key text used for most interactions with the customer, and, of course, the
contents of menus vary greatly from restaurant to restaurant. But, what is a
menu and what does it mean to have a literate understanding of one?

The restaurant menu is a genre unto itself. There is regularity and predictability 17
in the conventions used such as the listing, categorizing, and pricing of individual,
ready-made food items. The menu at Lou's contains ninety main course items, as
well as a variety of soups, salads, appetizers, and side dishes. In addition, there are
numerous selections where, for example, many main course items offer customers
a choice of their own starch item from a selection of four: spaghetti, ravioli, french
fries, or a baked potato. Some of the main course items, such as sandwiches,
however, only come with french fries—but if the customer prefers something such
as spaghetti, or vegetables instead of fries, they can substitute another item for
a small charge, although this service is not listed in the menu. In addition to the
food menu, there is also a wine menu and a full service bar meaning that hard
liquor is sold in this restaurant. There are twenty different kinds of wine sold by
the glass and a selection of thirty-eight different kinds of wine sold by the bottle,
and customers can order most other kinds of alcoholic beverages.

In one context, waitresses and waiters' knowing the meaning of the words in 18
the menus means knowing the process of food production in the restaurant. But
this meaning is generally only used when a customer has a question or special
request. In such situations the meaning of the words on the page are defined more
by the questions and the waiters or waitresses' understanding of specific food
preparation than by any standard cookbook or dictionary. For example, the *Better Homes and Gardens New Cook Book* (1996) presents a recipe for marinara
sauce calling for a thick sauce all sautéed and simmered for over thirty minutes.
At Lou's, a marinara sauce is cooked in less than ten minutes and is a light tomato
sauce consisting of fresh tomatoes, garlic, and parsley sautéed in olive oil. At a
similar restaurant nearby—Joe's Italian Diner—marinara sauce is a seafood sauce,
albeit tomato based. Someone who is familiar with Italian cooking will know that
marinara sauce will have ingredients like tomatoes, olive oil, and garlic, but, in
a restaurant, to have a more complete understanding of a word like *marinara*
requires knowing how the kitchen prepares the dish. Clearly, the meanings of the
language used in menus are socially and culturally embedded in the context of the
specific situation or restaurant. To be literate here requires something other than

a ninth-grade level of literacy. More than just a factual, or literal interpretation of the words on the page, it requires knowledge of specific practices—such as methods of food preparation—that take place in a particular restaurant.

On one occasion Harvey, the new but experienced waiter, asked me what 19
"pesto" sauce was. He said that he had never come across the term before, and explained that he had never worked in an Italian restaurant and rarely eaten in one. Pesto is one of the standard sauces on the menu, and like marinara, is commonly found on the menus of many Italian-American restaurants. I explained that it comprised primarily olive oil and basil, as well as garlic, pine nuts, Parmesan cheese, and a little cream. Harvey then told me that a customer had asked him about the sauce, and since he could not explain what it was, the customer did not order it.

On another occasion a mother asked Harvey if her child could have only car- 20
rots instead of the mixed vegetables as it said in the menu. Although he initially told her this was not possible, explaining that the vegetables were premixed and that the cooks would have to pick the carrots out one by one, the mother persisted. After a few trips from the table to the cooks' line, Harvey managed to get the carrots, but the customer then declined them because everyone had finished eating. Later, I explained to Harvey that it would have been possible to go to the back of the restaurant where he could find the vegetables in various stages of preparation. While the cooks only have supplies of pre-mixed vegetables on the line, Harvey could have gone to the walk-in refrigerator and picked up an order of carrots himself to give to the cooks.

Harvey's interactions with his customers highlight how much of what he 21
needs to know to be a good waiter is learned within the specific situations and social networks in which that knowledge is used. The instantiation of the meaning of words like *pesto* and *marinara* often occurs in the interaction between co-workers as well as with customers. Conversation becomes a necessary element in achieving an appropriately literate understanding of the menu.

Harvey's understanding and use of the menu and special requests also 22
involves more than his knowledge of food preparation. It involves the manipulation of power and control. Sociocultural theories of literacy consider the role of power and authority in the construction of meaning (Kress, 1993). From his perspective, the order of carrots was not simply an order of carrots, but a way of positioning one's self in the interaction. The customer saw her desire for the carrots as greater than what was advertised in the menu and thus exercised authority as a customer by requesting them despite Harvey's attempt to not make the carrots an option. While such a request might seem fairly innocuous in isolation, when considered in the specific situation of Lou's at that time— that is, peak dinner hour—it becomes more complex.

Special requests and questions can extend the meaning of the menu beyond 23
the printed page and into the conversation and interaction between the waiter or waitress and the customer. Furthermore, special requests and questions can be as varied as the individual customers themselves. The general public shares a diner restaurant menu, but it is used by each individual patron to satisfy a private appetite. How to describe something to an individual customer and satisfy

their private appetite requires not only the ability to *read* the menu, but also the ability to *read* the customer. This is achieved during the process of the dinner interaction, and it includes linguistic events such as greeting the customer or taking food orders and involves both verbal and non-verbal communication. In such events the meaning of the menu is continually reconstructed in the interaction between the waitress or waiter and the individual customer, and as a text functions as a "boundary object" that coordinates the perspectives of various constituencies for a similar purpose (Star and Griesmer, 1989); in this case the satisfaction of the individual patron's appetite. The degree to which private appetite is truly satisfied is open to debate, however. Virtually everyone who has eaten at a restaurant has his or her favorite horror story about the food and/or the service, and more often than not these stories in some way involve the menu and an unfulfilled private appetite.

In addition to being a text that is shared by the general public and used 24 by the individual patron to satisfy a private appetite, the menu is also a text whose production of meaning results in ready-made consumable goods sold for profit. The authors of a printed menu, usually the chefs and owners of the restaurant, have their own intentions when producing the hard copy. For example, it is common practice to write long extensively itemized menus in diner restaurants like Lou's. As was pointed out earlier, Lou's menu has over ninety selections from which to choose, and many of these can be combined with a range of additional possible choices. Printing a large selection of food items gives the appearance that the customer will be able to make a personal— and *personalized*—selection from the extensive menu. In fact, it is not uncommon for patrons at Lou's to request extra time to read the menu, or ask for recommendations before making a choice. The authors of the printed menu at Lou's constructed a text that appears to be able to satisfy private appetites, but they ultimately have little control over how the patron will interpret and use the menu.

The waiters and waitresses, however, do have some control. While customers 25 certainly have their own intentions when asking questions, waitresses and waiters have their own intentions when responding. When customers ask questions about the menu, in addition to exercising their own authority, they also introduce the opportunity for waiters and waitresses to gain control of the interaction. A good example of how this control could be manipulated by a waiter or waitress comes from Chris Fehlinger, the web-master of bitterwaitress.com, in an interview with *New Yorker* magazine:

"A lot of times when people asked about the menu, I would make it sound so elaborate that they would just leave it up to me," he said, "I'd describe, like, three dishes in excruciating detail, and they would just stutter, 'I, I, I can't decide, you decide for me.' So in that case, if the kitchen wants to sell fish, you're gonna have fish." He also employed what might be called a "magic words" strategy: "All you have to do is throw out certain terms, like guanciale, and then you throw in something like saba, a reduction of the unfermented must of the Trebbiano grape. If you mention things like that, people are just, like, 'O.K.!'" (Teicholz, 1999)

The use of linguistic devices like obfuscating descriptions and "magic 26 words" is not unusual—particularly for waiters in fine dining restaurants. In *The World of the Waiters* (1983), Mars and Nicod examined how English waiters use devices to "get the jump" and gain control of selecting items from the menu. Their position of authority is further substantiated in fine dining restaurants by the common practice of printing menus in foreign languages, such as French, because it shifts the responsibility of food ordering from the customer, who often will not understand the language, to the waiter.

While diner restaurants generally do not print their menus in incomprehen- 27 sible terms, they do, as at Lou's, tend to produce unusually long ones that can have a similar effect. But, diner menus like Lou's which offer Italian-American cuisine do use some language that is potentially unfamiliar to the clientele (e.g., *pesto*). The combination of menu length and potentially confusing language creates frequent opportunities for waiters and waitresses to get a jump on the customer. Customers at Lou's tend to ask questions about the meaning of almost every word and phrase in the menu. Not being able to provide at least a basic description of a menu item, as shown by Harvey's unfamiliarity with pesto, usually results in that item not being ordered.

Knowing what a customer wants often goes beyond simply being able to 28 describe the food. It also involves knowing which descriptions will more likely sell and requires being able to apply the menu to the specific situation. For instance, in the following transcription I approach a table to take a food order while one customer is still reading the menu (Customer 3b). She asks me to explain the difference between veal scaloppini and veal scaloppini sec.

Tony:	(to Customer 3a and Customer 3b) hi
Customer 3b:	what's the difference between scaloppini and scaloppini sec?
Tony:	veal scaloppini is a tomato based sauce with green onions and mushrooms / veal scaloppini sec is with marsala wine green onions and mushrooms
Customer 3b:	I'll have the veal scaloppini sec.
Tony	ok / would you like it with spaghetti / ravioli / french fries
Customer 3b:	ravioli
Customer 3a:	and / I'll get the tomato one / the veal scaloppini with mushrooms
Tony:	with spaghetti / ravioli / french fries
Customer 3a:	can I get steamed vegetables
Tony	you want vegetables and no starch? / it already comes with vegetables / (.) (Customer 3a nods yes) ok / great / thank you
Customer 3a:	thanks

The word *sec* functions not unlike one of Fehlinger's "magic' words. Cus- 29 tomers who are interested in ordering veal frequently ask questions about the distinctions between the two kinds of scaloppini. I discovered over time that my description of the veal scaloppini sec almost always resulted in the customer ordering the dish. It seemed that mentioning marsala wine piqued customer interest more than tomato sauce did. One customer once quipped that marsala is a sweet wine and wanted to know why the word *sec*—meaning *dry*—was used. I replied that since no fat was used in the cooking process, it was considered "dry" cooking. In situations like this the menu is situated more in a conversational mode than a printed one. The transition from print to spoken word occurs due to the customer's inability to understand the menu, and/or satisfy his or her private appetite which results in a request for assistance. As a result the waiter or waitress can become the authority in relation to not only the printed text, but within the interaction as well. Eventually, I began to recommend this dish when customers asked for one, and the customers more often than not purchased it.

This particular food-ordering event also is interesting with regard to the cus- 30 tomer's request for steamed vegetables. When I asked what kind of pasta she would like with her meal, she asked for steamed vegetables. The menu clearly states that vegetables are included with the meal along with the customer's choice of spaghetti, ravioli, or french fries. When she requested steamed vegetables, I simply could have arranged for her to have them and persisted in asking her which pasta she would like, but instead I anticipated that she might not want any pasta at all. I knew that, while it was not printed on the menu, the kitchen could serve her a double portion of steamed vegetables with no pasta. Most importantly, this customer's ability to order food that would satisfy her private appetite depended almost entirely upon my suggestions and understanding of the menu. Mars and Nicod (1984: 82), discussing a situation in a similar restaurant, noted a waiter who would say, "You don't really need a menu . . . I'm a 'walking menu' and I'm much better than the ordinary kind . . . I can tell you things you won't find on the menu." Examples like this illustrate not only how waitresses and waiters gain control of their interactions with customers, but also how other modes of communication—such as conversations—are used to construct complex forms of meaning around printed texts like menus. Thus, the meaning of words in a menu are embedded in the situation, its participants, and the balance of power and authority, and this meaning manifests itself in more than one mode of communication.

Reading menus and reading customers also involves a myriad of cultural 31 distinctions. Although there is not the space to discuss them here, age, gender, race, and class are all relevant to interactions between customers and waiter or waitress. The argument can be made that diner restaurants like Lou's promote a friendly, family-like atmosphere. Historically diners in the U.S. have been recognized as being places where customers can find a familial environment. Popular media today support this characteristic—particularly via television—where restaurant chains explicitly advertise that their customers are treated like family, and a number of television situation comedies have long used restaurants, diners, bars, and cafés as settings where customers and employees interact in very personal and intimate ways. This cultural atmosphere can have a tremendous impact on interactions with the customers. There is sometimes miscommunication or resistance where a customer may or may not want to be treated like family, or the waitress or waiter may or may not want to treat a customer like family. At Lou's, in addition to having an intimate understanding of food production and being able to describe it to a customer in an appealing fashion, reading a menu and taking a customer's food order also requires the ability to perform these tasks in a friendly, familial manner.

The following example reveals the complexity of meanings involved in tak-   32
ing a customer's food order and the expression of "family." Al is a regular customer who almost always comes in by himself and sits at the counter in front of the cooks' line. He also always has the same thing to eat, a side order of spaghetti marinara, and never looks at the menu. Perhaps more important to Al than the food he eats are the people he interacts with at Lou's. He will sit at the counter and enjoy the badinage he shares with the other customers who sit down next to him at the counter, the waitresses and waiters as they pass by his seat, and the cooks working just across the counter. On this particular evening, however, he was joined by his son, daughter-in-law, and young adult granddaughter, and rather than sitting at the counter, he sat in a large booth. Although I immediately recognized Al, I had never waited on him and his family before, and I was not sure how informal he would like the interaction to be. So I began with a fairly formal greeting saying "hello" instead of "hi" and avoided opportunities to make small talk with Al and his family:

Tony:	hello::=
Customer 2d:	=hello
Al:	hey(.) what they put in the water? / I don't know / is it the ice or what is it?
Customer 2s:	(chuckles from Customer 2d, Customer 2s, and Customer 2c)
Tony:	does the water taste strange?
Customer 2s:	no
Tony:	do you want me to get you another water?
Al:	no / I don't want any water
Tony:	ok
Al:	I had a couple of drinks before I came
Customer 2s:	(chuckles)=
Tony:	(in reference to the water tasting strange) =it could be / it could be / I don't know
Customer 2d:	(to Customer 2s) are you having anything to drink?
Customer 2s:	I'll have a beer / American beer / you have miller draft?
Tony:	(while writing down the order) miller genuine
Customer 2d:	and I'll have a tequila sunrise
Al:	(to Customer 2d) what are you having?
Customer 2d:	tequila sunrise
Al:	oh / you should fly / you should fly

Tony:	(to Customer 2a) al / you want anything?
Customer 2s:	(to Customer 2a) a beer? / or anything?
Al:	no / I've had too much already
Customer 2s:	are you sure
Customer 2d:	we'll get you a coffee later
Tony:	(nod of affirmation to daughter-in-law)
Al:	I've been home alone drinking
Tony:	ugh ogh:: / (chuckles along with Customer 2s)

Al's comment about the water tasting funny and his drinking at home alone 33 both provided opportunities for me to interact more intimately with Al and his family, but instead I concerned myself solely with taking their drink orders. Al's desire for me to interact in a more familial manner became more apparent when I returned to take their food order.

Customer 2d:	(as the drinks are delivered) ah / great / thank you
Tony:	(placing drinks in front of customers) there you go / you're welcome
Al:	(to Customer 2s) so we're flying to vegas (mumbles)
Tony:	all right / you need a few minutes here?
Customer 2s:	no / (to Customer 2a) are you ready or do you want to wait?
Customer 2d:	you made up your mind yet?
Al:	(mumble) made up my mind yet
Customer 2d:	oh / ok
Tony:	al / what can I get for you?
Al:	I said I haven't made up my mind yet
Tony:	oh / ok (everyone at the table chuckles except Al)
Al:	I always have pasta you know / I would walk out there (points to the counter) the guy says / I know what you want
Tony:	ok / I'll be back in a few minutes
Customer 2d:	come back in a few minutes / thanks

While I misunderstood Al when I asked if he was ready to order, for him the 34 greater transgression was simply asking if he was ready to order. Al expected me to know what he was going to eat because he's a regular; he's like family. He wanted a side order of spaghetti marinara and didn't want to have to speak regarding his food order. To be successful in fulfilling Al's private appetite required more than the ability to describe food according to individual customer preferences. A side order of spaghetti marinara represents not merely a food item on a menu, nor a satisfying mix of pasta and tomatoes, but also, depending on the way it is ordered and served, a gesture of friendliness: "I always have pasta you know / I would walk out there (points to the counter) the guy says / I know what you want." To be literate with a menu also means knowing when and how to express emotion (or not express emotion) to a customer through its use.

Being able to take a customer's order without him or her reading the menu 35 are important ways of expressing friendliness and family at Lou's. John, the most experienced waiter on staff, often can be found running to get an order of homemade gnocchi from the back freezer and delivering them to the cooks when they are too busy to get back there themselves. Or, he might step in behind the bar to make his own cappuccino when the bartender is busy serving other customers. On one occasion. like many others, John had a customer request a special order called *prawns romano*, a pasta dish consisting of fettuccine with prawns in a white sauce with green onions, tomatoes, and garlic. This is not listed on any menu in the restaurant. but it is something that the cooks occasionally offer as an evening special. John politely asked whether or not the cooks could accommodate his customer's request, and they complied. One can frequently hear John greeting many of his customers with some variation of, "Can I get you the usual?" Alternatively, in the case of special requests, some variant of, "That's no problem" is an often used phrase. Just like a friend for whom it would be no problem, John attempts to satisfy his customer's special requests in a similar fashion.

Yet, friendliness is often a feigned performance. Being friendly is an experi- 36 ential phenomenon that is learned through participation. To be a good waitress or waiter generally requires being able to perform friendliness under any number of circumstances. To be successful at the practice of being friendly requires performing certain techniques over and over until they can be performed on an unconscious level. Referred to as *emotional labor* (Hochschild, 1983: 6–7), this kind of work "requires one to induce or suppress feeling in order to sustain the outward countenance that produces the proper state of mind in others." Emotional labor also is an integral part to how a waitress constructs meaning in a menu. While emotional labor may not yield the same monetary results in restaurants like Lou's, it is still essential to the work. For example, John is masterful in the way he utilizes emotional labor. On one particularly busy evening John was trapped in a line at the bar waiting to place his drink order. He was clearly anxious, and was looking at his food order tickets to see what he needed to do next. The crowd of customers waiting to be seated spilled out of the foyer and into the aisle near where the waitresses and waiters were waiting to place their drink orders. One customer, who recognized John, caught his attention:

John:	hi=
Customer:	=hi can I get a glass of wine
John:	sure (.) what do you want
Customer:	are you busy
John:	NO (.) I got it (.) what do you want

John's friendly "hi" and overemphatic "no" were intended to suggest to the 37 customer that he was not busy, when he clearly was. As he later explained, he knew that the customer knew he was really busy, but he also knew that if he was friendly and accommodating, the customer probably would give him a nice tip for his trouble, which the customer did. His feigned amiability in agreeing to get the customer a drink was more or less a monetary performance. John had learned to use language for financial gain. One should not be fooled by the apparent simplicity in the preceding interaction. While it may be brief, being able to be friendly and accommodating under extreme circumstances like the "dinner rush" requires years of practice in a real work setting learning to be able to say, "hi—sure—NO, I got it."

Although interactions with customers have been presented individually, the reality of how these events occur is quite different. Unlike fine-dining restaurants where the dinner experience can extend over a few hours, diners operate on high volume, serving to a great number of patrons in a short amount of time. George Orwell, reflecting on the difficulty involved in this work, wrote, "I calculated that [a waiter] had to walk and run about 15 miles during the day and yet the strain of the work was more mental than physical. . . . One has to leap to and fro between a multitude of jobs—it is like sorting a pack of cards against the clock" (Orwell, 1933). Because one person may be serving as many as ten tables or more at one time, the process of serving each individual table will overlap with the others. Food orders are taken numerous times in a half-hour period during busy dinner hours at Lou's. The preceding transcriptions were taken from tape-recorded data collected on Friday evenings around 7 o'clock. My own interactions were recorded during a period when I had what is referred to as a *full station,* meaning that all of the tables under my supervision were filled with customers. By this point in the evening I had two customers at the counter, a party of four and six parties of two, for a total of eighteen customers—all of whom were in the process of ordering their meals within the same half-hour to forty-five minute period.

Literacy practices in this environment are nothing like those found in traditional classrooms, but they might be more comparable to those found in the emergency ward of a hospital or an air-traffic controller's tower. Interaction with texts and participants takes place in a rapid succession of small chunks. During the dinner hours, there are no long drawn out monologues. Time is of the essence during the busiest dinner hours for all participants involved: from the waiters and waitresses to the cooks, bartenders, and busboys. In two hundred lines of transcribed dialogue during a busy dinner period, for example, I never paused longer than thirty-nine seconds, and no participant spoke more than forty-one words in one turn. Even these pauses were usually the result of other work being completed, such as preparing a salad or waiting to order a drink. During this period, virtually all the conversation, reading, and writing were related to the immediate situational context. As this research has shown, language use was far more complex than one might assume in situations and events that involve taking a customer's food order. In addition to knowing how food is prepared, what will appeal to specific customers, and how to present this information in a friendly manner, the waiter or waitress must also remain conscious of the number of other tables waiting to have their orders taken and the amount of time that will take. Reading menus and reading customers requires the ability to think and react quickly to a multitude of almost simultaneously occurring literate events.

Conclusion

Menus at Lou's are texts that are catalysts for interaction between staff and 40 customers, and their meaning is firmly embedded in this interaction. Meaning is constructed from the menu through more than one mode of communication and between a variety of participants. This process involves knowledge of food preparation, use of specific linguistic devices like magic words and other ways of describing food, the ability to read individual customers' tastes and preferences, the general expectation to perform in a friendly manner, and all during numerous virtually simultaneous and similar events. Yet, there is much left unconsidered in this chapter, particularly regarding the nature of power and control. While waitresses and waiters are frequently able to manipulate control over customer decisions while taking a food order, this control is often tenuous and insignificant beyond the immediate interaction.

Little also has been said in this chapter about the role of management. Exten- 41 sive research has already been done in the area of management control, literacy, and worker skills (Braverman, 1974; Hochschild, 1983; Kress, 1993; Leidner, 1993; Hall, 1993; Hull et al., 1996; MacDonald and Sirianni, 1996; Gee, Hull, and Lankshear, 1996). These researchers consider how literacy practices are manipulated by management to maintain control over the worker. Whether it be scientific management where workers are deskilled and routinized, or Fast Capitalism where forms of control are more insidious and shrouded in the guise of "empowering" the worker, there is little research on interactive service work beyond the fast food industry that explores how this rhetoric plays itself out in a real world situation. This leaves open to debate questions regarding the effectiveness of Fast Capitalism as a form of control over the worker. While my research has shown that waiters and waitresses can exercise some level of authority, skill, and wit through their use of language with customers, they must also interact with management and other staff where authority and control play out in different ways.

In the end, however, the customer has ultimate authority over the waiter or 42 waitress. Diner waitressing has a long history of prejudice dating back to the beginning of the industrial revolution and involves issues of gender regarding our general perceptions and ways of interacting (Cobble, 1991; Hall, 1993). Waitressing is integrally tied to domesticated housework and likewise has historically been treated as requiring little skill or ability. In fact, the stigma of servitude that plagues waitressing and other similar kinds of work are not only the result of less than respectable treatment from management, but from customers as well. In her sociological study of diner waitresses in New Jersey, Greta Paules sums it up best:

> That customers embrace the service-as-servitude metaphor is evidenced by the way they speak to and about service workers. Virtually every rule of etiquette is violated by customers in their interactions with the waitress: the waitress can

be interrupted; she can be addressed with the mouth full; she can be ignored and stared at; and she can be subjected to unrestrained anger. Lacking status as a person, she, like the servant, is refused the most basic considerations of polite interaction. She is, in addition, the subject of chronic criticism. Just as in the nineteenth century servants were perceived as ignorant, slow, lazy, indifferent, and immoral (Sutherland 1981), so in the twentieth century service workers are condemned for their stupidity, apathy, slowness, incompetence, and questionable moral character. (1991:138–39)

The low status of waitressing and waitering belies the complex nature of 43 this kind of work and the innovative and creative ways in which such workers use language.

Endnotes

1. Some of the more than 20 websites I have found so far like waitersrevenge.com are award winning. They include sites for taxi drivers, hotel workers, and the like.
2. How to appropriately refer to waitresses and waiters is not a simple decision. Terms like *server* and *food server* are alternatives, but all are problematic. I personally do not like *server or food server* because they are too closely related to the word servitude. The waiter/waitress distinction is problematic not simply because it differentiates genders, but also because it is associated with a kind/class of service. Often in fine-dining restaurants today both men and women are referred to as waiters, but it is more commonly the practice in the "diner" style restaurant to maintain the distinctive terms. This is historically connected to the diner waitressing being regarded as inferior to fine-dining waitering because it was merely an extension of the domesticated duties of the household.
3. Pseudonyms have been used throughout this chapter.

Works Cited

Better homes and gardens new cook book. (1996). New York: Better Homes and Gardens.

Braverman, H. (1974). *Labor and monopoly capital: The degradation of work in the twentieth century.* New York: Monthly Review Press.

Bureau of Labor Statistics. (1996).Washington, D.C.: U.S. Department of Labor.

Cobble, S. (1991). *Dishing it out: Waitresses and their unions in the 20ᵗʰ century.* Urbana: University of Illinois Press.

Drucker, P. (1993). *Innovation and entrepreneurship: Practice and principles.* New York: Harperbusiness.

Gee, J. (1991). *Sociolinguistics and literacies: Ideology in discourses.* New York: Falmer.

Gee, J., Hull, G., and Lankshear, C. (1996). *The new work order: Behind the language of the new capitalism.* Sydney: Allen & Unwin.

Gowen, S. (1992). *The politics of workplace literacy.* New York: Teachers College Press.

Hall, E. (1993). Smiling, deferring, and good service. *Work and occupations,* 20 (4), 452–471.

Hochschild, A. (1983). *The managed heart.* Berkeley: University of California Press.

Hull, G. (Ed.). (1997). *Changing work, changing workers: Critical perspectives on language, literacy, and skills.* New York: State University of New York Press.

Hull, G. et al. (1996). *Changing work, changing literacy? A study of skills requirements and development in a traditional and restructured workplace. Final Report.* Unpublished manuscript. University of California at Berkeley.

Kress, G. (1993). Genre as social process. In B. Cope and M. Kalantzis (Eds.), *The powers of literacy: A genre approach to teaching writing* (pp. 22–37). London: Falmer.

Kress, G. (1995). *Writing the future: English and the making of a cultural innovation*. London: NATE.

Lave, J. and Wenger, E. (1991). *Situated learning: Legitimate peripheral participation*. New York: Cambridge University Press.

Leidner, R. (1993). *Fast food, fast talk: Service work and the routinization of everyday life*. Berkeley: University of California Press.

MacDonald, C. and, Sirianni, C. (Eds.). (1996). *Working in the service society*. Philadelphia: Temple University.

Mahiri, J. and Sablo, S. (1996). Writing for their lives: The non-school literacy of California's urban African American youth. *Journal of Negro Education*, 65 (2), 164–180.

Mars, G. and Nicod, M. (1984). *The world of waiters*. London: Unwin Hyman.

New London Group. (1996). A pedagogy of multiliteracies: Designing social futures. *Harvard Educational Review*, 66 (1), 60–92.

NSSB (National Skills Standards Board). (1995). *Server skill standards: National performance criteria in the foodservice industry*. Washington, DC: U.S. Council on Hotel, Restaurant and Institutional Education.

Orwell, G.(1933). *Down and out in Paris and London*. New York: Harcourt Brace.

Paules, G. (1991). *Dishing it out: Power and resistance among waitresses in a New Jersey restaurant*. Philadelphia: Temple University Press.

Reich, R. (1992). *The work of nations*. New York: Vintage.

Star, L. and Griesmer, J. (1989). Institutional ecology, translations and boundary objects: Amateurs and professionals in Berkeley's Museum of Vertebrate Zoology, 1907–1939. *Social Studies of Science*, 19.

Street, B. (1984 April 5). *Literacy in theory and practice*. London: Cambridge University Press.

Questions for Discussion and Journaling

1. Mirabelli begins his article quite differently from the ways in which the other authors in this chapter begin. What is different about it? What are the rhetorical effects of the way he begins? What can you infer from it about his intended audience(s) and purpose(s)?

2. While Johns focused on participation in academic Discourses and Wardle focused on participation in a white-collar, professional Discourse, Mirabelli chooses to focus on participation in a restaurant Discourse. Why? What is he contributing to the conversation on Discourses by doing so?

3. What is the "traditional" view of literacy, according to Mirabelli, and what is the view of literacy that New Literacy Studies takes? What are *multiliteracies*?

4. What seems to be Mirabelli's research question and where does he state it? What kind of data did Mirabelli collect to analyze the diner discourse community? What seem to be his primary findings in answer to his research question?

5. Mirabelli spends a good deal of his analysis focusing on the **genre** of the menu, and in doing so, he also discusses the diner's **lexis** and methods of **intercommunication**. All of these, as you should remember, are aspects of a

discourse community as defined by Swales. Why does Mirabelli focus on the genre of the menu? Is this an effective focus for him as he attempts to answer the research question you identified above? Why or why not?

6. Mirabelli argues that literacy in the diner includes not only reading the menu but also reading the customers. Do you agree that reading customers is a form of literacy? Why or why not?

7. Do you now or have you ever participated in a discourse community that is strongly stereotyped in the ways that restaurant work is stereotyped (for example, a football team or a sorority)? What are the stereotypes? Using Mirabelli, consider the various "multiliteracies" of this discourse community.

Applying and Exploring Ideas

1. Consider a nonschool discourse community that you are a member of, and answer the following questions about it:

   a. What are the shared goals of the community; why does this group exist and what does it do?

   b. What mechanisms do members use to communicate with each other (for example, meetings, phone calls, e-mail, text messages, newsletters, reports, evaluation forms)?

   c. What are the purposes of each of these mechanisms of communication (for example, to improve performance, make money, grow better roses, share research)?

   d. Which of the above mechanisms of communication can be considered genres (textual responses to recurring situations that all group members recognize and understand)?

   e. What kinds of lexis (specialized language) do group members use? Provide some examples.

   f. Who are the "old-timers" with expertise? Who are the newcomers with less expertise? How do newcomers learn the appropriate language, genres, and knowledge of the group?

2. Select a Discourse or community of practice you're interested in and develop a research question on it. What would you want to know, for example, about how the Discourse works, what it takes to enculturate or gain membership in it, and how it differs from other Discourses?

Meta Moment

Have any of the readings in this chapter changed any of your views on writing? Have any made you feel more powerful as a writer, or less? Have any helped you find ways of dealing with the double-edged sword of discourse communities—the fact that they simultaneously empower and disempower their members?

Coaches Can Read, Too:
An Ethnographic Study of a Football Coaching Discourse Community

SEAN BRANICK

Framing the Paper

Sean was a first-year student at the University of Dayton when he wrote this paper. He was enrolled in a two-semester composition sequence that allowed him to work on this ethnography for a year. His paper was chosen as one of the best from two such courses and was published in a one-time-only university publication called *Looking for Literacy: Reporting the Research*. Sean's interest in the discourse community of football coaches arose from his own experience as a high school football player and as a student in college. At the time of the publication of *Writing about Writing*, Sean was a student football coach at the University of Hawai'i at Manoa.

Branick 1

Sean Branick
Dr. Wardle
English 102
April 19, 2007

Coaches Can Read, Too:

An Ethnographic Study of a Football Coaching Discourse Community

The profession of coaching football is one of the most influential professions that exists in today's world. It is a profession essential to the game whether it is a third-grade team or a pro team. Coaches may range from parents volunteering with a child's youth program to people who dedicate every waking hour to the game. Coaches are made up of both everyday Joes and legends that will live in memory as long as the game is played. It is a profession that requires putting the athletes first:

> *In his introduction Sean includes the three "moves" that John Swales identified in his CARS model (see pp. 6–8)— establishing the territory, establishing a niche, and explaining how he will fill the niche. Find and mark these moves.*

"The main responsibility of the coach is to enable their athletes to attain levels of performance not otherwise achievable" (Short "Role," S29). It is a profession very visible to the public yet it has many behind-the-scenes factors that may be often overlooked that directly relate to success. Among these are the idea of goal-focused coaching, coaching with confidence, and the characteristics of effective coaches.

Goal-Focused Coaching

Whether on the football field or off the football field, people have always used the process of setting and chasing goals to achieve a desired outcome. A goal is often the universal starting point in many things, including football. Anthony Grant, a sport psychologist, takes an in-depth look at the process of effectively setting a goal in order to achieve a desired result. He talks about how the coach should help facilitate the entire process of using goals, which consists of the following: "an individual sets a goal, develops a plan of action, begins action, monitors his or her performance (through observation and self-reflection), evaluates his or her performance (thus gaining insight) and, based on this evaluation, changes his or her actions to further enhance performance, and thus reach his or her goal" (751).

Grant explains that there are five important parts to this goal-focused coaching concept. The first part is setting good goals. The coach must help the player set goals that coincide with his values, are well defined, and are realistically achievable. The second part is developing a strong working relationship between the coach and player. This means that a coach must work to develop an honest relationship to help create an environment conducive to growth where the player will feel comfortable being open and honest with the coach. The third aspect is developing a solution focus,

Branick 3

which means helping the athlete develop solutions to help him achieve his goals. The fourth part is managing process. This includes developing actions steps and holding the athlete accountable for completing the agreed steps. The fifth and final aspect is achieving the desired outcome.

Characteristics of an Effective Coach

While successful coaches have been exposed to the spotlight throughout history, certain personal qualities of these coaches have emerged as essential to success in the coaching business. Sports psychologist Sandra Short explores five specific qualities of effective coaches. The first of these qualities is being a teacher. This is important because coaches must be able to teach their players about the game and what to do during competition.

The second quality is being organized. Being organized is typically a behind-the-scenes job but it is important because a coach must be organized to keep track of players, competitions, and practice schedules. It is important to organize a plan for success and be able to stick to it. Coaches in team sports must be organized before stepping onto the playing field so that they will know how to handle specific situations such as substitutions and timeout management.

The third quality is being competitive. Coaches must have an inner desire to compete and work to instill that desire to compete in their athletes. Being competitive must be a foundational quality in athletes. It doesn't matter how gifted an athlete is or how much he knows, if he does not have the desire to compete then he will not be successful.

The fourth quality is being a learner. Coaches must continue to learn every day they are on the job. They must learn about their players' personality and they must learn about the newest trends, philosophies, and strategies in the sport that they coach.

The fifth and final quality mentioned is being a friend and mentor. It is important to be a positive role model for their players to look up to. A coach should also offer support and counseling when a player may need it. Fulfilling this role can bring about a deeper level of satisfaction for both the coach and the athlete.

Confidence in Coaching

Another aspect of coaching that has been studied is coaching confidence and its relationship with imagery. Sports psychologist Sandra Short argues that imagining being confident helps increase real confidence and the feeling of effectiveness. During pregame preparations, if a coach pictures himself as a confident, successful coach, he is more likely to exude real confidence.

Another point Short made is that coaches who use imagery to put together game plans feel more comfortable with the plans that they come up with. Coaches who make their plans and play out the game using their imaginations are more likely to see strengths and weaknesses in their plans and adjust their plans accordingly.

A third point made is that coaches who imagine in a "cognitive specific way," that is through clear specific examples, will have more confidence in their teaching abilities. In other words, coaches who specifically imagine teaching skills and techniques will acquire confidence in teaching these attributes and therefore be more effective teachers: "The confidence a coach portrays affects the confidence athletes feel . . . . The coach acting confident is one of the most effective strategies coaches can use to increase athletes' 'feelings of efficacy'" (Short, "Relationship" 392).

There have been many articles written on the X's and the O's (specific strategies) of the game. Seminars have been held on the newest strategies.

Branick 5

Books have been written on the characteristics of good coaches. Studies have been done on confidence in coaching, the method of setting goals, and the role of the coach in coach-athlete relationships; however scholars have yet to study a coach's ability to read his players and the game as a form of literacy. Many people may think that literacy is not part of the responsibilities that go with coaching. However, they couldn't be farther from the truth. Tony Mirabelli gives an unorthodox definition of literacy, arguing that "Literacy extends beyond individual experiences of reading and writing to include the various modes of communication and situations of any socially meaningful group" (146). He talks about reading people and knowing when to do something to help them as forms of literacy.

This idea of multiple literacies can be applied to football coaching staff as well. Coaches need to be able to do so much more than just read. They need to know how to read people. They need to know how to read their players so that they can find out how to get the most out of them. They must also know how to read and teach the plays. The coaches must know their plays because many plays have certain "reads" or "progressions" that the coach must be able to teach the players. Coaches also must be able to read the game so that they can call the best plays that suit certain situations properly.

Here Branick makes an important connection between literacy and coaching. Are you persuaded by his connection? Why or why not?

Coaching as a complex literacy practice has not been examined. How do football coaches, as members of a specific discourse community, go about reading their players and the game in order to get optimal performance and a positive end result? To figure this out, I conducted an ethnographic study on how the coaches at the University of Dayton go about reading people and reading the game.

Methods

I recorded football coaches at the University of Dayton during their
pregame speeches and interviewed those coaches afterwards; I also
interviewed a coaching graduate assistant at the University of Cincinnati
via email. The recording of the pregame speeches took place before a
home game on a Saturday afternoon. In the pregame speeches, Coach
Kelly and Coach Whilding attempted to bring out the best in their
players. I conducted an interview with Coach Whilding, the offensive
coordinator, the following week, and with Coach Kelly, the head coach
at the time, during the winter of the following season. Each interview
took place in the coachs' offices. The email interview with Coach Painter,
the graduate assistant at the University of Cincinnati, took place in
the winter as well. In it, I asked similar questions to those used for
the University of Dayton coaches. (Interview questions are attached as
Appendix A). I asked questions about how coaches go about reading their
players and the game and also about the coach's personal history and
motivation for coaching.

I used these methods because they allowed me to take a direct look at
what the coaches were saying and then get a look at the thought process
behind it. The interviews involved open-ended questions that helped
bring out coaching philosophies on many different issues, including the
issue of reading their players and the game. This idea of reading players
and the game is directly reflective of Tony Mirabelli's idea of multiple
literacies.

I analyzed the data collected by applying John Swales's six
characteristics of a discourse community. The characteristics I focused on
are the set of common goals, the genres, and the specific lexis used.

*Has Branick
mentioned Swales
previously in his
paper? Do you
think he needs to?
Why or why not?*

Branick 7

Results

Because we are studying the multiple literacies of football coaches by looking at coaching as a discourse community, it will be clearest to separate the results for the characteristics of a discourse community and the results for multiple literacies.

Characteristics of a Discourse Community

A football coaching staff is an excellent example of a discourse community. The characteristics are clearly defined and easy to recognize. The clearest characteristics to pick up on are the goals, lexis, and genres.

Goals. Coach Kelly and Coach Whilding helped make up one of the most successful coaching staffs in the history of division 1 college football. This is mainly due to their ability to set and achieve goals, both team and personal goals. There is always the goal of winning the game. The University of Dayton had goal charts with a list of about 10 goals for every game, for offense, defense, and special teams. They use these charts with stickers to help monitor how well they achieve these goals and figure out the goals they need to work on.

Coaches also have many individual goals. Many of these goals include getting the most out of their players physically and mentally. Coaches always strive to make their players push themselves to heights that they never thought they could reach. Coaches also have the goal of seeing their players develop as people. Coach Whilding talked about how he enjoyed seeing his players succeed in real-life situations after football: "It's good to see those guys mature and go on and get good jobs and raise families and be very responsible people in their communities."

Along with these goals, there are many rewards. While many big time college coaches may receive a hefty paycheck, Coach Whilding explained that

Branick is using a fairly complex system of primary headings, secondary headings, and tertiary headings. How helpful are these to you as a reader? What alternative organizational strategies might he have used?

some of the rewards are not monetary: "I know guys who just hate to get up in the morning and hate to go to work, and I have just never felt that way."

Lexis. Another important characteristic of discourse communities is that there is a specialized lexis, or set of terms that is unique to the community. There are many terms that are involved in football coaching communities that may not make sense to most people but, among a team, make perfect sense and help the community better do its work and achieve it goals.

Some of the more common terms might make more sense to the public, such as touchdown or tackle. There are, however, terms that might not make sense to anybody outside the team. Examples of these may be passing routes such as "Y corner," "Follow," or "Green Gold." They could also be things like blocking schemes such as "Bob," "Sam," or "Combo." There are terms for everything, and it takes many repetitions during practice to learn all of this lexis. The lexis helps save time because one word may describe several actions. This lexis is also important because the lexis varies from team to team, so if the opposing team hears it, they will not know what it means. Without many hours spent preparing and practicing, the players and the coaches would not have this advantage in communication.

Genres. A genre is a text that helps facilitate communication between people, and in this example all communication takes place within the discourse community. There are certain genres that help a football team and football coaching staff operate efficiently. Genres often use the unique lexis that was previously mentioned.

Note how Branick links elements of one characteristic (genre) to a previously discussed characteristic (lexis).

Perhaps the most essential genre is the playbook. The playbook is created by the coaches and shows all the plays that they plan on running and the proper way that the players are supposed to run them. The players

Branick 9

get the playbooks at the beginning of the season and need to learn the plays before they are "installed" during practice. The players must guard these books and make sure that no members from opposing teams get the information. The playbook is essential to success because there are many plays and without a playbook the players would become confused and make mistakes that could be disastrous to the outcome of the football game.

Another genre is a scouting report. The scouting report is also made up by the coaches for the players. It shows the other team's personnel, what plays they like to run, and when they like to run them. It helps the players know what to expect going into the game so they can prepare accordingly. The coaches will usually spend the day after a game putting together a scouting report and distribute the report to their players at the beginning of the week.

A third genre is a play-calling sheet. This is made up by the coaches and is only for the coaches, mainly the offensive coordinator. The play-calling sheet helps the coach remember all the plays that they have and what situation that the plays are favorable in. Without a play-calling sheet, the coach would have to remember the names of all the plays on his own, and that is something that could be a distraction to calling the proper plays, and could effectively cost a team a game.

Now that we understand what exactly a football coaching discourse community is and what it is made up of, we can learn exactly how the concept of literacy applies to this group.

What do you think of Branick's strategy here for transitioning to a new section/topic?

Multiple Literacies

Many people do not see the concept of literacy as something that would apply to a football coaching staff. However, Mirabelli defines literacy as not just reading and writing but things such as reading people. He uses the example of a waiter reading his customers in his article. This same idea can be applied to a football coaching discourse community.

Interpersonal Literacies. One of the literacies for a football coach is the ability to read the players. This can be described as an interpersonal literacy. There are two types of reading the coach needs to do. First, coaches must be able to read players to know when they are ready to play; second, coaches must be able to read their players to know how to motivate them properly to get the most out of them.

Throughout his paper, Branick gives an overview of his claims and then uses those claims to organize his content. How well do you think this strategy works?

There are different characteristics to look for when it comes to knowing when players are ready to play. Two are comfort and knowledge. Coach Painter from Cincinnati emphasized player comfort: "Knowing their personality is a big part of reading them. When a player is ready to play they will be in a comfortable mode. Whether that is listening to music, jumping around, or even reading, when a player is loose and comfortable they are ready to compete." Coach Kelly emphasized knowledge of the game: "Do they have the knowledge to perform? What we try to do is put them in as many stressful situations as possible from a mental point of view to see if they can handle that in practice. If they can handle that in practice . . . then we cut 'em loose and let 'em play." He went on to state that another way of finding out whether or not a player has that knowledge and is ready to play is by sitting down one on one with him. Coach Kelly elaborates, "I can get a good feel for a young man when I'm sitting in a room with him, watching practice or game tape, asking him questions. . . . If there is a lot of hesitation or if they are totally off then I know we're not there yet."

Note how Branick integrates direct quotations from his interviews in order to support his claims rather than simply listing one long quotation after another.

Coaches must be able to read their players in order to motivate them properly. Every coach emphasized that each player is unique and will

Branick 11

respond to different types of motivation in different ways. This can be done by taking an emotional, fiery approach or a calm and collected approach. Coach Kelly emphasized the importance of motivation, explaining,

> That's a key element in becoming a coach. Can they motivate? Can they identify what makes this guy go? Can you hit that button and how fast can you hit that button? The sooner you find that motivational tool the better off you're going to be. You can tell immediately if it works or not.

Finding out what motivates each individual is no easy task, but Coach Whilding explains, "You have to be able to understand 'How do I reach that player . . . that young man?' And there are a lot of ways to do that. Through the years, you figure it out." He went more in depth and explained that you have to be able to reach everybody as an individual player and that there are many types of players: "There are some that like to yell and scream and get excited. There are others who don't play well like that, who are a little quieter and keep it within themselves but are still very motivated." Coach Painter from Cincinnati points out the balance between these two opposing motivational styles: "You have to use both and know when to use them. . . . Too much fire and you will lose the team and its effectiveness. Too much calm and you will lose control over the environment."

These explanations show that reading players to know when they are ready to play and reading players to know how to motivate them are two very difficult parts of the coaching profession. They require balance, patience, and perseverance. Coach Whilding sums it up, saying, sometimes "it just doesn't work and you find out you have to just use another method."

Branick 12

Situational Literacies. A second essential coaching literacy is being able to read a game. The coaches must be able to actively read a game in order to put their players in the best possible situations to attempt to win the game. Reading a game can be broken down into two categories: pregame and in-game.

The week leading up to a game is a week filled with preparation. Preparation is important because it "will allow you the ability to put players in the places they need to be at the times they need to be there to make plays. From there it's out of your hands" (Painter). Coaches study the opposing team in and out and then formulate a game plan. They consolidate this game plan along with information on the opposition into a packet, make copies of the packet, and distribute the copies to the team. This helps players stay on the same page as the coaches and prepare mentally for the game. This mental preparation will make players feel more comfortable as to what to expect during the game: "You do a lot of preparation during the week, getting ready for the week. We watch a lot of tape. You have to have an idea of what their base defense is, what their coverage is going to be, when they're going to blitz, what down they're going to blitz, what are their favorite ones" (Whilding). Coach Kelly elaborated on the importance of preparation by explaining that you have to get a good idea of what the coach likes to do in certain situations and when you feel like you know the opposing coach, it becomes a game of feel: "It's really important to me to know what's going on in that coach's mind" (Kelly).

It is also important to be able to read the game in real time. Ways of reading and reacting during the game may be as simple as knowing when to call timeouts, call certain plays, or make substitutions, or may be more complicated such as knowing what type of halftime adjustments to make.

> Note that Branick keeps coming back to his overall claims about literacy and reading, weaving those terms into his sections.

Branick 13

Coach Whilding explains that a key aspect of making these adjustments is that "You have to get a feel on the field for what is working, and I think that's something you develop through the years . . . and it changes from week to week, from year to year sometimes, depending on your personnel. You have to know your personnel. What you're good at, what you're not good at."

Because coaches don't always have the best view and are not in a position to be heard by all the players when they are on the field, sometimes they will delegate this responsibility to their players. Coach Painter explains, "Our players are allowed a small amount of freedom on the fly. We ask our quarterback to check us out of plays when necessary, but we have established what and when he can make such checks." These checks (changing the play at the line) give the team a better chance of calling a play that will be more likely to be successful.

Halftime adjustments are also very important. Sometimes a team will come out in the first half and do something that was not expected or maybe a certain strategy is not working the way the coach expected it to. The coaches will come together at the end of the half and discuss possible changes that might help the team. They then use halftime to explain these changes and make sure everyone is on the same page. This can turn into a chess match because sometimes one team will adjust to something that another team does, but at the same time the other team changes up what they were doing. Coach Painter explains it best by saying, "Your opponent is going to adjust, if you do not then you will be at a disadvantage. No matter how much preparation you have put in, there are going to be things you did not expect. This is where your on the field adjustments give you the final edge."

Branick 14

Relationship between Textual, Situational, and Interpersonal Literacies.

Coaching functions as a discourse community that uses a variety of complex literacies, textual, interpersonal, and situational. All of these literacies can be seen functioning together in a game situation.

Before the game the coach had to spend time evaluating his players and deciding who was going to play. To do this he used interpersonal literacies. Now fast forward to a game situation. Let's say that the team we are looking at is on offense. While the players are playing the game, there are assistant coaches in the press box watching to see how the defense reacts to what the offense does. They are looking for any keys or tips that could give the offense an advantage. This is an example of situational literacies. The assistant coaches in the press box will then communicate what they see to the coach calling the offense. This process involves using lexis. The coach will then process what the assistant coaches told him and will look at his play-calling sheet and decide what play to run. The play-calling sheet is an example of a genre. He will then tell the quarterback what play to run. The name of the play consists of lexis as well. The quarterback will tell the team the play and then they will line up. The quarterback will then look at the defense and see if anything needs to be changed. This is an example of situational literacies. If he decides to "check" (change) the play based on what he sees in the defense, he will use lexis to do so. The quarterback will then call "hike" (lexis) and the ball will be snapped and the play will be run with the hopes of scoring a touchdown, which is the goal on any given play.

Conclusion

The world of coaching is more complicated than it may seem to the public eye. Whether it is looking at some of the characteristics of a coaching

> Note that Branick makes an overall claim here. He is not simply summarizing but, rather, he has worked up to a large claim and knows that now the reader has enough information to understand that claim.

Branick 15

community or looking at the tasks that coaches partake in, such as reading players and the game, there are still many characteristics and responsibilities that are unexplored to those outside of these communities. After looking in depth at some of the behind-the-scenes factors that go into coaching, I hope to have helped increase knowledge on the literacy aspects involved in coaching. I hope this helps spark interest in the connection between literacy and sports. This connection will now help people have a better sense of empathy with what the coaches are thinking when they make a specific call on the field or partake in an action off the field, and hopefully I have brought people closer to being able to answer the common question asked at any sporting event: "What was that coach thinking?!"

What do you think of Branick's conclusion? Do you find it effective? What else might he have done here?

Branick 16

Works Cited

Grant, Anthony M. "The Goal-Focused Coaching Skills Questionnaire: Preliminary Findings." *Social Behavior & Personality: An International Journal* 35.6 (2007): 751–60. Print.

Hasbrouck, Jan and Carolyn Denton. "Student-Focused Coaching: A Model for Reading Coaches." *Reading Teacher* 60.7 (2007): 690–93. Print.

Mirabelli, Tony. "Learning to Serve: The Language and Literacy of Food Service Workers." *What They Don't Learn in School*. Ed. Jabari Mahiri. New York: Peter Lang, 2004. 143–62. Print.

Short, Sandra E. "Role of the Coach in the Coach-Athlete Relationship." Spec. issue of *Lancet* 366 (2005): S29–S30. Print.

———. "The Relationship Between Efficacy Beliefs and Imagery Use in Coaches." *The Sport Psychologist* 19.4 (2005): 380–94. Print.

Swales, John. "The Concept of Discourse Community." *Genre Analysis: English in Academic and Workplace Settings*. Boston: Cambridge UP, 1990. 21–32. Print.

Appendix A

Interview Questions for Coaches

Interpersonal Literacies

1. How do you tell when a player is ready or not ready to play? Are there specific things that you look for (body language and attitude, etc.) or is it more intuitive?

2. In what ways do you go about motivating your players? Do you prefer a calm or a fiery approach? How did your coaches go about motivating you when you played? Do you feel like you have become an effective motivator?

3. Do you focus more on motivating players during the week or during a pregame speech? When do you think is more effective? Are there any

Branick 17

specific examples that stick out of when you made an attempt to motivate a player and it was either very successful or unsuccessful? If you were unsuccessful how did you change your approach?

4. Would you consider your approach to correcting athletes more of positive reinforcement or negative reinforcement? Do you think that players respond better to one method better than the other? Is it better to correct mistakes publicly or privately? How do the players react to each method?

Situational Literacies

1. What do you feel are the most important factors to reading and calling a game? Do you use any specific methods to help you mediate reading the game (scripting plays, play-calling sheet with specific situations)?

2. Do you put any of this on your players (system of checks or audibles, plays that are run differently depending on the defense's look)?

3. How much of the outcome of a game do you feel is attributed to pregame coaching preparations (game planning, watching film)?

4. How important are in-game decisions such as halftime adjustments, substitutions, and when to gamble on big plays? Do you go with the overall feel of the game or do you look for specific details when it comes to making a game-time decision?

Some Other Questions to Consider

-   On pages 560–61, Branick claims "There have been many articles written on the X's and O's . . . of the game. . . . however scholars have yet to study a coach's ability to read his players and the game as a form of literacy." Does Branick convince you that these abilities are, in fact, a form of literacy? Explain why or why not.
-   Branick's methods include analyzing the coaches' discourse community using John Swales's six characteristics. How well does he conduct this analysis? What, if anything, would you change or expand?
-   How does Branick define "situational literacies"? Are you convinced that this is a real skill? Are you convinced it is a form of literacy? Why or why not?

Writing about Discourses: Assignments and Advice

One of the assignments that I learned the most from would be about discourse communities. I learned that getting involved in a new community can be tough for an outsider. John Swales explains how each discourse community exists differently from others and offers six characteristics to define how each community "tends to be a specific interest group." Analyzing a discourse community is important because understanding the functions of a certain group will enhance an outsider's ability to cooperate effectively.

—Natasha Gumtie, Student

To help you learn and explore the ideas in this chapter, we are suggesting two Assignment Options for larger writing projects: Discourse Community Ethnography and Mushfaking the Dominant Discourse: An Analysis of Gee's Claims.

Assignment Option 1. Discourse Community Ethnography

Choose a discourse community that has made an impact on you or one that interests you and find a preliminary answer to this research question: "What are the goals and characteristics of this discourse community?" Write a four- to five-page report that tries to answer your research question based on careful observation of the community.

Data Collection

- *Observe members of the discourse community* while they are engaged in a shared activity; take detailed notes. (What are they doing? What kinds of things do they say? What do they write? How do you know who is "in" and who is "out"?)
- *Collect anything people in that community read or write* (their genres)—even very short things like forms, sketches, notes, IMs, and text messages
- *Interview at least one member of the discourse community.* Record and transcribe the interview. You might ask things like, "How long have you been here? Why are you involved? What do *X, Y,* and *Z* words mean? How did you learn to write *A, B,* or *C*? How do you communicate with other people [on your team, at your restaurant, etc]?"

Data Analysis First, try analyzing the data you collect using the six characteristics of Swales's discourse community:

- What are the shared goals of the community; why does this group exist and what does it do?
- What mechanisms do members use to communicate with each other (meetings, phone calls, e-mail, text messages, newsletters, reports, evaluation forms, and so on)?

- What are the purposes of each of these mechanisms of communication (to improve performance, make money, grow better roses, share research, and so forth)?
- Which of the above mechanisms of communication can be considered *genres* (textual responses to recurring situations that all group members recognize and understand)?
- What kinds of specialized language (*lexis*) do group members use in their conversation and in their genres? Name some examples—ESL, "on the fly," "86," and so on. What communicative function does this lexis serve (that is, why say "86" instead of "we are out of this"?)
- Who are the "old-timers" with expertise? Who are the newcomers with less expertise? How do newcomers learn the appropriate language, genres, knowledge of the group?

Then, use Gee, Johns, Wardle, and/or Mirabelli to analyze your data further:

- Are there conflicts within the community? If so, why?
- Do some participants in the community have difficulty? Why?
- Who has authority here, and where does that authority come from?
- What are the "modes of belonging" that newcomers are attempting to use?
- What sorts of "multiliteracies" do members of this community possess?
- Are members of this community stereotyped in any way in regard to their literacy knowledge? If so, why?

Planning and Drafting   As you develop answers to some of these questions, start setting some priorities. Given all you have learned above, what do you want to focus on in your paper? Is there something interesting regarding goals of the community? Types of literacies in the community? Lexis and mediating genres? Decide what your refined research question is and how you will answer it. (Consult the articles by Wardle and Mirabelli in this chapter for examples of how you might do this.)

Your paper ought to have the following parts or make the following moves (unless there's a good reason not to):

- Begin with a very brief review of the existing literature (published research) on the topic ("We know X about discourse communities" [cite Swales, Gee, Johns, Mirabelli, and/or Wardle, as appropriate]).
- Name a niche ("But we don't know Y" or "No one has looked at X").
- Explain how you will occupy the niche.
- Describe your research methods.
- Discuss your findings in detail (use Mirabelli and Wardle as examples of how to do this—quote from your notes, your interview, the texts you collected, and so on).
- Include a Works Cited page.

What Makes It Good?   Your assignment will be most successful if you've carefully followed your instructor's directions in collecting the required data and if you've really focused on your research question in trying to answer it. The assignment asks you to show a clear understanding of what discourse communities are and to demonstrate your ability to analyze them carefully and thoughtfully. And, of course, your paper should be a strong example of craft: thoughtfully organized, readable, fluent, and well edited.

Assignment Option 2. Mushfaking the Dominant Discourse: An Analysis of Gee's Claims

Write a four- to five-page essay exploring some of Gee's claims about Discourses *empirically*—that is, by doing your own firsthand research and comparing what you observe with what Gee's theory *predicts* you'll observe. The point of your essay is to compare his theory and your observations.

Theory
Step One: In Gee's article on Discourses, he makes a distinction between dominant and nondominant Discourses. Mastering dominant Discourses, he claims, can bring money, prestige, and status. What does Gee mean by *dominant Discourse*? Is he referring to the language used by people of a particular social class or race? Create a working definition of *dominant Discourse*, making absolutely certain that your working definition builds on Gee's and does not contradict his claims.

Step Two: Gee claims that once you have "fossilized" into a Discourse without becoming fully fluent in it, you "can't be let into the game." He claims that "true acquisition is probably not possible" and people who are not a part of the dominant Discourse can only "mushfake" it. Gee appears to be claiming that people who don't become fluent in the dominant Discourse early are never able to become a part of that Discourse. His claim seems to contradict what is commonly seen as the "American Dream"—the idea that in the United States anyone who works hard can become whatever they want. Using your working definition of dominant Discourse, challenge or support Gee's claim here. If you need additional help, you might want to read some of the research by the sociolinguists that Gee references (Milroy, for example).

Research   Spend a few hours hanging out with or near a discourse community of your choice—sorority, store, gaming community, and so on. Write down every use of specialized language that you hear—whether it is an unusual word or phrase, or simply an unusual use of a fairly common word or phrase.

Once you have a good list of terms, conduct a short interview with an "old-timer" in that discourse community. Ask the person about the different words, specifically things like "Why do you use this word or phrase instead of a different one?" "What does this word or phrase mean?" or "Why do you think this group uses this word or phrase? How does it help you achieve your objectives better than using a different word or phrase?"

Planning and Drafting   Build your essay by explaining your understanding of Gee's theory of Discourse (whatever aspects of it you have found interesting to test with your research) and showing how your own findings relate to the theory.

- Do your findings support his theory, contradict it, or do some of both?
- Can you see places where, by your research, Gee is likely right, and where he may be wrong? As an example, Gee's theory predicts that Discourses will have specialized languages. Based on your observations, do they?

You can also use your observations to add to or build on Gee's theory. For example, if you do find specialized language in the Discourse you observe, you might consider whether or not specialized language is intended to exclude people, whether it serves a more practical function, or whether it does both.

What Makes It Good?   You can see in the various elements of the analysis the basic ideas for what really makes your paper work:

- Since it's supposed to summarize and explain Gee's theory, a good paper will do that very well: accurately, concisely, and with good insight into both what Gee *says* and what the implications of his Discourse theory are.
- At the same time, your analysis shouldn't overreach, by (for example) trying to cover everything in Gee's theory in four or five pages, or trying to make unsupportable claims.
- Since the analysis is supposed to test Gee's theory against actual observations you make, a good paper should have very good observations and *explanations* of those observations.
- And then, in the hardest move of your paper, your analyses should compare the observation and theory in ways that help us understand each better.

As always, your paper should also be well written in terms of fluent and readable sentences, good organization and flow, and careful editing and proofreading.

Suggested Additional Readings and Resources

Bucholtz, Mary. "'Why Be Normal?' Language and Identity Practices in a Community of Nerd Girls." *Language in Society* 28.2 (1999): 203–23. Print.

Krohn, Franklin B. "A Generational Approach to Using Emoticons as Nonverbal Communication." *Technical Writing and Communication* 34.4 (2004): 321–28. Print.

Moss, Beverly, ed. *Literacy across Communities*. Cresskill: Hampton Press, 1994. Print.

Orwell, George. "Politics and the English Language." *Horizon* April 1946: 252–65. Rpt. in *A Collection of Essays*. San Diego: Mariner, 1970. 156–70. Print.

Sohn, Katherine Kelleher. *Whistlin' and Crowin' Women of Appalachia: Literacy Practices since College*. Carbondale: Southern Illinois UP, 2006. Print.

Steinkuehler, Constance A. "Learning in Massively Multiplayer Online Games." *Embracing Diversity in the Learning Sciences, Proceedings of the Sixth International Conference on Learning Sciences*. Ed. Yasmin B. Kafai, et al. Mahwah: Lawrence Erlbaum, 2004. 521–28. Print.

5 | Authority: How Do You Make Yourself Heard as a College Writer?

I hope that you have gained insight into the world of literacy sponsorship.

The final chapter in this reader continues the discussion of **discourse communities** from Chapter 4, but adds the wrinkle of exploring how writers become **authorities** in the discourse communities they join. By *authority*, we mean a mix of membership, expertise, and, most important, an ability to be *listened to* and *heard*. It might help to think of *authority* as a sort of position or platform from which writers can speak and, in doing so, gain respect.

In Chapter 4 we tried to illustrate how people join new discourse communities, primarily in nonacademic settings, and asked you to consider questions like these: In a sorority or a workplace, how do people learn to use language as people *who belong* in that community? How do newcomers become authorities in new communities,

In her composition course, student Emily Kopp (pictured above) drew on her expertise and authority as a musician to create a multimodal musical text discussing the concept of literacy sponsorship.

and what happens when they fail? In this chapter we ask you to take these ideas into a realm where it's often assumed (by students, teachers, and onlookers) that students *cannot* be authorities or experts: college. How do you, as a college student, develop authority to speak into, or contribute to, the various communities you join (or look in on) in your studies? How can you learn the languages, customs, and knowledge values of different academic disciplines in order to become, and sound like, a member of them? And what do you do when new discourses compete with old ones or when school discourses devalue "home" discourses?

This chapter begins with Joseph Harris's discussion of *discourse community* and the problems with moving among **Discourses** that sometimes conflict or compete. His article, and the journalistic piece by Josh Keller that follows, ask you to consider what is happening to you as you enter the university and begin writing in various classrooms:

- Do you feel conflicted about the ways in which you are asked to use language?
- Are you asked to write in ways that aren't comfortable for you?
- Do the writing tasks you are faced with here have implications for your identity?
- Do you feel that your home Discourse is devalued here? Or are you pretty comfortable with the ways in which you are asked to use language?
- Does your social writing using technology seem more important or useful to you than your school writing?

In short, we could ask, how does moving into new academic discourses affect the authority with which you've been able to write before? If you lose authority as you move into college writing, what does it take to regain it?

The following four readings in this chapter proceed from the understanding that finding a position from which to speak in the new Discourses that you move among can be difficult, but the authors offer practical suggestions for moving beyond this problem. These authors look at specific uses of language in different classrooms and disciplines, and they consider how students navigate these various communities. They also look explicitly at some texts in different disciplines and give you tools for figuring out what, for example, philosophers do differently from historians and engineers. Here's a bit more detail on what each reading does, specifically:

- Ann M. Penrose and Cheryl Geisler consider two students in one discipline— a first-year student and a graduate student—writing about the same subject and suggest very specifically how their writing differs because of their experience level and sense of authority regarding the material.
- Christine Pearson Casanave focuses on some of the **literacy games** that nonnative speakers of English have to learn to play in order to write in their college classrooms.
- Lucille McCarthy considers why one student has trouble writing in different classrooms and asks what teachers in three different classrooms value in writing.
- Ken Hyland shows how researchers in different disciplines cite their sources differently.

The readings in this chapter ask you to consider what your experience with writing has been and will be in the academy, and then try to arm you with some tools for tackling new kinds of academic writing in ways that let you make yourself heard within the conventions of these new Discourses. When you go into a new classroom, you should have some specific tools in your "writing toolkit" to help you figure out how to write with authority there. And if you don't succeed, you should be able to understand why.

Chapter Goals

- To understand how discourse is used in the university
- To understand how and why discourse conventions differ across disciplines
- To understand knowledge of disciplines' language and Discourses as a way of being heard
- To acquire tools for successfully responding to varied discourse conventions and genres in different classes
- To improve as a reader of complex, research-based texts

The Idea of Community in the Study of Writing

JOSEPH HARRIS

Harris, Joseph. "The Idea of Community in the Study of Writing." *College Composition and Communication* 40.1 (1989): 11–22. Print.

Framing the Reading

Joseph Harris received a Ph.D. from New York University in 1986 and has been teaching writing and directing college writing programs ever since. He spent six years at the University of Pittsburgh before leaving in 1999 to direct the University Writing Program at Duke, where he continues to teach today. He has written two important books about teaching writing. *A Teaching Subject: Composition since 1966* (published in 1997) and *Rewriting: How to Do Things with Texts* (published in 2006). He edited *College Composition and Communication,* the premier journal in composition, from 1994 to 1999, and he continues to serve as editor for *Studies in Writing and Rhetoric,* an important books series in the field.

In the article you are about to read, Harris participates in the conversation about what James Gee called **Discourses** and what John Swales called **discourse communities** (see Chapter 4). Harris argues that the word *community* is "empty and sentimental" and that it has no "positive opposing term" (in other words, there does not seem to be a positive word that is the opposite of *community*). He ends the article by arguing that the term *community* should only be used to describe what happens in very "specific and local groups."

While this is an important point to the theorists who discuss such things for a living, the most important part of this chapter for students is probably what Harris has to say from the section headed "Williams and the Problem of Community" through "Writing as Repositioning" (pp. 584–590). In those pages, Harris argues that people don't leave one discourse community to become a part of another one but, rather, are "adding to" their range of Discourses. So, for example, by learning to write in college you aren't leaving one Discourse to be a part of a new one but figuring out how to be a part of "a number of discourses, a number of communities, whose beliefs and practices conflict as well as align" (para. 23).

The hardest part about reading this article is sorting through all the viewpoints that Harris represents here. He pulls in a lot of the scholars who have contributed to the conversation about discourse communities—David Bartholomae, Linda Brodkey, James Porter, John Swales, and Patricia Bizzell. He agrees with them, questions them, argues with them, and then tries to make his own claims about discourse communities. If you have a hard time sorting out who is saying what, you might try making a kind of "conversation map" as you read—writing down what each of these people has to say about discourse communities and then trying to figure out where Harris is in this conversation.

Getting Ready to Read

Before you read, do at least one of the following activities:

- Consider how you felt when you first came to college. Did you feel that you were leaving your "old self" behind, or were you adding to your identity?
- If you read John Swales or Ann Johns in Chapter 4, refresh your memory on their definitions of *discourse community*.

As you read, consider the following questions:

- Which scholars does Harris cite? What views does each of them hold? (Take notes as you read.)

If you stand, today, in Between Towns Road, you can see either way; west to the spires and towers of the cathedral and colleges; east to the yards and sheds of the motor works. You see different worlds, but there is no frontier between them; there is only the movement and traffic of a single city.
—**RAYMOND WILLIAMS**
    Second Generation (9)

In *The Country and the City*, Raymond Williams writes of how, after a boy-   1
hood in a Welsh village, he came to the city, to Cambridge, only then to hear "from townsmen, academics, an influential version of what country life, country literature, really meant: a prepared and persuasive cultural history" (6). This odd double movement, this irony, in which one only begins to understand the place one has come from through the act of leaving it, proved to be one of the shaping forces of Williams's career—so that, some 35 years after having first gone down to Cambridge, he was still to ask himself: "Where do I stand . . . in another country or in this valuing city?" (6)

A similar irony, I think, describes my own relations to the university. I was   2
raised in a working-class home in Philadelphia, but it was only when I went away to college that I heard the term *working class* used or began to think of myself as part of it. Of course by then I no longer was quite part of it, or at least no longer wholly or simply part of it, but I had also been at college long enough to realize that my relations to it were similarly ambiguous—that here

too was a community whose values and interests I could in part share but to some degree would always feel separate from.

This sense of difference, of overlap, of tense plurality, of being at once part 3 of several communities and yet never wholly a member of one, has accompanied nearly all the work and study I have done at the university. So when, in the past few years, a number of teachers and theorists of writing began to talk about the idea of *community* as somehow central to our work, I was drawn to what was said. Since my aim here is to argue for a more critical look at a term that, as Williams has pointed out, "seems never to be used unfavourably" (*Keywords* 66), I want to begin by stating my admiration for the theorists—in particular, David Bartholomae and Patricia Bizzell—whose work I will discuss. They have helped us, I think, to ask some needed questions about writing and how we might go about teaching it.[1]

Perhaps the most important work of these theorists has centered on the 4 demystifying of the concept of *intention*. That is, rather than viewing the intentions of a writer as private and ineffable, wholly individual, they have helped us to see that it is only through being part of some ongoing discourse that we can, as individual writers, have things like points to make and purposes to achieve. As Bartholomae argues: "It is the discourse with its projects and agendas that determines what writers can and will do" (139). We write not as isolated individuals but as members of communities whose beliefs, concerns, and practices both instigate and constrain, at least in part, the sorts of things we can say. Our aims and intentions in writing are thus not merely personal, idiosyncratic, but reflective of the communities to which we belong.

> We write not as isolated individuals but as members of communities whose beliefs, concerns, and practices both instigate and constrain, at least in part, the sorts of things we can say.

But while this concern with the power of social forces in writing is much 5 needed in a field that has long focused narrowly on the composing processes of individual writers, some problems in how we have imagined those forces are now becoming clear. First, recent theories have tended to invoke the idea of community in ways at once sweeping and vague: positing discursive utopias that direct and determine the writings of their members, yet failing to state the operating rules or boundaries of these communities. One result of this has been a view of "normal discourse" in the university that is oddly lacking in conflict or change. Recent social views of writing have also often presented university discourse as almost wholly foreign to many of our students, raising questions not only about their chances of ever learning to use such an alien tongue, but of why they should want to do so in the first place. And, finally, such views have tended to polarize our talk about writing: One seems asked to defend either the power of the discourse community or the imagination of the individual writer.

Williams and the Problem of Community

In trying to work towards a more useful sense *of community*, I will take both   6
my method and theme from Raymond Williams in his *Keywords: A Vocabulary
of Culture and Society*. Williams's approach in this vocabulary reverses that of
the dictionary-writer. For rather than trying to define and fix the meanings of
the words he discusses, to clear up the many ambiguities involved with them,
Williams instead attempts to sketch "a history and complexity of meanings"
(15), to show how and why the meanings of certain words—*art, criticism, culture, history, literature*, and the like—are still being contested. Certainly *community*, at once so vague and suggestive, is such a word too, and I will begin,
then, with what Williams has to say about it:

> *Community* can be the warmly persuasive word to describe an existing set of
> relationships, or the warmly persuasive word to describe an alternative set of rela-
> tionships. What is most important, perhaps, is that unlike all other terms of social
> organization (*state, nation, society*, etc.) it seems never to be used unfavourably,
> and never to be given any positive opposing or distinguishing term. (66)

There seem to me two warnings here. The first is that, since it has no "posi-   7
tive opposing" term, *community* can soon become an empty and sentimental
word. And it is easy enough to point to such uses in the study of writing, particularly in the many recent calls to transform the classroom into "a community of interested readers," to recast academic disciplines as "communities of
knowledgeable peers," or to translate standards of correctness into "the expectations of the academic community." In such cases, *community* tends to mean
little more than a nicer, friendlier, fuzzier version of what came before.

But I think Williams is also hinting at the extraordinary rhetorical power one   8
can gain through speaking of community. It is a concept both seductive and
powerful, one that offers us a view of shared purpose and effort and that also
makes a claim on us that is hard to resist. For like the pronoun *we, community*
can be used in such a way that it invokes what it seems merely to describe.
The writer says to his reader: "We are part of a certain community; they are
not"—and, if the reader accepts, the statement is true. And, usually, the gambit
of community, once offered, is almost impossible to decline—since what is
invoked is a community of those in power, of those who know the accepted
ways of writing and interpreting texts. Look, for instance, at how David Bartholomae begins his remarkable essay on "Inventing the University":

> Every time a student sits down to write for us, he has to invent the university
> for the occasion—invent the university, that is, or a branch of it, like history or
> anthropology or economics or English. The student has to learn *to speak our
> language, to speak as we do*, to try on the peculiar ways of knowing, selecting,
> evaluating, reporting, concluding, and arguing that define *the discourse of our
> community*. (134, my emphases)

Note here how the view of discourse at the university shifts subtly from the
dynamic to the fixed—from something that a writer must continually reinvent

to something that has already been invented, a language that "we" have access to but that many of our students do not. The university becomes "our community," its various and competing discourses become "our language," and the possibility of a kind of discursive free-for-all is quickly rephrased in more familiar terms of us and them, insiders and outsiders.

This tension runs throughout Bartholomae's essay. On one hand, the university is pictured as the site of many discourses, and successful writers are seen as those who are able to work both within and against them, who can find a place for themselves on the margins or borders of a number of discourses. On the other, the university is also seen as a cluster of separate communities, disciplines, in which writers must locate themselves through taking on "the commonplaces, set phrases, rituals and gestures, habits of mind, tricks of persuasion, obligatory conclusions and necessary connections that determine 'what might be said'" (146). Learning to write, then, gets defined both as the forming of an aggressive and critical stance towards a number of discourses, and as a more simple entry into the discourse of a single community.

Community thus becomes for Bartholomae a kind of stabilizing term, used to give a sense of shared purpose and effort to our dealings with the various discourses that make up the university. The question, though, of just who this "we" is that speaks "our language" is never resolved.[2] And so while Bartholomae often refers to the "various branches" of the university, he ends up claiming to speak only of "university discourse in its most generalized form" (147). Similarly, most of the "communities" to which other current theorists refer exist at a vague remove from actual experience: The University, The Profession, The Discipline, The Academic Discourse Community. They are all quite literally utopias—nowheres, meta-communities—tied to no particular time or place, and thus oddly free of many of the tensions, discontinuities, and conflicts in the sorts of talk and writing that go on every day in the classrooms and departments of an actual university. For all the scrutiny it has drawn, the idea of community thus still remains little more than a notion—hypothetical and suggestive, powerful yet ill-defined.[3]

Part of this vagueness stems from the ways that the notion of "discourse community" has come into the study of writing—drawing on one hand from the literary-philosophical idea of "interpretive community," and on the other from the sociolinguistic concept of "speech community," but without fully taking into account the differences between the two. "Interpretive community," as used by Stanley Fish and others, is a term in a theoretical debate; it refers not so much to specific physical groupings of people as to a kind of loose dispersed network of individuals who share certain habits of mind. "Speech community," however, is usually meant to describe an actual group of speakers living in a particular place and time.[4] Thus while "interpretive community" can usually be taken to describe something like a world-view, discipline, or profession, "speech community" is generally used to refer more specifically to groupings like neighborhoods, settlements, or classrooms.

What "discourse community" means is far less clear. In the work of some theorists, the sense of community as an active lived experience seems to drop out almost altogether, to be replaced by a shadowy network of citations and references. Linda Brodkey, for instance, argues that:

> To the extent that the academic community is a community, it is a literate community, manifested not so much at conferences as in bibliographies and libraries, a community whose members know one another better as writers than speakers. (12)

And James Porter takes this notion a step further, identifying "discourse community" with the *intertextuality* of Foucault—an argument that parallels in interesting ways E. D. Hirsch's claim, in *Cultural Literacy*, that a literate community can be defined through the clusters of allusions and references that its members share. In such views, *community* becomes little more than a metaphor, a shorthand label for a hermetic weave of texts and citations.

Most theorists who use the term, however, seem to want to keep something 13 of the tangible and specific reference of "speech community"—to suggest, that is, that there really are "academic discourse communities" out there somewhere, real groupings of writers and readers, that we can help "initiate" our students into. But since these communities are not of speakers, but of writers and readers who are dispersed in time and space, and who rarely, if ever, meet one another in person, they invariably take on something of the ghostly and pervasive quality of "interpretive communities" as well.

There have been some recent attempts to solve this problem. John Swales, for 14 instance, has defined "discourse community" so that the common space shared by its members is replaced by a discursive "forum," and their one-to-one interaction is reduced to a system "providing information and feedback." A forum is not a community, though, so Swales also stipulates that there must be some common "goal" towards which the group is working (2–3). A similar stress on a shared or collaborative project runs through most other attempts to define "discourse community."[5] Thus while *community* loses its rooting in a particular place, it gains a new sense of direction and movement. Abstracted as they are from almost all other kinds of social and material relations, only an affinity of beliefs and purposes, consensus, is left to hold such communities together. The sort of group invoked is a free and voluntary gathering of individuals with shared goals and interests—of persons who have not so much been forced together as have chosen to associate with one another. So while the members of an "academic discourse community" may not meet each other very often, they are presumed to think much like one another (and thus also much *unlike* many of the people they deal with every day: students, neighbors, coworkers in other disciplines, and so on). In the place of physical nearness we are given like-mindedness. We fall back, that is, on precisely the sort of "warmly persuasive" and sentimental view of community that Williams warns against.

Insiders and Outsiders

One result of this has been, in recent work on the teaching of writing, the pit- 15 ting of a "common" discourse against a more specialized or "privileged" one. For instance, Bartholomae argues that:

> The movement towards a more specialized discourse begins . . . both when a student can define a position of privilege, a position that sets him against a "common" discourse, and when he or she can work self-consciously, critically, against not only the "common" code but his or her own. (156)

The troubles of many student writers, Bartholomae suggests, begin with their inability to imagine such a position of privilege, to define their views against some "common" way of talking about their subject. Instead, they simply repeat in their writing "what everybody knows" or what their professor has told them in her lectures. The result, of course, is that they are penalized for "having nothing really to say."

The task of the student is thus imagined as one of crossing the border from one community of discourse to another, of taking on a new sort of language. Again, the power of this metaphor seems to me undeniable. First, it offers us a way of talking about why many of our students fail to think and write as we would like them to *without* having to suggest that they are somehow slow or inept because they do not. Instead, one can argue that the problem is less one of intelligence than socialization, that such students are simply unused to the peculiar demands of academic discourse. Second, such a view reminds us (as Patricia Bizzell has often argued) that one's role as a teacher is not merely to inform but to persuade, that we ask our students to acquire not only certain skills and data, but to try on new forms of thinking and talking about the world as well. The problem is, once having posited two separate communities with strikingly different ways of making sense of the world, it then becomes difficult to explain how or why one moves from one group to the other. If to enter the academic community a student must "learn to speak our language," become accustomed and reconciled to our ways of doing things with words, then how exactly is she to do this? 16

Bizzell seems to picture the task as one of assimilation, of conversion almost. One sets aside one's former ways to become a member of the new community. As she writes: 17

> Mastery of academic discourse must begin with socialization to the community's ways, in the same way that one enters any cultural group. One must first "go native." ("Foundationalism" 53)

And one result of this socialization, Bizzell argues, may "mean being completely alienated from some other, socially disenfranchised discourses" (43). The convert must be born again.

Bartholomae uses the language of paradox to describe what must be accomplished: 18

> To speak with authority [our students] have to speak not only in another's voice but through another's code; and they not only have to do this, they have to speak in the voice and through the codes of those of us with power and wisdom; and they not only have to do this, they have to do it before they know what they are doing, before they have a project to participate in, and before, at least in the terms of our disciplines, they have anything to say. (156)

And so here, too, the learning of a new discourse seems to rest, at least in part, on a kind of mystical leap of mind. Somehow the student must "invent the university," appropriate a way of speaking and writing belonging to others.

Writing as Repositioning

The emphasis of Bartholomae's pedagogy, though, seems to differ in slight but 19 important ways from his theory. In *Facts, Artifacts, and Counterfacts*, a text for a course in basic writing, Bartholomae and Anthony Petrosky describe a class that begins by having students write on what they already think and feel about a certain subject (e.g., adolescence or work), and then tries to get them to redefine that thinking through a seminar-like process of reading and dialogue. The course thus appears to build on the overlap between the students' "common" discourses and the "academic" ones of their teachers, as they are asked to work "within and against" both their own languages and those of the texts they are reading (8). The move, then, is not simply from one discourse to another but towards a "hesitant and tenuous relationship" to both (41).

Such a pedagogy helps remind us that the borders of most discourses are hazily 20 marked and often travelled, and that the communities they define are thus often indistinct and overlapping. As Williams again has suggested, one does not step cleanly and wholly from one community to another, but is caught instead in an always changing mix of dominant, residual, and emerging discourses (*Marxism* 121–27, see also Nicholas Coles on "Raymond Williams: Writing Across Borders"). Rather than framing our work in terms of helping students move from one community of discourse into another, then, it might prove more useful (and accurate) to view our task as adding to or complicating their uses of language.

I am not proposing such addition as a neutral or value-free pedagogy. 21 Rather, I would expect and hope for a kind of useful dissonance as students are confronted with ways of talking about the world with which they are not yet wholly familiar. What I am arguing against, though, is the notion that our students should necessarily be working towards the mastery of some particular, well-defined sort of discourse. It seems to me that they might better be encouraged towards a kind of polyphony—an awareness of and pleasure in the various competing discourses that make up their own.

To illustrate what such an awareness might involve, let me turn briefly to 22 some student writings. The first comes from a paper on *Hunger of Memory*, in which Richard Rodriguez describes how, as a Spanish-speaking child growing up in California, he was confronted in school by the need to master the "public language" of his English-speaking teachers and classmates. In her response, Sylvia, a young black woman from Philadelphia, explains that her situation is perhaps more complex, since she is aware of having at least two "private languages": a Southern-inflected speech which she uses with her parents and older relatives, and the "street talk" which she shares with her friends and neighbors. Sylvia concludes her essay as follows:

> My third and last language is one that Rodriguez referred to as "public language."
> Like Rodriguez, I too am having trouble accepting and using "public language."

Specifically, I am referring to Standard English which is defined in some English texts as:

> "The speaking and writing of cultivated people . . . the variety of spoken and written language which enjoys cultural prestige, and which is the medium of education, journalism, and literature. Competence in its use is necessary for advancement in many occupations."

Presently, I should say that "public language" is *becoming* my language as I am not yet comfortable in speaking it and even less comfortable in writing it. According to my mother anyone who speaks in "proper English" is "putting on airs."

In conclusion, I understand the relevance and importance of learning to use "public language," but, like Rodriguez, I am also afraid of losing my "private identity"—that part of me that my parents, my relatives, and my friends know and understand. However, on the other hand, within me, there is an intense desire to grow and become a part of the "public world"—a world that exists outside of the secure and private world of my parents, relatives, and friends. If I want to belong, I must learn the "public language" too.

The second passage is written by Ron, a white factory worker in central Pennsylvania, and a part-time student. It closes an end-of-the-term reflection on his work in the writing course he was taking.

> As I look back over my writings for this course I see a growing acceptance of the freedom to write as I please, which is allowing me to almost enjoy writing (I can't believe it). So I tried this approach in another class I am taking. In that class we need to write summations of articles each week. The first paper that I handed in, where I used more feeling in my writing, came back with a (✓-) and the comment, "Stick to the material." My view is, if they open the pen I will run as far as I can, but I won't break out because I have this bad habit, it's called eating.

What I admire in both passages is the writer's unwillingness to reduce his or her options to a simple either/or choice. Sylvia freely admits her desire to learn the language of the public world. Her "I understand . . . but" suggests, however, that she is not willing to loosen completely her ties to family and neighborhood in order to do so. And Ron is willing to run with the more free style of writing he has discovered, "if they open the pen." Both seem aware, that is, of being implicated in not one but a number of discourses, a number of communities, whose beliefs and practices conflict as well as align. And it is the tension between those discourses—none repudiated or chosen wholly—that gives their texts such interest. 23

There has been much debate in recent years over whether we need, above all, to respect our students' "right to their own language," or to teach them the ways and forms of "academic discourse." Both sides of this argument, in the end, rest their cases on the same suspect generalization: that we and our students belong to different and fairly distinct communities of discourse, that we have "our" "academic" discourse and they have "their own" "common" (?!) ones. The choice is one between opposing fictions. The "languages" that 24 our students bring to us cannot but have been shaped, at least in part, by their experiences in school, and thus must, in some ways, already be "academic." Similarly, our teaching will and should always be affected by a host of beliefs and values that we hold regardless of our roles as academics. What we see in the classroom, then, are not two coherent and competing discourses but many overlapping and conflicting ones. Our students are no more wholly "outside" the discourse of the university than we are wholly "within" it. We are all at once both insiders and outsiders. The fear (or hope) of either camp that our students will be "converted" from "their" language to "ours" is both overstated and misleading. The task facing our students, as Min-zhan Lu has argued, is not to leave one community in order to enter another, but to *reposition* themselves in relation to several continuous and conflicting discourses. Similarly, our goals as teachers need not be to initiate our students into the values and practices of some new community, but to offer them the chance to reflect critically on those discourses—of home, school, work, the media, and the like—to which they already belong.

Community without Consensus

"Alongside each utterance . . . off-stage voices can be heard," writes Barthes   25
(21). We do not write simply as individuals, but we do not write simply as members of a community either. The point is, to borrow a turn of argument from Stanley Fish, that one does not *first* decide to act as a member of one community rather than some other, and *then* attempt to conform to its (rather than some other's) set of beliefs and practices. Rather, one is always *simultaneously* a part of several discourses, several communities, is always already committed to a number of conflicting beliefs and practices.[6] As Mary Louise Pratt has pointed out: "People and groups are constituted not by single unified belief systems, but by competing self-contradictory ones" (228). One does not necessarily stop being a feminist, for instance, in order to write literary criticism (although one discourse may try to repress or usurp the other). And, as the example of Williams shows, one does not necessarily give up the loyalties of a working-class youth in order to become a university student (although some strain will no doubt be felt).

In *The Country and the City*, Williams notes an "escalator effect" in which   26
each new generation of English writers points to a lost age of harmony and organic community that thrived just before their own, only of course to have the era in which they were living similarly romanticized by the writers who come after them (9–12). Rather than doing much the same, romanticizing academic discourse as occurring in a kind of single cohesive community, I would urge, instead, that we think of it as taking place in something more like a city. That is, instead of presenting academic discourse as coherent and well-defined, we might be better off viewing it as polyglot, as a sort of space in which competing beliefs and practices intersect with and confront one another. One does not need consensus to have community. Matters of accident, necessity, and convenience hold groups together as well. Social theories of reading and writing

have helped to deconstruct the myth of the autonomous essential self. There seems little reason now to grant a similar sort of organic unity to the idea of community.

The metaphor of the city would also allow us to view a certain amount of change and struggle within a community not as threats to its coherence but as normal activity. The members of many classrooms and academic departments, not to mention disciplines, often seem to share few enough beliefs or practices with one another. Yet these communities exert a very real influence on the discourses of their members. We need to find a way to talk about their workings without first assuming a consensus that may not be there. As Bizzell has recently come to argue: 27

> Healthy discourse communities, like healthy human beings, are also masses of contradictions. . . . We should accustom ourselves to dealing with contradictions, instead of seeking a theory that appears to abrogate them. ("What" 18–19)

I would urge an even more specific and material view of community: one that, like a city, allows for both consensus and conflict, and that holds room for ourselves, our disciplinary colleagues, our university coworkers, *and* our students. In short, I think we need to look more closely at the discourses of communities that are more than communities of discourse alone. While I don't mean to discount the effects of belonging to a discipline, I think that we dangerously abstract and idealize the workings of "academic discourse" by taking the kinds of rarified talk and writing that go on at conferences and in journals as the norm, and viewing many of the other sorts of talk and writing that occur at the university as deviations from or approximations of that standard. It may prove more useful to center our study, instead, on the everyday struggles and mishaps of the talk in our classrooms and departments, with their mixings of sometimes conflicting and sometimes conjoining beliefs and purposes. 28

Indeed, I would suggest that we reserve our uses of *community* to describe the workings of such specific and local groups. We have other words—*discourse, language, voice, ideology, hegemony*—to chart the perhaps less immediate (though still powerful) effects of broader social forces on our talk and writing. None of them is, surely, without its own echoes of meaning, both suggestive and troublesome. But none, I believe, carries with it the sense of like-mindedness and warmth that make community at once such an appealing *and* limiting concept. As teachers and theorists of writing, we need a vocabulary that will allow us to talk about certain forces as social rather than communal, as involving power but not always consent. Such talk could give us a fuller picture of the lived experience of teaching, learning, and writing in a university today. 29

Notes

1. This essay began as part of a 1988 CCCC panel on "Raymond Williams and the Teaching of Composition." My thanks go to my colleagues on that panel, Nicholas Coles and Min-zhan Lu, for their help in conceiving and carrying through this project, as well as to David Bartholomae and Patricia Bizzell for their useful readings of many versions of this text.

2. One might argue that there never really is a "we" for whom the language of the university (or a particular discipline) is fully invented and accessible. Greg Myers, for instance, has shown how two biologists—presumably well-trained scholars long initiated into the practices of their discipline—had to reshape their writings extensively to make them fit in with "what might be said" in the journals of their own field. Like our students, we too must re-invent the university whenever we sit down to write.

3. A growing number of theorists have begun to call this vagueness of community into question. See, for instance: Bazerman on "Some Difficulties in Characterizing Social Phenomena in Writing," Bizzell on "What Is a Discourse Community?" Herzberg on "The Politics of Discourse Communities," and Swales on "Approaching the Concept of Discourse Community."

4. See, for instance, Dell Hymes in *Foundations in Sociolinguistics*: "For our purposes it appears most useful to reserve the notion of community for a local unit, characterized for its members by common locality and primary interaction, and to admit exceptions cautiously" (51).

5. See, for instance, Bizzell on the need for "emphasizing the crucial function of a collective project in unifying the group" ("What" 1), and Bruffee on the notion that "to learn is to work collaboratively . . . among a community of knowledgeable peers" (646).

6. Bruce Robbins makes much the same case in "Professionalism and Politics: Toward Productively Divided Loyalties," as does John Schilb in "When Bricolage Becomes Theory: The Hazards of Ignoring Ideology." Fish too seems recently to be moving towards this position, arguing that an interpretive community is an "engine of change" fueled by the interaction and conflict of the various beliefs and practices that make it up. As he puts it: "Beliefs are not all held at the same level or operative at the same time. Beliefs, if I may use a metaphor, are nested, and on occasion they may affect and even alter one another and so the entire system or network they comprise" ("Change" 429).

Works Cited

Barthes, Roland, *S/Z*. Trans. Richard Miller. New York: Hill, 1974.

Bartholomae, David. "Inventing the University." *When a Writer Can't Write*. Ed. Mike Rose. New York: Guilford, 1985. 134–65.

Bartholomae, David, and Anthony Petrosky. *Facts, Artifacts, and Counterfacts: Theory and Method for a Reading and Writing Course*. Upper Montclair: Boynton/Cook, 1986.

Bazerman, Charles. "Some Difficulties in Characterizing Social Phenomena in Writing." Conference on College Composition and Communication. Atlanta, March 1987.

Bizzell, Patricia. "Foundationalism and Anti-Foundationalism in Composition Studies." *Pre/Text* 7 (Spring/Summer 1986): 37–57.

——. "What Is a Discourse Community?" Penn State Conference on Rhetoric and Composition. University Park, July 1987.

Brodkey, Linda. *Academic Writing as Social Practice*. Philadelphia: Temple UP, 1987.

Bruffee, Kenneth A. "Collaborative Learning and the 'Conversation of Mankind.'" *College English* 46 (November 1984): 635–52.

Coles, Nicholas. "Raymond Williams: Writing Across Borders." Conference on College Composition and Communication. St. Louis, March 1988.

Fish, Stanley. *Is There a Text in This Class?* Cambridge: Harvard UP, 1980.

——. "Change." *South Atlantic Quarterly* 86 (Fall 1987): 423–44.

Herzberg, Bruce. "The Politics of Discourse Communities." Conference on College Composition and Communication. New Orleans, March 1986.

Hirsch, E. D., Jr. *Cultural Literacy: What Every American Needs to Know*. Boston: Houghton, 1987.

Hymes, Dell. *Foundations in Sociolinguistics: An Ethnographic Approach*. Philadelphia: U of Pennsylvania P, 1974.

Lu, Min-zhan. "Teaching the Conventions of Academic Discourse: Structures of Feeling." Conference on College Composition and Communication. St. Louis, March 1988.

Myers, Greg. "The Social Construction of Two Biologists' Proposals." *Written Communication* 2 (July 1985): 219–45.

Porter, James. "Intertextuality and the Discourse Community." *Rhetoric Review* 5 (Fall 1986): 34–47.

Pratt, Mary Louise. "Interpretive Strategies/Strategic Interpretations: On Anglo-American Reader Response Criticism." *Boundary 2* 11.1–2 (Fall/Winter 1982–83): 201–31.

Robbins, Bruce. "Professionalism and Politics: Toward Productively Divided Loyalties." *Profession 85:* 1–9.

Rodriguez, Richard. *Hunger of Memory.* Boston: Godine, 1981.

Schilb, John. "When Bricolage Becomes Theory: The Hazards of Ignoring Ideology." Midwest Modern Language Association. Chicago, November 1986.

Swales, John. "Approaching the Concept of Discourse Community." Conference on College Composition and Communication. Atlanta, March 1987.

Williams, Raymond. *Second Generation.* New York: Horizon, 1964.

———. *The Country and the City.* New York: Oxford UP, 1973.

———. *Keywords: A Vocabulary of Culture and Society.* New York: Oxford UP, 1976.

———. *Marxism and Literature.* New York: Oxford UP, 1977.

Questions for Discussion and Journaling

1. Harris agrees with David Bartholomae that we "write not as isolated individuals but as members of communities whose beliefs, concerns, and practices both instigate and constrain, at least in part, the sorts of things we can say" (para. 4). Later, Harris agrees with Roland Barthes, adding "We do not write simply as individuals, but we do not write simply as members of a community either" (para. 25). What are Harris, Bartholomae, and Barthes saying here? Can you think of some examples to illustrate what they might mean?

2. David Bartholomae and other scholars Harris cites believe that students must learn to write for the university, must learn to write "academic discourse," and that in order to do this, students must "invent the university for the occasion—invent the university, that is, or a branch of it, like history or anthropology or economics or English" (para. 8, quoted from Bartholomae). Do you agree that this is what happens when students write in the university? Can you think of a time when you had to do this? What were you "inventing" as you wrote?

3. Harris agrees with Raymond Williams that we don't "step cleanly and wholly from one community to another" (para. 20) but, instead, always experience a "changing mix" of discourses. Do you think that this view is accurate? Or would you argue that sometimes people must leave one discourse community to be a part of another one?

4. Harris argues that discourse communities are not neat, tidy, and in complete agreement. (This idea is also present in the readings in Chapter 4, particularly in the articles written by Johns and Ward e.) Harris uses this idea to suggest that both teachers and students are at the same time "insiders" and "outsiders"

in academic discourse communities. He even goes so far as to argue that "Our students are no more wholly 'outside' the discourse of the university than we are wholly 'within' it" (para. 24). Do you agree with his claims? Why or why not?

Applying and Exploring Ideas

1. In the section called "Writing as Repositioning," Harris includes passages written by two of his former students in which they discuss their struggles with competing discourses. Write a one- to two-page reflection in which you consider the same questions Harris's students considered: what "languages" you have and where you use them, how they do or don't conflict with the languages of the university, and how your teachers respond if you vary from the kinds of language they expect from you in the university.

2. In a one- to two-page freewrite, reflect on your own literacy practices as you've experienced and developed them, and compare these experiences with what formal, school-based literacy instruction asks of readers and writers.

3. In the "Writing as Repositioning" section, Harris refers to "our students' 'right to their own language'" (para. 24). He is making an implicit reference to a position statement written by the National Council of Teachers of English in 1974, called "Resolution on the Students' Right to Their Own Language." You can read this short resolution by searching online for "NCTE right to their own language." Read this statement and then write a short reflection in which you try to balance the values of academic disciplines, as you've experienced them so far, with the principles outlined in the position statement. As you write, consider Harris's claim that people can and do belong to multiple and competing discourse communities at one time.

Meta Moment

How can you use the ideas you read about in Harris's article to understand and better adjust to conflicts you have experienced, are now experiencing, or might experience in the future? Think of some specific examples.

Studies Explore Whether the Internet Makes Students Better Writers

JOSH KELLER

Keller, Josh. "Studies Explore Whether the Internet Makes Students Better Writers." *The Chronicle of Higher Education*. Chronicle.com, 15 June 2009. Web. 23 Feb. 2010.

Framing the Reading

Most of the articles you have read in this textbook have been scholarly—that is, written by academic researchers and theorists, published in peer-reviewed journals or scholarly books, and intended to be read primarily by academic researchers. Josh Keller's article is different because he is a journalist writing for *The Chronicle of Higher Education*, a newspaper about education. Thus, this article is a good deal shorter than most of the ones you have been reading, and it should be quite a bit easier for you to understand right away.

In this article Keller describes the argument over how the writing students do in online media impacts their school writing. He cites a number of well-known Writing Studies scholars in this piece—Jeffrey Grabill (Michigan State), Kathleen Blake Yancey (Florida State), Andrea Lunsford (Stanford), Paul M. Rogers (George Mason), and Deborah Brandt (University of Wisconsin at Madison). These scholars generally argue for the importance of online composing with new media and suggest that universities need to pay attention to this kind of composing and students' experiences with it. Mark Bauerlein (Emory University) holds an opposing view, contending that composing online is hurting student writing in school and that, as Keller puts it, "students should adapt their writing habits to their college course work, not the other way around" (para. 12). Bauerlein has elsewhere called today's students "the dumbest generation," and, in 2008, he published a book by that title. The argument among Bauerlein and these and other Writing Studies scholars is not confined to Keller's article; more evidence of this ongoing and extremely lively debate can easily be found through a quick Web search.

As you read Keller's article, try to focus on the claims being made about the nature of writing in the university and how it differs from the kinds of writing students seem to be doing elsewhere. In particular, note that several of the Writing Studies scholars Keller cites argue that students find their out-of-class writing to be more "meaningful" and more purposeful and audience-directed than their in-class writing. One student even argues that students who write in *and* out

of the classroom are the ones who really improve as writers. As you consider these claims, you should find it helpful to remember Joseph Harris's ideas from the preceding article in this chapter—that students are members of multiple **discourse communities** at one time, that students are legitimate members of *academic* discourse communities, and that they influence how discourse is used in the academy.

Getting Ready to Read

Before you read, try the following activity:

- Make a list of all the kinds of writing that you do online; remember to include even brief writing like text messaging.

As you read, consider the following question:

- How do the claims made by the scholars being interviewed compare to your own experiences? If, for example, a scholar says that online writing doesn't require sustained critical thought, ask yourself if your own experiences confirm or contradict that claim.

As a student at Stanford University, Mark Otu-teye wrote in any medium he could find. He wrote blog posts, slam poetry, to-do lists, teaching guides, e-mail and Facebook messages, diary entries, short stories. He wrote a poem in computer code, and he wrote a computer program that helped him catalog all the things he had written. 1

But Mr. Otuteye hated writing academic papers. Although he had vague dreams of becoming an English professor, he saw academic writing as a "soulless exercise" that felt like "jumping through hoops." When given a writing assignment in class, he says, he would usually adopt a personal tone and more or less ignore the prompt. 2

"I got away with it," says Mr. Otuteye, who graduated from Stanford in 2006. "Most of the time." 3

The rise of online media has helped raise a new generation of college students who write far more, and in more-diverse forms, than their predecessors 4 did. But the implications of the shift are hotly debated, both for the future of students' writing and for the college curriculum.

Some scholars say that this new writing is more engaged and more con- 5 nected to an audience, and that colleges should encourage students to bring lessons from that writing into the classroom. Others argue that tweets and blog posts enforce bad writing habits and have little relevance to the kind of sustained, focused argument that academic work demands.

A new generation of longitudinal studies, which track large numbers of students over several years, is attempting to settle this argument. The "Stanford Study of Writing," a five-year study of the writing lives of Stanford students — including Mr. Otuteye — is probably the most extensive to date.

In a shorter project, undergraduates in a first-year writing class at Michigan State University were asked to keep a diary of the writing they did in any environment, whether blogging, text messaging, or gaming. For each act of writing over a two-week period, they recorded the time, genre, audience, location, and purpose of their writing.

> The rise of online media has helped raise a new generation of college students who write far 6 more, and in more-diverse forms, than their predecessors did. But the implications of the shift are hotly debated, both for the future of students' writing and for the college curriculum. 7

"What was interesting to us was how small a percentage of the total writing 8 the school writing was," says Jeffrey T. Grabill, the study's lead author, who is director of the Writing in Digital Environments Research Center at Michigan State. In the diaries and in follow-up interviews, he says, students often described their social, out-of-class writing as more persistent and meaningful to them than their in-class work was.

"Digital technologies, computer networks, the Web—all of those things 9 have led to an explosion in writing," Mr. Grabill says. "People write more now than ever. In order to interact on the Web, you have to write."

Kathleen Blake Yancey, a professor of English at Florida State University 10 and a former president of the National Council of Teachers of English, calls the current period "the age of composition" because, she says, new technologies are driving a greater number of people to compose with words and other media than ever before.

"This is a new kind of composing because it's so variegated and because it's 11 so intentionally social," Ms. Yancey says. Although universities may not consider social communication as proper writing, it still has a strong influence on how students learn to write, she says. "We ignore it at our own peril."

But some scholars argue that students should adapt their writing habits to 12 their college course work, not the other way around. Mark Bauerlein, a professor of English at Emory University, cites the reading and writing scores in the National Assessment of Educational Progress, which have remained fairly flat for decades. It is a paradox, he says: "Why is it that with young people reading and writing more words than ever before in human history, we find no gains in reading and writing scores?"

The Right Writing

Determining how students develop as writers, and why they improve or not, is 13 difficult. Analyzing a large enough sample of students to reach general conclusions about how the spread of new technologies affects the writing process, scholars say, is a monumental challenge.

The sheer amount of information that is relevant to a student's writing 14 development is daunting and difficult to collect: formal and informal writing, scraps of notes and diagrams, personal histories, and fleeting conversations and thoughts that never make it onto the printed page.

The Stanford study is trying to collect as much of that material as possible. 15 Starting in 2001, researchers at the university began collecting extensive writing samples from 189 students, roughly 12 percent of the freshman class. Students were given access to a database where they could upload copies of their work, and some were interviewed annually about their writing experiences. By 2006 researchers had amassed nearly 14,000 pieces of writing.

Students in the study "almost always" had more enthusiasm for the writing 16 they were doing outside of class than for their academic work, says Andrea A. Lunsford, the study's director. Mr. Otuteye submitted about 700 pieces of writing and became the study's most prolific contributor.

The report's authors say they included nonacademic work to better investi- 17 gate the links between academic and nonacademic writing in students' writing development. One of the largest existing longitudinal studies of student writing, which started at Harvard University in the late 1990s, limited its sample to academic writing, which prevented researchers from drawing direct conclusions about that done outside of class.

In looking at students' out-of-class writing, the Stanford researchers say 18 they found several traits that were distinct from in-class work. Not surprisingly, the writing was self-directed; it was often used to connect with peers, as in social networks; and it usually had a broader audience.

The writing was also often associated with accomplishing an immediate, 19 concrete goal, such as organizing a group of people or accomplishing a political end, says Paul M. Rogers, one of the study's authors. The immediacy might help explain why students stayed so engaged, he says. "When you talked to them about their out-of-class writing, they would talk about writing to coordinate out-of-class activity," says Mr. Rogers, an assistant professor of English at George Mason University. "A lot of them were a lot more conscious of the effect their writing was having on other people."

Mr. Rogers believes from interviews with students that the data in the study 20 will help show that students routinely learn the basics of writing concepts wherever they write the most. For instance, he says, students who compose messages for an audience of their peers on a social-networking Web site were forced to be acutely aware of issues like audience, tone, and voice.

"The out-of-class writing actually made them more conscious of the things 21
writing teachers want them to think about," the professor says.

Mr. Otuteye, who recently started a company that develops Web applica- 22
tions, says he paid close attention to the writing skills of his peers at Stanford
as the co-founder of a poetry slam. It was the students who took their out-of-
class writing seriously who made the most progress, he says. "Everybody was
writing in class, but the people who were writing out of and inside of class, that
was sort of critical to accelerating their growth as writers."

Although analysis of the Stanford study is still at an early stage, other schol- 23
ars say they would like to start similar studies. At the University of California,
several writing researchers say they are trying to get financial support for a
longitudinal study of 300 students on the campuses in Irvine, Santa Barbara,
and Davis.

Curricular Implications

The implications of the change in students' writing habits for writing and litera- 24
ture curricula are up for debate. Much of the argument turns on whether online
writing should be seen as a welcome new direction or a harmful distraction.

Mr. Grabill, from Michigan State, says college writing instruction should 25
have two goals: to help students become better academic writers, and to help
them become better writers in the outside world. The second, broader goal is
often lost, he says, either because it is seen as not the college's responsibility, or
because it seems unnecessary.

"The unstated assumption there is that if you can write a good essay for 26
your literature professor, you can write anything," Mr. Grabill says. "That's
utter nonsense."

The writing done outside of class is, in some ways, the opposite of a tra- 27
ditional academic paper, he says. Much out-of-class writing, he says, is for a
broad audience instead of a single professor, tries to solve real-world problems
rather than accomplish academic goals, and resembles a conversation more
than an argument.

Rather than being seen as an impoverished, secondary form, online writing 28
should be seen as "the new normal," he says, and treated in the curriculum as
such: "The writing that students do in their lives is a tremendous resource."

Ms. Yancey, at Florida State, says out-of-class writing can be used in a class- 29
room setting to help students draw connections among disparate types of writing. In one exercise she uses, students are asked to trace the spread of a claim
from an academic journal to less prestigious forms of media, like magazines and
newspapers, in order to see how arguments are diluted. In another, students are
asked to pursue the answer to a research question using only blogs, and to create
a map showing how they know if certain information is trustworthy or not.

The idea, she says, is to avoid creating a "fire wall" between in-class and 30
out-of-class writing.

"If we don't invite students to figure out the lessons they've learned from that 31
writing outside of school and bring those inside of school, what will happen is

only the very bright students" will do it themselves, Ms. Yancey says. "It's the rest of the population that we're worried about."

Writing in electronic media probably does benefit struggling students in a   32 rudimentary way, says Emory's Mr. Bauerlein, because they are at least forced to string sentences together: "For those kids who wouldn't be writing any words anyway, that's going to improve their very low-level skills."

But he spends more of his time correcting, not integrating, the writing habits   33 that students pick up outside of class. The students in his English courses often turn in papers that are "stylistically impoverished," and the Internet is partly to blame, he says. Writing for one's peers online, he says, encourages the kind of quick, unfocused thought that results in a scarcity of coherent sentences and a limited vocabulary.

"When you are writing so much to your peers, you're writing to other   34 17-year-olds, so your vocabulary is going to be the conventional vocabulary of the 17-year-old idiom," Mr. Bauerlein says.

Students must be taught to home in on the words they write and to resist the   35 tendency to move quickly from sentence to sentence, he says. Writing scholars, too, should temper their enthusiasm for new technologies before they have fully understood the implications, he says. Claims that new forms of writing should take a greater prominence in the curriculum, he says, are premature.

"The sweeping nature of their pronouncements to me is either grandiose or   36 flatulent, or you could say that this is a little irresponsible to be pushing for practices so hard that are so new," Mr. Bauerlein says. "We don't know what the implications of these things will be. Slow down!"

Deborah Brandt, a professor of English at the University of Wisconsin at   37 Madison who studies the recent history of reading and writing, says the growth of writing online should be seen as part of a broader cultural shift toward mass authorship. Some of the resistance to a more writing-centered curriculum, she says, is based on the view that writing without reading can be dangerous because students will be untethered to previous thought, and reading levels will decline.

But that view, she says, is "being challenged by the literacy of young people,   38 which is being developed primarily by their writing. They're going to be reading, but they're going to be reading to write, and not to be shaped by what they read."

Questions for Discussion and Journaling

1. Keller describes two competing points of view in this article: (1) the "new writing" students are now doing is "more engaged and more connected to an audience, and that colleges should encourage students to bring lessons from that writing into the classroom" (para. 5) versus (2) "tweets and blog posts enforce

bad writing habits and have little relevance to the kind of sustained, focused argument that academic work demands" (para. 5) Which view do you most agree with, and why?

2. This article and some of the research it reports suggest that students are doing quite a lot of writing outside of school. Do you believe that this is an accurate representation? Why or why not?

3. Researchers cited in this article found that out-of-class writing has a broader audience than in-class writing and accomplishes clear goals. For this reason, researchers like Paul Rogers believe that teachers should draw on what students do outside of class in order to help them with concepts like writing appropriately for a given audience. Do you agree that there is such a radical difference in audience and purpose between in-school and out-of-school writing? If so, why is this? Is it inevitable, or could (should?) this be changed?

Applying and Exploring Ideas

1. Go online and research more of Bauerlein's arguments about your generation's writing skills (you might start by searching on the title of his book, *The Dumbest Generation*). In two to three pages, describe some of the claims that Bauerlein makes and respond to them.

2. Bauerlein argues that the kinds of writing that students do online leads them to write school papers that are "stylistically impoverished," displaying "quick, unfocused thoughts." Why not test his claim? Look at a variety of kinds of online composing that students might do (blogging, Facebooking, texting, and so on). Pick three or four different kinds of online texts and compare them. Do they all use the same style? Do they use similar kinds of word choice? Do they share the same tone? Are they formatted similarly? Once you've done this brief analysis, write up what you find and then respond to Bauerlein: Does writing online lead to "stylistically impoverished" writing?

3. Respond to Paul Rogers's claim that out-of-class writing has broader audiences and accomplishes clearer goals than school writing: Think up three assignments teachers might give that you would see as meaningful, purposeful, and audience-driven. Describe them carefully, and then discuss what, if anything, makes them different from the assignments students are typically given in school. How do you think your current instructors would respond to your ideas? How would your classmates respond?

Meta Moment

Try to imagine some ways that you can use your skill as a writer of nonacademic, online texts to inform your school writing.

Reading and Writing without Authority

ANN M. PENROSE

CHERYL GEISLER

Penrose, Ann M., and Cheryl Geisler. "Reading and Writing without Authority." *College Composition and Communication* 45.4 (1994): 505–20. Print.

Framing the Reading

Ann Penrose is a professor of English at North Carolina State University, where she has taught since 1987. She earned a Ph.D. in Rhetoric from Carnegie Mellon in 1987, and she has written two books (*Hearing Ourselves Think: Cognitive Research in the College Writing Classroom* [1993] and, with Steven Katz, *Writing in the Sciences: Exploring Conventions of Scientific Discourse* [2004]) as well as numerous articles about writing. Cheryl Geisler also earned her Ph.D. at Carnegie Mellon (in 1986) and is now head of the Department of Language, Literature, and Communication and joint Professor of Rhetoric and Information Technology at Rensselaer Polytechnic Institute. Like Penrose, she has written several books (with Davida Charney and others, *Having Your Say* [2005]; *Analyzing Streams of Language: Twelve Steps to the Systematic Coding of Text, Talk and Other Verbal Data* [2003]; *Academic Literacy and the Nature of Expertise: Reading, Writing, and Knowing in Academic Philosophy* [1994]; and with David Kaufer and Christine Neuwirth, *Arguing from Sources: Exploring Issues through Reading and Writing* [1989]).

In the article reprinted in this chapter, Penrose and Geisler examine how the text of a first-year student (Janet) differs from a text on the same subject written by a doctoral student (Roger). Previous research has suggested that students like Janet simply need to gain more knowledge about a topic in order to write about it with more **authority**. In this study, Penrose and Geisler found that, while it would have been helpful for Janet to know more about the topic, her writing lacked authority for other reasons. Specifically, they argue that Janet and Roger had very different understandings of what knowledge is and how it is constructed.

(Their claims in this regard should be familiar to you if you read Chapter 1 of this textbook.)

Getting Ready to Read

Before you read, try the following activity:

- Consider a time when you wrote a research paper and felt like your sources were controlling you—in other words, when you felt like you didn't know what to do with the sources you found.

As you read, consider the following questions:

- How did Janet's and Roger's texts differ?
- What do Janet and Roger each believe about knowledge? (As always, it will be helpful for you to consider your own writing and your own view of knowledge as you read.)

By early March, Janet is ready to set aside the notecards she's been laboring over since midwinter. She begins to write: 1

> This paper will define paternalism and discuss its justification. Paternalism is the action of one person interfering with another person's actions or thoughts to help him. The person who interferes, called the paternalist, breaks moral rules of independency because he restricts the other person's freedom without that person's consent. He does it, however, in a fatherly, benevolent way, and assumes that the person being restrained will appreciate the action later.

Across town a few days later, Roger makes a similar decision. Setting aside his scrawled pages of notes, he, too, begins his text:

> Consider the following situations:
>
> Situation One: Mister N, a member of a religious sect which strictly forbids blood transfusions, is involved in a serious automobile accident and loses a large amount of blood. On arriving at the hospital, he is still conscious and informs the doctor that his religion forbids blood transfusions. Immediately thereafter he faints from loss of blood. The doctor believes that if Mister N is not given a transfusion he will die. Thereupon, the doctor arranges for and carries out the blood transfusion. Is the doctor right in doing this? [Two more cases are presented.] . . .
>
> Sometimes paternalistic actions seem justified, and sometimes not; but always, paternalism seems at least to be a bit disquieting . . . The authors whose efforts will be reviewed here have undertaken the task of trying to spell out conditions which must be satisfied for paternalistic actions to be justified . . . [S]o a preliminary task is that of giving an account of what are paternalistic actions; that of

settling on a definition in order to gain a clearer notion of what we are talking about, and of what, if anything, has to be justified.

The contrast between these two introductions is striking. Though they share a common focus on the definition and justification of paternalism, Janet's text views the definition and justificatory conditions as established truths, while Roger introduces them as matters yet to be resolved. Janet's text presents itself as a straightforward report about what paternalism "is" ("the action of one person interfering with another") and what a paternalist "does" ("breaks moral rules of independency"). Janet's only excursion into metadiscourse—discourse about the text itself and its context—is the opening noun, "this paper," which, by its very depersonalization, locates the authority for its claims in a material artifact rather than its human author, Janet herself. Roger's introduction, by contrast, makes no explicit claims about what paternalism is or isn't, although eventually making such claims is clearly his intent. Instead, his text foregrounds human agents: doctors, patients, and others in paternalistic relationships, the authors of other texts on paternalism, and a "we" who share an upcoming task of exploration. Roger's text only conditionally promises to arrive at a resolution to the "disquieting situation" upon which he and his readers have stumbled. Janet's text promises the facts, with no acknowledgement that there are, or ever were, matters to be resolved.

> The purpose of our study was to investigate how . . . differences in authority are played out in the academic sphere. We were particularly interested in how the lack of authority shapes the writing and reading practices students adopt.

Readers will not be surprised to learn that the differences between these two texts are rooted in differences between their authors' circumstances. At the time of this study, Janet was a college freshman; Roger was completing his doctoral work in philosophy. Janet knew nothing about the study of ethics; Roger had become steeped in the tradition. Roger had accumulated knowledge of the domain, its issues and its customs; Janet had not. Roger knew how to write as an authority inside the conversation of ethics; Janet was an outsider looking in.

We had recruited Roger and Janet for our study of academic expertise because their respective positions in the academy place them in different relationships with respect to academic knowledge. The basis for this difference is complex. Roger has authority in this domain not only by virtue of his disciplinary knowledge, but also by virtue of the educational credentials through which he has earned the right to speak in this community.[1] The distribution of this knowledge and these credentials is, in turn, related to factors such as age and gender. Confidence in one's own authority is assumed to increase generally with age, but gender may also influence this development. Recent studies provide strong evidence of contrasting epistemologies, one perspective valuing community and connection, the other emphasizing competition and separateness.

What it means to be an insider in the academic domain has largely been defined by the objective, competitive stance of mainstream academic argument at the expense of the personal knowledge and connective goals in which feminist epistemologies are grounded.[2] In short, a number of complex variables are likely to have influenced the differing degrees of authority assumed by Roger and Janet in this context. The purpose of our study was to investigate how such differences in authority are played out in the academic sphere. We were particularly interested in how the lack of authority shapes the writing and reading practices students adopt. We expected that Janet's position as outsider in the academic context would lead her to interact with academic texts in ways that would distinguish her from Roger, an insider, and further, that these process differences could not be explained simply by pointing to differences in topic knowledge.[3]

Observing the Effects of Authority

To observe the effects of differences in authority, we asked Janet and Roger to 5 work on the same academic task in the domain of philosophical ethics: Given a set of eight scholarly articles on paternalism by five different authors, they were to write a paper for an educated general audience "discussing the current state of thinking on paternalism." Each writer worked on the task at his or her own pace over the course of a semester, turning on a tape recorder and "thinking aloud" whenever they worked. They met with a member of the research team after each work session to discuss their goals, plans, progress and problems. Our profiles of these writers are based on our reading of their writing session protocols, interview transcripts, written notes and drafts.

We found Roger's reading and writing behaviors to be consistent with views 6 of knowledge as constructed. Roger seems to operate with an awareness that texts and knowledge claims are authored and negotiable. Janet's approach was consistent with a more traditional information-transfer model in which texts are definitive and unassailable. The specific differences we noticed led us to articulate four epistemological premises which seem part of Roger's worldview but not Janet's:

Texts are authored.

Authors present knowledge in the form of claims.

Knowledge claims can conflict.

Knowledge claims can be tested.

We organize our observations around these premises in the following sections. In brief, we found that Janet and Roger focused on different issues when reading, set different goals for writing, used evidence for different purposes, and developed quite different understandings of the subject matter they worked with. We will argue that these process differences are in large part a function of Janet and Roger's contrasting views of their own authority in this domain and of the role of human agents in the construction of knowledge generally.

Texts Are Authored

As the excerpts from his introduction indicate, Roger saw his task as one of 7
examining a set of alternative positions which had been put forward by prior
authors on paternalism. This focus on the authorship of knowledge claims per-
vaded Roger's reading, writing and thinking. In his notes, definitional features
are organized by author; his introductory section explicitly acknowledges the
role of author as claim-maker ("So each of our authors is forced in the nature
of the case to perform two tasks—each first provides a definition . . . and each
then provides an account of how paternalistic actions so defined are to be
justified"); and the 74 references to authors in Roger's final text each assert a
relationship between author and claim:

> First, nothing in [this definition] excludes actual consent at or before the time of
> action, though Gert and Culver clearly seem to think it does.
>
> Komrad . . . sees the problem quite differently, and seeks to give what appears to
> be intended as a small-blanket justification of specifically medical paternalism.

In essence, the names of the authors provided Roger with the basic categories
by which he organized his knowledge.

In contrast, Janet mentions none of the authors in her draft (although an 8
occasional set of quotation marks indicates she did have some sense of borrowing). The sections of her text are organized topically, as indicated by topic
sentences such as "Paternalism can exist between different kinds of people"
and "Paternalism does not always include actions that restrict the same people who are being helped." A transitional paragraph makes this arrangement
explicit:

> In the first part of this paper I gave descriptions of factors that make an act pater-
> nalistic. In this part I will discuss ways for a paternalist to determine if his acts
> are justified . . .

Janet's notecards were labeled by topic ("morality"; "consent"; "impure paternalism") and only sporadically included authorship information. In her tape
recordings, author names were mentioned an average of 4.6 times per thousand
words of transcript, only one-quarter as often as Roger (15.8 mentions/1000
words). The majority of these references occurred in the initial reading phase;
once Janet began to write her draft, she rarely referred to either the authors or
the articles.[4]

That Janet mentioned authors at all is significant. She occasionally used 9
author names as identifiers in her early notes (e.g., "G-C [Gert-Culver] definition") but began to pay more attention to authors around the time she read the
third article in the corpus, in which James Childress explicitly attacks the positions taken in the preceding articles (Childress' piece is subtitled "A Critique
of the Gert-Culver Definition of Paternalism"). Reading the Childress critique
seemed to sensitize Janet to the authorship issue; at this point in her think-
aloud transcripts she began to demonstrate a sense of authors "speaking" in
this literature. (Ellipses indicate pauses, not deletions.)

so Gert is saying that the only time that you can really call paternalistic . . . is when one person's qualified . . .

so Childress, the Gert Culver critique . . . says that example . . . um . . . young child helping drunk parent . . .

This sense of conversation was not consistently maintained, however, and is clearly not a central theme in Janet's transcripts. More typically, she referred to authors with a generic *it* ("on page twenty . . . it says . . .") or *they* ("I don't know what they're talking about"), though only one of the seven articles is co-authored. She often referred to the Childress article as "the critique" ("so for the critique . . . says that . . ."). These generic references suggest that Janet saw the corpus of articles (collected in a loose-leaf binder) as a single definitive source rather than as a set of multiple voices in conversation. This perception was brought home to us most dramatically in her transcripts and interview comments, where she often made reference to "the book" rather than to individual authors or articles: "I suppose I could steal [an example] from the book"; ". . . and they don't talk about that anywhere else in the whole book"; "I still don't think [my paper] really is [interesting] . . . but it's better than the book I read."[5]

Authors Present Knowledge in the Form of Claims

Roger saw the knowledge he gleaned from texts as claims to be argued for. For him, reading was a process of identifying, sorting, and evaluating the claims made by the various authors. This required him to analyze an author's claims into parts and to think about the validity of each part separately. It also required him to be able to assign a provisional truth status to a claim, a status that could change as his work progressed. In an early session, for example, Roger voiced the suspicion that his current definition of paternalism, which included two conditions—that it be against the beneficiary's will, and that it be for the beneficiary's good—was incomplete. By the next session he had tentatively decided to solve this problem by adding a third "morality condition" suggested by, but not the same as, the condition given by the authors Gert and Culver. In doing so, he was rejecting an alternative position put forward by the author Childress. Towards the end of the project, however, he reversed himself, arguing as he drafted his paper that the definition of paternalism should not include this third "morality condition." Thus, in his think-aloud protocols, we found Roger making distinctions, embracing or rejecting claims tentatively, and flatly changing his mind, all in ways consistent with his view of truth as multivalent.   10

Janet's goal, however, was not to evaluate claims but to search for facts. Claims and proposals in the readings often became "facts" in Janet's notes. For example, in response to a statement by Childress that "Some arguments for the legal prohibition of some sexual acts between consenting adults hold that such acts are wrong even if they do not harm others or violate principles of justice and fairness," Janet wrote a note that stripped away the rhetorical context: "Some acts are wrong even if they do not harm others." Similarly, Childress'   11 point, "Some arguments for the prohibition of contraception . . . sterilization and abortion contend that they are inherently immoral" became, in Janet's notes: "Things that are inherently immoral such as contraception sterilization and abortion." In ignoring both the original and current rhetorical contexts, Janet created a series of unauthored and undisputed facts.

This is not to say that Janet was unreflective. On the contrary, her protocol   12
transcripts contain numerous instances of evaluation and response:

> I don't think that that um . . . governments . . . governments should not interfere
> with parents and children . . . unless children are being abused or seek . . . seek
> seek help . . .
>
> If someone younger were reading this . . . younger were reading this thing would
> have different opinions.

Such comments demonstrate Janet's ability and inclination to exercise critical evaluation, but these reflections were uniformly absent from her written text, suggesting she did not consider them relevant to the task at hand. As a consequence, her final text not only stripped away any evidence of the role of other authors in constructing the domain knowledge of ethics, it also eliminated any evidence of her own role.

Knowledge Claims Can Conflict

Roger's goal of sorting and evaluating the various claims in the literature   13
enabled him to detect controversies in the readings and to recognize these controversies as critical areas for his own work. For example, issues such as the role of consent and the need for a "morality condition," alluded to above, are debated in the readings and became central concerns in Roger's thinking. An early interview comment indicates that he saw the debates in the literature as his starting points:

> you have to look at the literature first [. . .] [it] suggests to me ideas of what criticisms I might want to make . . . how I might want to view the different definitions
> say . . . or justifications in relation to one another . . . what's better . . . what's
> worse . . . who took what into account . . . um . . . it's just a matter of generating . . . as it were preliminary hints of what to say when you do the talking.

Janet reacted to controversy in the readings quite differently. She did notice   14
some disagreement among these authors, particularly when differences were clearly signaled as in the Childress critique. But it was clear from her interview comments that Janet was uncomfortable with controversy and had few strategies for dealing with it. She describes a disagreement over the issue of morality in the following interview excerpt:

> like one of them was saying that um . . . in order to do a paternalistic act you have
> to be immoral . . . and then I think somebody else said you don't necessarily . . . I
> don't understand that . . . like I don't understand why if you're doing something
> to help somebody . . . and when . . . what you're doing is going to bring about
> such a good consequence compared to what's going to happen if you don't act . . .

> I don't see that as being immoral . . . and they say well if you like do something against someone else's will . . . then it's immoral and in order to be paternalistic you have to always . . . like I don't understand that in paternalism . . .

Though Janet clearly sides with one of the two positions, the fact that the authors do not agree presented her with a dilemma. Her first inclination was to simply report both sides. She asked the interviewer, "do you want a definite decision . . . definition . . . can I like . . . say I don't know . . . and give both sides?" The interviewer told Janet she would need to resolve this issue and to build her own definition. Consequently, Janet began her next work session by announcing a plan to go through her notes and write down "only what I think I agree with and it's going to be my definition."

This approach helped Janet position herself in the ongoing conversation,   15 but unlike Roger who used such controversies as a springboard from which to develop his own position, Janet set out to align herself with one of the positions already available. Unfortunately, this strategy was not so straightforward. On the issue of whether or not the paternalist must be "qualified" in some way in order for an act to be considered paternalistic, Janet had trouble deciding which view to agree with:

> so ah . . . I . . . I agree . . . with critique . . . that the Gert Culver definition number two . . . that paternalist is qualified . . . is a bunch of baloney . . . is stupid . . .

> so um . . . Childress, the Gert Culver critique . . . says that example . . . young child helping drunk parent . . . so the purpose of this example is to show that someone who's NOT qualified can help [. . .] it doesn't prove anything . . . cause . . . this doesn't prove anything . . . cause . . . um . . . I don't think that a child could do anything for a parent without the parent's consent [. . .] so I think that the critique is not good . . .

Janet was still puzzling over this point two sessions later as she reread her notes:

> so here I'm saying he doesn't have to be qualified . . . and here I'm saying . . . that you HAVE to be qualified . . . here I'm saying the critique is not good . . . here I'm saying I agree with the critique . . . so how am I supposed to write this paper if I keep changing my mind? . . . this is ridiculous . . .

At this point, Janet went through the alternatives once again and concluded that she agreed with Gert and Culver that the paternalist must be qualified to act, but with "a variation." She did not carry out this rather expert move, however; the "variation" was never articulated and the issue is not mentioned at all in Janet's final draft. This "choosing sides" strategy for handling controversy is consistent with Janet's "outsider" view of her own authorship—author as reporter rather than creator—and the corresponding goal to report only that which is true. In those cases when she was able to determine which of two conflicting positions was correct, the topic made it into her paper. If she was unable to make this determination, however, the topic was omitted. This strategy clearly leaves Janet on the outside looking in. Though she weighed each view carefully, was not afraid to disagree, and at one point even considered formulating a "variation" of her own, Janet made no sustained attempt to insert herself into this conversation when she wrote.

Knowledge Claims Can Be Tested

Janet's outsider position was also evident in her use of examples. While Roger continually tested authors' claims through the use of examples and test cases, Janet used examples only to clarify or illustrate. She viewed "the book" as something to be understood and reported, not questioned or elaborated on. Examples occupy an important position in the domain of ethics, a point Roger makes in his introduction: "Examples . . . play a great role in writings about paternalism. They serve both to inspire insight and to correct mistaken definitions." In this literature, cases of people paternalizing and being paternalized abound. Roger used cases not only to clarify issues raised in the readings, but to generate new issues and to test their limits, as in the following excerpt, where he considers the "morality condition" mentioned earlier: [16]

> I'll have to discuss whether there is really a need for a morality condition [. . .] you recall the case of the two competitors, A . . . and B, . . . where B doesn't want A to withdraw . . . but A does want to withdraw for B's good [. . .] I don't know whether that's paternalism or not . . . I'm inclined to think it isn't paternalism . . . though it's something closely related . . . similar in spirit . . . it's only similar insofar as it's intended for the other person's good and B is at clash with his will . . .
>
> now on some of the definitions we've got . . . that would count as paternalism . . . but I think this is enough to say . . . that that's too broad . . . because I don't think this is . . . not like a standard case of paternalism . . . though it does satisfy those conditions and is for that reason . . . to the extent we are tempted to think that perhaps it falls under the definition of paternalism . . .

Roger used the case of the two competitors to compare the various positions in the literature and explore the concept of paternalism itself. He had used this case before; it appeared a number of times in his text and transcripts. He was thus able to integrate a number of issues by relating them all to this and a handful of other instances. In all, only seven distinct cases figure prominently in Roger's work.[6]

In contrast, Janet used twenty-four distinct cases to think through her ideas, rarely considering any particular case more than once. She regularly inserted examples in her paper, one or two for each point she made, noting "examples are important cause if someone's reading it . . . they don't understand . . . that's like how [we] make them understand." In addition to this explanatory purpose, examples sometimes served a clarifying function for Janet herself. At one point, to answer a question prompted by one of the readings, "Do all paternalistic acts deceive, break a promise or cheat?" Janet consulted a list of examples she had generated, decided that forcing a child to eat vegetables didn't fit any of those categories, and concluded "all paternalistic acts do *not* deceive, break a promise or cheat." She did not seem to see, however, that she was taking issue [17] with a defining condition proposed by one of the authors; her goal was simply to determine the truth of the matter. She concluded that the condition didn't hold and therefore did not include it in her final paper. We found it encouraging that Janet thought to use examples to help her understand her source material, but because she didn't have the goal of responding to these authors she failed to take advantage of this generative practice. Because she created new examples for every point she covered, she was not able to use them to help examine connections and contrasts. The topic remained for Janet a series of isolated facts and issues. Examples helped her move down the ladder of abstraction but never up, whereas they enabled Roger to run up and down the ladder at will, constructing categories at one moment, testing and illustrating key features the next.

Reading and Writing Without Authority

On close examination, Janet's reading strategies were more "expert" than we would have predicted: She did develop some sense of authors speaking to one another in these readings; she often reflected on and evaluated the illustrative examples they offered; she even developed examples of her own to clarify, and in one case to test and reject a defining condition proposed by one of the authors. Granted, these strategies were used haphazardly, but what is more striking is that none of this rhetorical sophistication was reflected in Janet's writing. Janet's approach to this task revealed that she saw no role for herself in this conversation. She responded to sample cases or proposed definitions only in passing as she read; these responses did not become central to her work and do not appear in her paper. Not even when her examples clearly "disproved" another author's position did she step into the conversation to say so. 18

As we noted earlier, feminist theorists have questioned the validity of the adversarial, "monologic" mode of argument that dominates academic discourse, offering alternative models which value connection and negotiation over confrontation, the personal and contextual over the impersonal and abstract. But Janet's approach to the paternalism task cannot be said to fulfill either of these models. She has not rejected argumentative discourse in favor of personal response or consensus building but has kept herself out of the discussion altogether. Both discourse modes assume a basic sense of personal identity and authority on the part of the writer. In the confrontational mode, writers rely on their own authority to form judgments about the work of others; in the collaborative mode, writers must value their own experiences and responses in order to connect with others (Lamb 16). Janet is reluctant to do either. 19

Janet seemed well aware of the customary split between public and personal, and continually resisted inserting herself in the text. In one session, she changed an example from first to third person ("it's not supposed to be in first person . . . that's silly"), rejected a campus example as frivolous ("I mean requiring freshmen to go on the fifteen or nineteen meal contract is a silly example"), and complained about how hard it was to come up with alternative examples ("I'm thinking of examples I can relate to . . . [un]fortunately they're different from 20 the examples that the readers can relate to . . ."). And in perhaps the most obvious instance of excluding herself from the conversation, Janet deleted from her draft a pair of terms she had developed to help explain a complex distinction proposed by one of the authors, saying "Why did I bring in 'indirect' [paternalism]? . . . That's my own word . . . I don't think I can just do that."

Janet's approach illustrates the degree to which such personal authority is 21 denied in school contexts. It is generally acknowledged that students enter college classrooms with extensive experience in, and often a strong commitment to, an information-transfer model of education which clearly clashes with current constructivist views of knowledge (Bizzell, "Cognition"; Bruffee; Witte). Certainly these contrasting views have personal and political implications: they shape learner attitudes and self-concepts and determine the extent of the power that individuals are willing to claim within the educational and larger social system. But our analyses of Janet and Roger suggest as well a more direct influence on reading and writing processes. These contrasting theories of knowledge and their corresponding assumptions about individual authority shape the way individuals approach intellectual tasks. Students like Janet who see all texts (except their own) as containing "the truth," rather than as authored and subject to interpretation and criticism, will of course see the objective report as the only conceivable response to a reading-writing assignment. Janet's "objective report" interpretation can in fact be extracted from our task directions, which stated that readers "will want to understand what paternalism is" and "under what conditions it can be justified." But she ignored other components of the task: "Summarize and evaluate the definitions of paternalism given in the first part of the corpus, and formulate your own definition." She selectively attended to those guidelines that fit with her information-transfer model, ignoring those that didn't.

The information-transfer model leaves little room for provisional or hypo- 22 thetical thinking. Roger, speaking as an authority, can be playful, tentative, exploratory. He can, and does, change his mind as his examples point up inconsistencies in his thinking. Janet has no such luxury. She must find the truth. And, while she acknowledges no authority of her own, she must speak authoritatively. Examine the tone of her conclusion:

> The methods mentioned throughout the second part of this paper can be used by the paternalist to decide when to act and how much to act. They can also be used by others to determine whether or not the paternalist is justified.

Janet writes the definitive text, a handbook for potential paternalists.

Teaching Towards Authority

Writing teachers, ourselves included, would be quick to describe Roger's 23 approach to this task as the more sophisticated of the two, but notice that Janet's was by far the more difficult—she sought to extract truth on an issue that cannot be so reduced. Once this truth-reporting goal was set, Janet did not have the option of discussing these authors as individuals in her paper; she could not address the inconsistencies she noticed in the readings; she was not free to present an opinion or response of her own. Her view of the academic enterprise, and of her role in that enterprise, precludes all these options.

At first glance it would seem that the solution, the way to help students like 24 Janet enter these academic conversations, lies not in the writing curriculum but in the content areas. The traditional response to the problem of lack of authority is to try to increase the domain knowledge upon which authority is supposedly founded. Indeed, cognitive research has demonstrated the critical influence of domain knowledge on comprehension and recall (see Wilson and Anderson for a review) and on such components of writing performance as topic choice (Gradwohl and Schumacher), organization (Langer), and coherence (Newell and Winograd). Under the domain knowledge explanation, the novice's poor command of the subject matter discourages him or her from adopting the sense of authority needed to question or respond to the texts of others. It is certainly the case that Roger's knowledge of the domain afforded him great advantages in this situation. He was familiar with common assumptions and stock issues in the field of ethics and could easily draw analogies to related topics. But we oversimplify if we attribute all of the novice writer's difficulties to a lack of domain knowledge. Simply teaching Janet more about the issue of paternalism or the field of ethics will not help her engage more productively with these texts. She is already sensitive to nuances in this discussion, as evidenced by her recognition of inconsistencies, and she already has a storehouse of relevant examples she could use to explore these issues. What she doesn't have is an understanding of the academic enterprise in which this personal knowledge has value. When we argue that the remedy for students' problems with authority is an increase in their domain knowledge, we implicitly accept their version of the information-transfer model, in which personal knowledge is denied.

We would instead argue for the role of rhetorical knowledge in the devel- 25 opment of authority. In order for Janet to take authority in this or any other situation, she needs to believe there is authority to spare—that there is room for many voices. She needs to understand the development of knowledge as a communal and continual process. Thus an alternative to the information-transfer model would be to insist on more interactive models of education in which a genuine rhetorical perspective is not only taught but enacted. One such model aims to encourage and value students' individual voices in class discussion, conferences, and written feedback, often restructuring the classroom to include peer interaction and group decision-making. The basic writing course developed by Bartholomae and Petrosky at the University of Pittsburgh, for example, explicitly aims to distribute authority more evenly in the classroom by having students decide on the topics to be explored, the concepts to be valued, even the terminology to be used—practices which require students to participate as insiders by creating the community around themselves, rather than trying to "break in" from the outside. Restructuring the environment in these or other ways seems essential if we are to help students come to see themselves as participants in, rather than observers of, the construction of knowledge.

Students can also come to recognize that knowledge develops through 26
conversation and debate by actively analyzing authors' assumptions and
motivations and the situations in which they work. Some pedagogies aim to
develop this understanding through the rhetorical analysis of texts, others
through self-conscious exploration of writers' processes and contexts. Haas
("Facts"), for example, asks students to interview members of particular discourse communities about how they choose, read, evaluate and acknowledge
other authors' texts. Greene has students analyze citation practices, structural
conventions, and other discourse features for clues to disciplinary patterns of
inquiry, and encourages students to "mine" the texts they read for strategies
they may in turn employ in their own writing. Grounded in both traditional
rhetorical theory and recent sociocognitive research, such activities aim to
create a context in which students see themselves as authors, reading and
writing alongside other authors in the development of community knowledge
and norms. In such a context we can build on Janet's developing rhetorical awareness by asking her to look for places where authors are speaking
to one another—that is, by placing value on those disagreements she has
noticed in reading. Some recent instructional approaches offer explicit support for the complex task of negotiating multiple positions. Higgins has students study and practice the synthesizing strategies of experienced writers,
which she demonstrates via think-aloud protocol transcripts of writers at
work. The textbook by Kaufer, Geisler, and Neuwirth, based on the research
program that includes these case studies, teaches students to construct tables
of agreements and disagreements and then synthesis trees from which they
develop their own contributions to the literature. We can build on Janet's use
of examples in this context too, by encouraging her to compare authors via a
common set of examples or principles.

Belenky and her colleagues report that the received knowledge perspec- 27
tive rarely persisted for long among their college-aged subjects, whose selective colleges provided the sort of "pluralistic and intellectually challenging
environments" that tend to "dislodge" this perspective (43). The instructional
approaches mentioned here are designed to create such environments in individual classrooms—to help students become aware of ongoing textual conversations and take part in those conversations. Helping students see themselves as
insiders enables them to engage in types of thinking that are denied them under
the information-transfer model. Only when a student such as Janet sees herself
and others as authors negotiating meaning will she think to acknowledge and
build upon the inconsistencies she notices, to use her store of examples genera-
tively, to examine and value her own responses to the claims of others.

Acknowledgments

We are grateful to several anonymous reviewers whose comments influenced
our thinking about academic authority and our understanding of the writers
we describe in this piece. These writers were participants in the WARRANT
Project, a research and curriculum development project at Carnegie Mellon

University, sponsored in part by a grant from the Fund for the Improvement of Postsecondary Education. Principal investigators were D. S. Kaufer, C. M. Neuwirth, C. Geisler, and P. K. Covey. This component of the project included four case study subjects, paid volunteers recruited from freshman writing classes at CMU and from the philosophy departments at CMU and the University of Pittsburgh. See Geisler (*Academic Literacy;* "Sociocognitive") and Kaufer and Geisler for further discussion of this writing task and research methodology.

Notes

1. We recognize that from a poststructuralist perspective Roger's entry into this community could be described as a move away from, rather than toward, personal authority, as his discourse and thinking are increasingly constrained by the conventions of the community. In these comparisons, however, we have taken the concept of authority at face value, focusing on the right to speak as established by the community's expressed values—that is, through the attainment of sanctioned knowledge, experience, and credentials. See Collins, Freidson.
2. See Belenky et al., Frey, Gilligan ("Adolescent"; *Different Voice*), Gilligan et al., and Tompkins.
3. Both Bartholomae and Bizzell ("Basic Writers") have argued that attributing basic writers' "failures" to a simple lack of writing skill ignores the actual lack of authority in these students' social circumstances and the influence of this outsider position on their ability, and willingness, to adopt the writing strategies of the insider. We believe this analysis applies more generally. Even relatively skilled freshman writers, like Janet, are unlikely to view themselves as authorities in the academic context. College students' deference to the authority of textbooks and teachers has been described in observational studies (Wall; Haas, "Biology") and figures prominently in autobiographical accounts of educational experiences (Rose, Rodriguez).
4. The presence or absence of author names is not a straightforward index of dependence on outside authority. For example, the other expert subject in our study mentioned none of the authors by names in his draft, but his protocol transcripts contained significantly more author references than either of the novice subjects. What distinguished experts from novices on this dimension was the role that individual authors played *during the writing process.* See Chapter 10 of Geisler's *Academic Literacy* for a full report of these analyses.
5. Haas ("Biology") observed similar patterns of generic reference in the freshman year in a longitudinal study tracing a student's college career.
6. See Chapter 11 of Geisler's *Academic Literacy* for more extensive analysis of the use of cases in the work of all four case study subjects.

Works Cited

Bartholomae, David. "Inventing the University." *When a Writer Can't Write.* Ed. Mike Rose. New York: Guilford, 1986. 134–65.

Bartholomae, David, and Anthony Petrosky. *Facts, Artifacts and Counterfacts: Theory and Method for a Reading and Writing Course.* Upper Montclair: Boynton, 1986.

Belenky, Mary Field, Blythe McVicker Clinchy, Nancy Rule Goldberger and Jill Mattuck Tarule. *Women's Ways of Knowing: The Development of Self, Voice and Mind.* New York: Basic, 1986.

Bizzell, Patricia. "Cognition, Convention and Certainty: What We Need to Know about Writing." *Pre/Text* 3 (1982): 213–43.

———. "What Happens When Basic Writers Come to College?" *CCC* 37 (1986): 294–301.

Bruffee, Kenneth A. "Social Construction, Language, and the Authority of Knowledge: A Bibliographical Essay." *College English* 48 (1986): 773–90.

Childress, James. *Who Should Decide? Paternalism in Health Care.* New York: Oxford UP, 1982.

Collins, Randall. *The Credential Society: An Historical Sociology of Education and Stratification.* New York: Academic, 1979.

Freidson, Eliot. *Professional Powers: A Study of the Institutionalization of Formal Knowledge.* Chicago: U of Chicago P, 1986.

Frey, Olivia. "Beyond Literary Darwinism: Women's Voices and Critical Discourse." *College English* 52 (1990): 507–26.

Geisler, Cheryl. "Toward a Sociocognitive Model of Literacy: Constructing Mental Models in a Philosophical Conversation." *Textual Dynamics of the Professions.* Ed. Charles Bazerman and James Paradis. Madison: Wisconsin, 1990.

——. *Academic Literacy and the Nature of Expertise.* Hillsdale: Erlbaum, 1994.

Gert, B. and C. Culver. "Paternalistic Behavior," *Philosophy and Public Affairs* 6 (1976): 45–57.

Gilligan, Carol. *In a Different Voice.* Cambridge: Harvard UP, 1982.

——. "Adolescent Development Reconsidered." Gilligan et al. vii–xxxix.

Gilligan, Carol, Janie Victoria Ward, Jill McLean Taylor, and Betty Bardige. *Mapping the Moral Domain.* Cambridge: Harvard UP, 1988.

Gradwohl. Jane M. and Gary M. Schumacher. "The Relationship Between Content Knowledge and Topic Choice in Writing." *Written Communication* 6 (1989): 181–95.

Greene, Stuart. "Exploring the Relationship Between Authorship and Reading." Penrose and Sitko. 33–51.

Haas, Christina. "Beyond 'Just the Facts': Reading as Rhetorical Action." Penrose and Sitko. 19–32.

——. "Learning to Read Biology: One Student's Rhetorical Development in College." *Written Communication* 11 (1994): 43–84.

Higgins, Lorraine. "Reading to Argue: Helping Students Transform Source Texts." Penrose and Sitko. 70–101.

Kaufer, David, and Cheryl Geisler. "Novelty in Academic Writing." *Written Communication* 8 (1989): 286–311.

Kaufer, David S., Cheryl Geisler and Christine M. Neuwirth. *Arguing from Sources: Exploring Issues through Reading and Writing.* San Diego: Harcourt, 1989.

Lamb, Catherine E. "Beyond Argument in Feminist Composition," *CCC* 42 (1991): 11–24.

Langer, Judith A. "The Effects of Available Information on Responses to School Writing Tasks." *Reading Research Quarterly* 19 (1984): 468–81.

Newell, George E. and Peter. N. Winograd. "The Effects of Writing on Learning from Expository Text." *Written Communication* 6 (1989): 196–217.

Penrose, Ann M., and Barbara M. Sitko, eds. *Hearing Ourselves Think: Cognitive Research in the College Writing Classroom.* New York: Oxford UP, 1993.

Rodriguez, Richard. *Hunger of Memory.* New York: Bantam, 1983.

Rose, Mike. *Lives on the Boundary.* New York: Macmillan, 1989.

Tompkins, Jane. "Me and My Shadow." *New Literary History* 19 (1987): 169–78.

Wall, Susan. "Writing, Reading and Authority: A Case Study." Bartholomae and Petrosky. 105–36.

Wilson, Paul T., and Richard C. Anderson. "What They Don't Know Will Hurt Them: The Role of Prior Knowledge in Comprehension." *Reading Comprehensions: From Research to Practice.* Ed. Judith Orasanu. Hillsdale: Erlbaum, 1986. 31–48.

Witte, Stephen P. "Context, Text, Intertext: Toward a Constructivist Semiotic of Writing." *Written Communication* 9 (1992): 237–308.

Questions for Discussion and Journaling

1. Penrose and Geisler point to a number of reasons that Roger wrote with more authority than Janet. What are these reasons?

2. Penrose and Geisler point to a number of ways in which Roger's text was written differently than Janet's. What are these differences?

3. The authors argue that the differences between Roger's and Janet's texts stem from a difference in their views of knowledge. They argue that Janet has been trained in an *information-transfer model* of knowledge while Roger sees "the development of knowledge as a communal and continual process" (para. 25, also known as a *constructivist model* of knowledge). Explain the differences between these two views of knowledge.

4. Janet did not seem to trust herself and always deferred to the authors she was reading, even when their claims conflicted and when the examples she thought of refuted the author's claims. Why do you think this was the case?

5. Is your writing more like Roger's or Janet's? Do you think you hold more of an information-transfer model of knowledge or a constructivist model of knowledge?

Applying and Exploring Ideas

1. Penrose and Geisler note that Janet sees texts as objective and unauthored; she doesn't seem to realize that texts are written by human beings who are in conversation with other human beings. In her paper, Janet almost never refers to the authors who wrote the texts she is discussing. Instead, she makes claims without noting who made them, refers to the authors as "it" or "they," and refers to "the book." Look at a research paper you have written recently and do a quick analysis. How often do you refer to authors by name in the ways that Roger does, and how often do you refer to texts or claims, as Janet does? What can you conclude about your own sense of *authority* in the writing you examined?

2. Ask a professor teaching in your major (or prospective major) if she would be willing to speak with you for about thirty minutes. In this interview, ask the professor (1) how she decides which authors to read when writing a research paper; (2) how she evaluates the claims that authors make; (3) what she does when authors disagree with one another; and (4) what she does when she disagrees with an author. Write up the professor's responses in a one- to two-page report to share with your classmates.

Meta Moment

Name two specific ways that having read this article can help you the next time you have to write a research paper.

The Beginnings of Change:
Learning and Teaching Undergraduate Academic Literacy Games

CHRISTINE PEARSON CASANAVE

Casanave, Christine Pearson. "The Beginnings of Change: Learning and Teaching Undergrad-uate Academic Literacy Games." *Writing Games: Multicultural Case Studies of Academic Literacy Practices in Higher Education*. Mahwah: Erlbaum, 2002. 35–81. Print.

Framing the Reading

Christine Casanave is a linguist who earned a Ph.D. from Stanford University in 1990. She has taught at Teachers College in Tokyo as well as at Temple University in Tokyo. She is interested in academic literacy and the professional development of language educators. Her books include *Writing Games*, from which the selection reprinted here is taken, and *Controversies in Second Language Writing* (2003).

This reading is the second chapter of her *Writing Games* book, and it is quite long. All of it is interesting, but it is divided into two basic parts that each serves a different purpose: a review of the studies conducted by others and a description of Casanave's own study. It is possible that your teacher might want you only to read a portion of the chapter, so pay attention to the directions you are given.

As you begin reading, you will see that (after a short personal story) Casanave almost immediately begins outlining the conversation on her topic, a strategy that Penrose and Geisler discussed in the preceding reading. In fact, a good half of Casa-nave's chapter is what you might call a "map" of the conversation among scholars regarding how best to help students learn to write in the university. This kind of "map" is also often called a **literature review**. In the first part of her review, Casanave synthesizes what a lot of other scholars have said. Beginning with the section headed "Sternglass' and Ivanič's Case Studies," she begins to focus in on just five of them, summarizing their findings in more detail. (One of the research-ers she focuses on is Lucille McCarthy, whose study of Dave is included in this chapter.) Starting with the section headed "Case Study: Communities of Practice?" Casanave moves from describing the research conducted by others to describing her own experience and study. Beginning with the section headed

"Game Strategy I," she makes some conclusions about the **game strategies** that the teachers she studied tried to teach their students.

In this chapter, Casanave focuses on **case studies**, which are in-depth studies of only a few people rather than large groups. Case studies are considered **qualitative research**, and the information gained from case studies can't be generalized and applied to everyone. Casanave notes that when scholars conduct case studies, "[W]e probably end up learning more than we want to: The case study invariably immerses the scholar in so much detail and so much complexity that the basic questions simply can't be answered unambiguously" (para. 15). As you read the case studies that Casanave describes, ask yourself how, if at all, case studies can be useful even though the information gained from them cannot be generalized. (Perhaps the easiest way to consider this question is to ask what you are getting from the experience of reading these case studies.)

As you read, remember that Casanave is a linguist who is particularly interested in helping nonnative speakers of English. As a result, she uses some terminology that might be unfamiliar to you: **L1** and **L2** *speakers* (people who speak using their first or second language, respectively) and L1 and L2 *scholars* (people who study the previous groups) and **EAP** (English for Academic Purposes), which she defines toward the beginning of the section headed "Published Studies."

Getting Ready to Read

Before you read, consider the following questions:

- If you had to think about the writing you do for school as a game, how would you explain it to someone else? What "games" do you play when you write in school? What are some of the "rules" for these games?

As you read the review of the literature, try the following activities:

- Note the ways in which Casanave describes the views of other authors. (Notice, for example, that she calls them by name directly and explains how their findings and claims relate to or are questioned by the findings and claims of others. This is very different from how Janet refers to authors in Penrose and Geisler's study reprinted in this chapter.)
- Try to get a handle on the "moves" in the conversation that Casanave is relating. (What claims are being made? Who made them? Who refuted them? What are the problems that seem to be unsolved?)

Clueless

Every now and then I am reminded of how wretchedly difficult my first writing experience was in college. I didn't know how to play any of the academic writing games, not the textual ones or the social and political ones, nor did I 1 imagine the existence of the latter at the time. I had to write a 5-page paper on some topic in ancient thought and history about which I clearly knew little and in which I had no interest. I sat up all night (I am not a night person) in an armchair in our dorm study room, pulling out sentences and phrases so slowly and painfully that I thought I would never finish. The night seemed endless. I turned in the paper, such as it was, at 7:55 A.M. the next morning, 5 minutes before it was due, and got a C– as I recall. Luckily my imperfect memory has saved me from a lifetime of recurring nightmares about this experience, but even without the details, the sensations still haunt me.

It's not that I was ever a bad writer. In fact, I occasionally got high praise 2 from junior high and high school teachers for my writing (Miss Wilson, my 8th-grade English teacher, had written in my year-end autograph book: "I hope English will be your forte," but she would not tell me what "forte" meant). I also passed a college writing test that exempted me from any English courses. But that first college writing experience shriveled all confidence I might have had, or might have nourished, in my undergraduate academic persona. I saw it as clear evidence that I correctly had chosen to be an art major, that I was not focused or bright enough to succeed in classes requiring extensive reading and writing on bookish topics. That I had passed the school's writing test was little consolation, and indeed this fact was buried so deeply in my memory that it did not find its way into the first draft of this chapter. I wonder how many undergraduates, including those in the privileged White middle and upper class, struggle with their early college

> Learning to write in academic settings is about change in ways of thinking, using language, and envisioning the self.

writing experiences this way, and later find they can, with some confidence, consider themselves writers. I wonder, too, how much of the struggle has to do with lack of practice, or with lack of knowledge of a writing topic, with simple lack of interest in the assigned tasks, or with lack of mentoring. I was the none-too-proud possessor of all four of these lacks.

Learning to write in academic settings is about change in ways of thinking, 3 using language, and envisioning the self. I see that now, but then I think I saw it as a matter of survival. I have queried some of the very bright undergraduate students at my Japanese university about their attitudes toward writing, and some of them echoed my sentiments of decades ago: We just want to survive, to turn in (not learn from) this report, to pass the class, to put it behind us. One student who had been raised in the United States told me that she had tried in her first semester to write "real" papers, but had quickly learned a different game. "Nobody writes real papers," she said, "because there's just no time." She continued by describing how students pulled things from the Internet and from books and pasted them together, without revision, since the teachers never gave feedback or returned the papers anyway. These students no doubt experienced change, but I am guessing that the changes concerned developing better survival strategies.

I don't know if I changed much during my undergraduate years as a result 4
of writing. I have no memory of developing a sense of identity as an academic
writer until I began graduate studies some years later. But of course then I was
choosing what to study with a much greater sense of awareness, interest, and
focus. Could this transformation have happened earlier? Or is there something
about being an undergraduate—a novice at writing and at almost everything
else as well, a self-conscious postadolescent who fantasizes about social life
and not about Roman history, a partially formed personality that doesn't know
what it really wants or why it is writing—that makes writing such a torturous
tooth-pulling blood-sweating task? Or was it just me?

I escaped my undergraduate years as quickly as I could, repressing most 5
memories of classes except those held in the art studios. What remained of
those times were social and artistic, not intellectual, lessons. Now, after teaching writing in undergraduate and graduate settings in Japan for some years, I
am astounded at how easy it is for me to be on the other side of the torture
chamber, at how rarely I recall my own past pain, and at how hard it is to
know what is really going on inside the minds of the kids who sit in my classes.
How many of my own students have gone through the all-night agony I went
through, and this in a foreign language? Among the bilingual students, how
many of them write as fluently and confidently as some of their drafts suggest
they do? And why am I making the undergraduates write, anyway, if in their
other classes they just need to survive, to turn in unrevised reports in Japanese,
and where their writing techniques are unabashedly electronically plagiarized?
I don't know the answers to these questions, but my experience and reading of
the literature as well as my research and teaching convince me that writing at
the undergraduate level is just plain hard partly because every undergraduate
writer needs to reinvent the writing wheel for him- or herself. In particular, the
case studies I have read and conducted have made me reevaluate my expectations for undergraduate writers and for myself as a writing teacher. They have
also made me ask more pointed questions about my novice writing students'
needs and goals, and the extent to which these arise and evolve from them as
individuals and from influences outside the classroom, or in interaction with
me and others in the context of specific practices in particular classes. When I
was an undergraduate I certainly did not know what I wanted as a writer, and
indeed had no sense of myself as a writer until many years later. But like other
writing teachers, I persist in wanting my students to achieve in a semester what
it took me a decade to learn, even though many of my students may never have
to write again in the ways I'm asking them to write. No wonder I'm sometimes
confused and frustrated.

Published Studies

Before looking more closely at some published case studies, I want to review 6
some of the issues that have been explored in undergraduate writing, particularly in the second language education "EAP" (English for Academic Purposes)
literature. Although this chapter concerns undergraduate education, many of

the issues I review here apply also to graduate level EAP courses and their influence on students' academic enculturation. Scholars in EAP seek ways to help a multicultural, multiclass population of students make the transition into English-medium universities and to link issues these students face with broader issues of literacy across the curriculum that all students confront (Matsuda, 1998; Zamel 1995, 1996). Many of these studies have tried to figure out specifically what game rules, strategies, and practices students need to learn in order to write successfully in their academic classes. The findings show that disciplinary discourse practices cannot be characterized in any unambiguous sense, thus making it difficult for EAP teachers to know what to teach. Those studies that presume a relatively unified discourse community into which students need to be integrated by adopting known sets of discourse or genre practices can be critiqued for not addressing the actual diversity and possibilities for agency in disciplinary discourse practices (e.g., Bartholomae, 1985; Berkenkotter, Huckin, & Ackerman, 1988; Bhatia, 1993; Walvoord & McCarthy, 1990).

Nevertheless, perhaps because it is their livelihood, many writing teach- 7 ers, materials developers, and researchers advocate explicit teaching of some kind, believing that some aspects of what students learn in a writing class can be transferred to discipline-specific content classes or become part of novice academic writers' permanent repertoires of knowledge and strategies. This belief exists in spite of ongoing debates about the value of explicit instruction and awareness in areas of language education such as form-focused grammar instruction in second language acquisition (e.g., Ferris, 1999; Truscott, 1996, 1998, 1999) and genre instruction in writing (Freedman, 1993a, 1993b; Williams & Colomb, 1993). We also have not resolved the question about what the content of EAP writing courses should be: language, genre, subject matter content, ideological and political issues, critical thinking tasks, or some combination (see, e.g., discussions on genre in Bhatia, 1993; Freedman & Medway, 1994; and Swales, 1990; on critical thinking in ESL by Atkinson, 1997 and Pally, 1997; on content by Gosden, 2000 and Parkinson, 2000; and on ideological, cultural, and pragmatic issues by Allison, 1996; Atkinson, 1997, 1999; Benesch, 1993, 1996, 2001; Ramanathan & Atkinson, 1999; and Santos, 1992).

In an early piece by Ruth Spack (1988), the message was that writing teach- 8 ers should leave the discipline-specific aspects of writing to the teachers in the disciplines. Her point at that time that we hear echoed in different forms in later work by other scholars was that students need to be "immersed in the subject matter" by attending lectures and seminars, reading, discussing, and observing professional writers (p. 40). "English teachers cannot and should not be held responsible for teaching writing in the disciplines," she said then. Rather, they should teach general inquiry strategies and rhetorical principles, helping students to learn to evaluate and synthesize data and reading sources (p. 40). Another second language researcher who has studied the demands that academic literacy makes on students is Pat Currie (1993). In her study of a social science class, she identified the following potentially generalizable skills in the class writing assignments: finding and recording information, using a concept to find and report observational details, using a concept to analyze data, classifying according to a concept, comparing and contrasting, determining causal relationships, resolving an issue, and speculating (p. 107).

However, in another study by Currie (1998), such skills were not explicitly 9 highlighted by the professor in a content class. In that study, Currie followed "Diana," a native speaker of Cantonese, throughout a one-semester undergraduate course in Management and Organizational Behavior at a Canadian university. Although Diana did have language and reading problems in spite of a high TOEFL (590), she faced even greater difficulties understanding the ways of reasoning and problem solving that her writing tasks required. In interviews with the professor of this class, Currie learned that the professor was not able to articulate explicit guidelines for writing and reasoning tasks because much of this conceptual knowledge was tacit, and deeply embedded in social practices within his field (see also Leki, 1995b).

Another potentially teachable and generalizable aspect of academic writ- 10 ing in Western cultural settings is awareness of plagiarism. The less pejorative notion of textual borrowing has been identified as a survival strategy for both first and second language students in academic settings who often need to write from their readings (Campbell, 1990). Indeed, Currie (1998) found that Diana eventually resorted to extensive "textual borrowing" because she was so distressed by her low grades in her weekly writing assignments. Her copying went undiscovered by the teaching assistant who read her papers, and her grades indeed went up. Can students in EAP classes be taught the serious game of textual borrowing, including how to recognize and avoid plagiarism, then apply this knowledge to their content classes? Deckert (1993) for one hopes so, since his first year students at a Hong Kong university seemed to have little concrete sense of what it was or why it might be considered a serious problem. Pennycook (1996) was not surprised at this, given what he learned about the complex history of the culture-loaded notion of plagiarism and the inconsistent uses of the words of others by published scholars in the West (see also Scollon, 1995). Discussions about textual borrowing as a cultural practice continue, with questions about how and what to teach undergraduate students unresolved. One thing we can do is to help both undergraduates and graduates understand that citation conventions are not just formalisms but one of the many serious game-like social practices within particular academic communities. We are learning more about these practices through fascinating sociolinguistic analyses of how and why the authors of research articles cite the words of others (Hyland, 1999; Paul, 2000). However, the findings have as yet had little impact on undergraduate academic writing courses, which tend to focus on the formal aspects of citation and oversimplified sanctions against copying. The social and political game rules and strategies are perhaps too complex to be taught explicitly and unambiguously and may more appropriately find their way into graduate level writing texts (Swales & Feak, 1994, 2000).

Ilona Leki (1995b) is not sanguine either about what explicit aspects of 11 academic writing within specific disciplines might be taught by EAP teachers. One of her questions, reflected in the discussion above, concerns the ability of writing teachers to teach genre-specific writing, given that so many disciplinary differences exist and that so much of what disciplinary insiders know is tacit, lying out of reach even of the probing questions of researchers. It is not reasonable, Leki (1995b) claims, to expect "those who do not participate as conversation partners in a discourse . . . to teach the explicit, let alone implicit, rules of that conversation to others" (pp. 236–237). For this reason, Bhatia (1993) and genre specialists in Australia and North America (see Cope & Kalantzis, 1993, Hyon, 1996, and the introduction to Freedman & Medway, 1994) suggest that special purpose English courses (ESP) follow a genre-based approach in which broad similarities of structure and function of writing across disciplines be taught.

In a related but somewhat different approach, Ann Johns (1988) claimed 12 that "generalized English skills, usable in any academic class" (p. 55) could be taught in special purpose writing classes. However, on closer examination of how skills such as summarizing and research paper writing were used in specific fields, she found more differences than similarities among disciplines (p. 55), as did Paul Prior (1998) in his studies of graduate level writing. Johns (1988) partially solved this problem by trying to "train students to become ethnographers in the academic culture," to discover for themselves what knowledge and skills were required in the specific academic communities they were involved in (p. 57). In later work Johns (1990, 1995) continued espousing an ethnographic approach to academic enculturation, recommending that students already enrolled in academic courses be trained to become aware of the social and textual conventions in their classes. Pat Currie (1999) experimented with this approach in two of her undergraduate EAP classes in Canada by asking the students to observe specific practices within their content classes and to report their findings in a "journalog." Alan Hirvela (1997) similarly recommended that students learn about literacy activities in their own disciplines and compile a portfolio of their findings. His study concerned graduate students but applies to undergraduates as well. In short, a partial solution to the dilemma of writing teachers trying to assist students with their disciplinary enculturation has been for teachers to set up tasks that ask students to discover the game strategies in their fields.

Even though my discussion has focused on specialized EAP courses, which 13 tend to be offered only to nonnative speakers of English, mother-tongue English speaking undergraduates are thought to need special help with writing, too. This help is expected to take place in their freshman composition classes in the typical North American university setting. In this context, just as in the undergraduate EAP class, the purposes and value of general academic writing instruction for native English speaking college freshmen have been questioned by a number of authors, such as those in Petraglia (1995) and debated by L1 scholars such as Bartholomae (1995) and Elbow (1995, 1999a). Although a detailed review of the issues from an L1 perspective is beyond my goal in this chapter, I want to point out that it is increasingly difficult to use an L1–L2 dichotomy in discussions of undergraduate academic writing, where students of all kinds often find themselves in the same freshman composition or remedial writing classes (Matsuda, 1998; Silva, Leki, & Carson, 1997). As will be clear from the case studies described below, the diversity of academic writing games in undergraduate settings raises challenges for all teachers of writing who wish to coach students effectively, not just for those teaching so-called nonnative English speakers.

Case studies, whether of students whose mother tongue is English or some other language, complicate the picture. What they show us is that even if we do consult disciplinary experts on college campuses and examine actual successful samples of reading and writing assignments from students' classes, each teacher and each student differ greatly and interact in ungeneralizable ways with context-bound academic literacy activities. The picture is further complicated when we consider the many students who are not yet taking classes in their disciplines—full time students in EAP or ESL classes—or those who are studying in undergraduate programs in non-English-medium universities (see the case study of David and Yasuko, below). It is not clear, under conditions of such diversity, local exigence, and complexity, how to encourage students' engagement in specialized academic literacy practices (Bazerrnan, 1995). Nor is it clear whether to urge students to take a pragmatic, accommodationist approach (assuming we know what we are accommodating to), a culturally appropriate approach (assuming we know what is culturally appropriate), or a critical resistant approach (assuming we know what to resist and question; e.g., Allison, 1996; Atkinson, 1997; Benesch, 1996; Canagarajah, 2001; Elbow, 1999b; Ramanathan & Atkinson, 1999; Santos, 1992). It may be that none of these approaches reflects the realities in many undergraduate students' lives. As Leki's (1999b) case study of Polish undergraduate student Jan showed and that some of the case studies I discuss below show in less extreme ways, the name of the undergraduate writing game may be Survival Strategies. Jan shocks readers with his wily and even illegal ways to get through the sometimes senseless writings and exams in his undergraduate years. Situations like Jan's cause Leki to ask whether writing is "overrated" in undergraduate education (Leki, 1999a).

There are not a great many case studies in print about college students and college writing teachers. One reason may be that case studies generally take more time than other kinds of studies such as surveys, cross-sectional sampling, or quasi-experimental studies. Most teachers who also do research do not have the luxury of much research time in their busy lives or the money to fund long-term studies. Sternglass (1997) talked about this problem in the introduction to her 6-year study of undergraduate writing development. Another reason for the paucity of case studies may be that qualitative studies, especially those including narratives and stories (Clandinin & Connelly, 1991; Connelly & Clandinin, 1990), are not accepted in some quarters as "scientific" enough (Herndl & Nahrwold, 2000; Miller, Nelson, & Moore, 1998). As a result, scholars in "fuzzy" fields, especially if those scholars are not yet well-established, may hesitate to take chances with research that does not follow a traditional model (Bridwell-Bowles, 1992, 1995). Still, the big questions in studies of academic reading and writing seem to be shared by most people interested in L1 and L2 literacy practices: Why is it difficult for different kinds of students to learn to read and write in college? What kinds of literacy activities do students and their teachers actually practice in different disciplines? How do students' academic literacies and identities change over time? What factors contribute to changes? Case studies can help answer these questions. A disturbing aspect of case studies, however, is that we probably end up learning more than we want to: The case study invariably immerses the scholar in so much detail and so much complexity that the basic questions simply can't be answered unambiguously. Once someone becomes a real person in a study she can no longer be an abstract subject, simplified and tidied up in the interest of objectivity and generalizability.

Let me turn now to some of the influential case studies of L1 and L2 under- 16 graduate writers. My mention of two of these studies, those of Sternglass (1997) and Ivanič (1998), is reluctantly brief, since their participants were older, mature undergraduates and I wish to focus on studies of younger students, similar in age and experience to those that the teachers in my own case study worked with.

Sternglass' and Ivanič's Case Studies

Marilyn Sternglass' (1997) study is billed as a true longitudinal study encom- 17 passing 6 years of interaction with nine students at City University of New York. The students who stayed with her for the duration of the study were primarily African American and Latino, with one Asian, and one White (all Sternglass' terms) as well. Students' personal lives, such as family relationships, work obligations, and gender identity influenced many aspects of their writing including their developing ability to integrate personal knowledge and interests with academic writing tasks. This ability to integrate aspects of their personal identities into their writing helped push some of the students toward greater control of their academic writing. Unlike Chiseri-Strater's (1991) Nick and Anna (below), we do not see them as silenced in their academic writing, but as liberated, through their own efforts and through some powerful mentoring efforts by concerned teachers. Moreover, Stemglass' study covered many years in her participants' lives as undergraduates. It is the longitudinal portrayal, Stemglass claims, that allows us to see the changes in students' academic literacies and identities and to recognize the fundamental need for students to interact with interested and engaged teachers over time. Their identities as competent players in academic writing game practices evolve over time, in other words, as they engage with more competent players (Wenger, 1998).

Roz Ivanič's (1998) shorter term case study of the academic literacy experiences 18 of eight mature (over age 25) undergraduate students—her "co-researchers"— deals primarily with what she refers to as the dlscoursal construction of identity in academic writing. She does not want to view academic enculturation as students' passive acquisition of dominant discourses. Instead she sees it as an experience involving tension and struggle between people and institutions in which students have opportunities to resist, take advantage of slippages in the system, and bring about change (Ortner, 1996).

Ivanič's (1998) study focused on linguistic text analyses and students' dis-   19
cussions about their linguistic choices. Although she interviewed eight students
about the construction of one major academic essay, her detailed case study of
"Rachel" shows how complex the discoursal construction of identity is. Rachel,
a social worker student, wrote a paper on a "Family Case Study," attempting to
blend disciplinary, course-specific, and personal voices. The tensions she experienced and choices she made highlight the many possible identities available
to student writers within particular disciplines, departments, and courses and
in interaction with specific people such as tutors (British usage) and teachers.
Ivanič emphasizes that Rachel's identities as evidenced in her essay were multiple, complex, and partial and that Rachel was not able to position herself confidently as a contributor to knowledge in her field rather than as a student:

> Rachel was caught in a web of sincerity and deception as she attempted to take
> on social roles and to portray qualities which were valued by her different read-
> ers and, whenever possible, to be true to herself. This process was complicated
> by the fact that Rachel was not a very adept writer: she had difficulty in playing
> these games and, sadly, even more difficulty in challenging the conventions and
> presenting herself as she ideally would like to appear, (p. 168)

In both Ivanič's and Sternglass' studies we see students doing much more   20
than learning a set of formal game rules. Instead, we see them learning to participate in game-like practices, sorting through and blending different values,
behaviors, and beliefs that they hold and that the institutions they write for
seem to espouse. From positions on the periphery and the margins (Wenger,
1998) they forged identities through their writing that were inevitably multivocalic and riddled with conflict and inconsistencies but that could potentially
contribute richly to their own knowledge-construction.

Both Sternglass and Ivanič provide numerous examples of students' writ-   21
ing; Sternglass incorporates examples into her discussion of research issues,
and Ivanič does detailed linguistic analyses. The amount and kind of focus
on actual writing differentiates the case studies discussed below as well as my
own, as does the extent of researchers' focus on teachers or students. Sternglass
and Ivanič, like the authors of most case studies in language education, focus
on students including the studies of Anna and Nick (Chiseri-Strater, 1991),
Dave (McCarthy, 1987), and Yuko (Spack, 1997) discussed below. My own
case study in this chapter focuses on two teachers of undergraduate EAP writing, with students playing background roles.

Anna and Nick

Elizabeth Chiseri-Strater (1991) revised her dissertation into a smooth-flowing   22
ethnographic study of two mother-tongue English speaking undergraduate college students, Anna and Nick, over two semesters. In this case study, the author
is fundamentally interested in the two students as individuals. She paints a
broad portrait of them in their college lives during this school year, drawing
on journals, dialogue in and out of class, observation, and the students' notes

and papers to document their responses to a variety of reading and writing activities. Chiseri-Strater captures some of the real-life drama of the students' lives: Nick, a prolific and expressive doodler, with his earring and torn jeans, combative and resistant in one class, cooperative in another; Anna the dancer, Anna the artist, and Anna the writer. Each of these very different undergraduate students was faced with the challenge so common in undergraduate education, that of learning to survive the demands of many different writing games across a diverse curriculum.

Both Anna and Nick seemed to thrive in a Prose Writing class taught by   23
the same teacher, Donna. Donna set up a writing community that allowed for "students' exploration of personal and intellectual literacy development" (p. 1). Students read essays and stories, wrote response journals and a final paper, discussed and collaborated in groups, and participated in several different feedback arrangements (group, individual conference, journal writing) that ensured their personal involvement in the literacy activities. The processes of talk, reading, writing, and discipline-specific thinking all supported students' learning (p. 12).

These literacy-related practices were valued differently in other classes that   24
Anna and Nick took. Anna revealed herself to be an artistic young woman who doubted her academic competence, yet rebelled against the formal ways of learning in her art history classes. She talked to Chiseri-Strater about the "tension in her academic life between fields that require distance, detachment, and objectivity and those that welcome intimacy, engagement and subjectivity" (p. 56). In the art history class that Chiseri-Strater visited, Anna was not able, for the most part, to connect the polished lecture and slide shows or the dense readings to her own interests, partly because the teacher had set up no classroom practices to promote feedback and engagement. Whatever connections Anna made by the end of the semester she managed on her own.

As for Nick, Chiseri-Strater describes him as a bored and troubled young   25
man who had changed majors several times and who rebelled against the idea of leading a "normal" life after graduation that would be characterized by "a profession, a wife, and a dog named Spot" (p. 96). He persisted in playing relatively nonserious academic roles and games in his junior and senior years and in distancing his personal life from his academic literacy practices. "School is what I *do*," he said, "Not what I *am*" (p. 97). Still, in Donna's Prose Writing class, he was confident, articulate, and expressive, dominating many of the class discussions. He wrote long response journals, in two voices—one formal and one personal—that demonstrated he had potential to push himself to think and write and rewrite in more complex and challenging ways, a goal that his teacher urged him to pursue in revisions. Nick, however, resisted all suggestions, revised none of his work, and continued to avoid difficult topics. The one real change that Nick saw in his writing in this class was a new appreciation for his audience, which now consisted of peers and a responsive teacher in addition to himself, no doubt as a result of the interactive practices that Donna involved the students in.

The game practices in Nick's class on Political Thought were interactive,   26
too, but not in the egalitarian and narrative style of the Prose Writing class. In

the Political Thought class the professor exhibited the persona of an expert and an authority, challenging students to debate and argue and to compete with his own authoritative views. Intimidated at first, as were the other students, Nick believed that the game in this class required that he come up with interpretations in his papers that matched those of his professor (p. 128). Unable until the final paper to connect his personal interests and his flair for expressive writing to the work in this class, Nick claimed to have "lost his tolerance for the formality of political science writing" (p. 131). The final paper, however, was opened up to different styles including the personal after Chiseri-Strater suggested to the professor that he encourage alternate forms of writing. This freedom allowed Nick to write in journal form and to express his view that education had limited rather than expanded his growth by channeling his ideas into narrow categories (p. 138). Chiseri-Strater concludes her portrait of Nick with the comment that he liked himself better in the Prose Writing class, where he played a cooperative, collaborative game than in the Political Thought class, where he took on the identity of an intimidated combatant.

Chiseri-Strater brings alive the issues of what it means to behave in literate ways in college, demonstrating how the students' personal lives interact with more traditional literate activities, how "literacy codes and conventions"—part of what I refer to as writing games—differ from one undergraduate class to another, and how little nourishment these two young people received from the academy. Nick and Anna, struggling with issues of relationships, intimacy, job fears, gender stereotypes, and identity as they tried to get through class assignments, simply did not respond to the sometimes hierarchical and competitive game practices in the academy in ways that contributed to their personal and intellectual development. As Wenger (1998) might put it, their academic identities were defined as much by their nonparticipation as by their participation. Not wishing to generalize from these two case studies, Chiseri-Strater tells us that the portrayals can help educators recognize the multiple ways that students enact literate behaviors, and the complexity of the development of their identities within academic settings. 27

Dave

As Chiseri-Strater's (1991) study of Nick and Anna showed, a student does not need to be a second language speaker or a member of an oppressed minority to find the academy a strange place. "Dave," the college student that Lucille McCarthy (1987) described as a "stranger in strange lands," is another nonminority student who probably led a college life similar to that of many undergraduate students in North American colleges. This life consisted of traveling from one "land" (i.e., discipline) to another during his first 2 years as he went about fulfilling the undergraduate requirements at his college. As was the case for Jan in Leki's (1999b) study, the game for him involved figuring out what his teachers expected from him in each course's writing assignments. In general, as a newcomer to academia, he faced an academic challenge in which each course and each teacher introduced a field and a way of writing that was new to him. 28

Dave, according to McCarthy, was typical of students at his college in that 29
he was young (18) when the study began, had comparable SAT scores and
high school grades, lived not far from the school, and was White. Dave told
McCarthy that he was a "hands-on" person who did not particularly care for
reading and writing, although he believed that "writing was a tool he needed"
(McCarthy, 1987, p. 238). By the time the study ended when Dave was a junior,
he had been working as a lab technician in a local hospital for about a year,
work that he enjoyed greatly and that did not involve any reading or writing.

McCarthy documented Dave's writing experiences in three different classes 30
over three semesters: a freshman composition class, a sophomore poetry class,
and a sophomore cell biology class. She visited the freshman composition class
once a week for 9 weeks, collected all the class documents from the composition and the poetry classes, and interviewed all the professors once or twice.
She conversed often with Dave and two of his friends, and interviewed them
at least once a month during the poetry and biology semesters, taping and
transcribing the longer interviews. McCarthy collected several protocols—
audiotaped and transcribed think-aloud sessions during writing—from Dave
as he wrote one draft of several papers in each class. From these she categorized what she called the "writer's conscious concerns" (p. 241). She also analyzed the papers that resulted and the teachers' written responses according to
Grice's (1975) Cooperative Principle.

We do not know from this article the details of all of Dave's writing assign- 31
ments for each of the three classes, but we do know that he wrote a series of
short papers in each one. In his freshman composition class, the paper that
McCarthy looked at was a discussion of the wrongs of abortion. In the poetry
class, Dave had to analyze the "true meaning" of one poem. In the cell biology
class, he had to write a review of a published scientific journal article. From the
think-aloud protocols, McCarthy learned something about what Dave believed
each of these writing games was about. Dave understood that his composition
teacher was interested in coherence—how ideas tied together—and seemed to
care little for content. Dave found this concept valuable. In the poetry class,
the teacher asked students to follow strictly a specific form for quoting poetry,
and conveyed the impression that there was one correct interpretation that
their analyses were to aim for, a task that Dave found meaningless. In the biology class, the teacher required that the students' reviews follow the standard
organization of a scientific article and that students incorporate the language
and concepts of the article into their summaries, a task he found useful when
considering his future in a scientific field. It is little wonder that an inexperienced writer like Dave could not see commonalities across the diversity of
game practices he was exposed to. Even though all three papers required similar skills of summarizing, analyzing, and of organizing, and all three papers
were "informational" texts written for the teacher-as-examiner, Dave believed
that each writing assignment asked for totally different things.

What stands out in this early study in light of much later work on the social 32
and political aspects of academic literacy practices is that Dave was doing more
than learning to write different kinds of texts. He also needed to negotiate his

way through very different role relationships between teacher and students in each class, showing that it is difficult to generalize about the function of the key players in academic writing games. In the composition class, the teacher portrayed herself as a writer herself, working alongside students, who themselves worked together. In the biology class, the teacher played the role of expert and professional, a mentor who was helping students learn to do what scientists do (he told McCarthy that "it often comes as a rude shock to the students that the way biologists survive in the field is by writing" [p. 257]). In the poetry class, the teacher seemed to play the role of a distant all-knowing insider with little interest in bringing students onto his playing field. Dave, then, might be seen as playing the roles of collaborator in the freshman composition class, of newcomer to a discipline in the biology class, and of outsider in the poetry class. On each of these playing fields the rules differed in Dave's view and his participation and his academic identities differed accordingly.

As an undergraduate learning how to write in his academic setting, Dave 33 thus seemed to be pulled in widely different directions, socially, intellectually, and textually, the rules of the game apparently differing widely in each specific context. It is possible that in this conflicted environment he may have begun to see himself as a writer, thanks to his composition class, and as a legitimate newcomer to a professional field, thanks to his cell biology class. But in his junior year the transition that he talked about was that of having learned the strategic game of survival. In recounting advice he would give new freshmen about writing in college he told McCarthy that "first you've got to figure out what your teachers want. And then you've got to give it to them if you're gonna get the grade" (p. 233). McCarthy (1987) realized that teachers concerned with the development of students' academic literacy may not like Dave's answer, but she insists that it reflects Dave's sensitivity to the social (and political?) realities of learning academic writing games in college:

> Successful students are those who can, in their interactions with teachers during the semester, determine what constitutes appropriate texts in each classroom.... They can then produce such a text. Students who cannot do this, for whatever reason—cultural, intellectual, motivational—are those who fail, deemed incompetent communicators in that particular setting. They are unable to follow what Britton calls the "rules of the game" in each class (1975, p. 76). As students go from one classroom to another they play a wide range of games, the rules for which, Britton points out, include many conventions and presuppositions that are not explicitly articulated. (pp. 233–234)

In short, the diversity of settings and the often unstated game rules in an 34 undergraduate context, combined with students' lack of identity as writers and their often uncertain purposes and interests make the task of learning to write seem even more difficult than it is in graduate and professional settings. It is no wonder that many of us floundered back then, myself included. This floundering seems normal in its inevitability. If so, it is astounding that so many young people, including students whose mother tongue is not English, manage to survive their undergraduate writing games as well as they do.

Yuko

In all of these case studies, we see how centrally important the situated local lit-   35
eracy practices were (Barton, Hamilton, & Ivanč, 2000), in contrast to general
skills students might have learned in special preparation classes. We also see
the beginnings of changes in identity as the students described by the authors
found their way into their majors and found ways to survive—to meet their
professors' expectations, with or without good mentoring. In the few case studies of second language learners in the academy, we see examples of strategies
that novice readers and writers not yet familiar with English academic discourse develop to survive on unfamiliar academic playing fields. Ruth Spack's
(1997a) study of "Yuko" is just such a study.

Spack's study of Yuko is a richly detailed longitudinal narrative, covering   36
Yuko's experiences in 9 undergraduate courses over 3 years and documenting
Yuko's beliefs and interpretations of her experiences in relation to her education in Japan. Yuko came from a small town in Japan, some distance from
Tokyo. In her childhood she learned to read before starting school, and later
left home to board at a competitive high school in Tokyo where she learned
the Tokyo dialect. During her school years in Japan she studied the books
authorized by the Ministry of Education but did little other reading. She also
recalled doing no writing except some 1-page "reaction papers" in a literature
class. As for English, she studied the required 6 years in Japan, according to the
grammar-translation methods used there, spent a year as an exchange student
in a U.S. high school, studied several nights a week in her junior and senior
years at a U.S.–British sponsored English school, and spent 10 weeks in a summer English program in England. These experiences, plus a great deal of extra
preparation, Yuko believed, helped her score so well on the TOEFL (640).

Spack undertook this study when Yuko, at that time a freshman, begged to   37
be let into one of Spack's ESL composition classes at her East coast university
in spite of demonstrated proficiency on the standardized test of English. Yuko
was one of those students whose high TOEFL score did not give her confidence
that she could survive her first semester at the U.S. university where Spack was
teaching. In halting speech, Yuko told Spack that in Japan she had not learned
what she needed to learn in order to compete in a U.S. university, such as
essay writing and efficient reading. Her many cross-cultural comparisons show
that she believed that the games of academic writing differed in Japan and the
United States. In her view, acquiring and memorizing information were needed
to succeed in the Japanese educational context, and creativity and originality
of opinion were needed in the U.S. context. She also seemed convinced that her
silence in class, ingrained in her from her many years in the Japanese system,
was holding her back. Pulled in conflicting directions, she was "attracted to
what she perceived to be the 'American style' because, in the American way,
'I can have my own point of view,' " yet felt unable to participate actively and
"superficially" in her classes as she thought many Americans did (p. 16).

At first Spack became curious about Yuko's literacy experiences in Japan and   38
how those would compare to her experiences in her freshman college classes.

But within a few weeks, Yuko was asking Spack for specific help with one class in International Relations that she was having trouble with. Spack decided to interview Yuko over the first year, to collect materials from the International Relations class, and to observe and take notes on Yuko in Spack's own English classes. Continuing the data collection into Yuko's third year, Spack held interviews and conversations with Yuko about her reading and writing experiences, observed Yuko in Spack's English class, and collected documents from Yuko's other classes and drafts of Yuko's papers.

We learn from Spack's study that perhaps the hardest aspect of Yuko's stu-   39
dent life in her first year was what Yuko herself called her lack of background knowledge and vocabulary. In her first International Relations class, she simply could not understand the readings in her textbook. Spack provided us with an excerpt from the book which suggested that the fault was not entirely Yuko's. Still, when her professor then asked the students to write an "original," "aggressive" paper applying course materials to a choice of topics, she gave up and dropped the course, not having developed at this point any survival game strategies. In her second semester, she had a similar experience in a Philosophy of Religion course, finding she "didn't have a clue" what the readings were about. Having dropped two courses, she went home for the summer, wondering whether to change majors.

However, Yuko's experiences in Spack's English courses during that same   40
difficult first year seemed to be those of another person. Although Yuko did not recognize fully the changes that Spack saw, she did in fact become a more fluent and fearless writer, and took on (in Spack's eyes) the identity of a person who could defend herself in class when challenged intellectually by classmates during debates and write clearly and coherently. Yuko did not yet see herself in these terms.

At home in Japan that summer, Yuko read novels in English. She came back   41
for her second year refreshed, determined not to give up, more confident in her reading ability, and armed with new game strategies. For example, she told Spack that she had stopped worrying about not being able to understand every word of every reading, was avoiding difficult readings when she had a choice of topics, and read differently according to the kind of text and to the treatment that text was given in her classes. She also learned to choose paper topics to which she could apply some of her background knowledge of Asia, and she learned as well to string together passages of text, with page numbers given, taken from her sources. The teaching assistants and teachers who read her papers, and even Spack herself at first, did not notice the extent of Yuko's "textual borrowing." Yuko remained torn about these papers, believing that her job was to come up with original ideas and phrasings throughout her papers as well as in introductions and conclusions. She was surprised that the "Japanese style" of textual borrowing and repeating information that she had hoped to leave behind actually worked to improve her grades (p. 32; cf. Currie's [1998] Diana). However, she was still convinced at the end of the second year that "there was a Japanese way of writing and an American way of writing, the former being a repetition of the ideas contained in a reading and the latter being

an original opinion provided by the (student) writer" (p. 39). Spack saw that Yuko was amply rewarded for repeating ideas from her readings, and recognized that student writers in the United States face the same dilemma—that of trying to write from sources and to be original at the same time. For her part, Yuko saw her confidence increase as she began to get As and Bs in her classes, a result, she believed, of "practice," of consulting with professors and TAs, and of learning to selectively ignore what she did not know (pp. 38–39). Yuko retook the International Relations course that she had dropped her first year, as well as a sociology course where the professor guided students to a deeper understanding of the material through reading response journals and systematic assignments. In her third year, Yuko continued taking more control of the reading and writing activities in ways that suited her abilities and interests and that integrated her own knowledge with what she was learning.

In the conclusion of her article, Spack describes some of the changes that   42 Yuko went through in her freshman, sophomore, and junior years. For example, she describes Yuko's early model of reading this way:

- Good students grasp meaning the first time they read.
- Good students understand every word of every reading assignment.
- Good students read everything assigned.
- Good students read everything on schedule. (p. 45)

Yuko gradually began to dispel these myths as she learned to read strategically and purposefully (see Haas's [1994] case study of Eliza, an undergraduate student learning to read biology texts), and to recognize that "American writing" was not original in the way she had believed at first. Writers, she learned, drew on other sources all the time. Critical thinking was based on what writers understood from published authorities.

Yuko believed, according to Spack, that she had learned to read and write   43 in an "American style," and that she had finally overcome her "Japanese style." Not having access to data on Yuko from Japan, Spack wisely refrains from commenting on the accuracy of Yuko's belief. What she does tell us is that Yuko's perception of her educational background in Japan influenced her approach to and her theorizing about the development of her academic literacy in the United States (p. 47) and that her background knowledge of Japanese culture became important in helping her develop topics for writing. Yuko, in other words, did not give up her Japanese identity, nor did she fully take on the identity of her mythical American student, but perhaps she discovered new aspects of her self, integrated them with the old, and played one off against the other. With time and maturity and with greater understanding of the complexity of academic environments and practices, she also lost some of her idealism. More realistic by the end of her third year, she had learned through situated practice in a wide variety of very different courses how to read and write strategically in ways that ensured her survival in a competitive foreign language academic environment. In the end, Yuko learned how to play the different writing games in her academic setting in her own way and crafted a complex academic identity that matched no stereotypes (even her own) of passive Japanese learners who supposedly depend on rote memorization for their success (see Kubota [1997, 1999] for critiques of these stereotypes). She was beginning to reconcile, in other words, her different forms of membership, what Wenger (1998) calls "multimembership," into a coherent and complexly negotiated identity that did not require that she give up any aspects of her past self. As part of her survival games strategies, she was learning instead to reinterpret her role and location of herself within the undergraduate community.

The Beginning of Change: Situated Survival?

The diverse and complex academic literacy games that the undergraduates in 44 these case studies were learning required that the students develop survival strategies in multiple local contexts rather than expertise as academic writers in focused disciplinary communities. Students who might have been able to identify themselves as successful academic writers based on their early experiences in some classes (e.g., Sternglass' students in their composition classes, Yuko in her ESL classes, Dave in his biology and composition classes) apparently did not recognize these successes as ones that could influence their literacy activities or their academic identities in other settings. Rather, they saw them as isolated responses to particular teachers and assignments. They did not see the undergraduate setting as part of a larger enterprise in which embedded communities of practice might have shared goals and practices (Wenger, 1998).

Of course they may have had trouble seeing the commonalities in academic 45 literacy games across the broad spectrum of classes they took because there weren't many. Indeed, research has revealed many disciplinary differences in academic writing, but equally importantly many differences according to particular teaching–learning situations. The key to the students' survival in academic settings thus involved their ability to figure out what was expected in each class—strategic social and interpretive skills rather than just formal academic writing skills. Moreover, as Brown, Collins, and Duguid (1989) pointed out some time ago, because much school learning takes places without immersing students in "authentic activity" in disciplinary domains, students are "asked to use the tools of a discipline without being able to adopt its culture" (p. 33). The systemic constraints of undergraduate education, with its brief forays into multiple disciplines and their concomitant literacy practices, make it unlikely that many students will come to identify with one or more of these disciplinary subcultures or will come to see coherence in the larger educational enterprise.

Although it is not clear that the undergraduate students I discussed in these 46 case studies came to see themselves as participants in a community of academic writers or as experts within the academy rather than as just survivors, their evolving identities as survivors on a wide range of academic playing fields will stand them in good stead. They developed a sense of what kinds of games were played, who some of the key players were, and what strategies they needed to employ to—literally—get the grade. With or without a local academic village (Geertz, 1983) in which to situate themselves, they had learned that academic writing games involve more than learning sets of formal game rules, and this lesson is foundational to the development of academic literacy.

Case Study: Communities of Practice? Game Strategies in Two Teachers' EAP Classes in a Japanese University

In this section I wrestle with the question of what a "communities of practice" [47] (Lave, 1996; Lave & Wenger, 1991; Wenger, 1998) EAP classroom might look like in an undergraduate English-as-a-foreign language setting and explore what kinds of game strategies might be practiced in such a setting. Given issues that have been raised in the literature discussed earlier, can such a framework be rationalized? What kinds of practices, identities, and transitions do teachers envision for their undergraduate EAP students, and what is it that students believe they are learning and practicing? In particular I hoped to learn what the two teachers I studied believed the most important aspects of academic writing were and how they introduced students to them in a brief one-semester course. Moreover, as proponents of versions of a "communities of practice" framework in our own teaching, all three of us wondered how such communities of practice could be enacted in a structurally constrained EAP foreign language setting in ways that would help students become participants in academic conversations (Casanave & Kanno, 1998) and help them begin to see themselves as writers with something to say. We could not send them out to become "ethnographers" of English-language academic literacy practices on our own university campus (Currie, 1999; Hirvela, 1997; Johns, 1990, 1995) because nearly all work was done in Japanese. Nevertheless, by the end of the study, I knew I would be able to present the study as a success story, one that demonstrated what was possible given hard work and engagement with challenging tasks (Bazerman, 1995; Leki, 1995a), in spite of my unresolved questions about academic literacy games.

Two Teachers, Two Communities of Practice

Background to the Study

In the spring of 1997, one of the teachers (Yasuko) and I undertook a semester- [48] long research project on our Japanese university campus to find out what the attitudes and practices were of five teachers of a newly established Academic Reading and Writing course for our undergraduates. The course was originally conceived by me and the second teacher (David) as a step in helping prepare our junior and senior students for future graduate work in English-medium universities. Many of our undergraduate students are advanced users of English, and some of these and other students as well dream of one day studying abroad (meaning outside Japan). Much to our surprise, in spite of a course description emphasizing graduate preparation and a course enrollment limited to 15, more than 100 students tried to enter the first two sections taught by David that were opened the semester before this study was undertaken. Clearly many of the students wanted more than a narrowly defined course in graduate preparation; they wanted more academic English as well, or perhaps just more English, regardless of their plans for future study. We opened more sections the next semester.

Yasuko and I worked together to help set up the multiple sections of the course. The other teachers of the new sections requested some guidance about what and how to teach this course, so we provided a broadly defined template of the course on Academic Reading and Writing that David had written, one that emphasized that we hoped to prepare students for critical reading and writing that they might need in graduate school and that students should design their own writing projects. All the teachers had the freedom to redesign the course in whatever way they saw fit, with the proviso that we wanted students to have a hands-on writing experience with topics chosen by them and not just to learn *about* writing. For the study, Yasuko and I observed five sections and took detailed field notes three times (beginning, middle, and end of the semester), interviewing the teachers after each observation, transcribing those interview tapes, and collecting class syllabuses and handouts. We also distributed a questionnaire in Japanese two times (beginning and end of the semester) to all students (about 140) asking them about their reasons for taking the class, their paper topics, and their responses to the class. Students responded in Japanese or English, as they wished; I had the Japanese responses from David's and Yasuko's students translated to English by two Japanese assistants. We did not collect student papers since our project was not focusing on text analysis. For my part of this project, I observed and interviewed David and Yasuko. Because I knew David and Yasuko quite well, our conversations about academic literacy didn't stop when the tape recorder went off, so some of my "data" and my interpretations slide off the field note and transcript pages and into the fuzzy realm of remembered lunches, dinners, and phone and e-mail chats. I also taped an interview with five of Yasuko's students mid-semester in English, and kept copies of the first month of e-mail conversations among David's students and between them and him. I used the questionnaire information to compile a general profile of students from that semester and to learn more about the goals and responses to the class of David's and Yasuko's students in particular. 49

We began the project with questions that the three of us continued to explore throughout the semester about what we should be doing in an undergraduate academic literacy course in a foreign language setting, our responses becoming more complex with the accumulation of experience in our particular setting. I believe that similar questions can be asked of any course that aims to help prepare undergraduate writers for more advanced academic work. Here are some that underlay our project and that I continue to wrestle with: To what extent were these classes about teaching and learning aspects of the English language or about teaching and learning some of the social and political values and practices associated with writing in academic settings? Does the argument that students need to get a head start in possible future graduate work in English-medium settings make sense, given our belief in the situated learning framework 50 and in the preeminent role of our own *in situ* academic enculturation? A head start in what? Does the apprenticeship metaphor work here, where EAP teachers are seen as mentors and expert models for novice practitioners, or does this metaphor work better at graduate levels? In what ways can the foreign language EAP classes of the two teachers I observed, David and Yasuko, be considered "communities of practice"? As "coaches" of academic writing games, how did David and Yasuko seem to understand and practice various academic writing games in their respective sections? In the discussion that follows, I first introduce David and Yasuko and their classes, then touch on some of these questions through a discussion of some of the classroom game strategies that David and Yasuko seemed to feel were relevant to their young students' development of academic literacy. I also bring in some of their students' views, in particular as documented in their open-ended responses in Japanese and English to questionnaires. The games were played in quite different ways in the two classes; some of the differences can be attributed to the two teachers' own experiences with academic literacy practices in their graduate school enculturation and in their current writing activities.

David

By the time I interviewed and observed David as part of the larger research   51
project on our campus about academic writing, I had known him for almost 6 years. A colleague of mine and I had interviewed him for a 3-year position in 1992, for which he was hired. We both liked his sense of humor and his energy in addition to his CV. Tall and athletic, sandy hair beginning to thin, David was in his mid-thirties at the time. He had traces of a southern U.S. accent that made a nice addition to the collection of Englishes in our program. When he arrived on our campus David was just finishing his dissertation in language education from a university in Georgia. I didn't think he could finish in a year and work full time, but he did. Since that time he had taught, read, presented, and written in areas such as foreign language education, cross-cultural pragmatics, and intercultural communication.

Fluent in Japanese, married to a Japanese, and the father of two young   52
"doubles" (he refused to refer to his children as "half Japanese and half American"), he had special interests and experience in Japan that made him a particularly committed teacher. He saw and resisted the constraints and limitations imposed by aspects of the Japanese educational system and worked hard to help talented young students see a larger academic world. At the same time, he understood and respected other aspects of the Japanese culture and educational system, and so seemed to me to feel pushed and pulled by conflicting understandings and goals. On our campus, David was particularly committed to helping high English proficiency students develop academic literacy. He had taught many conversationally fluent, seemingly bilingual English students in his undergraduate classes and believed these students could develop their full potential as bilinguals if they could become as literate in English as they were fluent in conversation. Moreover, some of these students wished to join

graduate programs in English-medium universities, and one way to help prepare them was to introduce them to North American practices of academic reading and writing that he was familiar with. He was instrumental in designing the original template for the reading and writing course, three semesters before our project took place—a course that because of institutional constraints was limited to one semester. At the time we worked together on this template we both knew that a one-semester course could barely scratch the surface of what students needed: lots of writing and reading practice, in-depth discussions, and designing and carrying out their own writing projects. What we didn't talk about explicitly at the time were the harsh realities of academic enculturation, where learning to participate in the many kinds of academic practices seems to take place through immersion in academic settings, in sometimes highly politicized interactions with different professors and colleagues, over many years. We were familiar with these realities from our own graduate educations.

David had taken a number of courses in his own graduate program that 53 dealt with literacy issues, and had been teaching aspects of academic literacy for a number of years. He himself was reading and writing whenever his tight schedule permitted, in Japanese (a lecture series course he was teaching) as well as in English. He wrote papers for conferences at least once a year, and whenever we talked, had several papers in the hopper waiting to be revised for publication. Talk about his research and writing was punctuated with acerbic though humorous comments about his heavy schedule, lack of time, and the dilemma of how to balance all of his obligations. David mentioned in his first interview that he felt he was not reading and writing enough, but that the manuscript reviews he did for academic journals and the masters thesis advising he did for an American university in Tokyo helped him understand what students needed in an academic reading and writing class. In other interviews he talked about designing his class activities and responses from "intuition." His high energy, intensity, and perfectionist tendencies kept him in a state of uncertainty throughout the semester, but also ensured that he did everything possible to conduct what he and students could assess as a successful class— one that resulted in students' production of a "good paper" and in everyone's sense of accomplishment. From my observations and interviews, I got a sense of what David thought the academic writing game was all about, and of what aspects of the practice he intuitively, as well as overtly, believed undergraduates needed to know in order to begin participating.

Yasuko

I first met Yasuko when she came to our campus for an interview for a posi- 54 tion in our English section. A native Japanese, she was still finishing up the last details of her PhD program in Canada where she had specialized in bilingual education and qualitative research methods. I remember sitting at a lunch table with her and several other colleagues and being struck by how tiny she was. I felt clumsy, large, and bulky next to her. She seemed half my height and weight, and I wondered where she was able to find clothes that fit her. The second surprise was how articulate and firm she was in her discourse with us, in her slightly British-accented English. I wondered at the time where all this confidence had come from in someone so young and tiny when I, at 20 years her senior, was still experiencing unsettling ups and downs in professional identity and in my relationship with the academic world. Was it an act, the kind we all perform when we are on stage in the serious game of the job interview? Or did she really have a comfortable sense already of who she was? Or, a third possibility, had she just not yet been burned by any of the political games in academia that tend to sap one's enthusiasm for the job? At any rate, I was taken with her freshness, her commitment to continuing her research, and her excitement, tempered with questions and inexperience, about teaching undergraduates. I sensed that the students would respond to her with enthusiasm, which they did.

At the time I observed her classes as part of our project she had been teach- 55 ing English at our university in her first full time job for about a year. She was teaching the Academic Reading and Writing course for the second time, two sections of it, plus regular required freshman and sophomore English classes. Throughout the semester in which I observed and interviewed her, she was doing her own academic reading and writing in addition to teaching her regular English classes, including "freewriting" that she did with her students and on her own, work on a paper from her dissertation for future publication, and reading in the areas of academic literacy, cultural readjustment, and Japanese minority children. She had had no formal training in the teaching of writing, although she had once taken an EAP-Iike course which she claimed had helped her understand what would be expected of her in her PhD program. Before arriving on our campus, as was the case for David, she had been immersed in nonstop reading and writing experiences for the 6 or so years of her doctoral work. As had David, Yasuko mentioned throughout the semester in which I observed her that her previous and current academic literacy experiences at the graduate level greatly influenced her class practices and reflected aspects of her own academic enculturation that she felt were important.

The Students and the Course

On our campus, an old private university, students came from all over Japan, 56 many entering through the grueling entrance exam process (see Brown & Yamashita, 1995; Frost, 1991) and some through Admissions Office processes involving special applications and interviews. Quite a few students were "returnees"—students who had spent several years in foreign countries where their businessmen fathers were stationed. All students were required to take a foreign language in their freshman and sophomore years, and could take some of the few elective language courses once their language requirement was fulfilled.

From the questionnaire data gathered from all of the students (136 responded 57 to the first one) at the beginning of the semester, we learned that most were sophomores (about 61%) and about 25% were juniors, even though the course was intended for juniors and seniors Seventy percent were women, and more than half had lived abroad for 1 year or more. Over 80% had learned something about writing in Japanese in their past schooling, and more than 50% had studied some kind of writing in English. About half of the students said they would seek full-time jobs after graduating, and about one third said they would pursue graduate study abroad. Most students claimed they liked to write or at least felt neutral about it (83% for Japanese, 75% for English). Moreover, many of the students said they read books and magazines outside of class in Japanese (88%) and just over half claimed to do so in English (52%). These last two sets of figures say something important about the students who chose to take the Academic Reading and Writing course—most enjoyed and practiced reading and writing in both their first and second languages.

In the open-ended responses to the first questionnaire, students explained 58 why they had decided to take the course and described what their goals were. David's and Yasuko's students, for the most part, stated that they hoped to maintain or "brush up" their English. About one third of their students said they needed academic English because they wished to study abroad some day or that they needed English for their future jobs. These figures accord with the general profile of the whole group. Specifically they said they hoped to learn aspects of basic writing skills, learn how to write good "high level" academic reports and papers, and to learn to express their ideas clearly and fluently. Some students, particularly those in David's very high level class, expressed a desire to learn specific techniques of writing, such as how to structure papers, how to collect reference materials, and how to write their opinions persuasively and logically. (Several of David's students had taken his class before and were aware of what they would be doing this particular semester.) In general, however, the students' personal goals for the class were quite general.

David and Yasuko taught two sections each, roughly considered the two 59 highest levels. In the sections that I observed, one for each teacher, there were 15 students in David's class and 6 students, all women, in Yasuko's class. Yasuko's class included as well one student from the newly opened graduate school on our campus. The classes met once a week for 90 minutes for 14 weeks. Except for the few students in David's class who had taken this same class before, none of the students had had a class in the development of academic literacy in English, and none had worked for a full semester on a major single-authored paper on a topic of their own choice in English or in Japanese even though some of them had done quite a bit of writing in freshman and sophomore English courses. In both David's and Yasuko's classes, most of the students had very high TOEFL scores, in the mid-500 to low 600 range, and some had spent more time living outside Japan than inside. These were "returnee" students, children of businessmen who had been stationed abroad by their Japanese companies and who had grown up bilingually. However, in some cases their English development had come to a halt in junior high school when they returned to Japan in order to enter the competitive race for entrance into a prestigious university. As Cummins (1981) and others have noted, fluency in oral conversation may be unrelated to competence in the text-related proficiencies required by people who need to read and write in the academy. Some students themselves were aware of and wished to close this gap.

The challenge facing David and Yasuko, and other teachers including me 60 (I had taught a section the previous semester), was where to start, and what to do in just one short semester of 13 or 14 class meetings. It seemed to all of us that students needed so much. We ourselves had learned to write in academic settings over many years, and most of that in graduate school. The one thing David and Yasuko and I did agree on was that we wanted to consider the undergraduate students in the classes to be inexperienced academic writers rather than just students lacking proficiency in English. All of us, after all, had once been novice academic writers and David and I could recall developmental experiences even in our native languages that made us squirm with discomfort. (Yasuko on the other hand continually surprised me by her love of writing.) We agreed, too, that we wanted students to "own" their topics, and to have ongoing support and interaction with teacher and peers as they struggled through their first writing experiences in these academically oriented classes. And as Bazerman (1995) advised, we wanted them to feel motivated enough to work very hard. To these ends, David had his students read and respond orally and in writing to academic journal articles and write a paper supported by at least five published sources. Yasuko had her students read and respond orally and in writing to nonfiction stories written by people who had done fieldwork, and then do their own ethnographic-style fieldwork project about which they were to write their own nonfiction story and give a class presentation. Amidst these broadly similar goals, what specific practices did these two teachers set up for their students? After briefly describing the setting for the two classes, I group my observations under several categories that I label "game strategies."

The Setting

To my eye, our campus is not conducive to encouraging student motivation, 61 study, and interaction. It was built on farm and forest land, opened in 1990, and was hailed as Japan's new innovative computer campus. It strikes me as gray and cold, built as it is of concrete slabs and a lot of glass. The landscaping in part makes up for the coldness; there are more trees and expanses of lawn than one usually sees at universities in the wider Tokyo area, and there is even a duck pond where an occasional snowy egret visits. On a rare clear day we can see Mt. Fuji from the fourth floors of the classroom buildings. But there are few places for the more than 4,000 students to sit, chat, study, and concentrate. The only outside seating consists of 10 card-table sized tables with a few metal chairs around each just outside the cafeteria and bookstore area. Weather permitting, some students sit on lawns. There are no dormitories, no general student center, and few quiet spaces in the media center-library, which is often crowded with noisy groups of students chatting behind a computer monitor or at one of the library study tables. Other than the rare empty classrooms, there are no other places for students to collaborate and study together. The classrooms themselves are square or rectangular gray concrete and glass rooms with bare walls, crowded with desk-chairs or heavy two-person tables with the teacher lectern or podium up front and close to the black or white board. Unless a teacher decides to take the noisy step of moving chairs and tables, all students face front in the regular 35–50 person rooms. Except for the smallest of the seminar rooms, chalk dust covered equipment abounds—large television monitor, VCR, OHP, tape system under the hinged desk top, and some with full computer-projecting systems.

David's and Yasuko's classrooms were designed to accommodate about 35   62 students. Like the design of the rest of the campus, the physical setting communicated that teaching and learning happens by transmission within classroom walls, from teachers-knowers to listening students, not around seminar tables or in lounges, cafes, and student centers. It did not convey the sense, in other words, that communication, engagement, and collaborative practice were central to the educational process. David and Yasuko, within these physical constraints, did what they could to create an atmosphere of engaged practice, warmth, and support for students, often leaving the front podium, rearranging seating, and joining student discussion groups. The "game strategies" they practiced in each of their classrooms differed in emphasis, but appeared in some form in both classes. I discuss six of these strategies below.

Game Strategy I: Interact with Texts and with Others about Texts

David and Yasuko hoped that their students would begin to see texts as enti-   63 ties with which they needed to interact constructively and about which they routinely interacted with peers and teachers. They both wanted students to read extensively, respond to what they read in writing and in discussion with them and peers, and to begin to see themselves as participants in conversations with authors and with each other about authors. The students in David's and Yasuko's classes had not conceptualized their relationships with texts in this way before. How did these two teachers set up games practices that might encourage students' changing relationship with texts? Reading response journals, discussion, and teacher feedback helped instigate this change.

Reading Response Journals and Follow-Up Discussion. Both David and Yasuko   64 asked students to read one or more common articles, write responses in a journal, and discuss their responses later in small group and whole class discussions. David also had his students read, respond to, and discuss articles each had found through an extensive literature search on an individual paper topic. David and Yasuko participated in discussions, sometimes as listeners, sometimes as commentators on the subject matter, and sometimes as guides to help students construct deeper, more critical and questioning responses, particularly in the case of a common reading article that they themselves knew well.

In my first observation very early in the semester, David was helping stu-   65 dents learn the serious game of how to respond to academic articles in writing and in talk and to interact with him and with each other in their discussions of readings, activities that he himself had learned to do in graduate school and that he was actively pursuing in his own current work. He had set up a small-group activity with reading response journals designed to get students interacting with each other through the texts they had read. He explained to them why this response activity was helpful. "It gives writers a sense that there are readers," he told the students, "that people are listening." At the end of class, in which the students had sat in their groups reading each others' journals and chatting quietly, he reminded them once again about the conversational nature of this academic activity: "These journals," he reiterated, "should be a conversation," not just between teacher and student but "sideways" too, between and among student readers and writers.

In revealing where this goal had come from, and his sense of how it could be 66
achieved, David said, "It came from my experience. It came from what I think is useful. Where else could it come from?" (Interview 1, 4/22/97). He clarified that this experience included not only his academic experiences in and out of graduate school, but also "peer advice and social interaction," his experience with Japanese schools, and his own theoretical orientations toward learning that he had developed through his own reading and study:

> The idea about reading and responding to a journal [article] was in part from my
> own theoretical interpretation about acquiring literacy, or acquiring language,
> through interaction, and by actually using the language. . . . I mean the practice
> develops out of that theory or theoretical interpretation. (Interview 1, 4/22/97)

Sometimes it was difficult to get students to direct their reading responses 67
to each other rather than just to the teacher. In my first observation of Yasuko at the beginning of the semester, she had asked her small group of women students to talk about the nonfiction readings they had chosen from her reserve list—a collection of well-written narratives she had put on reserve that were models of good nonfiction storytelling. She had chosen readings that she herself had found especially engaging and hoped that students, too, would become caught up in the stories about autistics, a male prostitute, or a well-known singing group, and find themselves getting to know the characters as well as the textual structure of the stories themselves. Her instructions to her small group of women students on this day were to talk about what they had read and about how they felt about what they had read. Her goal was to have students interact with each other about these readings, not just with her, and to respond to the descriptions and dilemmas of the characters and to the authors' manner of telling their stories.

The students did not yet know each other well, but I was struck in this 68
early class by how hesitant and teacher-oriented this small group of advanced English-speaking young women seemed to be. The talk tended to be directed at Yasuko in the beginning of this activity, more like an informal presentation than interaction among group members. Like most students, these young women were more familiar with a transmission model of education where information from a text was to be displayed back to a teacher, not used as a basis for interaction with classmates or with the text itself. Students had written in their response journals on their chosen readings, so referred to their papers as they

talked, but the first young woman to speak about her Oliver Sacks article on autism made eye contact only with Yasuko. Before the second student began to talk, Yasuko stood up suddenly and commented that students should be talking to each other. She then moved out of the circle and back to a seat behind a large teacher's desk. Just after the student began talking, again maintaining eye contact only with her, Yasuko quietly left the room. The speaker continued talking, looking down at her paper and now making eye contact primarily with the student who was sitting directly across from her. When Yasuko returned a few minutes later, the speaker continued without a break while two other women in the group nodded and backchanneled occasionally. Yasuko, at the teacher's desk, kept her gaze down at her own notebook of freewriting, flipping a page from time to time. Several other students talked about the articles they had read, fielding a few questions, and managing to interact with each other rather than with Yasuko, whose generally lowered eye gaze did not invite interaction with her.

However, Yasuko did participate actively in response to a pair of students 69 who had both read the same article—the second of two Oliver Sacks stories that were on reserve, this one on the effects of L-Dopa, the theme of the film "Awakenings." Both women spoke from a handout, which the other students followed as they spoke. Yasuko once asked, "So what can we learn from this?" In the discussion that followed, Yasuko was trying to get students to link the two texts by Sacks, to compare their structures, and to help them learn more about Sacks as a person and an author with extra information she was able to provide them. The discussion picked up. The students seemed curious about Sacks and wanted to know what was in the "rest of his book" and about "why he didn't insist anything, about what we should do." Yasuko filled these gaps as best she could in the limited time, trying to shape the author into a real person with whom students could communicate. The class laughed when Yasuko told them that Sacks "really likes footnotes" (some had complained about this characteristic of his writing) and that some of his articles devoted up to half a page to them. Yasuko talked about Sacks in the way she might talk about a colleague she knew, as someone with whom she had interacted over time through the many essays of his she had read. Students were getting a sense from this discussion that it was possible to relate to the authors they read as people with whom they could interact and that a serious expectation of academic literacy games was that readers interact with authors in just this way.

In this early class activity, I did not observe Yasuko explaining to students 70 how to communicate about the texts they had read, how to interact with the texts themselves through their journals (a required writing activity), or how to communicate with each other about texts. Yasuko chose instead to arrange the activity so that students would not be able to communicate in the traditional unidirectional way with her or just receive information transmitted from her, but would be forced to talk to each other. She also modeled how becoming familiar with an author's body of work could allow readers to see authors as people with a coherent agenda that could be discussed from the perspectives of their different writings. In particular in her descriptions of "inside information" on author Sacks, she showed students (did not teach them) that for her reading meant getting to know authors, becoming familiar with their quirks and personal styles, and finding in them tricks of the trade to apply to her own writing. I had the feeling as observer that the students had not practiced these kinds of interactions before, with texts, and with each other about texts, and that in their "presentations" and discussions they could not yet relate to the authors as people with or about whom they might have a conversation. They were just beginning to practice this interaction game, and in some cases did this through the back door: By mid-semester, I saw that Yasuko had begun to acquaint students with the interactive aspects of academic reading and writing by modeling a way of relating to reading and writing that she had acquired in graduate school and that was evident in how she herself talked about texts and their authors.

Feedback and Response.   Part of the practice of interacting with and about 71 texts, for both teachers, involved extensive teacher involvement through written and oral feedback, both on reading response journals and on student papers. These activities conveyed the sense that oral and written interaction with texts of all kinds was a normal practice that had less to do with grading and evaluation than with what David called the practice of "engaged discussion" between novice and more experienced academic writers.

For his part, David responded in depth in writing to students' reading 72 response journals and to their paper drafts, modeling in sometimes excruciating detail his belief in the role of an involved listener in the development of academic literacy. This was one of his ways of "talking to" individual students. He felt particularly strongly about the mentor role of a teacher, noting that ongoing teacher-student interaction was essential for helping students produce a good paper—his main goal in this class. "The teacher has responsibility," he said. "A teacher's part of this whole construction. We're part of the conversation, and if we don't respond enough to the students, or motivate them, encourage them enough so they can produce a good paper, then we haven't really done enough work ourselves" (Interview 1, 4/22/97). In explaining his commitment to teacher involvement in the revision process, for example, he drew on his own experiences with publishing and the value for him of feedback and response from reviewers:

> And then the activity of writing the paper, the revision so necessary, that's not just theoretical. I've seen how students' papers have just changed after revision. And producing a paper—the one big journal article that I've had came out of intense negotiation with—back and forth with the editor. And any papers that I've had published have always been out of that revision process. The activities are doing what it takes to get a good paper published, my experience, what other people go through, this is in Lave and Wenger's—I mean this is actually the practice instead of the theory about it. Actually doing it. (Interview 1, 4/22/97)

Later in the semester David also provided numerous opportunities for stu- 73 dents to read each other's paper drafts and respond with questions (especially of clarification) and suggestions. During these sessions he would circulate around the room, visiting each group as listener and commentator. Additionally, David and his students interacted by e-mail throughout the semester, although those interactions dealt primarily with formal and practical matters such as searching for journal articles and developing appropriate descriptors for an Internet search. For her part, Yasuko often met with students individually to discuss issues and ideas related to their fieldwork project. These practices, along with David's and Yasuko's extensive written commentary on journals and drafts, demonstrated for students the social and inquiry-oriented nature of the academic writing game and the role of readers and listeners as active participants in the construction and interpretation of ideas.

Game Strategy 2: Blend Voices

Another common practice that novice academic writers wrestle with is that of   74
learning the serious game of merging the voices of published authorities with their own—to rely on others' voices and at the same time to stamp their written work with what Spack's (1997a) Yuko believed was creativity and originality. This challenge of merging voices loomed large for David's students, who were required to use at least five references with proper APA documentation to help support their arguments in their papers but who were not allowed to copy more than a few consecutive words from their sources without citing them. Yasuko's students, who wrote from a fieldwork experience, did not need to learn the citation game at this time.

In the mid-semester class observation, I watched David set up an activity   75
whereby students were to figure out how two authors of published papers they had collected were interacting. An exercise in how to merge voices—students' and those of two authors, David asked students in small groups to "compare and contrast" the two articles they had read by trying to put the key information from both authors into one sentence. As each student summed the ideas from two authors, the other students were to listen closely, make notes that would allow them to paraphrase what each speaker had said, and ask appropriate questions, especially to clarify meaning.

Students had never tried to merge the voices of two authors before, nor to   76
blend those voices with their own writing without the kind of textual borrowing that Westerners call plagiarism (Deckert, 1993; Pennycook, 1996). In this compare-contrast activity, and in students' papers, as reported by David, students found their first experience with multivocality extremely difficult. This conforms with my own experiences with undergraduate writers. In my mid-semester class observation, I watched David's students working together in small groups and was not sure whether they grasped how to carry out the practice that David had set up. At the end of the class, two of the students presented their multivocalic summaries to the whole class, pulling expressions from their readings and sounding authoritative. However, as one student said after presenting her brief but confident-sounding commentary on her two authors, "I didn't know what I was talking about." Kenny, the student who

"didn't know what she was talking about," may have just been going through the motions of knowing how to play this particular game, but she and the other students had at the very least experienced their first tries at showing how authors "converse" and how they as novice writers could interact with these interacting authors.

At the same time, the students were encouraged to blend David's editorial 77 voice with theirs without needing to acknowledge him as a source, a different game strategy altogether. In a final interview at the end of the semester, David talked about inter- and intratextual interaction, and the blending of voices. He noted that in his own editing of students' drafts, he did not consider students' use of his own words to be plagiarism:

> So that my comments to students when I gave them editorially on their rough drafts were designed in that way, so that I would instead of trying to correct students' writing, I see it as rephrasing, adopting their point of view and talking in their voice, and they can use my words to pick them up and incorporate into their own writing. That's a theoretical notion of what I'm trying to do in interacting with students, responding to their writing and helping them to coconstruct a paper. (Interview 3, 7/18/97)

For David, the major issue was not plagiarism. "The major issue," he said in the final interview, "is in terms of dialogicality, or heteroglossia, multivocality." A copied argument, he explained, was unevaluated and underdeveloped, and therefore needed to be rephrased and explained in students' own words—which themselves were a paradoxical blending of theirs and his—as well as paraphrased and cited from sources. David wanted students to own their topics and papers, yet believed theoretically and in practice in the necessity, the inevitability, of the multivocality of academic discourse. He had no intention of resolving this paradox one way or the other. As he did in his own writing, students needed to learn to wrestle with this paradox themselves with their new awareness that in academic writing games in English, writers tried to distinguish between words they owned and words they borrowed from others (Pennycook, 1996).

In Yasuko's class, the task of blending voices differed in that students' main 78 writing project was not a library research paper but an experiential "ethnography," involving fieldwork observations and interviews that students then needed to craft into a well-told story. The voices that needed to be blended were those of people they had met, with their own voices as storytellers. Yasuko told me that she purposely did not ask students to consult library resources for this project because she did not want to deal with the problem of plagiarism and because one of her primary goals was to help students learn to tell a good nonfiction story from their own experiences and interactions with particular people in a particular setting. Such a story might, however, include direct quotes from her informants. The project, in other words, was set up so that the voices of others that found their way into students' work formed a natural part of the narratives that students constructed. Yasuko provided a handout to students on how to include these voices in their stories. I found it interesting that she did not consider this type of writing to be "academic," as is evident in the following quote from our mid-semester interview:

> We talked about citations a bit, although I don't focus too much on citations and APA style. Actually I don't focus on APA style at all because I don't think of this [project] as academic—academic reading and writing. Um, but then I thought you know if they want to quote their participants' own words, it would be useful to know how to cite people's words. So I prepared a little handout on that, and talked about that. (Interview 2, 6/10/97)

The only exercise in blending textual voices was in the first part of the semester in which students read and responded to nonfiction articles, described under Game Strategy 1. Moreover, unlike in David's class, Yasuko's students were not required to turn in drafts of their papers, but about a third did. In those cases, Yasuko provided extensive comments but without actually editing students' words. In all other cases, the first full draft that Yasuko saw was the final one. Yasuko's own voice, therefore, did not appear in students' papers in the way it did in David's. (See Game Strategy 3.)

Game Strategy 3: Own Your Research Experiences and Tell a Good Story from Them

A goal in both David's and Yasuko's classes was for students to pursue a topic of their own choice that had been developed and narrowed in discussion with teacher and peers. This they did. But because Yasuko's students did a fieldwork project in the second half of the semester, Yasuko felt they would be able to own their topics in ways that would be difficult to achieve with a library paper. The fieldwork, she explained in our last interview, was what gave students something to talk about, and was something uniquely owned by them. She talked in the mid-semester interview about some of these projects, which turned out to capture her own interest as well as that of classmates:

> Ok one woman is doing a study on a tea ceremony. [Yasuko describes the process briefly.] Another person is really interested in the interface between human beings and gadgets. And for that she is observing physically disabled people using computers. (...) And actually that's turning out to be really quite interesting. Because she's actually talking to one disabled person who communicates with her on e-mail, that way, because he actually cannot talk, or he has a hard time talking. But you know he uses the computer to talk with her. (...) And ah oh, what else are they do—oh another girl is observing a law firm. (Interview 2, 6/10/97)

Students then began to construct their stories in the form of informal class presentations soon after they had begun their fieldwork. Yasuko also provided instruction in how to structure a good story, including an exercise in which students analyzed the story structure of the readings they had done in the first part of the semester, and how to write a coherent paragraph (see Game Strategy 6). In the presentations of their final papers, a session that I observed, the students told structured stories about these real settings and people, using a variety of visuals that added another personal touch, such as their own PowerPoint displays and video clips.

By virtue of the fact that each of the students' fieldwork experiences was 80 unique and incapable of being checked as one might check students' cited sources, students owned their projects in ways that differed from David's students. The sense that students had come to own their experiences and their tales of them was evident to me in the last class in which the students were giving their final presentations. Their stories, uniquely theirs, captured the attention of their peers, teacher, and me in ways that summaries and analyses of previously told stories could not.

Game Strategy 4: Speak with Authority

The practices that novice readers and writers engage in influence how they 81 identify themselves within their academic settings and the authority with which they learn to express their knowledge and their identities. As we have seen from Chiseri-Strater's (1991) study of Anna and Nick, there is no guarantee that students will come to see themselves as academic writers in the way that more mature students might (Ivanič, 1998; Sternglass, 1997). On the other hand, from my own studies of journal writing I found that students can indeed come to see themselves as writers and thinkers in a university setting even without writing conventional academic papers (Casanave, 1992, 1995). In both David's and Yasuko's classes, in different ways, this was one of the goals that the two teachers had for their students. David and Yasuko wanted their students to begin to see themselves as writers who had something to say and who were aware that someone (peers, teachers) was reading and responding.

David saw this partly as an issue of voice. As I mentioned in a previous sec- 82 tion, David felt that the students needed to learn to do more than just report on an article. In the mid-semester interview after the class in which he had asked students to merge the main ideas in two of their reading articles he said:

> The big issue is the authorial voice. They're finding articles, and they're pursuing a topic, so with five articles in less than ten weeks, I think topic development is great. The question is, you know, do they, in the words of a student who came to me after class today, do they know what they think. And the question is, are they able to handle all of this, and to merge it, and to pull it together. Are they able to deal with it. . . . I see that as issues of voice and interpretation. (Interview 2, 5/27/97)

In asking students to do this kind of exercise in merging voices, David hoped to help students develop their own voices by helping them learn to be critical readers:

> It's built on something that last semester and the semester before that I noticed, that the students in developing their authorial voice that they need to be able to evaluate. That puts them in a position that lets them judge the advantages disadvantages, good points weak points. It's strengthening their voice in a sense. (Interview 2, 5/27/97)

Students learn to mimic an authorial voice as part of the writing games they 83
become familiar with in college. Bartholomae (1985) discussed this aspect of
learning academic literacies, as did Ivanič (1998) in her study of adult undergraduate writers, all of whom took on different voices that distanced them
from or identified them with voices in the academy. In Penrose and Geisler's
(1994) case study comparison of authorial voice in a freshman and PhD level
writers in philosophy, the novice freshman writer seemed to believe that an
authorial voice was one that presented "facts" as gleaned from her sources.
However, she had only a minimal sense of how the voices in her sources were
speaking to each other, and no sense of her own role in this conversation. In my
study, however, David seemed concerned with helping students develop confidence in themselves as writers who actually could speak with some authority.
After all, they had researched their own topics in areas in which David himself
and classmates as well were not necessarily authorities. Nevertheless, knowing
how long the practice of learning to speak authoritatively takes to develop
when young writers are relying on published sources (the "real" authorities,
some students believe, by virtue of having claims in print), David felt he had
barely scratched the surface of this practice with his students. He and his own
students (as expressed in their final questionnaire) both knew that one semester
provides too little time for inexperienced writers to take on authoritative roles
as participants in academic conversations.

Yasuko's students, on the other hand, in their final presentations and papers 84
spoke with the authority of "researchers" who owned their knowledge and
experiential resources. No one else in the class, neither peers nor teacher, were
experts on their topics, nor could expertise be accrued from published sources.
Yasuko had helped her students find a formal structure for their stories, but
the stories themselves were told by the students with the authority of writers who have first-hand knowledge. In our last interview, Yasuko described at
length some of the presentations from her other class that I had not witnessed,
indicating how much she and classmates had learned from each one. It seemed
to me, in other words, that David's more formal academic exercise of writing from sources helped students own their topics and develop an authoritative voice (a textual phenomenon?), whereas Yasuko's project helped students
develop authoritative personae (a social role?). As we know from work by
Ivanič (1994, 1998), a writer's identity, which I believe includes both voice
and persona, is constructed by and represented in texts, a most serious game
indeed. (See Ivanič, 1994, for a discussion of Goffman's terms for the different
ways identity can be represented in texts.)

Game Strategy 5: Learn to Love Writing (or at Least to Become Fluent)

Becoming a fluent, nonhesitant writer is a goal that some of us continue to 85
carry with us into our gray-haired years even if we have given up hope of ever
being able to say we love writing. Like me, David often struggled with his own
writing even though he seems to me to be a fluent and accomplished writer in
English and a budding academic writer in Japanese. Like most academic writers,

he ties his writing practices closely to his reading practices. The two kinds of fluency go together. From his perspective, then, he sympathized with students greatly and understood how much reading and writing his class entailed. In his interviews he did not talk about helping students learn to love writing. Nevertheless, the weekly reading response journals and multiple paper drafts that he required ensured that students who completed the course would develop fluency they had not had before. In their final questionnaires, some students commented on how valuable the regular and extensive reading and writing activities had been.

Yasuko, on the other hand, hoped her students would learn to love writing, 86 to become close observers of a setting and of the people in it, and to tell a good story, all intertwined aspects of qualitative research that she had learned in her PhD program. She wanted them, in other words, to come to see themselves as writers and as storytellers. In addition to the fieldwork experience, she also asked students to write often and write a lot in class, following the practice of freewriting that she herself benefitted from and paralleling in some ways the practice of regular journal writing that some of them had done in freshman and sophomore English classes. She also wanted her students to see her as a practicing writer. In one class early in the semester that I observed, she asked students to write nonstop for 10 minutes, as she herself wrote in her own journal, a Peter Elbow (1973) practice. As I both watched and participated, I marveled at the amount of writing that these Japanese students were producing in English and noted that some of them, as well as Yasuko herself, wrote faster than I did.

Yasuko explained that her goals for her writing class came very strongly 87 from her own experience, not so much from being taught, but "by doing it" (Lave & Wenger, 1991), an experience she tried to replicate with her own students that semester. Believing that "you improve if you write a lot," she had asked her students to do what she herself had been asked to do in graduate school, where she had developed her own identity as an academic writer:

> I learned that from personal experience, mostly in grad school, when I was writing a PhD dissertation. Because I was—Oh because when I first went to Canada, I took a course, I think it was Merrill Swain's course on applied linguistics or something. And part of the requirement was that every week there was a talk by someone, and you had to read an article on reserve by that person, and you either have to write a summary of it, or write a critique of it. And so every week, you are supposed to write say two pages, three pages. And that was really really hard when I first went there. And maybe that was a three-day project for me? But then towards the end, after six years, I could probably sit down in an afternoon and do it. Because I had written so much by then. (Interview 1, 4/28/97)

At the end of that semester, she spoke about whether she felt her goals 88 for her class had been achieved, goals that paralleled her own goals for her research and writing. She said that her goal of getting students interested in the process of writing came through in the final papers, an ambition that was close to her heart, as she had expressed in our first interview:

I guess the reason why that's so important to me is because that's really what I learned to do in the course of my PhD. And that's really changed my life, my professional life, and my personal life too, in that now— I mean I used to follow the last minute shot, last minute writing pattern, too. But then after learning to do journal writing and writing narrative way, I learned to integrate writing into my life, and my life is so much richer for it? . . . So I guess I'd like my students to have that experience too. (Interview 1 4/28/97)

Yasuko believed that her students had begun to see themselves as writers who could communicate their "owned" knowledge and experiences to an interested audience in an academic setting. In their final questionnaires, her students, like David's, commented on the value to them of the extensive opportunities for writing, reading, and discussion. I don't know if her students learned to love writing more than they might already have, but they learned not to dread it, and they learned that by practicing it regularly it did get easier. These are essential game strategies for academic writers.

Game Strategy 6: Make the Paper Look Right

Much has been written about the role of genre conventions and rhetorical 89 structure in academic writing, and arguments persist about whether we should teach students to conform to or resist formal conventions (see comments in the previous section). In different ways, Yasuko and David both taught students some formal features of academic writing that they expected to see in the final papers, partly for reasons of convention and partly for reasons of readability (requiring coherence of paragraphs, transitions between them, and so on).

David, for one, provided students with a great deal of detailed informa- 90 tion about rules and computer commands for formatting text and for citing and referencing in the very first class I visited, spending a full 10 minutes on these details. He insisted that students follow APA citing and referencing style, for example, and labored at length with examples on overhead transparency, handouts, and board to point out the dozens of details that he himself now used automatically (see Bazerman, 1987; Lynch & McGrath, 1993). David's focus on form as well as content from an early stage in the writing project communicated to me and to students a sense of his own values about the professional look of a paper, and about the need for formatting conventions to be practiced repeatedly (game-practice style) until they become second nature. The drafts of his own papers that I had seen in the past had all followed APA formatting conventions, those that he was teaching his students. Attention to these formal requirements at the earliest stages of writing, a much disparaged activity by some "process-oriented" scholars, might be thought of as attention to some of the sociolinguistically appropriate language game conventions that writers use when they communicate via academic texts.

In Yasuko's more formal teaching, to prepare students for structural analy- 91 ses of some of the narratives they had read and to help them structure their own narratives later, Yasuko talked about technical aspects of nonfiction story writing (paragraph writing, topic sentences, the characteristics of a good story). Unlike David, she had explicit lessons on paragraph writing and did structural analyses of the published readings but presented almost nothing on how to cite sources from readings. In interviews she talked about how important she felt it was for students to learn to write a well-structured paragraph and was continually amazed at how difficult this task—now second nature for her— was for students.

In their editorial comments on students' drafts as well as in class activities, [92] both David and Yasuko included comments that communicated to students the need to make their papers look right, although the formal features they emphasized differed. Neither teacher waited until the last stages of students' project write-ups to have students practice certain formal features of their writing, as so-called process approaches have suggested, but worked on them at different points throughout the semester, including in David's case from the very beginning.

Neither Yasuko nor David discussed their teaching in terms of strategies and [93] games. However, as I reflected on my experiences in their classrooms and on my discussions with them, the game analogy helped me to conceptualize what I saw and learned as structured, interactive, rule-governed practices. It also helped me understand that novice writers in undergraduate settings require a great deal of practice in the company of more expert players in order to learn to participate in such literate activities.

Students' Perspectives

The students in David's and Yasuko's classes struggled with a variety of aca- [94] demic game practices that these two teachers had set up. The students found David's class, in which reading and responding to academic journal articles formed a foundational practice in students' construction of their own papers, particularly difficult. In informal written evaluations that David asked students to write, they commented on specific difficulties: how difficult the reading and responding was, how limited their vocabulary, and how faulty their grammar. But these students and others also wrote that they felt they were learning how to think critically, that learning how to write in the way David was instructing them was essential for being able to communicate in a world where English was the dominant language of business and the Internet, and that the class was difficult but important. In the final questionnaire David's students said that by far the most difficult task in his class was finding appropriate journal articles, a literature search task that required that some of them travel to other university libraries. Several students commented on how difficult it was to blend voices: "[The most difficult thing was] combining all 5 or more articles and my opinion into one essay" and "Bringing the paper together at the end." For this last student, "Gathering the information was not at all difficult, but trying to mesh all the ideas together at the end" was. Looking back over the whole semester, students in both classes commented that classes were very hard work, but worth the effort.

The benefits, from the students' perspectives, were many. Five students from 95 Yasuko's classes whom I interviewed at the end of the semester spoke little of the traditional student concerns in school (i.e., grades) but seemed much more absorbed in the new interactive practices and ways of thinking that they were learning. In both classes, a majority of students commented in the final questionnaire on how valuable the small class discussions had been and many noted the value of regular reading and informal presentations. A student in David's class wrote that he or she had become consciously aware of readers, and another noted the value of learning how to avoid plagiarism and how to use references to back an opinion. One of Yasuko's students said that in this class it was possible to learn "formal writing," and "how to present ideas in a coherent and intellectual way."

Quite a few students in both classes commented in the final questionnaire 96 on the value of feedback and critical comments from teacher and peers. For example, as e-mail records from the interactions among David's students show, the students were consulting each other and David about various aspects of their projects, from descriptors needed to search for literature on their topics to technical and formal questions. Regular teacher and peer interaction occurred routinely in small group peer discussions and written commentary from the two teachers on journals and drafts. Yasuko's students as well shared fieldwork experiences and problems not just with Yasuko but also with each other. Lave and Wenger (1991) point out that in apprentice-type relationships it is quite typical that "apprentices learn mostly in relation with other apprentices" (p. 93).

A final question on the semester-end questionnaire asked students to give 97 advice to a friend who might be thinking about taking the course. Nearly all students in David's class commented on how much work the class was, and only those motivated students willing to "stick to it" should take the class, such as those determined to study abroad. Unlike some of the expectations they expressed in the first questionnaire, some students noted that this was not a general English course: "If you just want to brush up your English, don't take it." A student in Yasuko's class said, "If you really want to learn something and think hard, I recommend this class," and one in David's class said, "There is no other class that makes you think deeply."

In short, these students did not appear to view their classes in the same way 98 they viewed their other undergraduate classes or other foreign language classes. Yes, they were being graded and yes, they had to turn in a final paper (called "reports" in their other classes), but they could not cut and paste at the last minute. In interaction with each other and with their teachers, they had to involve themselves in reading, discussing, and writing activities, and in Yasuko's case in fieldwork, throughout the semester in order to achieve the final goal. Although David and Yasuko set up different academic literacy practices in their respective sections, both seemed to me to have established what could be called a mini-community of practice in which all students were participating in one sense or another as novice academic writers. The games they were learning involved far more than textbook exercises in grammar and writing. This finding parallels that by Freedman, Adam, and Smart (1994), who found that even "wearing suits to class" did not turn school writing into professional writing, but that the simulation activities they observed in a third-year financial analysis class did differ in important ways from more traditional class activities.

Communities of Practice in These Undergraduate EAP Classes?

David and Yasuko, looking mainly to their own backgrounds in and current 99 experiences with academic writing for guidance, had tried to figure out what their students needed and to create a community of practice in academic writing in English in a foreign language setting—a challenge by any stretch of the imagination. They hoped that the students would come to view themselves as participants in this classroom community of practice where writing and reading activities helped shape participants' identities. David hoped his students would develop an authorial stance—a sense of self as author—and knew this was particularly challenging for undergraduates (Ivanič 1998; Penrose & Geisler, 1994). His goal was similar to that of the teacher in Stuart Greene's (1995) case study of the development of authorship in the practices of two students in a beginning college writing class. By authorship Greene means what David intended: "the critical thinking skills that students use in their efforts to contribute knowledge to a scholarly conversation, knowledge that is not necessarily found in source texts but is nonetheless carefully linked to the texts they read"—an interpretive not a reporting activity (p. 187). David's students, as well as one of the two students in Greene's study, found this activity extremely difficult. It is thus questionable to what extent students' identities and participation practices can change in just one semester, which was all that David and Yasuko had, particularly in a foreign language setting. David sensed the beginnings of change, as did Yasuko with her students, who had learned to own and narrate a nonfiction story based on their fieldwork experiences.

However, using a "communities of practice" metaphor for interpreting 100 David's and Yasuko's classes is complicated by the fact that Lave and Wenger (1991; Wenger, 1998) do not consider a school to be a site where learning usually happens in the ways they conceptualize in their work in apprentice-style or organizational settings. In school settings, they point out, learning is usually viewed as internalization—in a cerebral sense—of bodies of knowledge as a result of students' being taught. They, on the other hand, are more interested in how learning happens inevitably as a result of learners' changing patterns of participation in the practices of specialized communities. This kind of learning, they note, results in ongoing changes of identity as newcomers become increasingly involved in the community's practices, including "new forms of membership and ownership of meaning" (Wenger, 1998, p. 219). Lave emphasizes that "learning is ubiquitous in ongoing activity, though often unrecognized as such" (Lave, 1993, p. 5). In a physics class, however, it is often not the community of physicists that students are learning to participate in, but the community of "schooled adults" except perhaps later at the graduate level (pp. 99–100). In this sense, students learn how to "do school" (Scribner & Cole, 1981)—learn how (as McCarthy's [1987] Dave concluded) to give teachers what they want and how to play the game well enough to get themselves through the system. In this view of school, students and teachers have clearly distinguished identities and participation practices.

In the communities of practice metaphor, however, learning happens and 101 identities are constructed through ongoing participation by all members in specialized practices. In this view, teachers and students cannot be neatly divided. As Lave (1996) points out, "the social-cultural categories that divide teachers from learners in schools mystify the crucial ways in which learning is fundamental to all participation and all participants in social practice" (p. 157). Wenger (1998) emphasizes that cross-generational encounters are essential features of communities of learning and that all participants are involved and changed. The question that arises in school settings is what activities take place in particular local settings and what it is that students, and indeed teachers, learn by participating in them.

In David's and Yasuko's Academic Reading and Writing classes, it is clear 102 that students were not participating in authentic, domain-specific academic literacy practices in apprentice relationships with their teachers (Brown, Collins, & Duguid, 1989). They might have done so if they had been involved as research assistants or coauthors on work that David and Yasuko were currently engaged in themselves. As do some graduate students, they could have done literature searches for a common teacher-directed project, read and written summaries of what they found, constructed reference lists, or helped analyze data. Perhaps such activities distinguish graduates from undergraduates. Still, the students in both David's and Yasuko's classes were certainly not just absorbing bodies of codified knowledge or learning only the formal mechanics of writing, and in neither class were tests of any kind used to evaluate their learning. Rather, students had to actually engage in the practices used by academics in both English-medium and Japanese settings in order to fulfill the class goals. The students' participation was indeed peripheral, but it was participation nonetheless. Following Lave and Wenger (1991) and Rogoff (1990), Freedman and Adam (1996, 2000) distinguished between "guided participation," which involves conscious attention to teaching and learning and "attenuated authentic participation," which does not. This distinction might be applied here. As described by Rogoff (1990) in the case of children's learning from caretakers and extended to the case of adults by Freedman and Adam, students can be viewed as guided by David and Yasuko into new practices in a conscious effort at scaffolding (Wood, Bruner, & Ross, 1976) in students' zone of proximal development (Vygotsky, 1978, 1986).

In terms of the game strategy metaphor, David and Yasuko helped their stu- 103 dents learn games strategies that focused, in Wenger's (1998) terms, on both participation and reification in communities of practice. The students engaged in techniques of participation through their reading response journals and their interactions with peers and teacher, and through the academic practices of literature searches and fieldwork. They also learned some of the academic games that revolve around the academy's reification—its genre conventions and documentation styles such as citation practices, its guidelines for interview and fieldwork research, its ways of using language, and its tools such as libraries, databases, and web sources. These game strategies were meaningfully connected to planned lessons because they linked the students to their individual projects. Moreover, game strategies such as the systems of interactive oral and written discussion, feedback, and response allowed students to interact cross-generationally with David and Yasuko, who as practicing academics were adults who "'represent their communities of practice in educational settings" (Wenger, 1998 p. 276). These teachers were not just textbook teachers of writing. They themselves were academic writers. In short, the students were learning writing game strategies that encouraged them to view their academic literacy activities as a form of negotiated engagement with expert community members and with the repertoire of tools, artifacts, and language that typify academic literacy practices. Although it is not clear from this short study how the teachers' identities or practices may have shifted, I believe that the one-semester experience contributed to the beginnings of a shift in the students' views of themselves as emerging participants in academic practices. As owners of their individual projects, for one, they were able to practice agency as writers and to recognize as well that their authority as writers was tied partly to the academic writing game of incorporating fieldwork experiences and voices from published sources into their own texts. At the very least, the students' awareness of practices of writing had changed, and with those changes they were beginning to learn new games, characterized by new sets of rules and values that involved reading, talking, listening, inquiring, and observing as integral practices to the sociopolitical practice of academic writing. And all of this, to my surprise, in a foreign language setting.

Chapter Reflections

As Wenger (1998) points out, "when we come in contact with new practices, 104 we venture into unfamiliar territory and don't know how to participate competently" (p, 153). The case studies in this chapter show that undergraduate students who are learning to participate in academic literacy practices indeed venture into unfamiliar territory. Those of us interested in academic writing and disciplinary enculturation want to learn more about specifically what undergraduates find unfamiliar, why, and how to help them make easier transitions onto the academic playing field.

What is it that novice undergraduate readers and writers need to learn about 105 texts and text-related practices beyond the widespread belief by undergraduates that they are primarily sources of information to be learned and then displayed back to teachers as another kind of text? If we follow Lave's and Wenger's work, a key sign of undergraduates' developing expertise in academic literacy games is their changing relationship to the texts they read and write. Their relationship to texts becomes more complex and layered, involving more aspects of themselves and of the people around them. All novice academic readers and writers, in other words, must learn to treat their readings and writings as media through which they are interacting with authors, professors, peers, and gatekeepers and to recognize the paradox of ownership and multivocality in their own writing. Such a view implies further that they need to learn to view themselves as communicators and builders as well as displayers of knowledge, taking on what Ivanič (1998) calls a contributor role not just a student role.

In enacting more complex roles and in expanding their view of academic writing to include reading and discussion as inseparable from it, undergraduate students are faced with the possibility that their academic identities will evolve in even more fragmented ways than the already fragmented undergraduate curriculum predicts. This may be what happened to Anna and Nick (Chiseri-Strater, 1991), Dave (McCarthy, 1987), and Yuko (Spack, 1997a) in the first year of her program. Following Giddens (1991) and others (Linde, 1993; Polkinghorne, 1991; Wenger, 1998), I surmise that a major challenge for novice academic writers is to figure out how to survive what may be an inevitable period of relative incoherence as they face a wide array of writing games that differ greatly in their local peculiarities. Because it takes time to construct a coherent identity as an academic writer and, as Ortner (1996, p. 12) notes, to learn to play the game with "skill, intention, wit, knowledge, [and] intelligence," the primary challenge for teachers may be to help students survive within the bounds of academic playing fields (Leki, 1999b), and then to become aware that academic literacy games eventually consist of more than games of survival. It is not clear how much of a head start in constructing academic identities students can get in short-term EAP classes like David's and Yasuko's, or whether time and immersion (as in the case of Spack's [1997] Yuko) and time and maturity (Ivanič, 1998; Sternglass, 1997) suffice. My observations of David and Yasuko convince me not to give up on the idea of EAP classes in foreign language settings. Something happened in both classes that worked: I saw motivation, hard work, engagement with texts, peers and mentors interacting, ownership, shifting identities and growing awareness, and a great deal of instruction in English that served larger purposes than language teaching. In these classes, the writing game definitely involved more than writing. 106

In this chapter I have discussed a number of undergraduate writing experiences from the perspectives of students and teachers that took place in different academic settings, not with the intention of generalizing about them, but of establishing a variety of connecting points, some of which I hope will resonate with readers' own experiences. The specific experiences of each of the students and teachers I discussed in this chapter cannot be replicated nor will they resonate in their entirety. However, each case can be reflected upon in terms of the serious games that were being learned, transitions that were or were not happening, and identities that were beginning to be constructed. All undergraduates (all newcomers to a community of practice) need to learn to figure out what to do and what their roles will be, as do newcomers to the teaching of academic literacy. Similarly, those who remain on the playing field will inevitably experience change of one kind or another as what was strange becomes more familiar, as they build background knowledge and skills, or as they resist and reject aspects of their academic literacy practices. Identities, always multiple, interacting, and often conflicting, and involving teachers as well as students, will take on some new facets, perhaps as strategic survivor as in the cases of Yuko and Dave, as 107 sometime rebel and resister as in the cases of Anna and Nick, or as champions and mentors for newcomers of a practice in which they themselves are still developing expertise as in the cases of David and Yasuko.

What strikes me about all these cases is the asymmetry between the ways that [108] teachers seem to perceive their worlds—full of complexity, detail, and purposeful rhetorical practices—and the confusion yet relative lack of complexity in students' perceptions. Certainly David and Yasuko could not easily put aside their post-PhD-level perceptions of what academic literacy is all about even though they were working with young undergraduates who could not at first perceive what the issues were or why they were important. I think that in some sense teachers of EAP want students to quickly become like us, to think and write in ways that have taken us years to learn how to do. Our lessons, our expectations are based on our own immersion experiences and our own drawn out learning of the serious academic literacy games we encounter, and these cannot be duplicated with students. After all, when faced with a new game, none of us can perceive its rules. We can certainly help students write papers that resemble the academic writing of more mature writers and that in some ways (as the case studies show) begin to initiate changes in practices and personae, particularly if as teachers we are practicing academics who are playing our own linguistic, social, and political academic writing games. However, the undergraduate students' sense of investment in their academic literacy practices probably cannot match the sense of investment or coherence that their teachers feel. This may be inevitable. There is probably not enough time or singularity of purpose, partly because of the fragmented nature of undergraduate education and partly because many undergraduates simply don't know what they want to do or who they want to be. Within their tentative beginnings, however, undergraduate students need to find a way to make some order out of the diversity of academic literacy games they are engaged in if only to survive. Perhaps a deeper sense of investment and coherence comes only later. I am reminded of composition scholar Min-Zhan Lu (1987), who came to understand the various writing conflicts and personae that she struggled with during her school years in China only much later, after time, experience, and reflection.

Acknowledgments

Special thanks to Yasuko Kanno and David Shea for participating in the research reported in the third section of this chapter, and for their insightful comments on earlier drafts of the chapter.

References

Allison, D. (1996). Pragmatist discourse and English for academic purposes. *English for Specific Purposes.* 15(2), 85–103.

Atkinson, D. (1997). A critical approach to critical thinking in TESOL. *TESOL Quarterly, 31*, 77–94.

Atkinson, D. (1999). TESOL and culture. *TESOL Quarterly, 33*, 625–654.

Bartholomae, D. (1985). Inventing the university. In M. Rose (Ed.), *When a writer can't write* (pp. 134–165). New York: Guilford.

Bartholomae, D. (1995). Writing with teachers: A conversation with Peter Elbow. *College Composition and Communication, 46*(1), 62–71.

Barton, D. Hamilton, M., & Ivanič, R. (Eds.). (2000). *Situated literacies: Reading and writing in context.* London: Routledge.

Bazerman C. (1987). Codifiying the social scientific style: The APA Publication Manual as behaviorist rhetoric. In J. S. Nelson, A. Megill & D. N. McCloskey (Eds.), *The rhetoric of the human sciences: Language and argument in scholarship and public affairs* (pp. 125–144). Madison: University of Wisconsin Press.

Bazerman, C. (1995). Response: Curricular responsibilities and professional definition. In J. Petraglia (Ed.), *Reconceiving writing, rethinking writing instruction* (pp. 249–259). Mahwah, NJ: Lawrence Erlbaum Associates.

Benesch, S. (1993). ESL, ideology, and the politics of pragmatism. *TESOL Quarterly, 27,* 705–717.

Benesch, S. (1996). Needs analysis and curriculum development in EAP: An example of a critical approach. *TESOL Quarterly, 30,* 723–738.

Benesch, S. (2001). *Critical English for academic purposes: Theory, politics, and practice.* Mahwah, NJ: Lawrence Erlbaum Associates.

Berkenkotter, C., Huckin, T. N., & Ackerman, J. (1988). Conventions, conversations, and the writer: Case study of a student in a rhetoric Ph.D. program. *Research in the Teaching of English, 22,* 9–45.

Bhatia, V. K. (1993). *Analysing genre: Language use in professional settings.* London: Longman.

Bishop, W. (1995). Responses to Bartholomae and Elbow: If Winston Weathers would just write me on e-mail. *College Composition and Communication, 46*(1), 97–103.

Bridwell-Bowles, L. (1992). Discourse and diversity: Experimental writing within the academy. *College Composition and Communication, 43,* 349–368.

Bridwell-Bowles, L. (1995). Freedom, form, function: Varieties of academic discourse. *College Composition and Communication, 46,* 46–51.

Brown, J. D., & Yamashita, S. O. (1995). English language entrance examinations at Japanese universities: 1993 and 1994. In J. D. Brown & S. O. Yamashita (Eds.), *Language testing in Japan* (pp. 86–100). Tokyo: Japan Association for Language Teaching.

Brown, J. S., Collins, A., & Duguid, P. (1989). Situated cognition and the culture of learning. *Educational Researcher, 18*(1), 32–42.

Campbell, C. (1990). Writing with others' words: Using background reading text in academic compositions. In B. Kroll (Ed.), *Second language writing: Research insights for the classroom* (pp. 211–230). Cambridge, England: Cambridge University Press.

Canagarajah, S. (2001). Addressing issues of power and difference in ESL academic writing. In J. Flowerdew & M. Peacock (Eds.), *Research perspectives on English for academic purposes* (pp. 117–131). Cambridge, England: Cambridge University Press.

Casanave, C. P. (1992b). Educational goals in the foreign language class: The role of content-motivated journal writing. *SFC Journal of Language and Communication, 1,* 83–103.

Casanave, C. P. (1995a). Journal writing in college English classes in Japan: Shifting the focus from language to education. *JALT Journal, 17,* 95–111.

Casanave, C. P., & Kanno, Y. (1998). Entering an academic conversation: Learning to communicate through written texts. *Keio SFC Review, 3,* 141–153.

Chiseri-Strater, E. (1991). *Academic literacies: The public and private discourse of university students.* Portsmouth, NH: Boynton/Cook.

Clandinin. D. J., & Connelly, F. M. (1991). Narrative and story in practice and research. In D. A. Schön (Ed.), *The reflective turn: Case studies in and on educational practice* (pp. 258–281). New York: Teachers College Press.

Connelly, F. M., & Clandinin, D. J. (1990). Stories of experience and narrative inquiry. *Educational Researcher, 19*(5), 2–14.

Cope, B., & Kalantzis, M. (Eds.). (1993). *The power of literacy: A genre approach to teaching writing.* London: The Falmer Press.

Cummins, J. (1981). The role of primary language development in promoting educational success for language minority students. In California State Department of Education (Ed.), *Schooling and language minority students: A theoretical framework* (pp. 3–49), Los Angeles, CA: Evaluation, Dissemination and Assessment Center, California State University.

Currie, P. (1993). Entering a disciplinary community: Conceptual activities required to write for one introductory university course. *Journal of Second Language Writing, 2,* 101–117.

Currie, P. (1998). Staying out of trouble: Apparent plagiarism and academic survival. *Journal of Second Language Writing, 7,* 1–18.

Currie, P. (1999). Transferable skills: Promoting student research. *English for Specific Purposes, 18*(4), 329–345.

Deckert, G. (1993). Perspectives on plagiarism from ESL students in Hong Kong. *Journal of Second Language Writing, 2,* 131–148.

Elbow, P. (1973). *Writing without teachers.* New York: Oxford University Press.

Elbow, P. (1995). Being a writer vs. being an academic: A conflict in goals. *College Composition and Communication, 46*(1), 72–83.

Elbow, P. (1999a). In defense of private writing: Consequences for theory and research: *Written Communication, 16*(2), 139–170.

Elbow, P. (1999b). Individualism and the teaching of writing: Response to Vai Ramanathan and Dwight Atkinson. *Journal of Second Language Writing, 8*(3), 327–338.

Ferris, D. (1999). The case for grammar correction in L2 writing classes: A response to Truscott (1996). *Journal of Second Language Writing, 8,* 1–11.

Freedman, A. (1993a). Show and tell? The role of explicit teaching in the learning of new genres. *Research in the Teaching of English, 27*(3), 222–251.

Freedman, A. (1993b). Situating genre: A rejoinder. *Research in the Teaching of English, 27*(3), 272–281.

Freedman, A., & Adam, C. (1996). Learning to write professionally: "Situated learning" and the transition from university to professional discourse. *Journal of Business and Technical Communication, 10*(4), 395–427.

Freedman, A., & Adam, C. (2000). Write where you are: Situating learning to write in university and workplace settings. In P. Dias & A. Paré (Eds.), *Transitions: Writing in academic and workplace settings* (pp. 31–60). Cresskill, NJ: Hampton Press.

Freedman, A., Adam, C., & Smart, G. (1994). Wearing suits to class: Simulating genres and simulations as genres. *Written Communication, 11*(2), 193–226.

Freedman, A., & Medway, P. (Eds.). (1994). *Teaching and learning genre.* Portsmouth, NH: Boynton/Cook.

Frost, P. (1991). Examination hell. In E. R. Beauchamp (Ed.), *Windows on Japanese education* (pp. 291–305). New York: Greenwood Press.

Geertz, C. (1983). *Local knowledge: Further essays in interpretive anthropology.* New York: Basic Books.

Giddens, A. (1991). *Modernity and self-identity: Self and society in the late modern age.* Stanford, CA: Stanford University Press.

Gosden, H. (2000). A research-based content course in EAP for graduate students. In A. S. Mackenzie (Ed.), *Content in language education: Looking at the future* (pp. 102–106). Proceedings of the JALT CUE Conference 2000, Tokyo: Japan Association for Language Teaching College and University Educators Special Interest Group.

Greene, S. (1995). Making sense of our own ideas: The problems of authorship in a beginning writing classroom. *Written Communication, 12*(2), 186–218.

Grice, H. (1975). Logic and conversation. In P. Cole & J. Morgan (Eds.), *Syntax and semantics* (Vol. 3: *Speech acts*) (pp. 41–58). New York: Academic Press.

Haas, C. (1994). Learning to read biology: One student's rhetorical development in college. *Written Communication, 11*(1), 43–84.

Herndl, C. G., & Nahrwold, C. A. (2000). Research as social practice: A case study of research on technical and professional communication. *Written Communication, 17*(2), 258–296.

Hirvela, A. (1997). "Disciplinary portfolios" and EAP writing instruction. *English for Specific Purposes, 16*(2), 83–100.

Hyland, K. (1999). Academic attribution: Citation and the construction of disciplinary knowledge. *Applied Linguistics, 20*(3), 341–367.

Hyon, S. (1996). Genre in three traditions: Implications for ESL. *TESOL Quarterly, 30*(4), 693–722.

Ivanič, R. (1994). I is for interpersonal: Discoursal construction of writer identities and the teaching of writing. *Linguistics and Education, 6*, 3–15.

Ivanič, R. (1998). *Writing and identity: The discoursal construction of identity in academic writing.* Philadelphia: John Benjamins.

Johns, A. M. (1988). The discourse community dilemma: Identifying transferable skills for the academic milieu. *English for Specific Purposes, 7,* 55–60.

Johns, A. M. (1990). Coherence as a cultural phenomenon: Employing ethnographic principles in the academic milieu. In U. Connor & A. M. Johns, (Eds.), *Coherence in writing: Research and pedagogical perspectives* (pp. 209–226). Alexandria, VA: Teachers of English to Speakers of Other Languages.

Johns, A. M. (1995). Teaching classroom and authentic genres: Initiating students into academic cultures and discourses. In D. Belcher & G. Braine (Eds.), *Academic writing in a second language: Essays on research and pedagogy* (pp. 277–291). Norwood, NJ: Ablex.

Kubota, R. (1997). A reevaluation of the uniqueness of Japanese written discourse. *Written Communication, 14*(4), 460–480.

Kubota, R. (1999). Japanese culture constructed by discourses: Implications for applied linguistics research and ELT. *TESOL Quarterly, 33*(1), 9–35

Lave, J. (1993). The practice of learning. In S. Chaiklin & J. Lave (Eds.), *Understanding practice: Perspectives on activity and context* (pp. 3–32). Cambridge, England: Cambridge University Press.

Lave, J. (1996). Teaching, as learning, in practice. *Mind, Culture, and Activity, 3,* 149–164.

Lave, J., & Wenger, E. (1991). *Situated learning: Legitimate peripheral participation.* Cambridge, England: Cambridge University Press.

Leki, I. (1995a). Coping strategies of ESL students in writing tasks across the curriculum. *TESOL Quarterly, 29,* 235–260.

Leki, I. (1995b). Good writing: I know it when I see it. In D. Belcher & G. Braine (Eds.), *Academic writing in a second language: Essays on research and pedagogy* (pp. 23–46). Norwood, NJ: Ablex.

Leki, I. (1999a, March). *Is writing overrated?* Paper presented at the Conference on College Composition and Communication, Atlanta, GA.

Leki, I. (1999b). "Pretty much I screwed up": Ill-served needs of a permanent resident. In L. Harklau, K. M. Losey, & M. Siegal (Eds.), *Generation 1.5 meets college composition: Issues in the teaching of writing to U.S.-educated learners of ESL* (pp. 17–43). Mahwah, NJ: Lawrence Erlbaum Associates.

Linde, C. (1993). *Life stories: The creation of coherence.* New York: Oxford University Press.

Lu, M. Z. (1987). From silence to words: Writing as struggle. *College English, 49*(4), 437–448.

Lynch, T., & McGrath, I. (1993). Teaching bibliographic documentation skills. *English for Specific Purposes, 12*(3), 219–238.

Matsuda, P. K. (1998). Situating ESL writing in a cross-disciplinary context. *Written Communication, 15,* 99–121.

McCarthy, L. P. (1987). A stranger in strange lands: A college student writing across the curriculum. *Research in the Teaching of English, 21,* 233–265.

Miller, S. M., Nelson, M. W., & Moore, M. T. (1998) Caught in the paradigm gap: Qualitative researchers' lived experience and the politics of epistemology. *American Educational Research Journal, 35*(3), 377–416.

Ortner, S. B. (1996). *Making gender: The politics and erotics of culture.* Boston: Beacon Press.

Pally, M. (1997). Critical thinking in ESL: An argument for sustained content. *Journal of Second Language Writing, 6*(3), 293–311.

Parkinson, J. (2000). Acquiring scientific literacy through content and genre: A theme-based language course for science students. *English for Specific Purposes, 19*(4), 369–387.

Paul, D. (2000). In citing chaos: A study of the rhetorical use of citations. *Journal of Business and Technical Communication, 14*(2), 185–222.

Pennycook, A. (1996). Borrowing others' words: Text, ownership, memory, and plagiarism. *TESOL Quarterly, 30*, 201–230.

Penrose, A. M., & Geisler, C. (1994). Reading and writing without authority. *College Composition and Communication, 45*(4), 505–520.

Petraglia, J. (Ed.). (1995). *Reconceiving writing, rethinking writing instruction*. Mahwah, NJ: Lawrence Erlbaum Associates.

Polkinghorne, D. E. (1991). Narrative and self-concept. *Journal of Narrative and Life History, 12*(2 & 3), 135–153.

Prior, P. (1995). Redefining the task: An ethnographic examination of writing and response in graduate seminars. In D. Belcher & G. Braine (Eds.), *Academic writing in a second language: Essays on research and pedagogy* (pp. 47–82). Norwood, NJ: Ablex.

Prior, P. A. (1998). *Writing/disciplinarity: A sociohistoric account of literate activity in the academy*. Mahwah, NJ: Lawrence Erlbaum Associates.

Ramanathan, V., & Atkinson, D. (1999). Individualism, academic writing, and ESL writers. *Journal of Second Language Writing, 8*, 45–75.

Rogoff, B. (1990). *Apprenticeship in thinking: Cognitive development in social context*. New York: Oxford University Press.

Santos, T. (1992). Ideology in Composition: L1 and ESL. *Journal of Second Language Writing, 1*, 1–15.

Scollon, R. (1995). Plagiarism and ideology: Identity in intercultural discourse. *Language in Society, 24*, 1–28.

Scribner, S., & Cole, M. (1981). *The psychology of literacy*. Cambridge, MA: Harvard University Press.

Silva, T., Leki, I., & Carson, J. (1997). Broadening the perspective of mainstream composition studies. *Written Communication, 14*(3), 398–428.

Spack, R. (1988). Initiating ESL students into the academic discourse community: How far should we go? *TESOL Quarterly, 29*, 29–51.

Spack, R. (1997a). The acquisition of academic literacy in a second language: A longitudinal case study. *Written Communication, 14*, 3–62.

Sternglass, M. S. (1997). *Time to know them: A longitudinal study of writing and learning at the college level*. Mahwah, NJ: Lawrence Erlbaum Associates.

Swales, J. M. (1990). *Genre analysis: English in academic and research settings*. New York: Cambridge University Press.

Swales, J. M., & Feak, C. B. (1994). *Academic writing for graduate students: A course for nonnative speakers of English*. Ann Arbor: University of Michigan Press.

Swales, J. M., & Feak, C. B. (2000). *English in today's research world: A guide for writers*. Ann Arbor: University of Michigan Press.

Truscott, J. (1996). The case against grammar correction in L2 writing classes. *Language Learning, 46*, 327–369.

Truscott, J. (1998). Noticing in second language acquisition: A critical review. *Second Language Research, 14*, 103–135.

Truscott, J. (1999). The case for "The case against grammar correction in L2 writing classes": A response to Ferris. *Journal of Second Language Writing, 8*, 111–122.

Vygotsky, L. S. (1978). *Mind in society: The development of higher psychological processes* (M. Cole, V. John-Steiner, S. Scribner, & E. Souberman, Eds.). Cambridge, MA: Harvard University Press.

Vygotsky, L. S. (1986). *Thought and language* (A. Kozulin, Trans. & Ed.). Cambridge, MA: The MIT Press.

Walvoord, B., & McCarthy, L. (1990). *Thinking and writing in college: A naturalistic study of students in four disciplines.* Urbana, IL: National Council of Teachers of English.

Wenger, E. (1998). *Communities of practice: Learning, meaning, and identity.* Cambridge, England: Cambridge University Press.

Williams, J. M., & Coiomb, G. G. (1993). The case for explicit teaching: What you don't know won't help you. *Research in the Teaching of English, 27*(3), 252–271.

Wood, D., Bruner, J. S., & Ross, G. (1976). The role of tutoring in problem solving. *Journal of Child Psychology and Psychiatry, 17,* 89–100.

Zamel, V. (1995). Strangers in academia: The experiences of faculty and ESL students across the curriculum. *College Composition and Communication, 46*(4), 506–521.

Zamel, V. (1996). Transcending boundaries: Complicating the scene of teaching language. *College ESL, 6*(2), 1–11.

Questions for Discussion and Journaling

[Note that discussion and journaling questions are primarily intended to address "Game Strategy 1: Interact with Texts and with Others about Texts" as described in that section of Casanave's selection (pp. 643–647).]

1. The focus of this reading, and of Casanave's entire book, is the "games" that students must learn to play in order to write successfully in the university. Go through this selection and jot down every type of "game" that Casanave mentions. Which of these "games" do you feel you play the most often? Are there any games you would add to this list?

2. Many of the concepts and authors mentioned in this selection should be familiar to you if you have read any of the preceding chapters in this textbook. Go through the selection and highlight every name and concept that is familiar to you from other readings and activities. (For example, Casanave cites Wenger frequently, as does Wardle in "Identity, Authority, and Learning to Write in New Workplaces.") Choose one concept from this list and write one or two sentences in which you compare and contrast what Casanave has to say about it with what another researcher in this book has to say about it.

3. At the end of this selection, Casanave notes that the term **community of practice** (which should already be familiar to you from readings in Chapter 4 of this textbook) is usually used to refer to workplaces, not school settings. Lave and Wenger, the originators of the term, argue that learning in school and work are very different. What are the differences between them?

4. Casanave and the other researchers she cites note that "plagiarism" is **constructed** differently in different countries. Explain some of the different

understandings of plagiarism or "textual borrowing" that are described in this reading.

5. David, one of the teachers Casanave studied, argues that plagiarism is not "the major issue" (para. 77). Instead, he thinks that plagiarism is the sign of a different set of problems. What are these problems? How is David's view of plagiarism different from the common American understanding of plagiarism as a black-and-white case of stealing?

Applying and Exploring Ideas

1. [For working further on "Game Strategy 2: Blend Voices," as described in that section of Casanave's article.] In the "map" or **"literature review"** section of this selection, Casanave sometimes mentions other authors directly in a sentence (**integral citation**), and sometimes mentions them only parenthetically (**nonintegral citation**). Analyze some instances where she uses each type of citation and try to figure out why she cited in the way that she did. What was her rhetorical purpose in citing Leki directly, for example, while citing a whole group of people parenthetically on the very next page? Next, look at a research paper you have written recently. Which kind of citation do you use the most (integral or nonintegral)? Do you ever cite long strings of names in parentheses like Casanave does? Why or why not? (If you want, you can jump ahead to the selection in this chapter by Ken Hyland, who provides a chart showing that some fields use more integral citation than others).

2. [For working further on "Game Strategy 2: Blend Voices," as described in that section of Casanave's article.] Casanave concludes by noting that as undergraduate students change, their "relationship to texts becomes more complex and layered" (para. 105). To succeed, they need to learn to "view themselves as communicators and builders as well as displayers of knowledge, taking on . . . a contributor role, not just a student role" (para. 105). This claim is very similar to that made by Penrose and Geisler in the preceding reading in this chapter. In one page, discuss the kinds of changes in attitude toward texts that students need to learn to make in this regard, being sure to compare and contrast the views of Penrose and Geisler with those of Casanave.

3. Drawing on Casanave and any of the preceding articles in this textbook that seem relevant, write a letter to a first-year college student in which you explain what it means and looks like to write with authority in the university.

Meta Moment

How does Casanave's article shed light on an experience you have had in school? What does it help you understand differently about that situation? What might you do differently when you write a research paper in the future as a result of having read Casanave's article?

A Stranger in Strange Lands:
A College Student Writing across the Curriculum

LUCILLE P. McCARTHY

McCarthy, Lucille P. "A Stranger in Strange Lands: A College Student Writing across the Curriculum." *Research in the Teaching of English* 21.3 (1987): 233–65. Print.

Framing the Reading

Lucille McCarthy earned her Ph.D. from the University of Pennsylvania, and she is currently a professor of English at the University of Maryland-Baltimore County, where she has taught since 1988. Her many articles and books demonstrate her interest in pedagogies that help promote student learning and writing. Five of her six books and many of her articles focus on student classroom experiences and have won awards such as the James N. Britton Awards for Research in the English Language Arts and a National Council of Teachers of English award for Research Excellence in Technical and Scientific Communication. Her books include *John Dewey and the Challenge of Classroom Practice* (1998), *John Dewey and the Philosophy and Practice of Hope* (2007), and *Whose Goals? Whose Aspirations? Learning to Teach Underprepared Writers across the Curriculum* (2002), all co-authored with her frequent collaborator, philosopher Stephen Fishman; and *Thinking and Writing in College: A Naturalistic Study of Students in Four Disciplines* (1991; with Barbara Walvoord).

McCarthy published the article reprinted here in 1987. At that time, researchers in other fields had used **case studies** and **ethnographic research** extensively, but researchers in the field of Writing Studies had only begun to consider what we could learn about writing by using those methods. In writing this article, McCarthy notes that researchers know that writing is strongly influenced by **social context**—that, for example, some people write well in one setting (e.g., at home alone) and not very well in another (e.g., on a timed exam), or that some people write well in one **genre** (e.g., poetry) but not very well in another genre (e.g., a literary criticism essay). But McCarthy wanted to know more about *how* writing is influenced by social settings in particular, she wanted to know how college writers and their writing are influenced by their different classroom settings.

At the time that McCarthy conducted her study, no one else had followed individual students as they wrote across the

university. Since McCarthy published her study, a number of such **longitudinal studies** have been published (Christine Casanave cites many of them in the preceding reading in this chapter). While no single case study can produce **generalizable** results, a number of case studies taken together can do so. Thus, if you are interested in making claims about how writers write in college, you should read the longitudinal studies that followed McCarthy.

McCarthy followed a student named "Dave" as he wrote in three different classes—composition, biology, and poetry. Dave got good grades in the first two classes, but struggled in poetry. McCarthy tried to find out why Dave was so unsuccessful in poetry and ultimately concluded that even though the writing tasks across all the classes had some similarities, Dave *thought* they were very different, and he had very different kinds of support for the writing in each of the classes.

Getting Ready to Read

Before you read, try the following activity:

- Consider a class where you have an easy time writing, and a class where the writing is hard for you. Think about why you might have different levels of success with these writing tasks.

As you read, consider the following questions:

- What research question(s) does McCarthy set out to answer?
- What major findings does McCarthy discover in answer to her research question(s)?

Dave Garrison, a college junior and the focus of the present study, was asked how he would advise incoming freshmen about writing for their college courses. His answer was both homely and familiar.

"I'd tell them," he said, "first you've got to figure out what your teachers want. And then you've got to give it to them if you're gonna' get the grade." He paused a moment and added, "And that's not always so easy."

No matter how we teachers may feel about Dave's response, it does reflect his sensitivity to school writing as a social affair. Successful students are those who can, in their interactions with teachers during the semester, determine what constitutes appropriate texts in each classroom: the content, structures, language, ways of thinking, and types of evidence required in that discipline and by that teacher. They can then produce such a text. Students who cannot do this, for whatever reason—cultural, intellectual, motivational—are those who fail, deemed incompetent communicators in that particular setting. They are unable to follow what Britton calls the "rules of the game" in each class (1975, p. 76). As students go from one classroom to another they must play a wide range of games, the rules for which, Britton points out, include many conventions and presuppositions that are not explicitly articulated.

In this article, writing in college is viewed as a process of assessing and adapting to the requirements in unfamiliar academic settings. Specifically, the study examined how students figured out what constituted appropriate texts in their various courses and how they went about producing them. And, further, it examined what characterized the classroom contexts which enhanced or denied students' success in this process. This study was a 21-month project which focused on the writing experiences of one college student, Dave, in three of his courses, Freshman Composition in the spring of his freshman year, and, in his sophomore year, Introduction to Poetry in the fall and Cell Biology in the spring. Dave, a biology/

> Successful students are those who can, in their interactions with teachers during the semester, determine what constitutes appropriate texts in each classroom: the content, structures, language, ways of thinking, and types of evidence required in that discipline and by that teacher.

pre-med major, was typical of students at his college in terms of his SAT scores (502 verbal; 515 math), his high school grades, and his white, middle-class family background.

As I followed Dave from one classroom writing situation to another, I came to see him, as he made his journey from one discipline to another, as a stranger in strange lands. In each new class Dave believed that the writing he was doing was totally unlike anything he had ever done before. This metaphor of a newcomer in a foreign country proved to be a powerful way of looking at Dave's behaviors as he worked to use the new languages in unfamiliar academic territories. Robert Heinlein's (1961) science fiction novel suggested this metaphor originally. But Heinlein's title is slightly different; his stranger is in a *single* strange land. Dave perceived himself to be in one strange land after another.

Background to the Study

The theoretical underpinnings of this study are to be found in the work of sociolinguists (Hymes, 1972a, 1972b; Gumperz, 1971) and ethnographers of communication (Basso, 1974; Heath, 1982; Szwed, 1981) who assume that language processes must be understood in terms of the contexts in which they occur. All language use in this view takes place within speech communities and accomplishes meaningful social functions for people. Community members share characteristic "ways of speaking," that is, accepted linguistic, intellectual, and social conventions which have developed over time and govern spoken interaction. And "communicatively competent" speakers in every community recognize and successfully employ these "rules of use," largely without conscious attention (Hymes, 1972a, pp. xxiv–xxxvi).

A key assumption underlying this study is that writing, like speaking, is   7
a social activity. Writers, like speakers, must use the communication means
considered appropriate by members of particular speech or discourse communities. And the writer's work, at the same time, may affect the norms of the
community. As students go from one class to another, they must define and
master the rules of use for written discourse in one classroom speech community after another. And their writing can only be evaluated in terms of that
particular community's standards.

Some recent practical and theoretical work in writing studies has empha-   8
sized that writers' processes and products must be understood in terms of their
contexts, contexts which are created as participants and settings interact (Bazerman, 1981; Bizzell, 1982; Cooper, 1986; Faigley, 1985; Whiteman, 1981).
Studies of writing in non-academic settings have shown just how complex
these writing environments are and how sophisticated the knowledge—both
explicit and tacit—is that writers need in order to operate successfully in them
(Odell & Goswami, 1985). And classrooms offer no less complex environments for writing. As Ericson (1982) points out, the classroom learning environment includes not only the teacher and the student, but also the subject
matter structure, the social task structure, the actual enacted task, and the
sequence of actions involved in the task. In addition, in many classrooms students may be provided with too few instructional supports to help them as
they write (Applebee, 1984). Specifically, college classroom contexts for writing, Herrington (1985) argues, must be thought of in terms of several speech
communities, viewed "in relation not only to a school community, but also to
the intellectual and social conventions of professional forums within a given
discipline" (p. 333). These overlapping communities influence the ways students think and write and interact in college classrooms, and will shape their
notions of what it means to be, for example, an engineer or a biologist or a
literary critic.

Research which has directly examined particular classroom contexts for   9
writing has provided insight into their diversity (Applebee, 1984; Calkins,
1980; Florio & Clark, 1982; Freedman, 1985; Herrington, 1985; Kantor, 1984).
Though these studies suggest that an individual student is likely to encounter
a number of quite different classroom writing situations, there is also evidence
that individual student writers may employ consistent patterns across tasks
as they interpret assignments, reason, and organize their knowledge (Dyson,
1984; Langer, 1985, 1986).

What has not yet been done, however, is to follow individual college students   10
as they progress across academic disciplines. In this study I offer information
about how one college student fares in such a journey across the curriculum.
That is, I detail how this student's behavior changed or remained constant
across tasks in three classroom contexts and how those contexts influenced
his success. Though this study is limited in scope to the experiences of a single
student as he wrote for three college courses, it addresses questions central to
much writing across the curriculum scholarship:

1. What are the tasks students encounter as they move from one course to another?
2. How do successful students interpret these tasks? Further, how do students determine what constitutes appropriate texts in that discipline and for that teacher, and how do they produce them?
3. What are the social factors in classrooms that foster particular writing behaviors and students' achievement of competence in that setting?

The ultimate aim of this study is to contribute to our understanding of how students learn to write in school. Findings from this study corroborate the notion that learning to write should be seen not only as a developmental process occurring within an individual student, but also as a social process occurring in response to particular situations.

Methods

The research approach was naturalistic. I entered the study with no hypotheses to test and no specially devised writing tasks. Rather, I studied the writing that was actually being assigned in these classrooms, working to understand and describe that writing, how it functioned in each classroom, and what it meant to people there. My purpose was to get as rich a portrait as possible of Dave's writing and his classroom writing contexts. To this end I combined four research tools: observation, interviews, composing-aloud protocols, and text analysis. The data provided by the protocols and text analysis served to add to, crosscheck, and refine the data generated by observation and interviews. Using this triangulated approach (Denzin, 1978), I could view Dave's writing experiences through several windows, with the strengths of one method compensating for the limitations of another.

11

The Courses

The college is a private, co-educational, liberal arts institution located in a large, northeastern city. Of its 2600 students nearly half are business, accounting, and computer science majors. Yet over half of students' courses are required liberal arts courses, part of the core curriculum. Two of Dave's courses in this study are core courses: Freshman Composition and Introduction to Poetry. The third, Cell Biology, is a course taken by biology majors; it was Dave's third semester of college biology. All three were one-semester courses. In the descriptions of these courses that follow, I use pseudonyms for the teachers.

12

In Freshman Composition, which met twice a week for 90 minutes, students were required to write a series of five similarly structured essays on topics of their choice. These two or four page essays were due at regular intervals and were graded by the professor, Dr. Jean Carter. Classes were generally teacher-led discussions and exercises, with some days allotted for students to work together in small groups, planning their essays or sharing drafts. Dr. Carter held one individual writing conference with each student at mid semester.

13

Introduction to Poetry is generally taken by students during their sophomore   14
year, and it, like Freshman Composition, met for 90 minutes twice a week. In
this class students were also required to write a series of similar papers. These
were three to six page critical essays on poems that students chose from a list
given them by their professor, Dr. Charles Forson. These essays, like those in
Freshman Composition, were due at regular intervals and were graded by the
professor. The Poetry classes were all lectures in which Dr. Forson explicated
poems. However, one lecture early in the semester was devoted entirely to writing instruction.

Cell Biology, which Dave took in the spring of his sophomore year, met three   15
times a week, twice for 90-minute lectures and once for a three-hour lab. In
this course, like the other two, students were required to write a series of similar short papers, three in this course. These were three to five page reviews of
journal articles which reported current research in cell biology. Students were to
summarize these articles, following the five-part scientific format in which the
experiment was reported. They were then to relate the experiment to what they
were doing in class. These reviews were graded by the professor, Dr. Tom Kelly.

The Participants

The participants in this study included these three professors, Drs. Carter,   16
Forson, and Kelly. All were experienced college teachers who had taught these
courses before. All talked willingly and with interest about the writing their
students were doing, and both Dr. Carter and Dr. Forson invited me to observe
their classes. Dr. Kelly said that it would not be productive for me to observe in
his Cell Biology course because he spent almost no time talking directly about
writing, so pressed was he to cover the necessary course material.

The student participants in this study were Dave and two of his friends. I   17
first met these three young men in Dr. Carter's Freshman Composition class
where I was observing regularly in order to learn how she taught the course,
the same one I teach at the college. As I attended that course week after week,
I got to know the students who sat by me, Dave and his friends, and I realized
I was no longer as interested in understanding what my colleague was teaching as I was in understanding what these students were learning. As the study
progressed, my focus narrowed to Dave's experiences, although none of the
three students knew this. The contribution of Dave's friends to this study was
to facilitate my understanding of Dave. At first, in their Freshman Composition class, these students saw my role as a curious combination of teacher and
fellow student. As the study progressed, my role became, in their eyes, that of
teacher/inquirer, a person genuinely interested in understanding their writing.
In fact, my increasing interest and ability to remember details of his writing
experiences seemed at times to mystify and amuse Dave.

At the beginning of this study Dave Garrison was an 18 year old freshman,   18
a biology pre-med major who had graduated the year before from a parochial
boys' high school near the college. He described himself as a "hands-on" person
who preferred practical application in the lab to reading theory in books.

Beginning in his sophomore year, Dave worked 13 hours a week as a technician in a local hospital, drawing blood from patients, in addition to taking a full course load. He "loved" his hospital work, he said, because of the people and the work, and also because difficulties with chemistry has made him worry about being accepted in medical school. In the hospital he was getting an idea of a range of possible careers in health care. The oldest of four children, Dave lived at home and commuted 30 minutes to campus. He is the first person in his family to go to college, though both of his parents enjoy reading, he said, and his father writes in his work as an insurance salesman. When Dave and I first met, he told me that he did not really like to write and that he was not very good, but he knew that writing was a tool he needed, one that he hoped to learn to see better.

Instrumentation and Analytic Procedures

I collected data from February, 1983, through November, 1985. A detailed, 19 semester by semester summary is presented in Table 1.

Observation

I observed in all three classes in order to help me understand the contexts for 20 writing in which Dave was working. During the observation I recorded field notes about the classroom activities and interactions I was seeing, and as soon as possible after the observation I read my notes and fleshed them out where possible. Returning to fill out the notes was particularly important when I had participated in the classroom activities as I did in Freshman Composition. In that class I participated in Dave's small group discussions of drafts and did the in-class writing exercises along with the students. I wrote my field notes on the right-side pages of a spiral notebook, leaving the pages opposite free for later notes.

Interviews

I interviewed Dave, his two friends, and the three professors in order to elicit 21 their interpretations of the writing in each class. Questions were often suggested by the participants' earlier comments or by emerging patterns in the data that I wanted to pursue. Interviews with professors generally took place in their offices and centered on their assignments, their purposes for having students write, and the instructional techniques they used to accomplish their purposes.

The interviews with the students took place in my office on campus and 22 lasted one hour. I chose to interview Dave and his friends together in a series of monthly interviews because I believed I could learn more from Dave in this way. The students often talked to and questioned each other, producing more from Dave than I believe I ever could have gotten from one-on-one sessions with him. I did on two occasions, however, interview Dave alone for one hour when I wanted to question him in a particularly intensive way.

Table 1

Data Collection Record

Observation

Freshman Composition (Freshman year. Spring, 1983)
- Participant observation in 1 class per week for 9 weeks.
- All class documents were collected and analyzed.

Introduction to Poetry (Sophomore year. Fall, 1983)
- Observation of the 90-minute lecture devoted to writing instruction.
- All class documents were collected and analyzed.

Cell Biology (Sophomore year. Spring, 1984)
- Observation of a lab session for 15 minutes.

Interviews

Freshman Composition
- Frequent conversations and 2 hour-long interviews with the professor, Dr. Carter.
- Frequent conversations with the students before and after class.

Poetry
- 1 hour-long interview with the professor, Dr. Forson.
- 4 hour-long interviews with the students at one-month intervals.

Cell Biology
- 2 hour-long interviews with the professor, Dr. Kelly.
- 4 hour-long interviews with the students at one-month intervals.

Junior Year Follow-up (Fall, 1984)
- 2 hour-long interviews with the students.

Protocols with Retrospective Interviews

Freshman Composition
- 1 protocol and interview audiotaped as Dave composed the first draft of his fourth (next to last) essay.

Poetry
- 1 protocol and interview audiotaped as Dave composed the first draft of his third (last) paper.

Cell Biology
- 1 protocol and interview audiotaped as Dave composed the first draft of his third (last) review.

Text Analysis

Freshman Composition
- Dave's fourth essay with the teacher's responses was analyzed. All drafts of all essays were collected.

Poetry
- Dave's third paper with the teacher's responses was analyzed. All drafts of all essays were collected.

Cell Biology
- Dave's third review with the teacher's responses was analyzed. All drafts of all essays were collected.

During all interviews I either took notes or made audiotapes which I later tran-   23
scribed and analyzed. All hour-long interviews with the students were taped.

Analysis of the Observation and Interviews

I read and reread my field notes and the interview transcripts looking for patterns   24
and themes. These organized the data and suggested the salient features of writing
in each context, its nature and meaning, and of Dave's experiences there. These
patterns and themes then focused subsequent inquiry. I was guided in this process
by the work of Gilmore and Glatthorn (1982) and Spradley (1979, 1980).

Composing-Aloud Protocols and Retrospective Interviews

Late in each of the three semesters, I audiotaped Dave as he composed aloud   25
the first draft of a paper for the course we had focused on that semester. Dave
wrote at the desk in my office, his pre-writing notes and his books spread out
around him, and I sat nearby in a position where I could observe and make
notes on his behaviors. The protocols lasted 30 minutes and were followed
by a 30-minute retrospective interview in which I asked Dave to tell me more
about the process he had just been through. I reasoned that in the retrospective
interviews Dave's major concerns would be reemphasized, whereas the smaller
issues that may have occupied him during composing would be forgotten.
Because I followed Dave across time and collected all his written work for each
assignment, I could examine what preceded and what followed the composed-
aloud draft. I could thus see how the protocol draft related to Dave's entire
composing process for a task.

The information provided by the protocols generally corroborated what he   26
had said in the interviews. Of particular interest, however, were the points at
which the protocol data contradicted the interview data. These points spurred
further inquiry. Though composing-aloud was never easy for Dave, who characterized himself as a shy person, he became more and more comfortable with
it as the semesters progressed. He did produce, in each of the protocol sessions,
a useful first draft for his final paper in each course.

Analysis and Scoring of the Protocols and Retrospective Interviews

I analyzed the transcripts of the protocols and interviews, classifying and count-   27
ing what I called the *writer's conscious concerns*. These concerns were identified as anything the writer paid attention to during composing as expressed by
(1) remarks about a thought or behavior or (2) observed behaviors. I chose to
focus on Dave's conscious concerns because I expected that they would include
a broad range of writing issues and that they would reflect the nature and
emphases of the classrooms for which he was writing. The protocols would
thus provide the supporting information I needed for this study. In identifying
and classifying the writer's conscious concerns, I was guided by the work of
Berkenkotter (1983), Bridwell (1980), Flower and Hayes (1981), Perl (1979),
and Pianko (1979).

The analysis of the transcripts was carried out in a two-part process. First I   28
read them several times and drew from them four general categories of writer's
concerns, along with a number of subcategories. Then, using this scheme, I classified and counted the writer's remarks and behaviors. The first protocol was, of
course, made during Dave's writing for Freshman Composition. The categories
from that composing session were used again in analyzing the protocols from
Poetry and Cell Biology. To these original categories were added new ones to
describe the concerns Dave expressed as he composed for the later courses. In
this way I could identify both concerns that were constant across courses as well
as those that were specific to particular classroom writing situations.

I carried out the analyses of the protocols alone because of the understand-   29
ing of the writing context that I brought to the task. I viewed this knowledge as
an asset in identifying and classifying Dave's writing concerns. Thus, instead of
agreement between raters, I worked for "confirmability" in the sense of agreement among a variety of information sources (Cuba, 1978, p. 17).

Text Analysis

The final window through which I looked at Dave's writing experiences was   30
text analysis. I analyzed the completed papers, with the professors' comments
on them, of the assignments Dave had begun during the protocol sessions. If
Dave is understood to be a stranger trying to learn the language in these classroom communities, then his teachers are the native-speaker guides who are
training him. In this view, students and teachers in their written interactions
share a common aim and are engaged in a cooperative endeavor. Their relationship is like that of people conversing together, the newcomer making trial efforts
to communicate appropriately and the native speaker responding to them.

Thus, in order to examine the conventions of discourse in each classroom   31
and get further insight into the interaction between Dave and his professors,
I drew upon the model of conversation proposed by Grice (1975). Grice says
that conversants assume, unless there are indications to the contrary, that they
have a shared purpose and thus make conversational contributions "such as
are required . . . by the accepted purpose or direction of the talk exchange in
which they are engaged" (p. 45). He terms this the "Cooperative Principle."
From the Cooperative Principle Grice derives four categories or conditions
which must be fulfilled if people are to converse successfully: Quality, Quantity,
Relation, and Manner. When conversation breaks down, it is because one or
more of these conditions for successful conversation have been violated, either
accidentally or intentionally. On the other hand, people conversing successfully fulfill these conditions, for the most part without conscious attention.
Grice's four conditions for conversational cooperation provided my text analysis scheme. They are

1. *Quality.* Conversants must speak what they believe to be the truth and
   that for which they have adequate evidence.
2. *Quantity.* Conversants must give the appropriate amount of information,
   neither too much nor too little.

3. *Relation*. The information that conversants give must be relevant to the aims of the conversation.
4. *Manner*. The conversants must make themselves clear, using appropriate forms of expression.

In my examination of Dave's last paper for each course, I considered both his work and his professor's response as conversational turns in which the speakers were doing what they believed would keep the Cooperative Principle in force. Dave's written turns were taken to display the discourse he believed was required in each setting so he would be deemed cooperative. I identified which of Grice's four conditions for successful conversation Dave paid special attention to fulfilling in each context. In this process I drew from the interview and protocol data as well as from the texts. I then counted and categorized Dave's teachers' written responses to his papers according to these same four conditions. A response was identified as an idea the teacher wanted to convey to Dave and could be as short as a single mark or as long as several sentences. Of particular interest were, first, the extent to which Dave and each teacher agreed upon what constituted cooperation, and, second, what the teacher pointed out as violations of the conditions of cooperation, errors that jeopardized the Cooperative Principle in that setting. Further, the form and language of each teacher's response provided insight into the ways of speaking in that particular discipline and classroom. **32**

The text analysis data added to and refined my understanding of Dave's classroom writing situations. And, conversely, my analyses of Dave's texts were informed by what I knew of the classroom writing situations. For this reason, I again elected to work alone with the texts. **33**

Validity of the findings and interpretations in this study were ensured by employing the following techniques. (1) Different types of data were compared. (2) The perspectives of various informants were compared. (3) Engagement with the subject was carried on over a long period of time during which salient factors were identified for more detailed inquiry. (4) External checks on the inquiry process were made by three established researchers who knew neither Dave nor the professors. These researchers read the emerging study at numerous points and questioned researcher biases and the bases for interpretations. (5) Interpretations were checked throughout with the informants themselves. (See Lincoln & Guba, 1985, for a discussion of validity and reliability in naturalistic inquiry.) **34**

Results and Discussion

Information from all data sources supports three general conclusions, two concerning Dave's interpretation and production of the required writing tasks and one concerning social factors in the classrooms that influenced him as he wrote. First, although the writing tasks in the three classes were in many ways similar, Dave interpreted them as being totally different from each other and totally different from anything he had ever done before. This was evidenced in the interview, protocol, and text analysis data. **35**

Second, certain social factors in Freshman Composition and Cell Biology   36
appeared to foster Dave's writing success in them. Observation and interview
data indicated that two unarticulated aspects of the classroom writing contexts
influenced his achievement. These social factors were (1) the functions that
writing served for Dave in each setting, and (2) the roles that participants and
students' texts played there. These social factors were bound up with what
Dave ultimately learned from and about writing in each class.

Third, Dave exhibited consistent ways of figuring out what constituted   37
appropriate texts in each setting, in his terms, of "figuring out what the teacher
wanted." Evidence from the interviews and protocols shows that he typically
drew upon six information sources, in a process that was in large part tacit.
These information sources included teacher-provided instructional supports,
sources Dave found on his own, and his prior knowledge.

The Writing Assignments: Similar Tasks, Audiences, and Purposes

My analysis of the assignments, combined with the observation and interview   38
data, showed that the writing in the three classes was similar in many ways. It
was, in all cases, informational writing for the teacher-as-examiner, the type of
writing that Applebee found comprised most secondary school writing (1984).
More specifically, the task in Cell Biology was a summary, and in Freshman
Composition and Poetry it was analysis, closely related informational uses of
writing. Dave's audiences were identified as teacher-as-examiner by the fact
that all assignments were graded and that Dave, as he wrote, repeatedly wondered how his teacher would "like" his work.

Further similarities among the writing in the three courses included the pur-   39
pose that the professors stated for having their students write. All three said
that the purpose was not so much for students to display specific information,
but rather for students to become competent in using the thinking and language of their disciplines. Dr. Kelly, the biologist, stated this most directly when
he explained to me why he had his students write reviews of journal articles:
"I want students to be at ease with the vocabulary of Cell Biology and how
experiments are being done. . . . Students need to get a feeling for the journals,
the questions people are asking, the answers they're getting, and the procedures
they're using. It will give them a feeling for the excitement, the dynamic part
of this field. And they need to see that what they're doing in class and lab is
actually *used* out there." Students' summaries of journal articles in Cell Biology were, in other words, to get them started speaking the language of that
discourse community.

Learning the conventions of academic discourse was also the purpose of stu-   40
dents' writing in Freshman Composition. Dr. Carter was less concerned with
the content of the students' five essays than she was with their cohesiveness.
She repeatedly stated that what would serve these students in their subsequent
academic writing was the ability to write coherent prose with a thesis and subpoints, unified paragraphs, and explicitly connected sentences. In an interview
she said, "Ideas aren't going to do people much good if they can't find the

means with which to communicate them. . . . When these students are more advanced, and the ability to produce coherent prose is internalized, then they can concentrate on ideas. That's why I'm teaching the analytic paper with a certain way of developing the thesis that's generalizable to their future writing." Dr. Carter's goal was, thus, to help students master conventions of prose which she believed were central to all academic discourse.

And likewise in Poetry the purpose of students' writing was to teach them how people in literary studies think and write. In his lecture on writing, early in the semester, Dr. Forson stated this purpose and alluded to some of the conventions for thinking and writing in that setting. He told students, "The three critical essays you will write will make you say something quite specific about the meaning of a poem (your thesis) and demonstrate how far you've progressed in recognizing and dealing with the devices a poet uses to express his insights. You'll find the poem's meaning in the poem itself, and you'll use quotes to prove your thesis. Our concern here is for the *poem*, not the poet's life or era. Nor are your own opinions of the poet's ideas germane."

Dr. Forson then spent 20 minutes explaining the mechanical forms for quoting poetry, using a model essay that he had written on a poem by Robert Herrick. He ended by telling students that they should think of their peers as the audience for their essays and asking them not to use secondary critical sources from the library. "You'll just deal with what you now know and with the poetic devices that we discuss in class. Each group of poems will feature one such device: imagery, symbolism, and so forth. These will be the tools in your tool box."

Thus in all three courses Dave's tasks were informational writing for the teacher-as-examiner. All were for the purpose of displaying competence in using the ways of thinking and writing appropriate to that setting. And in all three courses Dave wrote a series of similar short papers, due at about three-week intervals, the assumption being that students' early attempts would inform their subsequent ones, in the sort of trial-and-error process that characterizes much language learning. Further, the reading required in Poetry and Cell Biology, the poems and the journal articles, were equally unfamiliar to Dave. We might expect, then, that Dave would view the writing for these three courses as quite similar, and, given an equal amount of work, he would achieve similar levels of success. This, however, is not what happened.

Dave's Interpretation of the Writing Tasks

The Writer's Concerns While Composing. In spite of the similarities among the writing tasks for the three courses, evidence from several sources shows that Dave interpreted them as being totally different from each other and totally different from anything he had ever done before. Dave's characteristic approach across courses was to focus so fully on the particular new ways of thinking and writing in each setting that commonalities with previous writing were obscured for him. And interwoven with Dave's conviction that the writing for these courses was totally dissimilar was his differing success in them. Though he worked hard in all three courses, he made B's in Freshman Composition, Ds and Cs in Poetry, and As in Cell Biology.

The protocol data explain in part why the writing for these classes seemed so different to Dave. Dave's chief concerns while composing for each course were very different. His focus in Freshman Composition was on textual coherence. Fifty-four percent of his expressed concerns were for coherence of thesis and subpoints, coherence within paragraphs, and sentence cohesion. By contrast, in Poetry, though Dave did mention thesis and subpoints, his chief concerns were not with coherence, but with the new ways of thinking and writing in that setting. Forty-four percent of his concerns focused on accurately interpreting the poem and properly using quotes. In Cell Biology, yet a new focus of concerns is evident. Seventy-two percent of Dave's concerns deal with the new rules of use in that academic discipline. His chief concerns in Biology were to accurately understand the scientific terms and concepts in the journal article and then to accurately rephrase and connect these in his own text, following the same five-part structure in which the published experiment was reported. It is no wonder that the writing for these classes seemed very different to Dave. As a newcomer in each academic territory, Dave's attention was occupied by the new conventions of interpretation and language use in each community. (See Table 2.)   45

The same preoccupations controlled his subsequent work on the papers. In each course Dave wrote a second draft, which he then typed. In none of these second drafts did Dave see the task differently or make major changes. He is, in this regard, like the secondary students Applebee (1984) studied who were unable, without teacher assistance, to revise their writing in more than minor ways. And Dave revised none of these papers after the teachers had responded.   46

We can further fill out the pictures of Dave's composing for the three classes by combining the protocol findings with the observation and interview data. In his first protocol session, in April of his freshman year, Dave composed the first draft of his fourth paper for Freshman Composition, an essay in which he chose to analyze the wrongs of abortion. To this session Dave brought an outline of this thesis and subpoints. He told me that he had spent only 30 minutes writing it the night before, but that the topic was one he had thought a lot about. As he composed, Dave was most concerned with and apparently very dependent upon, his outline, commenting on it, glancing at it, or pausing to study it 14 times during the 30 minutes of composing. Dave's next most frequently expressed concerns were for coherence at paragraph and sentence levels, what Dr. Carter referred to as coherence of mid-sized and small parts. These were the new "rules of use" in this setting. Dave told me that in high school he had done some "bits and pieces" of writing and some outlines for history, but that he had never before written essays like this. The total time Dave spent on his abortion essay was five hours.   47

In Dave's Poetry protocol session seven months later, in November of his sophomore year, he composed part of the first draft of his third and last paper for that class, a six-page analysis of a poem called "Marriage" by contemporary poet Gregory Corso. To this session he brought two pages of notes and   48

Table 2

Concerns Expressed During Composing-Aloud Protocols and Retrospective Interviews

	Percent of Comments		
Concerns Expressed in All Three Courses	Freshman Composition	Poetry	Cell Biology
Features of Written Text			
Coherent thesis/ subpoint structure	22	18	0
Coherent paragraph structure	15	13	3
Cohesive sentences	17	8	3
Editing for mechanical correctness	9	3	3
Communication Situation (assignment, reader-writer roles, purpose)	8	6	5
On-Going Process	18	6	12
Emerging Text	11	2	2
Concerns Specific to Poetry			
Appropriately using quotes from poem	0	32	0
Making a correct interpretation of the poem	0	12	0
Concerns Specific to Cell Biology			
Following the 5-part scientific guidelines	0	0	20
Correctly understanding the content of the article being summarized	0	0	37
Rephrasing & connecting appropriate parts of the article	0	0	15
Total	100	100	100
Number of comments	64	62	60

his *Norton Anthology of Poetry* in which he had underlined and written notes in the margins beside the poem. He told me that he had spent four hours (of an eventual total of 11) preparing to write: reading the poem many times and finding a critical essay on it in the library. During his pre-writing and composing, Dave's primary concern was to get the right interpretation of the poem, "the true meaning" as he phrased it. And as Dave wrote, he assumed that his professor knew the true meaning, a meaning, Dave said, that "was there, but not there, not just what it says on the surface." Further, Dave knew that he must argue his interpretation, using not his own but the poet's words; this was his second most frequently expressed concern.

As Dave composed, he appeared to be as tied to the poem as he had been   49 to his outline in Freshman Composition the semester before. He seemed to be almost *physically* attached to the *Norton Anthology* by his left forefinger as he progressed down the numbers he had marked in the margins. He was, we might say, tied to the concrete material, the "facts" of the poem before him. Dave never got his own essay structure; rather, he worked down the poem, explicating from beginning to end. In the retrospective interview he said, "I didn't really have to think much about my thesis and subs because they just come naturally now. . . . But anyway it's not like in Comp last year. Here my first paragraph is the introduction with the thesis, and the stanzas are the subpoints." Dave's preoccupation with the poem and the new conventions of interpreting and quoting poetry resulted in a paper that was not an analysis but a summary with some interpretation along the way. His focus on these new rules of use appeared to limit his ability to apply previously learned skills, the thesis-subpoint analytical structure, and kept him working at the more concrete summary level.

This domination by the concrete may often characterize newcomers' first   50 steps as they attempt to use language in unfamiliar disciplines (Williams, 1985). Dave's professor, Dr. Forson, seemed to be familiar with this phenomenon when he warned students in his lecture on writing: "You must remember that the poet ordered the poem. *You* order your essay with your own thesis and subtheses. Get away from 'Next. . . . Next'." But if Dave heard this in September, he had forgotten it by November. Dave's experience is consonant with Langer's (1984) finding that students who know more about a subject as they begin to write are likely to choose analysis rather than summary. And these students receive higher scores for writing quality as well.

In his writing for Cell Biology the following semester, Dave's concerns were   51 again focused on the new and unfamiliar conventions in this setting. Before writing his last paper, a four-page review of an experiment on glycoprotein reported in *The Journal of Cell Biology*, Dave spent three hours preparing. (He eventually spent a total of eight hours on the review.) He had chosen the article in the library from a list the professor had given to students and had then read the article twice, underlining it, making notes, and looking up the definitions of unfamiliar terms. To the protocol session Dave brought these notes, the article, and a sheet on which he had written what he called "Dr. Kelly's guidelines," the five-part scientific experiment format that Dr. Kelly wanted students to follow: Background, Objectives, Procedures, Results, and Discussion.

In his composing aloud, Dave's chief concerns in Biology were, as in Poetry   52 the semester before, with the reading, in this case the journal article. But here, unlike Poetry, Dave said the meaning was "all out on the table." In Poetry he had had to interpret meaning from the poem's connotative language; in Biology, by contrast, he could look up meanings, a situation with which Dave was far more comfortable. But as he composed for Biology, he was just as tied to the journal article as he had been to the poem or to his outline in previous semesters. Dave paused frequently to consult the article, partially covering it at times so that his own paper was physically closer to what he was summarizing at that moment.

Dave's first and second most commonly expressed concerns during the Biology protocol session were for rephrasing and connecting parts of the article and for following Dr. Kelly's guidelines. These were, in essence, concerns for coherence and organization, what Dave was most concerned with in Freshman Composition. But the writing for Biology bore little relation in Dave's mind to what he had done in Freshman Composition. In Biology he was indeed concerned about his organization, but here it was the five-part scientific format he had been given, very different, it seemed to him, than the thesis/subpoint organization he had had to create for his freshman essays. In fact, until I questioned him about it at the end of the semester, Dave never mentioned the freshman thesis/subpoint structure. And the concerns for coherence at paragraph and sentence levels that had been so prominent as he wrote for Freshman Composition were replaced in Biology by his concern for rephrasing the article's already coherent text. In Freshman Composition Dave had talked about trying to get his sentences and paragraphs to "fit" or "flow" together. In Biology, however, he talked about trying to get the article into his own words, about "cutting," "simplifying," and "combining two sentences." Again, it is no wonder that Dave believed that this writing was totally new. It took one of Dave's friend's and my prodding during an interview to make Dave see that he had indeed written summaries before. Lots of them.

The Nature of Cooperation in the Three Courses.

The text analysis data provide further insight into why Dave perceived the writing in these courses as so dissimilar. The data provide information about what was, in Grice's terms, essential to maintaining the Cooperative Principle in these written exchanges. Analyses of the teachers' responses to Dave's papers show that his concerns in each class generally did match theirs. Put differently, Dave had figured out, though not equally well in all classes, what counted as "cooperation" in each context, and what he had to do to be deemed a competent communicator there. (See Table 3.)

Analysis of Dave's finished essay for Freshman Composition suggests that his concerns for textual coherence were appropriate. Dave knew that to keep

Table 3

Teachers' Responses to Dave's Papers

	NUMBER OF RESPONSES INDICATING VIOLATIONS OF CONDITIONS FOR COOPERATION				
	QUALITY	QUANTITY	RELEVANCE	MANNER	GRADE
Composition	0	0	0	2	18/20
Poetry	8	0	0	11	C+
Cell Biology	0	0	0	14	96

the Cooperative Principle in force in Dr. Carter's class, he had to pay special attention to fulfilling the condition of *Manner,* to making himself clear, using appropriate forms of expression. He succeeded and was deemed cooperative by Dr. Carter when she responded to his contribution with a telegraphic reply on the first page: "18/20." Apart from editing two words in Dave's text, she made no further comments, assuming that Dave and she shared an understanding of what constituted cooperation in her class and of what her numbers meant. (She had explained to students that she was marking with numbers that semester in an attempt to be more "scientific," and she had defined for them the "objective linguistic features of text" to which her numbers referred.) Dave did understand the grade and was, of course, very pleased with it.

In an interview, Dr. Carter explained her grade to me. "Though his content   56 isn't great," she said, "his paper is coherent, not badly off at any place. . . . He gave a fair number of reasons to develop his paragraphs, he restated his point at the end, and there is no wasted language. It's not perfectly woven together, but it's good." Though Dr. Carter mentioned the "reasons" Dave gave as evidence for his contentions, she was concerned not so much with their meaning as with their cohesiveness. Cooperation in this setting thus depended upon fulfilling the condition of *Manner.* Dave knew this and expected only a response to how well he had achieved the required form, not to the content of his essay.

In his writing for Poetry the following semester, Dave was attempting to   57 keep the Cooperative Principle in force by paying special attention to two conditions, *Quality* and *Manner.* That is, first he was attempting to say what was true and give adequate evidence, and, second, he was attempting to use proper forms of expression. This is evidenced in the interview and protocol as well as the text data. Analysis of Dr. Forson's 19 responses to Dave's paper shows that Dave's concerns matched those of his teacher, that Dave had figured out, though only in part, what counted as cooperation in that setting. Dr. Forson's responses all referred to violations of the same conditions Dave had been concerned with fulfilling, *Quality* and *Manner.* In seven of his eight marginal notes and in an endnote, Dr. Forson disagreed with Dave's interpretation and questioned his evidence, violations of the *Quality* condition. Mina Shaughnessy (1977) says that such failure to properly coordinate claims and evidence is perhaps the most common source of misunderstanding in academic prose. The ten mechanical errors that Dr. Forson pointed out were violations of the condition of *Manner,* violations which may jeopardize the Cooperative Principle in many academic settings. Dave's unintentional violations in Poetry of the *Quality* and *Manner* conditions jeopardized the Cooperative Principle in that exchange, resulting in the C+ grade.

Dr. Kelly's responses to Dave's writing in Biology were, like those in Freshman   58 Composition, much briefer than Dr. Forson's. Dr. Kelly's 14 marks or phrases all pointed out errors in form, unintentional violations of the Gricean condition of *Manner.* But these were apparently not serious enough to jeopardize the aims of the written conversation in Biology; Dave's grade on the review was 96.

This application of Grice's rubric for spoken conversation to student-teacher   59 written interaction gives further insight into the differences in these classroom contexts for writing. It is evident that successfully maintaining the Cooperative Principle was a more complicated business in Poetry than in Freshman Composition or Biology. In Biology, Dave was unlikely to violate the condition of *Quality*, as he did in Poetry, because he was only summarizing the published experiment and thus only had to pay attention to the condition of *Manner*. In Poetry, by contrast, he was called upon to take an interpretive position. This assumed that he had already summarized the poem. He had not. Thus his analytical essay took the form of a summary as we have seen. In Biology, on the other hand, the writing was supposed to be a summary that then moved to a comparison of the summarized experiment to what was going on in class.

For Dave, the latter assignment was more appropriate. Novices in a field   60 may need the simpler summary assignment that helps them understand the new reading, the new language that they are being asked to learn. They may then be ready to move to analysis or critique. One wonders if Dave's success in Poetry would have been enhanced if he had been asked to write out a summary of the poem first. He could then have worked from that summary as he structured his own critical essay.

Similarly, in Freshman Composition, Dave was unlikely to violate the condi-   61 tion of *Quality*, to say something untrue or provide inadequate evidence for his claim. Though Dave did have to provide evidence for his subpoints, he was not evaluated for his content, and thus he concentrated on the condition of *Manner*. Further, the writing in Freshman Composition did not require Dave to master unfamiliar texts as it did in both Poetry and Biology. And for Dave the task of integrating new knowledge from his reading into his writing in those courses was his salient concern, as we have seen.

The apparent absence of attention paid in any of these classes to fulfilling   62 the conditions of *Quantity* or *Relation* is puzzling. Perhaps Dave's prior school writing experience had trained him to include the right amount of information (*Quantity*) and stay on topic (*Relation*).

The text analysis data, then, show that what counted as cooperation in these   63 three classes was indeed quite different. Dr. Forson, in his extensive responses, apparently felt it necessary to reteach Dave how people think and write in his community. This is understandable in light of Dave's numerous unintentional violations of the Cooperative Principle. Further, though Dr. Forson told students that he was being objective, finding the meaning of the poem in the text, he told me that his responses to students' papers were to argue his interpretation of the poem and, thus, to justify his grade.

The differing language and forms of these professors' responses probably   64 also added to Dave's sense that in each classroom he was in a new foreign land. Response style may well be discipline-specific as well as teacher-specific, with responses in literary studies generally more discursive than in the sciences. Further, Dr. Forson's responses were in the informal register typically used by an authority speaking to a subordinate (Freedman, 1984). His responses to Dave's paper included the following: "You misfire here." "I get this one. Hurrah for me!" "Pardon my writing. I corrected this in an automobile." The informality, and the word "corrected" in particular, leave little doubt about the authority differential between Dr. Forson and Dave. By contrast, Dave seemed to interpret the numerical grade in Biology as more characteristic of a conversation between equals. In a comment that may say more about their classroom interaction than their written interaction, Dave spoke of Dr. Kelly's brief responses to his review: "Yeah. He's like that. He treats us like adults. When we ask him questions, he answers us." Dave's apparent mixing of his spoken and written interaction with Dr. Kelly emphasizes the point that students' and teachers' writing for each other in classrooms is as fully contextualized as any other activity that goes on there.

Before Dave turned in his last papers in Poetry and Biology, I asked him   65 to speculate about the grade he would get. When he handed in his six-page paper on the Corso poem, "Marriage," on which he had spent eleven hours, he told me that he hoped for an A or B: "I'll be really frustrated on this one if the grade's not good after I've put in the time on it." A week later, however, he told me in a resigned tone and with a short laugh that he'd gotten a C+. By contrast, when he turned in his last review in Biology, he told me he knew he would get an A. When I questioned him, he replied, "I don't know how I know. I just do." And he was right: his grade was 96. Dave obviously understood far better what constituted cooperation in Biology than he did in Poetry.

Social Aspects of the Classrooms That Influenced Dave's Writing

Why was Dave's success in writing in these classrooms so different? The   66 answers to this question will illuminate some of the dimensions along which school writing situations differ and thus influence student achievement. It would be a mistake to think that the differing task structure was the only reason that Dave was more successful in Biology and Freshman Composition than he was in Poetry. Assignments are, as I have suggested, only a small part of the classroom interaction, limited written exchanges that reflect the nature of the communication situation created by participants in that setting. Two unarticulated qualities in the contexts for writing in Freshman Composition and Biology appeared to foster Dave's success in those classes. These were (1) the social functions Dave's writing served for him in those classes, and (2) the roles played by participants and by students' texts there.

The Functions Dave Saw His Writing as Accomplishing.   It has been argued that   67 the social functions served by writing must be seen as an intrinsic part of the writing experience (Clark & Florio, 1983; Hymes, 1972a, 1972b; Scribner & Cole, 1981). Evidence from interviews and observations indicate that the writing in Freshman Composition and Biology was for Dave a meaningful social activity, meaningful beyond just getting him through the course. Further, Dave and his teachers in Freshman Composition and Biology mutually understood and valued those functions. This was not the case in Poetry. The data show a correlation not only between meaningful social functions served by the writing and Dave's success with it, but also between the writing's social meaning and Dave's ability to remember and draw upon it in subsequent semesters.

In Freshman Composition Dave's writing served four valuable functions for   68
him. He articulated all of these.

1. Writing to prepare him for future writing in school and career
2. Writing to explore topics of his choice
3. Writing to participate with other students in the classroom
4. Writing to demonstrate academic competence

In Biology Dave also saw his writing as serving four valuable functions: 69

1. Writing to learn the language of Cell Biology, which he saw as necessary to his career
2. Writing to prepare him for his next semester's writing in Immunology
3. Writing to make connections between his classwork and actual work being done by professionals in the field
4. Writing to demonstrate academic competence

Evidence from interviews and observation shows that Dr. Carter and Dr. Kelly saw writing in their classes as serving the same four functions that Dave did.

On the other hand, in Poetry, though Dave's professor stated four func-   70
tions of student writing, Dave saw his writing as serving only one function for him: writing to demonstrate academic competence. Dave, always the compliant student, did say after he had received his disappointing grade in Poetry that the writing in Poetry was probably good for him: "Probably any kind of writing helps you." Though he may well be right, Dave actually saw his writing for Poetry as serving such a limited function—evaluation of his skills in writing poetry criticism for Dr. Forson—that he was not really convinced (and little motivated by the notion) that this writing would serve him in any general way.

Dave contended that any writing task was easy or difficult for him accord-   71
ing to his interest in it. When I asked him what he meant by interesting, he said, "If it has something to do with my life. Like it could explain something to me or give me an answer that I could use now." Writing must have, in other words, meaningful personal and social functions for Dave if it is to be manageable, "easy," for him. These functions existed for Dave in Freshman Composition and Biology, providing the applications and personal transaction with the material that may be generally required for learning and forging personal knowledge (Dewey, 1949; Polanyi, 1958).

Dave's Poetry class, however, served no such personally meaningful func-   72
tions. Six weeks after the Poetry course was finished, I asked Dave some further questions about his last paper for that course, the discussion of the Corso poem on which he had worked 11 hours. He could remember almost nothing about it. When I asked him to speculate why this was, he said, "I guess it's because I have no need to remember it." By contrast, when I asked Dave in the fall of his junior year if his Cell Biology writing was serving him in his Immunology course as he had expected, he said, "Yes. The teacher went over how to write up our labs, but most of us had the idea anyway from last semester because we'd read those journal articles. We were already exposed to it."

Of course the functions of his writing in Biology served Dave better than   73
those in Poetry in part because he was a biology major. The writing for Cell
Biology fit into a larger whole: his growing body of knowledge about this
field and his professional future. The material in Cell Biology was for Dave a
comprehensible part of the discipline of Biology which was in turn a comprehensible part of the sciences. Dave was, with experience, gradually acquiring
a coherent sense of the language of the discipline, how biologists think and
speak and what it is they talk about. And his understanding of the language of
biology was accompanied by an increasing confidence in his own ability to use
it. Both of these are probably necessary foundations for later, more abstract
and complex uses of the language (Piaget, 1952; Perry, 1970; Williams, 1985).

In the required one-semester Poetry class, however, the poems seemed to   74
Dave to be unrelated to each other except for commonly used poetic devices,
and his writing about them was unrelated to his own life by anything at all
beyond his need to find the "true meaning" and get an acceptable grade. Dave's
different relationship to the languages of these disciplines was shown when he
said, "In Biology I'm using what I've *learned*. It's just putting what I've learned
on paper. But in Poetry, more or less each poem is different, so it's not *taught*
to you. You just have to figure it out from that poem itself and hope Dr. Forson
likes it." Nor, in Poetry, was Dave ever invited to make personally meaningful
connections with the poems. And he never did it on his own, no doubt in part
because he was so preoccupied with the new ways of thinking and speaking
that he was trying to use.

In Freshman Composition the social function of writing that was perhaps   75
most powerful for Dave was writing to participate with other students in the
classroom. In his peer writing group Dave, for the first time ever, discussed his
writing with others. Here he communicated personal positions and insights to
his friends, an influential audience for him. That an important social function
was served by these students' work with each other is suggested by their clear
memory, a year and a half later, both of their essays and of each others' reactions to them.

The four social functions that Dave's writing in Freshman Composition   76
accomplished for him enhanced his engagement with and attitude toward the
writing he did in that class. This engagement is reflected in Dave's memory not
only of his essays and his friends' reactions to them, but also in his memory and
use of the ideas and terms from that course. When Dave talked about his writing during his sophomore and junior years, he used the process terms he had
learned in Freshman Composition: prewriting, revision, and drafts. He also
used other language he had learned as a freshman, speaking at times about his
audience's needs, about narrowing his topic, about connecting his sentences,
providing more details, and choosing his organizational structure. This is not
to say that Dave had mastered these skills in every writing situation nor that
he always accurately diagnosed problems in his own work. In fact, we know
that he did not. It is to say, however, that Dave did recognize and could talk
about some of the things that writing does involve in many situations. Thus,
the value of this course for Dave lay not so much in the thesis/subpoint essay

structure. Rather, Dave had, as a result of his experiences in Freshman Composition, learned that writing is a process that can be talked about, managed, and controlled.

Thus the social functions that writing served for Dave in each class were   77
viewed as an intrinsic part of his writing experiences there. Where these functions were numerous and mutually understood and valued by Dave and his teacher, Dave was more successful in figuring out and producing the required discourse. And then he remembered it longer. In Poetry, where his writing served few personally valued ends, Dave did less well, making a C on the first paper, a D on the second, and a C+ on the third. It should be noted, in addition, that grades themselves serve a social function in classrooms: defining attitudes and roles. Dave's low grades in Poetry probably further alienated him from the social communication processes in that classroom community and helped define his role there.

The Roles Played by the Participants and by Students' Texts.   Other social aspects   78
of these classroom contexts for writing which affected Dave's experiences were the roles played by the people and texts in them. Such roles are tacitly assigned in classroom interaction and create the context in which the student stranger attempts to determine the rules of language use in that territory. Here we will examine (1) Dave's role in relation to the teacher, (2) Dave's role in relation to other students in the class, and (3) the role played by students' texts there.

Dave's Role in Relation to the Teacher.   This is a particularly important role   79
relationship in any classroom because it tacitly shapes the writer-audience relation that students use as they attempt to communicate appropriately. In all three classes Dave was writing for his teachers as pupil to examiner. However, data from several sources show that there were important variations in the actual "enactments" (Goffman, 1961) of this role-relationship.

In Composition, both Dave and his professor played the role of writer.   80
Throughout the semester Dr. Carter talked about what and how she wrote, the long time she spent in prewriting activities, the eight times she typically revised her work, and the strategies she used to understand her audience in various situations. She spoke to students as if she and they were all writers working together, saying such things as "I see some of you write like I do," or "Let's work together to shape this language." And, as we have seen, she structured the course to provide opportunities for students to play the role of writer in their peer groups. She also asked them to describe their writing processes for several of their essays. Dave told me in an interview during his junior year, "In high school I couldn't stand writing, but in Comp I started to change because I knew more what I was doing. I learned that there are steps you can go through, and I learned how to organize a paper." As a freshman, Dave understood for the first time something of what it feels like to be a writer.

In Biology both Dave and his teacher, Dr. Kelly, saw Dave as playing the   81
role of newcomer, learning the language needed for initiation into the profession. Dr. Kelly played the complementary role of experienced professional who

was training Dave in the ways of speaking in that discipline, ways they both assumed Dave would learn in time.

In Poetry, on the other hand, Dave played the role of outsider in relation- 82 ship to his teacher, the insider who knew the true meanings of poetry. And Dave stayed the outsider, unable ever to fully get the teacher's "true meaning." This outsider/insider relationship between Dave and Dr. Forson was created by a number of factors: (1) Their spoken and written interaction, (2) the few meaningful social functions served for Dave by the writing in that class, (3) the demanding nature of the analytic task, combined with (4) the limited knowledge Dave commanded in that setting, (5) the limited number of effective instructional supports, and (6) the low grades Dave got, which further alienated him from the communication processes in that class. (To the instructional supports provided in Poetry we will return below.) Because Dave's outsider role was not a pleasant one for him, he seemed increasingly to separate his thinking from his writing in Poetry, saying several times that he had the right ideas, the teacher just did not like the way he wrote them.

Dave's Role in Relationship to Other Students.   Students' relationships with 83 each other, like those between students and teachers, are created as students interact within the classroom structures the teacher has set up. These classroom structures grow out of teachers' explicit and tacit notions about writing and learning. What specifically were the relationships among students in Freshman Composition, Biology, and Poetry?

In Composition, as we have seen, students shared their writing and responded 84 to each other's work. The classroom structure reflected Dr. Carter's perhaps tacit notion that writing is a social as well as intellectual affair. However, in neither Poetry nor Biology was time built into the class for students to talk with each other about their writing. Dave lamented this as he wrote for Poetry early in his sophomore year, because, he said, he now realized how valuable the small group sessions had been in Freshman Composition the semester before.

In Biology, Dave told me students did talk informally about the journal 85 articles they had selected and how they were progressing on their summaries. Dr. Kelly, who circulated during lab, was at times included in these informal talks about writing. And it is no surprise that students discussed their writing in this way in Biology in light of Dr. Kelly's notions about writing. It is, he believes, an essential part of what scientists do. He told me that it often comes as a rude shock to students that the way biologists survive in the field is by writing. He said, "These students are bright, and they can memorize piles of facts, but they're not yet good at writing. They know what science *is*," he told me, "but they don't know what scientists *do*." Thus, writing up research results is seen by Dr. Kelly as an integral part of a biologist's lab work. No wonder his students talked about it.

In Poetry, however, there was little talk of any kind among students. Classes 86 were primarily lectures where Dr. Forson explicated poems and explained poetic devices. Only occasionally did he call on one of the 22 students for an opinion. This lack of student interaction in Poetry was in line with the image of the writer that Dr. Forson described for students, an image that may be widely shared in literary studies: A person alone with his or her books and thoughts. Dr. Forson did, however, tell students that he himself often got his ideas for writing from listening to himself talk about poems in class. Yet, in conversation with me, he said that he did not want students discussing the poems and their writing with each other because he feared they would not think for themselves. Dave picked up on this idea very clearly. It was not until the fall of his junior year that he admitted to me that he and his girlfriend had worked together on their papers. They had discussed the interpretations of the poems and how they might best write them, but, he told me, they had been careful to choose different poems to write about so that Dr. Forson wouldn't know they had worked together. This absence of student interaction in Poetry may have contributed to the outsider role that Dave played in that class.

Throughout this study I was amazed at the amount of talk that goes on all the time outside class among students as they work to figure out the writing requirements in various courses. What Dave's experience in Poetry may suggest is that where student collaboration in writing is not openly accepted, it goes on clandestinely.   87

The Roles Played by Students' Texts.

   What were students' texts called and how were they handled? Interview and observation data show that students' texts were treated quite differently in these three courses, and this affected how Dave saw the assignments, and, perhaps more important, how he saw himself as writer.   88

In Freshman Composition Dave wrote what he referred to as "essays"; in Biology, "reviews"; in Poetry, "papers." This latter term is commonly used, of course, but it is one that Emig (1983, p. 173) says suggests a low status text: "Paper"—as if there were no words on the sheet at all. In Poetry the high status texts, the ones that were discussed and interpreted, were the poems. Students' works were just more or less successful explications of those. Furthermore, in Poetry the one model essay the students read was written by the teacher. Though students were told they should think of their peers as their audience, in fact they never read each other's essays at all. Students' texts were, rather, passed only between student and teacher as in a private conversation.   89

In Biology, student texts enjoyed a higher status. Excellent student reviews were posted and students were encouraged to read them; they were to serve as models. Some student writers were thus defined as competent speakers in this territory, and the message was clear to Dave: This was a language that he too could learn given time and proper training.   90

And in Freshman Composition, of course, student texts were the *objects* of study. The class read good and flawed student texts from former semesters and from their own. This not only helped Dave with his writing, it also dignified student writing and elevated his estimation of his own work. Student texts were not, in short, private affairs between teacher and student; they were the subject matter of this college course.   91

Thus the roles that were enacted by teachers, students, and students' texts   92
were quite different in each classroom and were an integral part of Dave's
writing experiences there. The participants' interaction and the social functions that writing serves are important factors working to create the communication situation. And this communication situation, it has been suggested, is
the fundamental factor shaping the success of writing instruction (Langer &
Applebee, 1984, p. 171).

The Information Sources Dave Drew Upon

In a process that was in large part tacit, Dave drew upon six sources for infor-   93
mation about what constituted successful writing in Freshman Composition,
Poetry, and Biology. These included teacher-provided instructional supports,
sources Dave found on his own, and his prior experience. Many of these have
been mentioned above. They are summarized in Table 4.

Of particular interest are the information sources Dave drew upon (or failed   94
to draw upon) in Poetry, the course in which the writing assignment was the

Table 4

Information Sources Dave Drew Upon in Assessing Required Discourse

Information Sources	Freshman Composition	Poetry	Cell Biology
What teachers said in class about writing	Constant lectures & exercises about process & products	-One lecture -General statements to the class about their papers when returning them	-Ten minutes giving "guide-lines" when returning 1st set of reviews of reviews -Informal comments in lab
Model texts	Many, including flawed models	-One, written by teacher -One, written by professional (from library)	-The articles being summarized served as models. -Posted student reviews
Talk with other students	Frequent groups in class	With friend outside class	Informal, in class
Teachers' written responses to writing	Read responses & revised early essays accordingly	Read. No revision required	Read. No revision required
Dave's prior experience	The extent to which Dave drew upon prior experience is difficult to say. In each class he believed he had no prior experience to draw from. However, we know he had had related prior experience.		
Personal talk with teacher	One conference with teacher	None	None

most demanding and in which Dave did least well in assessing and producing the required discourse. The information source that Dr. Forson intended to be most helpful to students, the instructional support on which he spent a great deal of time, was his response to their papers. However, his extensive comments did not help Dave a great deal in learning how to communicate in that setting. Dave said that the comments on his first paper did help him some with his second, but he really did not refer to Dr. Forson's responses on the second paper as he wrote the third. Nor did Dave use the comments on the third paper when preparing for the essay question on the final exam. Dr. Forson required no revision in direct response to his comments, and the expected carry-over of his responses from one paper to the next did not occur. Rather, Dave repeated similar mistakes again and again. The assumption that trial and error will improve students' writing across a series of similar tasks did not hold true for Dave's work in Poetry.

Neither was the model text in Poetry, Dr. Forson's analysis of the Herrick   95 poem that he went over in lecture, as useful an information source for Dave as Dr. Forson had hoped it would be. Dave told me that though he had looked at Dr. Forson's model critical essay as he wrote his first paper, it had not helped him a great deal. "Seeing how someone else did it," he said, "is a lot different than doing it yourself." In Freshman Composition and Biology, however, the model texts, both excellent and flawed ones, were more numerous. And in Biology, the model provided by the article Dave was summarizing was virtually inescapable. Model texts are, it seems reasonable, particularly important to newcomers learning the conventions of discourse in a new academic territory.

An information source which Dave was not adept at using in any course   96 was direct questioning of the professor, the native-speaker expert in each setting. Dave never voluntarily questioned a teacher, though in October of his sophomore year, when he was doing poorly in Poetry, he did make an attempt to speak with Dr. Forson at his office. But when Dr. Forson was not there, Dave waited only a short time and then left—relieved, he said. He did not return. In Freshman Composition, however, Dave was required to interact with Dr. Carter individually in his mid-semester conference. That interview provided an additional information source upon which Dave could draw as he assessed and adapted to the writing requirements in that class.

Discussion

What, then, can we learn from Dave's experiences? First, this study adds to   97 existing research which suggests that school writing is not a monolithic activity or global skill. Rather, the contexts for writing may be so different from one classroom to another, the ways of speaking in them so diverse, the social meanings of writing and the interaction patterns so different, that the courses may be for the student writer like so many foreign countries. These differences were apparent in this study not only in Dave's perceptions of the courses but in his concerns while writing and in his written products.

Second, the findings of this study have several implications for our under-   98
standing of writing development. This study suggests that writing development
is, in part, context-dependent. In each new classroom community, Dave in many
ways resembled a beginning language user. He focused on a limited number of
new concerns, and he was unable to move beyond concrete ways of thinking
and writing, the facts of the matter at hand. Moreover, skills mastered in one
situation, such as the thesis-subpoint organization in Freshman Composition,
did not, as Dave insisted, automatically transfer to new contexts with differing
problems and language and differing amounts of knowledge that he controlled.
To better understand the stages that students progress through in achieving
competence in academic speech communities, we need further research.

Dave's development across his freshman and sophomore years, where he   99
was repeatedly a newcomer, may also be viewed in terms of his attitude toward
writing. Evidence over 21 months shows that his notion of the purpose of
school writing changed very little. Though there were, as we have seen, other
functions accomplished for Dave by his writing in Freshman Composition and
Biology, he always understood the purpose of his school writing as being primarily to satisfy a teacher-examiner's requirements. A change that did occur,
however, was Dave's increased understanding of some of the activities that
writers actually engage in and an increased confidence in his writing ability.
As a freshman, he had told me that he did not like to write and was not very
good, but by the fall of his junior year he sounded quite different. Because of
a number of successful classroom experiences with writing, and an ability to
forget the less successful ones, Dave told me, "Writing is no problem for me. At
work, in school, I just do it."

Whether Dave will eventually be a mature writer, one who, according to   100
Britton's (1975) definition, is able to satisfy his own purposes with a wide range
of audiences, lies beyond the scope of this study to determine. We do know,
however, that Dave did not, during the period of this study, write for a wide
range of audiences. Nor did he, in these classes, define his own audiences, purposes, or formats, though he did in Freshman Composition choose his topics
and in Poetry and Biology the particular poems and articles he wrote about.
What this study suggests is that college undergraduates in beginning-level
courses may have even less opportunity to orchestrate their own writing occasions than do younger students. Balancing teachers' and students' purposes is
indeed difficult in these classrooms where students must, in 14 weeks, learn
unfamiliar discourse conventions as well as a large body of new knowledge.

The findings of this study have several implications for the teaching of   101
writing. They suggest that when we ask what students learn from and about
writing in classrooms, we must look not only at particular assignments or at
students' written products. We must also look at what they learn from the
social contexts those classrooms provide for writing. In Freshman Composition, Dave learned that writer was a role he could play. In Biology, writing was
for Dave an important part of a socialization process; he was the newcomer
being initiated into a profession in which, he learned, writing counts for a great

deal. From his writing in Poetry, Dave learned that reading poetry was not for him and that he could get through any writing task, no matter how difficult or foreign. This latter is a lesson not without its value, of course, but it is not one that teachers hope to teach with their writing assignments.

This study also raises questions about how teachers can best help student 102 "strangers" to become competent users of the new language in their academic territory. Because all writing is context-dependent, and because successful writing requires the accurate assessment of and adaptation to the demands of particular writing situations, perhaps writing teachers should be explicitly training students in this assessment process. As Dave researched the writing requirements in his classroom, he drew upon six information sources in a process that was for him largely tacit and unarticulated. But Dave was actually in a privileged position in terms of his potential for success in this "figuring out" process. He had, after all, had years of practice writing in classrooms. Furthermore, he shared not only ethnic and class backgrounds with his teachers, but also many assumptions about education. Students from diverse communities may need, even more than Dave, explicit training in the ways in which one figures out and then adapts to the writing demands in academic contexts.

For teachers in the disciplines, "native-speakers" who may have used the 103 language in their discipline for so long that is it partially invisible to them, the first challenge will be to appreciate just how foreign and difficult their language is for student newcomers. They must make explicit the interpretive and linguistic conventions in their community, stressing that theirs is one way of looking at reality and not reality itself. As Fish (1980) points out, "The choice is never between objectivity and interpretation, but between an interpretation that is unacknowledged as such and an interpretation that is at least aware of itself" (p. 179). Teachers in the disciplines must then provide student newcomers with assignments and instructional supports which are appropriate for first steps in using the language of their community. Designing appropriate assignments and supports may well be more difficult when the student stranger is only on a brief visit in an academic territory, as Dave was in Poetry, or when the student comes from a community at a distance farther from academe than Dave did.

Naturalistic studies like the present one, Geertz says, are only "another 104 country heard from . . . nothing more or less." Yet, "small facts speak to large issues" (1973, p. 23). From Dave's story, and others like it which describe actual writers at work in local settings, we will learn more about writers' processes and texts and how these are constrained by specific social dynamics. Our generalizations and theories about writing and about how people learn to write must, in the final analysis, be closely tied to such concrete social situations.

References

Applebee, A. (1984). *Contexts for learning to write: Studies of secondary school instruction.* Norwood, NJ: Ablex.

Basso, K. (1974). The ethnography of writing. In R. Bauman and J. Sherzer (Eds.), *Explorations in the ethnography of speaking* (pp. 425–432). New York: Cambridge University Press.

Bazerman, C. (1981). What written knowledge does: Three examples of academic discourse. *Philosophy of the Social Sciences, 11*, 361–87.

Berkenkotter, C. (1983). Decisions and revisions: The planning strategies of a publishing writer. *College Composition and Communication, 34*, 156–169.

Bizzell, P. (1982). Cognition, convention, and certainty: What we need to know about writing. *PRE/TEXT, 3*, 213–243.

Bridwell, L. (1980). Revising strategies in twelfth grade students' transactional writing. *Research in the Teaching of English, 14*, 197–222.

Britton, J., Burgess, T., Martin, N., McLeod, A., & Rosen, H. (1975). *The development of writing abilities 11–18*. London: Macmillan.

Calkins, L. (1980). Research update: When children want to punctuate: Basic skills belong in context. *Language Arts, 57*, 567–573.

Clark, C., & Florio, S., with Elmore, J., Martin, J., & Maxwell, R. (1983). Understanding writing instruction: Issues of theory and method. In P. Mosenthal, L. Tamor, & S. Walmsley (Eds.), *Research on writing: Principles and methods* (pp. 236–264). New York: Longman.

Cooper, M. (1986). The ecology of writing. *College English, 48*, 364–375.

Denzin, N. (1978). *Sociological methods*. New York: McGraw-Hill.

Dewey, J. (1949). *The child and the curriculum and the school and society*. Chicago: University of Chicago Press.

Dyson, A. (1984). Learning to write/learning to do school: Emergent writers' interpretations of school literacy tasks. *Research in the Teaching of English, 18*, 233–264.

Emig, J. (1983). *The web of meaning: Essays on writing, teaching, learning, and thinking*. Upper Montclair, NJ: Boynton/Cook.

Ericson, F. (1982). Taught cognitive learning in its immediate environments: A neglected topic in the anthropology of education. *Anthropology & Education Quarterly, 13*(2), 148–180.

Faigley, L. (1985). Nonacademic writing: The social perspective. In L. Odell & D. Goswami (Eds.), *Writing in nonacademic settings* (pp. 231–248). New York: Guilford Press.

Fish, S. (1980). Interpreting the Variorium. In J. Tompkins (Ed.), *Reader response criticism: From formalism to post-structuralism*. Baltimore: Johns Hopkins University Press.

Florio, S., & Clark, C. (1982). The functions of writing in an elementary classroom. *Research in the Teaching of English, 16*, 115–130.

Flower, L., & Hayes, J. (1981). The pregnant pause: An inquiry into the nature of planning. *Research in the Teaching of English, 15*, 229–244.

Freedman, S. (1984). The registers of student and professional expository writing: Influences on teachers' responses. In R. Beach & L. Bridwell (Eds.), *New directions in composition research* (pp. 334–347). New York: Guilford Press.

Freedman, S. (1985). *The acquisition of written language: Response and revision*. New York: Ablex.

Geertz, C. (1973). *The interpretation of cultures*. New York: Basic Books.

Gilmore, P., & Glatthorn, A. (1982) *Children in and out of school: Ethnography and education*. Washington, DC: Center for Applied Linguistics.

Goffman, E. (1961). *Encounters: Two studies in the sociology of interaction*. New York: Bobbs-Merrill.

Grice, H. (1975). *Logic and conversation*. 1967 William James Lectures, Harvard University. Unpublished manuscript, 1967. Excerpt in Cole and Morgan (Eds.), *Syntax and semantics, Vol. III: Speech acts* (pp. 41–58). New York: Academic Press.

Guba, E. (1978). *Toward a method of naturalistic inquiry in educational evaluation*. Los Angeles: Center for the Study of Evaluation, University of California at Los Angeles.

Gumperz, J. (1971). *Language in social groups*. Stanford, CA: Stanford University Press.

Heath, S. B. (1982). Ethnography in education: Defining the essentials. In P. Gilmore & A. Glatthorn (Eds.), *Children in and out of school: Ethnography and education* (pp. 33–55). Washington DC: Center for Applied Linguistics.

Heinlein, R. (1961). *Stranger in a strange land*. New York: Putnam.

Herrington, A. (1985). Writing in academic settings A study of the contexts for writing in two college chemical engineering courses. *Research in the Teaching of English, 19*, 331–359.

Hymes, D. (1972a). Introduction. In C. Cazden, V. P. John, & D. Hymes (Eds.), *Functions of language in the classroom* (pp. xi–lxii). New York: Teachers College Press.

Hymes, D. (1972b). Models of the interaction of language and social life. In J. Gumperz & D. Hymes (Eds.), *Directions in sociolinguistics* (pp. 35–71). New York: Holt, Rinehart, & Winston.

Kantor, K. (1984). Classroom contexts and the development of writing intuitions: An ethnographic case study. In R. Beach & L. Bridwell (Eds.), *New directions in composition research* (pp. 72–94). New York: Guilford.

Langer, J. (1984). The effects of available information on responses to school writing tasks. *Research in the Teaching of English, 18*, 27–44.

Langer, J. (1985). Children's sense of genre: A study of performance on parallel reading and writing tasks. *Written Communication, 2*, 157–188.

Langer, J. (1986). Reading, writing, and understanding: An analysis of the construction of meaning. *Written Communication, 3*, 219–267.

Langer, J., & Applebee, A. (1984). Language, learning, and interaction: A framework for improving the teaching of writing. In A. Applebee (Ed.), *Contexts for learning to write: Studies of secondary school instruction* (pp. 169–182). Norwood, NJ: Ablex.

Lincoln, Y., & Guba, E. (1985). *Naturalistic inquiry*. Beverly Hills, CA: Sage Publications.

Odell, L., & Goswami, D. (1985). *Writing in nonacademic settings*. New York: Guilford Press.

Perl, S. (1979). The composing process of unskilled college writers. *Research in the Teaching of English, 13*, 317–336.

Perry, W. G. (1970). *Forms of intellectual and ethical development in the college years*. New York: Holt, Rinehart, and Winston.

Piaget, J. (1952). *The origins of intelligence in children*. New York: International Universities Press.

Pianko, S. (1979). A description of the composing processes of college freshman writers. *Research in the Teaching of English, 13*, 5–22.

Polanyi, M. (1958). *Personal knowledge: Towards a post-critical philosophy*. Chicago: University of Chicago Press.

Scribner, S. & Cole, M. (1981). Unpackaging literacy. In M. F. Whiteman (Ed.), *Variation in writing: Functional and linguistic-cultural differences* (pp. 71–88). Hillsdale, NJ: Lawrence Erlbaum.

Shaughnessy, M. (1977). *Errors and expectations*. New York: Oxford University Press.

Spradley, J. (1979). *The ethnographic interview*. New York: Holt, Rinehart and Winston.

Spradley, J. (1980). *Participant observation*. New York: Holt, Rinehart and Winston.

Szwed, J. (1981). The ethnography of literacy. In M. F. Whiteman (Ed.), *Variation in writing: Functional and linguistic-cultural differences* (pp. 13–23). Hillsdale, NJ: Lawrence Erlbaum.

Whiteman, M. F. (1981). *Variation in writing: Functional and linguistic-cultural differences*. Hillsdale, NJ: Lawrence Erlbaum.

Williams, J. (1985, March). *Encouraging higher order reasoning through writing in all disciplines*. Paper presented at the Delaware Valley Writing Council-PATHS Conference, Philadelphia.

Questions for Discussion and Journaling

1. What are McCarthy's research questions? What research methods did she use to find answers to these questions? What were her primary findings? How might her findings have been shaped by her methods? What other methods might she have used, and how might they have altered her findings?

2. McCarthy analyzed Dave's experiences using Grice's "Cooperative Principle." Explain what this principle is and how it helped McCarthy understand Dave's struggles and successes.

3. Why did Dave struggle in his poetry class? What might Dave and his teacher have done to improve Dave's chances of success in that class?

4. Reread Carol Berkenkotter's "Decisions and Revisions: The Planning Strategies of a Publishing Writer" in Chapter 2 (pp. 216–30). How would you connect Berkenkotter's findings on the importance of settings for writing with McCarthy's findings on the importance of *social* setting to the shape writing takes?

5. If you read Chapter 4, you read a lot about the importance of **Discourses** or **discourse communities** for the ways people do—and don't—use language. How might these concepts shed light on Dave's experience in McCarthy's study?

6. In the preceding reading in this chapter, "The Beginnings of Change," Christine Casanave describes what she calls **literacy games**. Does this concept help shed light on Dave's experiences in McCarthy's study? If so, how?

7. How does Dave's experience writing in college compare to your own? What aspects of writing in college frustrate or puzzle you? What has been hardest for you about writing in college? Why?

8. Do you find the same variance in expectations of your writing from class to class that Dave experiences, or are the expectations you encounter more consistent? What have been your strategies so far for handling any differing expectations you're finding? Does McCarthy's work give you any ideas for different strategies?

Applying and Exploring Ideas

1. For several weeks, keep a writer's journal about your experiences writing in different classrooms. What are you asked to write? What instruction are you given? What feedback are you given? Do you talk with others about the assignments? What genres are you asked to write? How well do you do? Do you understand the grades and comments your teachers give you? At the end of the weeks of journaling, write about your findings and share them with the class.

2. Write an informal, two-page analysis of McCarthy's article that answers these questions:

- Outline McCarthy's **rhetorical situation**: Who was McCarthy's audience? What was her purpose? What do you think her **exigence** was? What **genre** was she writing in? Where was her article published? (Keep in mind that this article is considered a "seminal" article in the field and has since been reprinted in a book called *Landmark Essays on Writing across the Curriculum*.)
- How does McCarthy put together her article in order to meet the needs and expectations of her audience and her genre?
- Are the strategies McCarthy uses effective for her audience and genre?

Disciplinary Discourses:
Social Interactions in
Academic Writing

KEN HYLAND

Hyland, Ken. *Disciplinary Discourses: Social Interactions in Academic Writing*. Ann Arbor: U of Michigan P, 2004. Print.

Framing the Reading

Ken Hyland is a linguist and currently a Reader in the School of Culture, Language, and Communication at the Institute of Education, University of London, where he is also the head of the Centre for Academic and Professional Literacies. In addition to the book from which the following reading is adapted, Hyland has written *Second Language Writing* (2003), *Academic Discourse: English in a Global Context* (2009), *Metadiscourse: Exploring Interaction in Writing* (2006), *English for Academic Purposes: An Advanced Resource Book* (2006), and *Genre and Second Language Writing* (2004), among others.

Rather than ask you to read a chapter from Ken Hyland's book on citation in the university, we are including a brief summary of his claims. Hyland analyzes how academic texts are **constructed**. Whereas other linguists you have read in this book, like Christine Casanave, conduct case studies, Hyland conducts **corpus analysis**. This means that he uses a computer program to analyze thousands of texts and make conclusions about how various groups of people use language in very specific ways. In this summary we include some of his findings regarding how researchers in different disciplines cite their sources. If you've read this far in the chapter, you can guess why this information might be important. Learning to cite like professionals in your field can help you to better play the **literacy games** that Casanave discusses and to write with more **authority**.

Research is a social activity, it requires researchers to engage with their colleagues and it happens within social institutions. There are some features that all academic discourses share: acknowledging sources, rigorous testing, intellectual honesty, etc. But there are many ways that texts differ across disciplines, beyond obvious content differences. These differences are appropriate to the "academic tribe" that uses them. Each academic "discourse community" or "community of practice" has different goals, tools, and expertise. Their language demonstrates these goals, tools, and expertise.

Similarities in All Academic Research Articles

Hyland argues that in research articles, writers' attempts to be persuasive involve:

- establishing the novelty of one's position,
- making a suitable level of claim,
- acknowledging prior work and situating one's claims in a disciplinary context,
- offering warrants for one's view based on community-specific arguments and procedures, and
- demonstrating an appropriate disciplinary **ethos** and willingness to negotiate with peers (12).

There is more than one way to interpret a piece of data. Readers can always reject a claim. Thus, the writer makes rhetorical choices to:

- galvanize support,
- express collegiality,
- resolve difficulties and
- avoid disagreements in ways which most closely correspond to the community's assumptions, theories, methods, and bodies of knowledge (13).

Readers reject statements for

- Failing to meet adequacy conditions (claims don't seem plausible given the beliefs of the discipline). Writers respond by using the specialized vocabulary and argument forms of the discipline.
- Failing to address acceptability conditions (meet the expectations of participants with a credible attitude toward readers and the information being discussed). Writers respond by demonstrating disciplinary credentials, showing themselves to be reasonable, intelligent co-players in the community's efforts to construct knowledge and well versed in its tribal lore. They display proper respect for colleagues and balance the need to demonstrate their own expertise with humility as a disciplinary servant. (13)

Differences across Disciplines

There are many. Hyland focused primarily in differences in citation, including number of cites, how they are incorporated, and what verbs are used.

Numbers of citations

Table 1

Rank Order of Citations by Discipline

Rank	Discipline	Av. Per Paper	Per 1,000 Words	Total Citations
1	Sociology	104.0	12.5	1040
2	Marketing	94.9	10.1	949
3	Philosophy	85.2	10.8	852
4	Biology	82.7	15.5	827
5	Applied linguistics	75.3	10.8	753
6	Electronic engineering	42.8	8.4	428
7	Mechanical engineering	27.5	7.3	275
8	Physics	24.8	7.4	248
	Totals	67.1	10.7	5372

How outside work is incorporated (quote, block quote, summary, generalization)

Table 2

Presentation of Cited Work (%)

Discipline	Quote	Block quote	Summary	Generalization
Biology	0	0	72	38
Electronic engineering	0	0	66	34
Physics	0	0	68	32
Mechanical engineering	0	0	67	33
Marketing	3	2	68	27
Applied linguistics	8	2	67	23
Sociology	8	5	69	18
Philosophy	2	1	89	8

What verbs are used to introduce citations

Table 3

Reporting Forms in Citations

Discipline	Reporting Structures		Most Frequent Forms
	Per Paper	% of Citations	
Philosophy	57.1	67.0	say, suggest, argue, claim, point out, propose, think
Sociology	43.6	42.0	argue, suggest, describe, note, analyse, discuss
Applied linguistics	33.4	44.4	suggest, argue, show, explain, find, point out
Marketing	32.7	34.5	suggest, argue, demonstrate, propose, show

(*Continued*)

Table 3   *(continued)*

Biology	26.2	31.7	describe, find, report, show, suggest, observe
Electronic engineering	17.4	40.6	propose, use, describe, show, publish
Mechanical engineering	11.7	42.5	describe, show, report, discuss
Physics	6.6	27.0	develop, report, study
Totals	28.6	42.6	suggest, argue, find, show, describe, propose, report

Type of citation—integral (cited within the sentence) versus nonintegral (cited in parenthesis). For example:
   Integral: "John Jones claims that X is true (31)."
   Nonintegral: "X is thought to be true (Jones 31)."

Table 4

Surface Forms of Citations (%)

DISCIPLINE	NON-INTEGRAL	INTEGRAL	SUBJECT	NON-SUBJECT	NOUN-PHRASE
Biology	90.2	9.3	46.7	43.3	10.0
Electronic engineering	84.3	15.7	34.2	57.6	8.2
Physics	83.1	16.9	28.6	57.1	14.3
Mechanical engineering	71.3	28.7	24.9	56.3	18.8
Marketing	70.3	29.7	66.9	23.1	10.0
Applied linguistics	65.6	34.4	58.9	27.1	14.0
Sociology	64.6	35.4	62.9	21.5	15.6
Philosophy	35.4	64.6	31.8	36.8	31.4
Overall Averages	67.8	32.2	48.3	32.7	19.0

Questions for Discussion and Journaling

1. Hyland's work is meaningful only if you remember and understand that all written practices are **rhetorical** and *constructed* (ideas discussed in detail in Chapter 1 of this volume). In one or two paragraphs, explain what this means.

2. If written practices are rhetorical and constructed, they demonstrate values and conventions of a **Discourse** (James Gee's term) or **discourse community** (John Swales's term). Explain how written practices can demonstrate a community's values or conventions, and give several examples from your own experiences.

3. Hyland argues that, in their research articles, scholars try to be persuasive by making **rhetorical** *moves* such as "making a suitable level of claim" or acknowledging previous research conducted by other scholars. How do these persuasive rhetorical moves differ from what you are used to thinking of as "persuasive" writing? Do you agree with Hyland that citing previous research can be considered an attempt to be persuasive? Find an example of some of these persuasive moves in articles in this textbook, and explain how they are persuasive even if they don't immediately appear intended to persuade.

4. Because every piece of researched data can be interpreted differently, academic researchers make some common rhetorical moves in their writing in order to try to persuade other scholars that their interpretation is the most effective one. Explain what a few of these rhetorical moves are, and try to find some examples of them in articles you have read in this textbook.

Applying and Exploring Ideas

1. If all written practices are rhetorical and constructed, demonstrating values and conventions of a Discourse or discourse community, they serve a purpose. Try to figure out why the disciplines Hyland studied use some of their rhetorical conventions. For example, why do you think that sociologists use so many more citations than physicists? Why do you think that philosophers are the only academics who routinely use more **integral citation** than **nonintegral citation**? Why do different disciplines use different verbs when introducing quotations and paraphrases?

2. Ask a professor in your major if they would be willing to spend thirty minutes talking with you (make an appointment). Ask them questions related to Hyland's findings, such as these: (1) When you write a research article, how many citations do you usually include? Why do you do this? (2) When you relate information from others in your research papers, do you generally quote them directly, paraphrase them, or just refer generally to their ideas? Why? When you cite someone in your paper, do you usually mention them by name directly in the sentence (i.e., "John Jones says X") or do you just state their ideas and cite them in parentheses? Why?

3. Using some of Hyland's categories, analyze papers from two different disciplines. How do these two disciplines compare in terms of their citation practices? Do your findings agree with Hyland's findings?

4. Hyland notes that research papers do share some things in common, even though they are quite different in many respects. Find a scholarly research

paper on a topic in your major and analyze the ways that the author tries to create credibility, using the categories that Hyland outlined on the first page of this handout. For example, how does the author acknowledge the work of other people and then try to situate his or her own claim in relationship to it? How does the author try to suggest that his or her own work is novel and important? How does the author try to pay "proper respect" to his or her colleagues?

Meta Moment

Name two specific ways that the information from Hyland can help you when you have to read or write research papers in the future.

Seven Ways High School Prepares You for Failure

KELSEY DIAZ

Framing the Paper

Kelsey Diaz wrote this letter in her English Composition 1101 course at the University of Central Florida in fall 2009. Her assignment was to explain what she'd learned in the course to other students who would take it next. Her class did not use a final portfolio; instead, she wrote this as a final reflection on her learning for the course. Diaz's work gives you a chance to think about audience, tone, message, and the choices writers can make to speak their minds while also engaging their readers. We think more drafting would have refined this message significantly—but we also think the message is well worth considering.

Diaz 1

Kelsey Diaz
Professor Uttich
English Comp 1101
November 11, 2009

Seven Ways High School Prepares You for Failure

Welcome to the new mythical world of higher education: Lecture upon

lecture, crazy parties, intense study sessions, and social dramas that put

Who does Diaz seem to be writing to? Are you part of that audience? If so, do you think she understands you well?

your virtual Facebook arguments to shame. I know you're excited; I was

too, but before you start planning your Greek life, remember you're here to

learn. And not only are you here to learn, but you are blissfully unaware of

a major disadvantage that affects all incoming freshman: Most of what they

taught you in high school English was a lie!

Shocking, yes. Now, before you begin to doubt me, know this: I've

been there, and I've done that. I went to high school. Every day in senior

English was blissfully easy: reviewing the 5 paragraph essay, learning about

Diaz 2

literature in the Victorian age, doing a "picture essay." Senior English was fun. I was an eager freshman in English composition, waiting for the next challenge. Boy, did I get one! I had to learn a new way of writing.

As kind and caring or harsh and cruel as your high school teacher may have been, there's no way that they could have prepared you for college, especially with all of the "standardized test" bullcrap. Now, I'm not saying that you didn't learn anything in your English class; you probably learned a lot! All I'm saying is that the writing you did in high school and the writing you will do in college are two totally different things.

The 5-Paragraph Essay

Ever since the No Child Left Behind act, it seems that teachers aren't teaching the same material. I can't remember a time when the teacher didn't start a lesson with "Now, you'll need this for the FCAT. . . . " The problem is that apart from standardized tests, you will never write another 5-paragraph essay again.

How often do you read any serious writing that has an introduction with a thesis, 3 body paragraphs, and a conclusion that restates the thesis? If you were writing a letter to your grandmother asking for her famous homemade cookies, you wouldn't use a 5-paragraph essay. Don't do it in college. Your professor will most likely laugh at you.

Write Objectively

Remember all of those assignments when you weren't allowed to use "I," "we," or "us"? It turns out that not only can you break this rule, but you may never write "objectively" again! (Once you learn the technique.) Think of it this way: No two writers write alike. After all, we are all just individual,

Florida high school students must pass the "FCAT," Florida's Comprehensive Assessment Test, in order to graduate. FCAT is a response to the federal No Child Left Behind (NCLB) act, intended to improve pre-college educational standards. A common criticism of NCLB is that teachers are forced to "teach to the test," but the tests don't really measure what students (need to) know.

Do you recognize the 5-paragraph essay format that Diaz describes? How do your thoughts about it compare to Diaz's?

Diaz 3

unique people. Everyone has their own way of saying what they need to say, and it's okay to just say it how you need to say it.

Diaz sometimes writes in all-or-nothing terms. Here, she seems to completely dismiss the value of objectivity in writing. Do you think Diaz has considered her audience carefully enough in this letter?

You Have to Cite a Resource for Every Single Part of Your Paper

In high school, the teachers wanted to know if you can think hard enough to gather sources with similarities and use them to back up a statement, usually not chosen by you. The standard procedure for papers was to make up a (usually obvious) point, turn it into a thesis, google your topic for "resources," copy and paste quotes, and finish with your own "original" sentences, tying everything together so it wasn't just one big block of quotation marks.

In college, you're the one trying to prove something, not your sources. Not nearly as many are used, and they are used for actual research and learning, not restatement. Of course, different papers will use different numbers of sources, but you're analyzing the meaning of the source, not regurgitating quotes.

Ideally, Diaz would have talked about sources in terms of kinds of writing. For instance, can you give some examples of how scholarly writers use sources differently from the way Diaz describes high school writing?

Turn in a Rough Draft and Your Final Draft

Honestly, how many of you in high school actually revise your papers? Typing up a version of scribbled notes and putting it through a spell check doesn't count. You will need to learn to write lots of drafts. You will have to completely restart a paper even though you think you're almost done. Chances are, after all editing and revising is finished, you'll likely have less than a quarter of content from your first draft, if any at all.

Editing is a whole new beast in college; you're not just looking for typos. You're looking for audience, style, restated information, off-topic content, and most importantly, ideas. If you ever get stuck, just start writing;

Diaz 4

chances are you'll be throwing most of it out in a revision anyway. As a rule: the more drafts, the better the paper.

Your Resources Are Right and True

In high school, you've probably learned how to determine a "good" resource from a "bad" one. They taught you at least one thing right; at least for the most part. Remember that all writing, even if it's from a professional, even if it's by a researcher who has been studying a subject for years on end, is by writers who are still just people. They all have their own way of writing, and more importantly, they all have their own reason for writing.

You must learn to *analyze* the content of your source, not just read it. Who wrote it? Why? What are they trying to accomplish? What are their intentions for the reader? Is the writer biased? Do two different sources disagree? Why? Remember that you are the one writing the paper, so you are the one in control; you are the one that has to prove what you've learned.

Use One Book Source and Three Internet Articles

Here's a fun one. You might actually get the chance to interview a professional. More than likely, you'll be required to interview one sometime in your college career. Don't goof off, though it can be very easy to do so.

Research your topic, your interviewee, everything you possibly can. There may be special words or "lingo" that you just don't understand. Learn about the profession's, organization's, or group's goals and background information; it can give you ideas for introductory questions. And for the sake of all that is good, don't try to write everything down!

What do you think of Diaz's certainty here? Have you seen evidence so far for what she's saying?

How would you characterize Diaz's attitude toward high school teaching about writing? Does she give sufficient reasons for her attitude?

Can you tell why it's so important to Diaz that academic writers are "still just people"?

Diaz here explicitly addresses a concept that much of her critique has circled around: control. Can you read each of the "myths" Diaz explores in this letter as a different element of control by or over a writer?

You're going to want to ask open-ended questions, with lots of follow-ups in order to get the maximum amount of useful information in your interview.

You're on Your Own in College

Simply lies. Most likely, you'll be in a class with plenty of students who are just as confused as you are. It takes a while to learn a whole new writing style, and your professor is there to teach you; not to be an evil sadistic torturer who gives nothing but F's. Your professor knows you are a freshman, and that you are treading new waters. If you ever need help, just ask!

If you're like me—lazy, tired, and not willing to read bulleted points with long paragraphs—just remember one thing: You are not alone. Learning a whole new way of writing may seem a daunting task, but you're not the first freshman ever, you're not the only one to do it, and there will always be someone to help you when you need it. And just to make sure you get the point, I'll "restate the thesis" like you're used to: Write in your own words. You're the writer writing, not your sources, so just grab a pencil and have at it!

Diaz seems to be saying that, when you're interviewing, you need to conduct a conversation instead of asking rote questions and writing down answers. Did this come through for you? If not, how could she revise?

This is the second time Diaz has used the term "lies." Do you think Diaz is justified in using the term? Is her use of it appropriate for her audience and purpose?

What does the first sentence of her last paragraph do to Diaz's ethos?

Some Other Questions to Consider

- Sometimes writers use an uncompromising, "no-holds-barred" tone. Other times they find it better to write in a more measured tone that may not say exactly what they think but may sound more reasonable or acceptable to an audience. In your opinion, does the tone Diaz adopts help her accomplish her purpose? Would it have helped her to use a gentler tone, or does her purpose demand the bluntness she uses here?
- How does Diaz's title connect to the material in her letter? She never discusses "failure" at all—to what, then, does her title refer?
- What do you suppose high school teachers would say in response to Diaz's letter? (Note that Diaz doesn't seem to address it to teachers; they would be reading it as a third-party audience.) Has Diaz been fair to high school teachers? What could they say back to her? And what, then, might she say back to them?

Writing about Authority: Assignments and Advice

In addition to making multiple drafts, one must always revise the writing task. Revising refers to the content of the paper as opposed to the grammar and structure of it. A good way to revise is to try reading from the audience's point of view as you write. It's a difficult way to revise, but once understood fully, it will aid you in observing the rhetorical situation as you write. Knowing this information in high school would have helped me tremendously in my college English courses. I wish that I would have had more time to study them before arriving at college but now it has made me a better writer. Combining the concept of rhetorical situations with the understanding of first drafts and revisions is an excellent way to better understand the way college writing differs from that of high school.

—**Sam Greenberg, Student**

To help you learn and explore the ideas in this chapter, we are suggesting three Assignment Options for larger writing projects: Do Students Have a Right to Their Own Languages?; What Does It Mean to "Write with Authority" in College?; and Analysis of Science Accommodation.

Assignment Option 1. Do Students Have a Right to Their Own Languages?

In this essay, you will consider what students' languages are, and how those languages coincide and conflict with the languages of the university.

Brainstorming   In the first reading in this chapter, "The Idea of Community in the Study of Writing," Joseph Harris refers to "our students' 'right to their own language'" (p. 589). Harris is making an implicit reference to a position statement written by the National Council of Teachers of English in 1974, called "Resolution on the Students' Right to Their Own Language."

- First, find this resolution by searching on "NCTE right to their own language." Read the background on the statement and then the statement itself.
- Jot down your initial reactions to this statement. Is there anything in the statement that confuses you? What do you think is meant by "the dialect that expresses their family and community identity, the idiolect that expresses their unique personal identity"? What would you say your own personal idiolect is? Or do you have more than one? What about your classmates? What are the varieties of personal idiolects you see? Are there conflicts between the language(s) you are asked to use in school and your home language(s)? If so, how do you resolve them?

- Now go back to essays in this textbook that you think might be useful in illuminating this problem of home versus school languages. Some possibilities include Harris or Donald Murray (Chapter 1); Sondra Perl (Chapter 2); Shirley Brice Heath (Chapter 3) John Swales, James Gee, or Ann Johns (Chapter 4); and Christine Casanave or Lucille McCarthy (Chapter 5). Decide which of these articles you think would be most helpful for you to draw from in writing an essay on this topic. Looking at two or three of them, pull out claims and findings from these articles that can speak to the issue of conflicting home and school languages.

Planning and Drafting   Begin to plan an essay in which you consider the goals of schooling and the values of academic writing and how those conflict and coincide with the home languages that students bring with them to school. Should the goal of school be to teach everyone the same language practices? What is gained or lost in this? Is it possible to balance home languages and school languages? Is it possible that home languages can inform and enrich school languages?

Consider your claim(s) in answer to these questions and draft an essay that draws on both your own experiences as well as the two or three articles you've opted to work on.

Your essay should be approximately four to seven pages. Be sure to cite your sources and include a Works Cited page at the end.

Revising   Exchange drafts with a classmate. Read your classmate's essay and do two things: (1) make a note of some things they did well that you would like to work on in your own writing; and (2) mark places in your peer's essay where they could make stronger claims, expand claims, and/or bring in additional sources to support claims.

What Makes It Good?   This essay should demonstrate that you have thought carefully about the issues of student and academic language, and should make some insightful claims about the issues involved. Your essay should pull in sources from this textbook to support or expand claims. This essay is successful if your teacher and classmates read and gain some insight into the issues at hand.

Assignment Option 2. What Does It Mean to "Write with Authority" in College?

For this assignment, you will try to gather up what you have learned about writing with authority and use that knowledge to give some advice to incoming college students.

Brainstorming   Try the following:

- Freewrite for a few minutes about what you think it means to have "authority" over texts in college. What *is* authority? How do you know when you or someone else does—or doesn't—have authority with texts?
- Set your freewrite aside, and now begin considering what some of the authors in this book have said about authority. Begin to make a list of

strategies that help readers and writers gain authority with texts. Some readings you might consider looking at include Margaret Kantz, and Christina Haas and Linda Flower (Chapter 1); Carol Berkenkotter (Chapter 2); John Swales and Elizabeth Wardle (Chapter 4); and Joseph Harris, Ann Penrose and Cheryl Geisler, and Christine Casanave (Chapter 5).

Drafting   Write a first draft that is entirely for the purpose of exploration. Drawing on your freewrite and notes from brainstorming, write a definition of *authority* and describe some specific things college students can do in order to gain more authority with texts—both as readers and as writers.

Revising   Go back to your draft now with your audience and purpose firmly in mind. You are writing to new college students to help them understand what it might mean to write with authority in college, and then to provide them with useful advice about how to gain this authority. Given this purpose, what should your text look like? What genre will it be—could it be a letter, a memo, a Web site, a traditional essay? How should it be organized so that these readers will pay attention and get the most out of it? What tone should you take? How can you gain credibility with your readers? Revise your draft to act on the answers to these questions.

What Makes It Good?   Your text will be effective if it accurately and thoughtfully draws on what you have learned and communicates that knowledge usefully to brand-new incoming college students. If your younger friends or siblings could read this and have a better chance of succeeding as readers and writers in college, then you have done a good job.

Assignment Option 3. Analysis of Science Accommodation

One way to better understand the kinds of writing and thinking valued in the university is to compare them to more popular forms of writing and thinking with which you are familiar. Toward this end, this assignment asks you to find a mass media report or discussion about a scientific finding and then trace it back to the original report from which it was taken in order to analyze the differences between the two types of discourse.

Brainstorming   Find an interesting mass media report or discussion about science (e.g., a CNN headline, a blog entry, and so on). Trace the science back to the original research report from which it was taken. Make some initial observations about how they're different. Are there any obvious similarities?

Researching and Analyzing   Analyze the differences between the original scientific report and the mass media report of the scientific finding. The technical name for what happens when a scholarly source becomes popularized is **accommodation**. (If you would like to read more about the accommodation of science before you begin, check out Jeanne Fahnestock's article "Accommodating Science" listed in the "Suggested Additional Readings and Resources" section at the end of this chapter.)

As you analyze each text, consider questions such as:

- What is the **rhetorical situation**—**exigence**, **rhetors** (writers/speakers), **audiences**, purpose, and so forth—for each text? (If necessary, turn to Grant-Davie in Chapter 1 for assistance.)
- What are the **genres** for each text (e.g., is one a peer-reviewed research article and the other a two-minute news report)? Is there a genre shift between the original presentation of the scientist's work and its popularization? Why was one genre not appropriate or useful in the other rhetorical situation?
- How subtly or obviously are claims stated in each? How accurately are they stated? How do the scientists state the significance of their claims? How does this compare to how the media account reports on their significance?
- How are nonspecialists accommodated in the mass media piece—for example, through language change, tone change, more overt statements of significance, the use of more sweeping claims (i.e., "the only kind" or "the first kind"), placement of information in the paragraph or sentence, removal of qualifiers or hedges (i.e., taking out "appears" or "suggests"), other changes in phrasing? Why were these changes made? Do they change the meaning of the original?
- What sources are used in the original science report and in the media accommodation of it? Does the accommodation go beyond the published research to include interviews or quotations from the scientists not found in the original article? Do these interview quotations include observations and conclusions not found in the original published article? Why are these changes made? What is their effect?
- Is contradictory evidence omitted in the accommodation? If so, why?
- Are unsupportable or unsupported claims included in the accommodation? If so, why?
- Is there any evidence that the scientists tried to refute claims in the accommodation? Given your analysis of information published about this research, did the scientists succeed in changing the claims made about their work?
- To your knowledge, did other scientists refute the claims of the original scientists after the original publication? If so, were those counterarguments ever publicized?

Now step back and consider what values are suggested by the scientists' language and what values are suggested by the media's language. For example, do scientists value objectivity and caution more than the media? What do the media seem to value? How can you explain the differences?

Planning   Consider what you found by asking yourself the following:

- What are the differences between the writing done by scientists and the writing done by those in the popular media? What do these differences tell us about the values of academic writers?
- What is hard or unfamiliar to you about the scientific writing?

- How do scientists support their claims? How does this compare to how the media support their claims?
- What are the strengths and weaknesses of each type of writing?

Now plan an essay written for incoming first-year college students in which you outline how academic discourse differs from more popular discourse. In this essay, you should note various levels of difference, from values to length to tone to sources used. It might be helpful to frame your advice in terms of the values, conventions, and purposes of different **activity systems** or **discourse communities**. Why and how is language used differently in the university, and particularly in the sciences?

Drafting   You have a variety of options for presenting the information you have gathered to your audience of incoming students:

- You might consider writing a fairly formal and traditional research paper, starting off by making the three "moves" that John Swales outlines (see the **CARS model** in the Introduction to this text, pp. 6–8).
- You might present your information in a less formal way, perhaps as a magazine article that includes tables or visual representations of some of the differences you've found or as an interactive Web site where you and your classmates can share your findings.

As always, discuss your options with your instructor before beginning.

Revising   Share a rough draft with several of your classmates:

- Ask them whether you have answered this question effectively: How and why does academic discourse differ from more popular discourse?
- Ask them if you make clear claims and have enough support for each claim.
- Ask them to mark places where they are confused, and other places where they are particularly interested.
- Ask them to provide one or two specific ideas for revision. (Note that these ideas should not be about correcting grammar and punctuation, but rather working on larger claims and organization.)

What Makes It Good?   Once you know the differences between the science article and its accommodation, your job is to educate other students about what you have learned. You should be able to explain to them how scientific academic writing differs from more popular kinds of writing, and you should be able to help them understand *why* these two kinds of writing are so different. (You'll need to use everything that you have learned about **Discourses**.) A really good analysis will not just explain *what* is different but *why* those differences exist and what they *mean*.

Suggested Additional Readings and Resources

Bartholomae, David. "Inventing the University." *Cross-Talk in Composition Theory: A Reader.* Ed. Victor Villanueva, Jr. Urbana: NCTE, 1997. 623–54. Print.

Carr, Nicholas. "Is Google Making Us Stupid?" *The Atlantic.* The Atlantic Monthly Group, July/Aug. 2008. Web. 23 Feb. 2010.

Ervin, Elizabeth. "Encouraging Civic Participation among First-Year Writing Students; or, Why Composition Class Should Be More Like a Bowling Team." *Rhetoric Review* 15.2 (1997): 382–99. Print.

———. "Academics and the Negotiation of Local Knowledge." *College English* 61.4 (1999): 448–70. Print.

Fahnestock, Jeanne. "Accommodating Science." *Written Communication* 3.3 (1986): 275–96. Print.

Gutierrez, Kris. "Unpackaging Academic Discourse." *Discourse Processes* 19.1 (1995): 21–37. Print.

Kain, Donna, and Elizabeth Wardle. "Building Context: Using Activity Theory to Teach about Genre in Multi-Major Professional Communication Courses." *Technical Communication Quarterly* 14.2 (2005): 113–39. Print.

Reither, James. "Writing and Knowing: Toward Redefining the Writing Process." *College English* 47.6 (1985): 620–28. Print.

Glossary

accommodation

In this book, *accommodation* is used to refer to the ways that writers from one group understand and write about texts written by another group—for example, how journalists write about ("accommodate") scientists' research articles.

activity system

In his 1997 article "Rethinking Genre in School and Society: An Activity Theory Analysis," David Russell describes an *activity system* as "any ongoing, object-directed, historically conditioned, dialectically structured, tool-mediated human interaction." In simpler terms, an *activity system* consists of a group of people who act together over time as they work toward a specific goal. The people in the system use many kinds of tools, both physical (like computers or books) and symbolic (like words), to do their work together. The group's behaviors and traditions are influenced by their history, and when one aspect of the system changes, other aspects of it change in response.

apprenticeship

Apprenticeship is a term used to describe the relationship between a master and a student, or a mentor and a mentee, in which the student or mentee undergoes training in order to become an expert in a profession or group.

In his 1998 book, *Communities of Practice*, Etienne Wenger argues that apprentices move from peripheral participation to more central participation in a group as they become engaged with and more skilled at the group's practices. (See also **community of practice**.)

argument

Argument can describe any of the many ways by means of which people try to convince others of something.

Mathematically, arguments are the individual propositions of a proof. In a legal context, formal arguments are used to persuade a judge or jury to rule in favor of a particular position. In everyday use, or on talk radio or cable news shows, arguments tend to consist of people yelling at each other but rarely convincing or being convinced. We call all these forms of argument *agonistic*, meaning that they pit people against each other in a win/lose contest.

In an *intellectual* or *academic* context, argument is *inquiry-based* or *conversational*, and it describes the attempt to *build knowledge* by questioning existing knowledge and proposing alternatives. Rather than aiming simply to show who is right or wrong, inquiry-based argument aims to *cooperatively find the best explanation* for whatever is in question.

audience

An *audience* is anyone who hears or reads a text — but it is also anyone a writer *imagines* encountering his or her text. This means that there is a difference between *intended* or "invoked" audience and *actual* or "addressed" audience.

For example, when Aristotle composed *On Rhetoric* in about 350 BC, his intended audience was his students, and for a time they were also his actual audience. (We would also call them his *primary* audience, the ones who first encountered his text.) Today, Aristotle's actual audience — the people who read him in coursepacks, on iPads, and on Kindles — are *secondary* audiences for Aristotle's work.

authority

An *authority* is an accepted source, an expert, or a person with power or credibility. *Authority* (as an abstract noun) denotes confidence and self-assurance.

In this book, the term is generally used to refer to people who understand the **conventions** or accepted practices of a **discourse community** and thus are able to speak, write, or act with credibility and confidence. A writer's **ethos** is based in part on his or her authority.

authorship

To "author" a text is to create or originate it; the *authorship* of a text then is a question of *who* created or originated it. Most traditional Western notions of authorship presume that **originality** is one key component of authorship.

The term is seen by some scholars as problematic if it assumes *sole* authorship — invention by just one person — because it seems to discount the importance of social interaction and the fact that virtually every idea we can have already draws from other ideas authored by other people. The question becomes, where do we draw the line on who has authored what? For a related discussion, see **plagiarism**.

autobiography

Literally, *autobiography* is writing about one's own life. ("Auto" = self, "bio" = life, and "graphy" = writing.) The **genre** of autobiography is a book-length text containing a retrospective account of the author's life.

More broadly, *autobiographical* means simply about, or having to do with, one's own life. Donald Murray and others contend that all writing is autobiographical — that is, that one's writing always has some connection to one's own life and that a writer can never completely remove all traces of her life from her writing.

autoethnography

Autoethnography is an **ethnography**, or cultural study, of one's own experiences and interaction with the world.

CARS ("Create a Research Space") model

John Swales's description of the three typical "moves" made in the introductions to academic research articles. Swales conducted an analysis of research articles in many disciplines and discovered that most introductions in all disciplines do the following:

1. establish a territory (by describing the topic of study);
2. establish a niche (by explaining the problem, gap, or question that prompted the current study); and
3. occupy the niche (by describing the answer to the question or problem, and/or outlining what will be done in the article).

case studies

Case studies are detailed observations and analyses of an event, situation, individual, or small group of people. Case study research, according to Mary Sue MacNealy in her book *Strategies for Empirical Research in Writing*, refers to "a carefully designed project to systematically collect information about an event, situation, or small group of persons or objects for the purpose of exploring, describing, and/or explaining aspects not previously known or considered." Case studies are considered to be **qualitative research**.

claim

A *claim* is an assertion that a writer tries to convince his or her readers of. For example, "*Wired* magazine is great." To believe or accept a claim, readers need to know the *reasons* why a writer believes the claim or wants readers to accept it. For example, "*Wired* includes really interesting articles about people in the technological world." Readers may also need *evidence* to believe the claim or its reasons, like, "Every month *Wired* has several stories that interview the people who invented netbooks, the iPhone, cloud computing, and the most cutting-edge technological innovations."

cognition

Cognition describes anything having to do with *thought* or *mental activity*.

In Writing Studies, *cognitive* and *cognition* have to do with the internal thinking processes that writers use to write. Scholars in Writing Studies have contrasted the *internal, private, personal* nature of cognition with the *social* aspects of writing — that is, with the writer's *external* interactions with their surroundings, culture, and audience. Most research about cognition in Writing Studies was conducted in the 1980s and sought to find and describe the mental processes that writers use to solve problems related to writing.

community of practice

Community of practice is a term coined by sociologists Jean Lave and Etienne Wenger to describe groups of people who participate in a shared activity or activities. In his 1998 book, *Communities of Practice*, Wenger argues that participating in a community of practice also involves "constructing *identities* in relation to these communities" (4).

This term is similar to, but not exactly the same as, the terms **activity system** and **discourse community**.

conflict
Conflicts are disagreements, fights, struggles, clashes, or tensions, usually resulting from perceived differences in interests, needs, values, or goals.

constraints
Constraints are factors that limit or otherwise influence the persuasive strategies available to the rhetor. More precisely, in "Rhetorical Situations and Their Constituents," Keith Grant-Davie defines constraints as "all factors in the situation, aside from the rhetor and the audience, that may lead the audience to be either more or less sympathetic to the discourse, and that may therefore influence the rhetor's response to the situation" (273).

construct (CONstruct, conSTRUCT)
Construct, the verb (pronounced conSTRUCT), means *to build* or *to put together* ("con" = with, and "struct" = shape or frame). By turning the verb into a noun (pronounced CONstruct), we make the word mean, literally, *a thing that has been constructed*. In everyday use, we use the noun *CONstruct* only in the realm of *ideas or concepts*. The ideas of *freedom, justice, wealth,* and *politics*, for example, are all constructs, or ideas that we have *built up* over time.

   What is important to remember about constructs is that, while they may seem to be "natural" or "inevitable," they're actually unchallenged **claims** that can be questioned, contested, redefined, or reinvented.

context
Literally, a *context* is the substructure for a woven fabric ("con" = with/together, "text" = weaving, fabric). In Writing Studies, *context* typically refers to where a text comes from or where it appears. (A *written work* first started being called a *text* because it's "woven" from words in the same way that *textiles* are woven from threads.) Contexts can consist of other text(s) as well as the circumstances or setting in which a text was created — for example, various contexts for the statement "We hold these truths to be self-evident" include the Declaration of Independence, the meeting of the Continental Congress in spring and summer of 1776, and the broader socio-historical environment that describes pre–Revolutionary War America.

contribution
In academic contexts, one makes a *contribution* by adding to an ongoing conversation on a given research subject, issue, problem, or question.

   In Writing Studies, *contribution* is commonly discussed in terms of Kenneth Burke's *parlor metaphor*, where Burke describes scholarship as an ongoing conversation at a party: You arrive late and other guests are already in conversation; you join one conversation by listening for a while and then, once you have something to add, making a contribution to the conversation; after a time, you join another conversation, while the first one continues without you.

conventions

In Writing Studies, writing is understood to be governed by *conventions* — that is, agreements among people about the best ways to accomplish particular tasks (such as starting new paragraphs, or citing sources, or deciding how to punctuate sentences). That people have to come to agreements about such questions means that there is no "natural" or pre-existing way to accomplish the tasks; rather, people simply agreed to do *A* rather than *B*. Tabbing the first line of a paragraph one-half inch is a convention. Ending sentences with periods is a convention. Citing sources in parentheses is a convention, as are parentheses themselves.

Conventions are a kind of **construct**, and like constructs, they can be questioned, challenged, and changed, if key decision makers agree to alter them or to establish another convention in their place.

corpus analysis

A *corpus analysis* is a detailed examination of a collection of related texts, phrases, utterances, etc. (*Corpus* means "body" — the word *corpse* derives from it.) For example, Ken Hyland conducted a *corpus analysis* of academic writing to discover how people in various fields cite their sources.

Create a Research Space Model: see CARS ("Create a Research Space") model

discourse/Discourse

At its most basic, *discourse* is *language in action*, or language being used to accomplish something. Discourse can describe either *an instance of* language (e.g., "His discourse was terse and harsh") or a collection of instances that all demonstrate some quality (e.g., "Legal discourse tries to be very precise"). Because groups of people united by some activity tend to develop a characteristic discourse, we can talk about communities that are identified *by* their discourse — thus, **discourse community**.

James Paul Gee uses *Discourse* with an uppercase D to differentiate his specialized meaning of the term, which you can read about in his piece in this book (pp. 481–495).

discourse community

Scholars continue to debate the meaning of this term, as the selections in this book suggest. For the sake of simplicity, we will use John Swale's definition from his 1990 book, *Genre Analysis: English in Academic and Research Settings*. According to Swales, a *discourse community* is a made up of individuals who share "a broadly agreed upon set of common public goals"; further, it has "mechanisms of intercommunication among its members," "uses its participatory mechanisms primarily to provide information and feedback," has and uses "one or more genres" that help the group achieve its shared goals, "has acquired some specific lexis," and has "a reasonable ratio" of "novices and experts."

drafting

Drafting is the writing-process activity that involves writing down what you're thinking. While a basic description of the writing process differentiates drafting and revision, any moment in which a writer is creating text can be seen as drafting, even if it's also revising. (Some writers, in fact, report that they revise *while* they draft.)

EAP: see **ESP**

editing
Editing is the correction of minor errors in a written text. Editing usually comes at the end of the writing process. It should not be confused with **revision**, which involves major rethinking, rewriting, and restructuring of texts.

enculturation
Enculturation refers to the process by which a newcomer learns to become a part of a group or "culture" (including an **activity system**, **discourse community**, or **community of practice**). Becoming successfully encultured usually requires gaining some level of competence in the activities and language practices of the group. See **apprenticeship** for a definition of a similar term.

error
Error is the term for "mistakes" in grammar (e.g., subject-verb agreement, like "Dogs barks loudly"), punctuation, or usage (e.g., using "that" where some readers would prefer "which"). *Mistakes* is in quotes here because such "errors" are as often differences of opinion regarding convention or taste as they are actual problems that every English speaker or writer would agree are violations of rules.

ESP, EAP
ESP stands for English for Specific Purposes and refers to a subfield of Applied Linguistics that examines how people learn to use language for specialized purposes. *EAP* is a subset of ESP and stands for "English for Academic Purposes." It refers to a field of study that teaches **L2** (non-native) speakers how to use their non-native language (English) appropriately in school settings.

ethnography, ethnographic research
Ethnography is a research methodology for carefully observing and describing people participating in some activity. At its broadest, ethnography can be written of entire cultures; more narrowly, ethnographies can be written of a class of students, a church and its members, or a videogame arcade and the gamers who play there.

ethos
Ethos is a Greek word usually used to describe the credibility, expertise, or competence that a writer or speaker establishes with an audience through his or her **discourse**. At its broadest, *ethos* is a term for the sense of "personality" that readers perceive about a writer. As a persuasive appeal, ethos derives from **authority**, character (the perceived

values, morals, and ethics of a writer), and goodwill (the readers' sense that the writer has the readers' best interests at heart and is not purely self-interested).

exigence

Exigence is the *need or reason* for a given action or communication. All communication exists for a reason. For example, if you say, "Please turn on the lights," we assume the *reason* you say this is that there's not enough light for your needs—in other words, the *exigence* of the situation is that you need more light.

game strategies

Game strategies is a term used by Christine Casanave to describe the plans or methods that students can (or should) use when they face the challenges of writing in the university. See also **literacy games**.

generalizable, generalize

Generalizable is a term used to refer to research findings that can apply to a larger group than the one that was studied. Generalizable research typically examines a group of statistically significant size under rigorous experimental conditions. **Qualitative research** is not generalizable, strictly speaking while **quantitative research** may be.

genre

Genre comes from the French word for "kind" or "type" and is related to the Latin word *genus*, which you might remember from the scientific classification system for animals and plants. In the field of rhetoric, *genres* are broadly understood as *categories of texts*. For example, poetry, the short story, the novel, and the memoir are genres of literature; memos, proposals, reports, and executive summaries are genres of business writing; hiphop, bluegrass, trance, pop, new age, and electronica are genres of music; and the romantic comedy, drama, and documentary are genres of film.

Genres are types of texts that are recognizable to readers and writers and that meet the needs of the **rhetorical situations** in which they function. So, for example, we recognize wedding invitations and understand them to be different from horoscopes. We know that when we are asked to write a paper for school, our teacher probably does not want us to turn in a poem instead.

Genres develop over time in response to recurring rhetorical needs. We have wedding invitations because people keep getting married, and we need an efficient way to let people know and to ask them to attend. Rather than making up a new rhetorical solution every time the same situation occurs, we generally turn to the genre that has developed—in this case, the genre of the wedding invitation.

Discourse theorists have suggested that the concept of *genre* actually goes well beyond texts; accordingly, some theorists use *genre* to describe *a typified but dynamic social interaction that a group of people use to conduct a given activity.* (*Typified* means it follows a pattern, and *dynamic* means that people can change the pattern to fit their circumstances as long as it still helps them do the activity.) In "Rethinking Genre. . . .," for example, David Russell says that genres are actually "shared expectations among some group(s) of people" (513).

heuristics

Heuristics are approaches or patterns for problem solving. For example, a heuristic for deciding what to have for dinner tonight might be the following: (1) check the fridge; (2) check the pantry; and (3) eat whatever can be assembled most quickly and palatably from the ingredients there.

identity

Identity comprises an individual's characteristics or personality; it consists of those factors that create a sense of "who you are." Recent theory suggests that individuals may not have one "true," stable identity but might have multiple and/or changing identities.

integral citation, nonintegral citation

Integral citation is the term used for citation in which the source is named directly in the sentence of an article or paper. For example, "John Jones claims that water is wet" (23). *Nonintegral citation* is the term used for citation in which the source is cited only parenthetically. For example: "Water is wet (Jones 23)."

intercommunication

Intercommunication refers to communication within a group (as opposed to communication between or among individuals in different groups).

intertextuality

Intertextuality refers to the idea that all texts are made up of other texts — and thus, to the resulting *network* of texts that connect to any given text or idea. At the most basic level, texts share *words*: that is, every text uses words that other texts have used. Sometimes texts use words that, in their combination, are considered unique; in those cases, following Western conventions, those words must be formally marked as *quotations*. *Intertextuality* can go beyond just language, however, by referencing the *ideas and events* that other texts have focused on. If, for example, I claim that people whose governments abuse them have the right to make a better government, I haven't used a quotation from the Declaration of Independence, but most people familiar with that document could "hear it" in my statement. Intertextuality thus is an effect even more than an intention — I don't have to *intend* to be intertextual in order to *be* intertextual.

invention

Invention comprises the processes, strategies, or techniques writers use to come up with what to say in their writing. While the term suggests the notion of "making things up," a significant part of invention is not saying brand-new things but rather combing one's memory and written resources for things that have already been said that will work. Ancient rhetorical theorists such as Aristotle thought carefully about how *stock arguments* they called *common topics* could help a speaker — for instance, the idea that "that which has happened frequently before is likely to happen again," which could be recalled through invention and included in many pieces of writing.

L1, L2

L1 is a term used in lingustics to refer to a native (or "first") language; it is commonly applied to people who are speaking or writing in their native language ("L1 speakers") and to those who study first-language acquisition ("L1 scholars"). *L2* refers to a second (or non-native) language, and it is commonly applied to people who are speaking or writing in their second (or non-native) language ("L2 speakers") and to those who study second-language acquisition ("L2 scholars").

lexis

Lexis is a term used for the specific vocabulary used by a group or field of study.

literacy, literate

Literacy denotes fluency in a given practice. In its original use, *literacy* referred to *alphabetic* literacy — that is, to fluency in reading and writing "letters," or alphabetic text. This kind of literacy was contrasted with **orality**, which was characterized as a *lack* of literacy. Over time, however, in academic circles, the meaning of *literacy* and *literate* has broadened to encompass fluency in other areas; most academics therefore now use the term *literacies* (plural) and discuss *digital, electronic, musical, visual, oral, mathematical,* and *gaming* literacies, among many other kinds.

literacy game

Literacy game is a term used by Christine Casanave to describe the strategies students use to negotiate the challenges they face when they write in the university.

literacy sponsor

Literacy sponsor is a term coined by Deborah Brandt to describe people, ideas, or institutions that help others become **literate** in specific ways. A sponsor could be a parent or sibling who taught you to read, a teacher who helped you learn to love books, or a manufacturing company that requires its employees to be able to read. The sponsors of *alphabetic* literacy in your life might be very different from the sponsors of *visual* literacy, *musical* literacy, or other forms of literacy in your life. (*Pandora*, for instance, can be a musical literacy sponsor for people who use it.)

literature review, review of the literature

A *literature review* (or *review of the literature*) is a text that explains the existing conversation about a particular topic. Literature reviews are usually found at the beginning of research articles or books, but are sometimes written as separate projects. Note that *literature* in this case refers to published research in an area, not to novels or short stories.

longitudinal study

A *longitudinal study* is a research study that examines an individual, group, event, or activity over a substantial period of time. For example, rather than studying a student's writing habits for just a few days or weeks, a *longitudinal study* might look at his or her habits over several years.

metaknowledge
Metaknowledge is knowledge about knowledge — that is, what we can determine about our learning, its processes, and its products.

methodologies
In an academic or scholarly context, *methodologies* are procedures for conducting research — the formalized, field-approved methods used to address particular kinds of research questions. Some examples of methodologies in Writing Studies are **case study**, **ethnography**, experiment, quasi-experiment, and **discourse analysis**. *Methodology* can also mean the particular combination of methods used in any particular study. For example, the methodologies used by Sondra Perl in "The Composing Processes of Unskilled College Writers" include case study and discourse analysis.

mindfulness
Mindfulness means thinking carefully about what one is doing — that is, purposefully and carefully paying attention. This term derives from Zen Buddhism and has become a key concept in modern psychology. It is often used by researchers interested in helping writers effectively **transfer** knowledge about writing. For a writer to be mindful, for example, means not just to come up with something to say, but to *pay attention to how* she came up with something to say. In the future, she may be able to *mindfully* try that procedure again, adapting it to the new situation.

multiliteracies
Multiliteracies is a term that reflects the recent, broader understanding of **literacy** as consisting of more than mastery of the "correct" use of alphabetic language. *Multiliteracies* includes the ability to compose and interpret *multimodal* texts (texts that include oral, written, and audio components, among other possibilities), as well as the ability to make meaning in various contexts. A group of scholars known as the New London Group is generally credited with coining the term *multiliteracies*.

mushfake
Mushfake is a term used by James Gee to describe a partially acquired **discourse**, a discourse that people use to "make do" when they participate in or communicate with a group to which they don't belong. Gee borrows the term from prison culture, in which *mushfake* refers to making do with something when the real thing is not available (490).

nonintegral citation: see **integral citation, nonintergral citation**

non participation
Non participation is a type of rebellion in which a person chooses not to engage in an expected activity or to abide by a particular code or rule.

orality

Orality is the condition of being spoken rather than written. An *oral culture* is one that has no system of writing (meaning that the language used in the culture has no alphabet or other way of being visually represented). Such cultures rely on oral **literacies** that, before being recognized as a kind of literacy, were thought by researchers such as Walter Ong to be the *opposite* of literacy.

originality

Originality is the quality of being singular, unique, and entirely made up or invented, as opposed to imitative or derivative. American culture presumes that writers will have originality—that they will invent work never seen before—and judges the quality of **authorship** in part on its originality. This simplified view of **invention** is assumed by many scholars to be inaccurate in that it fails to describe how people develop ideas through social interaction. This can lead to difficulties in defining and identifying **plagiarism**.

plagiarism

Plagiarism literally means *kidnapping* in Latin; in contemporary English, the word refers to the *theft* of a text or idea. (Authors sometimes think of their writings or ideas as their "children," thus the link to kidnapping.) Definitions of plagiarism tend to come down to *taking another's ideas without giving them credit and thus pretending that you invented the ideas yourself.* In cultures that highly value *intellectual property*—the idea that one's ideas are one's *own* and that use of those ideas by others deserves either credit or payment—plagiarism is an ethical violation punishable by community sanction (such as failing a class or losing one's job). Plagiarism's cousin *copyright infringement* is an actual crime punishable by fine or imprisonment.

A significant difficulty with the idea of plagiarism is that **originality** and **authorship** are technically quite difficult to trace in ways that new digital technologies are making impossible to miss or deny. In *sampling, re-mixing*, and *mash-up* cultures where ideas are freely reused and reincorporated to make new texts, authorship becomes very difficult to trace, and it becomes difficult to tell what counts as original work.

planning

While **invention** focuses on coming up with what to say in one's writing, *planning* focuses more broadly on *how to get a piece written*. Therefore, it includes not only invention but *arrangement*, which is the art of organizing what one has to say to present it most effectively. Planning also includes **process** considerations, such as considering what work needs to be done to complete a piece, what order to do it in, and when to do it in order to meet a deadline.

process

Process refers to the variety of activities that go into writing/composing, including, at minimum,

- **planning** (inventing and arranging ideas)
- **drafting** (creating actual text from previously unwritten ideas)

- **revising** (developing a text or a portion of a text further after an initial draft)
- **editing** (fine-tuning, polishing, or correcting problems in a text), and
- production (transferring a text to its final, "produced" form, whether in print, online, or in a portable digital format).

Process theory is the study of the methods by which various writers compose and produce texts. The *process movement*, which took place within the field of Composition Studies in the 1970s, was the widespread adoption by writing teachers of instruction that focused on teaching students successful writing processes rather than focusing solely on the quality of their written products.

qualitative research, quantitative research

The term *qualitative* refers to an event or object's *qualities* that can't be explained or measured numerically (that is, *quantitatively*). *Qualitative research* includes studies such as **case studies** and **ethnographies** designed to explore such qualities; it typically seeks explanations or answers to questions such as *who*, *what*, *how*, and *why*—for example, how some people go about writing, or why they write as they do. *Qualitative research* usually includes small, focused samples, as opposed to the large samples in *quantitative research*. As a result of qualitative findings, researchers formulate *hypotheses* (theories), which can often in turn be tested through further qualitative research or through larger data sets gathered through quantitative research (for example, surveys of large numbers of people or laboratory experiments). It should be noted, however, that there are many aspects of reading and writing that cannot easily be studied through quantitative studies.

rebellion

Rebellion is an act of defiance or a refusal to accept something (a rule, for example) that an authority or group has presented as appropriate or expected.

register

In the field of linguistics, *register* refers to a type of language used in a particular setting. Changing one's register might mean changing the kinds of words used, as well as the way one says the words. For example, a person might say, "I've finished my homework" to her parents, using one register, while she might say (or text), "I'm finally dooooooooooooone!" to her friends.

review of the literature: see literature review

revision

Revision is the act of developing a piece of writing *by* writing—that is, by adding additional material, shifting the order of its parts, or deleting significant portions of what has already been written. The purpose of revision ("re-vision") is to "see again," which is necessary because what one could see in originally drafting a piece has been changed *by* the drafting.

This might become clearer if you think of writing as driving at night. When you begin to write, you know a certain amount about where you're going in your project, just as, when you're driving at night, your headlights let you see two hundred yards (but only two hundred yards) ahead. Writing (or driving) further takes you to new places, where you continually see something different, rethink your position, and decide how to proceed.

Because revision can go on for some time, for many professional writers *most* writing time is actually spent revising, not creating the first draft. Also, it is important to distinguish revision from **editing,** the correction of minor mistakes in a near-final draft.

rhetor

Originally (in Greek) a *public speaker, rhetor* means *one who engages in rhetoric* or **discourse.** *Writer* and *speaker* are common synonyms.

rhetoric

Rhetoric is the study of human interaction and communication, or the product(s) of that interaction and communication. Because most human interaction is *persuasive* by nature — that is, we're trying to convince each other of things, even when we say something simple like "that feels nice"— one way to think of rhetoric is as the study of persuasion.

Rhetoric always has to do with these specific principles:

1. Human communication, or **discourse,** is *situated* in a particular time and place. That time and place are the **context** of the communication. A given instance of communication — say, a particular text — doesn't in a sense mean *anything* if considered in isolation from its context; knowledge of the context of the communication is necessary in order to understand its meaning. For example, "Help me!" means one thing when your mom is standing next to a van full of groceries and another when she's standing next to a van with a flat tire. Her *discourse* is *situated.*
2. Communication is *motivated* by particular *purposes,* needs, and values. There is no such thing as *unmotivated* communication — no neutral, non-persuasive, "just-sayin'" discourse.
3. Communication is *interactional* — that is, it develops in the "back-and-forth" between author and **audience.** This means that readers actually *complete* a writer's text. Successful writers think carefully about who their audience is and what the audience values and needs.
4. Communication is *epistemic,* which means that it *creates new knowledge.* We often talk about "reporting" or "transmitting" information as if all we do is pass it along. But rhetoric suggests that we can't just pass along knowledge without changing it as we pass it, so our communication makes new knowledge as it goes.
5. Communication is *contingent,* meaning that what we consider *good* communication depends on the circumstances and context in which it happens. Because communication depends on context, we can't make universal rules about what makes good communication.

rhetorical

Rhetorical describes an understanding of or approach to human interaction and communication as situated, motivated, interactive, epistemic, and contingent. (See the definition of **rhetoric**.) *Rhetorical study*, then, is the investigation of human communication as situated, motivated, interactive, epistemic, and contingent. *Rhetorical reading* involves reading a text as situated, motivated, etc. *Rhetorical analysis* is a way of analyzing texts to find what choices their **rhetor** (speaker or writer) made based on their purpose and motivation, their situatedness and context, and how they interact with and make new knowledge for their audience.

rhetorical situation

Rhetorical situation is the particular circumstance of a given instance of communication or **discourse**. The rhetorical situation includes **exigence** (the *need or reason* for the communication), **context** (the *circumstances* that give rise to the *exigence*, including location in time/history and space/place/position), **rhetor** (the originator of the communication — its speaker or writer), and **audience** (the auditor, listener, or reader of the rhetor's discourse).

social context

Social context is the environment, situation, or culture in which something is embedded. Key aspects of the social context of **discourse** might include participants, goals, setting, race, class, gender, and so on.

speech community

Speech community is a term from the field of sociolinguistics used to describe a group of people who share similar language patterns. According to John Swales, people are generally members of a speech community "by birth, accident, or adoption" (24). A speech community thus differs from a **discourse community**, where members are recruited "by persuasion, training, or relevant qualification" (24).

stases

Stases (we often say *the stases*) are a problem-solving pattern (a **heuristic**) that helps writers develop arguments by asking a set of specific questions about the subject. First described in the rhetorical theory of Aristotle, the word *stases* shares the same root as the words *state, status,* and *stasis* (the singular of *stases*), all of which denote *condition* or *being*. Stases have to do with *the state of things,* so that when we consider the stases, we are taking stock, or asking, "What is the state of things?" The stases include (1) questions of fact, (2) questions of value, and (3) questions of policy:

1. What is the *nature* of the thing in question? How would we define or name the thing? What caused the thing? For example, if a four-legged creature with a wagging tail shows up at your back door, your first question might be "What is [the nature of] that?" Your answer might be that it's a "stray dog."

2. What is the *quality* or *value* of the thing? Is it good or bad? Desirable or undesirable? Wanted or unwanted? Happy or sad? Liked or disliked? Your answer to this will depend on a complex set of calculations, taking into account the nature of the thing and the context in which it is encountered. To extend our example, let's say you decide the stray dog is good because you like dogs and this one is appealing.

3. What should *be done* about it? What policy should we establish toward it? What is the best thing to do with respect to it? In the case of our example, you might decide that the best policy would be to take in the stray dog, at least temporarily, and feed it.

tone

Tone is a reader's *judgment* of what a text sounds like, sometimes also termed the dominant mood of a text. It is important to note that tone is not a characteristic actually *in* a text but rather one constructed in the interaction among the writer, the reader, and the text. Tone emerges not just from the language (word choice and sentence structure) of a text but also from a reader's judgment of the **rhetorical situation** and the writer's **ethos** and motivation.

transfer

Now often called *generalization*, *transfer* refers to the act of applying existing knowledge, learned in one kind of situation, to new situations. For example, a writer who learns how to write a summary in her College Writing I class in English is expected to *transfer* that summary-writing knowledge to her "history of the telescope" project in Astronomy. Transfer, we are learning, is not automatic — people learn many things that they forget and/or don't or can't use in different circumstances. Research suggests that learning in particular ways (for example, being **mindful**) can increase the likelihood of later transfer.

voice

Voice is the way a writer "sounds" in a text, or the extent to which you can "hear" a writer in his or her text. The definition of this term has changed over time. It has been used to refer to **authenticity** in writing, as well as to a written text that seems to be "true" to who its author is and what he or she wants to say. Author bell hooks has argued that finding a voice or "coming to voice" can be seen as an act of resistance. In *Writing about Writing* we use the term *voice* to refer to a writer's ability to speak with some **authority** and expertise deriving from his or her own experiences and knowledge. According to this view, writers have multiple voices, any one of which may find expression, depending on the precise context of utterance.

Works Cited

MacNealy, Mary Sue. *Strategies for Empirical Research in Writing*. New York: Longman, 1999. Print.

Russell, David. "Rethinking Genre in School and Society: An Activity Theory Analysis." *Written Communication* 14.4 (1997): 504–554. Print.

Swales, John. *Genre Analysis: English in Academic and Research Settings.* New York: Cambridge UP, 1990. Print.

Wenger, Etienne. *Communities of Practice: Learning, Meaning, and Identity.* New York: Cambridge UP, 1998. Print.

Acknowledgments

Text

Alexie, Sherman. "Superman and Me." Original publication: *Los Angeles Times*, April 19, 1998, as part of a series, "The Joy of Reading and Writing." Copyright © 1998 Sherman Alexie FallsApart Productions. All rights reserved.

Baron, Dennis. "From Pencils to Pixels: The Stages of Literacy." *Passions, Pedagogies, and 21st Century Technologies*. Eds. Hawisher, Gail E. and Cynthia L. Selfe. Logan: Utah State University Press, 1999 (pp. 15–33). Reprinted by permission.

Berkenkotter, Carol. "Decisions and Revisions: The Planning Strategies of a Publishing Writer." *College Composition and Communication* 34 (1983):156–69.

Brandt, Deborah. "Sponsors of Literacy." *College Composition and Communication* 49.2 (1998): 165–185.

Casanave, Christine Pearson. "The Beginnings of Change: Learning and Teaching Undergraduate Academic Literacy Games," from *Writing Games: Multicultural Case Studies of Academic Literacy Practices in Higher Education* by Casanave, Christine. Copyright © 2002 by Taylor & Francis Group, LLC Books. Reproduced with permission of Taylor & Francis Group, LLC Books in the format Textbook via Copyright Clearance Center.

Dawkins, John. "Teaching Punctuation as a Rhetorical Tool." *College Composition and Communication* 46.4 (1995): 533–548.

DeVoss, Dànielle, et al. "The Future of Literacy." from *Literate Lives in the Information Age: Narratives of Literacy from the United States*, by Cynthia Selfe, Gail Hawisher, eds. Copyright © 2004 by Taylor & Francis Group LLC Books. Reproduced with permission of Taylor & Francis Group LLC Books in the format Textbook via Copyright Clearance Center.

Díaz, Junot. "Becoming a Writer." First published in *O, The Oprah Magazine* and reprinted by permission of Junot Diaz and Aragi, Inc.

Gee, James Paul. "Literacy, Discourse, and Linguistics: Introduction." *Journal of Education* 171.1 (1989): 5–17. Reprinted by permission.

Goodman, Allegra. "Calming the Inner Critic and Getting to Work." From *The New York Times*, Arts Section, 3/12/2001 issue. Reprinted by permission.

Grant-Davie, Keith. "Rhetorical Situations and Their Constituents." *Rhetoric Review* 15 (1997). 264–279. Reprinted by permission of Taylor & Francis Ltd. (http://www. informaworld.com).

Greene, Stuart. "Argument as Conversation: The Role of Inquiry in Writing a Researched Argument." Reprinted with permission from *The Subject Is Research: Processes and Practices* by Wendy Bishop and Pavel Zemliansky. Copyright © 2001 by Wendy Bishop and Pavel Zemliansky. Published by Boynton/Cook Heinemann, Portsmouth, NH. All rights reserved.

Haas, Christina, and Linda Flower. "Rhetorical Reading Strategies and the Construction of Meaning." *College Composition and Communication* 39.2 (1988): 167–183.

Harris, Joseph. "The Idea of Community in the Study of Writing." *College Composition and Communication* 40.1 (1989): 11–22. Reprinted by permission.

Haruf, Kent. "To See Clearly, Start by Pulling the Wool over Your Own Eyes" from *The New York Times*, Arts Section. 11/20/2000 issue, Section E, Page 1. Reprinted by permission.

Heath, Shirley Brice. "Protean Shapes in Literacy Events: Ever-Shifting Oral and Literate Traditions." In *Spoken and Written Language: Exploring Orality and Literacy*. Ed. Deborah Tannen. Norwood: Ablex, 1982. 91–117. Reprinted by permission of the author.

Hyland, Ken. "Disciplinary Discourses: Social Interactions in Academic Writing." Handout on differences in different disciplines' discourse. Adapted from tables 2.1, 2.2, 2.3, and 2.4 from *Disciplinary Discourses: Social Interactions in Academic Writing*. Ann Arbor: University of Michigan Press, 2004. Reprinted by permission.

Johns, Ann M. "Discourse Communities and Communities of Practice: Membership, Conflict, and Diversity." *Text, Role, and Context: Developing Academic Literacy*, pp. 51–70. Cambridge University Press, 1997. Reprinted with the permission of Cambridge University Press.

Art

of Carol Berkenkotter; (2) Copyright © Gary Samson, University of New Hampshire; (3) Courtesy of National Council of Teachers of English; **p. 236:** (1) Mike Rose; (2) Courtesy of National Council of Teachers of English; **p. 251:** Courtesy of Sage Publications; **p. 301:** (1) Mark Richards; (2) "Book Jacket" copyright © 1994 by Pantheon Books, a division of Random House, Inc., from *Bird by Bird* by Anne Lamott. Used by permission of Pantheon Books, a division of Random House, Inc.; **p. 305:** (1) AFP/ Getty Images; (2) Reprinted with the permission of Scribner, a Division of Simon & Schuster, Inc., from *On Writing: A Memoir of the Craft* by Stephen King. Copyright © 2000 by Simon & Schuster, Inc. All rights reserved; **p. 308:** (1) © Rick Friedman/Corbis; (2) From The New York Times, © 2010, The New York Times. All rights reserved. Used by permission and protected by the Copyright Laws of the United States. The printing, copying, redistribution, or retransmission of the Material without express written permission is prohibited; **p. 311:** (1) Copyright © Cathy Haruf; (2) From The New York Times, © 2010, The New York Times. All rights reserved. Used by permission and protected by the Copyright Laws of the United States. The printing, copying, redistribution, or retransmission of the Material without express written permission is prohibited; **p. 315:** (1) Chester Higgins Jr./*New York Times*/Redux; (2) From The New York Times, © 2010, The New York Times. All rights reserved. Used by permission and protected by the Copyright Laws of the United States. The printing, copying, redistribution, or retransmission of the Material without express written permission is prohibited; **p. 328:** *World of Warcraft*® and *Blizzard Entertainment*® are registered trademarks of Blizzard Entertainment, Inc., and *World of Warcraft*® is a copyrighted product of Blizzard Entertainment, Inc., and hereby used with permission. **p. 331:** Courtesy of National Council of Teachers of English; **p. 353:** "Book Cover (Ballantine edition)," copyright © 1992 by Ballantine Books, from *The Autobiography of Malcom X* by Malcolm X and Alex Haley. Used by permission of Random House, Inc.; **p. 362:** (1) Ulf Andersen/Getty Images; (2) Cover art by Randy Scholis, used with permission from Milkweed Editions; **p. 367:** Courtesy of ABC-CLIO LLC; **p. 395:** (1) Photo by L. Brian Stauffer, University of Illinois at Urbana-Champaign; (2) Courtesy of Joseph Johansen; (4) Photograph by Envera Dukaj; (5) Courtesy of Taylor & Francis; **p. 400:** From *Literate Lives in the Information Age: Narratives of Literacy from the United States*, by Cynthia L. Selfe and Gail E. Hawisher. Copyright © 2004 by Taylor & Francis Group LLC. Reproduced with permission of Taylor & Francis Group LLC via Copyright Clearance Center; **p. 402:** From *Literate Lives in the Information Age: Narratives of Literacy from the United States*, by Cynthia L. Selfe and Gail E. Hawisher. Copyright © 2004 by Taylor & Francis Group LLC. Reproduced with permission of Taylor & Francis Group LLC via Copyright Clearance Center; **p. 409:** From *Literate Lives in the Information Age: Narratives of Literacy from the United States*, by Cynthia L. Selfe and Gail E. Hawisher. Copyright © 2004 by Taylor & Francis Group LLC. Reproduced with permission of Taylor & Francis Group LLC via Copyright Clearance Center; **p. 414:** From *Literate Lives in the Information Age: Narratives of Literacy from the United States*, by Cynthia L. Selfe and Gail E. Hawisher. Copyright © 2004 by Taylor & Francis Group LLC. Reproduced with permission of Taylor & Francis Group LLC via Copyright Clearance Center; **p. 422:** (1) Photograph by Rachel Baron; (2) Copyright 1999 Utah State University Press. Used by permission; **p. 428:** Copyright © 2002 by Scientific American. Reprinted by permission. All rights reserved; **p. 431:** Rare Books Division, The New York Public Library, Astor, Lenox and Tilden Foundation; **p. 437:** Digital image by Jack Harris. Original photograph of Marilyn Monroe courtesy of Personality Photos, Inc.; **p. 440:** Cartoon by Dennis Baron; **p. 463:** Photofest; **p. 466:** Reprinted with the permission of Cambridge University Press; **p. 481:** (1) Suzanne Starr; (2) By permission of the *Journal of Education*; **p. 498:** (1) Ann M. Johns, Ph.D. Professor Emerita, San Diego State University; (2) Reprinted with the permission of Cambridge University Press; **p. 538:** Courtesy of Peter Lang Publishing; **p. 581:** Courtesy of National Council of Teachers of English; **p. 595:** Courtesy of The Chronicle of Higher Education; **p. 596:** Copyright © Tim Rue/Corbis; **p. 602:** (l) Edward T. Funkhouser; (2) Courtesy of National Council of Teachers of English; **p. 618:** (1) Photo by Martha Casanave, 2010; (2) Courtesy of Taylor & Francis; **p. 667:** Courtesy of National Council of Teachers of English; **p. 700:** (1) Courtesy of Ken Hyland; (2) By permission of University of Michigan Press.

Index